THE ENLIGHTENED CAPITALISTS

ALSO BY JAMES O'TOOLE

*Watts and Woodstock: Identity and Culture in the
United States and South Africa*

Work in America (principal author)

Work and the Quality of Life (editor)

Energy and Social Change (principal author)

Work, Learning, and the American Future

Tenure (principal author)

Making America Work

Working: Changes and Choices (principal editor)

Vanguard Management: Redesigning the Corporate Future

The Executive's Compass: Business and the Good Society

*Leading Change: Overcoming the Ideology of Comfort and the
Tyranny of Custom*

Leadership A to Z: A Guide for the Appropriately Ambitious

*Creating the Good Life: Applying Aristotle's Wisdom to
Find Meaning and Happiness*

The New American Workplace (co-author)

America at Work (co-editor)

Transparency: Creating a Culture of Candor (co-author)

Good Business: Exercising Effective and Ethical Leadership (co-editor)

The Practical Idealist: Gandhi's Leadership Lessons

Corporate Stewardship: Achieving Sustainable Effectiveness (co-editor)

THE

ENLIGHTENED CAPITALISTS

Cautionary Tales of Business Pioneers
Who Tried to Do Well by Doing Good

James O'Toole

HARPER
BUSINESS

An Imprint of HarperCollins*Publishers*

HarperCollins books may be purchased for educational, business, or sales promotional use. For information, please email the Special Markets Department at SPsales@harpercollins.com.

FIRST EDITION

Poem "King of the River" © 1971 by Stanley Kunitz, from *The Collected Poems* by Stanley Kunitz. Used by permission of W. W. Norton & Company, Inc.

Designed by Bonni Leon-Berman

Library of Congress Cataloging-in-Publication Data

Names: O'Toole, James, author.
Title: The enlightened capitalists: cautionary tales of business pioneers who tried to do well by doing good / James O'Toole.
Description: New York: HarperCollins, [2018] | Includes bibliographical references.
Identifiers: LCCN 2018024870 | ISBN 9780062880246 (hardcover)
Subjects: LCSH: Businesspeople—United States—Biography. | Entrepreneurship—United States—History. | Businesspeople—United Kingdom—Biography. | Entrepreneurship—United Kingdom—History.
Classification: LCC HC102.5.A2 O85 2018 | DDC 338.092/273—dc23 LC record available at https://lccn.loc.gov/2018024870

19 20 21 22 23   LSC   10 9 8 7 6 5 4 3 2 1

For Marilyn

CONTENTS

Preface: The Good Unearthed   *xi*

Introduction and Background: Why It Is Hard to Do Good   *xix*

PART I: THE PIONEERS

1   The First Business Reformer: Robert Owen (1771–1858)   3

2   Man with a Thousand Partners: James Cash Penney
    (1875–1971)   31

3   The Businessman Who "Cleaned Up the World":
    William Lever (1851–1925)   51

4   Kisses Sweeter Than Wine: Milton Snavely Hershey
    (1857–1945)   71

5   Creating an Enduring Enterprise: James Lincoln
    (1883–1965)   94

6   New Forms of Incorporation and Governance:
    John Spedan Lewis (1885–1963) and John Joseph Eagan
    (1870–1924)   120

7   Johnson & Johnson's Roller-Coaster Ride: Robert Wood
    Johnson (1893–1968) and James Burke (1925–2012)   145

8   Great Genes: Levi Strauss (1829–1902) and His Heirs   176

9   Marks & Sparks: Michael Marks (1863–1900) and
    the Marks and Sieff Families   206

PART II: THE GOLDEN ERA

10 Leadership as an Art: Max De Pree (1924–2017)   227

11 Too Much of a Good Thing: William C. Norris (1911–2006)   243

12 Business Mavericks: Ken Iverson (1925–2002),
    Robert Townsend (1920–1998), Herb Kelleher (1931–),
    Bill Gore (1912–1986), and Terri Kelly (1963–)   264

13 The Patricians: Thornton Bradshaw (1917–1988),
    J. Irwin Miller (1909–2004), Edwin Land (1909–1991),
    John Whitehead (1922–2015), and Roy Vagelos (1929–)   304

14 Environmentalists or Capitalists? Anita Perella Roddick
    (1942–2007) and Tom Chappell (1943–)   342

15 Lever Redux: Ben Cohen (1951–)   376

16 Capitalists of a Different Stripe: Yvon Chouinard (1938–),
    Jack Stack (1949–), Robert Beyster (1924–2014), and Others 395

PART III: YESTERDAY, TODAY, AND TOMORROW

17 Looking Back: What We Have Learned   423

18 Looking Forward: The Prospects for Enlightened Corporate
    Leadership   442

    Conclusion: *Difficile Est Bonum Esse*   473

Acknowledgments   479
Notes   483
Index   511

PREFACE

The Good Unearthed

...the good is oft interred with their bones.
—*Shakespeare,* Julius Caesar

One was a professional manager who during the bleakest days of the Industrial Revolution created Britain's most successful manufacturing business, the profits from which he used to provide decent working and living conditions for his workers and their families. For those efforts he was damned by his peers in industry—*and* by Karl Marx. One was a self-made American millionaire who enabled a thousand others to become successful business executives, only to lose his own fortune during the Great Depression on an ill-conceived investment.

Another, the inventor of bar soap and modern product advertising, shared his wealth with thousands of employees and then lost his giant global enterprise to his creditors. Yet another was the playboy heir to a great corporation, a self-styled military "general" who created a model code of ethics for his company that, later, was ignored by executives who succeeded him.

Then there was the brilliant computer scientist who single-mindedly dedicated his company to addressing some of the world's most intractable social programs, leading it to virtual bankruptcy in the process. And more recently there was the woman known as "the mosquito," who pestered the corporate world to pay attention to environmental and consumer health issues before selling her company to a large corporation that showed little interest in such matters.

For nearly five decades, I have been fascinated by the stories of these and a small group of other (mostly now forgotten) business leaders who attempted to do good while at the same time doing well. I call them the enlightened capitalists. I have identified some fifty American and British business leaders who, over the last two centuries, have introduced unusually admirable organizational practices that greatly benefited both their shareowners and society, the careers of roughly half of whom are profiled in these pages. Each attempted to address the world's most chronic and deeply entrenched problems: unemployment, poverty, unsafe and unhealthy working conditions, low-quality goods, and environmental degradation. By endeavoring to serve the needs of their employees, customers, and the broader community while at the same time successfully meeting the necessity of profit, those leaders hoped the organizations they created would serve as models their fellow capitalists would emulate.

Significantly, the enlightened capitalists sought to address social problems primarily through their business practices, rather than by acts of charity or philanthropy. Their ethical and responsible acts were not add-ons, afterthoughts, or atonement for bad behavior, but integral to the way they did business, incorporated in how they made products and delivered services. Their actions went far beyond the current executive affirmation that "our company serves the needs of all our stakeholders." Unlike practitioners of the "Davos Conscience"—executives who migrate to the Swiss Alps to speak high-mindedly for a few days a year, then go back to business as usual for the next eleven and three-quarter months—the enlightened capitalists have steadfastly attempted to practice what they preach.

I admire the moral courage these men and women have displayed when doing what they felt was right, whatever the personal cost. Some of them have been, I admit, a bit quirky and obsessive, and a few utterly eccentric; nonetheless, to the extent that I have heroes, they are mine. They represent the promise of a virtuous corporate capitalism that the idealistic side of me finds socially and economically desirable.

Yet as I have studied—and sometimes personally observed—the efforts of these pioneering individuals, the realist in me has been struck by the fact that in their companies few of their virtuous practices have been long maintained. At some point shortly after the enlightened capitalists retired, died, were forced out of office, or sold their companies, their successors abandoned the very practices that made those companies both financially successful and publicly admired. Among the two dozen companies we examine—the earliest dating back to the early 1800s—at only a handful did their founders' virtuous practices survive through as many as two successions in leadership.

That pattern has continued to the current day. In the mid-1980s I had pegged two dozen American firms as being in the vanguard of what I then believed would become a general movement toward the adoption of enlightened practices. Before the century was out, only three of those companies had maintained those practices. The others abandoned them as the result, variously, of being acquired by other firms, going bankrupt, or changes in leadership.[1]

Of course all companies change over time, forced to alter their products and strategies and adopt new technologies to meet competitive challenges. But the changes made at the enlightened capitalists' companies were of a different sort: they involved the deliberate cessation of successful, socially desirable practices—practices, moreover, that were often the cornerstones of company success. Indeed, over the last two centuries, precious few companies have managed to sustain enlightened practices—particularly corporations operating in economies characterized by the Anglo-American variety of laissez-faire shareholder capitalism. That is not to say all good companies inevitably come to bad ends; nonetheless, there has been an unmistakable historical pattern in that direction.

While the focus of this book is on the past—after all, that is the only way the sustainability of business practices can be evaluated—it should not be seen as a work of history. Rather, it is about economic, political, and social issues being debated today. As I have studied enlightened leaders and the companies they led, I have found my idealistic and realistic sides debating the question many citizens are asking today: Are socially virtuous business practices compatible with shareholder capitalism? I offer my personal (uncertain) answer to that question at the end of the book. But what ultimately will matter is the collective judgment of corporate executives: Do *they* believe it is possible—or sensible—to try to do good as they seek to do well?

There is now a special urgency for them to engage with this issue. Over the last decade, a growing number of citizens in America and Britain have begun to challenge the legitimacy of the current economic order—a central pillar of which is the private corporation. The role corporations play in that order is a major (albeit not the only) determinant of the degree to which economic systems are viewed as fair and legitimate. When giant businesses are seen as behaving ethically, responsibly, and in the public interest, the citizenry tends to be satisfied that the system of corporate capitalism is fair. But when corporate behavior is perceived as rapacious, narrowly self-interested, and insensitive to the needs of society, those citizens may demand radical changes to the system.

The threat of radical change may be what led CEOs attending the 2018 Davos meeting into earnest discussion about social responsibility. There, the chairman of Wall Street's Vanguard investment fund, Bill McNabb, called on his fellow executives to end their obsession with short-term profits and instead focus on addressing such major social problems as climate change and employee well-being. This came fast on the heels of a similar plea by Larry Fink, CEO of $6 trillion investment fund BlackRock, who had recently declared that "society is demanding that companies, both public and private, serve a social purpose . . . and benefit all their stakeholders." A few months earlier, the editors of the *Financial Times* concluded that "business must help fix the failures of capitalism."[2] Arguing that "capitalism needs a new social contract," a system more "competent, ethical and fair," they warned corporate leaders that "proposals for tighter reg-ulation, heavier legislation and even nationalization [in Britain] are winning support." Without offering the particulars of that new rela-tionship between business and society, the editors suggested that "a better social contract would be built on the idea of a humane, mutu-ally beneficial interdependence between the two."[3] In essence, busi-ness leaders are now being called on to decide if their corporations can, will, or should engage more deeply in efforts to solve social and environmental problems—or instead continue to concentrate on ful-filling their economic missions. As we see in the pages that follow, that decision is not an easy one to make.

It is important to note that McNabb, Fink, and the *Financial Times* editors were specifically referring to companies operating under the Anglo-American form of corporate capitalism. This differs in several historical and legal respects from Continental European and Asian forms. There, characteristically, large firms are far more likely to be owned and controlled by families and private foundations, and in cases where stock is publicly traded, shareholders traditionally have fewer rights and influence; in particular, it is more difficult to engage in hos-tile takeovers. Furthermore, European companies tend to be more heavily regulated and, at the same time, work more closely with their national governments to address social issues. In light of those and other analysis-complicating differences, our focus in these pages is on companies in the United Kingdom and the United States.

As today's executives in Britain and America struggle to decide whether their companies should attempt to address complex social problems, I believe it is instructive for them to review the careers of men and women who attempted to do business in ways that were, in the words of the *Financial Times*, "competent, ethical, and fair." In es-sence, those enlightened capitalists—in their own companies, and in their own ways—attempted to flesh out in practice the terms of a new social contract between business and society. We thus turn to the past not because we believe history will be repeated, or for answers we can apply willy-nilly to current problems; instead, we primarily examine historical experience to avoid repeating errors of the past. There is no excuse for doing that. As President Harry Truman—an astute student of history—noted when a skeptic asked why he spent so much time reviewing "old" news, "the only new thing in the world [is] the history you [have] not read."[4]

The individuals whose unusual business philosophies are reviewed in these pages attempted to prove to their peers in industry that profitable companies can, in fact, operate in ways widely perceived as being in the public interest. But to what degree does the record of their efforts support that contention? In the chapters that follow, we examine the practices of the enlightened capitalists—the strategies, programs, and policies they introduced—with an eye to discovering which were successful, which were not, and why. To the extent that the motivations of others can ever be fully understood, we try to fathom what compelled them to take the road less traveled. Were they in search of greater profit, public recognition, or the respect of their peers? Were they motivated by religious precepts, economic ideology, ethical principles instilled by their parents, or the ego satisfaction that derives from creating something new and unusual? Finally, we endeavor to understand why, in most cases, their practices were not sustained, and—in the few instances where they were—why and how they succeeded.

In conducting this review, my method is simple storytelling. Obviously any one of the stories told here, by itself, amounts only to anecdotal evidence. But when many stories are compiled, one on the other—and we look to see where they do and do not overlap—we then can analytically examine a rich body of data. This approach allows readers to make their own generalizations based on a substantial body of experience. For some readers, a few of these stories may be familiar; for most, I suspect that the names of the profiled individuals will largely be unknown. Indeed, it was said of one of these idealists that his "good works had been interred even before his bones." My task has been to unearth the records of forgotten men and women who struggled with challenges similar to the ones business leaders face today, and who, like them, experienced both successes and setbacks.

Typically, most business biographies have either been portraits of larger-than-life executives whose accomplishments are inflated and failures swept under the rug, or of robber barons, rogues, and fabulously wealthy tycoons whose practices were shady at best. In contrast, this look backward entails neither the heroic hagiography found in too many current business biographies nor the Enron/WorldCom/Bernie Madoff brand of corporate crime stories popular of late. Nor will I focus on the behavior of contemporary business executives; as one who wrote a glowing account of the practices of Enron's leaders just months before their criminal shenanigans were revealed, I am living proof of the foolishness of prematurely judging executive performance. Instead, I endeavor to depict these idealistic capitalists as objectively as I can, examining the careers of deceased or long-retired men and women who, like all other humans, had flaws as well as virtues.

What follows, then, are the stories of a few rare individuals who sought to create a good society through enlightened business management—stories replete with incredible characters, high drama, improbable twists, acts of impressive courage, rare feats of imagination and innovation, moments of elation and disappointment, displays of folly and wisdom, and marvelous dollops of inspiration. Their efforts represent what might be thought of as two hundred years of socioeconomic experimentation. I hope they encourage today's leaders of business—small or large, publicly traded or privately owned—to draw useful lessons from their experiments, then proceed to create profitable business organizations that address the most profound human needs.

Why It Is Hard to Do Good

If the water were clear enough
if the water were still . . .
you would see yourself,
slipped out of your skin,
nosing upstream,
slapping, thrashing,
tumbling
over the rocks
till you paint them
with your belly's blood . . .
you would surprise yourself
in that other flesh
heavy with milt,
bruised, battering toward the dam.
—*Stanley Kunitz, "King of the River"*

Call them salmon. Akin to the metaphorically finny humans in Stanley Kunitz's poem, the business leaders profiled in these pages are men and women who, "nosing upstream, slapping, thrashing, tumbling over the rocks," were ceaselessly driven on, bloodied, "bruised, battering toward the dam." They insisted on swimming against the current of received wisdom and, with long odds contrary to success, struggled to overcome formidable obstacles placed in their way by those opposed to the ends they pursued (and by those who simply thought them insane for making the attempt). Indeed, few succeeded in reaching the desired end of their improbable journeys, the goal of which was to spawn future generations of enlightened business executives who would transform the ways in which corporations are organized and led.

Traditionally, most businesspeople have viewed their work simply as a way to earn a living and accumulate wealth; thus, they have been motivated primarily, if not exclusively, by the prospects of material gain (and personal satisfaction). And a few have been inventors who entered business to profit from a product idea or technological creation. It makes sense, then, that their standard of success would be the profit they made in the short term and the wealth they generated in the long run. But the chapters that follow examine the atypical careers of men and women who also took up the greater challenge of addressing social problems through their business activities. They attempted to create profitable businesses while daring to differ from the vast majority of their peers in several significant ways:

- They developed fully fleshed-out philosophies of business in which they identified higher purposes for their enterprises than simply making a profit. Significantly, they were not philanthropists: the good they attempted to do was an integral part of their business practices.
- Strong ethical compasses guided their decision making with regard to meeting the diverse needs of their constituencies: customers, employees, shareholders, suppliers, host communities, the broader society, and the natural environment.
- Their primary ethical value was respect for people. Whether that value was rooted in the Bible's Golden Rule or in the humanistic values of the Enlightenment, these business leaders tried to use their organizations as vehicles for the aspect of human development that Thomas Jefferson called "the pursuit of happiness."

- They each maintained a commitment to their values through good times and bad. They also attempted—if too seldom successfully—to create sustainable business models buttressed by strong corporate cultures that institutionalized virtuous behaviors.

These commitments were at the foundation of the businesses these mindful managers created. But before we turn to an examination of their lives, careers, practices, and ideas, we need first to understand how businesses have historically been managed, why those practices have prevailed for so long, and how they differ from the philosophies of the enlightened capitalists. For what is most remarkable about our business iconoclasts is the extent to which they broke with long-established traditions, norms, and beliefs about the hows and whys of business that are traceable back to humankind's earliest trading activities. In essence, we first must understand the tenets of business orthodoxy before we can appreciate our enlightened capitalists' heresies.

Received Wisdom: The Practice of Business Throughout Most of History

COMMON TO ALL MANKIND, Adam Smith wrote, is "the propensity to truck, barter and exchange" goods. Indeed, at some point in prehistory, one of our ancestors may have swapped a bunch of apples for a joint of meat, and the species has been engaged in business ever since. Hence it might be said, contrary to competing claims, that the world's oldest profession is business. If you think about business in terms of stories, as I do, one story is as old as human society itself: the one about the division of labor, and the trading of goods to meet the necessities of life. For most of early human history "business" consisted solely of trading and bartering. To increase the odds of their survival, early humans learned that if they voluntarily cooperated—first in families, then in tribes, and later in communities—they would fare better than if each person sought to satisfy all of his or her own basic needs for food, clothing, and shelter. Although humans are patently self-interested creatures, they are, at the same time, "social animals," as Aristotle was the first to observe (his teacher, Plato, had earlier described the advantages of the division of labor). Since there could be no human progress without commerce and trade, businesslike activities were initial steps toward the creation of early societies.

Over the millennia, as human societies became formally structured, caste hierarchies arose in places like India, where each caste was assigned to a certain occupation; in other locales—Europe, in particular—feudal systems evolved in which serfs worked for noble lords who assigned them specific tasks, for which they were paid not in cash but by the use of plots of land on which to provide their own food and shelter. In medieval times, business in urban areas came to be conducted by traveling traders who brought goods from distant lands, and by skilled self-employed specialists—shoemakers, dyers, weavers, blacksmiths, silversmiths, potters, millers, and the like— aided, at most, by their own children and perhaps one or two apprentices. Sometimes members of those professions formed guilds, the main purpose of which was to protect their monopolies in their particular trades or crafts. As late as the fourteenth century, the only organizations employing more than a dozen or so individuals were armies, navies, churches, and states. Before that time, there is no history of business enterprises as we know them today for the simple reason that such organizations (companies) did not yet exist. And corporations—originally called joint-stock companies—did not come into being until the seventeenth century, although the seeds of modern enterprises were first sown in Europe at the dawn of the Renaissance. It was then that traders like the Italian Francesco Datini began to engage in what we would recognize as proto-capitalist activities.

The Merchant of Prato and the Dominant Mode of Business Thought

THROUGHOUT RECORDED HISTORY THERE have been markets, traders, craftsmen, and moneylenders, but not until the end of the medieval era did businesspeople, with an eye toward personal gain, begin to systematically organize their activities and hire paid workers. The earliest of such proto-capitalists about whom we have a detailed record was Francesco Datini, known as the Merchant of Prato. And what a complete picture we have of Datini's personal and business life between 1335 and 1410! The merchant's story is not only the most thoroughly documented business history surviving from those times but also among the most complete such records of any era. He consciously left behind five hundred ledgers and account books, three hundred deeds of partnership, insurance policies, countless bills of exchange and lading, a slew of checks, and 503 files of business letters (as well as some 140,000 personal letters). Printed at the top of many of those documents was his motto: "In the name of God and of profit." The record confirms that those two concerns were the only deep, abiding ones in his life—with a strong accent on the latter.[1]

Datini's documents have been an invaluable resource for business historians since they were discovered in the 1870s, providing insights into accounting, finance, marketing, and strategic methods of the distant past—a past that looks remarkably like the present. What his vast archive demonstrates is that Datini was quite nearly a modern businessman. According to Charles Handy, Datini used double-entry bookkeeping a century before it is said to have been invented by an Italian monk.[2]

Datini began his career as an importer in his Tuscan hometown of Prato, eventually expanding his operations internationally with offices as far away as France, Spain, Belgium, and England. For most of his career he was a workaholic. An astute, shrewd, ambitious, ruthless, and greedy entrepreneur, he was filled throughout his life with constant anxiety: fear that the ships carrying his silks from Venice, wool from England, spices from the Black Sea, wine from Catalonia, salt from Ibiza, and pilgrim's robes from Romania would sink or be captured by pirates; worry about paying too much in taxes, about the soundness of his investments, and about collecting money from his debtors. He was a micromanager so distrustful of those who worked for him in his far-flung enterprise that he labored long into every night penning detailed letters of instructions, seeking to control his employees' every act. To his best (and only) friend, Ser Lapo Mazzei, he confessed, "I am not feeling well today on account of all the writing I have done in these two days, without sleeping either by night or by day, and in those two days eating but one loaf."[3] He constantly scolded and berated his managers, telling one, "You cannot see a crow in a bowlful of milk."

Datini was neither simply a good nor a bad man, although his competitive tactics might be considered a bit unethical by modern standards, and his incidental trade in slavery is hard to condone today (or, perhaps, even in his own time). Avid for gain, he was never satisfied with the amount of his fortune. So devoted was he to the pursuit of more that he seldom felt at peace, always laboring to make himself richer and, in the process, alienating himself from the affections of his wife and adopted daughter, as well as those of his mistresses and illegitimate children. "Destiny has ordained that from the day of my birth I should never know a whole happy day," he wrote to his wife.[4] And to his friend, the wise Ser Lapo Mazzei, he complained, "In May it will be two years since I slept at ease for more than four hours a night." Mazzei, in turn, warned the soon-to-be sixty-year-old merchant about the corrosive effects of such materialism on his character:

> I have already known, from your letters, of your tribulations and the hindrances caused to you by the things of this world; but now that I have seen them with my own eyes, they are far greater than I had believed. When I think of the cares you are building, of your branches in far-off lands, your banquets and your

accounts, and many other matters, they seem to me so far beyond what is needed. . . . In short I wish you would wind up many
of your matters, which you yourself say are in order, and desist
from any more building, and give away some of your riches in
alms with your own hands, and value them at their true worth,
that is, own them as if they were not yours.[5]

As an old man in his seventies, a guilt-ridden Francesco Datini finally listened to his friend's advice and, in an act of contrition, left his
entire fortune of 70,000 gold ducats (tens of millions in today's dollars)
to endow a foundation for the betterment of social conditions among
the poor of Prato. After his death, Prato's grateful citizenry erected a
statue of him in the town's main square. It is still there today, along with
the foundation he endowed.

The Merchant of Prato may have been unique in his meticulous doc-
umentation of every activity; nonetheless, his basic business behavior
was, if obsessive, not unusual among the millions of entrepreneurs,
managers, and executives who would follow—especially the practice
of late-career philanthropy.

Less than a hundred years after Datini's death, another merchant,
the German Jacob Fugger, accumulated a fortune importing pepper
and other spices, luxurious textiles, and exotic foods. Fugger then took
capitalism to its next stage by recognizing that there was greater profit
in finance than in trading. Using his influence to convince Pope Leo X
to issue a papal bull that ended the long-standing prohibition against
Christians charging interest on loans, he put his capital to work financing the entrepreneurial activities of European businessmen, aristocrats,
monarchs, and popes—often demanding a proprietary interest in their
businesses as collateral. As banker to Holy Roman emperors Maximilian I and his successor, Charles V, Fugger was granted highly profitable
monopolistic privileges in key commodities. Financing, and eventually
controlling, silver and copper mines in Europe and gold and silver ones
in the New World, he earned an annual increase in capital of over 23

percent per year over his long business life, ultimately becoming, so his biographer claims, "The richest man who ever lived."[6] He owned several estates and a sumptuous palace filled with rare books, manuscripts, and fine art, to the point that his extravagant lifestyle outshone those of the monarchs he bankrolled. Moreover, he became politically more powerful than the kings and popes he then deigned to treat as peers. Apparently it all went to his head. Before death, he composed his own brazen obituary:

> TO GOD, ALL-POWERFUL AND GOOD! Jacob Fugger, of Augsburg, ornament to his class and to his country, Imperial Councilor under Maximilian I and Charles V, second to none in the acquisition of extraordinary wealth, in liberality, in purity of life, and in greatness of soul, as he was comparable to none in life, so after death not to be numbered among the mortal.[7]

During his lifetime Fugger financed the foundations of the great wealth later displayed by European princes and potentates. He left his own fortune to heirs who continued for generations to bankroll commerce across the continent and the globe. Fugger, like Francesco Datini, endeavored to save his soul in old age through charitable donations to the poor.

The Philanthropic Search for Atonement: The Preferred Course

IN THE CENTURIES FOLLOWING Fugger's death, most businesspeople continued to view their work solely as a means to accumulate wealth for themselves and their families. To the extent they also sought to contribute to the betterment of their fellow humans, it was through philanthropic acts, most of which, as with Datini and Fugger, were late-in-life occurrences. In the modern era, stories about business moguls who, after working careers characterized by unethical and ruthless behavior, sought redemption through acts of charity have become the stuff of legend—notably, the grandiose philanthropic acts of John D. Rockefeller (1839–1937), Henry Ford (1863–1947), and Andrew Carnegie (1835–1919).

Here's what William Warden, president of the Atlantic refinery, wrote in 1887 to his boss, John D. Rockefeller, when the latter's Standard Oil Trust had a virtual monopoly in the domestic petroleum market:

> We have met with a success unparalleled in commercial history, our name is known all over the world, and our public character is not one to be envied. We are quoted as the representation of all that is evil, hard hearted, oppressive, cruel . . . , we are pointed at with contempt, and while some good men flatter us, it is only for our money. . . . There is a bitter cry in the oil regions, and the curse is laid at our door and if we listen to it and are wise enough to try to mitigate it, we may turn the tide in our favor.[8]

Warden went on to offer a series of practical proposals for fairer treatment of Standard Oil's suppliers, customers, and employees, ending his letter with this plea: "Now Mr. Rockefeller, let me ask you to give this much thought and careful consideration and do not cast it to one side or let it pass into the wastebasket as a thing unworthy to be considered." There is no evidence Warden's letter was ever answered; however, five years later the courts issued what was to be the first of many adverse rulings against the Standard Oil Trust, culminating in the US Supreme Court's 1911 decision declaring the trust illegal, which in turn led to its ultimate breakup. In 1905 John D. Rockefeller Jr.—like his father a devout Baptist—told his Bible study class that he had challenged his father with regard to Standard Oil's business practices. He told his father that the fortune he was about to inherit from him was morally "tainted." Many years later, the aged Rockefeller dedicated what was left of his life to giving away his fortune to make amends for what he had by then come to regard as his business sins.[9]

Henry Ford's story, like his life, was one of contradictions and paradoxes. The automotive pioneer was visionary, innovative, rational, wise, honest, and a committed pacifist, and at the same time shortsighted, rigid, irrational, dissembling, and belligerent. He presented himself to the world as a model of domesticity, yet had a decades-long relationship with a mistress who bore his love child (conveniently, he put his second family up in a comfortable home near the one in which he lived with his legal wife and son). Henry owned the lion's share of Ford Motor Company stock, yet he cultivated a folksy image of himself as Everyman: once, asked by a reporter what it felt like to be the world's first billionaire, feigning homespun humility he replied, "Oh, shit!"[10]

Ford was briefly the greatest friend African American workers had in big business (in 1926, some ten thousand blacks were employed in his plants, often supervising whites); at the same time he was a virulent anti-Semite. He hired and promoted women, immigrants, and disabled workers decades before other large companies, while supporting nativist political movements. Famously, he introduced the $5-per-day wage when the average industrial worker was making half that amount, yet his infamous Sociology Department snooped into his workers' private lives, dismissing those who drank, gambled, or cheated on their spouses. As welcome as Ford's $5 a day was to his workers, the gesture should not be mistaken as a sign of virtue: he made it perfectly clear that his motive was to increase car sales by making it possible for factory workers to afford his Model A. He was notorious for firing workers when they gained seniority, replacing them with younger, lower-paid employees. In 1928 he established Fordlandia, a 2.5-million-acre rubber plantation in the Amazon on which he built a model community for his Brazilian workers, providing them with comfortable housing and public amenities unknown in South America at the time. But when the rubber business proved insufficiently profitable, he lost all interest in that utopian "social experiment," sorely neglecting Fordlandia, which was eventually sold to the Brazilian government for pennies on the dollar.

Because of his rigid thinking, Ford failed in the 1920s to respond to the challenges General Motors presented to his dominance of the auto industry. He waited so long to meet those challenges that he was forced to shut down all production between 1927 and 1929 during an unplanned, disruptive, and mind-bogglingly expensive transition from Model Ts to Model As—a retooling that caused pandemonium among Ford's managers and engineers and left scores of thousands of workers on the street without incomes. By the time he reached old age, the increasingly autocratic Ford was hated by his employees. Thanks to his opposition to America's entry into World Wars I and II, his public persona was nearly as reviled as those of the detested robber barons who had preceded him. However, at age seventy-three, he engaged in a highly publicized philanthropic act that burnished his badly tarnished reputation, establishing the Ford Foundation "for scientific, educational, and charitable purposes, all for public welfare and for no other purposes." In fact, there was another purpose, and it was the main one as far as Ford was concerned: the foundation was a colossal tax dodge that saved the Ford family $321 million in inheritance levies while keeping Ford Motor Company's voting stock in their hands.[11]

Andrew Carnegie, who once hired goons to open fire on his striking employees, became the most generous philanthropist of his era as an old man—doing so neither to appease his Maker nor to evade the taxman but, instead, for convoluted philosophical reasons. Born to a working-class Scottish family, Carnegie rose from the obscurity of relative poverty to become a respected world figure, as much a player in the fields of international politics, philanthropy, and literature as in the world of big business. He started his career as an underage telegraph operator, but never became interested in technology. By age nineteen, though, he found a calling he would embrace with avid enthusiasm: the making of money. His business dealings were frequently shady or unethical by today's standards, although not necessarily illegal at the time. He capitalized on—perhaps profiteered from—the Civil War, and as a result he was worth more than $5 million (in current dollars) before he was thirty.[12]

After a few unsatisfying stints of paid employment, Carnegie, following in the footsteps of Jacob Fugger, surmised that it was far better to let money work for him than to labor himself. Work, he concluded, was an activity that needed to be minimized so he had ample leisure time to enjoy the good life of reading, writing, horseback riding, traveling, concertgoing, and engaging in long conversations with thoughtful friends at his palatial homes in Scotland and Manhattan. The young, newly rich Carnegie once candidly admitted that the source of his vast wealth was found not in his "labour, nor skill. No, nor superior ability, sagacity, nor enterprise, nor greater public service."[13] Instead, he confessed, he had merely been the right man at the right time to capitalize on the nation's growing demand for steel—first for building railroads, and then for constructing giant skyscrapers. He later would have a startling change of mind regarding the source of his wealth.

Early in his career, Carnegie found himself owning the controlling interest of what would one day become US Steel, the world's largest company in its industry. Better than his competitors, he understood the advantages of economies of scale: in the game of efficiency, bigger was not just better; it was the winner. His Carnegie Steel company grew rapidly as it gobbled up market share and competitors and drove into bankruptcy those it didn't digest. His giant Pittsburgh mills operated 24/7, but he rarely bothered to visit them. He didn't go to the office either. He seldom put in more than four hours a day at his desk, wherever that happened to be. Living comfortably in New York during the social season, and for up to six months in Scotland when the weather was conducive, he saw no reason to waste time in sooty Pittsburgh, or to bother with his company's day-to-day business operations. Carnegie, in fact, was neither manager nor leader of the giant enterprise he owned and had named to honor himself. He turned those dreary "details" over to Henry Clay Frick. This odd couple—the cosmopolitan, loquacious Carnegie and the factory-bound, taciturn Frick—had a fraught relationship, but one in which they understood that each needed the other: Carnegie supplied the vision, Frick the managerial chops.

That Andrew Carnegie would become known as one of America's most virulent (and successful) union busters was more than a bit strange. Raised in a family of militant trade unionists, he personally suffered exploitation as a young worker, and early in his business career he spoke out in favor of unions and in solidarity with the laboring class. Putting those beliefs into practice, he proposed to the union representing his steelworkers a farsighted deal in which wage increases would be tied to company profits, so both employer and employees would share in good times and bad. The union bought into the proposal and, during a recession, made good on their word by agreeing to cut wages and increase working hours. However, when the postrecession boom arrived, Carnegie reneged on his own deal, refusing to cut his worker "partners" in on the upside. Strikes ensued. When workers accused him of being a liar, hypocrite, and scoundrel, he replied that he had merely had an important insight that they failed to understand.

Carnegie wrote that he had experienced a philosophical epiphany while reading Herbert Spencer's theory of social Darwinism, which, in brief, claimed that "the laws of civilization decree that wealth must accumulate in the hands of those with the greatest talent for organizational management."[14] In his famous essay "The Gospel of Wealth," Carnegie credits Spencer with changing his mind about good luck and timing having been the source of his fortune. Once enlightened by Spencer, he saw that it was the duty of those with his manifestly rare talent at making money to also administer those funds as a kind of public trust, dispensing them in ways he deemed most beneficial to the community. Therein lay his logic for reneging on his deal with the union: it ran afoul of "the laws of civilization" to permit the unwashed laborers who produced his wealth to decide for themselves how to spend it. Employing social Darwinist logic, Carnegie also concluded that if he continued to pay his workers more than the minimum they needed to survive, he would "encourage the slothful, the drunken, the unworthy." Ergo, instead of dividing his profits into "trifling amounts" as higher wages that then would be "wasted in the indulgence of appetite," he would accumulate his wealth and put it to higher purposes. With supreme self-confidence (and self-delusion) he concluded that "even the poor can be made to see this."

They couldn't. Carnegie's workers thought they needed more and better food, clothing, and shelter. However, their blithely paternalistic employer knew better: what they *really* needed, he assured them, were libraries, hospitals, museums, and vocational schools. Not only did the laws of political economy dictate that he must not share profits with his workers; it also was his sacred duty to *reduce* their wages so he would have more to give to those charities he had the superior capacity to understand would serve their true needs. The self-righteous Carnegie displayed no hint of empathy for the men who toiled long hours with no breaks in the inferno of his mills. Instead, for their sake, and the sake of others like them, he paternalistically cut their wages in order to fund public baths, parks, and churches.

In 1892, when the workers at his gargantuan Homestead facility violently rebelled against their treatment, Carnegie allowed manager Frick to call in Pinkerton guards, who then fired on the strikers. While Homestead burned, Carnegie was away in Scotland fishing. When a reporter later asked him if he cared to comment on the strike, he condescendingly replied that he had given complete control of the company to Frick and wouldn't think of interfering with his managerial prerogatives. The Great Scot, his friend Samuel Clemens noted, sadly lacked the capacity for self-reflection: "Mr. Carnegie is not any better acquainted with himself than if he met himself for the first time the day before yesterday."[15] With the union broken, Carnegie's resulting cost advantage enabled him to drive out unionized competitors.

In 1901 the sixty-six-year-old Carnegie sold his controlling interest in the steel company to J. P. Morgan, pocketing $226 million in gold bonds, a staggering amount worth at least twenty times that today. He was then said to be the richest man of all time, perhaps surpassing Jacob Fugger's vast fortune. He then dedicated the last two decades of his life to giving that money away, in the end almost making good on his promise to die without a penny to his name. For the most part he gave more carefully, thoughtfully, and wisely than perhaps any philanthropist prior to Bill Gates, his largesse benefiting millions of people over the last century. Nonetheless, President Theodore Roosevelt offered this final assessment of the man: "If Andrew Carnegie had employed his fortune and his time in doing justice to the steelworkers who gave him his fortune, he would have accomplished a thousand times what he has accomplished" in his public and philanthropic works.[16]

Was T.R. Right?

ROCKEFELLER, FORD, AND CARNEGIE frequently harmed their employees, competitors, customers, business partners, and the communities where their companies operated—yet they later did great good through philanthropic activities and the foundations they created, which to this day continue to make significant contributions to society. Those paradoxical facts illustrate how difficult it is to assess the careers of unethical business moguls who engage in philanthropic sin-washing. Even more complicated is the assessment of the social contributions made by great inventors and entrepreneurs such as Robert Fulton and John Deere at the turn of the nineteenth century, Thomas Edison and Cornelius Vanderbilt a century later, and Steve Jobs and Bill Gates in our day. They each made significant business and technological contributions that improved the lives of ordinary men and women, yet while they were far from being robber barons—their business sins were relatively peccadilloes—none is particularly remembered for his business virtue or enlightened practices. Their biographers' recourse has been to provide evenhanded accounts of the pros and cons of their various activities and accomplishments, recognizing that no simple, final assessments are possible.

It is harder still to offer valid generalizations about the great business figures of history, in toto, because their motivations, careers, and actions have been so varied. It seems the only thing they all have had in common is the primary, if not exclusive, motivation to succeed for their own personal gain and satisfaction. For a few individuals like Deere and Edison, a great deal of that satisfaction was derived from the acts of creating new and useful products (whatever material gain they received was seen as public confirmation of those contributions). That caveat registered, the protagonists of most stories about great business leaders have been self-interested individuals whose metrics of success were profits and wealth creation. Moreover, the goal of profit has long been accepted by most citizens in capitalist societies as both appropriate and sufficient.

The Realists' Case Against Business Enlightenment

IN 1776 ADAM SMITH laid the foundation for the case against business idealism in *The Wealth of Nations*: "It is not from the benevolence of the butcher, the brewer, or the baker that we expect our dinner, but from their regard to their self-interest."[17] Baldly stated, Smith thus reminds us that the motivation bakers have in baking bread is making money, not feeding us. That helps us to understand why the measure of success of business leaders historically has been, and still is, the yardstick of profit. At a basic level, there is the general recognition that businesspeople who fairly and ethically earn great profits are those who best provide customers with goods they want at prices they are willing to pay. In other words, profits are widely seen as just rewards for efficiently providing us with the food we eat, the clothes we wear, and the luxuries we purchase.

At a subtler level of economic analysis, business enterprises create wealth for the broader society; indeed, capitalist organizations have proved to be the best mechanisms for providing the financial wherewithal needed to advance civilization. (Pharaohs, kings, and Marxist dictators have used state-owned and -controlled enterprises as mechanisms of wealth creation, but they did so far less efficiently, and at a considerable loss of human freedom, equality, and quality of life.) Since the formation of publicly traded corporations in the seventeenth century, the economic history of market-oriented societies reveals a general long-term trend of economic growth and an overall increase in the standard of living of most citizens—recessions, depressions, wars, and persistent relative poverty notwithstanding. Whether that long-term upward trend is nearing its end in the world's most developed nations is best left to economists to discern; what we can say is that until recently, the material standards of living of citizens in developed, market-oriented nations have improved with each subsequent generation. And the primary engines of those remarkable increases in wealth have been businesses engaged in competition with each other for customers, market share, and profit. In that vein, John Maynard Keynes made what may be the strongest case against business virtue. In his 1930 essay "The Economic Possibilities of Our Grandchildren," Lord Keynes speculated that the day when everyone would be rich might not be far off. When that day arrived, he believed, we might

> once more value ends above means and prefer the good to the useful.... But beware! The time for all this is not yet. For at least another hundred years we must pretend to ourselves and to everyone that fair is foul and foul is fair; for foul is useful and fair is not. Avarice and usury and precaution must be our gods for a little longer still. For only they can lead us out of the tunnel of economic necessity into daylight.

Hence, until universal prosperity is achieved, Keynes argued, greed is good and the road to heaven is paved with bad intentions, because the profit motive creates the wealth of nations and civilizations.

That is a major reason why leaders of companies who have sought to engage in social activities not directly intended to produce profit have been viewed, at best, as overly idealistic or misguided. The accepted wisdom has been that business leaders who take their eyes off the singular goal of profit will ultimately fail at the hands of competitors who stay focused on serving their customers. Moreover, it is widely assumed that the primary skill of businesspeople is to organize their companies to efficiently and effectively serve those customers; thus even the most admired corporate leaders are not considered to be social reformers, deep philosophical thinkers, government administrators, or political leaders. Nor are corporate leaders retained by their shareholders to undertake such roles. Addressing criticism leveled against film industry executives for their alleged failure to promote racial diversity, legal scholar Stanley Fish writes that "doing good is not the business they are in and no one is paying them to do it."[18] That argument is even stronger when applied to more mundane enterprises and industries.

It is cogently argued that business executives who allow themselves to be distracted by issues outside their traditional financial remit will end up producing less wealth, and therefore there will be fewer resources on which elected government officials, educators, and nonprofit administrators can draw. Hence the paradoxical net effect of corporate do-gooding will be to make the very social problems that well-intentioned business leaders attempt to address grow worse. Furthermore, as Milton Friedman famously argued, in democratic societies no one wants or expects business leaders to do the job of elected officials (or, in publicly traded companies, to "tax" their shareholders in order to address social problems that they, hired managers, personally identify as needing attention).[19] For all those logical reasons, investors have resisted the efforts of corporate managers to address social problems, preferring that profits be paid out to them so that they, the company's legal owners, can decide for themselves which, if any, charities or social causes to support.

The historical skepticism about, and opposition to, business social activism is rooted in the ages-old philosophical divide between realists (those who take things as they are) and idealists (those who imagine things as they believe they should become). Realists see the way business has historically been conducted as the natural product of market forces, and thus to be tampered with only at great risk, while idealists believe that conscious human actions can reshape corporate conduct for the better. This is not an ideological divide in the classic left-versus-right construct. Opposition to corporate do-goodism has come not only from conservative investors and economists but also from labor leaders, civil libertarians, and progressive scholars realistically concerned about the consequences for democracy when business leaders try to impose their personal moral, ethical, and social values on employees, customers, and the public.

Indeed, as we see in the chapters that follow, there is a fine line between business activities clearly in the long-term interest of all affected parties, on the one hand, and the brand of paternalism famously practiced by Henry Ford, on the other. Further, do-gooders open the door to charges of hypocrisy. As Adam Smith either cynically or realistically concluded, "I have never known much good done by those who affected trade for the public good. It is an affectation."[20] Regardless of ideology, few citizens in modern democracies are comfortable when powerful individuals tell others how to live their lives—especially when they tell *us* what is "good for us." Even paternalism exercised in a worthy cause is experienced as an effort to impose their will on others by those, such as Andrew Carnegie, with an elevated sense of moral superiority. Hence, paternalism invariably generates resistance.

For all such reasons, the realist critics of executive social activism would conclude that Francesco Datini acted virtuously by maximizing his fortune, and then leaving his accumulated wealth for Prato's future generations to decide how to use it. By that same logic, the most virtuous twentieth-century business leaders could be said to have been philanthropists in the mold of Carnegie, Rockefeller, Ford, and Gates, whose careers were devoted to amassing great wealth and not to solving social problems by way of enlightened business practices. In other words, the Gates Foundation could be said to do more good for the world than Microsoft might have done under Gates's leadership if, to address social problems, he had diverted his attention from the company's economic and technological functions. Oracle's chairman Larry Ellison goes further, arguing that "the Ford Motor Company did more good than the Ford Foundation" by providing jobs, tax revenues, and mobility to millions.[21] And even the likes of Thomas Edison and Steve Jobs—who evidenced not only little to no interest in addressing social problems during their business careers, but also no desire to engage in philanthropy—are said by some to have made greater social contributions through their technological innovations than they could have made through any acts of social engagement.

That is the received wisdom, notwithstanding the arguments of such notables as Theodore Roosevelt and, today, the politicians, environmentalists, academics, and leaders of religious and nonprofit organizations who aver that large corporations can, and must, behave in more socially responsible ways.

The Idealists' Retort (in Brief): "It's Different This Time"

TODAY'S ADVOCATES OF GREATER corporate social engagement acknowledge that most past efforts by enlightened business leaders did not succeed in the long term. Nonetheless, those advocates are not deterred by experience, believing that conditions have changed to the point where socially beneficial and environmentally sustainable business practices have become practical necessities. In particular, they cite the problem of global warming as an issue corporate leaders can no longer avoid facing (indeed, there has been a marked shift among today's responsible corporate executives away from the enlightened capitalists' primary focus on meeting the needs of employees and customers toward addressing environmental issues). Furthermore, critics offer evidence of a marked shift in social expectations with regard to the behavior of business: consumers, employees, scholars, nongovernment institutions, and the public in general now demand greater social accountability on the part of large global corporations. Indeed, increasing numbers of business leaders—and a growing cadre of business students—have begun to search for new ways to manage that will enable companies to do well financially while at the same time doing good socially. Some advocates of social engagement claim that addressing social problems will improve business performance, if only by enhancing a corporation's reputation. More encouraging yet, the leaders of a few companies in America and Britain as well as Continental Europe and Asia have begun to turn those good intentions into practice, as we see in this book's concluding chapters.[22]

Indeed, there is currently a spontaneous movement in which a few politically progressive corporate leaders have begun to see themselves as "stewards" of their organizations and of the physical environment— almost as trustees charged not simply with responsible management of resources belonging to others (their shareholders) but also with responsibility to leave their companies, and the communities and environments they inhabit, in good stead for use by future generations.[23] On a separate track, leaders of some American companies have joined together in the so-called Conscious Capitalism movement, which is designed to encourage other executives to adopt enlightened employment, consumer, and environmental practices. It is notable that most of the executives participating in this movement tend to be from the *right* of the political spectrum—a hopeful sign that ideology may not prevent business executives from agreeing on a common agenda with regard to the social role that publicly traded corporations should play in the future.[24]

And calls for increased social engagement are becoming more global in scope. Sunil Bharti Mittal, founder of Bharti Enterprises and chairman of the International Chamber of Commerce, argues that the business community needs to do more to address the concerns of workers adversely affected by globalization, as well as those of environmentalists worried about global warming. He suggests that those concerns are best addressed not through philanthropy but through business actions and investments, "to show that business is a genuine force for good in society [and to] demonstrate that profit comes with a real social purpose."[25] Agreeing with Mittal, the prestigious Business and Sustainable Development Commission recently estimated that sustainable business strategies could create up to 380 million new jobs and $12 trillion in economic opportunities by 2030. In 2017, the commission's blue-ribbon international board of directors—composed of chief executives from multinational corporations and leaders of major nongovernmental agencies—issued its report *Better Business, Better World*, which predicted that "companies that see the business case—as well as the moral imperative—for achieving [high social and environmental goals] will take a 'Global Goals Lens' to every aspect of their business strategy to change the way they operate." In light of such recent developments, optimists believe we have entered into a new age in which enlightened corporate behavior will become the norm.

Can Business Leaders Be Both Profitable and Virtuous?

YET, REALISTS NOTE, THE majority of businesses have not joined in those movements, and the few who have often discover that it is difficult to sustain their efforts, finding it nearly impossible to advance beyond relatively inexpensive and easy to implement initial steps—such as shifting from incandescent to LED lighting—in their environmental practices. Many companies that have pledged to become carbon neutral, to use only recycled and recyclable materials, and to source only fair-traded commodities have discovered after years of trying to meet those goals that they are still decades away from doing so. More significantly, a number of companies committed to social engagement have come under attack by activist investors claiming that such efforts reduce the profits belonging to *them*, the legal owners of those corporations.[26] Indeed, a leitmotif running through all the enlightened capitalists' stories is conflict over the control of company ownership. That is because, in capitalist systems, those who control a corporation's stock have the final say in setting its policy.

In sum, members of the business community seem more open than ever to the idea of expanding beyond their traditional economic role, yet they are uncertain how to do so in practice, not sure if it is possible to do so effectively and efficiently, and greatly concerned about doing so in a way that is profitable enough to satisfy investors. The enlightened capitalists were, as we shall see, *practical* idealists, who sought to create and maintain a delicate balance between profit and virtue. But practical idealism sounds oxymoronic to the ears of many business leaders today—graduates of business schools where they were instructed in "the primacy of shareholder value," and readers of business publications reporting the fates of underperforming executives at the hands of shareholder activists.

Questions, and More Questions, Business Leaders Need to Ask

IN LIGHT OF THE powerful arguments offered in opposition to socially enlightened business practices, it is therefore legitimate for executives to ask why businesses should engage in activities that possibly detract from producing the wealth on which social, technological, and material progress is predicated (and on which government taxation and the funding of nonprofit universities, cultural institutions, and community-based charities depend). And because unprofitable businesses are of use to no one, if a corporation's leaders opt to assume greater social responsibilities, it is sensible for them to ask how they can do so while remaining profitable. It is also understandable for executives to ask why they should personally risk engaging in nonbusiness social activities, given that few business leaders who have attempted to do so in the past have succeeded in the long run. And if executives do choose to engage in enlightened business practices, will they put themselves at a disadvantage against competitors who do not? Roughly a century after Francesco Datini's death, his fellow Tuscan, Niccolò Machiavelli, offered these realistic words of caution to political leaders inclined toward idealistic acts of virtue: "how we live is so far removed from how we ought to live, that he who abandons what is done for what ought to be done will rather learn to bring about his own ruin than preservation. A man who wishes to make a profession of goodness in everything must necessarily come to grief among so many who are not good."[27]

The uber-realist Machiavelli could just as well have been advising today's business leaders. In the modern business context, his point becomes: Can ethical business leaders succeed if their competitors behave unethically? Will investors look kindly on companies in which executives address social problems? Or, to offer a specific example: Can retail businesses offering health care benefits to employees successfully compete against companies like Walmart that do not? And if business leaders are bent on virtue, how are they to know if their actions will be welcomed as increasing the general welfare, or reviled as paternalistic? There is also the overarching philosophical question of whether it is possible for virtuous business managers to align their ethical principles with their self-interest (or the self-interest of their shareholders). In Robert Bolt's play *A Man for All Seasons*, the character Sir Thomas More observes, "If we lived in a State where virtue was profitable, common sense would make us good, and greed would make us saintly." Clearly, business leaders need to consider whether More and Machiavelli were correct in concluding that moral men and women are doomed to fail in an amoral, if not immoral, world.

Or is that view too cynical? To answer that question, one would need to find examples of ethically principled leaders who succeeded in the rough-and-tumble world of competing interests. For example, John Bunn, a Whig political ally of the young Abraham Lincoln, was convinced that the Great Emancipator was both a principled and an effective politician: "Lincoln's entire career proves that it is quite possible for a man to be adroit and skillful and effective in politics, without in any degree sacrificing moral principles."[28] And that great admirer of Lincoln, Theodore Roosevelt—who realistically understood the limits to what imperfect individuals can accomplish in an imperfect world—nonetheless believed business leaders like Andrew Carnegie could make a difference for the better, at least in those arenas over which they had some control (their businesses). Which brings us to the purpose of the stories we are about to review: Do the experiences of past business leaders support the contentions of the realists or idealists? My guess is that readers will find that the historical record tempers the arguments of both.

"Difficile Est Bonum Esse"

THE EXPERIENCES OF THE enlightened capitalists confirm one of the oldest truths: "Difficile est bonum esse." It is, indeed, hard to be good, as an adviser to the notoriously corrupt fifteenth-century papal curia once observed.[29] It is even harder to *do* good, as the virtuous business leaders profiled in these pages each discovered. The question then becomes, Will it be easier in the future? To gain a broad, practical perspective on that current question, we will examine it through the prism of the past.

Readers will note that this book is divided into three sections. Part 1 deals with the daring individuals who pioneered enlightened capitalism between 1815 and 1970; part 2 describes the efforts of corporate leaders in the period between 1970 and 1990, a time when many thought socially responsible corporate behavior was destined to become the norm; and part 3 summarizes the lessons that can be drawn from the stories of the enlightened capitalists, assesses the current state of business virtue, and offers a speculative perspective on what might be expected from corporate leaders in the coming decade.

In essence, the book is intended as a dialogue between the past and the present about the future, while keeping in mind that lessons drawn from history are inherently limited guides to what is to come.[30] As historian Kate Maltby cautions, historical perspectives, at best, "point us to new ways of thinking, or new questions to ask, rather than providing easy answers."[31] And often they point to important old questions that have remained unresolved and thus need to be raised anew. For example, in 2002 the editors of the *Harvard Business Review* wrote, "It's time—again—to ask ourselves the most fundamental question," specifically the one posed by business philosopher Charles Handy: What's a business for?[32] That question had first been raised by British businessman Robert Owen nearly two hundred years earlier. As we see in the next chapter, Owen's answer shocked the economic, political, and intellectual leaders of his time. Indeed, it is a question all the enlightened capitalists who would follow Owen attempted to answer.

PART I

THE PIONEERS

1

The First Business Reformer

ROBERT OWEN (1771–1858)

In 1742, shortly after large-scale manufacturing began in the mid-eighteenth century, the Lombe brothers established a giant mill in England. Daniel Defoe, author of *Robinson Crusoe*, described the incredible interior of that vast six-story building, with its "26,586 Wheels and 97,746 Movements, which work 73,726 Yards of Silk-Thread every time the Water-Wheel goes round, which is three times in one minute." Defoe failed to mention that the children who worked in such mills "tended the machines round the clock for twelve to fourteen hours at a turn . . . [and] were boarded in shifts in barracks where, it was said, the beds were always warm."[1] Those children were as young as five years of age, but in the eighteenth century that was more likely to be considered a sign of progress than exploitation. Writing to the US Congress in 1789 about the economic advantages of British textile mills, Secretary of the Treasury Alexander Hamilton proposed the enactment of policies to encourage the construction of large manufacturing facilities in America. In addition to the material wealth created by industrial factories in Britain, Hamilton cited the advantage of "employment of persons who otherwise would be idle and, in many cases, a burden on the community. . . . It is worthy of particular remark that, in general, women and children are rendered more useful, and the latter more early useful, by manufacturing establishments, than would otherwise be. Of the number of persons employed in the cotton manufactures of Great Britain, it is computed that four-sevenths, nearly, are women and children, and many of them of a tender age."

To spur American economic growth and military security, Hamilton thus advocated the establishment of William Blake's "dark, satanic mills" in America—and was more than willing to pay the price in terms of child labor. When the ever-economizing Hamilton saw young American children playing on their parents' farms, he saw underutilized factors of production who could be employed more "usefully." In distinction, his lifelong rival, humanist Thomas Jefferson, saw such children as potentially virtuous, self-sufficient citizens in need of an education to prepare them for democratic participation in their communities. By and large, Hamilton's view would prevail in America and Britain over the subsequent century.

Britain, circa 1800

The mid-eighteenth-century introduction of such laborsaving devices as James Hargreaves's spinning jenny, Richard Arkwright's water frame, and Samuel Crompton's spinning mule greatly reduced the time it took to spin thread from cotton and to make it into cloth, functions previously performed at home by women using distaffs and spindles and, later, spinning wheels. By 1800, cotton cloth would be more efficiently mass-produced in gigantic mills far larger even than the one Defoe had described six decades earlier. The effect of industrialization on Britain's economic and social order was staggering. By 1816, machines were spinning cotton, wool, flax, and silk into thread and turning out millions of yards of cloth annually. The productivity of those mills created vast wealth for their owners and for the British nation. In that year, it was estimated that the machines in one enormous mill produced the labor equivalent of eight million women spinning at home. John Quincy Adams, while a member of the House of Representatives, estimated that, during the War of 1812, machines in Britain had produced the equivalent of the labor of two hundred million people. A dozen years later, another member of Congress calculated that, even if such estimates were inflated by a factor of two, "every British workman, on the average, has but *forty* inorganic slaves to help him."[2] Consider the numbers: in 1769, Britain had exported only about £212,000 worth of cotton goods per year; in 1829, over £37 million was exported. New, efficient methods also were developed for making iron and steel, and steam-driven machines were substituted for animal and human power in other industries as well. The net effect of the Industrial Revolution was to transform Britain into the wealthiest and most militarily powerful nation on the globe.

It is thus easy to understand why Hamilton's view of British industrialism had been so benign: he wanted America to have the mother country's wealth and power. What he failed to anticipate were two terrible consequences of the Industrial Revolution: the growth of large cities and the creation of slums within them. As British workers left the farmlands where their forefathers had toiled for generations, they made their way to cities such as Manchester, where jobs awaited them in the new mills. In the early 1840s German expatriate Friedrich Engels (Karl Marx's co-author, friend, and patron) managed a cotton mill in Manchester owned by his father, where he observed what he and Marx would later call the "immiseration" of the men, women, and children who labored in factories like his father's. In his classic 1845 analysis *The Condition of the Working Class in England*, Engels meticulously documented how Manchester's mill workers and their families lived, often six to ten huddled in one small, filthy, unsanitary, unheated room without the benefit of running water. Most wore rags, many suffered from tuberculosis, all breathed foul air and endured the stench of open sewers. They were paid subsistence wages on which they could afford only meager meals of bread, the occasional piece of mutton, and a mug of cheap gin. The little food they had was often as contaminated as the water they drank. In the mills, men and women labored twelve hours a day under horrendous conditions alongside children, often "of a tender age." Those children—typically orphans living in workhouses—slept on straw and, like cattle, were fed from troughs. Engels noted with disapproval that such conditions existed at the very time Britain was experiencing the greatest increase in wealth, and the largest outpouring of scientific advancement and technological invention, in the history of the human race.

Enter Robert Owen

Thirteen years after Hamilton issued his report to Congress, and forty years before Engels wrote his own report drawing quite different conclusions, a British industrialist with a Jeffersonian philosophical bent observed the terrible conditions in Manchester's mills and then asked himself how he could make manufacturing pay without dooming his workers to misery and degradation.[3] That manufacturer, Robert Owen, famously succeeded in doing just that between 1800 and 1824. Yet despite his example, over the next century only a handful of industrialists in Britain and America saw fit to adopt Owen's practices—in effect turning their backs on methods manifestly more profitable and more virtuous than their own. In exploring the mystery of why they chose to act as they did, we discover that in numerous ways the last two hundred years of business history reads like a sequel to the puzzling story of Robert Owen's New Lanark textile mills.

Among the business leaders profiled in these pages, none has been written about more than Robert Owen.[4] Yet despite all the ink devoted to analyzing his beliefs and actions, no consensus has emerged on how history should evaluate his significant, albeit odd, career. To some observers he was a thoughtful, benevolent, farsighted manager and thinker whose pioneering reforms at the New Lanark mills addressed the worst by-products of the Industrial Revolution, thus demonstrating that capitalism need not be exploitative. Yet to Marx and Engels, Owen was a profit-mongering capitalist who exploited his own workforce. To others, he was an insane, utopian socialist dedicated to the abolition of capitalism, a radical free thinker hell-bent on the destruction of traditional societies, and a dotty, impractical do-gooder in the mode of Dickens's Mrs. Jellyby. To his admirers he was an infidel, to his critics a prophet. The British historian and politician Thomas Macaulay described Owen as "a gentle bore" from whom he "fled at the first sound of his discourse," but prominent scientists, philosophers, monarchs, and presidents considered him a valued friend. Especially, he was much loved by those who knew him best: the workers and schoolchildren of New Lanark.[5] He was, in short, a most unusual man.

Owen was born in Wales in 1771, the sixth of seven children in a lower-middle-class family that, unusually for the era, had the wherewithal to send Robert and his siblings to the village school. Owen's first four years of childhood were passed at home with his loving family (at roughly the time Adam Smith was furiously penning *The Wealth of Nations* in Edinburgh). Beginning at age five, Owen attended the school taught by a certain Mr. Thickness, whose improbable Dickensian name was an accurate description of his mental capabilities. Despite schoolmaster Thickness's shortcomings, Owen proved himself to be something of a prodigy, learning to read, write, and do arithmetic sums by the time he was seven. As incompetent as Thickness was, he nonetheless was capable of recognizing talent, and thus enlisted Owen—before the latter was eight years old—to serve as his assistant teacher, instructing younger children in the three Rs. Over the next two years, Owen "acquired the itch to learn and still more the itch to teach." In his own words, "I thus acquired the habit of teaching others what I knew," a habit that would serve him for both good and ill in his subsequent career.[6] Socially awkward, he compensated by mastering the art of dancing, a "habit" he acquired at age seven.

At age nine, realizing he had no more to learn from Thickness, Owen dropped out of school to work in a draper's shop. At ten, he borrowed forty shillings from his father—the last financial support he would re-ceive from his parents—and set off to London to make his fortune. But after only six weeks at his brother's home in the British capital, he again was off by carriage, this time to Stamford, a small town in Lincolnshire where he apprenticed himself for three years to Mr. McGuffog, a lace maker with another marvelously Dickensian moniker. Many years later, Owen wrote that he had been "fortunate in obtaining such a man for my first master," for McGuffog was "thoroughly honest, and a good man of business—very methodical, kind, liberal and much respected by his neighbors and customers."[7] From his experience working for McGuffog, Owen concluded that ethical business practices could cre-ate satisfied customers, and treating employees well could foster a pro-ductive, loyal workforce. Indeed, as a young employee, Robert Owen was exceptionally well looked after by McGuffog, who allowed his ap-prentice to spend as many as five hours a day reading in his extensive library.

At the end of the apprenticeship, Owen returned to London, where he went to work as an assistant in a drapery house. There the thirteen-year-old worked long hours, often from eight in the morning until two a.m., seven days a week (on Sundays there was a welcome break for a good dinner, the only meal during the week Owen didn't take while standing and working). At fifteen he decided he'd had enough of such treatment—in that era, not only factory workers labored un-der bad conditions—so he quit and moved to Manchester, where for the next three years he worked in decent circumstances for a success-ful draper. There, Owen's workday was short enough to allow him to continue his self-education, and he used the spare time to read widely, if not deeply. Manchester was then, along with London and Edinburgh, a prime center of Enlightenment thinking. During the seventeenth and eighteenth centuries Europe had given birth to that intellectual movement predicated on the assumption that humans could find knowledge and happiness—and advance civilization—

through the application of reason. Two luminaires of the Enlightenment, John Locke and Jean-Jacques Rousseau, reasoned that, because existing political, social, and economic constructs had been created by humans, ergo, humans had the power to change them. As Rousseau famously argued in *The Social Contract*, God did not create social classes, nor were those in the lowest classes inherently inferior to their "betters" (contrary to what aristocrats and popes had long claimed). Hence, the fact that most extremely poor people at the time didn't bathe, couldn't read, lived in hovels, and demonstrated little ambition was due not to their nature but their nurture, to use the modern lexicon. Locke's and Rousseau's writings encouraged subsequent generations of men and women to attempt to change the unjust structure of society through either reform or revolution. Those ideas were in the smoky air of late-eighteenth-century Manchester, and Robert Owen absorbed them.

But Owen's mind at the time was more attuned to business than philosophy. On the job, he quickly mastered most aspects of business from bookkeeping to the ins and outs of the fabric trade. Manchester in 1789 was the Silicon Valley of its time, and Owen found himself at the innovative center of the Industrial Revolution. Not surprisingly, he wanted to play a part in the exhilarating technological and business changes going on around him. By the time he was eighteen, he was junior partner in a firm that manufactured the latest technologies of the era—such as Arkwright's water frame, Hargreaves's spinning jenny, Crompton's mule, and Edmund Cartwright's power loom—all used in the production of high-quality cotton cloth. He soon went off on his own and established himself as a successful self-employed businessman. But he was ambitious, and when he read a notice soliciting applicants for the post of factory manager at a large mill, he applied. He went in person to meet the mill's owner, a wealthy merchant and manufacturer named Drinkwater. Taking one look at Owen, Drinkwater curtly said, "You are too young." Owen explained that he might look young for his age, but he had years of business experience. Drinkwater then asked, "How often do you get drunk in the week?" Owen indignantly replied, "I was never drunk in my life." That apparently impressed Drinkwater, who asked what salary Owen was looking for, as recounted by the latter's eldest son, Robert Dale Owen:

> "Three hundred a year" [around $200,000 in today's dollars].
> "Three hundred a year! Why, I've had I don't know how many others after the place here, this morning; and all their askings together wouldn't come up to what you want."
> "Whatever others may ask, I cannot take less. I am making three hundred a year by my own business."
> "Can you prove that to me?"
> "Certainly. My books will show."[8]

Owen got the job, and within a year he had turned Drinkwater's underperforming mill into a highly profitable enterprise employing five hundred workers.

About that time, Owen joined the prestigious Manchester Literary and Philosophical Society, where he became friends with the chemist John Dalton (originator of atomic theory), the poet Samuel Taylor Coleridge, and the American inventor Robert Fulton. (Owen briefly shared quarters with Fulton, who borrowed £160 from him to finance his fledgling "steamboat project." Fulton later repaid Owen £100, then neglected to remit the remainder.) Based on how Owen conducted himself in debates with the great minds of the society, they dubbed him "the reasoning machine."[9] He delivered at least one well-received learned paper there, which indicates that these distinguished men accepted him as their social and intellectual equal. His extensive reading had thus equipped him not only with a sound education but with social mobility unusual for that era. He was now widely accepted as "a gentleman."

The New Lanark Mills

Among other gentlemen in Manchester at that time were many who were growing rich thanks to booming industrialization. Those with money to spare were eager to invest in promising business ventures. Thus, when the twenty-seven-year-old Owen heard of a large, unprofitable mill for sale in New Lanark, Scotland, he had little trouble raising the capital to buy it. Nonetheless, the mills' owner, David Dale, could not believe such a young manager had the wherewithal to make a major financial investment of £60,000 (perhaps $60 million now). Furthermore, the cheeky lad had the temerity to ask Dale not only to sell him the mills but, in the next breath, also for the hand of his daughter, Caroline, in marriage. Dale was not amused. He was a wealthy, socially well positioned Scottish Presbyterian of the strictest Calvinist sect, and no lover of the English (or the Welsh, for that matter). In addition, he was a rabid Tory who believed poverty was the consequence of working-class vice and sloth. He saw in Owen a moderately well-off social upstart, a Welsh deist who, although not active politically at that time, had evident Whig leanings. It had taken Dale little time to discover that the core of Owen's social and political philosophy was his conviction that Britain's social and economic structure needed to be changed, and all the prayers and sermons advocated by all the Dales of the world would not help a bit. Finding Owen an improper match for either his mills or his daughter, Dale rejected both of the young man's proposals.

Ah, but money has a way of overcoming seemingly immovable obstacles. Dale was in such deep financial debt that, much to the surprise of Owen and his financial backers, when he learned that the £60,000 offer for the mills was real, he made a quick about-face and accepted it. (Owen's personal capital contribution was only £3,000.) Owen then spent time getting to know Dale, and the latter surprised himself by growing not only to like the former but also willing to let him marry his daughter. A cynic might conclude that Robert Owen then simultaneously relieved David Dale of two sources of continuing financial drain.

In January 1800 Robert Owen took possession of the New Lanark mills and the company town in which they were situated on the falls of the river Clyde, a day's carriage ride from either Edinburgh or Glasgow. While David Dale had a well-deserved reputation for being a kind and good man, Owen found little evidence of such benevolence when, for the first time, he toured his new possessions. What he found was a village in which drunkenness was strife, theft common, and fighting in the streets a regular occurrence. According to Owen, "They were a very wretched society: every man did that which was right in his own eyes, and vice and immorality prevailed to a monstrous extent. The population lived in idleness, in poverty, in almost every kind of crime; consequently, in debt, out of health, and in misery."[10]

The workers' homes, the village streets, and the water-powered mills themselves were disgustingly filthy. Of the 1,700 people then living in New Lanark, about 400 were pauper children who had been assigned to work there by public agencies seeking to free themselves of the burden of feeding and housing them.[11] The well-intentioned Dale had believed he was doing the children—"foundlings" like Oliver Twist—a favor by getting them out of overcrowded almshouses where they likely would have been abused and underfed. Hence, children as young as six found themselves employed in the New Lanark mills, where they stood at their tasks for eleven hours a day in eighty-degree heat, all the while breathing unhealthy cotton dust.[12]

Owen was appalled by the conditions in both the village and the mills, but he did not blame Dale for what he found. His father-in-law had been an absentee owner, leaving management of New Lanark in the hands of others. Initially, Owen attempted to work with those managers, trying to convince them of the need for reform. He quickly learned that the old guard had no interest in changing their methods, so he relieved them of their duties and began to institute a series of reforms. His first actions at New Lanark were to end the practice of hiring pauper apprentices, and to cease employing child labor, in general. Instead, he placed all the village preteens in a school that he provided. At the same time, he took actions to remove filth from the village and mills, ordering the streets to be swept daily and the garbage neatly piled, collected, and properly disposed of. He "debugged" the pestilence-ridden community, paved its streets, and constructed a second story on workers' homes to reduce overcrowding. Almost from the day he arrived in New Lanark, Owen seems to have been resolved to create a model mill town where workers and their families would be provided with clean, decent housing in a community free of controllable disease, crime, and gin shops. Schooling was at the top of his reform agenda. He built a new schoolhouse, a spacious, well-heated and -lighted building that even by today's standards is an inviting learning environment (it still stands as a museum). There he invented preschool, day school, and a progressive philosophy of education based on making learning a pleasurable experience (the school may have been the first in Britain to abolish "the rod"). He also started the world's first adult night school.

In the mills themselves, workers would come to enjoy relatively short working hours, a grievance procedure, guaranteed employment during economic downturns, and contributory health, disability, and retirement plans—all unprecedented and, for all intents and purposes, unimaginable at the time. He made certain the mills were well ventilated in summer and heated in winter, and that not a speck of cotton was to be found on the factory floors. Although Owen was resident manager of the mills, his absentee senior partners did not grant him free rein in its "government." As Owen wrote many years later, "I say government for my intention was not to be a mere manager of cotton mills, as such mills at this time generally [were] managed, but to . . . change the conditions of the people who, I saw, were surrounded by circumstances having an injurious influence upon the character of the entire population of New Lanark."[13] Unfortunately, Owen's partners had other ideas: they had bought the mills to make a handsome profit, not to conduct a social experiment. Thus, from 1800 to 1809, Owen was forced to introduce reforms slowly, quietly, and without seeming to challenge accepted practices of the era: "The changes were to be made gradually, and to be effected by the profits of the establishment."[14]

From a twenty-first-century perspective, it is surprising to learn that Owen's employees also resisted his efforts to improve their working and living conditions. As he introduced new laborsaving machinery, the workers interpreted his actions as a traditional manufacturing speedup despite the fact that he reduced their working hours while keeping their pay at previous levels. According to Owen, the untrusting workers "were systematically opposed to every change which I proposed, and did whatever they could to frustrate my object."[15] Determined to improve a system he described as "wretchedly bad," Owen set out to win the trust of his workforce: "I therefor sought out the individuals who had the most influence among them from their natural powers or position, and to those I took great pains to explain my intentions for the changes I wished to effect. . . . By these means I began slowly to make an impression upon the least prejudiced and most reasonable among them; but the suspicions of the majority, that I only wanted to squeeze as much gain out of them as possible, were long continued."[16]

The workers were finally won over in 1806, when an American-imposed trade embargo on British goods led to the closing of mills throughout Britain. Owen's partners insisted that the New Lanark mills also shut down for the duration of the embargo. He agreed on the condition that all workers were retained and paid to keep the factory's machinery in good working condition until business conditions improved. During that four-month period, New Lanark's workers were paid a total of £7,000, the equivalent of several million dollars today.[17]

A Force of Nurture

In the several books he wrote, Owen outlined the philosophy that influ-enced all his actions at New Lanark, the core of which was what today would be called human development. "Man's character is made for, not by him," he wrote, believing that character is formed by way of nurture and not nature—that is, by education and opportunity. He believed a primary purpose of his mills was not simply to make cloth and money but to form the characters of the men and women who worked in them by providing an environment in which, because their bodies and minds were cared for, their better natures would be encouraged to grow.[18] He believed it wrong to blame the poor for the miserable lives they led; in-stead, he argued, it was better to provide them with an environment in which they could become industrious, prosperous, virtuous, and happy.[19] And better not only for the workers but also for the mills' owners, and for society in general. In 1816 Owen summarized his philosophy in four essays on "the formation of character": "Any general character, from the best to the worst, from the most ignorant to the most enlightened, may be given to any community, even the world at large, by the application of proper means: which means are to a great extent at the command and under the control of those who have influence in the affairs of men."[20]

In essence, Owen thought the workplace was where the foundation of a just and reasonable social order could be laid. His commitment to human development stemmed from the same Enlightenment-era sources that had inspired Jefferson, forty years earlier, to propose a right to the pursuit of happiness. In granting that right to his workers, Owen also anticipated the modern economic concept of "human cap-ital." A major application of that concept is a calculation of returns on investment in education, along with the overall savings to society, of having a workforce productively employed, as opposed to being on the dole or engaged in crime. As Owen asked his fellow industrialists,

Will you continue to expend large sums of money to procure the best devised mechanism of wood, brass, or iron; to retain it in perfect repair; and to save it from falling into premature decay? Will you also devote years of intense application to understand the connection of the various parts of these lifeless machines, to improve their effective powers? And when you estimate time by minutes, and the money expended for the chance of increased gain by fractions, will you not consider whether a portion of your time and capital would not be more advantageously applied to your living machines?[21]

Although Owen sought to improve the lives of his workers, he was also a practical businessman determined to make the mills profitable. Thus he proceeded with due economic deliberation as he introduced his reforms: "These changes were to be made gradually and to be effected by the profits of the establishment. . . . I found it necessary . . . to make the establishment not only self-supporting, but also productive of sufficient surplus profit to enable me to effect the changes of the improved conditions which I contemplated."[22]

Nonetheless, Owen's partners grew impatient with his investments in the company school and improvements to the lot of its workforce. Owning eight-ninths of the company, they had ultimate control of its purse strings; in 1809, they decided to tighten them. Owen was presented with an ultimatum: either pay out more of the company's earnings to its owners, or buy them out. Owen chose the latter, and his partners walked away having doubled their investment over nine years. Owen immediately entered into a second partnership, which proved as problematic as the first. His new partners soon criticized him for investing too much in peripheral activities they claimed reduced their profits, expressing "disapproval of the mixture of philanthropy and business." They were, as one Owen biographer noted, "men who wanted not merely a moderate return on their money, but the largest return that could be expected in those halcyon days of low wages, high profits, and rapid accumulation of capital."[23] Even though they were making handsome profits, the partners calculated how much more they could be making if Owen would quit mollycoddling workers with benefits no competitors had any intention of matching.

In 1812, when Owen's second group of partners prohibited him from erecting a new school building, he resigned as manager. The partners promptly put the mills up for sale at auction. While they were preparing for the sale, Owen traveled to London, where he formed a third partnership with a group of wealthy Quakers and other prominent churchmen willing to invest in the mills on the understanding they would earn 5 percent interest annually on their capital investments—all profits beyond that would be reinvested in the business and the school. Owen arrived back in Scotland in the midst of protracted bidding for the mills. He then shocked his former partners by offering the winning bid at the auction: an astonishing £114,000. At the same time, it pleased them greatly to have realized a handsome profit on the £84,000 they had invested four years earlier.[24] On his return to New Lanark, he was greeted at the outskirts of town by a parade and band that escorted him home to the cheers and hurrahs of the mills' normally dour Scottish workforce.

Until 1808 Owen and his wife, Caroline, lived in a modest house in New Lanark as their family grew, but the arrival of their seventh child necessitated leasing a larger home in the country about a quarter mile from the mills. Owen's relations with his own children were as affectionate as his interactions with the village children. He seemed to have a natural rapport with all children, and to be more comfortable with them than in the company of adults. Indeed his oldest son, Robert Dale Owen, described him as an affectionate, indulgent father emotionally closer to his children than was their stern mother. The Owens might well have had a perfect family life if it weren't for one topic that, over time, would create great distance between Caroline and Robert: religion. Throughout her life, Caroline Dale Owen would remain a faithful adherent to her father's strict Calvinist beliefs, while her husband would grow more and more adamant in his deism (which to her, and to most of society, was tantamount to atheism). Robert Dale reported a conversation he once had with his mother: "'Pray to God, my child,' she would say, 'that he will turn your dear father's heart from the error of his way and make him pious like your grandfather.' Then, with tears in her eyes, 'O, if he could only be converted, he would be everything my heart could desire; and then when we die he would be in heaven with us all.'"[25]

Over the years, as Owen grew increasingly obsessed with the need to propagate his ideas, he paid less and less attention to his wife. With regard to his relationship with Caroline, historian Margaret Cole wrote, "Owen was not so much neglectful as apt to forget she existed at all."[26] Nonetheless, Caroline Owen supported her husband's reform efforts until the bitter end—and, the end turned bitter, indeed.

In 1813, however, all seemed right with the world as Owen found himself free for the first time to run the mills as he believed they ought to be managed. When he initially arrived in New Lanark, the adult mill workers had been laboring as long as fifteen hours a day, often standing for the entire duration. As time progressed, Owen reduced the workday to ten and three-quarter hours, the lowest in the world at the time. He ended the practice of summary dismissal, and provided job security (the only people he fired were cruel supervisors and chronic drunks). As the company town grew to a population of three thousand, he provided free showers and baths for all, established a credit union, and opened a company store that sold healthy food at a 25 percent discount (although a teetotaler himself, he recognized that his business was, after all, in Scotland, and thus permitted the sale of quality whisky— albeit in wee quantities). Because most of the women in the village worked in the mills, it was difficult for them to prepare good meals for their families, so Owen opened a communal kitchen where everyone was provided with healthy food. He also established a retirement home for aged workers. Farsightedly, Owen built parks for the community, thus becoming a proto-environmentalist and town planner whose efforts to beautify the village anticipated the much later greenbelt and garden city movements in Britain and the United States.

Inside the factory, Owen improved physical conditions and "extinguished government by fear" by prohibiting corporal punishment of workers and retraining their supervisors in the arts of humane disciplinary practices.[27] He believed that education, moral suasion, and peer pressure were more powerful disciplinary tools than physical force. Loathing punishment, Owen sought to establish discipline in the mills by way of his system of "silent monitors." At each worker's station he hung a block of wood painted a different color on each side. Depending on the worker's conduct, the plant superintendent would turn the block to the appropriate color: black for bad, blue for mediocre, yellow for good, and white for excellent. If the worker disagreed with the superintendent's ranking, he or she had the right to appeal to Owen. Significantly there were neither rewards nor punishments attached to the rankings; nonetheless, peer pressure, along with the innate human desire to please, apparently were effective in changing worker behavior. As Owen explained, "At the commencement of this new method of recording character, the great majority were black, many blue, and a few yellow; gradually the black diminished and were succeeded by the blue, and the blue were succeeded by the yellow, and some, but at first very few, were white."[28] This method may strike the modern reader as paternalistic, but we should recall that a large part of the New Lanark workforce consisted of teenage labor.

Owen extended his ethical practices to his other business constituencies, as well: "It was Owen's habitual practice that when he foresaw a fall in the price of yarn [he asked] his customers whether they would not wish any orders which might be in hand to be deferred so that they might take advantage of the lower prices; and in the same way, he would write to his correspondents before a [price] rise, and urge them to buy."[29]

Owen initially sought to win his fellow industrialists over to his practices with appeals to their self-interest. He argued that well-treated workers were not only more productive but, if they also were better paid, would be better customers for the products sold by their employers: "No evil ought to be more dreaded by a master manufacturer than low wages of labor.... [Workers], in consequence of their numbers, are the greatest consumers of all articles, and it will always be found that when wages are high the country prospers; but when they are low all classes suffer from the highest to the lowest, but more particularly the manufacturing interest."[30]

Owen thus anticipated by a hundred years Henry Ford's famous rationale for paying his autoworkers the then-unheard-of sum of $5 a day: it gave them the wherewithal to buy his and other manufactured goods.

So unusual were Owen's methods, and so great the profits reaped, that the story of New Lanark was met with near-universal disbelief. At the time, the conventional wisdom was that it was impossible to do good *and* earn a profit. That apparent conundrum drew twenty thousand visitors to New Lanark between 1815 and 1824 to see for themselves how Owen turned the trick. Among those who signed the mills' guest book were leading politicians and industrialists from Britain, America, and the Continent, including the future czar of Russia. For a while, Owen's work was admired by the British aristocracy and nobility, who disdained the rising class of "uncouth" manufacturers—that is, Owen's competitors, who viewed him as their bête noir (illustrating the truth of the adage "the enemy of my enemy is my friend"). The Duke of Kent, Queen Victoria's father, was Owen's greatest champion, having become convinced by what he observed at New Lanark that capitalism should, and could, be humanized. Owen's ideas gained further traction with the founding of the *Economist* in 1821, which was first published as an Owenite newspaper.[31] The mills' fame spread so widely that Owen was certain other industrialists would follow his example, and thus the long era of mass poverty would end in general prosperity. He asked: "What then remains to prevent such a system from being immediately adopted into national practice? Nothing, surely, but a general distribution of the knowledge of the practice."[32]

Owen's Critics

When Owen wrote those words in his forties, everything he could foresee pointed to the dawning of a new age of humane and effective industrial practices. Indeed, had he then continued to concentrate his efforts on running the mills, it seems possible that the practices he pioneered might have been adopted by at least a few other industrialists. But his optimism proved misplaced, and the outcome he so desired was not to be. Instead of diffusion of the knowledge he created, he was met with a barrage of criticism from left and right and, ultimately, near total public rejection. Owen was attacked as a socialist by his fellow industrialists, on the grounds that he broke two sacred laws of economics: profit maximization and the iron law of wages. Nonetheless, he was, in fact, a believer in Adam Smith's free market, arguing, "The natural course of trade, manufactures and commerce should not be disturbed except when it interferes with measures affecting the well-being of the whole community."[33] Acting on that belief, he twice led the efforts of British industrial free-traders to put an end to mercantilist tariffs. And as far as business management was concerned, a prominent historian who examined the New Lanark mills' records concluded, "Owen was an extraordinarily good organizer and businessman; and he made of his mills a model of business efficiency."[34] Under Owen's management, the New Lanark mills earned a reputation for producing the highest-quality goods on the market, and as Owen practiced what came to be called "the economy of high wages," his workers became more and more productive, and the mills ever more profitable. The record shows they may have become the most profitable mills in Britain. The most famous of Owen's partners, utilitarian philosopher Jeremy Bentham (much admired by today's libertarians), called the New Lanark venture his "only successful investment." In all, Owen seems personally to have accumulated a fortune of at least £60,000 over the quarter century he managed it. But those facts didn't stop critics who claimed that the quirky and often self-absorbed Owen "hardly cared a rap whether he made money or not."[35]

In fact, Owen's fellow industrialists actually despised him for publicly challenging them to follow his lead, for showing them up by having a more profitable business than their own, and for criticizing the way they treated their workers. By all accounts, Owen was a courteous man with a gentle disposition—yet he was supremely confident that his beliefs were correct and that those who disagreed with him were ill-informed. Thus, when challenged, he would repeat his arguments slowly and clearly until his interlocutors "saw the light" and accepted them. That approach worked well with New Lanark's children, but his fellow industrialists found it patronizing.

During the first fifteen years of his New Lanark reforms, Owen had kept a relatively low public profile. But as word of his efforts spread, and important political figures increasingly took notice of what he was doing, he became more and more evangelical about the need for industrial reform. He might have been more successful in that endeavor had he limited his appeals to his fellow industrialists' self-interest, stressing that the New Lanark mills' enormous profits of some £15,000 annually were due to its readily replicable practices. Instead, Owen ill-advisedly made a well-publicized tour in 1816 to examine the working conditions in British factories, where he documented that children as young as five were working twelve- to fourteen-hour days in sordid conditions. He then made his manufacturer peers look bad by publishing those findings. By thus going public, Owen built resistance among the very men he hoped to convert to his way of thinking. Even an Owen admirer had to admit he was a "political lunatic."[36] His actions led his business peers to make outrageous claims: the inordinate success of Owen's mills was the by-product of the unique air at New Lanark; the mills were productive thanks to the unusual Scottish work ethic; and it was impossible to replicate the Lanark plant site.

When it became clear that his fellow industrialists had no intention of adopting his methods, Owen grew frustrated and turned to Parliament in a badly managed attempt to win legislation designed to end the use of child labor. Had the bill passed, it would have banned employment of children younger than ten, provided thirty minutes of education each day for workers under the age of eighteen, abolished night shifts for all children, shortened their workdays to ten and a half hours, and been enforced by government inspectors in factories. That prospect so alarmed Britain's industrialists that they fired back with their own parliamentary lobbying, claiming that there was a lack of scientific evidence that it was injurious for children to work night shifts, stand for twelve hours a day at their tasks, eat their meals while standing, go out into the cold night thinly clad after laboring all day in a hot factory, and continually breathe air heavy with cotton fluff. They prevailed in getting the bill scuttled.

Although he failed to win support for his reforms among industrialists, Owen continued to make farsighted changes at New Lanark. Between 1816 and 1824, he greatly improved working conditions in the mills, increased medical care for workers and their families, and expanded educational opportunities. If anything, Owen's educational reforms were more progressive (even radical) than his industrial ones. In the early nineteenth century, the majority of Britons were illiterate, education a privilege largely enjoyed by the aristocracy and professional classes. Moreover, one historian argued that "the overwhelming majority of manufacturers resisted every attempt to educate [the working class], not merely because their fortunes were built on child labor, but on the deliberate ground that educated workers would be less docile."[37] Owen completely disagreed, believing that character could be molded, and that children were the clay of human development. He doted on the children of New Lanark, lavishing on them the benefits and attention he felt they needed and deserved in order to grow into healthy, civilized adults. He enrolled all New Lanark's children under the age of twelve (starting at age one) in the school formally known as "The Institute for the Formation of Character." He had colorful maps, paintings of animals, and other instructional materials made for use

in the school, such as an engaging poster depicting competitions between General Noun, Colonel Adjective, and Corporal Adverb. All the
children—boys and girls—were dressed in clean, lightweight classical tunics that kept them cool in summer and comfortable when the
schoolhouse was heated in winter. When they performed Highland
dances, they were costumed in tartans, the boys clad in kilts. The children were neither punished nor rewarded for how they fared in their
lessons; instead, they were left to discover that learning is its own reward. All the children were instructed in reading, writing, arithmetic,
history, and geography—and, unprecedented in that era, also in drawing, painting, music, and especially dance.

Owen loved dancing, encouraging not only New Lanark's children but their parents as well to participate in his favorite pastime.
This harmless eccentricity was used against him by some of his fellow
manufacturers, who found a few disgruntled New Lanark employees willing to state publicly that Owen was a paternalistic tyrant in
the guise of a benefactor, an employer who, according to one worker,
"had got a number of dancing-masters, a fiddler, a band of music; that
there were drills and exercises, and that [workers] were dancing together till they were more fatigued than if they were working." Thus,
Owen stood accused of abusing his workers by the inhumane method
of excessive dancing![38]

In 1822 the pious members of Owen's third partnership decided
they could no longer support a school in which religion was not taught;
thus, they demanded that New Lanark's children be instructed in the
scriptures. They also called for an end to dancing and singing (except
"psalmody"), and insisted that the boys wear trousers, and the girls,
long, heavy dresses. When the matter came to a crisis in 1824, Owen
lost managerial control of the mills. For all intents and purposes, his
great New Lanark experiment then came to a whimpering end. Although Owen retained a minority financial interest in the mills until
1828, by then his partners had undone his reforms and reintroduced
most of the accepted industrial practices of the era. In a matter of time,

the mills were once again as unprofitable as they had been when Owen first arrived in New Lanark.

As if that weren't enough, Owen's critics on the left were claiming that his reforms were intended to divert the working class from achieving broader political aims. When he advocated a public works program for the chronically unemployed, radicals called his proposed worksites "a community of slaves." Labor leaders sought to dismiss his reforms as mere paternalistic salve intended to preserve the status quo, one claiming that New Lanark was "really a capitalist enterprise with an infusion of business ethics and paternalism," which, in many ways, it was.[39] Years later, Marx and Engels attacked Owen for being a bourgeois capitalist who "acted with great injustice towards the proletariat." Indeed, Owen was opposed to communistic "class struggles" and to the state ownership of the means of production. He felt that proletarian revolutions were not only morally wrong but unnecessary because societies had the power to enact progressive legislation that would end the growing antagonism between labor and capital. Engels countered that Owen profited to the tune of some $6 million during his time at New Lanark, which was true, arguing that the sum had been "expropriated" from the workers, which was false. Believing private property to be theft, Engels damned Owen for doing what capitalists had damned him for not doing: getting rich. Never mind that Engels himself was a wealthy capitalist who managed British mills owned by his German father.[40]

Marx and Engels doubtless were right to fear the spread of Owenism. With great prescience, Owen repeatedly warned his fellow industrialists that if they failed to reform, they would fuel nascent movements in Europe calling for proletarian revolutions. He predicted that if those radical movements ever were to succeed, their leaders would become tyrants. Alas, Europe's capitalists failed to embrace Owen's benign prescriptions for reform, thus allowing social conditions to fester to the point where, as he predicted, they eventually led to calls for Marxist revolutions.

A Sad, Bad End

Finding himself under attack on all fronts, a despairing Owen abandoned all hope that his fellow industrialists could be convinced to follow his lead, reluctantly accepting the fact the industrial reforms he sought would not occur in Britain during his lifetime: "I thought previous to experience, that the simple, plain, honest enunciation of truth, and its beautiful application to all the real business of life, would attract the attention and engage the warm interest of all parties; and that the reformation of the population of the world would be comparatively an easy task. But as I advanced I found superstitions and mistaken self interest . . . deeply rooted and ramified throughout society."[41]

As opposition to his ideas grew over time, Owen became increasingly rigid in his thinking, unwilling to accept the smallest of compromises, ultimately refusing to accept reform in stages. He lost the support of the aristocracy—his last remaining advocates—when he blamed the ills of society on organized religion and became an outspoken champion of feminism, divorce, birth control, a graduated property tax, and universal suffrage—in an era when those causes were utterly unthinkable to the vast majority of British subjects. By the mid-1820s, he had turned away from industrial reform to champion the establishment of utopian, self-sufficient communities in which Britain's countless unemployed would find useful work. Abandoning all elements of practicality in his schemes, he wholly embraced the ethereal realm of idealism by offering detailed plans for "villages of co-operation" in which five thousand people, their homes neatly arranged in parallelograms, would work communally and share equally in the fruits of their labor. Such impractical schemes only invited ridicule. As one critic famously wrote, Owen was "for establishing *communities* of paupers! . . . Wonderful peace, happiness, and national benefit are to be the result. How little matters of black eyes, bloody noses, and pulling of caps are to be *settled*, I do not exactly see."[42]

As criticism mounted, Owen grew increasingly deaf to the opinions of others, convinced he alone was possessed of truth. Even one of his greatest admirers, Harriet Martineau, once quipped that he was "not a man to think differently of a book for having read it." His father-in-law, exasperated by Owen's unwillingness to entertain ideas other than his own, once told him "Thou needst to be very right, for thou art very positive."[43] The philosopher R. H. Tawney, who shared Owen's values, nonetheless described him as "an exacting, and at times imperious chief. Modest in manner and intransigent in beliefs, he claimed with a mild, impersonal arrogance, regardless of such trifles as majority votes, the obedience due to the voice of the inspired—or as he would have termed it, rational truth."[44]

Owen's son Robert Dale—who knew his father the most intimately, and whom Owen had trained to be his successor as manager of New Lanark—perhaps offered the fairest and most objective criticisms of the man he loved and respected. Bemoaning the influence of Jeremy Bentham's utilitarian philosophy on his father's thinking, Robert Dale concluded that Owen's "mistakes as a practical reformer" resulted from his conviction that all rationally educated people would be honest, moral, and put the public interest above their own self-interest. He admired his father's predilection to always assume the good in humankind, but he "over-zealously" embraced that notion and "ran to extremes" with it.[45]

After Owen left New Lanark, his countless failures and rejections appear to have totally unhinged him. He adopted more extreme views and offered them, unsolicited, to the likes of Napoleon, Santa Anna, and seven sitting, or former, US presidents. Utterly dejected, in 1824 Owen immigrated to America with his oldest children (tellingly, Caroline stayed put in Scotland, their marriage long since having become meaningless). There, Owen would lose 80 percent of his entire fortune in an unrealistic attempt to create a utopian community in New Harmony, Indiana. Purchasing twenty thousand acres of farmland from a religious sect, he invited all comers to join the commune in 1825; eight hundred did so in the first few months. Believing in the basic goodness of all humans, he failed to screen those to whom he granted plots of land, among whom were, alas, a few rascals, thieves, freeloaders, and others more than willing to cheat and bilk their naive benefactor. New Harmony ceased operating as a community in 1827. One bright spot of Owen's American sojourn was his visit with eighty-year-old Thomas Jefferson at his farm in Monticello, where those two sons of the Enlightenment probably discussed their common faith in the efficacy of education.

Owen's Legacy

Financially ruined and behaving in an increasingly eccentric manner, Owen returned to England in 1828, where he lived to see the rise of the violent anticapitalist sentiment he had feared. Fortunately for America, his son Robert Dale remained behind, where he became a prominent member of Congress best remembered for having introduced the bill in the House of Representatives establishing the Smithsonian Institution. Throughout his life in America, Robert Dale worked for the emancipation of slaves, and ended his distinguished public career as a diplomat representing the United States in Italy.[46]

His father spent the rest of his long life alone and occupied with a series of failed idealistic ventures. At age sixty-three, he helped to launch—and briefly chaired—the Grand National Consolidated Trades Union, a forerunner to the modern British trades union movement. In effect, he joined forces with those who had been vocal critics of his practices at New Lanark. Curiously, he then made the same appeal to industrial workers that he previously had made to their employers: "Men of industry, producers of wealth and knowledge, and all that is truly valuable in society! Unite your powers now to create a wise and righteous state of human existence—a state in which the only contest shall be, who shall produce the greatest amount of happiness for the human race."[47]

Owen soon discovered that British workers were no more prepared than their bosses to create what he called a "New Moral World." Owen and the unionists soon parted company. As Robert Dale noted, his father's greatest legacy was one he never acknowledged: after the failure of New Lanark, a group of Owenites created the cooperative movement in Britain. Although Owen vaguely supported the movement during his dotage, he did not see it as an outgrowth of his philosophy. But in 1877, when Robert Dale learned there were over a thousand cooperatives in Britain, he had "sober second thoughts" leading him to conclude that cooperatives were, in fact, the most practical way to achieve the reforms in society his father had failed to achieve in large investor-owned industries.[48] That legacy continues to this day, as we shall later see.

His dreams unfulfilled, Owen died in 1858 at the age of eighty-seven after a sad last few years in which he ruined what was left of his reputation by turning to the practices of spiritualism and phrenology. One of his earliest biographers concluded that "Owen's good works had been interred even before his bones."[49]

Today, New Lanark is a UNESCO World Heritage site. The mills, company store, workers' houses, and the Owens' modest first home have been restored to how they looked in the early 1820s. A few of the original water-propelled spinning mules have been returned to working order, and the mills now produce a small quantity of Scottish wool for sale to the thousands of tourists who visit New Lanark's idyllic setting on the banks of the river Clyde in what has become a beautiful nature preserve. But long before that happened, Owen had died a defeated man. In Owen's old age, Ralph Waldo Emerson asked him, "Who is your disciple? How many men possessed of your views will remain after you to put them into practice?" Owen answered, sadly, "Not one."[50]

He was right at the time, but were he alive today, he doubtless would be pleased to learn that the practices he pioneered at New Lanark had been adopted, in one form or another, in several successful businesses founded in Britain and America over the next century and a half. Yet as we shall see, over that same long stretch of time most business leaders resisted his enlightened philosophy, for reasons ranging from ideological to practical, Owen's ideas had been rejected in his day. Doubtless, human nature in the form of greed, ego, and honest self-interest played a part. John Stuart Mill (like Owen, a friend and disciple of Jeremy Bentham) wrote his famous treatise *On Liberty* in an effort to explain why the sensible ideas of "eccentrics" like Owen seemed always to be rejected by society. According to Mill, a part of the reason is that most men and women are satisfied with status quo and simply do not desire changes that will discomfit them. Simply put, Mill concluded that the "tyranny of custom" hinders, and in most cases prevents, useful social reforms—even new ideas that would benefit those who most oppose them.

2

Man with a Thousand Partners

JAMES CASH PENNEY (1875–1971)

Samuel Clemens called the post–Civil War era in America "The Gilded Age." It was a time when immense fortunes were made, and virtue went missing in the practice of businesses large and small: robber barons bribed corrupt politicians who granted them vast swaths of public land on which to lay their railway tracks, while the stock-in-trade of small-town businessmen was flimflam, snake oil, and the confidence game. An angry populace took notice. In 1877, wide-scale rioting erupted in protest against the practices of capitalists in the wake of five years of economic depression that caused hundreds of thousands of working-class Americans either to lose their jobs or to see their wages severely diminished.

James Cash Penney was born in 1875 in the midst of that era of excessive greed, venality, and unfettered self-interest, yet over the next nine decades he led a life in opposition to Gilded Age values, his business conduct the antithesis of robber-baron behavior. In several profound (and a few rather strange) ways, the story of James Cash Penney is similar to Robert Owen's—although the sources of their motivation to create morally virtuous businesses differed as night from day. Penney was born into working-class poverty in rural Missouri, his father a minister in the Primitive Baptist Church, a strict Calvinistic sect that prohibited paying its preachers. Hence, little Jimmie Penney and his eleven siblings were forced to work on the family's farm to put bread on the table, a necessity that limited the amount of schooling they received. Penney's father shaped the values Penney would carry with him into his business career, starting at age eight, when young Jimmie demonstrated a natural entrepreneurial aptitude by selling pigs he raised to buy his own clothes. When neighbors complained of porcine odor, his father made him sell the pigs because "you have no right to make money at the expense of others."[1]

A few years later, Jimmie sold watermelons outside the entrance of the local fairgrounds to avoid paying the fee for a concession inside. When his father learned what he had done, he explained to his son that such behavior was unethical. As Penney recalled many years later, "Paw said, 'You were getting trade away from others without paying for the privilege on a par with them. That's unfair dealing.'"[2] From then until he died in 1971, James Cash Penney Jr. would live his life by the Golden Rule. As he put it: "Money is important; but the practice of the golden rule in making money—as in every other aspect of human relations—is the most substantial asset of civilized man."[3]

In his later life, Penney would adopt many of his father's fundamentalist religious beliefs and traditional midwestern social values. Yet by no means could the senior Penney simply have been characterized as "conservative." Throughout his son's youth and adolescence, James Cash Penney Sr. was actively engaged in Democratic Party politics. When the Democrats did not prove progressive enough in representing the interests of small farmers and the working class, Penney Sr. lent his considerable energies to advancing the causes of the left-leaning Populist Party and, later, the People's Party. Although the senior Penney failed to win on the few occasions he ran for public office, his son came to embrace his father's political and economic views with regard to the evils of excessive economic inequality. Throughout Penney Jr.'s life, his beliefs would remain an

unusual admixture of his father's religious conservatism and economic progressivism.

At age fifteen, while still in high school, Penney apprenticed himself
to a local merchant where he soon discovered that he "had a flair for trading."[4] Nonetheless, he resisted the urge to drop out of high school (at that
time only about 5 percent of Americans had diplomas), and went on to
complete a rigorous secondary curriculum that included Latin, history,
literature, algebra, geometry, and rhetoric. He also spent hours reading
the "city story" genre of literature popularized by Horatio Alger, which
emphasized the entrepreneurial opportunity open to all young American men willing to pull themselves up by their bootstraps and turn rags
into riches.[5] Although he was academically qualified to enter the University of Missouri, his family could not afford to send him to college, a fact
he so regretted later in life that he spent months in private study to gain
the higher education he had missed in his youth.

After high school, Penney went to work full-time for $2.27 per
month in Hale's Dry Good Store in Hamilton, Missouri (population
1,800), where he quickly learned the ins and outs of retail trade, eagerly
absorbing lessons about sales, merchandising, purchasing, and bookkeeping that he would build on during the rest of his business life.[6] He
was influenced, in particular, by the ethical philosophy of proprietor
John Hale, who, according to Penney, "had the proper contempt of the
spiritually honest man for the adage Caveat emptor—'Let the buyer be-
ware!'"[7] It was from Hale, Penney recalled, that he learned to apply his
father's religious and social ethics to the world of commerce, adopting
Hale's unswerving dedication to "fair dealing" and customer service:
"Slowly I was acquiring a pattern of moral and ethical values."[8] After
a year on the job, Penney had been promoted and was earning $200 a
year (with the promise of $300 in the near future) when his father, age
fifty-three, died of tuberculosis. Shortly thereafter, Penney himself was
diagnosed with a possible case of the same disease and urged by his
doctor to move to a healthier climate.

The Golden Rule Stores

At the close of the nineteenth century, Penney headed west in search of healthy climes, settling down in booming Denver, where he took a job as a store clerk for $6 a week. But he had higher ambitions, and soon bought a butcher shop/bakery in nearby Longmont, where he went into business for himself. He promptly lost the store (and his life savings) when he refused to pay a weekly bribe of a bottle of whiskey to the buyer for his best commercial customer. It is not clear whether Penney found the bribery or the whiskey more offensive. At any rate, he was broke at age twenty-three. He then went to work for Tom Callahan and Guy Johnson, owners of a chain of six clothing and dry goods stores located in small towns in the Rocky Mountain region. In their employ, Penney displayed his retailing acumen, so proving himself that in 1902 the company's owners offered to make him a partner in a new branch of the business they planned to open in Kemmerer, Wyoming (population 900). The Golden Rule store opened with $6,000 in capitalization—two-thirds of which was contributed by Callahan and Johnson, the remaining $2,000 by Penney (who borrowed $1,500 to make the investment).[9] Amid all that activity, Penney somehow found time to woo and wed Berta Hess, a divorcée a few years older than himself. That marriage—in an era when divorce was rare and considered morally scandalous—revealed a streak of unconventionality Penney would occasionally manifest in his largely conventional life and career.

J. C. and Berta Penney worked side by side, twelve to fourteen hours a day, seven days a week, to make a go of their Golden Rule store. Although Penney had long been living by the principle of the Golden Rule, he did not claim credit for naming the store. In fact, stores all over the West in that era were similarly named because the Golden Rule signified fair dealing to customers who, even if illiterate, had learned that basic moral tenet while attending church. Late in life, Penney wrote of the opening of the first Golden Rule store that "I wish it could be recorded that we had a moment of prayer before we opened the door for business. . . . The fact is we were thinking that morning only of business."[10] He also said he felt guilty about keeping the store open on the Sabbath.[11]

The store operated with a policy of "cash and carry"; that is, no credit was offered, which allowed Penney to keep his prices low for the sheep farmers and coal miners who were his main customers. The store was so successful that Penney and his partners were soon able to finance the opening of two additional small-town Wyoming stores. Nonetheless, the chain wasn't growing fast enough for the increasingly ambitious Penney: in 1907 he bought out his partners for $30,000. He soon opened three more branches in rural Idaho and Utah, creating a chain known as the Golden Rule Syndicate.

Manager Partnerships

Penney did not invent chain stores. Nearly two thousand years earlier a merchant named Los Kass had operated a large number of stores in China, and Mitsui began operating a chain in Japan in 1643. In the United States, the A&P grocery chain had been operating on the East Coast for years before Penney went into business.[12] Penney's unique contribution to chain retailing was his "manager partnership" method for financing and staffing store expansion. The idea came about when Earl Corder Sams, a clerk in Penney's first store, showed such great business potential that Penney made him its manager—thus freeing Penney to open and run a new store. Penney then told Sams that if he accumulated sufficient capital to finance a one-third ownership in yet another new store, Penney would put up the remaining two-thirds—provided Sams trained a successor to manage the first store. When Sams thought about the proposed partnership plan, he asked, "You mean, Mr. Penney, that you are willing to surrender a financial interest in properties that may be valuable?" Penney replied, "I don't look at it that way, Mr. Sams. . . . I will be getting something more valuable: managers who have caught the spirit of partnership." Sams insightfully replied, "What you are planning is an organization that will always be renewing itself from within."[13] From then on, the company would grow organically as each store generated enough capital to allow Penney to launch a new one, and the promise of partnerships became a strong motivational incentive to store managers (and to clerks who yearned to become managers). Years later, Penney wrote, "If I had insisted on keeping personal control of the Penney Company we would still be merely a small chain of stores scattered through the Middle West."[14] Indeed, thanks to the partnerships, the company expanded rapidly:

1908	4 stores and partners	gross sales = $218,000
1910	14 stores and partners	gross sales = $660,000
1916	127 stores and partners	gross sales = $8,428,144
1926	747 stores and partners	gross sales = $115,683,023
1928	1,023 stores and partners	gross sales = $176,700,000

In the early years, Penney often lent money to his managers to finance their one-third partnerships in expansion stores. When later asked why he had been so willing to expand the partnership, and thus dilute his own share of overall company ownership, he explained that "in a business such as ours the premier asset was, not money, not buildings, not land, but men."[15] And the men (for decades they were all males) whom Penney recruited for partnerships were, in the main, doppelgängers of Sams and himself: sons of farmers (or from small towns) and abstemious Christians of "good character," meaning men Penney could trust to enter the partnership based more on handshakes than legal documents. And Penney treated them as true partners. When he proposed that the company build a single warehouse to serve all its stores, his partners balked. On hearing this, a banker told Penney he should compel the partners to accept the idea; after all, Penney was the company's founder and president. Penney answered, "A man can't *compel* his partners. . . . My point is simply that partners are men working as one. . . . It is much more important that the partnership idea be kept intact than that I should make—or force—any point of mine."[16]

The Penney Principles

Penney and his early partners developed a formula that led to success in an industry crowded with competitors (including the mail-order catalog businesses of Sears, Roebuck and Company and Montgomery Ward). To compete against such better-funded national chains, Penney's stores were located in small towns, where rents were low; buying for the chain was centralized; and purchases were made directly from manufacturers, which led to economies of scale and the elimination of wholesale middlemen. The only products offered in Penney's stores were those for which there was clear demand (leading to rapid turnover of inventory), and store overhead was kept to a minimum by such means as an emphasis on frugality in window displays, and the recycling of packaging materials. The company never offered sales, discounts, "loss leaders," or credit (which resulted in predictable cash flow), and its emphasis on "carry" meant saving the expense of delivery of purchases. In particular, having store managers who were partner-owners provided motivation for them to work hard and efficiently. Consequently, the company was able to offer lower prices than both small, locally owned stores and large national chains like Sears, against whom it competed.

Penney believed his company's greatest competitive advantage was its customer service. He told his managers they would succeed to the extent they put themselves in the shoes of customers, counseling them to "study your customers' needs, study your markets, pay attention to your shelves, watch your inventory. If you do, you will learn to estimate your customers' buying habits."[17] Penney believed the highest purpose of a store was to serve customers, which meant providing them with the highest-quality goods at the lowest possible price. When one of his managers reported record profits, Penney investigated only to discover the manager had done so by charging an unusually high markup. Penney called on the man, telling him, "This isn't the way we do things in the Penney Company. We owe to our community the service of merchandise at a fair profit. We can't ever allow ourselves to make too much of a profit." Penney was also a stickler for quality. On a buying trip to New York in the company of several of his partners, he asked for samples of the clothing a manufacturer offered to sell to them. He then shocked the partners by taking the products back to his hotel room to wash, wring out, and let dry before agreeing to buy them. When one of his partners argued that the effort was unnecessary because the seller had guaranteed the colors were fast, Penney replied, "How can I tell my customers that unless I know?"[18]

Penney constantly stressed the value of selective, high-quality buying, handing out signs to his partners that read "Goods Bought Right Are Half Sold."[19] When purchasing children's cotton socks, Penney bought the more expensive of two grades that looked and felt identical to one of his partners, who then asked, "Why didn't you buy at the lower price and save ten cents?" Penney replied, "How then could I tell customers I was offering the best stockings I could buy?"[20] Penney was known to continually repeat pithy phrases he coined to summarize the company's principles in ways his partners would remember them. "Cheap goods are dear at any price" was one of his favorites.[21] His oft-repeated admonition "Respect yourself; respect others; work hard and continuously at some worthwhile thing" was both his philosophical mantra and the advice he offered to young managers.[22]

As early as 1913, Penney codified in a printed doctrine the ethical credo that would become known as the Penney Principles, which he intended as guidelines for the behavior of his partners and employees:

1. To serve the public, as nearly as we can, to its complete satisfaction.
2. To expect from the service we render a fair remuneration and not all the profits the traffic will bear.

3. To do all in our power to pack the customer's dollar full of value, quality and satisfaction.
4. To continue to train ourselves and our Associates so that the service we give will be more and more intelligently performed.
5. To improve constantly the human factor in our business.
6. To reward the men and women of our Organization through participation in what the business produces.
7. To test our every policy, method and act in this wise: "Does it square with what is right and just?"[23]

Penney gave this document life by engaging his partners in long conversations about the difficult ethical question raised by the seventh principle: How does one decide "what is right and just"?[24] He constantly reminded his partners that without customers they could not remain in business; hence, they should look on customers as their "real board of directors." In his words, "Making a customer is more important than making a sale."[25] Penney also made sure the notion of service wasn't idle talk by outlining the social responsibilities store managers had to their host communities:

1. A Penney manager joins in movements that build his town.
2. A Penney manager contributes from the store's funds to those agencies that help his town.
3. A Penney manager registers and votes in his town.
4. A Penney manager guards the reputation and good name of his company and store as zealously as he guards the capital investment entrusted to him.[26]

Those principles anticipated by decades the actions of enlightened leaders who, years later, would commit their companies to helping communities they served. Additionally, Penney found ways to share the wealth the company created with all its employees—not just partners—by adopting such New Lanark–inspired benefits as

paid vacations and sick days, life insurance, job security, profit sharing, and career-long training—most of which would not be offered by
other American companies for decades to come. Penney explained,
of course, that the entire system was based on the Golden Rule.
Nonetheless, in 1912, he acceded to Corder Sams's desire to change
the chain's name from Golden Rule to J. C. Penney after Sams explained that their company lacked a clear identity in the eyes of customers because so many competitors operated under "Golden Rule"
marquees.[27]

Incorporation

At the time of the name change, the fast-growing chain consisted of
thirty-four stores owned in complex arrangements between Penney
and his many partners, with Penney owning between one-third and
two-thirds of each outlet, and some partners owning shares of more
than one store (Sams was partner in ten).[28] That system had been
manageable when there were few partners and stores, but with the
rapid proliferation of outlets it was becoming an accounting night-
mare. With an eye toward further expanding the partnership, the J. C.
Penney Company was incorporated in 1913, with all preferred stock
divided among its partners according to the percentage of their ownership of the entire organization, and dividends paid to them based
on the earnings of the stores they managed (the remaining profits of
the entire corporation were allocated among the partners). All J. C.
Penney shares were held by partners, and in the event any of them
wished to sell their stock, they agreed to sell it back to the company.[29]
The company's articles of incorporation also included a provision
that, before the opening of any additional store, a new partner would
be trained to manage it. It seems the incorporation spurred and facilitated the intended growth: by the end of 1913, there were forty-eight
J. C. Penney stores operating in eight western states.[30]

During the year prior to incorporation, James Cash Penney had been at most a distracted participant in the management of the company, which in late 1910 was doing so well that Penney and Berta decided to travel to Europe for their long-postponed honeymoon. Prior to the trip, Berta was advised to undergo a precautionary tonsillectomy. Sadly, after the operation she developed pneumonia and died, leaving behind two young children. Penney went into deep mourning, suffering depression, if not despair. He withdrew from company affairs for months until he was persuaded by his minister to take his sons (ten and seven years old) on a long voyage to the Holy Land and Europe. The trip was healing for Penney, but the end was nearly disastrous. He and his boys had been booked to return home on the second voyage of the *Titanic* when word reached England that the ship had sunk on its initial sailing. That event appears to have shocked Penney out of his depression.

When Penney finally returned to work, he threw himself into the business of turning a small regional chain into what would soon become America's largest retail business. The company established its headquarters in Salt Lake City, where it would be closer to the banks from which it borrowed funds to fuel its expansion. Corder Sams, a more focused administrator than Penney, began to take an active role in company leadership as it introduced ever more efficient buying, distributing, merchandising, and financial processes. Penney, in turn, accelerated the pace at which he sold his stock to new partners, continually diluting his share of ownership of the company he now called "a profit-sharing co-operative." Increasingly, he concentrated his efforts on manager-partner recruitment and development, explaining that "I wanted to get away from administration and executive detail and concentrate on becoming, so to speak, a fisher of men."[31] He subsequently turned to the task of explicating the company's ethical principles and philosophy of service for the benefit of its next generation of managers, stressing the importance of what he called the "spirit of co-operation": "Co-operation in business means good team work, good team work means efficiency, and efficiency means success. . . . Every man is ready to help his brother manager at any time, and one man's idea or plan for the betterment of the business is the property of every other manager in the chain as soon as its practicality is proved."[32]

In 1914 Penney and Sams opened a purchasing office in New York City, closer to the garment manufacturers who were their prime suppliers. The allure of the big city proved irresistible for most of the company's other top managers as well. They soon relocated to Manhattan, and then it was just a matter of time before the J. C. Penney headquarters officially moved to New York.

In late 1916 the company's partners received a totally unexpected message from their president: "The day is now here when I should retire from the active leadership of this company and yield the presidency to one of my associates. It seems to me it will hurt the spirit of the partnership plan to let the idea grow in the minds of my associates, or in my own mind, that I am indispensable."[33] Thus, in order to demonstrate his faith in his partners, Penney became chairman of the company, and the partners then unanimously selected Corder Sams to succeed him as president. That choice turned out to be a brilliant one: Sams would lead the company through three decades of profitable growth while remaining faithful to Penney's principles.

Penney was just forty-one years old in 1917. But from that time until his death some fifty-four years later, he would play only two major roles in the company bearing his name: from the outset, he was its chief talent developer, and years later he became its public face. Anticipating the role Jack Welch would play at GE in the late 1980s, Penney turned his full attention in 1919 to the selection and training of managers, personally interviewing five thousand candidates, then selecting a hundred of them for partnerships (he later would become known as "the man with a thousand partners").[34] In the process of adding those partners, he further diluted his personal ownership share in the company, retaining only about 15 percent in 1920.

Prior to stepping down from the company's presidency, Penney had introduced a house organ, the *Dynamo*, intended to communicate his values to an ever-increasing number of "associates" (employees) spread across the North American continent. He used the publication as a vehicle to encourage those associates to engage in continual development of their knowledge and skills, advocating "study, more study, and then more study."[35] He followed his own advice. Increasingly called upon to write articles and give speeches, Penney was dismayed to discover that his "facility with English was weak, noticeably in the written word."[36] He thus hired a university lecturer to tutor him in reading, writing, and public speaking, embarking on an ambitious half-of-every-day program of tutorials that lasted for eighteen months, during which "nothing was permitted to break the appointments."[37] The tutor assigned Penney the works of such authors as Plato, John Ruskin, and William Makepeace Thackeray to read and then write reports about, which the tutor critiqued. Penney was so impressed by the process that he commissioned the tutor to design "a well-devised reading-and-study plan for Penney personnel as a whole."[38] At one point in the 1920s, some 90 percent of Penney employees were enrolled in the company's free correspondence courses.[39]

Losing Interest

In 1923 the company opened its five hundredth store—fittingly, in Hamilton, Missouri, where J. C. Penney had begun his life in retailing. He had always wanted a store in his hometown, but had refused to compete with his mentor, John Hale. But when Hale retired, Penney bought his store and turned it into a J. C. Penney outlet.[40] About that time, Penney remarried, and soon thereafter he was father of a third son. Then the unconventional streak in his character reemerged: seemingly losing all interest in the management of the Penney Company, he turned his attention to such diverse activities as farming, real estate, and banking. With money he had made selling company shares to his new partners, and from the ever-increasing dividends from the stock he still held, he bought a mansion on Belle Isle in Miami that became his family's principal home. So ensconced, Penney uncharacteristically adopted the lifestyle of a millionaire, buying expensive cars and investing in the breeding of some three thousand purebred cattle and hogs, along with four thousand prize chickens. He bought 120,000 acres of land in northern Florida, where he attempted to create a utopian farming community called Penney Farms, à la Robert Owen's failed Indiana venture. Penney recruited "men of good character"—churchgoers who neither smoked nor drank—to work the farm, giving them gratis use of plots of land with the opportunity of purchasing it with the profits they generated on it, in the manner of Penney Company manager-partnerships. Some of those men and their wives had never before set foot on a farm, a detail blithely overlooked by their benefactor.

Penney also generously established a foundation to support a variety of Christian causes, including a rent-free community for retired ministers and YMCA and YWCA leaders. He constructed twenty-two apartment buildings on his northern Florida land to house the retirees and their spouses at the cost of some $1.1 million, roughly two years of his Penney Company dividends. He also invested heavily in the City National Bank of Miami, becoming its principal shareholder and, ultimately, chairman of its board of directors. All this activity stretched his finances to the point that he was forced to borrow large sums from several banks, using his Penney Company stock as collateral.[41]

Bank Failure

Then things began to turn sour for Penney. In 1926, only seven years after they were married, his second wife passed away. The "men of good character" who had moved to Penney Farms began to quarrel and refuse to cooperate with each other when they saw that the land and climate of northern Florida were not suited for growing the crops that experts at the Penney-funded Institute of Applied Agriculture had recommended. Penney Farms soon went the way of all utopian communities. Then, when the stock market collapsed in 1929, Penney borrowed some $7 million to shore up the City National Bank of Miami, which, despite his efforts, went into federal receivership in 1930 (the legal and financial issues arising from the bank's failure were not resolved until 1943). Worse yet, his creditors called in his loans, and when he couldn't pay his debts, they began selling his Penney Company shares, which in a badly depressed stock market yielded a fraction of their true worth. In 1930 Penney was forced to sell the Belle Isle mansion, the last of his marketable assets. Financially devastated, fifty-eight-year-old Penney experienced what may have been a nervous breakdown after finding himself unable to pay a doctor who had treated him for shingles. He was left with no alternative but to start drawing a salary from the J. C. Penney Company for the first time since 1909.[42]

Penney subsequently engaged in a period of critical self-examination, concluding that he had "permitted the idea of the power of money to possess me."[43] He recalled that, when he had started in business in 1902, he had hoped to someday have $100,000 in net worth, but by 1920, "my sights were set on becoming worth a million dollars." Admitting he had succumbed to the twin evils of ego and greed ("As time went on I became big in my own mind"), he resolved for the rest of his life "to think more about the power of God and less about the power of money."[44]

The one bit of good fortune to come his way in that otherwise bleak era was the J. C. Penney Company's continued profitability throughout the Great Depression. Thanks to prudent leadership by Corder Sams and the many partners Penney had developed, between 1930 and the end of World War II the company grew into a nationwide chain of over 1,600 stores, in the process becoming the world's largest retailer of blankets, sheets, work clothes, men's shirts, and women's housedresses.[45] During that period the company adhered rigorously to the Penney Principles, offering low prices, quality goods, excellent customer service, and first-rate employment conditions. Although a few of its stores became unionized, the company never engaged in the virulent anti-union activities undertaken at many other businesses at the time. And throughout that era, the J. C. Penney Company prided itself on maintaining close, positive working relationships with its suppliers, much as it continued to emphasize its commitment to community service. Although he now owned only about 1 percent of J. C. Penney's stock,[46] its founder served as a member of the company's board of directors until his death, becoming its public spokesman, officiating at the opening of new stores, and constantly on the road, attending company events and dropping in on stores where he would remind employees that "we interpret the golden rule as the *mandate of service.*"[47]

Corder Sams retired from the presidency in 1946, and then served as the company's chairman until he died in 1950. Penney continued on the board for twenty-one years after Sams's passing, gradually losing influence with the board and officers. This was a consequence of his own earlier actions: when Penney's creditors sold his shares on the open market after his 1920s Florida follies, the sale had triggered the erosion, and ultimate demise, of the company's system of partner ownership. In subsequent decades, increasing percentages of J. C. Penney stock found their way into the hands of outside investors; by the time of Sams's death, the partnership amounted to little more than a profit-sharing scheme. Because it was the partnership that had served as the bedrock of the Penney Principles, the company then began to drift away from its philosophical underpinnings. By the time Penney died, in 1971, its operating philosophy differed little from that of its major competitors.

As we saw, Robert Owen's major challenge over the quarter century he managed the New Lanark mills was to satisfy the demands of his investors—all men he knew personally—for greater returns on their capital. As difficult as that was, Owen was spared the far greater challenge of satisfying the shareholders of a publicly traded corporation. Stock exchanges had begun to appear in Amsterdam in the sixteenth century when shares of the Dutch East India Company were first traded.

In 1801 stock dealers—who previously had traded in coffeehouses—established the forerunner of what eventually would become the London Stock Exchange. In America, a stock exchange was established in Philadelphia in 1791; a year later another followed in Manhattan, under a tree on Wall Street; and in 1817 brokers formally organized the New York Stock and Exchange Board. The long-term significance of those modest events proved far greater than they doubtless seemed at the time. Formal stock markets provided the funds entrepreneurs needed to allow their firms to grow, thus planting the seeds for the rise of large-scale enterprises (such as railroads) and manufacturing firms (such as steel mills) requiring vast amounts of capital. At the same time, the resulting separation of a publicly traded company's "ownership" from its professional management inevitably led to conflict between not-always-passive investors and those actively involved in organizational management. As we shall see, that tug of war over control bedeviled all the enlightened capitalists, starting with James Cash Penney.

The Inexorable Decline of the Penney Company

The slow, inexorable unraveling of the J. C. Penney Company—nearly complete today—was a long-term process with many complex causes, the most obvious of which were the disadvantageous locales of most of its early stores. Beginning in the 1950s, when its competitors were expanding into America's fast-growing suburbs, the company found itself badly situated strategically, most of its stores located either in shrinking small towns or deteriorating city downtowns. In the late 1950s the company began to follow the lead of Sears, Montgomery Ward, and other retailers who had a significant head start on locating stores in suburban shopping centers and malls. The world of retailing was also changing: while its competitors were focused on offering sales, style, credit, and mail-order convenience, Penney's continued to offer low everyday prices, quality, and cash and carry.

Slowly, and too often maladroitly, J. C. Penney Company's managers began to copy the practices of their competitors, building mega department stores and offering a full line of goods, including kitchenware, sporting goods, appliances, and automobile tires, but in the process the company lost its previous competitive advantage of low overhead. By the time the company introduced a catalog, even Sears and Montgomery Ward were aware that the heyday of that particular form of mail-order business had passed. And only long after its competitors started offering stylish, fashion-driven clothing did Penney's begin attempting to keep pace—for example, in the 1960s carrying British Mod designer Mary Quant's line of trendy clothing.

What the company's leaders failed to appreciate was that their traditional customers were looking for quality, not flash. To attract new customers, Penney began to offer sales and "loss leaders" and engage in costly print and television advertising. Some of those gambits were successful, at least for a time. The long-term problem was that me-too strategies seldom allow a lagging company to catch up with the leaders in its industry. In the case of J. C. Penney, the copycat strategy mostly succeeded in confusing customers about the company's identity. Clearly it was no longer aiming to be the first choice of working- and middle-class customers who wanted high-quality goods at low prices. But who *was* the intended customer?

In 1958 the Penney Company appointed its fourth president, William Batten, on the heels of a board decision to adopt his sweeping proposal to compete by aping the competition. His proposed plan included abandoning one of the company's most basic principles: on Batten's recommendation, the board voted to offer credit in its stores. The decision was almost unanimous, with the one "no" vote cast by James Cash Penney. Penney explained his reasoning to the board in ethical terms: "We all know there are times when sales and profits are hard to get and this puts pressure on management. It will come again. Without intending to do so you will get very aggressive in your selling, and you will end up encouraging people to buy things they cannot afford and should not buy. By offering them credit we encourage them to overbuy. With me, it is a moral issue of getting people in financial trouble."[48]

When he cast his dissenting vote, Penney was perhaps thinking about his own financial overextension in the 1920s. Whatever his innermost thoughts may have been, even at age eighty-three he had not lost sight of his father's belief in the Golden Rule. Throughout his career, Penney had always aimed to make a profit, but to the end, he would not do so at the expense of the customer. It can be argued that he was naive to believe the company could compete without offering credit, but a principle was a principle to the ever-virtuous James Cash Penney. It is also true that the company needed to make drastic changes in its business model to succeed in the dramatically altered retail industry, but it had lost its primary engine of change with the demise of its partnership system. Penney had believed, and he may have been right, that encouraging store managers to stay close to their customers—and then rewarding them for responding to new wants and needs—was the surest way to keep pace with a changing world. Thus, Corder Sams's dream of "an organization that will always be renewing itself from within" had faded along with the partnerships that once made it a reality.

In the decade that followed, Batten hewed to the strategy of duplicating the practices and strategies of Sears and Montgomery Ward—tactics that, ironically, would lead those two companies into eventual irrelevance. From that time on, the company focused on delivering more profit to shareholders, who, increasingly, were Wall Street investors. After Penney's death, the J. C. Penney Company lurched from strategy to strategy, never finding a core identity. By the beginning of the twenty-first century it was in a downward spiral of decline from which it has never fully recovered. A 2014 *Fortune* article concluded that in an era marked by epic corporate failures, greed, and incompetence, "for its stomach-churning mix of earnest ambition, arrogance, hope, and delusion—along with a series of tragic miscues—it's hard to top J.C. Penney."[49] The final irony came in 2012–13, when yet another Penney Company CEO, Ron Johnson, attempted to rescue the

floundering enterprise by reintroducing Penney's policy of low everyday prices and no sales. Johnson lasted only sixteen months before the
company's board heeded investor demands for his ouster.

Over a century ago, James Cash Penney founded his company on
the ethical principle of treating his customers, employees, partners,
suppliers, and host communities the way he would want to be treated
by them: in his words, "fair and square." But by the 1960s, the company had lost that moral focus and regressed to the practices of its
competitors—practices that would prove to be failures by whoever
employed them. One wonders what might have happened in the 1920s
had Penney not lost interest in his company, and had remained its active leader until he was certain his values and principles were irrevo-
cably part of its culture. Of course we will never know. What we can
say for certain is that the pioneers of business virtue on both sides of
the Atlantic, Owen and Penney, experienced similar fates in the end.
As the following chapter further illustrates, enlightened practices like
theirs have seldom proved sustainable.

3

The Businessman Who "Cleaned Up the World"

WILLIAM LEVER (1851–1925)

Returning to Britain, we consider the remarkable career of William Hesketh Lever, founder of Lever Bros. (today's multinational Unilever). Lever was the world's first soap magnate, the man who was said to have "cleaned up the world" after he began to mass-produce body soap during the sooty Industrial Revolution, when few people bathed regularly. In 1801 the average Briton consumed only 3.6 pounds of soap per year; thanks largely to Lever, they were buying 16 pounds by the end of the century—and doubtless smelling the better for it.[1] Lever was an innovator par excellence: he hit upon the idea of slicing up the large, solid bricks of soap produced in the 1870s into the manageable smaller bars still used today. He is thus the answer to the trivia question "Who invented bar soap?"

Lever was the seventh of ten children—eight girls and two boys—born to Eliza Lever and her grocer husband, James. The Levers were devout Congregationalists, yet religion seems not to have been the source of son William's later commitment to improving the lives of others. Where his loving mum and dad were pious, William enjoyed the occasional religious services he attended solely for their ceremony and feeling of community. Rather than religion, the source of William's social conscience appears to have been the physical environment in which he was raised: the industrial town of Bolton. In the same book in which Engels castigated Robert Owen for his supposed capitalist sins against the working class, the dour German singled out Bolton as one of Britain's "worst" towns, a stinking "dark, unattractive hole" with soot-infused air from the factories in which most of its sixty thousand residents—men, women, and children—labored long hours in hot, unsafe, and unsanitary conditions.[2]

Although William's middle-class father was far from being wealthy, the grocer provided his family with a decent home and sent his children to the local school. By all accounts, William was an indifferent student but an avid reader who, from an early age, displayed a prodigious curiosity about natural science. His formal education ended when he turned sixteen and began work as an apprentice to his father, who at the time was in the process of closing his grocery store to concentrate on the more profitable wholesale side of the food business. Within two years William—a charmer with the skills of a natural politician—was James's most successful traveling salesman. William also seems to have been born with an inordinate capacity for uxorious love: when he was twenty-one, he and his childhood schoolmate, Elizabeth Hulme, were betrothed, and theirs would become the happiest of marriages. For the next forty-one years, until Elizabeth's death in 1913, the Levers were a doting and devoted couple, a model of Victorian connubial bliss.

Gradually William took control of his father's business, making the two of them—and William's younger brother, James—wealthy by introducing efficient management practices. As Lever would years later explain, "There is a general impression that in making money you have to do something very wonderful, but believe me, there is much more money made in doing something better than it was done before than in doing something new."[3] By 1884 the family business was a roaring success when, in a surprising J. C. Penney–like gesture, at thirty-three William announced that he was ready to retire.

Of course he didn't; instead he decided to capitalize on the growing demand for soap for bodies and clothing, both uses becoming more prevalent in Victorian England, where cleanliness was increasingly linked to godliness among the middle class. William borrowed money from his father and other family members and then talked brother James into joining him in a new soap manufacturing enterprise to be known as Lever Bros. In 1886 the first bar of Sunlight soap was produced in a leased factory employing thirty workers. Lever Bros. soap was touted as being uniquely "pure." Their soap wasn't significantly different from other brands on the market, but it proved more successful than others thanks to William's genius for marketing. He invented attractive product packaging that appealed to those who made most personal and laundry soap purchases: women.

Although Lever didn't invent advertising, he was the first in Britain to perfect its use in the mass marketing of packaged goods. He informed the ladies who were his prime customers that if they mixed a third of a bar of his patented Sunlight soap with a teaspoon of brandy, they would have a dandy formula for cleaning silk dainties. It seems sexist today, but in the 1880s it was good business when Lever's ads promised that his gentle-on-the-hands product would improve marital relations: "Don't let steam and suds be your husband's welcome on wash days." Another ad boldly asked, "Why Does a Woman Look Old Sooner than a Man?" The answer: because housewives spent their days toiling in scalding water, trying to scrub the dirt out of the family washing using elbow grease. Ah, but Lever Bros.' Sunlight soap was guaranteed to take the hard work out of washing, leaving Mum less tired and looking years younger![4]

Lever also was the father of commercial jingles, unleashing the jingle genie that, when music was later added, would drive generations of radio listeners and television viewers crazy trying to get the "worm" out of their heads. Here's a jingle touting Lever's Brooke's dish soap:

Dirty pan
Supper late
Angry man
In Sad state
"What, no tea?"
Swears Big D
Wife, of course,
Gets divorce
Pistol shot,
Gone to pot.

Prudent wife
Tea in time;
Without strife
Life's sublime
Full of hope,
Brooke's soap
Keeps pans bright;
Meals all right
Married Bliss
Happiness.[5]

Such marketing proved magic. During its first week the Lever Bros.' factory turned out 450 tons of soap; two years later, it was at full capacity, producing three thousand tons per week.[6] But Lever had more in mind than merely selling soap. When he first went into business, he tried to engage his customers in corporate philanthropy, offering to donate £2,000 to the charity receiving the most votes from his soap purchasers.[7] However, when customers didn't bother to vote, he switched strategies and began using company profits to improve the lives of his workforce. In an era when most workers still lived in disease-ridden slums no more salubrious than those Robert Owen had encountered eighty years earlier when he first went into business, Lever created a model "new town." In many ways a modern version of Owen's New Lanark, Lever's Port Sunlight was situated on the banks of the Mersey River, not far from Liverpool and adjacent to Lever Bros.' new soap factory (capacity, sixteen thousand tons).[8] But instead of being a grimy, disease-infested mill town like Bolton, Port Sunlight offered Lever employees up-to-date, spacious homes designed by a leading architect, all with indoor plumbing, their rent heavily subsidized by the company (employees were offered financing to enable them to purchase the homes). Lever's intention was to create a close-knit community with company-sponsored schools, parks, shops, health care, sports fields, swimming pool, concert hall, gymnasium, library, and cultural clubs and events: "It is my hope, and my brother's hope, to build houses in which our work people will be able to live and be comfortable—semi-detached houses, with gardens back and front, in which they will learn more about the science of life than they can in a . . . slum, and in which they will learn there is more enjoyment in life than the mere going and returning from work and looking forward to Saturday night to draw their wages."[9]

Starting in 1890, Lever did just that at Port Sunlight—and more. He was a dynamo, energetically inserting himself into every aspect of the town and factory while attempting to make the town's ideal, "prosperity sharing," a reality. In the process, he simply ignored the presence of his incompetent—and perhaps mentally handicapped—younger brother, who was his partner in name only. But the tireless William more than compensated for any lack of contribution on James's part; indeed, he ran what amounted to a one-man show in Port Sunlight.

(It is worth noting that Lever and Owen were not the only nineteenth-century industrialists to have created model towns for their employees. In 1851 Titus Salt built a town he called Saltaire—now incorporated as a part of Bradford, West Yorkshire—where he provided high-quality housing for the workers in his five adjacent wool mills. The town had all the amenities found in New Lanark, and anticipated many to come in Port Sunlight. Like New Lanark, Saltaire is today a World Heritage site—and, incidentally, home to one of the largest collections of paintings by David Hockney, who was born and raised nearby. While Saltaire made a remarkable contribution to the state of worker housing, it is not at all evident that Sir Titus Salt's benevolence extended to the working conditions in his mills.)

As benevolent as William Lever was, he was also paternalistic and in many ways autocratic in his dealings with the company's board, managers, and employees. With supreme confidence in his own wisdom, he cheerily micromanaged every detail of Lever Bros.' operations. He didn't entrust his top managers with real authority, and didn't bother grooming a successor, assuming—incorrectly, as it turned out—that his only child, William Hulme Lever, would inherit and then head the company. Indeed, Lever listened only to his wife, Elizabeth, whom he called his "better two thirds" and who was, it seems, his only confidante. When Lever Bros. went public in 1894, William made certain to retain complete control of the company: the only stock he sold were preferred shares (carrying a fixed dividend as a percent of company profit), while he retained all the common voting shares—thus leaving him free to pack the company's board with relatives and friends whose loyalty, and obedience, he could count on. For years he was the absolute, albeit charmingly beneficent, ruler of his Sunlight Kingdom, beholden to no one save Elizabeth.

At work and at leisure, Lever was a man of great enthusiasms: from architecture to vegetarianism, from world travel to dandyish Savile Row suits, his interests were varied and extravagantly expressed. He was a certifiable health nut: he and Elizabeth slept in an open-air bedroom exposed to the inclement British weather 365 nights a year. After a chilly night's sleep, he started each morning with a frigid bath (also alfresco).[10] An early environmentalist, he favored nature preserves and encouraged fellow manufacturers to follow his lead by providing green spaces and clean air and water in the communities surrounding their plants and mills. Eventually Lever's efforts with regard to creating healthy garden communities were extended to his grimy hometown,

Bolton, where he offered to pay for a giant park in which he proposed to construct public buildings for the recreation and entertainment of the villagers. In an early example of shortsighted NIMBYism, the town elders turned down the offer.

Lever Bros. manufacturing plants were far ahead of their time, offering abundant daylight, ventilation, and heat in winter. Every effort was made to protect workers from unhealthy manufacturing conditions by providing a safety inspector and doctor in every plant. No children under age thirteen were employed, and all young workers were required to attend school. A firm believer in investing in the personal growth of employees, Lever wrote, "There is an awakening amongst the people for what they know they ought to have . . . and that means development."[11] And he provided it: Lever employees were offered free courses in such subjects as English, foreign languages, accounting, science, and engineering. As the company grew ever more profitable, Lever reduced the workday from eight to six hours—while paternalistically introducing two hours of compulsory education.

Perhaps Lever's most radical, and farsighted, employment practice was gender equality. The women who constituted a high percentage of his workforce were given equal pay for equal work and promoted to management alongside men. They also were provided with safe and sanitary working conditions, and secure separate housing was available for unmarried women. As early as 1903, Lever was a vocal supporter of women's suffrage, and thirteen years later—a dozen years before all British women over twenty-one were enfranchised—he was publicly backing the cause, saying "The old idea of woman has to go . . . and it can only be done if she receives an equal education in every way and an equal equipment with man."[12]

Then there was the dancing! Lever, like Owen before him, loved to dance at the company's frequent soirees, making a point of inviting the wallflowers (who otherwise might not have been asked to dance) to join him for a terpsichorean spin. He had an immense dance floor installed in his mansion, along with a balcony on which musicians played the latest tunes of the era. It is probable that he never heard them, as he was practically stone-deaf, but that handicap didn't prevent him from joining every dance, although it necessitated having someone inform him when the music stopped.[13] He also provided all-expenses-paid company excursions to places his employees were unlikely to visit on their own, but where he felt they would benefit from the cultural exposure, personally escorting groups of up to two thousand staff members on trips to London, Paris, and Brussels.[14]

Co-Partnerships

Thanks to the company's ever-increasing economies of scale and continuing stream of new products and innovations—soap flakes were introduced in 1899—Lever Bros. quickly grew to become the world's largest soap producer. In the process, William Lever became one of Britain's wealthiest self-made businessmen. Although he greatly enjoyed the privileges of wealth, he wanted others to prosper as well. In 1909 he introduced a scheme in which a defined share of company profits was distributed among Lever Bros. employees in the form of "Co-Partnership Certificates"—nonvoting "stock" entitling its bearers to annual dividends. To qualify, employees needed to complete five years of productive service during which they "loyally and faithfully further[ed] the interest of Lever Bros." The scheme provided the average "partner" with 2 to 5 percent of annual pay, and personally cost Lever on the order of £40,000 annually.[15] Over his lifetime, some eighteen thousand Lever Bros. workers—men and women—would become his "partners."[16] Characteristically, there was a paternalistic hitch: he retained the right to revoke shares if workers proved to be drunks or gamblers—or failed to keep their Port Sunlight gardens tidy.

As early as 1888, when the company was turning a profit of £50,000 a year, Lever had begun to ask himself, "Whose was that money? For I want to give it to that man that ought to have it."[17] He concluded it should be shared by those who produced it: management, investors, and workers. But Lever was no socialist. He argued that his enlightened labor practices were self-motivated: "The truest and highest form of enlightened self-interest requires that we pay the fullest regard to the interest and welfare of those around us, whose well-being we must bind up with our own and with whom we must share our prosperity."[18]

Lever was elected to Parliament in 1905 as a member of the pro-business Liberal Party at a time when *liberal* was synonymous with free-market economics (he and his fellow Liberal parliamentarian, the young Winston Churchill, were leading advocates of the same free-trade cause that Robert Owen had unsuccessfully championed eighty years earlier). Lever's high moment in the House of Commons came in 1907 when a bill he had introduced establishing government-sponsored old-age pensions was enacted into law. Nonetheless, Lever was a reluctant parliamentarian at best, spending as little time as possible in Westminster and giving up his seat at the first opportunity. As he became increasingly involved in activities unrelated to the management of Lever Bros., he was drawn away from Port Sunlight for long periods, leading him to worry about losing control of his company. For example, while ostensibly traveling on business, he and Elizabeth became world travelers, voyaging for months at a time. During one extensive trip to Australia and Hawaii he lost his managerial grip on the company for weeks on end.

By the early 1900s, Lever Bros. factories across Europe and North America were producing twenty brands of soap, including Lux, Lifebuoy, Rinso, and other brands still selling today, while successfully diversifying into the manufacture of margarine, made from many of the same raw materials as soap. To source the tallow, copra, resin, citronella, and cottonseed oil used to make soap, Lever created the world's first global corporation, with raw material operations in Asia, South America, and the Pacific Islands. The most remarkable were in West Africa, where, at the request of Albert, newly crowned King of the Belgians and colonial master of the Congo, Lever turned his personal attention. Albert's deceased uncle, the thoroughly detestable and degenerate monarch Leopold II, had run the Congo as his personal fiefdom, his cruel rule characterized by slavery, rape, and pillage. During Leopold's reign, tens of thousands of Africans were murdered, some shot by Europeans for sport. But young Albert was an enlightened ruler who, before assuming the throne, had traveled to England, where he had become so impressed by the way Lever Bros. was managed that he resolved to encourage such progressive practices throughout his kingdom when, and if, he became king. On the death of Leopold, Albert approached Lever with the proposition that he establish copra farms in the Congo in a fifty-fifty partnership with the Belgian government. Lever, then sixty, jumped at the idea, and set off with Elizabeth for what would be the first of several lengthy trips to Africa. In 1911 the joint venture was founded, eventually employing some seventeen thousand indigenous workers. Under Lever's direction, the company did itself proud, providing decent wages, clean housing, schools, and health care to people who recently had been treated almost as slaves by their colonial rulers, and who were still exploited routinely in the Congo and elsewhere in Africa by other Western businesses.

Lord Leverhulme

Lever wrote on the order of 130,000 letters during his lifetime (they are still in the company archives) and gave countless speeches in which he explained his philosophy of enlightened capitalism. "No employer-capitalist with a true feeling of brotherhood," he lectured in one of these numerous—and invariably turgid—public addresses, "can be quite happy in the fullest sense in the enjoyment of wealth (the product of his own hard work, intelligence, self-denial and thrift, every penny earned without committing injury to any man, and the acquisition of which has resulted in enormous benefits to his employee-workmen) without feeling a strong sense of dissatisfaction with present industrial conditions and a strong desire to improve them so that the employee-workman may be raised to a much higher level in social well-being."[19]

There it all is: a justification for his personal wealth, a commitment to ethics, and a desire to improve the lot of employees. At the height of the company's success, British prime minister William Ewart Gladstone praised Lever for seeking to "improve the material condition of the workman, to give him . . . an increase in wages and decrease in labor; but besides this to give him the sense of common interest with his employers."[20] In recognition of his remarkable achievements, King George V granted Lever a peerage in 1917. He then entered the House of Lords, and was henceforth known as Viscount Leverhulme—not bad for a grocer's son from Bolton. (In choosing that name, William honored his wife, Elizabeth, by combining his last name, Lever, with hers, Hulme.)

Yet, Lever was not universally admired. He was the particular bête noir of one Alfred Harmsworth—later Lord Northcliffe—publisher of the *Daily Mail* and *Daily Mirror*. Like Rupert Murdoch's tabloids today, these papers specialized in fomenting fabricated scandals about those whom Harmsworth suspected of progressive tendencies. On more than one occasion, they focused their venom on William Lever, accusing him in 1906 of such things as price-fixing and selling fifteen-ounce "pounds" of soap. In fact, Lever briefly *had* conspired with his competitors—but with the intent of keeping the price of soap *low*. As a consequence of the efficiencies of Lever's operations, his smaller competitors' profits had been squeezed to the point he felt the need to "conspire" with them to share sourcing and advertising costs, lest he drive them out of business. And, in fact, he *had* reduced the size of his soap bars—while publicly stating that his reason for doing so was to continue making the product affordable to those on meager budgets (for a quarter of a century, the price of Sunlight soap had been raised only once). Nonetheless, the actions smelled of scandal—indeed, the conspiracy would be illegal today—and Harmsworth pounced. In the words of Adam Macqueen, author of a marvelously accessible biography of Lever, Harmsworth "and his fellow editors finally had an opportunity to voice their long-held prejudices about this weird, progressive social experiment on the banks of the Mersey, and they weren't going to let Lever get away with it."[21] Over the course of the aptly named Harmsworth's long press campaign to discredit Lever, considerable damage was inflicted to the soap magnate's reputation—and to Lever Bros.' sales and profits. After a prolonged libel suit, Harmsworth eventually paid Lever the equivalent of several million in today's dollars to settle, but the damage had been done. Alas, the scandal-that-wasn't became the first of a series of heartbreaking setbacks Lever would suffer.

While Lever was still reeling from the press attack, his brother, James, died in his fifties after a long illness, and after several periods of confinement in a mental asylum (hushed up by William).[22] Three years later Lever's beloved wife, Elizabeth, died of pneumonia contracted while he was away on a business trip—sleeping in the Levers' open-air bedroom doubtless having hastened her end. William was devastated. He said of Elizabeth that "during the whole of our married life of 40 years, however early business called me, I never breakfasted alone; she was always up and saw that the breakfast was properly prepared, and I always knew that whatever might happen in the course of the day the great event for her would be my homecoming in the evening."[23] And that had been the great event of his days, as well. But now there would be no more of them, and Lever found himself alone without a close friend in the world.

A Sad, Bad End

In 1918 Lever made one of the riskiest—and most disastrous—personal investments of his life. He purchased two impoverished islands in the Scottish Outer Hebrides, home to Gaelic-speaking pre-industrial communities whose economies Lever intended to develop. By investing in new industries, he attempted to provide employment for the thirty thousand inhabitants then barely eking out a livelihood in harsh North Sea climes. With the goal in mind of replicating his Port Sunlight and Congo succès d'estime, he moved to the island of Lewis to oversee the transformation he envisioned. Everyone he knew warned him it couldn't be done; of course, he didn't listen. As he half-seriously said, "An advantage of being deaf is in business you can form your own plans and need not listen to anyone's advice."[24] He would stay on Lewis for some seven years, building factories, ports, and electricity and gas plants, and drawing up plans to create a new "garden town." All the while, he fired a steady barrage of some fifty thousand directives to his managers in England, in a desperate attempt to keep control of a business that day by day was slipping out of his hands. In the end, the Hebrides project turned out to be a disaster. Lever never understood the local culture, and the Scots never warmed up to the Anglo Lever, who they felt was patronizing in his attempts to destroy their traditions. Millions of pounds having been wasted in the effort, Lever eventually sold the islands, cut his losses, and went home.

While all that was transpiring outside company walls, Lever Bros. continued to be so successful that by 1920 its ever-dictatorial founder was diversifying wildly into such unrelated businesses as a paper mill, a colliery, a limestone quarry, an engineering firm, a sausage factory, and fisheries. The Lever Bros. board—beholden to the founder—authorized the equivalent of some $2 billion in today's currency to cover the investments. Then calamity struck in the form of a perfect storm: a worldwide speculative bubble burst, the prices of raw materials Lever Bros. produced collapsed, deflation followed rapidly on the heels of high inflation, and new, efficient competitors entered the soap trade. At the same time, Lever's £8 million purchase of an oilseed operation in Nigeria was found to have been made without sufficient due diligence, thus necessitating an additional £2 million to cover an overdraft that had gone undisclosed at the time of sale.

As demand for their products fell, several Lever Bros. companies lost significant sums at the very time that millions of pounds of loans were being recalled by the company's creditors. To cut costs, the company began to lay off workers and reduce wages for the first time in its history, which led to low morale and subsequent strikes. Trade unionists who once had praised Lever now turned against him with accusations of paternalism. Said one union leader, "No man of an independent turn of mind can breathe for long the atmosphere of Port Sunlight. . . . The profit-sharing scheme not only enslaves and degrades the workers, it tends to make them servile and sycophant, it lowers them to the level of machines tending machines."[25] As exaggerated as such criticism may have been, the reality was that the rapid growth and international expansion of the company had made it impossible to provide its tens of thousands of new employees with the housing and other benefits enjoyed by the eight thousand or so living in Port Sunlight. As a result, the sense of community Lever sought to create in the company began to erode.

As the seventy-year-old Lever found himself overextended, trying to micromanage his global empire and engage in such demanding civic activities as serving as mayor of Bolton (characteristically, he insisted on personally chairing every meeting of the town council), he lost focus, credibility, money, and—like J. C. Penney a few years later—the leadership of the company he founded. In 1921 he understatedly wrote, "We are not entirely our own masters at the present moment and I am not captain of my own ship."[26] Much like Owen before him, Lever was ultimately forced to cede control of his company to a profit-oriented accountant, Francis D'Arcy Cooper, who saved Lever Bros. but had little interest in Lever's broader social agenda. Over Lever's objections, Cooper moved the company's headquarters from Port Sunlight to London.

After an ill-advised trip to Nigeria—where he failed to rescue the troubled oilseed company—Lever returned to London a sick, lonely, and broken man. In 1925, at age seventy-three, he died of pneumonia as Elizabeth had done before him. He was buried beside her in Port Sunlight. His son then became the second Viscount Leverhulme, having also inherited his parents' big hearts and intelligence but not his father's love of business: young Lever would devote the rest of his life to philanthropy and writing his father's biography.

Unilever After Lever . . . and the Company Today

Four years after Lever's death, the company merged with a successful Dutch company, Margarine Unie, creating the modern Unilever. Almost immediately, the firm began to drift away from Lever's founding values, although it never did so entirely. Throughout its history, Anglo-Dutch Unilever has maintained a strong corporate culture that stresses the nurturing of community spirit among its employees. Equally, it has earned a reputation for ethical behavior. Harvard Business School historian Geoffrey Jones concludes that integrity has been one of the hallmarks of Unilever's culture throughout its history, and that "the concept of integrity was wider than honesty. 'Making money' per se was not seen as the exclusive goal within Unilever, either for individuals or for the company."[27] In the late 1940s and early '50s, Unilever's Dutch chairman Paul Rykens "was a prominent exponent of the philosophy" that the company had responsibilities to its various constituencies—employees, consumers, and local communities. In this he adopted the idea of corporate social responsibility that had recently been introduced by the American executive Robert Wood Johnson (see chapter 7). However, Unilever's commitment to that philosophy was muted considerably during the 1980s and '90s, when the company was led by executives whose focus was squarely on profit.

Today, Unilever's global workforce of over three hundred thousand is the world's largest producer of ice cream, tea, and margarine. The company's brands include Lipton, Birds Eye, Dove, Vaseline, Pond's, Lifebuoy, and Ben & Jerry's (the recent integration of the latter company's culture and values is a sui generis success story examined in chapter 15). Strikingly, in 2005 the company began to introduce a series of programs designed to align its strategies, products, and practices around environmentalism and to infuse social responsibility into all its activities—for example, certifying the sustainability of its sources of fish, palm oil, and tea, and reducing greenhouse emissions. The motivations for those efforts apparently were an admixture of a need to keep pace with more progressive competitors by appealing to socially conscious consumers, pressures to expand in underdeveloped markets—and, perhaps, some desire to return to the values of the founder.[28] In 2010, under the lead of its newly appointed CEO, Paul Polman, the company announced the Unilever Sustainable Living Plan, which set specific, ambitious social and environmental goals for the company over the next decade. It pledged to reduce the company's environmental impact by 2020, while improving the health of a billion people and the welfare of millions more—at the same time doubling the company's sales. Since then, the company has been engaged in a complex and lengthy process of aligning its business strategies with its commitment to meeting the broader needs of global society.

To achieve its self-imposed goal of halving its environmental footprint, Unilever has been changing its product mix and reducing its use of water and energy in manufacturing and distribution.[29] Harkening back to William Lever's admirable Congo operations, Unilever today is committed to addressing issues of land rights, pollution, and community development in Africa, Asia, and Latin America, and to adopting fair-trade sourcing of its raw materials and agricultural products. The company also says it will work with governments in developing countries to create policies and practices that address human and environmental needs. With a nod to the ghost of Lord Leverhulme, Unilever has returned to its feminist roots, pledging to make 50 percent of its managers women, and to introduce flexible working conditions to help make that possible. In order to fully integrate ethical practices, social responsibility, and environmental sustainability in Unilever's corporate strategies, CEO Polman has pledged to create an organizational culture built on "doing the right thing," rather than viewing such behavior as an inessential add-on. Perhaps the most radical aspect of Unilever's transformation is its decision to abandon the traditional goal of short-term profit maximization.

Polman acknowledged that transforming the culture of a £50 billion company with a thousand brands sold in 190 countries would not be easily accomplished. For example, the company has vowed to make the production of its Hellmann's mayonnaise certifiably sustainable. In an interview with the *New York Times*, Unilever managers illustrated how difficult reaching that seemingly simple goal will be.[30] For starters, there is no independent certification program for the soybeans used in the product, nor is there a standard measure of farm sustainability. Thus, the company must first cooperate with independent certifiers to establish such standards. Then there is the problem of sourcing cage-free eggs, a principal ingredient in mayonnaise. There simply are not enough such eggs available. And how should the company account for the recycling of the jars its mayonnaise comes in, or the amount of energy and water used in its processing? Unilever's challenge with regard to energy and water usage is particularly daunting, given that laundry soaps are among its top-selling products. As Polman explains, "A lot of the water usage in our value chain comes from cooking and showering, from heating up water. How do you halve that? It's very difficult."[31] All of this will take time, Unilever's managers say—a long time, in fact, because making their thousand other brands certifiably sustainable will be just as complicated as it is with soap and mayonnaise.

Polman has recently become the world's most vocal corporate advocate of socially responsible business practices, "something of a roving sustainability evangelist, calling out for stricter environmental regulations and speaking out against a fixation on short-term profits."[32] In the manner of Robert Owen, Polman frequently and publicly calls on his fellow business leaders to adopt practices similar to the ones his company is pioneering. As a result, Unilever today is considered among the world's most socially responsible global corporations, and Polman is widely lauded as an exemplary business leader; the company claims that reduction of energy use alone saved the company $430 million between 2008 and 2015.

Yet not everyone is satisfied with the company's performance. Unilever has been criticized by human rights advocates for the treatment of its workers in Kenya and for unsanitary conditions in an Indian factory, and by "green" competitors who question the purity of its products.[33] In 2015 Polman also came under pressure from investors to scale back his social efforts to increase Unilever's growth after the company missed financial analysts' sales forecasts during six out of eight quarters. Polman responded to his critics on Wall Street and in London's City, claiming they "have over-optimistic expectations. We would be hostage to the financial market if we ran this company judged on expectations."[34] He reemphasized his stated opposition to a ninety-day reporting cycle, arguing that the practice leads to a short-termism that would prevent Unilever from achieving the goals outlined in its Sustainable Living Plan. Executives typically don't succeed with that line of argument, and there are signs that Polman's unorthodox social and environmental stands are being met with increasing wariness by investors. Since Unilever announced the Sustainable Living Plan in 2010, its share price has lagged behind the FTSE index by a significant margin. Given that record, it has now become questionable whether Polman can succeed—where Owen, Penney, and Lever failed—in leaving behind a lasting legacy of organizational virtue. (We will return to Unilever's continuing saga in chapter 18.)

Coda: The Shavian Perspective

It might be said that Owen's and Lever's reform efforts bookended the Industrial Revolution in Britain. Yet during the century separating their efforts—an era when more wealth was created than at any other time in history—few other business leaders followed their examples, a paradox that puzzled such observers as George Bernard Shaw, the great Irish playwright and social critic. Shaw was a bit of a contrarian on the subject of enlightened capitalists. In his controversial 1905 play *Major Barbara*, Shaw's protagonist is a greedy munitions manufacturer who also happens to be a model employer with a mission to end world poverty. We recognize this character, Andrew Undershaft, as possibly a composite distant cousin of many of the business leaders profiled in these pages, most particularly Lever. Although Shaw's intent in the play was not to offer a critique of enlightened business leadership, the issues he raised illuminate the complexity and paradoxes involved in objectively evaluating the practices of those who use profit-making enterprises to achieve social good.

Undershaft, a shockingly politically incorrect, atheistic arms manufacturer, is a benevolent, perhaps even paternalistic employer who respectfully treats his workers as his social equals, and never issues harsh or arbitrary commands or punishments. At a time when the typical British worker toiled for pennies under terrible conditions and lived in unspeakably grim slums, Undershaft pays his employees well; they work in spotless factories, and he provides them and their families with comfortable living accommodations. Away from grimy London, he creates a "heavenly city" for his workers, complete with libraries, schools, hospitals, a nursing home, a ballroom, and a banquet hall where good meals are provided for pennies. He offers his workers generous insurance programs, home loans, pensions, and shares of company stock, at a time when such benefits were all but unimaginable for members of the working class.

When Undershaft is accused of doing all this to create loyal and productive workers, he unapologetically admits that those are his aims. When his daughter, Major Barbara of the Salvation Army, castigates him for being a merchant of death who profits from weapons of war, he tells her he is proud of that fact because the money made by capitalists—even ones like himself whose wealth derives from what many consider evil means—is the only source of the wherewithal needed to fight poverty, which he says is the greatest social evil. Charities like his daughter's have never solved poverty, he argues, but if he takes a "half-starved ruffian" from the slums of London and brings him to his model town, the man's life can be transformed, "Not by word and dreams; but by thirty-eight shillings a week, a sound house in a handsome street, and a permanent job. In three weeks he will have a fancy waistcoat [vest]; in three months a tall hat and a chapel sitting [a reserved church pew]; before the end of the year he will shake hands with a duchess at a Primrose League meeting, and join the conservative Party."

Undershaft argues that it is in the self-interest of capitalists to abolish poverty because poverty can lead to a Marxist revolution in which their wealth and property would be abolished. He tells his daughter not to be a hypocrite about the fact that his wealth comes from dirty money and his motives are materialistic, impure, and self-interested; instead, she should realistically accept that the source of the money collected by the Salvation Army is from the activities of capitalists like himself. If she wants charity in a capitalist society, she must accept that the wherewithal can come only from business. There is no other alternative but state ownership (which Shaw personally favored). Recognizing that alternative is unacceptable to the British electorate, Undershaft tells Barbara that the real choice then lies between capitalists like him who make the system work for themselves and their employees, and hypocritical capitalists who exploit their workers and then piously seek atonement by giving to charities, such as hers, which are totally ineffective in fighting poverty. In the end, Barbara turns in her Salvation Army uniform and marries her father's successor-owner of the family's munitions business. Shaw leaves the playgoer wondering if Undershaft's behavior is cynical or realistic.

Now, back to our story . . .

4

Kisses Sweeter Than Wine

MILTON SNAVELY HERSHEY (1857–1945)

Milton Hershey was to the milk chocolate bar what William Lever was to bar soap: if he didn't invent it, he most certainly perfected and popularized it. Hershey and Lever led remarkably parallel lives: both had as much passion for social engineering as they did for business. The legacies of both the chocolate magnate and the soap baron became current news in the early twenty-first century. However, in contrast to Unilever's promising rediscovery of Lever's practices, recent news about Hershey's legacy has threatened to stain what, for over seventy years, had been a sterling reputation.

There were, it seems, two M. S. Hersheys, and the genesis of that dual persona can be credited to his parents. Milton's father, Henry, was a renegade Mennonite—a dreamer, drinker, risk-taker, free thinker, and charmingly convivial wanderer. In the eyes of his wife, Fanny (née Snavely), Henry was an irresponsible, incorrigible, ne'er-do-well rogue—the kind of man a deeply religious, puritanically conservative, hardworking woman like herself would eject from her home and erase from her life. She accomplished the former task when their son, Milton, was not yet twelve years old; alas, she never quite succeeded with the latter. Significantly, both Henry and Fanny would live until Milton was well into middle age, and both would remain near and dear to him, their mismatched personalities the source of the two sides of his often contradictory character and behavior.

The Hersheys and the Snavelys were of Pennsylvania Dutch stock, both families anchored for generations in Lancaster County, home to large communities of Amish and Mennonites—"Old Church" Christian pacifists and Anabaptists who lived austerely while retaining the customs of forebears who had emigrated from German-speaking regions of Europe decades before Britain's thirteen American colonies declared independence. The Mennonite Hirsch (anglicized to Hershey) family left Switzerland in 1715, the Snavelys following a few years later. Henry Hershey's parents were practicing Mennonites; while not completely resisting the modern technology, culture, and lifestyle of "the English" around them, they nonetheless were pious and religiously observant. Henry, however, fully rejected Mennonite traditions, embracing instead the pursuit of the American dream and the joys of worldly pleasures.

The Snavelys were of a different ilk of Mennonite. Fanny's father was a Reformed Mennonite bishop—"reformed" in the sense that it was an orthodox sect rejecting the "modernist" tendencies of those Mennonites who had begun to vote and engage in such frivolous activities as attending county fairs.[1] The Snavelys' sole entertainment was hard work—and accumulating a bit of wealth as the result of that dedication. By marrying Henry in a Lutheran church, Fanny had shown signs of rejecting her family's values, but once rid of him, she reverted to "plain and simple" Mennonite self-denial, adopting the sect's modest black-and-gray dress. Photos of her son, Milton, at around age eight depict a young boy dressed in the long, dark wool coat and wide-brimmed hat that were the hallmarks of a traditional Mennonite upbringing (Fanny, in distinction, adhered to the sect's practice of not allowing herself to be photographed, believing that to be an exercise in shameful vanity).[2]

Milton was an indifferent student in his uncle's one-room schoolhouse, which he attended at his father's insistence—and over the objections of Fanny, who equated book learning with sinful putting on of airs. While Milton languished in school, Henry often was away from home engaging in a variety of unsuccessful entrepreneurial ventures, such as failing to strike it rich in the booming Pennsylvania oil fields where John D. Rockefeller would soon thereafter make his fortune. With Henry off chasing impossible dreams, the support of Milton and his little sister, Sorena, fell entirely on Fanny, who, working long hours seven days a week on the family farm, barely managed to make ends meet by selling eggs and butter (which she churned herself) to neighbors. Worse, with Henry absent, she was forced to deal alone with the tragedy of Sorena's death, from scarlet fever, at age five. That event, followed shortly thereafter by a final parting of the ways with Henry and the subsequent failure of their farm, drew Fanny closer to her spinster sister Mattie and the relatively well-to-do Snavelys. Fanny and Milton eventually moved in with Mattie—followed, rather bizarrely, by the estranged and penniless Henry, whom the Snavelys took in out of pity. Although Fanny and Henry never divorced, she shunned him even as they shared the same roof (but not the same bed). At any rate, Henry didn't spend much time at the Snavely house, mainly occupying himself with the development of a perpetual motion machine he was certain would make him rich, and telling amusing tales at the local saloon.

Milton's Early Career

Milton dropped out of school at age fourteen, apprenticing himself as a "printer's devil" to an Amish newspaper editor. As the story goes, one day, while manually setting type for that German-language publication, Milton dropped a galley. As he watched the letters spill to the floor—eliciting guttural curses from the editor—he realized the printing trade was not for him. Changing careers, as it were, he entered a field he loved: the confectionary business. Milton had a sweet tooth, and fortunately, the consumption of sugar was one of the few worldly pleasures Pennsylvania Dutch allowed themselves.

For the next five years, Milton worked at Roger's Ice Cream Parlor and Candy Store in Lancaster, learning all aspects of the confectionery business. In addition to mastering the making of candies (basically all were made by boiling sugar in those years before chocolate became widely available in America), he also absorbed the requisites of business success: making and selling high-quality goods to satisfy customers. Having accumulated that knowledge, he set off for Philadelphia, where, with money borrowed from Aunt Mattie and her brother Abraham, he opened a shop that sold penny candies. Mattie didn't simply provide capital for the venture; she and Fanny also moved to Philly to wrap the candies Milton made and sold. It soon became clear that Milton had a real talent for making sweets. Constantly experimenting with different recipes, he created a caramel goodie the very thought of which was said to cause customers to salivate. Because he couldn't make enough of the stuff, Fanny and Mattie found themselves slaving long hours in a back room trying to wrap enough caramels to satisfy growing demand. Regrettably, Milton's talent for innovation was insufficiently matched with skills in business management: he was unable to deal with the complexities of a booming trade, and his business rapidly ran out of cash. Uncle Abraham sent an infusion of capital from Lancaster that saved the day, but unfortunately, at the same time Milton's father also decided to go to Philadelphia. Against the Snavelys' wise council, Milton agreed to take Henry into the shop as partner. Within a year Milton was forced to buy out his hapless father for $350—which Henry happily pocketed, promptly setting off to Colorado looking to strike it rich in that state's booming silver mines.

When Milton's Philadelphia candy business ultimately failed—and Abraham was no longer willing to subsidize it—the Snavely sisters returned to Lancaster, while Milton followed his father to Colorado. There, Milton quickly realized he would be unable to find a place for himself in mining towns more accommodating to saloons and brothels than candy stores, so he soon headed back east. Now twenty-six years old, and again with borrowed funds, he next tried his entrepreneurial hand by opening a candy store in New York City on Sixth Avenue between Forty-Second and Forty-Third Streets—before the heyday of Broadway, and when the reputation of that now high-rent district was tainted by the nearby presence of the aptly named Hell's Kitchen. Fanny and Mattie again joined him as backroom laborers—and, to no one's great surprise, Henry later appeared on the scene. Ever an easy mark for his charming dad, Milton agreed to put up $10,000 to buy machinery Henry needed to enter the cough-drop manufacturing trade. History then repeated itself, this time as farce: Milton was again forced to beg the Snavelys for money to pay for equipment that never produced a single cough drop. Unwilling to keep investing good money in Hershey père or fils—both of whom Uncle Abraham now considered congenitally born to fail—the Snavelys refused the request for cash. Yet Milton remained the apple of Aunt Mattie's eye: she pledged property she personally owned as collateral for a bank loan that, when granted, bailed her nephew out and provided enough capital for him to start his third candy enterprise.

The Sweet Taste of Success

Now in business in Lancaster, Milton began to experiment with recipes for caramels that wouldn't stick to the teeth of his customers and pull out their fillings. Through trial and error with small batches of sugar, he eventually developed what became an irresistible treat (the secret ingredient: generous portions of milk, an abundant resource in dairy-land Lancaster County). He began by selling the caramels on the street from a pushcart; a few years later he was employing over a thousand workers in a 450,000-square-foot factory.[3] Milton Hershey's Lancaster Caramel Company gained a reputation for making the finest candies in America, so good he found markets for the product all over the East Coast, and even exported cases of the gooey stuff to England. After opening an additional plant in Chicago, and two more in Pennsylvania, Milton had the manufacturing capacity to reach customers almost everywhere in North America—and as far away as Australia and Japan.

By the early 1890s he was the esteemed and prosperous owner of a large manufacturing company employing some two thousand workers, capitalized at well over $750,000, and profitable enough to pay off debts incurred in his first two ventures.

Increasingly on the road, Milton began to cultivate a taste for certain costly pleasures unavailable—or frowned upon—in the provincial confines of Lancaster County, such as gambling, gourmet food, French champagne, and Cuban cigars. Moreover, he found himself wealthy enough to begin seriously considering the taking of a wife. He soon found the love of his life working, appropriately, behind the counter at a candy store in Jamestown, New York, where he was visiting on a sales trip. After a year of wooing, he proposed to the Irish Catholic Catherine "Kitty" Sweeney. She accepted, and they were married in Manhattan's St. Patrick's Cathedral without the presence of either friends or family. Not surprisingly, the Mennonite Snavelys did not approve of the redheaded daughter of Celtic immigrants, although Papa Henry was swept away by his daughter-in-law's informal manner, openness, ready laughter, and sharp wit—traits rarely found among women in Pennsylvania Dutch country.

For their honeymoon, Milton and Kitty decided to embark on a round-the-world trip, beginning in Mexico City. As the *New York Times* reported it, after a few days in the Mexican capital Milton told his bride, "I can't stand this; I've got to get back to work." They canceled the rest of their honeymoon so Milton could return to Pennsylvania to continue experiments with chocolate he had begun two years earlier. For the rest of his life, Milton Hershey would concentrate on the chocolate business.[4]

Milton's fascination with chocolate had begun just before he met Kitty, when he was an enthusiastic frequent attendant at the 1893 Chicago World's Columbian Exposition. There, awed by Daniel Burnham's farsighted "White City" design of the fairgrounds and buildings, Milton became an early advocate of the era's City Beautiful movement, vowing someday to create a model city for his employees with lush parks and wide boulevards. Furthermore, Milton enthusiastically embraced Burnham's famous advice, "Make no small plans." While in Chicago, it seems quite likely Milton also visited nearby Pullman, Illinois, where George Pullman provided housing for some twelve thousand of his railway-car factory workers and their families.[5] While that company town was well planned and offered its residents many modern amenities, Pullman went far beyond being paternalistic in the benevolent mode of Robert Owen and William Lever. Pullman was autocratic: exploiting the employees he pretended to befriend, he charged them excessive rents and attempted to police their private lives. In 1894 Pullman's workers rebelled, engaging in a violent strike that ended with the intervention of the US Army. Over the years, Milton Hershey would find himself teetering on the edge of Pullman-like behavior.

Even more than Burnham's planned fairgrounds, Milton's favorite thing about the Chicago expo was the giant Machinery Building, where he spent hours observing the magnificent devices developed by the German J. M. Lehmann to make the chocolate he sold to fairgoers. Because solid forms of chocolate are unstable at high and low temperatures, before the fair the closest most Americans had come to enjoying the treat had been a cup of hot cocoa. But some ten years earlier, Swiss confectioner and pharmacist Henri Nestlé had developed a process for making chocolate that didn't melt in the summer or turn brittle in winter. In 1879 another Swiss, Rodolphe Lindt, invented a machine that turned large batches of cocoa into liquid chocolate that was poured into molds in which, when left to cool, could be formed into bars. Building on those innovations, the Rowntree and Cadbury families, British Quakers, created large, profitable chocolate manufacturing businesses. Lehmann's machines were the culmination of those developments, and Milton Hershey decided he had to have them for his own. When the fair ended, he purchased Lehmann's equipment and shipped it off to Lancaster.

Once the machines were installed in his plant, Milton began experimenting with the roasting and grinding of cocoa beans, searching for a way to make naturally bitter chocolate palatable to Americans' taste for sugary sweets. For several years, that trial-and-error process yielded few positive results, but Hershey's caramel business was so profitable that he could easily afford the investment of time, money, and manpower in the development of a marketable chocolate bar. In fact, the caramel business was so successful that in 1900 a competitor bought Hershey out for $1 million. Hershey eventually succeeded in improving chocolate in much the same way he had improved caramels: by adding milk. Experimenting in the family kitchen—with Papa Henry offering encouragement—Milton developed a milk chocolate bar in the same year he sold the caramel business. Although he had no idea how to mass-produce the product, he was convinced that Hershey's Milk Chocolate was destined to become a wildly successful national brand along the lines of recently introduced Coca-Cola, Heinz beans, Wrigley gum, and Kellogg's Corn Flakes—each of which had become must-have products for consumers across the continent. With those examples in mind, Hershey began to "think big" à la Burnham.

He Bought the Farm, and Built a Town

With the $1 million from the caramel company sale as bankroll, Hershey bought 1,200 acres of farmland in rural Lancaster County near the property his mother and father had once owned. There, beginning in 1903, he set about constructing a giant modern factory, one of the first to be air-conditioned. The factory offered workers large, clean restrooms equipped with showers and a bright lunchroom. Employee safety was stressed, and a nurse was always in attendance. Adjacent to the factory, he began work on a model town to house the thousands of men and women he envisaged hiring. Drawing inspiration from Lever's Port Sunlight and Burnham's City Beautiful movement, Hershey hired engineers, architects, landscape gardeners, and others to design a model town, draw up a street grid, and begin to lay its infrastructure.

Hershey wanted the latest, best, and most beautiful of everything from sewer lines to community buildings. His well-planned town would have green open spaces, a public park, a zoo, a library, a swimming pool, and a hospital. All its two-story homes would have indoor plumbing, electricity, and central heating. Thanks to generous financing by the Hershey Chocolate Company, the workers would own their homes. Not only would the town have a trolley to take people from their homes to the factory where they worked, Hershey would also build a railroad to connect this remote locale to Lancaster and the nation's main railway lines.

The town he created was as quaint, precious, and antiseptic as Disneyland's faux Main Street. Every charming brick house in the self-styled "sweetest place on earth" had its own well-trimmed garden. The town's main intersection was the corner of Chocolate and Cocoa Avenues, and other streets were named after places where cocoa is grown—Caracas, Grenada, Trinidad, and Java—all illuminated by streetlights in the shape of Hershey's Kisses. The whole treacly town was beautifully landscaped, with a park rivaling Central Park in size. From its founding, it boasted a volunteer firehouse, post office, and school—but no jail or saloons. In subsequent years Hershey donated a community center, a theater, a golf club, and of course an enormous dance pavilion that accommodated four thousand dancers, enough to have made William Lever jealous. The city was meticulously clean and the ambience so artificially wholesome and saccharine that a visiting comedian was moved to wax poetic:

> Tell me truly, tell me please,
> Is Hershey a town, or a disease?

Even while occupied in utopian town planning, Hershey continued to work tirelessly alongside his employees to perfect the mass production of milk chocolate bars, often mercilessly driving them on during sixteen-hour shifts. He bought a herd of cows to ensure a ready supply

of milk—a key ingredient in his chocolate bars—eventually concluding that the skim milk of Holsteins was just the ticket. In the midst of
all this activity, in 1904 Papa Henry died after trudging home through
the snow following a night of rye and bonhomie at his favorite saloon.
Mama Fanny marked the occasion by burning her estranged husband's
considerable library of books. A year later, the Hershey chocolate factory began operations.

Milton found little time to grieve the passing of his father, occupied
as he was with his business and city planning ventures. Moreover, he
now had his wife Kitty's failing health to worry about. She suffered
from locomotor ataxia, a debilitating disease almost certainly caused
by syphilis she had contracted before meeting Milton.[6] Madly in love
with Kitty, Milton devoted his every free second to trying to find a cure
for her disease, sparing no expense. He frequently took her to New
York and Europe seeking advice and treatment from medical specialists. Whenever they traveled, it was always first class—the best hotels,
the finest restaurants, the most expensive clothing stores—anything
Milton could do to make Kitty comfortable and demonstrate his profound love. The Hersheys' glamorous lifestyle on their frequent travels
stood in sharp contrast to their modest living arrangements in puri-
tanical Lancaster County, where they endeavored to avoid displays of
conspicuous consumption that might cause them to stand out among
their "plain and simple" neighbors (as late as 1945, the New York Times
reported that bearded Amish and Mennonite men and traditionally
bonneted women were working in Hershey plants).[7]

Hershey's behavior as an employer was also a mass of contradictions. His recent biographer, Michael D'Antonio, describes his leadership as "schizophrenic," noting that "Hershey could be both generous
and short-fused."[8] Almost invariably he would speak to employees in
the factory as his peers and equals, and then suddenly and harshly criticize a loyal worker over a trivial offense. He made certain his workers
lived in comfortable homes in a spotlessly clean community with free
schools and hospitals, yet acted the miser when it came to paying their

wages. While Milton personally enjoyed fine wines and brandy on his travels, he fired employees caught drinking in his company town. The Hershey factory was clean, warm in winter, and well-ventilated in summer, yet its workers toiled under Frederick Winslow Taylor's "scientific management" system, which reduced their tasks to dulling, inhumane assembly-line routines that called to mind the soul-destroying work satirized in Charlie Chaplin's classic film *Modern Times*. Although Hershey lavished imported luxuries on Kitty, he harshly reprimanded employees who "wasted" electricity by turning on extra lights needed to do their tasks.[9]

Job security was the unquestioned norm in the chocolate factory, where most employees assumed they had lifetime employment; nonetheless, Hershey had a reputation for the occasional arbitrary firing. One such incident concerning the company's most skilled cocoa roaster became the stuff of legend. Just as a fire broke out in the oven where the roaster was working, Hershey happened to enter the room, accompanied by three touring guests, who suddenly found themselves confronted by a lava flow of flaming cocoa beans. They escaped safely. Nonetheless, Hershey summarily fired the roaster, despite explanations from his supervisor that the fire was due not to carelessness but to a faulty brick in the oven, and that furthermore, the roaster had done a heroic job in dousing the flames. Hershey would hear none of it.

Such foibles and contradictions aside, Milton Hershey was genuinely beloved by his employees and the residents of the town that came to be known as Hershey, Pennsylvania. After all, he provided them with a standard of living and quality of life unimaginable to most working-class Americans at the turn of the twentieth century. Whatever harm Milton's occasional bad judgment might have caused, in the public eye his behavior was saintly compared to the greedy disdain for workers displayed by such robber-baron contemporaries as John D. Rockefeller and Andrew Carnegie, or the self-serving paternalism of Henry Ford and George Pullman.

Hershey quickly became a renowned public figure, respected for both his philanthropic deeds and his entrepreneurial skills. The Hershey Chocolate Company made a great deal of money between 1905, the year the factory opened, and 1917, when the United States entered World War I, and its benevolent owner spent almost all of it creating his model town and funding charitable activities designed to improve the lives of its residents. It is difficult to say exactly how profitable the company was; in that pre-income-tax era, such information was known only to Hershey and his accountants. We do know the company's net sales in its first year of operation were about $1 million, growing to $20 million a dozen years later.[10] And based on the thousands of acres of land Hershey acquired during that era, the capital he reinvested in expanding the factory (five additional buildings), the impressive number of public works and buildings he erected (a hotel, amusement park, zoo, and convention hall), and the generous profit-sharing bonus (20 percent of salary) he began paying his employees annually in 1912, it is safe to conclude that the enterprise was highly profitable. And, unbeknownst to anyone other than Milton, Kitty, and their lawyer, in 1909 the Hersheys initiated a process by which they would give away the bulk of their fortune.

The School

Given the nature of Kitty Hershey's health problems, it is not surprising that she and Milton were unable to have children of their own. Nonetheless, the couple found a way to compensate for the family they profoundly felt they were missing. In 1909 they began to take in needy and orphan boys to live on Henry and Fanny's old homestead, which Milton had repurchased for his father in 1886, and which was now a working dairy farm. There, Milton and Kitty established a free boarding school for boys between four and fifteen years old, based on a pedagogical philosophy similar to that of Robert Owen's New Lanark school: play and physical activities were viewed as equally central to the development of healthy and happy children as was classroom learning. Much as those in Nebraska's Boys Town, the Pennsylvania orphans lived in relatively small homes headed by married couples, and they worked in the dairy with the intent of learning to become skilled farmers. As the number of boys in their care grew, the Hersheys officially established the Hershey Industrial School, offering up to twelve years of free foster care, clothing, education, and vocational training to orphaned and disadvantaged boys from Lancaster County. The boys were paid modest amounts for the work they did on the farm, enough for each to accumulate a nest egg with which to get started in life after graduation.

Milton genuinely loved the school and regularly visited the increasing number of boys living on his old farm, although Kitty's rapidly declining health made it difficult for her to join him on his visits. When she died in 1915, at forty-two, he went into a period of deep mourning that lasted nearly three years, ending only when he secretly put 500,000 of the 730,000 shares of Hershey Company shares he owned—valued then at some $60 million—into a trust benefiting the Industrial School. That donation was not made public until 1923, when the *New York Times* broke the story on its front page.[11]

Hershey explained his beneficence in the following way: "When a man gets very rich, he either gets very selfish or his money worries him." Later he added, "I never could see what happiness a rich man gets from contemplating a life of acquisition only, with a cold and legal distribution of his wealth after he passes away. . . . After all, what good is one's money unless one uses it for the good of the community and humanity in general?"[12] The source of Hershey's motivation to "do good" is not clear. He was a relatively apolitical supporter of Theodore Roosevelt's reformist brand of Republicanism, yet there is no evidence that he was an ideological progressive. For example, while he favored the taxation of inherited wealth, he also believed that taxing the income of rich Americans would inhibit the entrepreneurship needed for economic growth. He seems not to have had any deep religious motivations, either: Hershey considered himself a nonpracticing Christian who "found good in all religions."[13] Nonetheless, he may have had an ingrained touch of the Mennonites' dedication to a life of virtue. We will never know for certain; unlike most of the other business leaders profiled in these pages, he never made the effort to put his philosophical beliefs on paper.

There was, however, a curious religious connection in Great Britain to Hershey's life and career in Pennsylvania. As noted above, the Quaker Cadbury and Rowntree families pioneered the production of chocolate bars in Britain about the time Hershey was doing the same in the Quaker State. Moreover, British Quakers had been the first, perhaps only, British businesspeople to have adopted Robert Owen's practices while the great reformer was still alive. In 1845 the Quaker industrialist John Grubb Richardson built an iron mill in Northern Ireland alongside a model town he had created to house his four thousand workers, a town with many of the social amenities Owen had provided New Lanark's residents. In 1878 Quaker George Cadbury opened a chocolate factory near Birmingham, where he founded a model town, Bournbrook, to house his employees and other working-class people seeking decent housing in a clean, safe community in which to raise their children. And Hershey's contemporary Joseph Rowntree employed four thousand workers in a chocolate factory located in New Earswick, a village in Yorkshire where residents enjoyed a library and tuition-free schooling. According to journalist Mike King, author of *Quakernomics: An Ethical Capitalism*, in the late nineteenth century Rowntree's company provided employees with humane working conditions and such benefits as pensions and medical and dental care. Rowntree is reported to have said, "I do not want to establish communities bearing the stamp of charity but rather of rightly ordered and self-governing communities."[14] In that, Rowntree was more progressive than Milton Hershey.

¡Cuba, Si!

After his mother, Fanny, died in 1919, Milton began to spend less time in Pennsylvania and more in Cuba, where in 1914 he had purchased a sixty-thousand-acre sugar plantation and mill with the intent of securing a reliable—and inexpensive—source of sugar for his chocolate factory. When America entered World War I, and the price of a pound of sugar more than doubled, his prescient investment proved extremely profitable. In 1919 sixty-two-year-old Milton Hershey went all in with the Cuban investment, establishing a company mill town that he dubbed Central Hershey, connecting it to the port of Havana 120 miles away via a private railroad he had constructed. He then devoted much of the next decade to the task of turning Central Hershey into a utopian community modeled on the one he had created in Lancaster County: he built schools for the children of his workers and established an orphan school that eventually accommodated over a thousand Cuban boys. He also spent considerable time in Havana's fleshpots, gambling, drinking, and smoking Cuban cigars while enjoying floor shows in which young women, some of whom wore little or nothing in the way of costumes, danced to catchy Latin rhythms. He dropped as much as $50,000 per month in Havana's casinos—all the while resisting demands from his Cuban railway workers for living wages. As always, there were two sides to Milton Hershey.

Despite his love of gambling, Hershey was prudent when it came to the finances of his chocolate company, which he reorganized as the Hershey Chocolate Corporation in 1927 before offering a small amount of restricted stock to outside investors. He divorced ownership of the risky Cuban business from that of the predictably profitable chocolate company, and created yet a third entity to own the public utilities, trolley line, and department store of Hershey, Pennsylvania, and the large hotel, sports arena, office building, school, and amusement park he would later build. He flirted with selling all three companies to a New York bank in early 1929, but reconsidered the deal just prior to the Wall Street crash in October of that year. Instead, he placed all his stock in the three companies under control of the Hershey Foundation, designating the bulk of it for support of the Industrial School (with a smaller, separate foundation devoted to benefiting the company town).

Because Americans continued to purchase candy during the Great Depression, the Hershey company handily survived the horrendous decade during which tens of thousands of American businesses and banks closed their doors, and nearly a quarter of all employed Americans lost their jobs. Much as the company had done during World War I, it remained profitable during the 1930s, with all its employees maintained on the payroll. Some were put to work constructing the many buildings Hershey erected in his town as a means to counter the effects of the Depression. Hershey, although an inveterate gambler, nonetheless considered investing on the stock market to be far too risky; hence, he personally rode out the bad times with little economic loss. Moreover, he came out of the Depression with an enhanced national reputation due to the fact that Hershey, Pennsylvania, was one of the few places in America relatively unscathed by the economic plague that had afflicted most communities.

Hershey's Detractors

Despite his many virtues, Milton Hershey had detractors—and fairly so. *Fortune* magazine criticized him for retaining sole control over his company town: "Hershey has no mayor and no municipal government because it has never been incorporated. . . . Its inhabitants lead their daily lives in a relationship so close to Mr. Hershey as to be patriarchal."[15] For example, without informing the townspeople, he spent $100,000 to construct a department store he donated to them to run as a cooperative. Perhaps influenced by Robert Owen's old-age involvement with the cooperative movement, Hershey said, "Co-operation is the only true solution of many of our problems."[16]Alas, the townspeople were more interested in deciding for themselves what they needed, and in one of their rare rebellions against Hershey's paternalism, they refused his offer. The *Fortune* article further criticized Hershey's refusal to alter the rigid terms imposed on the school's trustees, which as early as the 1930s were making it difficult for them to change policies in response to a changing environment—for example, to allow Catholic boys to attend mass, or to admit nonwhites (and, later, girls). Moreover, even though the company accumulated some $45 million in retained earnings during the 1930s, Hershey refused to use any of it to increase his chocolate workers' wages.

In 1937 Hershey's autocratic rule led to a major effort by the Congress for Industrial Organizations (CIO) union to organize his factory's workforce. During the years when he had been off in Cuba—or cruising the Caribbean—he had turned a blind eye toward a managerial system characterized by favoritism with regard to hiring, promotions, and pay. He had ignored chronic discrimination against Italian American employees and failed to control managers who rejected the pleas of workers concerned about growing health and safety issues in the factory. Hence, when the CIO made its move, some 80 percent of the factory workers joined the union. An irate handful of them went so far as to engage in a strike that brought production to a halt, then dug in and occupied the plant. Hershey stayed above the fray, turning matters over to a tough anti-union executive who refused to recognize the union's right to bargain for the workers. With tensions running high, things stood at a standoff until hundreds of local dairy farmers—joined by townspeople employed at Hershey enterprises unrelated to the chocolate business—stormed the factory, attacking the strikers with "bats, hammers, and pitchforks," dragging them out of the building, where "they were kicked, beaten, pelted with stones and lumps of coal."[17] The strikers' occupation of the factory was broken in a matter of minutes.

The anti-union riot appears to have been spontaneous and un-prompted by either Hershey or his managers. The dairy farmers had been motivated by the simple fact that Hershey Chocolate was their prime customer, without whose milk purchases they would have gone under in the midst of the Depression, and the townsfolk who joined them had been recipients of Hershey's beneficence and were thus gen-uinely loyal to him. Nonetheless, seventy-nine-year-old Milton Her-shey was shocked by the turn of events, never having allowed himself to consider the possibility that his factory was anything other than a model workplace. Two years later the National Labor Relations Board ruled against the company, forcing it to change its pay policies relat-ing to overtime, vacations, and holidays, and to establish a grievance procedure—terms duly negotiated by the new, company-dominated union that two-thirds of the factory workers had elected to represent them.

In his declining years, Milton donated his home to serve as the Hershey employees' clubhouse at the company's golf course. He es-tablished a tuition-free Hershey community college and a fund to provide educational and cultural opportunities for town residents, and constructed a medical center, sports arena, and amusement park, ultimately giving away his entire fortune. Hershey was still at his desk at age eighty-four when America entered World War II, and the last major act he oversaw—from a distance—was the development of "Field Ration D," a nutritious chocolate bar some five hundred thou-sand US soldiers and sailors consumed during the course of the con-flict (although they often complained that its taste left something to be desired). By then, he had largely retreated from management of the chocolate company, devoting most of his time to the school bearing his name. Increasingly eccentric in his later years, he died in 1945 after celebrating his eighty-eighth birthday with a small number of friends at his parents' old homestead. Some twelve hundred people attended the funeral of the man revered by employees, townspeople, and the general public alike.

A Mixed Legacy

Throughout his long life, Milton Hershey did things his own way. During the rise of the consumer economy in early-twentieth-century America, he stood alone among food manufacturers in eschewing the use of mass advertising. Ignoring the growing influence of Madison Avenue on marketing practices, he insisted that he "always believed that the best advertising is to make the best kind of good and it would advertise itself."[18] Decades after Hershey's death, the company remained the last holdout against the practice in the consumer goods industry of competing in terms more of advertising than of product quality. To this day, the company remains profitable and independent despite several attempts by larger corporations to acquire it. It has a good reputation for socially responsible behavior and, on a lesser scale, for engaging in the kinds of global sustainability efforts pioneered by Unilever. The company's ownership remains controlled by the charitable trust Milton Hershey established to fund the Hershey Industrial School in perpetuity. The school, renamed the Milton Hershey School in 1951, now educates two thousand boys and girls of all races and creeds, offering both vocational and academic courses, and providing students with free tuition, food, clothing, and medical care. The trust's $12 billion endowment is the largest endowment of any private school in America, rivaling funds at some of the wealthiest major universities, and fed annually by some $160 million in Hershey company dividends.

When Hershey died, he no doubt was satisfied with all he had accomplished as a businessman and philanthropist, and confident his legacy would be maintained. That confidence proved well deserved until 2002, when the first outsider to head Hershey Foods (as the company was then known) began, at the urging of the school's trustees, to concentrate on increasing its profit margins. CEO Richard H. Lenny closed three plants and a warehouse while announcing that, henceforth, Hershey employees would have to pay more toward their health coverage.

Viewing these actions as a betrayal of Milton Hershey's benevolent practices, some 2,700 Hershey employees went on strike. One worker explained, "Milton Hershey worried about the workers. The new guy here is nothing but corporate greed."[19] Before the dust could settle, a much bigger threat to Hershey's legacy became front-page news: the Hershey School trustees were putting Hershey Foods up for sale.

Prompted by the Pennsylvania state attorney's office to exercise greater prudence with regard to the billions in assets they managed, the trustees decided that instead of keeping all those eggs in one basket—the 77 percent of Hershey Foods stock they controlled—they would accept a $12 billion acquisition bid from the Wrigley Company. Hershey's townspeople, however—some 6,700 of whom worked for the candy firm—fearing the loss of their jobs, their community's historic economic base, and their town's unique traditions, coalesced to stop the sale. The same state attorney's office that had prompted the sale then stepped in to halt it, requesting a court order to block any future sale unless it could be shown to do no harm to the community or school. That brouhaha led to several changes in the composition of the board of trustees, and to an agreement with the attorney general to revamp their governance practices. It also was the impetus for the first critical public examination of the terms of the Hershey Trust. What then became clear to all had been clear to many from the time the terms were drafted by Milton Hershey's lawyers: the trustees were charged with maximizing revenue for the school, not with being responsible to the company's workers or host community; they had been given too little flexibility to change the way the school was funded and governed as circumstances changed over time; they had too much control over the company, whose needs were subservient to the perceived needs of the school (to many trustees, the company was merely a cash cow); and they were an indecently overpaid body with what amounted to lifelong sinecures.

But little was done about any of those problems until 2016, when what had festered for so long erupted as a major scandal. The precipitating event was a $23 billion bid by food giant Mondelēz International to acquire Hershey Company.[20] It is worth noting that Mondelēz attempted to acquire Unilever a year later. The objections raised to both attempts were similar: Mondelēz was seen by employees, local communities, and informed observers as a conventionally managed company with little interest in maintaining the unique culture and high-minded practices of such companies as Hershey and Unilever.[21] Members of the school's trust had a different take: they believed selling the company would double the trust's current endowment of $12 billion. As members of the boards of both the trust and the company saw it, they had a fiduciary duty to maximize profits for stockholders (principally the trust, which now controlled over 80 percent of voting stock).[22]

Locals protested, concerned about the potential of losing their jobs and benefits, the negative effects on community financing, and the implications for tourism in the "sweetest place on earth" if it no longer was suffused with the aroma of chocolate. And alumni of the school worried about changes that might occur if it acquired a Yale-sized endowment. For some time, they had been alarmed by the proclivity of the trustees to amass a far bigger endowment than needed to support the school (its annual budget was far less than the annual dividend the trust received from its Hershey stock), and by the board's continuing heavy investment in unnecessary brick and mortar, rather than in expanding the number of children being served. The alumni then joined with concerned community members to cast a harsher spotlight on the same individuals they had identified as culprits in the 2002 failed company takeover: the school's trustees.

The bright lights revealed an unlovely sight. It turned out that the trustees had been gorging themselves at the Hershey trough for years. Each member of the self-serving, self-perpetuating board received $110,000 per year in compensation, but that was just the minimum: three members were also entitled to a $250,000 seat on the company board, another had a similarly lucrative seat on the board of Hershey Entertainment, and the trust's chairman was found to have $3.6 million in a deferred compensation account.[23] As if that weren't bad enough, the board had used trust money to purchase a golf course at $12 million, two to three times its appraised value, in the process bailing out a dozen investors who had financed its construction—including one Richard Lenny, the former Hershey Foods CEO who had created the 2002 stir and now served as a school trustee. For good measure, the board had kicked in an additional $5 million of trust money to build a fancy bar and restaurant at the golf course. The trustees had also hired a lobbyist to whom they paid $900,000 a year until he was convicted for bribing a state politician (albeit on behalf of a different client).[24]

With so much money at play, and so many opportunities for self-dealing and attendant conflicts of interest, the trust's boardroom had become toxic with intrigue and infighting. Members accused each other, variously, of using their influence to get jobs for their offspring at companies doing business with the trust; trading on insider Hershey Company information; betraying Milton Hershey's principles and philosophy; spending $1 billion on unnecessary brick-and-mortar projects at the school to enrich local contractors; and launching smear campaigns against each other. In 2015–16 the trust spent $4 million in legal fees just to investigate the charges board members had made against each other.[25] Again, the Pennsylvania attorney general stepped in to investigate. The company's prospects for remaining independent in the future are unclear.[26]

Of course Milton Hershey anticipated none of this, and would have been appalled by it all. Yet in some ways he inadvertently set the stage for the sorry spectacle. As his biographer D'Antonio muses, Hershey "could have let the industrial school trust have the flexibility to change with the times. He could have allowed Hershey to become a real town in which voters elected officials who could collect taxes and deliver services according to the will of the people. He could have paid his workers better wages, and let them decide what to do with the money."[27] Instead, Hershey had insisted on exercising sole, paternalistic control over the school trust, the governance of the town, and management of the company.

Probably the fairest way to assess Milton Hershey's career is to say that he *almost* got it right. His primary error was to mix conventional philanthropy with business, favoring the former at the expense of the latter. In the end, he was more concerned with his reputation for serving the broader society than he was with creating a great and sustainably virtuous company; hence, he paid insufficient attention to the business, the needs of its employees, and the values of those who lived in *his* company town. In sum, Hershey was a far better confectioner and philanthropist than businessman.

5

Creating an Enduring Enterprise

JAMES LINCOLN (1883–1965)

In 1914, James Finney Lincoln began to make a series of managerial decisions that, decades later, would allow his company to accomplish what
William Lever tried, but ultimately failed, to do: reconcile the antagonistic interests of workers and owners. Lincoln believed, as educator
Horace Mann had claimed in 1867, that "property and labor in different
classes are essentially antagonistic; but property and labor in the same
class are essentially fraternal."[1] Thanks to the system Lincoln created,
over the last century the owners, managers, and workers of the Lincoln
Electric Company have had strong incentives to cooperate in order to
meet the needs of their customers. In so doing, they have together forged
the world's largest manufacturer of electric arc-welding machines.

Even after numerous changes in Lincoln Electric's leadership, that
system remains in place today in what has become a highly profitable
$3 billion multinational enterprise which dominates its global markets
as the result of the enviable productivity and innovation of its 3,300
workers in the United States, and 6,000 in nineteen other countries.
Over the last century, Lincoln Electric consistently has ranked among
the most productive manufacturing enterprises in the United States.
Since 1947, it has not laid off a single permanent employee, and for
over eighty years it has paid bonuses to its workers averaging 40 to 100
percent of their annual salaries (in 2017 the company paid out about
$100 million in bonuses on $300 million in net profit). Over the years,

Lincoln workers have earned two to three times the average income of their fellow Americans, while enjoying top benefits and the rare guarantee of employment in good times and bad.

Americans, by and large, are so focused on today's business news and this quarter's results that few know much about Lincoln Electric, their nation's greatest continuing corporate success story. That story began in 1904 when John Cromwell Lincoln, son of a Congregationalist preacher, established the Lincoln Electric Company, which became the first to make and market an economically viable electric car. Despite John Lincoln's remarkable talent for invention, electric cars soon lost out in competition with more efficient internal combustion engines. Nonetheless, the resourceful Lincoln saw that the generator in his cars could be retooled to create an arc of electricity powerful enough to weld steel to steel—a far more effective bonding process than the then-dominant technology of riveting. After he switched industries, engineer Lincoln's arc-welding company became a financial success; however, he promptly realized he had no interest in managing it. He then recruited his younger brother, James, to run the business, himself retreating to the company's lab, where he would spend the rest of his career accumulating fifty-five patents.[2]

John Lincoln was an extremely tall, gaunt man of few words, a college dropout uncomfortable managing even the small team of fellow engineers in his lab. Brother James—seventeen years John's junior—was every bit as tall as his brother, yet the similarities stopped there. James was a solidly built, ruggedly handsome former star fullback on the Ohio State football team. By all accounts, he was a different breed of industrialist than his sibling: a true entrepreneur, charismatic leader, and brilliant capitalist with a singular focus on creating the finest business firm in America. Early on, he had a profound insight that would influence every decision the company made from the early 1920s until his death in 1965: "I knew that if I could get the people in the company to want to succeed as badly as I did, there would be no problem we could not solve together."[3]

James Lincoln approached business the way he had played football: he threw himself into the fray enthusiastically, working harder than everyone around him. He once said, "Successful management requires the intelligence of a genius, the patience of a Job, the fighting ability of a Spartan, and the enthusiasm of a nut."[4] He displayed all those traits—even the last—in spades. There seems to have been nothing on James Lincoln's mind he wouldn't say in public, and nothing he ever had thought about on which he didn't have a strong opinion. Over his long life he had something impolitic to say about Wall Street investors, his fellow industrialists, labor unions, his own managers, and especially the "high-minded incompetents" in government. He was an equal-opportunity offender, albeit a cheery and affable one.

In 1914, finding himself, with no prior business background, the general manager of his brother's manufacturing firm, James Lincoln was forced to pursue a self-taught crash course in how to run a company. Not knowing where to start, he made a thorough study of the industrial practices Henry Ford was then pioneering in Detroit, learning valuable lessons on how, and how not, to manage. Lincoln approached the practice of management with the same gung-ho attitude he had displayed as captain of his college football team, beginning every meeting with the salutation "Fellow workers." When he later went on the stump to persuade other business leaders to convert to his business philosophy, he undertook that task with "the messianic zeal of an Old Testament prophet."[5] His message to both his workers and his peers was clear and simple: business was all about serving customers by providing them with the highest-quality product at the lowest price—and the means to that end was to engage all employees in the task. In the tradition of Robert Owen, William Lever, and J. C. Penney, a deep commitment to "the development of latent ability" lay at the core of Lincoln's philosophy. He firmly believed the world's greatest untapped resources were the abilities of the millions of undereducated and untrained men and women trapped in social systems and work organizations in which they had no opportunity to develop, or exercise, their potential. Ergo, he concluded the task of business leaders was to create conditions under which those talents could be developed—and the extent to which leaders succeeded in utilizing that talent would determine the progress of industry and society.[6]

To make employee development a reality in his company, Lincoln worked diligently over four decades to create a unique system he called "incentive management." The system had four key elements: communication and participation; piecework compensation; merit-based bonuses; and guaranteed employment. It took him many years to fine-tune and align those four factors to his satisfaction, but when he had done so, he believed he had created a coherent system, at the same time highly productive *and* fair to workers. But he didn't stop there: he then became a secular prophet, preaching the merits of his system to other business leaders. He told them that if they all adopted his incentive system, they could create a just alternative to socialism. He proved to be a brilliant business leader, but a poor social and economic prognosticator.

Element I: Communication and Participation

James Lincoln believed that workers are motivated to cooperate with management when they are respected as human beings and given a chance to develop—and use—their talents on the job. He thus resolved to treat his employees as partners, giving them access to managerial data and allowing them to find ways to improve the company's productivity and efficiency. Most singularly, he was bent on rewarding them handsomely for doing so. He began in 1914 by establishing the annually elected Lincoln Electric advisory board, which now has met with the company's top management every two weeks for over a century. Over that period, workers and management jointly have made almost every major decision the company has taken. The board was, and still is, empowered to make suggestions, lodge complaints, criticize management, propose new ways to improve productivity and product quality, and raise any other concerns on the workers' minds. In 1929, when the board suggested closing the company at noon so employees could attend the opening day of baseball season, James Lincoln agreed—and off they all went to cheer on the Cleveland Indians. More recently, and far more significantly, Lincoln's domestic American workers agreed to create new jobs abroad, instead of at home, reasoning that foreign expansion was necessary for the long-term viability of their enterprise. That unprecedented decision doubtless represented a degree of employee cooperation with management found in no other American manufacturing enterprise.

Over the years, Lincoln workers have shown no interest in killing the goose that produces the abundant eggs in their compensation and benefits baskets. The company has granted its employees— all of whom are nonunion—with benefits found in the highest-compensated unionized shops, and many more: group life insurance, medical insurance, paid vacations, stock ownership, profit sharing, and pensions—almost all of which they received long before other American factory workers. They have enjoyed those benefits in egalitarian work environments with no executive parking lots or dining rooms, and in manufacturing facilities as safe and as clean as any found in American industry, each with a single entrance shared by executives, workers, and visitors alike.

From the day James Lincoln assumed leadership of the company, the door to the chief executive's office has been open to every employee. The intent of that openness has not been to encourage workers to bring decisions to the boss for him to make; instead, it has been to facilitate a free flow of information throughout the company so problems will be solved—and initiatives taken—at the operating level. In general, Lincoln production workers are self-managing and empowered to solve problems without supervisorial permission. Yet the company is not a democracy: top management retains the right to veto any decisions made by the advisory board. Tellingly, that residual power has never been exercised, because workers and management have come to share the same interests.

Although the company has enjoyed unusually harmonious industrial relations, it would be a mistake to overidealize that aspect of its culture. As in any organization, there have been conflicts, disagreements, and disgruntled groups and individuals. In the mid-1990s, dissident Lincoln Electric employees took part in a union-organizing campaign to "force management back to better lines of communication" with regard to decisions that had reduced the company's commitment to promoting from within, and altered the way its pension plan was funded. When management subsequently reversed those decisions, the employees promptly called off the organizing drive. The worker who had led the effort explained to journalist Frank Koller that his peers' intent had been simply to get management back in the habit of listening to them, and that in fact they never wanted a union: "Why would we want to hurt our livelihood?"[7] In all, it had taken Lincoln's leaders decades of hard work to build a culture in which its employees trust management's commitment to its oft-stated goal that "everybody wins."

Element II: Piecework Compensation

Unlike most industrial workers, Lincoln's one thousand domestic American manufacturing employees are not paid by the hour, by the week, or based on seniority. Instead, the company's managers and workers negotiate objective scales by which factory workers are compensated based on their actual, productive output—the more they produce, the more money they make. Factory pay at Lincoln Electric is thus calculated under a piecework system. The base rate for the average worker is set at approximately the going wage for unionized workers in the region—but no upper limit is placed on how much above that any worker, or all of them, can earn based on the amount, or number, of "pieces" they complete. In fact, there is an incentive for employees not only to earn as much as they can but literally to work themselves out of their jobs by finding ways to do their tasks through automation. When they do so, they are rewarded and promoted to jobs requiring higher human skills.

Calculating piece rates that are both fair and effective is no mean feat. Indeed, it is Lincoln Electric's major ongoing managerial challenge. To ensure fairness, every manufacturing worker has the right to challenge new rates when they are set, and such negotiations between workers and managers are common. In the end, piecework pay at Lincoln is effective because it is based on workers' trusting management not to exploit them—buttressed by average earnings that, at about $74,000 per annum, give workers little to complain about. Moreover, the system provides incentives for workers to invent new ways to improve the company's financial performance, thus justifying James Lincoln's abiding faith in the untapped abilities of production workers to contribute to the success of the company.

That faith stemmed from an advisory board meeting held during the darkest days of the Great Depression. At the meeting, a factory worker asked Lincoln, "If we did more, tried harder, and worked together as a real team, would the company pay us more?" The answer was obvious to Lincoln, who then set about creating a system in which the company could pay workers based on their contributions to its bottom line. In Lincoln's philosophy, all workers have deep reserves of "latent ability," and therefore it is the duty of managers to organize a system that fully uses those abilities. For example, by eliminating the need for most supervisors and middle managers—the prime source of costly, unproductive overhead in most companies—Lincoln Electric became the most efficient company in its industry, including companies in low-wage Asia. As one worker explained to journalist Koller, "I know I am doing a good job if I seldom see my manager, I'm working hard, I'm taking pride in my work. I don't need to be managed, and that's part of the merit-rating system, how well you work without supervision. It makes his job easier, and, in turn, he rewards me."[8]

Worker self-management allows Lincoln Electric to offer the highest compensation in its industry while, paradoxically, enjoying the lowest total labor costs. Their formula is simple: fewer highly paid, highly productive employees add more value than larger numbers of low-paid, less productive ones. In essence, James Lincoln understood the crucial difference between unit labor costs and total labor costs, a distinction most business leaders have historically failed to make, and many still do not grasp. For example, Walmart's Sam's Club has focused on keeping its unit labor costs low by offering minimum wages and few benefits to its relatively large, poorly trained, and underproductive workforce. In contrast, Sam's Club's prime competitor, Costco, concentrates on keeping its total labor costs low by offering higher pay and more generous benefits to its relatively smaller, better trained, and considerably more productive workforce, and hence is more profitable than Sam's Club. By using a similar formula, well-paying Lincoln Electric has been able to compete successfully against Asian manufacturers paying low wages.[9]

Element III: Merit-Based Bonuses

Only about a third of Lincoln Electric's domestic American employees are production workers paid by piecework. The two-thirds *not* paid that way could constitute a significant financial drag on the company were they not as motivated as their factory peers. Since it is almost impossible to effectively apply piecework to the compensation of employees involved in sales, finance, human resources, research and development, and other white-collar functions, the company motivates all its workers with a uniquely generous form of profit sharing. Annually, roughly one-third of total company profits are paid out to employees—including those in production—as merit-based bonuses. The bonus amounts awarded to production workers are based on their individual performance with regard to output, quality, adaptability, dependability, teamwork, ideas, cooperation, and adherence to environmental, health, and safety standards. The bonus metrics for white-collar employees are slightly different, including such factors as customer focus, innovation, decision-making judgment, and working without supervision. From the beginning, the bonuses have been generous: in 1941 James Lincoln granted bonuses ranging from $40,000 to $50,000 to members of his top management team, while also awarding a shop foreman $25,000.[10] In 2017 the typical Lincoln employee took home roughly $74,000 in total annual compensation, about $25,000 of that coming in the form of a bonus.[11] The total percentage paid in bonuses to individuals has varied over the years from as high as 120 percent of base pay to as low as 25 percent.

In 1992 the system was put to an acid test when Lincoln Electric's foreign operations ran such deep losses that, despite the continued profitability of its US business, the company as a whole was hemorrhaging red ink. Hence, there were no profits from which to pay the annual bonus that had been a staple at Lincoln Electric for some eighty years. The company's top management and board of directors then did the unexpected and unprecedented: they borrowed money to pay bonuses. The company's domestic workers had put in heroic efforts to keep the company afloat, they reasoned, and thus deserved to be rewarded accordingly. More important, not paying the bonus would have amounted to breaking the company's social contract, with subsequent negative consequences for the high level of trust accumulated over the decades.[12]

Managers at Lincoln find determining fair and effective individual bonuses to be almost as complex and time-consuming as setting piecework rates: the process requires establishing meaningful, objective standards, then following up with rigorous data gathering and analysis. Awarding merit bonuses probably would generate more controversy at Lincoln than it does were it not for the fact that the system has been managed so diligently—and, no less important, that it has paid out so handsomely. During World War II, James Lincoln found himself forced to defend the system in testimony before a congressional hearing at which skeptical Democratic representatives accused him of paying large bonuses to evade federal corporate taxes. Moreover, they accused him of allowing Lincoln Electric's bonus-earning workers to profiteer from the sale of goods purchased by the military. Controlling his tendency to attack those with whom he disagreed, Lincoln patiently explained that *because* of the bonus system, his company was able to sell its products to the government at a far lower price than its competitors, thus saving taxpayers some $35 million annually.[13] That congressional naysaying was not unusual; James Lincoln spent a great deal of time attempting to explain his company's unusual practices to all manner of doubters, skeptics, and critics, few of whom he appears ever to have convinced.

Element IV: Guaranteed Employment

While Lincoln Electric had a long history of avoiding employee layoffs during bad economic times—weathering the Great Depression with its workforce intact—that record was sorely challenged during severe recessions in 1954 and 1957, when company managers were forced to scramble to reassign underemployed workers to useful tasks, much as Robert Owen had done at New Lanark under similar economic conditions 150 years earlier, and Milton Hershey did during the Depression. When his managers successfully kept everyone employed by such judicious means as reducing the number of hours worked per week and giving paintbrushes to production workers, James Lincoln became convinced it was practical to institute a formal no-layoff policy. Hence, in 1958, the company introduced the guaranteed continuous employment plan that is still in place today. It is important to note that the plan does not guarantee jobs for life; instead, Lincoln's permanent domestic employees (those with three years of service in Cleveland) are guaranteed at least thirty hours of paid employment per week even when there is low demand for its products. Workers are not guaranteed their current jobs or pay rates, and the plan covers only those who have met the company's clearly defined standards of performance. In exchange for the guarantee, workers agree to work overtime when Lincoln products are in great demand. The plan has worked well over the six decades it has been in place, although the company was forced to go to a thirty-hour week at the bottom of the 2008–9 recession. Such exceptions notwithstanding, full employment (on average, forty-five-hour weeks) has been the norm at Lincoln Electric, where it has not been unusual for workers to put in fifty-plus-hour weeks.

To deliver on its unique promise of guaranteed employment, Lincoln's managers pay inordinate attention to staffing levels, work scheduling, job assignments, and hiring practices. Even though Lincoln Electric is the preferred employer among blue-collar workers in Cleveland, relatively few people qualify for its jobs, and among those chosen, a great number quickly find the hard work is not for them. As a result, the company's turnover rate in the first three months of employment was historically extremely high, between 30 and 50 percent. However, a new, highly selective hiring process was introduced in 2006 to help identify job candidates most likely to thrive in a system demanding so much of its workers. Since then, the company's ninety-day quit rate has been reduced to around 10 percent.[14]

Significantly, almost all workers who last through the initial three-year probationary period tend to stay on until retirement. Lincoln Electric is unusual in that it doesn't push older, higher-paid workers out the door in favor of younger, lower-paid new hires. As a result, on average, the company has a relatively mature workforce. It also has an unusually large number of employees who are related to each other—in some cases, multigeneration employee family members. This phenomenon probably is explained by the fact that the unusual work ethic needed to succeed at Lincoln stems from values shared in only a relatively small number of families. Moreover, not everyone is as willing as Lincoln workers to be so flexible in terms of the number of hours they work, and

what tasks they are asked to perform. For example, Lincoln employees agree to be moved to different jobs, even lower-paying ones, when
asked. Almost all Lincoln employees have experienced what they call
"the tap"—that is, when they are tapped on the shoulder and told they
are needed in another part of the company. As one worker explained,
"You gotta go and help where there is demand."[15] Almost every account
written about the company contains anecdotes concerning relatively
undereducated blue-collar workers who have hustled, sacrificed, and
used their brains and initiative to make James Lincoln's system work.

The same is true of the company's managers and white-collar employees. Much is expected of Lincoln's salaried engineers, researchers,
salespeople, and managers, who, in common with production workers,
enjoy guaranteed employment. In downtimes, when demand for arc-
welding machines is low, the pay of company managers and salaried
workers is reduced, and their prime task then becomes finding ways to
get the hourly production workers back on full-time. As Lincoln employees at every level say, "We are all in this together."

Trade Union Objections

On the face of it, one might assume that unions would be in favor of
James Lincoln's philosophy of management. After all, Lincoln Electric's hourly employees enjoy high incomes, generous benefits, job security, stock ownership, profit sharing, a say in management, and clear
grievance procedures—everything historically on the union agenda,
and more. Yet in fact unionists have been the harshest critics of the Lincoln model of employment, as they have been of almost every similar
effort made by industrial managers in the United States and Britain.
In the 1940s one labor organizer commented, "They work like dogs at
Lincoln, but it pays off," explaining that "there are plenty of people who
are willing to burn themselves out for the kind of money Lincoln pays."
Yet he suggested that James Lincoln may actually have *overemphasized*

financial rewards: "If the day comes when they can't offer those big bonuses, or his people decide there's more to life than killing yourself making money, I predict the Lincoln Electric Company is in trouble."[16]

In general, unions have opposed such managerial initiatives as profit sharing, employee engagement in the design and management of their work tasks, and employee participation in company-wide decision making. Similarly, they have rejected worker capitalism in the form of employee stock ownership as a clever ploy designed to fool workers into believing their interests are identical to those of management. One trade union objection to the Lincoln system stems from the absence of a collective employee "voice" in the workplace. Unionists believe that only through worker solidarity can labor generate sufficient power to present a counterbalance to the formidable weight of capital. They argue that unless there is a strong, independent union empowered to speak for all workers collectively, any benefits employees receive from a company will be arbitrary, in the self-interest of owners, and non-contractual and thus subject to being rescinded at the discretion of management. Hence, over the years, labor leaders have characterized Lincoln's advisory board as "a company union" (forbidden under federal law). In essence, unions argue that Lincoln's employee advisory board amounts to a company-controlled faux union that on the surface appears to represent the interests of workers, but in fact functions as a tool by which management can manipulate the workforce. Lincoln Electric has successfully answered that charge to the satisfaction of government regulators by portraying the role of the advisory board as a formal structure to facilitate employee-management communication and coordination.

But the unionists' strongest criticisms are directed at Lincoln's piecework method of compensation. That system has been the bane of unions since the "scientific management" era of the late nineteenth century, when infamous industrial engineer Frederick Winslow Taylor attempted to break down manufacturing tasks into discrete and measurable physical actions, calculate how many such actions workers could do in a given time period, and then establish a pay rate to reward workers for the number of actions they complete. Unions long have argued that such a system—the system Milton Hershey used in his chocolate factory—is simply a method designed to wring the last bit of productivity out of workers. Worse, unions argue, piecework creates invidious competition among workers when the herculean output of few highly productive "rate busters" able and willing to engage in hard toil at full speed for hours on end causes managers to alter the pay scale when those atypical workers begin to "make too much." Then, after the bar is raised, it becomes harder for average workers to earn fair wages. Unions say experience shows that management uses the efforts of rate busters to set the standards of performance for all other workers—standards impossible for the average worker to meet or maintain. Moreover, they say that piecework standards can be arbitrarily changed by management.[17]

James Lincoln was aware of such criticisms—and abuses of the piecework system—and pledged to find a way to reward individual performance while at the same time protecting workers from the relentless, inhumane pressure to constantly produce more. "Piecework has a bad name," he concluded, "not because of the worker, but because of management. The great difficulty was that as soon as a man started to increase his earnings, [the piece rate] was renegotiated and his earnings reduced. We feel it is essential that price [i.e., pay for piece] is guaranteed forever; regardless of how much a man makes it will stand. Only as a new method or a new machine, one that would make a real change in the job itself, is introduced is a new price set. And that [new] price is guaranteed forever."[18]

Even though Lincoln made good on this pledge, unions have remained adamant in their opposition to piecework, pointing to examples when they have been burned by executives who claimed to act in the interest of workers, only then to jack up the piece rate when workers started to gain "too much" benefit from the system. For example, in 1972, Sidney Harman, head of Harman International Industries, wrote that a business leader "cannot serve shareholders effectively if he does not act to make business itself an agent for human growth and fulfillment. For, unless the businessman-employer . . . recognizes this as a minimal obligation, he will in the long run (and more likely in the short term) participate in the destruction of the very instrument from which stockholders draw nourishment." Echoing James Lincoln, Harman went on to assert that "work satisfaction—which is to say the attainment of a sense of purposefulness in his or her work, the achievement of a sense of personal worth and dignity—should be seen as a fundamental obligation of employers."[19] It appeared that Harman was prepared to put into practice what he advocated when he enlisted the cooperation of the United Auto Workers in a highly publicized experiment to "humanize" work in an auto-mirror factory he had recently purchased. The plant, located in the economically depressed town of Bolivar, Tennessee, was plagued by low productivity and a history of poor labor relations, compounded by the fact that its workforce was largely composed of undereducated African Americans working under white supervisors. The idea of the experiment was for management and the union to negotiate a fair piecework rate—in this case, the number of mirrors produced per day. Then, whenever during the day the workers had achieved the standard, they were offered three choices: go home; stay on the job and earn overtime; or attend free classes in a company school offering a range of courses from business math to piano playing.

The workers were left to decide for themselves how best to organize their work, and it took several days of experimentation before they figured out how to meet the set standard by closing time. After that, they gradually improved their productivity almost daily. Soon they were reaching their daily quota in the early afternoon. When the company then demanded a reset of the piecework standard, the union and workers acceded. But when the workers again increased productivity, and the company called for yet another renegotiation, the union and workers balked. In effect, when management saw how productive (and profitable) the factory could be, they concluded the experiment had proved "too successful." Soon thereafter, owner Harman walked away from the experiment to accept a presidential appointment in the Carter administration; subsequently, he sold the Bolivar factory. In the eyes of the union and others who had been following the progress of the experiment, Harman appeared to have parlayed the positive press he received as "an enlightened business leader" into a subcabinet position. Again, it is impossible to know the motives of others, but Harman thereafter seemed to have lost interest in workplace reform and the corporate social responsibility he previously had championed. Thanks to the behavior of leaders like Harman, unions have interpreted managerial efforts to close the historically deep divide between labor and management as subtle forms of paternalism, the hidden purpose of which is to increase productivity and profitability and burnish the public image of managers and owners. That is why James Lincoln was never able to persuade them that his motivations were noble, and why they still oppose the company's piecework system.

Product Innovation

One key source of Lincoln Electric's long-term success has been the company's impressive record of product and process innovation, beginning with the contributions of founder John Lincoln. For the better part of a century, the company has dominated its industry in the introduction of new products and processes and, in particular, delivering high-quality and economic value to customers. Almost every arc-welding advance worldwide has come from Lincoln Electric's labs and factories. James Lincoln was as adamant about the need for the company to be the innovative leader in its industry as he was about the need to engage workers in that task. Historically, almost all the company's innovation and growth has been generated from within as the result of heavy reinvestment of profits. Lincoln continually resisted suggestions by his top management team to diversify the company's product line out of arc-welding, to engage in acquisitions, and to take the company public in order to raise capital for more rapid growth. More than one company executive argued that the company was financially underperforming because its rate of growth was below the average of large publicly traded, manufacturing firms. Lincoln adamantly disagreed. He was committed to the company's narrow product line, committed to financing growth through reinvestment, and totally opposed to selling shares to investors in order to become a giant Fortune 500 company. Above all, he wanted to avoid the boom-and-bust cycle that characterizes the record of most large, industrial enterprises. His preference was to grow slowly and steadily, even if that meant that his company would never be an industrial giant and thus could not pay its executives nearly as much as their peers in larger companies, nor create as much wealth for his family and employee-shareholders.

Lincoln didn't "think small," but he thought narrowly, focusing on the long-term benefits of private ownership that accrued to his employees and their community. One externalized benefit of the Lincoln system has been its effect on the communities in and around Cleveland, where the company's main plant is located. Even as that city suffered the fate of other rust-belt communities, Lincoln's three thousand employees provided a social and economic anchor to what otherwise would have been abandoned neighborhoods. Today, as Ohio's top exporter, Lincoln Electric remains the bright spot in Cleveland's otherwise troubled economy, its enormous, ultra-clean plant glowing under a giant wind turbine—the largest of its kind in an urban area—that provides power to the plant and keeps the community's air fresh and unpolluted.

The motivation for creating such a unique and enduring enterprise is clear: both John and James Lincoln wrote that their managerial beliefs were founded on their father's Christian values, notably the precept of the Golden Rule. Both quoted freely—and one senses, out of great familiarity—from Christian scriptures. James was an active member in the Presbyterian Church and fond of citing the Sermon on the Mount as the source of his managerial philosophy. Everything James Lincoln wrote, said, and did in his many books, articles, and recorded speech and actions manifests a fundamental desire to treat people well and with respect. He insisted on ethical behavior in all Lincoln Electric's policies and transactions: "Fair dealing and common honesty are not only legal but are fundamentally the best policy."[20] Yet he was careful to separate his personal religious convictions from the operational policies and practices of the company, invariably explaining the latter in secular, business terms. Moreover, in the several books he wrote to encourage other business executives to adopt incentive management, the arguments he advanced were couched in conventional economic terms and conservative political assumptions.

James Lincoln was a dyed-in-the-wool, rock-ribbed conservative, a vocal advocate of free-market capitalism, and a harsh critic of President Franklin Roosevelt's New Deal, which he dubbed "glorious larceny." He firmly believed that the Lincoln system was not only *the* just alternative to communism but also the most efficient alternative to Roosevelt's social welfare programs. In 1933 he publicly promoted his incentive management as an alternative to the New Deal, implying that if all businesses adopted the system, there would be no need for FDR's creeping socialism. "If the present attitude in Washington continues," he wrote to his brother in 1936, "this will not be a place where either you or I or our children can live with any degree of satisfaction."[21] Yet when he needed to be, James Lincoln was supremely pragmatic. When he made the case for guaranteed employment, it was neither in religious nor ideological terms but as sound, efficient management. What he would not—or could not—acknowledge was the reality that other business leaders were not interested in adopting his system.

Prior to World War II, James Lincoln's voluminous writings were full of anti-welfare-state vitriol, but later he produced thoughtful, well-reasoned expositions of his economic and managerial philosophy. "Incentive management," he concluded, "is more like a religious conversion. It is not a spur to the man to speed up; it is a philosophy of work. It is not a method of getting more work for less wages; it is a plan for making industry and all its parts more useful for mankind."[22] In the end, he advocated the creation of a classless society in which each individual would be able to rise to the level of his or her highest abilities: "We know that if a worker is treated as a 'hand' by his boss, as a 'common man' by the politician, and as a 'union man' by many labor leaders, he will never develop his latent abilities. If a man is put into a class and becomes class conscious, he thus becomes the same as his class and remains so. He will go to his grave a clod, even when he had the abilities of the genius latent in him."[23]

The Lincoln Electric Difference

During the first quarter of the twentieth century, numerous American companies began to introduce enlightened labor practices, including Eastman Kodak, General Electric, Sears, Roebuck and Company, Procter & Gamble, and, as we have seen, J. C. Penney. Driven largely by the distant threat of communism and the more immediate challenge of trade unionism, such companies experimented with profit sharing, pensions, group life and health insurance, and no-layoff policies. Thus, while not all of Lincoln Electric's practices were unusual for their time, James Lincoln's system has proved uniquely durable. While most major corporations have continued to provide employee health and life insurance, other enlightened labor practices they once offered have not been retained. Kodak and Sears followed J. C. Penney's pattern of shrinking into corporate insolvency and irrelevance, and the once-pioneering General Electric and P&G now offer only employment practices and benefits that are standard in global corporations of their size. In the 1990s, IBM became the last major corporation to end its policy of guaranteed employment.

James Lincoln's managerial thinking, as noted, was greatly influenced by the practices of Henry Ford—particularly those introduced in the early days of the Ford Motor Company, when its founder was seen not simply as a brilliant manufacturing innovator but also as an enlightened employer: for example, when he became the first employer to offer factory workers the then-unheard-of pay of $5 a day (at a time when the average industrial worker earned half that amount) and decent, company-provided family housing. Despite such progressive practices, as time progressed, Ford's faults began to far outweigh his virtues as he increasingly displayed maddening inconsistencies between what he said and how he behaved. In the process, his reputation as an employer changed for the worse: he came to be portrayed as an enemy of his own workers. As a result, the trust leaders earn through personal integrity and managerial consistency ultimately went missing at Ford Motor.

James Lincoln carefully observed those sad goings-on in Detroit, vowing not to follow Ford's path to self-destruction. Instead, he dedicated himself to creating a managerial system based on trust and a strong sense of community—virtues he would consciously and carefully nurture over decades of unwavering commitment to his stated values and practices. He saw that Ford's paternalistic acts had been a mistake; for instance, the day had long since passed when there was a need for company towns like New Lanark and Port Sunlight. He therefore resolved to treat his employees as adults, leaving them to decide how to spend the money they earned. He also learned a valuable lesson from one of the greatest challenges Ford faced: a lawsuit that to this day is cited by investors opposed to corporate managers placing the long-term needs of employees and customers above the short-term financial interests of shareholders. In 1916, when the Ford Motor Company had a capital surplus of some $60 million, Henry decided to forgo paying dividends to his shareholders to reinvest in plants and equipment, hire new employees, raise wages, and reduce the price of his cars. In his words, "My ambition is to employ still more men, to spread the benefits of this industrial system to the greatest possible number, to help them build up their lives and their homes. To do this we are putting the greatest share of our profits back in the business."

As the company's president and largest shareholder, Ford believed he had the authority to make such decisions. However, two brothers who owned 10 percent of the company, John and Horace Dodge, sued Ford on the grounds that he had a fiduciary duty to operate the company for the profit of its shareholders; hence, they claimed, he lacked authority to use "their" profits to engage in "charitable activities." In 1919 the Michigan Supreme Court ruled in the Dodge brothers' favor, denying Ford the wherewithal to lower car prices and raise employee wages, and ordering the company to pay investors a $19.3 million dividend. "A business corporation is organized and carried on primarily for the profits of the stockholders," the court held. "The powers of the directors are to be employed for that end. The discretion of directors is to be exercised in the choice of means to attain that end, and does not extend to a change in the end itself, to the reduction of profits, or to the non-distribution of profits among stockholders in order to devote them to other purposes."[24]

James Lincoln was outraged by the Michigan court's decision. Although an out-and-out capitalist, a staunch political conservative, and a firm believer in the profit motive, Lincoln couldn't accept the conclusion that the sole and higher purpose of a corporation was to maximize shareholder profits. Even while he railed against Franklin Roosevelt's New Deal and warned of threats to the American system from creeping socialism, he was equally a vocal critic of Wall Street and the short-term dictates of the stock market. Echoing almost verbatim the question William Lever had once raised with regard to the wealth his company created, Lincoln asked, "Where should such profits go?"[25] Characteristically, his answer was stated even more boldly than Lever's: "The present policy of operating industry for [the benefit of] stockholders is unreasonable. [The stock holder] gets income that should really go to the worker and the management. The usual stockholder contributes nothing to efficiency. He buys today and sells it tomorrow. He doesn't even know what the company makes. Why should he be rewarded by large dividends?"[26]

While there have been few, if any, cases after *Dodge v. Ford Motor Company* in which courts have forced companies to forgo the interests of their customers, employees, and host communities in order to enrich shareholders, the threat that they might do so has remained in the minds of generations of managers of publicly traded corporations.[27] In light of that reality, James Lincoln set out to structure the ownership of Lincoln Electric to shield it from short-term investor pressures. He did so by putting company shares in a family trust and by encouraging widespread employee ownership. As we see below, that protective shield is in the process of disintegrating, and the company may soon be subject to the Wall Street dictates Lincoln sought so assiduously to avoid.

Lincoln Electric's founder, John Lincoln, was as ambivalent about certain aspects of capitalism as his brother. John served on the company's board for many years, content to let his brother lead while quietly supporting his every action, no matter how unconventional. In 1931 John and his wife moved to Arizona, where he divided his time between working on inventions in the lab and investing in real estate. He proved as adept at the latter as he was at the former: when he died in 1959, at the age of ninety-two, he left an estate worth as much as $100 million, including such valuable properties as the Flamingo Hotel in Miami Beach, Florida, and the Camelback Inn in Scottsdale, Arizona. Throughout his long life, the politically conservative John Lincoln was an advocate of progressive economist Henry George's "single-tax" theory, designed to generate a fairer distribution of wealth. Curiously, landowner John Lincoln supported economist George's radical proposal to tax land ownership at a nearly confiscatory rate, despite the fact that George's tax was intended to discourage the kind of real-estate speculation in which Lincoln so profitably engaged.

Although John was the Lincoln company's founder and largest shareholder, from the get-go brother James managed it as if it belonged to him alone. James Lincoln listened carefully to everyone who worked for him, but there was never any doubt in their minds who the boss was.

And when he made up his mind, it was set in stone, and there was no use arguing against him. As a result, many promising executives who disagreed with James Lincoln regarding questions of strategy and the development of new products left the company to work elsewhere, including several who became successful CEOs of major corporations. Worse, James was never willing to pass the leadership of the company on to the next generation, staying on at its helm until the day he died in 1965, at age eighty-two.

James Lincoln's lifelong best friend, and pastor of his church, delivered the eulogy at his memorial service. Lincoln, he noted, "had faults and they were like everything else about him—big." For example, he often made intemperate public remarks: "I have known him to make statements with which I disagreed. I have heard him make extreme statements for the sake of argument: he would rather argue than eat. But I have never heard him make a statement with the intent to deceive. More than once I have heard him tell the truth to his own hurt—although in the long run I do not think a man ever tells the truth to his hurt. For a reputation for honesty is a priceless asset—and that Mr. Lincoln had."[28]

The pastor concluded that his friend had been a morally courageous, bigger-than-life leader who created wealth for his family, his workers, and his community, likening Lincoln's death to the felling of an enormous tree that "goes down with a great shout upon the hills and leaves a lonesome place against the sky."[29]

Lincoln Electric Today

The Lincoln Electric Company is still going strong today, serving its customers, employees, community, and shareholders by adhering to James Lincoln's unique managerial system, albeit with some modifications. Unfortunately, the ownership shield Lincoln erected to protect the company from investor demands for short-term profit appears at risk of possible dismantlement. Although the majority of Lincoln company stock may still remain in the hands of employees, the Lincoln family, and the family foundation, the company went public in 1995, and since then, increasingly larger percentages of its shares are being traded on NASDAQ. The result is that Lincoln Electric's executives now participate in quarterly phone calls with Wall Street analysts and in annual meetings with investors. Hence, they are under pressure to put the interests of investors ahead of the constituencies James Lincoln believed deserved precedence.[30] At the same time, most of the company's growth has been overseas, often in countries where laws and customs preclude the introduction of some, or all, of Lincoln's traditional employment practices. In his 2018 annual blog about the state of Lincoln Electric, Frank Koller notes that the company had recently acquired a number of smaller American firms at which employees were offered the opportunity to participate in Lincoln's unique system of incentive compensation, yet most declined, citing the risks of mandatory overtime during good years and a possible reduction in pay during bad times. Koller argues that it is not easy for a company to operate for long under two systems of compensation, concluding "I can't help but worry about the future." It is thus anybody's guess how long the culture created by James Lincoln can be sustained.

Were James Lincoln alive today, he doubtless would be troubled by the fact that, despite the demonstrable success of his system, and despite the thousands of Harvard Business School graduates who have studied it, no other major company has adopted it, and no corporate leader has claimed to be guided by his managerial philosophy.* If Lincoln were alive today and asked who his disciples were, he would be forced to reply, as Robert Owen did when asked the same question, "None."

---

* Southwest Airlines practices a form of piecework compensation, as described in chapter 12, and the founder of SAIC credited Lincoln Electric as the inspiration for its employee ownership plan and system of employee participation, as noted in chapter 16.

If Lincoln's system has been so successful, why don't other managers adopt it? Over the forty years in which I led discussions about the company with MBA students and senior corporate managers, I asked them that question. Here are some of the reasons they gave:

- Lincoln Electric Company is sui generis; what works there is unique and can't be replicated elsewhere.
- The Lincoln Electric system requires too much work on the part of management, and the financial results are not worth the extra effort.
- The Lincoln Electric system puts the company at high risk of losing out to a competitor who develops a new, more efficient technology for welding because Lincoln's employees are so wedded to what they have been doing for decades that they could not adapt to the change.
- Investors will not buy stock in companies offering Lincoln's employee-friendly policies and so focused on the long term.
- It is a mistake to offer promises—such as bonuses and guaranteed employment—that a company may not be able to deliver.
- Executives need more flexibility to hire and fire than the Lincoln system allows.
- There are not enough people to hire who have the work ethic needed in a system like Lincoln's.
- Few people today want to work at one company for their entire careers.
- Lincoln doesn't pay its executives enough to attract the best and the brightest (in 2008 its CEO earned sixty-five times more than the company's average worker, as opposed to three hundred plus times at Fortune 500 companies).
- Lincoln executives don't receive the generous perks enjoyed by their peers in other companies.
- Very few executives want to work jointly with an elected employee advisory board.

- Successful companies need to be focused on the bottom line, not on meeting the needs of employees and host communities. They also require the discipline that comes from being held accountable by investors.
- It is contrary to the capitalist system to pay a quarter of company profits to labor as bonuses.
- Employee development is an inappropriate central purpose for a publicly traded company.
- Widespread employee ownership limits a company's growth, innovation, and the managerial prerogatives needed for efficient operation.
- Founders want to leave their company stock to their heirs, not to their employees or to restricted charitable trusts.

Those are, of course, similar to the objections that were raised against the practices of Owen, Lever, Penney, and Hershey. As we shall see, such arguments have been offered against the practices of nearly all enlightened capitalists in America and Britain.

6

New Forms of Incorporation and Governance

JOHN SPEDAN LEWIS (1885–1963) *and*
JOHN JOSEPH EAGAN (1870–1924)

The John Lewis Partnership

The John Lewis Partnership—ranked today among Britain's largest retail chains—is one of those rare companies, like Lincoln Electric, in which enlightened practices have passed the test of sustainability over several generations. In 1864, John Lewis established a clothing shop on London's Oxford Street at which his eldest son, John Spedan Lewis, came to work as a nineteen-year-old in 1904. As Spedan soon learned, his father displayed a terrible temper at work, which he directed at employees (including his sons) if they made the slightest mistake. (A few years later, Spedan's brother would quit the business after one particularly nasty row with Lewis Sr.)

When Spedan was twenty-one, he began to realize that the family business was not nearly as successful as it could be, so he took the unheard-of step of establishing employee committees to solicit ideas about what might be done to improve its performance.[1] He experimented by putting a few employee suggestions into practice at Peter Jones, Limited, a store his father had recently acquired. Through trial and error, Spedan discovered that employees' performance improved when they were paid fairly and their ideas treated with respect. He also observed that the organization prospered when there was a strong sense of community, which he quaintly characterized as "general friendliness." When he told his father what he had done and learned, Lewis Senior was so alarmed by his son's "radical" notions that Spedan was forced to withdraw from the business for a matter of years while his father reconciled himself to the fact that Junior would never be a chip off the old block. Spedan's mother, "who was always in favor not only of fairness but of kindness," helped to restore peace between father and son, and he returned to the business in 1910.[2]

When Spedan examined the company books, he calculated that his family reaped a larger share of its total revenues than did all its employees combined. Believing that to be both unfair and damaging to morale, he committed to finding an efficient way to more equitably share the wealth the company created. He then spent the next four decades creating what he called "a far reaching experiment in industrial democracy."[3] The experiment took this long to effectuate due to the many obstacles he encountered over the years: two world wars, a depression, and the challenge of creating a viable legal framework for the company's governance and ownership. Most challenging was the presence of his ever-disapproving father, who lived on as, for all intents, the company's owner for nearly two decades after Spedan had assumed company leadership, thus effectively hamstringing the younger Lewis's efforts to introduce meaningful reforms. Spedan's brother, an absentee part owner, was also unenthusiastic about the "experiment."[4] Moreover, it took a long time for Spedan, a stickler for detail, to learn how to create the kind of practical organization that would achieve the higher purpose he intended for it. A sense of urgency was not to be found among Spedan's many virtues, nor was he in the habit of adopting the simplest way of doing things. Indeed, he seems to have embraced complexity, a trait manifested in his prolix writing style. Witness his description of the goal of his "far-reaching experiment": "The experiment may be summed up as an attempt so to organize and conduct a business that all the advantages whatsoever of owning it shall be shared as fairly as possible by all who are working in it and that the qualification for having a position in it shall be the ability (without overstrain) to fill that position in a way reasonably first rate for the service of the general community, the service in which the business has to live."[5]

That's a tall order, especially achieving it "without overstrain." Spedan's motivation to create a virtuous enterprise seems not to have stemmed from religious conviction. Instead, he was driven by secular business and moral reasoning that led him to believe that it was possible to create a business both efficient and ethical: that is, one large enough to enjoy economies of scale while at the same time maintaining the "general friendliness" of an intimate community. As he posited, "Suppose for a moment . . . it is really possible to have enough of the psychological advantages of small-scale ownership and yet to have at the same time genuine teamwork on any scale necessary for efficiency."[6]

Spedan Lewis sought to demonstrate that a company could make money by focusing on customer care and fair treatment of its employees. Much like Robert Owen before him, he was convinced that such an enterprise could become the model of a new type of capitalism that other business leaders would emulate. Indeed, Spedan explicitly stated that the purpose of his experiment was to create a *lasting* organization in "the direction in which Robert Owen achieved for a time so much and in the end so little."[7] Toward the conclusion of his long life, Spedan explained his motivations in a BBC interview: "The present state of affairs is really a perversion of the proper working of capitalism. It is all wrong to have millionaires before you have ceased to have slums. Capitalism has done enormous good and suits human nature far too well to be given up as long as human nature remains the same. But the perversion has given us too unstable a society. Differences of reward must be large enough to induce people to do their best but the present differences are far too great."[8]

In 1954, he wrote that the West was living "on a volcano" with a few wealthy people at the top, and millions of poor below ready to erupt in anger and frustration: "Moreover, apart from fears of a breakdown of society, more and more of the well-to-do are genuinely troubled because so many of their fellow citizens are so badly off. . . . The remedy may be in fairer sharing of the proceeds of work. What is fair? Nobody can say precisely. Mere equality is not the answer. . . . Wide differences of earnings seem necessary if possessors of uncommon ability are to discover it in themselves and to develop it as the common good requires . . . but the present differences are far too great."[9]

Like James Lincoln, Spedan dreamed of witnessing the dawn of a meritocratic "classless society," one that constituted "a possible advance in civilization and perhaps the only alternative to Communism." He had started working on that dream while his father was still alive, a period in which he was occupied in "an effort to see where my father had been right and where he had been wrong."[10] Shortly after his father's death, in 1928, Spedan wrote a formal constitution for the company that, henceforth, would be called the John Lewis Partnership. That 1929 covenant, or social contract, begins with this Jeffersonian statement of purpose: "The Partnership's ultimate purpose is the happiness of all its members, through their worthwhile and satisfying employment in a successful business. Because the Partnership is owned in trust for its members, they share the responsibilities of ownership as well as its reward—profit, knowledge and power."[11]

As the document states, the ethical aim of the partnership is to employ and maintain "people of integrity who are committed to working together and to supporting its Principles," an organization in which "relationships are based on mutual respect and courtesy." The intent of the partnership is to "deal honestly with its customers and secure their loyalty and trust by providing outstanding choice, value and service."

The company's constitution, titled "Principles and Rules of the

Lewis Partnership," delineates the firm's governance structure, the role of the executive, who has power to take what actions, how internal elections are to be held at various organizational levels, a bill of partners' rights and responsibilities, and a list of the firm's responsibilities to its stakeholders: customers, suppliers, competitors, local communities, the law, and the environment (the latter two constituencies added in later revisions to the document). Significantly, article 12 of the constitution requires the company's officers and directors to swear to uphold its principles.[12]

Even more unusual is the company's ownership structure as laid out in the binding legal documents that established the partnership trust in 1950: the John Lewis Partnership is indirectly owned by its employees, who all share in the profits it generates. The company shares those profits by way of an annual bonus that is a fixed percentage of each employee's salary—typically around 15 percent. Lewis partners are also issued nonvoting "bonus shares" in the company that it repurchases on their retirement (or in the case of debilitating illness).[13] The percentage of total company profits paid out to employees is also fixed by statute, with the remainder (the vast majority) earmarked for reinvestment in future growth. Intent on creating a lasting organization, Spedan understood the need for significant reinvestment.

Partner Participation

The company is legally owned by the John Lewis Partnership Trust Limited, the trustees of which are legally bound to manage the company in the long-term interests of its employees. Spedan created a complex system of checks and balances designed to limit the ability of those trustees to stray from that commitment. Similarly, the company's managers have the freedom to operate it efficiently—and the strategic flexibility needed for innovation and to meet future competitive challenges—but the constitution constrains them from taking actions counter to its "ultimate purpose" of serving the needs of employees and customers. After Spedan's death in 1963, his successor chairman of the partnership, Sir Bernard Miller, summarized how the company's system of governance functioned, and how it had evolved over the years: "The Partnership's democracy is based on the rule of law, the law here consisting of a written Constitution, legally binding through two Deeds of Settlement, Rules and Regulation developed in the light of experience, and the accumulation of precedents in the working of the system. As the nature of the Partnership has changed with the growth in the scale of the business, the 'law' upon which it is based has been adjusted to this growth. Changes in the original system have been mainly directed towards extending the sharing of power."[14]

Miller made it clear that the company was not a democracy in the political sense (Spedan had called it a "constitutional monarchy").[15] For example, the partner-employees were not entitled to choose the company's professional team of executives, were not empowered to make key managerial and strategic decisions, and did not have the right to vote on them. Instead, the constitution provides for partner participation in an extensive communication system that gives them full access to managerial information, and in an elaborate structure of committees, each with clearly defined roles, responsibilities, and authority. At the lowest level of the company, there are numerous elected committees for communication, with direct access, if need be, to the company's chairman. At the next level, each operating unit has an elected branch council, and above those, the entire partnership elects members to the central council, which serves as the company's "parliament," sharing powers in a tripartite system along with the operating central board of the company and with its chairman. The central council, with one seat for every 150 partners, has its own budget and appoints three "Trustees for the Maintenance of the Constitution" to serve on the board of the trust, and also elects five of the twelve members of the company's central board.[16] Nothing was ever simple with Spedan Lewis.

The structure Spedan created may have been extremely complex,

yet in practice the system has functioned a bit like "consensus management" in Japan: after much discussion at all levels of the company, general agreement on major issues has typically emerged without a need
for voting. If such an agreement emerges, top management then makes
its final decision. In the absence of such consensus, it is the prerogative
of management to act as they see fit. Typically, partnership committees have chosen not to become involved in day-to-day decision making, deferring those responsibilities to management; thus, for the most
part, the company has operated much like any other large, profession-
ally managed corporation. But on issues related to "the happiness of
its members," partnership committees have often become actively involved. For example, in the late 1950s, when British industry began to
adopt the five-day workweek, a major exception was the retail industry,
where shops remained open on Saturday, the day on which most working people traditionally shopped, and the day the Lewis company made
the most sales. The challenge for the partnership was to decide how to
allocate the time of store clerks—who worked five-day weeks—over
the company's six operating days in an efficient, fair, and economical
manner. The issue became pertinent when, over time, branch councils
adopted a range of local practices that, in turn, led to different store
opening days and hours across the chain. That anomaly was eventually
taken up by the central council, which, after considerable deliberation,
concluded that it was necessary for the company to have a uniform policy: all stores would be open six full days.

Nonetheless, one branch council took the extraordinary step of announcing that it would continue to close on Saturday afternoon. That
prompted a "constitutional crisis" when the chairman supported the
branch's decision, ruling the matter closed. Some partners interpreted
that as an abuse of executive power, but the ruling stood. Paradoxically, over coming years that executive decision would become the
precedent for increasing devolution of authority to lower levels in the
organization. From another perspective, the five-day-workweek issue
illustrated both the minuses and pluses of participative management.

The process was slow (nearly a decade elapsed between the time the issue was mooted until it was finally resolved); yet the very act of prolonged deliberation led to a productive increase in the general level of employee engagement, which had been the intent of the founder. The issue also highlights the inherent, and perhaps inescapable, tension Spedan struggled with between the necessity of maintaining managerial prerogatives, on the one hand, and authentic employee participation, on the other.

Spedan Lewis was an extremely serious fellow. Photos of him in a high Eton collar as stiff as his own ramrod posture bring to mind the stereotypical stern and proper Edwardian gentleman featured in period films and novels. In a recorded BBC interview he spoke—droned on at great length, actually—in a deep monotone about his philosophy.[17] As noted, his writing style was as humorless, stuffy, and careful as a lawyer's. In everything he wrote and said, he comes across as opinionated, obsessive, and sure of himself—doubtless no fun to be with at the company's annual "holiday gala," the employee-written, -acted, and -produced revue that, in Spedan's words, "mocked all parties, Partners and non-Partners, the managers and the managed."[18] While the founder may have been a bit of a sourpuss, the company he created nonetheless provided its employees with countless leisure and entertainment benefits: subsidized theater and concert tickets, paid holidays, sick pay, accident insurance, family allowances, and a well-funded adult education program. Yet, Spedan emphasized, the most valuable part of being a John Lewis partner was neither the generous employee benefits nor the profit sharing. Instead, he insisted that what made the company a special place to work was the sharing of power and knowledge. In support of that contention, he cited the results of an employee poll that found "most members felt the sharing of information was a more important part of co-partnership than profit sharing."[19]

Although employees were the Lewis Partnership's prime constituency, Spedan stressed the importance of ethical behavior with regard to its other stakeholders as well, insisting on the fair treatment of suppliers and customers. In 1925 he introduced the slogan "Never knowingly undersold," which would become the company's cardinal customer-service policy. The policy stated that if a customer could buy the same item cheaper at a competitor, the company would refund the difference. From then to today, the John Lewis Partnership has been known for providing exceptional service to customers in a nation where clerks in stores catering to the working and middle classes have traditionally been, at best, inattentive.

In 1933 the company began to expand nationally from its two London shops, and four years later it acquired Waitrose Limited, a chain of grocery stores. In subsequent decades, it expanded through the purchase of stores from the Selfridges, Safeway, and Bon Marché chains. Employees from those acquired companies became full John Lewis partners, participating in all the benefits shared by their fellow "owners" of the parent company. One of those benefits includes the right to post anonymous letters in the company's house organ, the *Gazette*. Spedan was committed to the right of free speech, believing employees should be encouraged to candidly voice their views about matters of company management, and also entitled to express their political views off the job, even radical ones. The company's policy was to publish every letter the *Gazette* received, no matter how critical of management, as long as it was neither obscene nor libelous. Top management made it a practice to respond, in print, to suggestions and criticisms, often putting forth plans to enact useful employee ideas and, when called for, offering mea culpas.

A Bit of "Science"

In 1964, as part of the partnership's Jubilee Celebrations, a team of British social scientists administered survey questionnaires among a sample of the company's employees to determine the extent to which Spedan's "experiment in industrial democracy" had succeeded.[20] There was no question the company had continued to grow over those five decades, from two locations employing a handful of people into a chain of seventeen thousand partners working in fifty-six stores and distribution centers across the United Kingdom. At the time, the company was doing £63.5 million in annual sales, and was the most profitable department-store chain in the UK. Thus the question the social scientists focused on was not the extent to which the company was a business success—that was clear—but whether it had realized Spedan's dream of providing for the "happiness" of its partners. With the blessing of company management, the researchers were left free to ask whatever questions they chose. They opted to pose some challenging ones. For example, they sought to discover if Lewis partners were better off than comparably employed unionized workers. The issue was pertinent because the 1960s was a time of considerable labor unrest in Britain, and trade unionists were adamant that workers' interests could be protected only through collective bargaining. Offering similar criticisms to the ones American union leaders raised in opposition to Lincoln Electric's practices, British trade unionists argued that "industrial democracy" in the form offered by the Lewis Partnership was a sham, nothing more than a clever form of paternalism designed to make employees work harder. They further claimed that the lack of a binding labor contract meant that worker benefits could be rescinded arbitrarily by management. Hence, in 1960s welfare-state Britain, the performance of the Lewis Partnership was widely viewed as a test case of the viability of capitalism itself: Could the private-enterprise system deliver a decent standard of living for the working class? Indeed, Spedan Lewis had set the stage for that challenge in 1954, when he declared that the partnership's enlightened practices were "the only alternative to communism."[21]

In general, the researchers found that the Lewis partners were materially better off than their unionized peers: they were better paid, had greater job security (becoming "tenured" after their seventh year of employment), enjoyed more and better benefits (for example, pensions), and had greater access to training opportunities. Almost all partners questioned were satisfied with their annual bonuses, although some expressed dissatisfaction that the amounts of such bonuses were linked to a percentage of their annual salaries, so that higher-paid workers took home bigger bonus checks. Not surprisingly, some partners felt that their allotted annual shares of bonus stock—which in effect amounted to a pension scheme—did not make them feel that they were, in fact, "owners of" or "partners in" the firm.

The researchers concluded that the company had yet to realize fully its founder's dream of securing "the fairest possible sharing by all the members of all the advantages of ownership—gain, knowledge and power." Although partners were, in general, satisfied with their pay, benefits, and working conditions, a significant portion of them expressed only slight interest in participating in the management of the company, and roughly the same percentage questioned management's sincerity with regard to employee involvement. As many as 20 percent reported that they wouldn't care if the three levels of elected councils were disbanded, and some offered negative comments about the degree to which employees' views were heeded in practice.[22] When partners were presented with the statement "The employees in this firm have a real say in many important decisions affecting the business," 45 percent agreed, 15 percent disagreed, and 38 percent were undecided. To the statement "The workers in this firm have a lot of power if they care to use it," 52 percent agreed, 19 percent disagreed, and 27 percent were undecided.[23] The researchers found that those workers who expressed the most interest in having a voice in management were also the most likely to say that their voices were heard, while those who expressed the least interest in participative management were also the least likely to express satisfaction with the company's commitment to employee involvement.

There are several reasonable interpretations of those findings. The researchers themselves concluded that the partnership was not suited to everyone, working best "for those who, to be really happy, need to feel they are giving good service to the general community and whom [the company's] particular character and methods suit well enough in other ways."[24] Today, that significant minority of dissatisfied partners would be seen as a product of poor recruiting practices; prior to the 1970s, the importance of having a sophisticated process of employee selection was not widely understood in industry, and few companies did much more than examine job applicants' school records and letters of recommendation. It wasn't until well into the twenty-first century that Lincoln Electric's managers understood that high-involvement companies needed to carefully select new hires whose values were consistent with their organizational cultures. Moreover, the Lewis Partnership had expanded greatly in the 1950s as the result of acquisitions, which meant that many of its employees had originally come from companies with quite different cultures. They then found themselves in a high-involvement organization requiring more commitment than they were prepared to give. In that light, the fact that some 80 percent of partners were satisfied with, and actively participating in, the company's unique system of shared decision making might well be seen as a positive affirmation of Spedan Lewis's legacy.

The Company Today

John Spedan Lewis had a remarkable mind. Although formally uneducated (he had rejected his father's offer to send him to Oxford), he was well-read and thoughtful, and over his long life developed a coherent business philosophy he outlined in two long, detailed (and aridly dry) tomes. Like Robert Owen and James Lincoln, Spedan produced a systematic political-economic philosophy, and like them he sought to use his business enterprise as the platform on which to build a just society. Despite that idealism, Lewis and Lincoln were not socialist egalitarians (and Owen only became one late in his life, after abandoning the business world). Instead, they were capitalists who firmly believed in private property, the efficiency of markets, and rewards for merit. They differed from their fellow capitalists largely in their commitment to the ethical concepts of fairness and treating fellow humans with respect and dignity. In essence, their philosophies were similar to that of the great champion of liberty John Stuart Mill, who believed capitalist practices could and should be made consistent with efforts to eliminate poverty, want, and rigid social-class distinctions. Hence, instead of calling for a Marxist redistribution of wealth, they sought to build productive enterprises capable of generating a higher standard of living and quality of life for all their constituencies. "But," as Spedan noted, "the supreme problem is not satisfaction of material appetites but prevention of a galling sense of needless inferiority of any kind and above all the sense of being exploited, victimized for somebody else's benefit."[25]

In 1954 Spedan wrote that the partnership couldn't be considered firmly established until some future time when his *successor's successor* was found supporting the company's constitution.[26] Although that document has been altered somewhat over the years—largely in the direction of giving more power to partners—it is still in effect and credited as the prime source of the John Lewis Partnership's extraordinary success and sustainability. In 2014 the company boasted of 93,000 partners working in 43 modern department stores and 305 Waitrose supermarkets. It is still employee owned, still manages with a long-term perspective, and is still known for its exceptional customer service. The partnership prides itself on being a "transparent democracy" in which employees, customers, suppliers, and the public have extraordinary access to information about the company; for example, the results of employee surveys are published in its annual report. It has become a national leader in environmental stewardship and community involvement, and a major innovator in electronic retailing. In 2014 the company had £10 billion in sales and paid £202 million in bonuses to its partners, approximately 15 percent of their annual pay.

Lewis Company Naysayers

Today, the Lewis company's commitment to living by its constitution seems as strong, if not stronger, than at the time of its 1964 Jubilee. Its growth, commercial success, and ability to change and innovate remain impressive. Yet not everyone is convinced of the merits of Spedan Lewis's system. A 2012 article in the *Economist* claimed that the company's "cuddly model of capitalism has been oversold." While acknowledging that its worker ownership "may have commercial benefits," the magazine challenged Spedan's "belief that the model could replace traditional capitalism," noting, factually, that "few have adopted it." Moreover, the article claimed, "there is little evidence that shared ownership makes capitalism socially and ethically more responsible," as the head of the British Liberal Democrat Party had recently attested. In sum, the *Economist* argued, "It is rash to put a worker's livelihood, savings and pension in one basket," and concluded that shared ownership was, in general, an unsustainable, unworkable, and impractical system: "Companies that are wholly-owned by their staff may face barriers to growth. Many firms need a flexible capital base to expand—one reason the partnership model in banking declined. Employee mobility promotes innovation. At base, it is unrealistic to expect many bastions of capitalism to turn their shares over to their workforce, reckons Ian Brinkley of the Work Foundation, a think-tank. It is, he says, hard to imagine someone like Sir Fred Goodwin, the acquisitive former Royal Bank of Scotland boss who oversaw its demise, 'being reined in by some worker's committee.'"[27]

Several ironic aspects of the *Economist*'s criticisms are noteworthy. In its early years, the magazine looked with favor upon the worker-cooperative philosophy of Robert Owen's disciples; and, according to its editors, it has long remained governed by a Lewis Partnership–like board of "independent trustees whose role is to safeguard our corporate and editorial independence."[28]

Although such eminent British scholars as E. F. Schumacher and Charles Handy have cited the Lewis Partnership as a business model deserving emulation, there has also been a competing chorus of naysayers in the United Kingdom—voices coming from trade unions, the media, academia, and business who remain skeptical about, if not critical of, the company despite its long record of evident success. As in the past, trade unionists argue that shared ownership at the Lewis Partnership is a form of paternalism, bemoaning the absence of an independent collective body (read, a union) strong enough to countervail arbitrary exercises of managerial power. Journalists and scholars often concede that the Lewis Partnership has been successful, yet they argue that the example is sui generis and thus not suitable for other companies or in different industries—concluding, in effect, "It may work there, but it won't work elsewhere." Business critics offer yet a different set of objections based on the system's perceived organizational inefficiencies, resistance to change and innovation, administrative impracticalities, and, in particular, absence of sufficient financial incentives to top management. Moreover, as suggested in the above quote from the *Economist*, if making money for themselves is the prime motivation of most corporate executives, it is naive to expect many of them to create organizations dedicated to serving the financial interests of employees. Relatedly, there is the question of executive ego: experience shows that most executives are uncomfortable sharing power with employees, let alone willing to be "reined in by some workers' committee." And when the unwritten rules of corporate capitalism dictate that the primary duty of a CEO is to serve the interests of investors, supposedly all-powerful executives might not be viewed as worth their salt if the ownership of companies they lead is in the control of employees. In sum, many British executives conclude that they would find insufficient career satisfaction creating a company like the John Lewis Partnership.

There is obviously a great similarity between British criticism of the Lewis Partnership and the arguments American critics level against the Lincoln Electric system. From an idealist's perspective, that is a discouraging finding, given that those two companies have had the longest records of sustainable success among US and UK firms with enlightened practices. Yet there are those who find great merit in John Spedan Lewis's "experiment in industrial democracy." In a 2002 BBC poll, Spedan Lewis was voted the greatest business leader in British history.

The American Cast Iron Pipe Company

John Joseph Eagan was an American businessman who left behind a business legacy that has endured as long as Spedan Lewis's in Britain. Although Eagan was fifteen years older than Lewis, they lived in such distant and distinct social environments, and led companies in such markedly different industries, that there is little reason to believe that Lewis knew of Eagan's earlier success in perpetuating enlightened management practices similar to the ones he would adopt two decades later. Today, the story of Eagan's unusual achievements is even less well known than it was during Lewis's lifetime.

Eagan was born in a small Georgia town a few years after the end of the Civil War. On his father's side, he was descended from Irish Catholic stock, but his mother was a devout Presbyterian, the religion to which her son would become a fervently faithful adherent. He grew up in Atlanta during the era of Reconstruction and the horrific days of Jim Crow segregationist laws and brutal lynchings of African Americans, all of which Eagan found morally abhorrent from an early age. Eagan's father died when he was quite young, which meant that John's family could not afford to give him much in the way of formal education. Forced to leave school around age fifteen, he went to work in his maternal uncle's store. Apparently the uncle was pleased with his nephew's performance, for when he died in 1899, he left Eagan an estate valued at some $6,000.[29] In addition to the store, the twenty-nine-year-old Eagan inherited real estate and a tobacco business, the latter of which he promptly divested himself of on religious grounds. He wrote that, instead of tobacco, it was his Christian "duty to get into a field where I can glorify Him the most."[30]

After investing in several ventures—each was successful, although none fully engaged his interest—Eagan found his field of Christian glory when he was approached by a businesswoman, Charlotte James, who was building a new plant to make cast iron pipe in Birmingham, Alabama. James was looking for investors, but in Eagan she also found the person who would lead the new American Cast Iron Pipe Company (ACIPCO) as its first president. When the company was chartered in 1905, Eagan knew nothing about metals manufacturing or the new "continuous process" technology employed in the plant. In a crash effort to learn about the metals industry, Eagan made careful study of the way Andrew Carnegie's steel business was managed. In his diary, Eagan approvingly quoted the words Carnegie supposedly wanted carved on his tombstone: "Here lies a man who became rich by drawing around him men brighter than himself."[31] And Eagan did as Carnegie claimed, hiring people who had mastered the new technologies for dealing with molten metal, and then leaving them free to manage ACIPCO's operations.

Informed by his reading of the New Testament, Eagan then developed his own philosophy of business stewardship in which he viewed himself as "trustee" of the wealth he had inherited and, subsequently, caused greatly to increase. He so closely welded his business and religious philosophies that they became inseparable not only in his mind but, more significantly, in the actions he would take at ACIPCO. Excerpts from Eagan's numerous business memos, papers, and letters reveal that he seldom made any managerial or financial point without specific reference to a supporting biblical passage, faithfully citing chapter and verse in full. In a memo to his board of directors, referencing Luke 12:42–46, he reminded them of their duties with regard to servant leadership: "And the Lord said, who then is that faithful and wise steward, whom his lord shall make ruler over his household, to give them their portion of meat in due season? Blessed is that servant whom his lord when he cometh shall find so doing."[32]

Like Penney's and Lincoln's, Eagan's business philosophy—as well as, eventually, the guiding principles of ACIPCO—was based explicitly on the Golden Rule. More unusual, given the southern locale and segregationist era in which Eagan worked, he extended to African Americans his commitment to treat others as he wished to be treated. But Eagan wasn't simply a man of God: he was equally a reformer. Throughout his career in Birmingham, and in his hometown of Atlanta, Eagan attempted to find ways to address not only the region's ingrained racism but such social problems as prostitution, inhumane prison conditions, lack of venues for public recreation, and the low quality of schooling available to the disadvantaged. In 1913 he began to play a public role in addressing the needs of African Americans, helping to fund a "colored" YMCA and donating large sums to support educational institutions serving blacks.

In 1919 Eagan helped to establish the Commission on Interracial Cooperation (CIC) in segregated Atlanta, on which both whites and blacks served with the goal of encouraging cooperation between, and greater equality among, the two communities. Remarkably, at a time when liberal whites were wont to treat blacks paternalistically by telling them what they needed, Eagan actually listened to what the non-white members of the CIC identified as their problems, and what they said they needed to live good lives. The commission advocated equal justice for all, starting with the two hundred thousand black soldiers returning to the South after serving in Europe during World War I.[33] Although the commission fought against mob violence directed at African Americans, and was vocal in its opposition to Jim Crow laws, it seems to have stopped short of advocating desegregation of schools and public places. Nonetheless, it took courageous stands in favor of voting rights for blacks, their right to serve on juries, and equal distribution of public funds for education, health, and educational institutions.[34] The Atlanta-based CIC spawned the creation of numerous branches throughout the South. Although noble in intent, those bodies eventually were disbanded long before they achieved their goals.

The legacy of ACIPCO is far more positive. During the company's initial years, Eagan began buying up shares held by its other investors and converting those he couldn't buy into nonvoting stock. When he eventually achieved control of the company, he announced that henceforth it would be managed on the basis of the Golden Rule. He then committed the company to following three basic principles: paying a living wage to its lowest-paid workers; continuous employment for all workers, even during depressed economic conditions; and the application of the Golden Rule in all employer-employee relations.[35] In practice, the latter principle led ACIPCO to provide its workers—white and black alike—with pensions, medical care, sick leave benefits, death benefits, group insurance, recreational facilities, housing, and a co-op store where they could purchase good food at reasonable prices. On the job, special attention was paid to worker safety, an issue of paramount importance given the dangers involved in pouring molten iron and steel. In the early 1920s, when ten-hour-plus days were the norm, ACIPCO's male employees worked eight hours, and women seven. Most unusual, women were paid enough to be self-supporting, even to support a family in the absence of a working spouse.[36] The average pay of ACIPCO workers in 1922 was $1,600 per annum, twice that offered by its competitors.[37] Years before Spedan Lewis and James Lincoln did so, Eagan established an elected board of employees to advise management on issues that workers themselves deemed important. Further, he decreed that workers had the right to elect two of their number to serve on the company's board of directors.

In order to "apply the teachings of Jesus Christ" to all ACIPCO's constituencies, "including customers, employees, stockholders, directors, officials and competitors," Eagan introduced a stakeholder approach to management, although he didn't call it that.[38] In reaction, one of his plant managers quit in disgust and, in 1921, started a competitor company in Birmingham, which he then managed in conformity with traditional business practices of the era. And that era was a harsh one for the vast majority of American workers. According to US Bureau of Health estimates, in 1917 some thirty million people in the country (out of a population of a hundred million) lacked the income needed to purchase the basic goods necessary for physical health and to live in decent conditions.[39] The bureau estimated that some 92 percent of Americans dying from disease in industrial towns, such as Birmingham, suffered from afflictions that were "wholly preventable," even by the crude health care and environmental safety measures available at the time.[40] The bureau also noted a strong correlation between mortality and morbidity rates, on the one hand, and levels of income, on the other—data Eagan was aware of, and found unacceptable "in a Christian nation."[41]

Eagan's own health was chronically poor, and because he had had early intimations of his mortality, in his late forties he began thinking about his legacy—specifically, how he could guarantee that ACIPCO's Golden Rule business practices would live on after him. With the goal of ensuring that all ACIPCO's workers received at least a living wage, he made binding legal arrangements for the company to pay no more than 6 percent of its profits annually to shareholders, the rest going to employees as profit sharing.[42] Around 1922 he penned a will in which he left all his own stock in a trust, the profits of which would be used for the benefit of the company's employees and "the public." His stated purpose was "to insure service to the purchasing public and to labor on the basis of the Golden Rule."[43]

Secular businesspeople might find Eagan's relentless religiosity offputting and inappropriate in today's workplace, but it should be noted that he balanced his piety with financial prudence: although he left ACIPCO to its employees, he left his real estate holdings and other investments to his family, an arrangement to which his wife generously consented. He stipulated that his ACIPCO stock was never to be sold because his employees were "not servants but friends," and thus the business's profits, in fact, "belonged" to them.[44] He made clear that his gift of stock was not an act of charity, any more than the many benefits ACIPCO's 1,200 employees enjoyed were the product of his largesse. Reasoning that stock in the trust would be worthless unless the company was successful in the marketplace, he concluded that nothing was being given to the workers. Instead, he was simply establishing a profit-sharing scheme in which employees would reap only what they earned—and in which they would bear most of the company's financial risk. In his will, he spoke directly to those workers: "This places before you a great opportunity. It puts upon you a grave responsibility. The amount of these dividends will depend largely upon your efforts. By faithful, efficient work, and careful saving for your Company you may largely increase the amount of the dividends. By wasting your time, or materials entrusted to you; or by careless breakage or by failure to promptly repair any machine, or stop any leak, you will decrease not only your own income, but the income of every other employee."[45]

In the same vein, Eagan stressed the need for employees continually to reinvest in new plants and equipment, even if it meant lower pay in the short term.[46] He counseled his workers to carefully explain the need for reinvestment to new hires, expressing his every confidence that, when those workers understood why it was in their self-interest to increase the company's productivity, they would act accordingly. As he explained, "In order to carry out the principles of service to the public it is necessary that we should be able to produce goods of at least equal quality and as cheaply as our competitors. My conviction is that a group working together on a co-operative basis will, over a period of years, produce goods of better quality and more cheaply than competitors operating under the old competitive system."[47]

Turning to matters of governance, Eagan penned a company constitution similar to the one being put in effect around the same time at the John Lewis Partnership. In it, he spelled out the roles and responsibilities of ACIPCO's board of directors, who also were to serve as trustees of his will. In addition to having two elected employee members, he stipulated that the board's composition also include a customer and a representative chosen by the Federal Council of Churches. The constitution also required the creation of board committees to deal with employee pensions, living conditions, working conditions, housing, and wages, prohibiting the board from taking actions with regard to those concerns without first consulting the elected employee advisory board. Eagan explicitly directed the board to use dividends from his shares in three ways: as profit sharing; as income to workers if the plant shut down for any reason; and as support to the widows and children of deceased workers.[48]

In ACIPCO's constitution Eagan articulated the company's basic ethical values and principles—honesty, justice, a square deal, and "doing right," illustrating each with a practical example (such as equal pay for equal work for black employees). Those who knew Eagan well recalled that his prime interest in writing the constitution was to ensure the future character development of the company's workforce.[49] His intention to use the workplace as the locus of human development thus parallels the efforts of Owen, Penney, and Lever.

"The real purpose of business is to serve acceptably and continuously all of the needs of all of the people all of the time," Eagan summed up his managerial philosophy, concluding that profit was the result of doing those things.[50] The record shows he had been right about the long-term financial benefits of ACIPCO's employment practices: between 1922 and 1930, the company's book value doubled, and when the Great Depression then struck a near fatal blow to many American businesses, ACIPCO was able to weather the storm, its practices and most of its workforce intact, until demand for its products soared again during World War II.

ACIPCO's Rediscovery

The company continued to prosper after the war, but stayed largely out of the limelight until 2003, when its prime competitor, the

Birmingham-based McWane Inc., found itself in the news after being cited for more than four hundred OSHA safety violations in the previous eight years—some four times more than its six major competitors combined. During the same period, nine of McWane's workers had died as the result of work-related injuries. When journalists looked into the matter, they discovered OSHA reports documenting that McWane workers had frequently suffered severe burns at work, often causing scars and disfigurations, some leading to the amputation of limbs. Workers had complained to OSHA about the company's failure to comply with safety and environmental standards, about the absence of training for handling five-thousand-pound molten pipes, and about chronically abusive treatment by supervisors. In relating those horrific working conditions to journalists, McWane employees claimed that the company's management cared only about greater productivity and profits, no matter the human cost. As a result, annual rates of employee turnover at McWane approached nearly 100 percent in one of its plants, leading the company to recruit convicts furloughed from local prisons to keep its furnaces burning.

In undertaking their investigations, journalists learned from Birmingham locals that there was another pipe manufacturer in town, one managed with almost exactly the opposite practices at McWane: ACIPCO. Thus, in 2003, ACIPCO was "discovered" by the media. The next year, it was ranked sixth on *Fortune*'s annual 100 Best Companies to Work For list. Actually, there was little new at ACIPCO. Over the years, the company had maintained founder Eagan's emphasis on worker health and safety—for example, its plant was air-conditioned, whereas at McWane even the ice cubes in water coolers were rationed in a facility where ambient temperatures could rise to 130 degrees. All ACIPCO employees received extensive on-the-job training, and they and their children were eligible for college tuition remission. Turnover among its 2,554 employees was less than 0.5 percent per year, and its workers, a third of them African American, enjoyed a state-of-the-art wellness center that was also open to their families. The company's workers, their families, and retirees had access to the company's on-site medical center staffed by twenty doctors and nurses, eleven dentists and hygienists, and four pharmacists. Employees paid only $10 for a doctor visit, and 25 percent of prescription costs.

Today, the company continues to operate for the benefit of its employees under the terms of its original constitution, continues to be a leader in occupational health and safety, and is the preferred place of employment in Birmingham for blue-collar workers of all races. There is a significant footnote to the story: the plant manager who quit ACIPCO in 1920 to start his own business when Eagan introduced the Golden Rule philosophy was named J. R. McWane.[51]

Eagan died in 1924 at the age of fifty-four, probably from cerebral meningitis (he may also have been a longtime tuberculosis sufferer). He was eulogized at a memorial service in Atlanta by Dr. Isaac Fisher, a minister and faculty member at Fisk University. Fisher spoke with great sadness about the premature loss of the white businessman who had once asked him two remarkably honest questions few whites in the South would have considered posing to a black man: "Dr. Fisher, why don't you hate all of us?" and "How can you trust even me?" At the service, Fisher documented the reasons why, in fact, he had trusted Eagan, noting that he was the rare white employer who visited the homes of his lowest-level black employees to learn firsthand what it was like to be poor and nonwhite in segregated Birmingham, and then took meaningful action to improve their lives. Fisher concluded, "And so with his great heart, but feeble body, he set himself to the task of making this a Christian nation in its relations with colored people."[52]

Good Endings at the Lewis Partnership and ACIPCO

John Spedan Lewis was more fortunate than John Eagan in having lived long enough to see the Lewis Partnership fully developed as a sustainable enterprise, and firmly committed to serving its customers and employees based on the principles outlined in its constitution. Had Eagan lived another thirty years, he would have had the pleasure of knowing his Golden Rule management was firmly in place at ACIPCO. In any event, Lewis and Eagan joined James Lincoln in creating lasting legacies of virtuous business practices in the companies they once led. They each did so as the result of devoting months of creative thought to the question of how best to ensure that their practices would outlive them. Unlike Milton Hershey, who seems to rather casually have dictated the terms of his will and trust, Lewis, Eagan, and Lincoln worked closely with lawyers, and at great expense, to draft wills capable of withstanding future legal challenges and the whims of trustees. Virtue requires hard work, indeed.

Most significantly, a key difference between Lewis's, Lincoln's, and Eagan's durable successes—and the long-term failures experienced by Owen, Penney, and Lever—was that the latter lost control of their companies to partners, investors, and creditors who did not share their values, whereas the former retained near-sole ownership of their respective companies, and hence were able to shape the futures of their organizations. Lewis and Eagan perpetuated their enlightened practices by passing control of their companies on to those who benefited most from them, and those least likely to change them: their employees.

Postscript: As this book went to press in late 2018, the John Lewis Partnership announced an unprecedented decline in the firm's profitability. Its ability to meet the growing challenge of e-commerce promises to be an acid test of Spedan Lewis's heretofore robust system.

7

Johnson & Johnson's
Roller-Coaster Ride

ROBERT WOOD JOHNSON (1893–1968) and
JAMES BURKE (1925–2012)

The makers of such familiar health-related products as Band-Aids and Tylenol might just as appropriately have been named Johnson&Johnson&Johnson&Johnson&Johnson. The company was founded in 1886 in New Brunswick, New Jersey, by the two brothers for whom it was eponymously named: James (Johnson number one), and Edward Mead (Johnson two). As things turned out, they were among the least significant Johnsons in the company's long history. Their brother, Robert Wood (Johnson three), joined the firm shortly after its founding, infusing it with both a dose of needed capital and medical knowledge—the latter informed by the latest thinking in the then-fast-developing field of medical science. Johnson was one of the first American disciples of Joseph Lister, the British surgeon who, in developing the art of antiseptic surgery, successfully applied Louis Pasteur's germ theory of disease to operating room practices. Johnson had become an advocate of antiseptics after attending a lecture given by Lister in 1876, at which the great scientist described the need for sterile surgical dressings to combat infection.[1] One of the first products J&J introduced under Robert Wood's leadership was sterile medicinal plasters (forerunner of

Band-Aids), followed in subsequent years by ligatures, maternity and obstetric products, and the still-marketed Johnson's Baby Powder.

Johnson also had an early understanding of the power of advertising, retaining the personal services of the young J. Walter Thompson, with whom he worked closely in developing the firm's first marketing efforts. About that time, Johnson met a local pharmacist, Fred Kilmer, who for the next forty-five years would serve as J&J's de facto head of research and development, in the process becoming "the most revered pharmaceutical chemist in the country," according to the editors of *Time*.[2] When Johnson met "Doc" Kilmer, the pharmacist was running a drugstore in New Brunswick frequented by Thomas Edison, whose laboratories were located in nearby Menlo Park. Over the years Kilmer would prove to be as prolific an inventor as his friend and customer Edison, starting with the creation of Johnson's Baby Powder in 1890. Kilmer later developed the surgical products J&J made available, gratis, to the US military during the Spanish-American War, and to victims of the devastating 1900 Galveston hurricane and 1906 San Francisco earthquake and fire (within hours of learning of the latter disaster, the company was loading boxcars full of cotton gauze, bandages, and plaster to be sent west).[3] In 1906 Kilmer played a significant role in shaping the landmark 1906 Pure Food and Drugs Act, setting a precedent for future J&J cooperation with government agencies.

Robert Wood Johnson II

With 2,500 employees, Johnson & Johnson was highly profitable and fast-growing when Robert Wood died unexpectedly of Bright's disease in 1910. He was succeeded by his brother, James (Johnson one), who made his mark on the company's history primarily by continuing with the precedents set by Robert Wood and depending on Doc Kilmer to develop new products. But the Johnson who created the giant global corporation known today as J&J was Robert Wood II, the son of Robert

Wood, who had been sixteen at the time of his father's death. Known as Bob, Johnson number four was born into a life of wealth and privilege in 1893; he and his two siblings would inherit a trust fund containing almost all of J&J's stock, worth some $2 million, in 1910. He joined the family business on graduation from high school, then worked his way up from a manual job in the company's power plant to the top of its hierarchy over a period of some two decades. He had been primed for a career in the company by his father, who often took him as a young boy to sit quietly and listen in on business meetings.

Bob Johnson was quite unlike the other corporate stewards profiled in these pages. He was not the entrepreneur-founder of the company he led, but a thrice-married playboy who enjoyed fast and expensive cars, planes, and boats. During his life he was both famous and widely respected, and after his death he has been remembered more for his philanthropy than his corporate leadership. Above all, he was a man of many contradictions: an archconservative Republican who championed much of Franklin Roosevelt's New Deal legislation; a Protestant who spent numerous hours in the company of Roman Catholic clerics and based his ethical thinking on the teachings of the church; a patrician completely at home in the company of the working class; a leader in the advance of medical science whose greatest skill was advertising; a CEO who touted J&J as "a family of companies" with a "family of employees," but who in his personal life was a poor and often absent husband and father; a demanding, hypercritical, micromanaging perfectionist who was also the foremost executive apostle of business decentralization and delegation; and a red-white-and-blue patriotic American whose proudest achievements included the internationalization of J&J to the extent that its foreign managers were allowed to run their national businesses with almost complete autonomy from the company's US headquarters.

At age twenty-one, Bob Johnson was elected to the board of J&J, a role with no management responsibilities. He soon became a protégé of Doc Kilmer, whose own son, Joyce, had died in battle during World

War I. (Joyce had been a highly successful writer, and his poem "Trees" is still recited—and frequently parodied—today.) While always remaining more than a bit the party animal, under Kilmer's tutelage Bob gradually matured and became dedicated to his work at J&J, ultimately becoming expert in the latest medical developments, and a vocal advocate of better hospital management. With an eye toward eventually leading the company, Bob convinced his sister to sell him all her shares, leaving him and his younger brother as the company's controlling shareholders. As he worked his way up the company ranks, he became known for his progressive business ideas and practices. In an era when American factories were dirty, dismal, and architecturally hideous, he built a state-of-the-art cotton mill in rural Georgia that was not only externally attractive to the eye but also a safe, clean, and comfortable place for those inside to work. The J&J workers were well paid by local standards, and the facility was the first in the region not to employ children.

Influenced by the recent example of William Lever, Johnson built a model company town near the mill, with modern, five-room brick houses for his workers and their families.[4] Although he soon abandoned the outmoded practice of creating company towns, in subsequent years he would build over a hundred beautiful, safe, and antiseptically sterile factories. He located all J&J facilities in landscaped, parklike settings on which he challenged the finest architects to design buildings that didn't look like factories. Typically, those buildings—constructed using a great deal of glass to bring in daylight—offered the then-unheard-of luxury of air conditioning and featured plush lobbies that production employees were urged to use as entrances on their way to work. Johnson said he wanted all J&J workers to feel they "owned" the handsome buildings: "We build not only structures . . . in which men and women will work, but also patterns of society in which they will work. We are building not only frameworks of stone and steel, but frameworks of ideas and ideals."[5] In 1924 Johnson supervised the opening of J&J's first foreign plant in Slough, England, followed by many more overseas as he led the company's rapid and successful international expansion. Unlike those of many global corporations, J&J's foreign facilities were of the same high quality as its domestic ones.

From an early age, Johnson was active in Republican politics, serving as an alternate delegate in the 1929 presidential convention that nominated Herbert Hoover. He would serve as mayor of the New Jersey town in which he lived, and remain a kingpin in that state's Republican Party for the next five decades. During the Roaring Twenties, Bob was one of the loudest lions, making a reputation for himself as a spoiled rich boy, the first to buy the latest sports car in which he sped to his favorite Manhattan speakeasies. A member of the horsey set, he "rode with the Stoney Brook Hunt" when he wasn't sailing in the Caribbean on one or another of the many yachts he would own during his long life.[6]

"Bob" in Charge

At the end of the 1920s, J&J's top executive, James Johnson, was in ill health. Bob gradually found himself taking on more of his uncle's leadership duties. In 1930, twenty years after the death of his father, J&J's board of directors named Bob the company's vice president and general manager. Two years later, they none-too-gently pushed James out of office, electing Robert Wood Johnson II as president.[7] On assuming leadership of J&J, Bob promptly adopted a high public profile, urging president-elect Franklin Roosevelt in 1932 to advocate legislation reducing the workweek and increasing wages as first steps toward recovery from the Great Depression. Within J&J, Johnson dealt with the economic crisis by reducing workweeks, shortening shifts, and eliminating Saturday work. As a result, no J&J employees were laid off; indeed, a few hundred new jobs were created when countless other American workers were queuing up in breadlines. Moreover, Johnson gave a 5 percent wage increase to all J&J employees, hoping that act would encourage other industrialists to follow suit; at the same time he reduced the pay of J&J executives by 15 percent.[8] A few years later, he would give his employees another raise when it became clear that the Depression wasn't abating. He publicly called on all American employers to pay their workers a living wage, arguing that such measures were, in fact, conservative and in the self-interest of business. Like James Lincoln, Johnson firmly believed that it was better for "business and free enterprise to generate its own sense of public responsibility instead of being dictated to by the government."[9] He was sorely frustrated when his peers rejected his plea. During a congressional hearing, a senator asked Johnson if he was a member of the National Association of Manufacturers. Echoing Robert Owen, he offered this reply: "Senator, I have been unable to find a sympathetic group of colleagues in organized business and I've tried very hard."[10] Johnson then established himself as the nation's leading business advocate of improved labor-management relations, shocking the business establishment by criticizing the National Association of Manufacturers for its rigid antilabor philosophy.

During the Depression, Johnson developed his philosophy of "corporate social responsibility." Indeed, he may have coined that phrase; if not, he was the first major American industrialist to use it. At the height of the Great Depression, he penned an essay provocatively entitled "Try Reality," addressed to his fellow capitalists:

> Out of the suffering of the past few years has been born a public knowledge and conviction that industry has the right to succeed where it performs a real economic service and is a true social asset.
>
> Such permanent success is possible only through the application of an industrial philosophy of enlightened self interest. It is to the enlightened self interest of modern industry to realize that its service to its customers comes first, its service to its employees and management second, and its service to stockholders last. It is to the enlightened self interest of industry to accept and fulfill its share of social responsibility.[11]

Johnson contended that it was in the self-interest of southern textile mill owners to adopt a forty-cents-an-hour minimum wage—if they didn't, either the government would mandate it or workers would unionize to win it. In response, Georgia newspapers labeled him the "stormy petrel" of the textile industry, and "a wild-eyed maverick." His biographer, Lawrence G. Foster, dubbed Johnson "the gentleman rebel." Actually, he must have seemed like an anarchist bomb thrower to his peers in industry. In the middle of bitter Depression-era wrangling between FDR and the business community, Johnson called for the resignation of the Republican Party's entire leadership.[12] His words were incendiary: "American businessmen are probably the most efficient in the world, but I am afraid they are nevertheless political morons. I find we have as astute a group of politicians as we have anywhere, but I am afraid they are business morons. But there are more politicians who know something about business than there are businessmen who know something about politics."[13]

While engaged in public battles, Johnson was also involved actively in the management of the company. He was, for all intents and purposes, J&J's head of advertising, approving every major ad campaign and in the process driving creative types at ad agencies crazy with his constant quibbles, carping, and second-guessing. He was particularly incensed when ad men misrepresented or oversold a product. He had a strict, if not obviously clear, formula for advertising success: "Dramatics+Simplicity+Continuity+Brand Name Dominates+Brief and Legible Copy+Corporation Signature Strong"—and woe to the agency professional who dared deviate from it. In all his managerial actions he was a stickler for doing things the right way (which, invariably, was his way), and totally intolerant of efforts not resulting in perfect quality, absolute cleanliness, and sterility. He was highly opinionated, cutting in his criticisms, and "made many mistakes, but rarely admitted them."[14] He was also deeply concerned with new product development, especially products with high social utility. For example, he encouraged company efforts to create inexpensive, effective sanitary napkins for use by women in the undeveloped world, personally hiring a nurse and charging her with traveling around the globe to discover what poor women needed in that regard.

In 1936 Johnson contributed twelve thousand shares of his J&J stock to form the Johnson New Brunswick Foundation, dedicated to alleviating the effects of the Depression in the city where the company's headquarters were located. Two years later, at age forty-five, he appointed himself J&J's first chairman of the board, a title he would hold for the next twenty-five years. About that time, he threw a party for some five thousand J&J employees at which he out-Levered William Lever, personally dancing until the wee hours of the morning with a steady stream of the most timid ladies on the staff.[15] Like Lever, Hershey, and Owen, Johnson prided himself on his abilities as a ballroom dancer, a pastime that would cause him great domestic difficulties: reports in the press that he was seen frequently on Manhattan dance floors in the arms of a woman to whom he was not married led to the second of his three divorces.

"General" Johnson

While the Depression didn't hamper the indefatigable Johnson's efforts to remake American industry, World War II did. In 1942 he was commissioned as an army colonel and assigned to an ordnance division responsible for supplying the military with equipment needed in the Atlantic and Pacific theaters of combat. His specific charge was to ensure that the nation's thousands of small businesses received their fair share of government contracts. He created a detailed plan to that end, but it met such a wall of resistance from the Pentagon that his friend President Roosevelt promoted him to the rank of brigadier general to increase his clout with the military. The promotion didn't help. Every effort Johnson made to steer contracts to small businesses was rebuffed by one federal agency or another. Exhausted by his futile efforts, he resigned his commission some sixty-four days after receiving it. His parting words, as reported by Walter Winchell, were "Washington is a magnet for mediocrity."[16] He then devoted the rest of the war to leading the home-front manufacturing effort that was, in many ways, key to the ultimate Allied victory. During the war, J&J provided the military not just with medical supplies but also with gas masks, artillery shells, and aircraft parts, mostly without profit to the company. Although he was only a general for two months, for the rest of his life he would be referred to as "the General" by his friends and Johnson & Johnson colleagues. If he was uncomfortable with that honorific, he did nothing to discourage those who addressed him by it.

In 1944 Johnson & Johnson became a publicly traded company, a decision that Johnson later would claim to regret.[17] His intent at the time had been to make it practical to grant large amounts of J&J stock to the company's senior managers. Indeed, in subsequent years almost all J&J executives would become major shareholders in the company. At the time of the initial public offering, Johnson emphasized that the stock listing would not change the company's managerial philosophy or practices. To that end, he continued to appoint only insiders to its board—managers who, like himself, had spent their entire careers in the unique J&J culture and were therefore committed to preserving it. In subsequent years the company would find itself subject to considerable criticism from the New York Stock Exchange, and others, for its failure to appoint outside board members. But Johnson held out until the end, never accepting a broader role for outsiders in the company's governance, thus presaging decades of tension in publicly traded companies between managers wishing to sustain an organization's enlightened practices and outside investors with no such commitment. Decades after his death, that tension would surface at J&J.

At the end of the war, Johnson returned to his interest in labor relations, penning a book in 1947 in which he laid out his philosophy of what a "just society" would look like in America, and the role business should play in creating it. The oddly named book, *Or Forfeit Freedom*, bore the supertitle "People Must Live—and Work Together."[18] It was, in many striking ways, an Owenite plea to Johnson's fellow industrialists to provide living wages, good working conditions, and a modicum of job security to their employees. If they failed to do so, Johnson warned, the American public would lose confidence in corporate capitalism—thus paving the way for the introduction of either a Marxist or fascist system. To preserve the freedom in his book's title, he contended, it was necessary for the country's business leaders to accept the legitimacy of labor unions, learning how to work with them (and with the government)—if not as partners, at least fairly and respectfully. Much of the book is dated, focusing on the issues dominating the headlines in the immediate aftermath of the war: widespread unemployment, low wages, strikes, shortages of food and consumer goods, and the lingering government controls and high taxes that had been introduced as emergency measures during the conflict.

Setting aside such material, the book reads as a thoughtful work of political economy, albeit one written in informal, often jarringly colloquial language. Johnson had no formal education after high school, yet he was clearly well-read, comfortable quoting Adam Smith, Thomas Macaulay, two Roman Catholic pontiffs, Henry Luce, Elton Mayo, and Peter Drucker (then a young, little-known author). He began his book with an analysis of what was wrong with the American system of private enterprise, specifically the problems that had led to the 1929 stock market crash, the subsequent Great Depression, and the failure of the economy to recover after the war. He accused the business community of being in denial about the underlying weaknesses of the American system: "because a few business leaders both talked and practiced nonsense, private enterprise is in disgrace with one part of the public and on probation with the rest."[19] He called for a rethinking of the system in a fashion reminiscent of President Theodore Roosevelt's Square Deal and Franklin Roosevelt's Four Freedoms: "It [the new system] will have its creature comforts, of course, for people will buy no stock in a future that does not at least promise higher standards of living. But it will also involve fair dealings between business, employers, and public; mutual effort and understanding; freedom from privation, fear, and the threat of insecurity. Thus it will replace the weaknesses that now threaten the economic system that also is our way of life."[20]

The book then outlines actions that each of the nation's key players—government, business, trade unions, workers, consumers, and citizens—needed to take to bring about the transformation Johnson envisioned. Johnson had strong views, and rock-ribbed confidence that he was right in what he advocated; yet he was neither a utopian dreamer nor an ideologue. His proposals were in the main practical and pragmatic, and he made every effort to recognize and address the legitimate interests of both labor and capital. Central to his philosophy was the need for fair treatment of all the nation's various constituencies—including business owners. Throughout his life he constantly called for lower taxes on income and wealth, reasoning that there was nothing morally wrong with becoming rich or inheriting great wealth. He even wrote an amusing article, "Dough Boy," about how hard it was to be born with a silver spoon in one's mouth! He also called for the end of unnecessary bureaucratic controls on business, while rejecting the laissez-faire doctrine that government should impose no regulations in the marketplace. In particular, he opposed the social Darwinist version of that philosophy elucidated by Herbert Spencer in Britain and William Graham Sumner in America, which, he wrote, "gave authority for competition as ruthless and impersonal as that waged by weeds and wild beasts. It also justified exploitation, made severity a prerequisite of progress, and dignified greed as part of the struggle for existence. Poverty was the normal result of weakness, while riches became evidence of fitness to survive."[21]

Instead of cut-throat winner-take-all laissez-faire—the dominant ideology in the English-speaking world among business leaders—Johnson aligned himself with the sentiments expressed by Pope Leo XIII in his landmark 1891 encyclical *Rerum Novarum*, subtitled "On the Condition of the Working Classes." The pope was no Marxist, yet he called on businesspeople to correct the economic and social wrongs of capitalism—principally, low wages and inhumane working conditions. Johnson was particularly drawn to the pope's belief in the dignity of labor and the God-given right of all workers to be treated with respect. Ever one to balance his statements, Johnson duly noted that the Protestant Federal Council of Churches had echoed the pope's themes in its Social Creed of 1908, which called on business to deal with the problems of poverty and to protect workers during the rapid technological changes occurring in the industrial order. Not to leave anyone out, he added that those "Christian leaders were joined by rabbinical bodies. Seeking modern application of Mosaic and Talmudic legislation, the rabbis supported bills guaranteeing workers the right to organize, outlawing child labor, establishing social security and old-age pensions, setting up fair employment practices, and so on."[22] Such religious appeals, he pointed out, had been largely rejected by business, and that was why, forty years after Leo XIII's call for reform, Pius XI felt compelled to return to the same themes in his 1931 encyclical *Quadragesimo anno*, subtitled "On the Reconstruction of the Social Order."

A Critic of Capital and Labor

While understanding the deep-seated reasons for union mistrust of management, Johnson nonetheless called the labor movement to task for "remaining indifferent to good government—in fact, they often allied themselves with the crookedest of local machines and the worst of racketeering bosses."[23] He scored organized labor for constantly demanding "more," even in instances where higher wages were economically unsupportable by levels of productivity. Such demands, he warned, would lead to the pricing of American goods out of world markets, and subsequent unemployment for the very workers for whom unions had sought to win unrealistic raises. He was particularly critical of union leaders who refused to cooperate with such well-meaning employers as James Lincoln in joint efforts to improve productivity. He called labor unions out for such unproductive practices as working-to-rule, featherbedding, and limiting the number of apprentices to produce artificial scarcities of skilled labor. He chastised union bosses for engaging in violence against their own members who dared speak in opposition to their dictates. At the same time, he recognized the rights of working people to organize, and of trade unions to represent them in collective bargaining, acknowledging that millions of Americans were laboring for less than a living wage. In the tradition of the best political economists, he offered an economic analysis of why so many workers were unfairly paid, and why they needed a decent income.

In the same vein as Theodore Roosevelt's famous 1910 "New Nationalism" speech, Johnson argued that millions of potentially productive but currently underemployed, undereducated workers were a drag on the American economy. It was therefore in the self-interest of business to employ those individuals more productively: if they were trained and put to work satisfying the pent-up material needs of consumers and repairing the nation's neglected infrastructure, they would create demands for the products of industry. He thus used the same reasoning earlier advanced by Robert Owen and Henry Ford: well-paid workers were the best customers of the companies in which they were employed. Furthermore, according to Johnson, better-compensated employees were more productive. And because America was underproducing, he advocated greater industry investment in new plants and technology to increase future economic growth. As a fillip, he added the same conservationist proviso Teddy Roosevelt had earlier raised: economic growth needed to be environmentally sustainable, which required the judicious use of all the nation's natural resources, including its air and water.

Much as J. C. Penney had, Johnson urged his business peers to pay attention to product quality, charge fair prices for the goods they made and sold, listen to the wishes of their consumers, engage in community-spirited activities, reduce air and water pollution, and accept all those concerns as part of their social responsibility.[24] Citing the Roman pontiff as his moral authority, he called on business leaders to provide challenging jobs that engaged not only the hands of workers but also their minds. He noted that many Americans believed that owner-managers were more open to accepting those responsibilities than corporate professional managers, expressing his personal belief that there were individuals in both categories "who love their work as a way of life," and that for such individuals to behave irresponsibly was "both a moral and commercial sacrilege."[25]

Although Johnson often cast his arguments for change in moral terms, invariably he would realistically turn to an appeal to the self-interest of the business community. He was convinced that those individuals, for all their faults, were more capable, effective, and efficient than government and labor leaders when it came to managing the industrial order. With regard to the issue of fair wages, he asked his peers to take the initiative: "Or do you prefer to have government do the job, add a stiff service charge, and compel you to pay the bill in the form of income taxes?"[26] He cited Lincoln Electric's system of compensation as an example of a method managers should consider adopting to improve their companies' productivity, and the economic well-being of their employees.[27] In all, he claimed that assuming such social responsibility was the surest way for managers to provide a sound profit to their stockholders in the long term.[28]

His Managerial Philosophy

Johnson was not only a social reformer but equally dedicated to advancing managerial practices. He was an early advocate of organizational decentralization, arguing, in effect, that it was more efficient for a company to have ten separate operating units, each with five hundred workers, than one giant facility employing five thousand: "Big business has been making one of the very mistakes for which it bitterly criticizes government. Under different names it piles bureau on bureau. . . . Thus the central management builds up a bureaucracy that buries the actual man on the job, robs him of authority, and relies on time-consuming conferences instead of quick decisions."[29]

"Business bureaucracy," Johnson claimed, "can give greater offense than government, since it directly affects customers and employees."[30] Furthermore, it was in the self-interest of corporate leaders to decentralize and delegate authority because workers are more likely to understand how they fit into the system of a small organization than a giant one. In small-scale organizations, workers and managers were also more likely to know each other by name, and thus see themselves as part of a common enterprise: "Since management and employees know each other, every worker becomes a person. There is mutual respect, regardless of position, and a strong feeling of dignity."[31] Although Johnson failed to mention it in Or Forfeit Freedom, his own company was, at the time of its writing, pioneering the practice of industrial decentralization; over the next four decades, that structure would become one of the three pillars on which its culture would rest. In effect, Johnson was using J&J as "his laboratory for the development of his many creative ideas for making business more responsible."[32]

Johnson also located J&J's numerous independent mini operating units in small towns and rural communities for the sake of creating greater employee engagement and work satisfaction. He felt workplaces should be organized so that employees could participate in the decisions affecting their own work, particularly as members of self-managing teams that would create a sense of community on the job.[33] As an integral part of that effort, Johnson believed that corporations had a responsibility to facilitate the personal development of workers, and that "training must go far beyond the job itself, to develop understanding, attitudes, and habits that will make the worker a better member of his plant community, his city, and his nation."[34] He encouraged employers to prepare workers with skills required to deal with emerging technologies, saying that training could occur in continuing education classes provided in workplaces, imagining at every workplace "an adult university keyed to the requirements of the changing business world."[35] In the spirit of Owen, Penney, and Lever, Johnson thus believed that employers had a responsibility for not only the training but also the education of their workforce.

In proper Jeffersonian fashion, Johnson wanted Americans to be not only productive workers but virtuous citizens as well, and he felt that the key to their moral and intellectual development was for managers to show them respect: "Dignity in employment is hard to define. It involves pride in the job one holds, pride in the work one produces, and pride in oneself as a worker and as a member of the community. It involves a subtle and complex personal relationship with employers and society as a whole. This relationship runs through the literature of the early American scene."[36]

Johnson found cultural displays of respect for American workers in the iconic paintings of Grant Wood, the Richard Rodgers and Oscar Hammerstein musical *Oklahoma!*, and the myth of Paul Bunyan. The benefits of showing workers respect, he believed, were underscored by findings of modern psychology: "Actually, the whole matter of dignity in employment boils down to this: Every worker, from chairman of the board to office boy or sweeper, is a human being. As such, he is endowed with an ego, which one dictionary defines as *the I who thinks, feels, and acts.* Modern business has reduced the size of that *I* by ignoring or grossly violating the innate requirements of workers."[37]

Taken as a whole, Johnson's philosophy looks back to the unfulfilled social agenda of the Progressive Era, and forward to the managerial theories of such humanist scholars as Douglas McGregor and Abraham Maslow. Although Johnson was putting in place at J&J the practices he advocated in his book, he made no specific mention of his own company in its pages. For example, he wrote that business leaders needed to adopt an "industrial credo; a statement of responsibility in the strictly business realm," a list of duties he claimed all companies had to their many constituencies. What he chose *not* to say was that the code outlined in his book was a generic version of a document that he had recently posted on the walls of his company's highly decentralized units, a document that would become the second pillar of the company's culture.

With the clear intent of creating a "moral business," in 1943 Johnson wrote a statement that he first titled "An Industrial Credo" (later changed to "Our Credo"), a litany of the company's responsibilities to its sundry constituencies: "the doctors, nurses, hospitals, mothers" who used its products; its employees and managers; its host communities; and finally its stockholders. To those who objected to putting owners last, he replied, "If we put our customers first and follow through on our other responsibilities, I assure you the stockholders will be well served."[38]

By all accounts, Johnson dedicated his tenure at J&J's helm to ensuring that the company bearing his name lived up to its credo. In 1957 he further elucidated its meaning in a single-page document entitled "Our Management Philosophy," one of the first calls for what later would become known as servant leadership. "Our concept of modern management," he wrote, "may be summarized by the expression 'to serve.' It is the duty of the leader to be a servant to those responsible to him." In addition, he recorded forty-four short audio programs to be broadcast to all J&J facilities, in which he explicated J&J's stewardship philosophy and explained its implications for employee behavior. For example, in the manner of Penney, he outlined each operating unit's responsibilities to its host community. He encouraged every J&J employee to become involved in community affairs, to vote, and even to run for office, regardless of the party they chose to support. Such efforts often were seen as sermonizing, leading some labor leaders to accuse him of paternalism.[39] In fact, he provided a constant flow of ideas and advice not only to his workers and managers but also to business, labor, military, medical, and government leaders.[40] Some of those ideas were quirky and eccentric: in the 1950s he advocated the building of bomb shelters, penning an article entitled "Dig, Son, Dig."[41] As his biographer notes, he "was highly opinionated and a staunch advocate of his fresh ideas, even after some of them went sour on him." Johnson himself admitted that even his own executives reacted negatively to one or more of his many notions.

As Johnson neared the end of his long reign as J&J's chairman and chief executive officer, finding a worthy successor became a major issue. Many of the company's executives favored the obvious candidate, his son, Robert "Bobby" Wood Johnson III. Sadly, Bobby (Johnson number five) had never been close to his father, having been raised from an early age by his mother after his parents divorced. Nonetheless, following two years of college Bobby joined the company, and like his father before him he spent his entire career working his way up the corporate hierarchy to become its president. He clearly had the qualifications—and the name—for the job, but when it came time to anoint him, his father balked. It seems that Johnson's obsessive perfectionism extended to the evaluation of his own son, whom he criticized often and severely. Moreover, Bobby was much like his father: obstinate and opinionated. The two clashed in private and at business meetings, and when Bobby had the bad luck to be hospitalized for a lengthy period, his father took advantage of his absence to abolish the position of president of J&J. Bobby appealed to his father to reconsider, but Johnson remained adamant. At age forty-five Bobby left the company, never to return.

Johnson retired in 1963 and died four years later, bequeathing all his $1.2 billion in J&J stock to the renamed Robert Wood Johnson Foundation, which made it the second largest private foundation in America. The foundation, originally established to support New Brunswick during the Depression, was repurposed to fund "the advancement of medical knowledge."

J&J After Johnson

Johnson's successor at the company's helm, Philip Hoffman, seems to have ignored "Our Credo," treating it with benign neglect. When he in turn retired in 1973, J&J's board of directors named Richard Sellars as the company's CEO. Sellars, by his own account, was as dedicated to the credo as Johnson had been, and found it unacceptable that it had fallen into desuetude under Hoffman. His commitment to its principles was soon tested. Shortly after Sellars assumed J&J's leadership, it was revealed that managers in its foreign divisions had engaged in bribery to secure overseas business. Sellars immediately put his foot down: and, citing the credo as his authority, fired those responsible. Shortly thereafter, the company's commitment was again challenged by mounting pressure to move its headquarters from the rapidly decaying urban core of New Brunswick and join the "white flight" to the suburbs. Before deciding to abandon the city, Sellars said he had looked "at the Credo's commitment to communities where we work and live" and then opted not only to keep J&J's headquarters in New Brunswick but to erect a modern headquarters building to serve as the core of what would become the company's ten-year revitalization of the city's center. Ultimately, hundreds of millions of J&J funds were invested in that effort.[42] Near the end of Sellars's relatively short tenure as CEO, the company's young president, James Burke, launched a program he called the Credo Challenge. In the years to come, that program would make Burke the first non-Johnson chief executive to leave an indelibly positive mark on the company.

James Burke

James Edward Burke is one of the few corporate stewards profiled in these pages who never explicated his business philosophy in a book, nor is he the subject of a published biography. Fortunately, he was featured in five informative videos and the subject of several in-depth Harvard Business School cases, and thus we can reconstruct his impressive career and discover the sources of the remarkably virtuous behavior he displayed as J&J's leader.

Born in Rutland, Vermont, in 1925, Burke grew up in a small town near Albany, New York, where his father was a bond and insurance salesman. His mother "loved intellectual ferment," Burke recalled; "She taught us to challenge everything. Our dinner table was constant arguing over anything and everything."[43] Years later, Burke's J&J career would be marked by one after another round of fruitful "challenging" and "constant arguing."

Burke attended a strict Catholic high school, where he was profoundly influenced by the ethical teachings of the Brothers of the Holy Cross of Notre Dame. He then enrolled at the College of the Holy Cross, but his higher education was interrupted by naval service in the South Pacific during World War II. After the war he returned to Holy Cross, graduating with a degree in economics, followed directly by a Harvard MBA. About that time, Harvard Business School published a new set of educational objectives for its students, a document that included two goals that, unfortunately, shortly thereafter disappeared from its mission: "Understanding of the useful generalizations of political economy and ability to develop at least the beginnings of an integrated social and economic philosophy"; and "Understanding of ethical considerations as an integral part of business administration and ability to develop a unified set of ethical concepts for personal guidance in administration." As a student, Burke seems to have met those objectives—and met them in a way that later made him particularly amenable to the business philosophy of Robert Wood Johnson II. In the late 1980s, Burke recalled his time at Harvard:

The thing that amazed me, and was totally unexpected, is that in everything we did, we were reminded of the moral values—the importance of moral values in our decision making. We all spent a lot of time talking about it, and many had some doubts. . . . I guess partly because of the way I was brought up, I had a set of values that I knew I was going to have difficulty compromising ever. And whether we like it or not, in our educational system, even at a place like Holy Cross, there is an underlying doubt about the enterprise system.[44]

After a short stint as a brand manager at Procter & Gamble, Burke tried his hand at creating three entrepreneurial ventures, each of which failed. Now deeply in debt, he returned to corporate life in 1953, taking a job at J&J as Band-Aid product director while Johnson was still in command of the company and the credo he'd written was fresh on its walls. Burke was soon a rising star, given the opportunity to develop and market a new product line of aspirin substitutes for children. Unfortunately, the line failed, at considerable cost to the company. Shortly thereafter, Johnson called Burke into his office. Burke had never been alone with the General and, convinced he was about to be fired, was certain the visit would also be his last. To his great surprise, Johnson congratulated him on his enterprising attempt to create a new business: "What business is all about is making decisions, and you don't make decisions without making mistakes. Now, don't make that mistake again, but please make sure you make other mistakes."[45] As Burke explained years later to researchers from Harvard Business School, "That incident was extremely important to me, and the General became important to me—first of all because he was tougher than hell; he was egocentric, but he was very creative. He loved to argue, almost as much as I do. On anything. I don't know that he was a mentor of mine, but he loved young people and he was very close to what was going on in the company."[46]

Burke was subsequently promoted to vice president of product management—coincidentally, at about the time J&J acquired McNeil Pharmaceuticals, the eventual makers of Tylenol, the product that one day would bring Burke to the attention of the American public. In 1962 he was named president of J&J's baby and proprietary products division, which he promptly reorganized, splitting its marketing and research functions. Subsequently, Johnson indicated his displeasure with the performance of the newly reshuffled division, letting it be known that he was considering replacing Burke. As Burke recalled, "I was furious." He demanded a meeting with Johnson and J&J's executive committee, at which he planned to make a formal presentation demonstrating that, in fact, his division was performing well. In the middle of that presentation, Johnson walked out of the room and didn't return. Although the committee ended up giving Burke a vote of confidence, he was nonetheless upset by the General's abrupt departure. Johnson later explained his behavior to another J&J executive: "It was perfectly obvious that the business was in complete control and well-managed. Why waste my time on it? You know, I don't think it really hurt Burke, do you?" When the executive related that conversation to Burke, he noted that Johnson had "a twinkle in his eye" when he mentioned that he hadn't hurt him. Burke recalled, "That made me start thinking. Not only didn't it hurt us, the business was much better managed as the result of the General's challenge. . . . We did a whole lot of things that never would have happened if the General hadn't challenged us, and I never forgot it."[47]

While Burke never became an intimate of the much older Johnson, he was supervised by Johnson's son, Bobby, who, before he was fired, had recommended Burke for several key promotions, including, in 1965, as head of J&J's domestic operations and member of the corporate executive committee. It was then that Burke had his first close view of what J&J's credo meant in practice. At the time, Bobby was manager of development for a promising new product, Baby Liquid Cream, which was to be marketed for use by infants and their mothers. Bobby was anxious to make the product a success; if it was, he felt his father might then look more favorably on his possible succession. Burke recalled it as "a beautiful product, beautifully packaged," and

Bobby was eager to put it on the market. But just as he prepared to do so, clinical results arrived, showing that the lotion caused minor skin irritation in some 5 percent of adult users. The tests also revealed that the only women who experienced such irritation were those with pre-existing skin problems and who, in addition, were extremely heavy users of the lotion. Given the routine practice of putting warnings about such potentially minor problems on product labels, some members of J&J's executive committee were in favor of proceeding with marketing the cream. But Bobby demurred: "We are not going ahead. Dump it in the Raritan River if you have to."[48] "What he meant was get rid of it," Burke explained, "and he did. He made the decision like that, and it cost the corporation a lot of money. I thought at the time that this was the kind of thing that made Johnson & Johnson different, and that thought returned many times over the years."[49]

The Credo Challenge

A few years later—after both the General and Bobby had left the firm—Burke, now J&J's president, decided to restore the credo's centrality to the company's culture. He was confident that his boss, Chairman Sellars, was a true believer in the document, but uncertain how deep support went down the ranks of J&J's management—particularly among younger members who had not served under Johnson. In 1975 Burke initiated the Credo Challenge, inviting some twenty top J&J corporate executives, several of whom were also members of the company's board of directors, to a two-day-long discussion to assess how useful they found the company's credo in their decision making. Sellars chose not to attend the meeting; in his words, "I feel so strongly about the Credo that I think I would have challenged each of those individuals to believe as I do. I would have found myself selling [it]." The meeting was filmed, and it stands as one of the few unscrubbed views business scholars and students have of how the forces of idealism and realism conflict in high-level corporate meetings. As captured on film, here is a verbatim sample of what was said at that first Credo Challenge:[50]

BURKE: The Credo sits in somewhere between 150–200 of our locations—hangs on the walls, at least. If the Credo doesn't mean anything, we really ought to come to that conclusion, and should rip it off the walls and get on with the job. If it is there as an act of pretention, it is not only useless, it has a negative effect. . . . You should all feel free to stir up some controversy. I don't think we will get much out of this unless you do. [Burke then asked the committee to recommend whether the company should (a) get rid of the Credo; (b) change it; or (c) commit to live by it. If they chose to change it, they were asked to provide specific, alternative language. He then left the meeting.]

EXECUTIVE 1: . . . [Every] decision is either good or bad; but good or bad against what? If you have every manager interpreting for himself what [the Credo] means, it is like playing golf and everyone has his own par. That's why I think it is meant as absolutes, and should be absolutes.

DAVID COLLINS (MCNEIL PHARMACEUTICALS DIVISION HEAD): I have trouble looking at the Credo as that kind of a regulation because I find the need to resolve inconsistencies between its principles when used to assess the performance of an individual in a job. Because he can rightly come back to you and say "Our Credo says to make a profit, and that is what I did. How can you possibly fire me for doing that?"

EXECUTIVE 2: Any guy who runs a business is, in our case, like a guy juggling five colored balls, four are white ones—the first four tenets of [the Credo]. The fifth is a bright red one, and it says "profit." Everyone in this room knows he better not drop that red one or he is going to be in deep trouble. What he really doesn't know is what it means in terms of the other four. Which one can I drop first? Can I fumble that one? Or where can I give a little? But he knows about that red one.

EXECUTIVE 3: Picking up [your] point, you can't kid yourself: The purpose of a business is to make a profit. We are capitalists. This country was built on it. This business is built on it. We can't let all this discussion degenerate into something that says fulfilling that objective [profit] is not very nice.

EXECUTIVE 4: I don't know if anybody is really saying that . . .

EXECUTIVE 3: Oh, I don't know . . . there's an undercurrent . . .

EXECUTIVE 5: We are losing sight of what the General was trying to say. . . . Unless we meet the demands of society, someone—number one, the government—is going to force us to do it. . . . Should we not therefore do what is best for the business—not only what is morally and ethically correct—but what is best for the business by following the concept of the Credo so that we meet the needs of society, and therefore are able to do things better and cheaper than the government? And do things that are basically right and decent and human.

EXECUTIVE 6: That's apple pie and motherhood. We are all in agreement about that. The question is, which of these things is a legitimate demand of society, and how many of these can we fulfill and stay in business?

EXECUTIVE 7: Making a profit all by itself is not the issue. What we are talking about is a set of principles that you can't make a profit at the expense of. . . . We must meet all of those things.

EXECUTIVE 3: I am not suggesting [otherwise]. I just don't want to see us unnecessarily diminish the importance of profit.

EXECUTIVE 8: We go around and around on this. We are not challenging whether the executive committee believes in [the Credo] or wants to practice it, but the question that Jim [Burke] put to us yesterday: "Do we sometimes get conflicting signals?" And I think we are saying "Yes, we do get some conflicting signals."

A few months after the meeting, J&J invited distinguished television journalist Edwin Newman to visit the company's headquarters, view the Credo Challenge video, and then critique it on camera in discussion with Sellars and Burke. When Newman expressed some cynicism about the credo's placement of profit fifth, and last, in the order of J&J's responsibilities, Sellars replied: "We learned long ago that if you can't run a business profitably while paying for your social responsibilities, you better get out of the business." Newman then noted that the credo would "be a pretension and self-serving if the company was not acting on it," leading Burke to reply that some individuals who took part in the Credo Challenge had implied that the company was "not always living up to the high principles of the Credo," suggesting that was because the document's numerous "priorities are difficult to balance, and the priorities are sometimes in conflict." Nonetheless, he said, the company's managers had no choice but to resolve those conflicts to maintain the public's trust. In light of the filmed exchange between McNeil head David Collins, in which he offered a subjective reading of the responsibilities enumerated in the credo, and the executive who interpreted it in absolute terms, Burke made it clear that he firmly believed that all five of the "balls" that managers juggled at J&J were red.

Sellars told Newman that the Credo Challenge had taught him that some J&J managers felt there was "insufficient understanding" of the document among the executive committee and members of the company's board. As a consequence, he had a copy of the credo enlarged and posted on all four walls of J&J's boardroom to serve "as a constant reminder that its principles are a part of our decision-making process." Concluding that the Credo Challenge had been a success, Sellars and Burke decided that the process should be repeated, in cascading fashion, down through every level of the company's hierarchy. Moreover, in order to institutionalize the practice, each unit in the company thenceforth would devote one day each year to a Credo Challenge. "I don't really think you can impose convictions or beliefs on someone else," Burke explained, but he believed that the Credo Challenge was not about forcing managers to accept the company's stated values; instead, "what they really are doing is challenging their own beliefs."[51]

"Beliefs," "values," and "corporate culture" were central concepts in Burke's leadership philosophy. As he explained, "The company functions as it does because of its value system.... Our culture really is it."[52] Thus, when Burke was named CEO in 1976, he viewed his major leadership task at the highly decentralized J&J as sustaining its strong value system, and the primary tool at his disposal as the Credo Challenge.

The Tylenol Crisis

When Burke instituted the Credo Challenge, he had no idea how powerful a tool it would prove to be until, in 1982, a psychopath laced Tylenol capsules with cyanide and then placed the tampered bottles on store shelves. Seven people died as a result of ingesting the capsules. Almost from the moment it was clear to Burke and his leadership team that the poisoned capsules threatened the lives of J&J's customers and its reputation as "a company that cares," the record shows they behaved in an exemplary fashion. Even before they had confirmed that the company was not responsible for the poisonings, J&J's executives ignored legal advice to remain silent and not say anything that might later be used against them in litigation. Burke even opened the doors of J&J's crisis management meeting room to the investigative newsman Mike Wallace and his *60 Minutes* television camera crew, at a time when the very name Mike Wallace struck terror in the hearts of managers who heard that he was at their office door requesting an interview. Wallace had never been known for never doing puff pieces; on the contrary, he was known for digging up dirt.

The crisis management process Wallace recorded was in many ways similar to the candid way in which the Credo Challenge had been conducted at J&J over the previous seven years. Burke assembled a cross-functional team of J&J executives who met twice a day for six weeks. In his words, "We let the debate rage." Perhaps drawing on what he had learned from his mother at the dinner table and his spirited debates

with the General, Burke declared "Let everybody say what they god-
dam believe." In one exchange aired on *60 Minutes*, Burke is seen in
heated discussion with McNeil division head David Collins over when
product advertising should begin as part of the process of restoring
consumer trust in Tylenol. Collins's beliefs about the lack of moral absolutes in the company credo appear unchanged from the subjective
position he expressed seven years earlier in the Credo Challenge video:
he is seen on camera disagreeing forcefully with Burke, suggesting
that considerations of profit should not be set aside while the company
addresses consumer safety issues. Significantly, Burke does not order
Collins to deal first with safety and trust issues; instead, he engages
with the McNeil head and the other assembled executives in a free-
flowing debate among equals designed to surface—and thoroughly
and logically analyze—all possible perspectives on how to deal with
the aftermath of the crisis. Later, Burke credited the Credo Challenge
for having prepared his managers to do "the right thing" when disaster
struck. A postscript: in the years after the Tylenol crisis, skeptic Collins
would become the company's leading public advocate of J&J's Credo
Challenge.

The stakes involved in the Tylenol crisis were high in terms not only
of loss of life but of financial impact on J&J. Tylenol had been the nation's top selling analgesic and J&J's most profitable product. Shortly
after the news of the Tylenol deaths reached Wall Street, the company's
stock price plummeted by 20 percent, amounting to a $2 billion paper
loss for its shareholders. Most experts predicted Tylenol was finished
as a consumer product, even though J&J was blameless in the deaths.
Madison Avenue advertising guru Jerry Della Femina predicted, "In
a year it will be difficult to find a product with the name Tylenol on
it." Thus, after the immediate crisis had passed, Burke was faced with a
dual task: meeting the needs of investors in the short term, and saving
the Tylenol brand in the long run. In Burke's view, the long run was
what counted. As the General had often stated, long-term thinking was
the third pillar of J&J's culture, and events proved him right. A year

after the poisonings, Tylenol was back on drugstore shelves, having regained its leadership position in the analgesic market. The reason was clear: with its admirable responses to the crisis, the company had been able to regain public trust. J&J had quickly recalled all Tylenol products from retailer shelves at a cost of some $100 million, earning high praise from the head of the FBI, who testified that the company had not only cooperated fully with the agency's investigations but proactively recalled Tylenol much faster than the feds recommended. More than that, Burke had offered to repurchase from customers any bottles of the product, open or not, on the off chance that some had been bought before the recall.

In the months following the crisis, J&J engaged in a series of socially responsible, candid, and prompt actions, culminating with the introduction of new safety packaging, including the "neck seals" now standard on bottles in the pharmaceutical industry (the ones that make it so hard to open plastic jars of medicine). Throughout the crisis and its aftermath, Burke, who had not previously appeared on television in his seven years as J&J's CEO, made himself readily available for on-air interviews. In each, he offered complete and factual answers to all questions asked, no matter how hostile or skeptical the interviewer. In the end, Burke and J&J won the admiration of even the congenitally negative Mike Wallace, who concluded: "Instead of stonewalling, they have been forthcoming." J&J's handling of the Tylenol incident still stands as a model for how corporations should deal with crises. Yet when later faced with major crises, executives at Exxon and Union Carbide in the 1990s, and at Volkswagen and Wells Fargo more recently, chose to reject J&J's transparent and candid approach in favor of stonewalling and denial.

After the Tylenol crisis passed, Burke returned to the routine of leading a giant multinational corporation. Over the decade he served as J&J's leader, he quadrupled its investment in research and development, doubled the number of its foreign divisions, and oversaw a threefold increase in sales, to $7 billion in 1986. Unfortunately, that year also witnessed another Tylenol-associated tragedy: a copycat poisoning of tampered capsules. After discussions with his staff, Burke concluded that there was no way to make capsules 100 percent safe, announcing that J&J would no longer offer over-the-counter capsule medications. At the cost of some $150 million, J&J recalled and destroyed all Tylenol capsules, replacing them with caplets, even though most consumers preferred the former form. In hindsight, Burke rued that the company had kept using capsules after the first incident.

If Robert Wood Johnson II was a man of many contradictions, James Burke stood as a model of consistency: he invariably practiced what Johnson had advocated. As he summed up the three pillars of J&J's philosophy and culture, "We believe the consistency of our overall performance as a corporation is due to our unique form of decentralized management, our adherence to the ethical principles embodied in our Credo, and our emphasis on managing the business for the long term."[53]

Burke retired from J&J in 1989, declining the offer of a seat on its board. With characteristic humility, he explained, "I wouldn't want to have the burden of me around if I were the new management."[54] He remained active in public life as a member of several prominent boards, including IBM's, where he convinced Louis Gerstner to become the company's CEO when it was suffering financially. Gerstner is widely credited with saving IBM from being dismantled and sold off piecemeal, if not from bankruptcy, largely by following Burke's example of focusing on revitalizing the company's culture. In 2000 President Bill Clinton awarded Burke America's highest civilian honor, the Presidential Medal of Freedom, citing his virtuous business record and chairmanship of the Partnership for a Drug-Free America. In 2003 *Fortune* placed him on its 10 Greatest CEOs of All Time list. He died in 2012 at the age of eighty-seven.

Yet Another Sad, Bad End

J&J's handling of the Tylenol crisis became famous. Yet, paradoxically, Burke's successor canceled the Credo Challenge, ostensibly to save the cost of the process. Finding that decision difficult to believe, in the 1990s I telephoned J&J's public relations department, where I was told by an anonymous manager that the new CEO had wanted "to make his own mark." When I asked if I could obtain a fresh copy of the company's Our Credo video to replace my badly worn VHS tape, the manager told me, "No such video exists." My conclusion was that the new CEO felt eclipsed by his eminent predecessor's shadow, and was attempting to erase his legacy.

After Burke's retirement, the emphasis of J&J's top management shifted from quality to cost control in order to boost short-term profits. Indeed, the company became more profitable under Burke's successors. However, those profits came at the loss of lives and, subsequently, the company's ethical reputation. Since 2000, when J&J withdrew its heartburn drug Propulsid from the US market after it was linked to more than eighty deaths, the company has been on an ethical and legal roller-coaster ride, with intermittent displays of social responsibility, followed by periods of regulatory compliance violations and embarrassing product recalls. Incredibly, several of those recalls were at its McNeil division, including two in 2009–10, related to lax quality and sterility controls in the manufacture of Tylenol.

In December 2010, J&J's directors were hit with a shareholder lawsuit citing a long list of "federal and state regulatory investigations, subpoenas and requests for documents, FDA warning letters, news articles, and the recall of products accounting for hundreds of millions of dollars of corporate losses."[55] The General would have been appalled.

8

Great Genes

The making of the first pair of Levi Strauss jeans is the stuff of legend. As the story goes, during the great California gold rush Levi Strauss, a Jewish immigrant tailor, made a pair of pants for a '49er out of fabric used to make tents, fastening parts of the sturdy material together with brass rivets. Like most legends, this one is more fiction than fact. What is true is that Levi Strauss was a Jewish immigrant from Bavaria who arrived in New York in 1847, accompanied by his brothers Louis and Jonas and sister Fanny, none of whom spoke English. Six years later, he sailed around Cape Horn at the southernmost tip of South America—the trip took three months—settling in the California boomtown recently named San Francisco. Levi was no tailor, but a budding merchant who promptly established a dry goods store near the city's busy waterfront in partnership with Fanny's husband, David Stern, and three others, including his brothers. There was never a question about who the senior partner was: Levi was the acknowledged business genius, the master entrepreneur, the *macher*. By the mid-1860s, Levi Strauss & Co. was an established, thriving business selling dry goods shipped from New York.

The Jewish immigrant tailor in the legend was, in fact, a certain Jacob Davis of Reno, Nevada—a failed brewer, tobacconist, and coal merchant who in 1869 bought duck cloth from Levi Strauss & Co. with which he made horse blankets, tents, and wagon covers. One day, a woman came to Davis's Reno shop to ask him to fashion a pair of pants for her husband, an obese teamster who had worn out the only pair she'd ever found that fit him. Since the poor man couldn't walk around town in just his drawers, she had brought his measurements to Davis so he could tailor something that was both sturdy and sufficiently capacious. Later, when other men in Reno saw the teamster's custom-made duck-cloth pants, they started visiting Davis's shop to order pairs for themselves. When Davis ran out of duck cloth—and Levi Strauss & Co. didn't have any in stock to send him—he ordered blue denim, instead. In the next eighteen months, he sold some two hundred pairs of handmade brass-riveted denim pants. Seeing the commercial potential of his creation, the semiliterate Davis approached the owners of Levi Strauss & Co., proposing that they help him obtain a patent for the riveting of pants and contract with him to sell the jeans he produced. Davis then sold them a half interest in the patent they had helped him win.

Soon Levi Strauss & Co. was in the manufacturing business, with Jacob Davis in its employ, overseeing a factory with 250 sewing machine operators. Davis directed the operators to sew two curved Vs on the back pockets of Levi's to distinguish the company's jeans from those of copycat competitors. He affixed an oil-cloth guarantee on the back of the pants, portraying two dray horses vainly trying to rip apart a pair of Levi's "Two-Horse Brand" denim trousers (a leather patch was later substituted). Over the next decade, as the company's fortunes grew, Levi Strauss's partners began to die off, beginning with brother-in-law David Stern in 1874. After Levi bought out his last living partner in 1886, he became the sole owner of the firm bearing his name. A lifelong bachelor, the childless Levi named his four Stern nephews as his heirs.[1]

The oldest of the Stern brothers, Sigmund, entered the family business when he came of age, and soon after, his uncle began turning over company operations to him. Sigmund had always been Levi's favorite nephew, the one who most shared his uncle's business sense and, in particular, his love of the good life (Sigmund brought his friend "Willie" Hearst to the lavish parties Levi loved to host at the swank St. Francis

Hotel).[2] He also shared his uncle's paternalistic concern for the company's employees, most of them immigrants, initially from Eastern Europe and then later from Italy. Although the company treated its workers with respect, in the early years it was far from a model employer. The hours worked in the plant were long, the pay poor, and the repetitive tasks physically taxing. Levi Strauss had been tempted to hire Chinese workers in the late 1870s because they were willing to work for even less than his European employees, but he bowed to pressure from customers, reluctantly agreeing to hire "none but white labor."[3] Unlike in most companies discussed in these pages, enlightened labor practices were not part of the company's initial DNA. Yet between the 1880s and 1970s, Levi Strauss's heirs gradually introduced practices that would earn the company a near impeccable reputation for socially responsible behavior.

By the late 1880s Levi Strauss had established himself among San Francisco's most prominent business leaders and citizens. He invested successfully in several other firms—helping to found the local gas company and to start a railroad intended to break the Southern Pacific's much-despised monopoly—and ably served on numerous public boards and commissions. He was respected as a generous philanthropist, funding the first scholarships at the fledgling University of California. Over the last twenty years of his life, those concerns came to occupy the bulk of his time and energy, and consequently, his visits to the Levi Strauss company offices became less frequent, and Sigmund's role there more important. When Levi died in 1902, he left an estate of $6 million, the bulk of which—minus generous bequests to Jewish, Protestant, and Catholic orphanages—went to the Stern brothers. That sum, enormous in an era when a salary of $100 a month was considered good pay, seems to have been derived as much from Levi's many outside investments as it was from pants-factory profits. A few days after Levi's demise, the *San Francisco Bulletin* eulogized him in an editorial urging its readers never to forget one of the city's most respected founders, "a credit to the race from which he sprung, and the country of which he was an honored citizen." Indeed, he would be remembered—although not for his civic leadership but instead for having created trousers that were, in fact, the work of another man.

In 1890, when Jacob Davis's rivet patent expired, more competitors started producing knockoff jeans. But that made little difference to the fortunes of Levi Strauss & Co., whose five hundred stitchers and sewers couldn't keep pace with demand for its expanding line of products. The company continued to grow under the management of Sigmund and his brothers, and the factory under the direction of Davis. Then, in 1906, disaster struck in the form of a calamitous earthquake, followed by a devastating fire that destroyed the core of San Francisco's business area—along with the factory, store, and offices of Levi Strauss & Co. The Sterns reacted to the disaster by announcing that the company would build a new factory (astonishingly, it opened six months later), pay salaries to its employees until they were back at work, and extend credit to their retail merchants who had lost everything in the disaster. That new factory, constructed under the direction of Simon Davis—the aging Jacob's twenty-nine-year-old son—represented a breakthrough in industrial design. It was clean, quiet, well-lighted, and situated in a largely residential neighborhood some distance away from the grimy, rat-infested areas where most of the city's manufacturing was conducted. The architecturally significant building is still in use today as a Quaker school in the city's now-trendy Mission District.

After Jacob Davis retired, his son became the firm's head of manufacturing, running the business as if he owned it. As creative as his father, Simon designed a one-piece button-up-the-front denim overall for toddlers called Koveralls, a product that became almost as popular as Levi's iconic 501 jeans. Unfortunately, Simon was headstrong and lacked business sense, a combination of traits that would eventually nearly bankrupt the company. Although Levi's sales increased each year well into the 1920s, its manufacturing costs increased at a faster rate. The Sterns—dependent on Simon's management of the factory— were reluctant to rein in his spendthrift tendencies. They were also getting old and preparing to retire, and like Uncle Levi before them, neither had a son old enough to succeed them in the firm.

Son-in-Law to the Rescue

But Sigmund had a daughter, Elise, who had made a wise marriage to Walter Haas in 1914. After he was demobilized from service in World War I, thirty-year-old Walter was lured into joining his wife's family firm in 1919. Two years later, now Levi Strauss & Co.'s vice president and treasurer, Walter was in a position to discover that Simon Davis's inventory numbers didn't compute; moreover, there was a serious problem with the quality of the products coming out of the factory the latter managed. Walter shared what he had learned with his father-in-law, who, torn between his loyalty to Simon and the desire to support his son-in-law, agonized for some time over how to act. Ultimately, Sigmund went to Simon's home. Confronted with the facts Walter had collected, the plant manager decided to bolt from the company—taking with him two key production managers, with the intent of establishing a rival firm. Walter and his newly recruited second-in-charge, his cousin Daniel Koshland, then set about tackling the problems Simon had created. Soon the company's finances were back in order and its profits rising. To celebrate, the company announced significant Christmas bonuses for its managers, clerks, and salesmen. On hearing this news from Walter, Milton Grunbaum, Simon's successor as head of operations, demanded to know why "I'm getting five hundred dollars and my [factory workers] are getting nothing," angrily adding, "I won't accept my bonus unless you give one to all the people at [the factory]." Walter, taken aback, had a sudden revelation that in many ways marked the true beginning of Levi Strauss & Co. Grunbaum was right; the hardworking sewers and stitchers had earned bonuses. As Walter later recalled, "Very secretly, so it would be a surprise, we got the money out of the bank . . . and gave everybody in the factory five dollars, a day's wages."[4] Over the next eight decades, ethical arguments would trump all other considerations in the company.

When Sigmund died in 1928, Walter was firmly in command of the firm, with cousin Koshland serving as its treasurer. A year later the stock market crashed, and one after another of the company's retail dealers started going out of business. Throughout most of the ensuing Great Depression, orders for Levi's products were insufficient to keep its factory operating at full production. Competitors in the garment industry closed their factories and laid off workers, who then joined millions of other unemployed Americans in breadlines and at soup kitchens. Although a hundred thousand unsold pairs of pants filled the company's stockroom—and even its restroom—Haas and Koshland opted not to lay off Levi's employees. Instead, they were put on a three-day workweek—painting the factory, refinishing its floors, anything to enable them to earn a paycheck large enough to feed their families.

The Depression was so devastating for American workers that many began to form trade unions. By the mid-1930s, almost every business in San Francisco had been organized. The one major exception, Levi Strauss & Co., then found itself targeted for organization by the United Garment Workers of America (UGWA). But when union organizers approached the Levi plant's employee entrance, they were largely ignored by the company's workers, who apparently were grateful to have been spared the curse of unemployment. Resolved to win the right to represent the workers, the UGWA began to picket the facility. The union had a significant point of leverage: it demanded that its members buy only products affixed with a "union-made" label. Because work clothes were the company's main products, and Levi's competitors (none of whom based in San Francisco) were unionized, if Haas and Koshland didn't sign a union contract, they would find themselves at a significant competitive disadvantage at a time when they and their employees desperately needed more orders for their jeans. The cousins were thus in a bind: they didn't want to tell their workers they *had* to join a union, yet they felt Levi's couldn't afford to be the largest nonunionized company in a union town like San Francisco. They signed the contract.

The Next Generation Enters the Pants Business

Walter and Elise had two sons, Walter Jr. (Wally) and the younger Peter, who grew up in the family's San Francisco mansion. Both siblings attended the University of California, the institution where their great-granduncle Levi had endowed scholarships and where the business school would one day be named after them. Wally later earned an MBA from Harvard Business School, then entered the family business. While serving an apprenticeship in Levi's factory, he observed two "retired" sewing machine operators washing dishes by hand in the company cafeteria. "My Harvard Business School training told me that was both unsanitary and inefficient," Wally later recalled, so he approached plant manager Grunbaum with the idea of replacing the two women with a mechanical dishwasher. Applying his B-school smarts, he prepared a quantitative analysis to demonstrate that such a machine would be both more efficient and more sanitary. After studying the report, Grunbaum told Wally, "Well, that's all very good. You know, these ladies are too young to get any garment union benefits, and too old to work [a sewing machine], and each has about thirty years in the factory. What am I going to do with them?"[5] Years later, when Walter Haas Jr. was chairman of what had become the world's largest garment manufacturer, he said he had learned a lesson from Grunbaum that day, one that hadn't been part of the Harvard B-school curriculum: a company has a responsibility to attend to the welfare of its lowest-paid workers. With evident pride, Haas Jr. explained, "And it was a good lesson."

Walter Haas Sr. lived until he was ninety, coming into his office almost every day until the end came in 1979, although he had turned over leadership of the company to his sons in 1958. Working side by side, Walter Jr. and Peter developed a philosophy of enlightened leadership that included not only serving the needs of Levi's employees but also meeting the company's ethical responsibilities to its suppliers, customers, and the communities in which it operated. Walter had learned his lesson from plant manager Grunbaum; one of his first executive actions in the 1940s was to declare the full day of the company's annual afternoon Christmas party a paid holiday for the entire workforce. He and Peter then began to hire African American and Asian American workers, and to grant Levi Strauss stock to key employees. The Haas brothers also began actively seeing to the care of company pensioners—for example, hiring recent Levi Strauss retirees to bring gifts of food to their older peers. Later, Levi Strauss began offering its retirees cost-of-living adjustments to their pensions, at a time when its competitors' blue-collar retirees received no pensions at all.

Company fortunes received a major boost in the 1950s, when jeans—traditionally sold as work clothes—were suddenly embraced as fashionable by young Americans. When matinee-idol James Dean appeared in popular films wearing Levi Strauss jeans, every teenager in America suddenly wanted a pair. To meet the growing demand, the company rapidly expanded sales far beyond its original markets in the western US, establishing manufacturing operations across America. Shortly after they had opened a plant in Blackstone, Virginia, the Haas brothers discovered that blacks applying for jobs there were being turned away. The small town was segregated, and its white citizens intended to keep it that way. Reluctant to impose "San Francisco values" on a small southern community, the company approached members of the local chamber of commerce with the argument that the plant made such a substantial contribution to the local economy that it was in their self-interest to integrate it in order to keep it open. The town elders came back with a counterproposal: build a wall between the areas where whites and blacks worked. The Haases refused. Then how about painting a white line down the middle of the factory? The Haases held firm. Well, then, at least segregate the water fountains! No dice. Ultimately the town relented, and the plant was integrated. Only one white employee refused to work in the integrated plant—a woman who said she agreed with the new policy, but her husband had insisted she quit.[6]

During the 1950s and '60s, the company doubled its sales every five years, thus finding itself in need of capital to fuel the rapid expansion. Walter Sr. was adamantly opposed to raising the needed money by floating a stock issue, fearing the family would lose control of the firm to financiers insufficiently committed to preserving its values and culture. Viewing the alternative course—borrowing money—as the lesser of two evils, the company took on $20 million in debt from the Metropolitan Life Insurance Co. Another by-product of the company's success was a growing problem with the quality of products made in its rapidly expanding number of plants. To meet that challenge, Walter and Peter created a product quality department whose manager reported directly to them. That unstinting commitment to quality underscored the brothers' stated goal of making Levi Strauss "the best darn corporation in America."[7]

Increasingly, the Haases came to believe that meeting their goal of all-around excellence required them to view the purpose of their company as broader than simple profit making. They began to speak—and act—as if the company were not just a business, but a *societal institution* with responsibilities to San Francisco and the two dozen communities across America in which it had facilities. They established a community affairs department to manage its growing number of civic-minded initiatives. The Haas family channeled increasing amounts of money into the Levi Strauss Foundation, appointing a professional director to manage the company's philanthropic activities independent of any business implications (or the influence of company executives with personal charitable agendas). Levi Strauss & Co. began supporting the formation of minority-owned clothing stores, and to contract with minority-owned manufacturers and suppliers, and Walter Jr. personally assumed a leadership role in the National Alliance of Businessmen (NAB), which was formed in the mid-1960s as a response to the urban riots then breaking out in central cities across the country.

Most significantly, the company authorized employees at its many facilities to create community involvement teams in which shop-floor workers—sewers and stitchers—were encouraged to volunteer time at local nonprofits of their choice. The company funded the teams by distributing a large tranche of Levi Foundation money to them, empowering the workers to use it to support local organizations of their choosing. In effect, Levi Strauss employees—most of them women and members of minority groups—were made into philanthropists. Those women, largely uneducated and typically inactive socially and politically, were thus transformed into respected citizens with voices in their communities. They were no longer just sewing machine operators; they were treated as equals by hospital administrators, school officials, and community leaders. Moreover, most of the workers' jobs were hard on the eyes and fingers, and tough on backs and necks—not the kind of work in which time flies. Thus, a by-product of the community teams was an improvement in the quality of life of workers whose routine, hard jobs were nearly impossible to enrich or make intrinsically satisfying in any other way. As one employee told a Levi's executive, "I never thought it was fun working before."[8]

As the company grew, and profits increased, it steadily added to the benefits offered employees, including generous health and insurance programs previously unheard of in the garment industry. Whenever a union won a concession in one of its organized facilities, the company extended it to those working in its nonunion locales. Women were hired to fill positions—such as plant mechanics—that previously had been all-male domains, and by 1976, 166 of the company's management positions were held by women.[9] In addition, handicapped workers were given rare employment opportunities (blind workers ran the cafeteria in a Texas plant). When automated equipment was introduced, workers were retrained for other tasks rather than being displaced. Employees were encouraged to find ways to organize their jobs to make them less monotonous, and rewarded for finding ways to improve productivity and efficiency. Nonetheless, the work itself remained extremely taxing

and demanding, and turnover was extremely high, averaging 75 percent annually (although, as at Lincoln Electric, most of it came within
the first year of employment). Making clothing was never turned into
a joy, but the company did what it could to mitigate the worst aspects
of the work. In all, by the 1960s, the Haas brothers were on their way
to realizing the dream of making their company "the best darn corporation in America."

The Best American Company?

In the period from the 1960s to the 1980s, Levi Strauss built a reputation
for being one of the nation's most socially engaged large corporations,
and Walter Haas Jr. came to play an increasingly public role in encouraging other companies to actively assume broader social responsibilities.
Beginning in the mid-1960s—when America experienced a prolonged
period of social unrest driven by the Vietnam War, the struggle for
civil rights and women's rights, growing environmental pollution, and
concerns about consumer and worker safety—many citizens blamed
corporations for some, or all, of those ills. In response, the Mobil Oil
Corporation launched a public campaign to address what they called
"public ignorance about the economic realities of the marketplace. We
think it [the criticism] reflects a basic lack of knowledge about economics itself . . . or more precisely, a *lack of economics education*."

Walter Haas Jr. analyzed the same situation, but arrived at a different conclusion: "Over the years, we've spent millions of dollars on
economic education. But these millions of dollars have not stemmed
the tide of business criticism. The thesis of this spending has been, 'If
only those people understood, they would be more sympathetic.' It is
my judgment that economic education—while it can be useful and
informative—has not and will not attack the mistrust problem."

Haas proposed addressing that problem by altering the corporate
behavior that caused mistrust. Proposing that business "make alliances

with many sectors of the public" and "deal ethically and openly" with employees, shareholders, customers, and not the least, the general public, he concluded, "The social responsibility of business requires establishing standards of excellence in all phases of operation—such as truth in advertising, quality of products, accuracy of labelling, appropriate disclosure, job content, working conditions, and upward mobility."

Walter Jr. and Peter did their best to live up to their public pronouncements. For example, their company's slogan was "Quality never goes out of style," so when they discovered in the 1970s that quality wasn't up to snuff in a Levi's factory, they shut down production for ten days until the problem had been corrected. In the company's dealings with retailers, its ethical standard became "What we do for one, we do for all," which led frequently to unhappiness among retail customers looking for deals to gain a competitive edge. At the risk of alienating those retailers, the company adamantly stood by the practice of treating its largest accounts the same as its smallest: pricing, terms, conditions, and marketing support would be the same for all, a highly unusual practice in the apparel industry. When the company was offered the opportunity to purchase thousands of yards of denim made of cotton blended with spandex on an exclusive basis soon after that "miracle material" first came to market, it passed on the offer. Such a purchase would have given Levi's a significant jump on competitors, but the company's leaders concluded that their customers should not bear the risk of buying a product for which there were no established quality standards. As a result, a competitor enjoyed a significant increase in sales for over six months while Levi's undertook testing to provide the quality benchmarks. Adherence to the ethical principle *primum non nocere*—"First, do no harm"—also led Levi's to invest a large sum to bring levels of formaldehyde in the finish of its patented Sta-Prest pants below government standards—even though there was no evidence of harm to consumers or employees.

The company did its best to avoid harm in all facets of its business activities, but no organization is perfect. In 1976 the Federal Trade Commission accused Levi's of price-fixing and restraint of trade because it prohibited retailers from discounting its products. The company settled the suit by agreeing to abandon the practice euphemistically called "suggested pricing." Although Levi Strauss was not required to admit wrongdoing, that slap on the wrist amounted to a painful lesson about the danger of moral arrogance. The Haases then vowed to create a culture in which employees were safe to question all company practices, and in which mistakes were publicly acknowledged. In the words of Walter Haas Jr., "One thing you can say for us: We learn from our mistakes."

Another thing one could say about Levi Strauss is that it had—and still has—a jaw-dropping capacity to undertake a corporate volte-face in company policy and strategic direction. A few years after firmly rejecting public sale of its stock, Levi's top management revisited the decision. It is a fact of business life that companies need capital to grow, and Levi Strauss was no exception. Since few companies are able to self-finance their own growth, most turn to capital markets for needed funds. It is possible, of course, for a company to grow without going public, but its owners may then have to be satisfied with lower profits and its employees settle for smaller salaries and fewer benefits, and the entire enterprise may be put at risk of losing market share—or entire markets—to better-funded competitors. Moreover, few business founders and executives can resist the temptation of going public in the hope of hitting the jackpot with a successful initial public stock offering. For such reasons, in April 1971 Levi Strauss & Co. announced an IPO of 13 percent of its total shares. Against the advice of its underwriters, the Haas family insisted on including this caveat in the stock prospectus: "The company's social responsibilities have for many years been a matter of strong conviction to its management. Well before legal requirements were imposed, the Company was an 'equal opportunity employer.'"

The Haases had wanted to make it clear to prospective investors that *they* intended to continue managing the company, and to do so in keeping with *their* values. To Levi's employees, the message offered was slightly different: going public would allow Levi Strauss to greatly increase the ranks of its 480 employees who owned shares. Moreover, going public would create a market for employee stock that, in all likelihood, would lead to an increase in the value of their shares. The Haases directed the underwriters to set aside 126,000 commission-free shares for purchase by employees who did not already own the company's stock. Some two thousand Levi's workers took advantage of the offer, buying stock at the list price of $47 per share (the maximum allowable purchase was 270 shares, and the average number purchased was 90). A year later, 20 percent of company stock was in the hands of Levi's employees not members of the Haas family.[10] However, only a small percentage of shop-floor workers became owners. There was nothing surprising about that; union leaders typically discourage blue-collar workers from making such purchases. Even workers with the wherewithal to do so are told it is "too risky" to invest in their employer's stock. Many objective financial experts say that is sound advice, while others claim that trade unionists' real concern is that blue-collar shareholders might start to see themselves as having the same interests as management. Doubtless, there is more than a modicum of truth in both positions.

Although Levi Strauss did little initially to encourage stock ownership among its blue-collar workers, the company endeavored to promote front-line employees into the ranks of management, and thereby into the middle class. In the early 1970s a Mexican American woman was promoted to manage a line of 130 operators in the company's Albuquerque plant at the annual salary of $14,500 (coincidentally, exactly what I was then earning as an assistant professor). Six of the twenty-four managers in that plant were Mexican American or Mexican nationals—all women who had begun their employment as sewing machine operators.

And Then Things Changed . . .

About the time of the IPO, the garment industry entered what would become a two-decade-long period of transformation during which nearly every aspect of Levi Strauss & Co.'s fortunes would be altered, mostly for the worse. The first change to occur had profound implications: the jeans market went from being a commodity business offering the same standard work clothes year in and out, into a high-fashion business where consumers expected an ever-changing variety of garments, in new styles, fabrics, and colors. That shift presented Levi's with a formidable challenge. Its business model was based on turning out tens of thousands of the same product: the more that were sold, and the fewer returned with quality defects, the higher its margins and the greater its profits. Indeed, that business model made it possible for the company to pay high wages and offer generous benefits to its American workforce.

In contrast, fashion houses turn a good profit when they design a hot product, then quickly contract with low-cost manufacturers in Asia to produce small runs of it. Suddenly, in the early 1970s, Levi Strauss found itself competing with numerous fashion houses doing just that. Levi's was paying its sewing machine operators $3.30 per hour, while its competitors paid their Asian contract workers forty cents.[11] Moreover, because Levi Strauss owned its manufacturing facilities, it had much higher overhead costs. To make matters worse, most of its key employees were experts in efficiently manufacturing and delivering the unchanging and unchangeable 501 jeans but were babes in the woods in the fashion world. The skills needed for one industry are different from those needed in the other, which made it nearly impossible for them to effectively compete in terms of the latest styles and trends. The company did what it could to cope, trying in every way possible to reduce costs and improve the efficiency of its operations. In 1971 Levi's top management considered the possibility of boosting profits by creating their own retail apparel outlets, going so far as to open several trial shops. When the small retailers who constituted the major outlets for Levi's products complained about the unwelcome competition, Levi's decided to close the company stores, stay out of the retail business, and continue to focus on manufacturing.[12] In all, the future appeared increasingly grim for Levi Strauss & Co.

The European Theater of Operation

There was, however, a glimmer of financial hope at the time, and it emanated from Europe. Demand for Levi's was strong on the Continent, particularly in France. The company's $100-million-a-year European operations were headquartered in Brussels, from which the thirty-two-year-old recently minted Stanford MBA Peter Thigpen oversaw seven production facilities and twenty-three sales affiliates and distributors, operating in thirteen countries. Thigpen was relatively new to the business, and the challenges he faced were great: the logistics involved in serving so many markets, the difficulties of operating in many languages, and a frustrating lack of inventory control systems to handle the rapid growth of the European business amounted to almost more than he could handle. But the fact that the company was selling everything it could make—sales had increased 400 percent in four years—masked the severity of the problems its European operations faced. To feed the beast of demand, Thigpen had stepped up production, turning out more and more denim goods. But the company's inability to deal with an increasing variety of products, and the complexity of responding to the different tastes of customers in the many European markets it was attempting to serve, caught up to it. Thigpen was suddenly stuck with piles of inventory he couldn't sell. He tried unloading it at bargain prices in developing markets such as South America, but there was just too much stuff no one wanted to buy. The net effect was a $12 million loss for Levi Strauss & Co. in the fourth quarter of 1973, and the price of its stock plummeted to $16.62 a share, down from a high of $59.75 a year earlier. That precipitous decline came as a shock to Levi's employees who had bought the stock for $47 just two years earlier—lending some credence to the trade union argument it is too risky for workers to own stock in the company employing them.

The shock was just as great for Walter Haas Jr., who flew off to Brussels to see if anything could be done to mitigate the effects of the catastrophe. Thigpen was waiting in his office when the boss arrived, expecting to be fired on the spot, a fate he felt he deserved. Instead, Haas reassigned him to a lower-level position managing southern Europe. Thigpen couldn't help but ask, "Walter, why didn't you fire me?" It was the company's fault for putting Thigpen in a job he wasn't ready for, Haas replied, adding "We've paid a lot in tuition for your education; now we want to get a return on that investment."[13] Walter's decision illustrated the behavior that potential investors had been duly warned about: he and brother Peter had no intention of straying from the company's values.

A footnote to the story: a few years later, a wiser, more experienced Peter Thigpen was appointed president of Levi Strauss USA, and the company then received its "return on that investment." But as we will see below, Thigpen was later involved in yet another company crisis.

The collapse of Levi's stock price led *Fortune* to run an unflattering article under the headline "Levi Strauss Burst Its Britches."[14] The Haas brothers, however, found nothing humorous about the situation. Nonetheless, several years after the debacle, Peter Haas would claim it had taught them a useful lesson: "It certainly made us think about Dad's philosophy, which has essentially been more conservative. I remember in years past he said, 'How big do you want to grow? Do you have to keep running so fast?'" There is no evidence that the Haases ever fully answered those questions.

Although company profits soared over the next two years, its stock price remained moribund in the $12.50 to $22.00 range. Levi Strauss was no longer a Wall Street darling, and investors were beginning to grow restless and critical of management. It began to appear that Walter Sr.'s concerns about going public had been well founded.[15] However, when Levi's sales surpassed the billion-dollar mark in 1975, that concern was temporarily forgotten. To celebrate the milestone, each of the company's 29,000 employees was rewarded with either shares of Levi's stock or a $50 bonus (2,700 opted for the stock, the price of which was showing signs of recovery). But bad news came again the following year with the revelation that several Levi's overseas employees had violated the Foreign Corrupt Practices Act, bribing officials to the tune of a total of $145,000—not a large sum, but for a company priding itself on its ethics, the besmirching of its reputation was treated as grounds for firing. Soon thereafter, the company pulled out of Indonesia, having determined that it was impossible to do business there ethically.[16]

In 1981 Levi Strauss moved to a new eight-acre campus on San Francisco's Embarcadero, the waterfront at the foot of Telegraph Hill, where half the area is given over to a public park and plaza with views of the Bay Bridge. The architecturally stunning three-story headquarters was constructed of brick in the style of neighboring buildings of historical note. The Haases had surprised nearly everyone when they announced plans for the campus shortly after having moved into another new high-rise office building. That multistory building had offered the latest modern conveniences, but, with employees working on many different floors, top management felt they were losing touch with "their people," meeting them only by chance in the elevator. Believing that "we belong on the ground, no higher than treetop level," Levi's top management decided to build an award-winning jewel of a building that enhanced the feeling that everyone in the company was family.

By the time its new headquarters opened, Levi Strauss & Co. had become the world's largest clothing manufacturer, but once again it was feeling growth pains. Its retired president, Daniel Koshland, remarked, "We know that the company has grown so much that we've lost humanistic values."[17] No longer Koshland's and Walter Sr.'s paternalistic, caring company, it was fast becoming an impersonal corporate behemoth, no matter how much the Haases fought the trend. Kit Durgin, who had worked her way up in the company from a secretarial position to an executive one, remarked that the old culture was quickly vanishing: "Those days are gone, but I think Walter and Peter hope they aren't, and still try to operate that way. Maybe they're a little bit naïve in that. We have more high-powered executives than we had in those days, men who are more political and maybe take advantage."[18] To remain competitive, the company had recruited managers from the fashion industry, as well as experienced finance and marketing professionals from other industries. Few of those indispensable newcomers had deep commitments to the company's traditional values, and that greatly worried long-tenured employees.

The Fifth Generation of Family Leadership

Conditions were changing rapidly in the garment industry during the late 1960s and early 1970s, and perhaps that is why Peter and Walter Jr. decided to step aside in favor of Wally's son Robert. Bob Haas had been a bearded history major at UC Berkeley, where he was class valedictorian. After graduation, he spent two years with the Peace Corps in Africa, then shaved off the beard and enrolled at Harvard Business School, an experience he found less than enjoyable. After getting his MBA, he served a year as a White House Fellow, followed by a brief stint with the abortive presidential campaign of "peace candidate" Eugene McCarthy. In 1969 he took a position as management consultant with McKinsey & Co. in its San Francisco office. (Disclosure: Bob Haas and I started working there at the same time, and have remained friends ever since.) Worried that employees would feel he had inherited his position rather than earned it, Bob had never planned on entering the family business: "What changed my mind was the yawns I received from women at cocktail parties when I told them I worked at McKinsey; but when they learned my family was connected to Levi Strauss, they suddenly became interested, and couldn't wait to tell me what a great company it was, or to relate the story of their favorite pair of jeans." Bob decided he wanted to work for a company he could be proud of, and so in 1973 he accepted a job in inventory management, near the bottom ranks of the family business. That job was followed by a spell in Levi Strauss's international division, where he rose to assistant general manager for the Far East. In 1977, when he was elected company vice president, it became apparent to all that Levi Strauss's great-great-grandnephew was heir apparent to the firm's leadership. His concern that his name would be a burden proved unwarranted; his ascendency was well received by employees, many of whom were relieved to learn that another Haas family member would be at the helm. They found it especially reassuring that the CEO-to-be was firmly committed to preserving the values that had made the company special.

The origin of the Haas family's values is a mystery, even to the Haases. Some believe that these values are rooted in the family's Jewish faith. Although five generations, dating back to Levi Strauss, have been members of San Francisco's Reform temple Congregation Emanu-El, there is no evidence that many, if any, of them were particularly religious. As Bob Haas explained to me, their attachment to the temple was a way of "meeting social expectations," and at most, some Haases may have been "semi-observant." Nonetheless, it is probable that their values were influenced by aspects of secular Jewish culture that stress the virtue of philanthropy.

Shortly after Bob Haas was named Levi's CEO, in 1984, I visited him in his office, where he immediately turned our conversation to the subject of the company's values, the most important of which, he believed, was treating people with respect. That meant several things to him, he explained: offering consumers high-quality products at good value; providing reliable, responsive service to retailers; and negotiating fairly with suppliers. He stressed that the company was committed to being exemplary citizens in the communities where it had facilities, and observing the highest legal and ethical standards. He spoke proudly of its record with regard to the diversity of its workforce—the most diverse found in the professional ranks of a major corporation. He was especially concerned with showing respect for the lifeblood of the company, the thousands of sewing machine operators working in the dozens of Levi's facilities located in seventeen countries. Most of those employees were undereducated women from underprivileged backgrounds—African Americans in the American South, Hispanics in the West, Chinese immigrants in Hong Kong, and working-class folk in Scotland. Showing respect for them meant offering fair wages, excellent benefits, and opportunities to learn and develop additional skills. Having said that, Haas then emphasized that the company was a business, not a charity. Moreover, it was one with the stated goal of giving its stockholders optimal *long-term* return on their investments. Echoing his father, who insisted that "the moral position usually turns out to be good business," he saw no inherent reason why the company could not meet both its social responsibilities and its financial goals.

To accomplish both its financial and social goals, Haas explained that it was critical for his top management team to effectively execute the corporation's strategy of "catering to middle America," which meant leaving the low-profit budget end of the apparel business to discounters, and the market for trendy designer jeans to companies whose goods were sold on Rodeo Drive and Fifth Avenue. Serving the broad middle market had required the acquisition of several companies that filled holes in Levi's product line—for example, in 1981, purchasing San Antonio–based Santone, makers of men's sports jackets and suits. Haas acknowledged that Wall Street hadn't always reacted positively when such acquisitions didn't immediately pay off, but he was confident that the investments would prove sound in the long term: "Many apparel companies live for the moment, for the season. We've grown because we've kept our long-term goals intact. We're not jumping out windows because some of our selective diversification efforts didn't meet our [immediate] goals. Our goals are to steadily increase our position over a five- or ten-year period. Because we're patient, we can make mistakes, take risks, and still mature a business. We were in women's wear for ten years before we got the formula right. We were in menswear for almost ten years. . . . Patience pays off in the long run."

When I left Bob Haas's office, I was convinced the company was on the right course.[19] What I didn't know then—and no doubt Haas was not fully aware of himself—was that when he inherited Levi Strauss's top job, he also inherited what would turn out to be two decades of *tsuris*—a useful Yiddish word meaning "trouble." The company's troubles were many, various, and all seemed to converge shortly after Bob moved into the executive suite. The trend toward manufacturing abroad was by then intensifying as trade continued to become ever more global, and the tariffs and quotas once protecting US-based manufacturers were being slashed or ended altogether. Consequently, the flow of inexpensive imported jeans into the country had gone from a trickle to a flood. The countless small main-street department stores and haberdasheries that had been Levi's prime retail outlets were being either acquired by a few large national chains such as Macy's, or forced out of business in the face of relentless competition from powerful, national discounters like Walmart (and, later, Costco) that were interested in buying Levi's products only at prices too low for the company to meet, given its high-paid workforce. At the same time upscale department stores such as Nordstrom and Bloomingdale's were becoming national chains, catering to the designer-jean tastes of affluent consumers. "In sum," as Bob Haas explained to me some thirty-two years after our first discussion, "we were pinched from above and below: 'The Jaws of Death,' as a former Levi's executive dubbed it."

Moreover, as all those untoward changes were occurring, the character of Wall Street was being transformed. Once home to patient investors who held stock for the long term, now it was the domain of restless speculators demanding high (and quick) financial returns from companies they assumed they "owned." In effect, Wall Street had come to expect exactly what Levi Strauss was unable to deliver in the early 1980s—high quarterly profits—and that failure caused Levi's investors to demand drastic changes in the corporation's strategy, practices, products, and governance. Were he to meet those demands, Bob Haas knew, it would be necessary to violate fundamental Levi Strauss values he was committed to protect. So instead, in 1985 he took the company private by way of a $1.4 billion leveraged buyout, a record amount at the time. Members of the extended Haas family, along with a number of Levi's officers and directors, were then owners of the company.

What happened next wasn't always pretty. Over the following dozen years, Levi Strauss would shut down one after another of its many manufacturing plants around the world, permanently closing the last one in the late 1990s. Over that period, some twenty thousand blue-collar workers would lose what, for most of them, had been the best job they had in their entire lives. Bob Haas and his team agonized over each plant closing, scrambling to find ways to avoid it. They tried everything possible to reduce costs and increase efficiency, often buying time, but ultimately it was to no avail. For example, in 1985 their introduction of a successful product line, the Dockers brand, offered temporary respite, but not a permanent one.

In 1989 the market for the sports jackets and suits made at the San Antonio Santone factory Levi's had purchased seven years earlier vanished, and no alternative outlets for those products were to be found. The jobs of Santone's 1,150 employees might have been saved if the plant could have switched to producing much-in-demand Dockers products. That turned out to be impossible, however; the methods and skills required to manufacture the Dockers line were completely different from those used in making sports jackets. Moreover, contractors in Central America and the Caribbean, where the average wage was one-sixth that paid to workers in San Antonio, were bidding for the Dockers work. Managers at the San Antonio plant made a desperate effort to find cost-effective ways to compete with those foreign contractors, but they could not make their plant's economics viable. There was simply no getting around it: the factory was losing money, with no prospect of again becoming profitable. The decision of when, and how, to close the plant was placed in the hands of Levi's chief of operations, Peter Thigpen.[20]

Thigpen had been reluctant to close the plant, but once he was convinced that he had no choice, he began to think about what kind of termination package the company should offer the San Antonio workers. The workers had rights the company had an obligation to honor, he felt, but he was less certain what those rights and obligations amounted to in practice. As he later explained, he was forced to find an answer to an extremely difficult moral question: What responsibilities do employers have to employees when the work they do is no longer profitable? Thigpen considered many factors. A majority of the San Antonio operators were relatively uneducated Hispanic women for whom English was a second language, and thus he worried that simply laying them off with the legally required sixty-day notice would leave most unemployed, in dire financial straits, and with little chance of quickly finding new jobs. Moreover, the company had a history of helping employees in bad times—for example, saving jobs during the Depression—and he wanted to remain true to its stated values. Unfortunately, given Levi's current financial condition, it was impossible to be as generous as he and Bob Haas might wish. Also, Thigpen feared that the closure was likely to be just the first of many in coming years; whatever the company offered its San Antonio workforce would set a precedent for future closures. The calendar was also a consideration: with the holiday season drawing near, it would be cruel to spoil Christmas for the workers, so he decided to postpone announcing the plant closure until the New Year.

In January 1990, Thigpen informed workers that the company had no choice but to close the plant, reassuring them that they were not responsible for the economic realities forcing the decision. He gave them ninety days' notice, and told them they would be receiving one week's severance for each year they had been employed—including any time they had worked for Santone before the plant's purchase by Levi's. Their health benefits would be extended three months beyond the plant's closing date, and outplacement services would be available for fifteen months. The company would provide GED and English classes for those who wished to take them. Arrangements would also be made to provide job fairs and access to government-sponsored retraining agencies and programs. Finally, a $1 million fund was set aside to cover job training, counseling, child care, transportation, and emergency assistance. (In the end, the company would spend nearly $2 million on those activities.) The company kept its part of the agreement, providing training or education for 680 of the workers, and finding immediate employment for 103. Nonetheless, fifteen months after the closing many former workers remained unemployed.

Shortly after the plant closed, a group called Fuerza Unida called for a boycott of Levi's products, and then sued the company in federal court on grounds that it had closed the plant to deprive workers of benefits, severance pay, and incentive bonuses they were due. The boycott never got off the ground, and a judge dismissed the suit, affirming that the company had treated its workers in a "fair and responsible fashion," and that the claims had "no basis in fact." Indeed, the facts were undeniable: Levi Strauss had more than met its ethical obligations to its former employees, as it would do time and again over the next few years with each lamentable plant closing.

The net cost of the numerous severance packages Levi's provided over two decades was staggering; yet today, Bob Haas says the money—much of it out of his own pocket—was well spent, and nothing has made him prouder about his tenure as CEO than the way those closures were handled. For example, when the company closed its plant in Blackstone, Virginia—the town that had so strenuously resisted integration—the town's mayor praised Levi Strauss for all it had done for his community, saying the company had a standing invitation to return to the city if that were ever possible. At another plant closing, the Levi's manager who announced the terms of severance was actually applauded by the workers he had just terminated. In all the closings, the company made the very best it could out of unavoidably heartbreaking circumstances.

Creating a New Levi Strauss & Co.

It wasn't simply the influx of cheap, imported goods that bedeviled Levi Strauss in the 1980s and '90s: the company's ownership structure wasn't working as intended at the time of the LBO. Coping with the varied agendas of members of the large Haas clan, and responding to the second-guessing and demands of shareholding company executives and directors—many now retired—proved almost as exasperating as dealing with Wall Street. Mounting frustration with what had become a can't-win situation led Bob Haas and a few of his closest relatives to borrow a large sum to buy out all but a handful of those who, a decade earlier, had participated in taking the company private.

The numerous plant closings had done serious damage to Levi Strauss's once-golden reputation, but Haas was determined to try to win it back. As a first step, in 1987, the company issued mission and aspirations statements that, together, reaffirmed the company's values: "We all want a company that our people are proud of and committed to, where all employees have an opportunity to contribute, learn, grow, and advance based on merit, not politics or background. We want our people to feel respected, treated fairly, listened to, and involved. Above all, we want satisfaction from accomplishments and friendships, balanced personal and professional lives, and to have fun in our endeavors."[21]

The pledge was put to a test in the 1980s during the emerging AIDS epidemic, the epicenter of which was San Francisco, home to Levi's headquarters as well as to America's largest gay community. The likelihood of a Levi's employee contracting AIDS was high, and increasing, a point brought home to Haas when a group of concerned company employees asked him for permission to distribute information to fellow employees about the disease. At this time, even in liberal San Francisco, few large employers were open to acknowledging that some, if not many, of their employees were homosexual. Haas immediately recognized the danger of stigmatization those Levi's workers faced if they went public with their informational campaign. Not all Levi's employees were San Francisco liberals, he realized; some company managers harboring antigay prejudices might react in ways that harmed the careers of employees who came out of the closet. Nonetheless, because he meant what he said about the need to respect all Levi's employees, he authorized the production of a video about AIDS and the introduction of a mandatory training session that dealt openly with facts about the disease—the purpose of both being to ease the unwarranted fear some heterosexuals had about how the disease is spread, and to create an environment in which gay and lesbian workers would no longer feel the need to hide their sexual orientation. Levi Strauss was thus the first large American corporation to openly address the AIDS crisis and to fully accept homosexual employees, distinctions not likely to have won the company many friends among religious conservatives.

More *Tsuris*

To compete with its competitors' cheaper imported goods, Levi Strauss had begun to rely heavily on offshore subcontractors to manufacture its products. The company soon discovered the perils of Asian subcontracting. In 1991, Levi's pants bearing a "Made in the USA" label, supposedly manufactured in the Northern Mariana Islands—an American territory—were found to have been actually made in China, and under "slave-like" conditions, according to the US Labor Department. The next year, Levi's became the first company in the apparel business—and one of the first in any industry—to issue guidelines for global product sourcing. It set rigorous standards for the hours per week employees were allowed to work, a minimum age for workers, and stringent safety and environmental standards, insisting that all its foreign manufacturers comply fully or risk losing their contracts. Levi's guidelines later became benchmarks for the entire apparel industry—

although only after revelations appeared in the media about horrific working conditions in Asian plants manufacturing Nike products.

Long before other companies, Levi's had inspectors in place at its six hundred overseas contractors closely monitoring compliance. Shortly after issuing its guidelines, the company terminated contracts with 5 percent of its Asian suppliers, and required significant improvements in the performance of an additional 25 percent. When two contractors were found to employ children under the age of fourteen, Levi's immediately moved to void their contracts. However, when Levi's inspectors learned that those children were major contributors to their impoverished families' incomes, the company said it would agree to retain the contractors if they met certain conditions: first, the children were to be sent to school, at Levi Strauss's expense; second, the contractors would continue paying the children while they were in school; and third, the contractors agreed to offer to rehire the children after they had graduated. Initially, Levi's global sourcing guidelines were opposed by many in the apparel industry—including some of Levi's own managers—who felt the added costs contractors were being forced to shoulder would drive up their goods' prices. As things turned out, any cost increases incurred were easily borne by Levi Strauss and the rest of the American apparel industry.

Bob Haas continued as Levi's CEO until 1998, then chaired the company's board until he retired in 2013. In 2016, he told me that the company had paid a price over the years for the progressive stands it had taken, beginning with the decision to hire Asian American workers. He had often told the story of the furor caused when his father hired the company's first Filipino secretary: "A number of employees, including the highest ranking woman, protested that they didn't want to use the same toilet facilities; my father refused to meet their demands."[22] Looking back, Haas said that he was proud Levi Strauss had a history of taking such unpopular positions long before they became accepted practices—whether it was hiring minorities, resisting investor pressure for short-term profits, refusing to give discounts to selected retailers, paving the way for the acceptance of homosexual employees, or nudging other apparel companies to introduce tougher employment and safety standards in Asia. He then directed my attention to a poster on his office wall depicting hundreds of white sheep all heading in one direction. In the middle of the herd was a single black sheep resolutely going the other way. "That black sheep was Levi Strauss and Co.," he explained, "and we wouldn't have had it any other way."

Over the four decades during which Bob Haas was associated with Levi Strauss, the company went from being a manufacturer to being in the fashion business. Toward the end of his career it was transformed yet again, this time becoming the retailer that, in 1971, Walter Haas Jr. had decided it should never be. In some ways those transformations have been positive and in keeping with the rapidly, and radically, changing times. Because so few Americans today are willing to do the hard work of sewing and stitching no matter how much they are paid, it might be said that Levi Strauss has upgraded the quality of the jobs it now offers its domestic workers. Instead of having a low-skilled, undereducated workforce, the company now employs educated designers, marketers, buyers, and managers in well-paying jobs. The downside of hiring such people has been that many are not fully committed to the company's historic values. As early as the 1990s, when I spoke with the company's chief operating officer—who had been brought in from the outside—I was surprised to discover that he believed profit maximization was the only legit-imate business goal, privately confessing his discomfort with many of the company's enlightened practices. Nonetheless, he assured me that, when needed, he was willing to publicly pay lip service to the stated values! At the time, it probably made little difference how he felt about the company's values, because Bob Haas was on the scene to reinforce them. However, in 2016 Levi Strauss was being led by its third nonfamily CEO, and responsibility for managing the company was completely in the hands of its professional executives, although it was still owned by the Haas family.

Today, philanthropy has become the Haases' prime focus, but their family values are still posted on walls at the headquarters of Levi Strauss & Co., and the company has recently acquired a positive reputation for enlightened environmental practices. Nonetheless, company old-timers have told me that working there is increasingly like employment at other well-managed giant corporations. They also suspect that the company's executives would like nothing more than to take Levi Strauss public yet again. After all, don't most MBAs have visions of stock options floating around in their heads?

From my perspective, Bob Haas deserves credit for having taken the company through the complex transition from labor-intensive manufacturing to talent-intensive retail marketing. He deserves to be proud of the ethical ways in which he managed that extremely rare accomplishment, particularly how he minimized the horrendous side effects of the transition on its blue-collar workforce. Nonetheless, he had his critics both within and outside the business, including some of his relatives. In a 1999 *Fortune* feature article, his "benevolent management" was blamed for "having trashed a great American brand." The authors called his idealistic approach "a failed utopian management experiment" in which "group decision making usually degenerates into endless meetings, task forces, memos and e-mails," and doubted he would still be CEO if the company were publicly traded. Haas, with characteristic candor, agreed: "I wouldn't be CEO because I wouldn't want to work in the company" if it were publicly owned.[23] Doubtless, he now joins many others in looking back in sadness at the company's history over the last quarter century. Today, no one would rate Levi Strauss as "America's greatest company." Having always tried to do what was right, the Haases have learned how difficult an endeavor that is.

9

Marks & Sparks

MICHAEL MARKS (1863–1900) *and* THE MARKS AND SIEFF FAMILIES

In 1882, nineteen-year-old Michael Marks immigrated to England from Białystok, a village in the Pale of Settlement—the region of Imperial Russia in which Jews were allowed to live—in what was then Russian Poland. That was a particularly bad era for Jews in Eastern Europe (not that there was ever a particularly good time), and Marks had been driven from his homeland by pogroms. When he arrived in London—nearly penniless, illiterate, and speaking no English—he was dismayed to learn that the one person he had counted on finding in England, his brother Barnet, had recently set sail to North America to join the Yukon gold rush. Alone, and looking to find a toehold in a strange country, Michael headed north to the industrial town of Leeds, where a community of some seven thousand Jews had established themselves, predominantly in what was called "the rag trade."

England, then at the height of the Industrial Revolution, was undergoing profound technological, social, economic, and political transformations. The world of business was being turned topsy-turvy as large-scale manufacturing concerns drove traditional skilled craftsmen out of business. Independent ironmongers, shoemakers, tailors, potters, and furniture makers who owned their own small shops were being replaced by an emerging system of mass production, distribution, and merchandising. That new world of business was closed to

Michael Marks, who, lacking capital, perforce had to make his way in the old economy as an itinerant peddler of buttons, pins, needles, and socks. The most likely prospect for such a "licensed hawker" in that era was a lifetime of living hand to mouth.

But Marks got lucky. One of his suppliers, I. J. Dewhirst, was willing to lend him £5 (several hundred dollars today), largely to serve as credit to buy goods from Dewhirst's warehouse to stock his stall in the Leeds market, a covered hall where food, homeware, and clothing merchants rented space for their pushcarts and makeshift display tables. Within months, Marks was profitably selling a constantly expanding range of merchandise: clothing, earthenware, hardware, household goods, toys, and paper products—dozens of items, each offered for the price of a penny. Marks's English skills being insufficient for the then-traditional merchant's practice of haggling with customers, he placed a large sign above his stall that read "Don't Ask the Price, It's a Penny." Similarly, his poor English forced him to lay out all his wares and let customers pick for themselves the items they wished to purchase, in lieu of the established practice in which store clerks stood behind counters and filled customer orders from a stock of goods on shelves and in cupboards located behind them. Those novel practices—fixed prices and self-service—were so well received by customers that within two years Marks was able to establish "branch" stalls in covered markets in several nearby towns. His stalls soon built a reputation for fair dealing among working-class customers.

By 1886, Marks's business was so successful that he found himself in the category of eligible bachelor. That status soon changed to recent bridegroom when he wed Hannah Cohen, changing again a year later to proud papa on the birth of their son, Simon. In the meantime, Michael's business expanded so extensively that he was spending most of his time scouting additional stall locations, opening branches, and negotiating with distributors and wholesalers. In 1894 he realized that he needed a partner to help him manage a warehouse he had just opened and, equally important, to contribute an infusion of capital to fund the business's rapid growth. He found both in a cashier then employed at Dewhirst's warehouse. Thomas Spencer was an excellent bookkeeper with an eagle eye for numbers, an efficient organizer, and familiar with the ins and outs of the wholesale business. Moreover, he was honest, hardworking, easy to get along with, and best of all, had access to the requisite £300 to buy a half interest in the business.[1]

They were perfect partners, albeit opposites in every way. Gentile Tom, forty-two years old when the partnership was formed, was skilled at office management and dealing with suppliers, although he suffered from excessive fondness for food and drink and lacked all ambition to lead; Jewish Michael, thirty-one, was abstemious, relished the opportunity to head a growing business, and "had a gift of sympathy and imagination which enabled him to understand the needs and wants of his working-class customers."[2] Michael's "gift of sympathy" for Britain's disadvantaged stemmed, apparently, from the travails and hardships he had faced in anti-Semitic Mitteleuropa.

Some fifty yards away from the Marks residence in Leeds was the domicile of another family of East European Jewish immigrants, the Sieffs. Ephraim Sieff had emigrated from Lithuania in the early 1880s, successfully establishing himself as a merchant in the clothing trade. He had married and fathered two sons and a daughter, all around the same age as the Marks children. The oldest Sieff son, Israel, had met Simon, the oldest of the Marks siblings, in school where they became fast friends—a friendship that would last throughout their lives. From then on, the history of the Sieff and the Marks families would be intertwined.

By 1900, Marks and Spencer's Penny Bazaars were operating profitably as stalls in twenty-four market halls, but, more significantly, also as twelve independent shops, which would be the format for all the company's subsequent growth. In 1903 the company moved its headquarters to the larger, more prosperous city of Manchester, where it incorporated as Marks & Spencer. Then the unambitious Tom Spencer retired, looking forward to many years of living off his anticipated share of Marks & Spencer's profits. Unfortunately, neither Marks nor Spencer made provisions for succession after their deaths, which, as fate would have it, occurred all too soon for both. In 1905, Spencer died at the age of fifty-three; three years later, he was followed to the grave by Marks at the even younger age of forty-four.

At the time Michael Marks died, Spencer's son, Thomas Spencer Jr, had been working in the company for several years; however, like his dad, he had neither the ability nor the desire to lead it. Michael's son, Simon, nineteen at the time, was too young and inexperienced to manage what was now a thriving chain, with over sixty locations spread across England. Control of the company thus fell to a minority shareholder, William Chapman, the sole remaining member of the company's original board of directors. For the next seven years, Marks & Spencer continued to grow and evolve under Chapman's direction, introducing new lines of business, many of them failures, while trying a variety of merchandising strategies, none of which was successful. As years progressed, increasing areas of conflict arose on the board between, on the one hand, Chapman and Spencer Jr., and on the other, Michael Marks's heirs. As Simon Marks grew older, he had begun to purchase company stock as it became available; by 1915, he and his family had acquired a sufficient number of shares to command a majority of seats on the board. In 1917 both Chapman and Spencer retired, and from that year until 1968, the company would be headed by Simon—closely aided by his friend Israel Sieff—in total, a remarkable half century of leadership continuity.

Brothers-in-Law

Simon and Israel had remained friends since childhood, and their relationship had grown even closer after they each married the other's sister: Simon Marks wed Miriam Sieff, and Israel Sieff wed Rebecca Marks. Moreover, they shared the same economic philosophy—that of "Michael Marks, not Karl Marx," as Simon liked to joke—and both became disciples of Chaim Weizmann, a professor of biochemistry at Manchester University and a leading advocate of Zionism, social responsibility, and the application of science in all aspects of society, including business—causes to which Simon and Israel became deeply committed in their work and private lives.

In the early 1920s, Israel became a director of Marks & Spencer. He later served as the company's vice chairman and, after Simon's death, its chairman. The brothers-in-law were in total agreement about their company's business model: providing the working class with a great variety of inexpensive, high-quality goods. They shared the belief that high turnover on low margins would make the company profitable. They were also committed to maintaining Michael Marks's high ethical standards—in particular, the benevolent treatment of employees. Following Weizmann, they "came to see in their business a means to creating what is essentially a social service to the consumer."[3]

In the 1920s, Marks & Spencer found itself in competition with Woolworths, the formidable American retail chain. When it became apparent to Simon and Israel that they could not match the American company's deep financial resources, sophisticated management processes, and retailing expertise, they concluded they would either have to follow its lead or go out of business. Thus, as Simon later recalled, he embarked for America in 1924. "It was there that I learned many new things," he would recall. "It was my first serious lesson in the chain store art. I learned the value of more imposing, commanding [store] premises, modern methods of administration and the statistical control of stocks [inventory] in relation to sales. I learned that new accounting machines could help to reduce the time to give the necessary information to hours instead of weeks."[4]

Simon also brought home from America the concept he called "super stores," a reconceptualization of the small, traditional English shop that would transform retailing in Britain and vault Marks & Spencer to the forefront of its industry. The company then started to do things the American way: "thinking big." Taking his cue from Sears and J. C. Penney's, Simon began to eliminate wholesalers and distributors and deal directly with manufacturers. Over subsequent decades, the maintenance of close and mutually beneficial relationships with manufacturers—many of whom became its sole suppliers—became a hallmark of Marks & Spencer's ethical business practices. (As late as the 1970s, the Dewhirst firm was still a major M&S supplier.) Because Simon and Israel were able to work closely in trusting relationships with suppliers—providing them with large, secure markets for their products—the company was continually able to lower its prices and thus offer a greater range and number of consumer goods to the working class. Influenced by Weizmann, they introduced industrial research to their industry, establishing first-rate laboratories in which knowledge about the production of synthetic fabrics was advanced. At the same time, the company was able to steadily raise the wages of its workers, reduce the number of hours they worked, and provide many of the pioneering employee benefits introduced by J. C. Penney across the Atlantic.

In 1926 the company went public as a limited liability corporation, and the capital generated from that initial offering was reinvested in opening new stores and modernizing existing facilities. Simon and Israel, recalling what had happened after the death of the company's founders, kept tight control by insisting that any shares owned by the public were nonvoting (in 1966, acting under pressure from investors, all M&S shareholders were granted voting rights). Between 1927 and 1939, the number of Marks & Spencer stores increased from 126 to 234; by then, almost every midsize town in Britain had its own "Marks and Sparks," as the chain of clean, well-lighted stores affectionately came to be known. In 1939 the company's eighteen thousand employees sold some three hundred million separate items, making it Britain's dominant retailer of clothing and food products.[5] In 1953 M&S introduced the slogan "The customer is always completely right!," backing it with the guarantee that any purchase could be returned for a full cash refund no matter when it had been bought, provided a receipt was shown—a practice unheard of at the time.

The diet of the average Briton in those days was grossly unhealthy by today's standards, acknowledged as subpar even by nutritionists back then. Working-class meals, in particular, lacked the basic elements of a balanced diet. In response to that problem, one of the most significant employee benefits M&S introduced was heavily subsidized employee lunchrooms in which staff were provided with healthy, well-prepared meals. As Israel Sieff later explained, "When we first introduced staff canteens in our stores, long before the [second world] war, we were astonished and horrified to find that some of the girls were actually hungry."[6]

Because their employees also didn't have adequate health care, Israel and Simon inaugurated regular physical examinations for the staff, along with subsidized medical, dental, and optical insurance. (After the postwar introduction of socialized medicine in Britain, M&S provided supplemental health insurance.) The company was the first, perhaps only, to offer the services of chiropodists to its staff—after all, clerks who stand all day get sore feet! Additionally, M&S provided in-store hairdressers for the convenience of its predominantly female workforce; retirees were later made eligible for that unusual benefit. It was also one of the first British companies to offer retirement benefits and, in 1977, began a profit-sharing-cum-stock-ownership program. Most significantly, the company led in the provision of a wide range of training and education opportunities for its employees, and was a pioneer in the development of women managers.[7] Marcus Sieff, Israel's son and future M&S chairman, explained the philosophy behind the company's employment policies in an article published in the *Sunday Times* in 1982: "Human relations in industry should cover the problems of the individual at work, his or her health, well-being and progress, the working environment and profit sharing. Full and frank two-way communication and respect for the contributions people can make, given encouragement—these are the foundations of an effective policy and a major contribution to a successful operation."[8]

Portrait of Robert Owen, circa 1799, when he and his partners purchased the New Lanark mills from Robert Dale, and Owen married Dale's daughter, Caroline. (*Public domain*)

A view of New Lanark in 1818, with cotton mill buildings to the right and Owen's school at the front left. (*Public domain*)

J. C. Penney's Golden Rule Store in Kemmerer, Wyoming, in the early twentieth century. (*Courtesy of DeGolyer Library, Southern Methodist University*)

James Cash Penney in his later years after he had lost influence in the company he founded. (*Courtesy of DeGolyer Library, Southern Methodist University*)

Soap magnate William Hasketh Lever, aka "Lord Leverhulme." (*Courtesy of Unilever from originals in Unilever's Collection, Unilever Art, Archives and Records Management, Port Sunlight*)

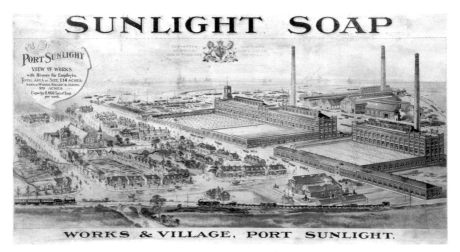

Port Sunlight, home of Lever Bros.' soap works and model village. (*Courtesy of Unilever from originals in Unilever's Collection, Unilever Art, Archives and Records Management, Port Sunlight*)

Chocolate bar baron Milton Hershey with his wife, Catherine "Kitty" Sweeney, dressed for their favorite pastime, world travel. (*Courtesy of Hershey Community Archives, Hershey, Pennsylvania*)

James Finney Lincoln, head of
the Lincoln Electric Company
and creator of America's longest-
running industrial success story.
(*Courtesy of Lincoln Electric,
Cleveland, Ohio*)

John Spedan Lewis in his
customary Edwardian
collar—a business leader
nowhere near as rigid as he
appeared. (*Courtesy of the John
Lewis Partnership*)

Michael Marks, the immigrant peddler who founded Britain's Marks & Spencer. (*Courtesy of Marks & Spencer company archives*)

Marcus (later, Baron) Sieff—grandson and, oddly, also grandnephew of Michael Marks—the last member of his family to lead Marks & Spencer. (*Courtesy of Marks & Spencer company archives*)

Robert Wood Johnson—"the General" who authored Johnson & Johnson's influential credo. (*Courtesy of Johnson & Johnson Archives*)

James Burke, the chief executive who led J&J successfully through the Tylenol crisis. (*Courtesy of Johnson & Johnson Archives*)

Levi Strauss, the denim merchant who, contrary to popular belief, did not sew the first pair of jeans that would come to be known as Levi's. (*Courtesy of Levi Strauss & Co. Archives*)

Strauss family descendants Walter Haas Jr. (*center*) and Walter Haas Sr. (*right*), ever ready to accommodate all their customers, even their biggest. [Man on the left unidentified.] (*Courtesy of Levi Strauss & Co. Archives*)

Herman Miller's avuncular chief executive Max De Pree, who practiced leadership "as an art." (*Courtesy of Herman Miller Archives*)

The Body Shop's environmentalist founder Anita Roddick, with friends in the Amazon. (*Courtesy of photographer Christine Burrill*)

Despite that claim, it was said that Simon Marks and Israel Sieff were paternalistic employers; indeed, they seemed often to have decided what was good for their employees without consulting them.[9] At the same time, critics claimed that M&S's attention to its workforce was simply a sensible way to increase productivity and profits. Israel agreed, but said the critics had it backward: "Every single thing we've done because we felt we had a moral obligation has also, within five or ten years, turned out to be good business, even though we didn't start out with that idea."[10]

Beginning in the 1930s, M&S became active in community affairs, making generous contributions to medical institutions, the arts, research, and other charitable causes. During the Great Depression, a Baptist minister in an impoverished Welsh mining town wrote to M&S inquiring if the company could provide inexpensive shirts for the local men, 30 percent of them unemployed, the majority of whom owned only one shirt. Israel and Simon sent the minister a gift of six thousand shirts.[11] Perhaps the company's greatest social contributions came from employees who engaged in volunteer work in community organizations in which they often took leadership roles. M&S frequently seconded its employees to nonprofits, paying their salaries while they helped to organize and manage them. Starting in the 1970s, the company became deeply involved in counseling small businesses, training immigrants, and providing skills development to members of minority groups. All those practices were unusual, if not unique, in Britain when they were introduced.

Serving the Masses

More than anything else, Marks & Spencer became known for catering to the needs of common men and women. In 1928 the company introduced the first private brand in British retailing, St Michael, named in honor of Michael Marks, thus "canonizing" its Jewish founder, as his grandson Marcus Sieff joked.[12] The brand became synonymous with guaranteed high quality and low prices. In the words of Peter Drucker, "Marks & Spencer redefined its business as the subversion of the class structure of nineteenth-century England by making available to the working and lower-middle classes goods of better than upper-class quality."[13]

The company also made inexpensive, high-quality food available to the masses. For example, it imported fresh grapefruits from Israel—which necessitated a campaign to teach working-class customers how to eat what to them was an exotic food. Thanks to M&S's sale of nutritious groceries tested for purity, freshness, and cleanliness, grocery shoppers in Britain no longer ran a high risk of contracting disease through food contamination. The company also worked with its suppliers to develop products that working-class people needed and wanted, such as new fabrics, thus enhancing their standard of living and quality of life. By the 1950s, most British women had access to affordable, rather fashionable St Michael clothing, and their children could be dressed for school in ways that didn't invidiously mark them as working class. The company also supported British manufacturing firms: during World War II, it was able to advertise that 99 percent of M&S products were domestically sourced—a practice it did its best to continue after the conflict ended.

As with other leaders profiled in these pages, the tale of the Marks and Sieffs is not one of unalloyed virtue. By all accounts, Simon Marks was not an easy man to work for. A diminutive five foot seven (in heeled shoes!), he was feisty, hypercritical, and verbally punched far above his weight. He had a nasty temper, did not suffer fools gladly, and was convinced of his own brilliance. As his double-nephew Marcus Sieff wrote, "Virtually nobody around Simon, whether a member of the family or a colleague in the company, was spared his criticism or his occasional irascibility . . . but the one exception was Father [Israel]; he could do no wrong. Simon respected his views and his judgement; a gentle word from him could swiftly bring relief to a victim of Simon's wrath."[14]

Another explanation may be that brother-in-law Israel had no ambition to succeed Simon. The situation was far different with regard
to the firm's heir apparent, nephew Marcus, who often suffered harsh
criticism from his uncle when they disagreed about company policy.
"I think that how he treated me was partly, if not mainly, due to his
growing feeling that one day I would succeed him as chief executive,"
Marcus explained. "He did not have any personal objections to me as a
potential Marks & Spencer chief executive; it was more that, like many
leaders of genius, he did not like the idea of being succeeded *by anybody*."[15]

Marcus, as strong-willed as Simon, seriously considered resigning
from the company after several angry clashes with his uncle. Nonetheless, Marcus later wrote, Simon's harsh criticisms were almost always
aimed at managers—himself included—who had acted contrary to
company policy and values with regard to matters central to maintaining the organization's culture, customer and employee relations, product quality, and store cleanliness. Following his ill-tempered outbursts,
Marcus added, Simon quickly and invariably forgave and forgot.

In the decades after World War II the company constantly revised
its product line, working hand in glove with suppliers to produce a
constant stream of better products at lower prices. It reduced the range
of products it sold to concentrate on those items it was better able to
provide, and at lower cost, than its competitors: underwear, women's
clothing, men's shirts, and sweaters for all ages and both genders. It
also kept prices low by minimizing its spending on advertising; like
Hershey's, M&S's marketing consisted mainly of maintaining its reputation for quality.[16] The company was the first in Britain to introduce
the latest management ideas and business techniques, a great many of
which had been developed in America. During the post–World War II
era—when the UK's domestic industries suffered from what was called
the "British disease": stagnant productivity, low levels of investment,
incompetent management, and poor labor relations—Marks & Spencer took their lead from the best-managed American firms, striving

diligently to reduce bureaucracy, eliminate paperwork, simplify operations, do away with restrictive company rules, and stress speed in product development and restocking of store shelves. To better serve customers, M&S employees at the lowest levels were trusted to make decisions that in most British firms would have required supervisorial approval. In effect, Marks & Spencer brought the efficiencies and benefits of American discount shopping to the shores of Britain, and in some instances outdid the Yanks at their own game. From the 1960s to the 1980s, for example, shopping for Marks & Spencer's inexpensive, high-quality wool sweaters was a part of the American tourist's standard itinerary when visiting Britain. (Personal aside: My wife and I often shopped at M&S when we lived in England in the late 1960s. When I recently asked my wife what she recalled about the store, she replied, "It reminded me of the great J. C. Penney's store where I had my first job." High praise, indeed.)

In sum, under Israel's and Simon's four decades of leadership, M&S developed philosophies and practices that distinguished it from its competitors, specifically:

- Offering customers a selected range of high-quality, well-designed, and attractive merchandise at reasonable prices under the St Michael brand.
- Encouraging suppliers to use the most efficient production methods based on the latest developments in science and technology.
- Cooperating with suppliers to enforce high standards of quality control.
- Simplifying management procedures to enhance efficiency and reduce bureaucracy.
- Fostering good relations with employees through fair wages, good benefits, excellent developmental opportunities, and participation in decision making, profit sharing, and stock ownership.
- Serving local communities and society in general.[17]

Simon Marks, knighted by King George VI in 1944, then raised to the peerage by Queen Elizabeth in 1961 as Baron Marks of Broughton, served as M&S's chairman until his death in 1964. In a dramatic end to his life and career, Simon died of a heart attack in his office, collapsing in the arms of his nephew Michael, Israel's youngest son. He was succeeded as chairman by Israel, also elevated by the Queen in 1966, as Baron Sieff. Israel briefly led the company until his retirement in 1967 when his brother, Edward, followed him as chairman and chief executive until 1972. In that year, Israel's son Marcus assumed leadership of the firm.

The Itinerant Peddler's Grandson

Marcus Sieff (who was named Lord Sieff of Brimpton in 1980) grew up in conditions of such astounding affluence that his grandfather, the company's immigrant founder, would have found them immorally excessive. A child of privilege, Marcus enjoyed all the benefits of an aristocratic upbringing. He attended the finest public (private) schools, and earned a degree in economics from Cambridge University. During World War II, he served in the British army with great distinction, rising to the rank of lieutenant colonel while serving directly under General Montgomery. In that capacity he came into contact with many prominent British political leaders. Like Simon before him, he became active in the Conservative Party and throughout his life hobnobbed with presidents and prime ministers, effortlessly moving in the highest social circles. In his candid and chatty 1986 autobiography *Don't Ask the Price*, Sieff casually dropped the names of famous men and women with whom he socialized: celebrities like Cary Grant, Mary Astor, and Danny Kaye; sports figures such as Olympics ice-skating champion Sonja Henie and Davis Cup tennis victors Bill Tilden and Fred Perry (the latter Marcus's frequent doubles partner); British prime ministers Winston Churchill, James Callaghan, Harold Wilson, Edward Heath, and Margaret Thatcher; American political figures Franklin D. Roosevelt, Dwight D. Eisenhower, and Henry Kissinger; and every significant Israeli politico from David Ben-Gurion to Golda Meir.

Like his father and uncle before him, Marcus became a protégé of Chaim Weizmann, aiding him in the successful effort to establish a Jewish state and then spending several years in newly created Israel as an adviser to its government. As Marcus explained, "As a youth I was perhaps more conscious of being a Zionist than a Jew."[18] Indeed, Marcus often wondered to what extent the Marks & Spencer culture had been influenced by Judaism and Judaic culture. His grandparents and parents had been relatively observant Jews, but none even remotely orthodox. Although Marcus was nearly secular himself, at the end of his career he made pointed reference to how a fundamental Jewish text had influenced his own sense of social responsibility: "As it says in *The Ethics of the Fathers*, 'It is not your responsibility to finish the task, nor are you permitted to desist from it.'"[19] He was proud to claim that he never desisted from the task of trying to improve society.

Marcus, like his uncle Simon, was a complicated man, and no saint by a long shot. He had a taste for fine clarets and expensive cigars, and a reputation as a ladies' man (he married four times). When I met him in 1975, I recall being struck by his patrician speech and demeanor—no one would have assumed he was the grandson of an itinerant peddler. As he acknowledged in his autobiography, he much enjoyed the sound of his own plummy voice and "was never modest."[20] Nonetheless, as chairman of Marks & Spencer he faithfully adhered to his uncle's and father's ethical, humanistic business practices, greatly expanding the company's community activities, and sought to improve the quality of the working lives not only of his own employees but of British workers in general. Despite his aristocratic demeanor, he dressed in off-the-shelf M&S clothing, insisting that the company sell only goods of such quality that the wealthy members of its board would buy and use them. There is no record of the board members following his example.

Marcus Sieff inherited his uncle Simon's obsessions with caring for customers and employees, along with his overweening self-confidence. He made regular visits to company stores, where he talked with customers and took lunch with the clerks who worked there, listening attentively to the ideas and complaints of both constituencies. He created employee welfare committees in each company store, empowering staff members to run them. Marcus funded the committees to meet exigent and unusual financial needs of employees, such as caring for elderly relatives, coping with long illnesses, and settling crippling debts. One welfare committee sought his advice on how to handle the case of a cheerful cleaning lady who had worked for the company for over twenty years. She had always displayed a sunny disposition, but had recently become severely depressed, heartsick that her son, who lived in South America, was about to be wed there, and she and her retired husband could not afford to attend the nuptials. The committee was concerned that paying for their plane tickets was not in keeping with the intended purpose of the welfare fund, but Marcus advised them to pay. When the head of a major British business firm learned of the decision, he told his friend Marcus, "You must be mad to do it for a cleaner."

"Would you do it for an executive?" asked Marcus.

The man answered, "Ah, that would be different."

"Please tell me," Marcus said, "why such a privilege should be given to an executive and not to a cleaner who has given many years' loyal and faithful service?"[21]

Marcus readily admitted that often in his career, "Many people, including my friends, thought I was 'soft' on industrial relations, naïve, obsessive, paternalistic and/or boring. I came in for criticism."[22] Despite those critics, Marcus Sieff continued the company's enlightened employment policies, expanding them beyond what his father and uncle had offered, even undertaking a public crusade to persuade other British chief executives to follow suit. Like Robert Owen and Spedan Lewis before him, he failed in that cause, generating only resentment among his peers.

A Sad, Bad End (or Nearly So)

Although Marks & Spencer continued to be profitable under Marcus Sieff's leadership, several decisions made during his tenure proved ill-advised in the long term. The 1973 decision to open forty-seven M&S stores across Canada turned into a two-decade drain on company profits, and in 1999, after years of losses, the company was forced to abandon those operations. The company had similar problems with many of its Continental European stores. And Marks & Spencer suffered its first ethical lapse when Marcus and several other members of the M&S board sold their houses to the company and then leased them back on favorable terms.[23] A badly embarrassed Sieff admitted to an error in ethical judgment when the transactions were publicly revealed.

Marcus would be the last member of the Marks-Sieff family to lead the company when he retired in 1984. His successor, Derek Rayner, became M&S's first nonfamily leader since 1917. A longtime company employee, Rayner attempted to continue its traditional, enlightened practices; nonetheless, he made a disastrous foray into the American market by acquiring the Brooks Brothers clothing company and the New Jersey–based Kings Food Markets chain. Neither investment panned out, and both were subsequently sold. The company briefly reached its financial peak in 1998 under Rayner's successor, Richard Greenbury, who departed radically from the business model established by Simon and Israel eight decades earlier: to boost profit margins, he raised the prices of goods in M&S stores significantly, and in the process eroded customer loyalty that had accumulated over those many years. By then, the Marks-Sieff family had lost most of its influence in the company (the last link to the founder's family, Marcus's son David, had retired after serving two decades as a nonexecutive member of the board). In addition, the ownership of company stock had become increasingly dispersed over the thirty years since its voting shares were first sold to the public: in 1985, M&S shares were owned by some 235,000 individuals and entities, the largest single shareholder, the Prudential Corporation, holding less than 7 percent of the total. Although 22,000 M&S employees owned company stock, their total holdings represented only a fraction of a percentage of the millions of shares owned by investors; thus they had relatively little influence with the board.[24]

About that time, British investors began to behave like their Wall Street counterparts, demanding higher short-term earnings. The challenge of meeting those demands was compounded by the rising cost of the British-made goods that had been the company's staple, and by increasing competition from retailers offering cheaper products made in Asia.

Marks & Spencer went into a tailspin in 1999. The company's profits fell precipitously, from £1 billion in 1998 to £145 million in 2001, its stock losing two-thirds of its value. Long-term managers and executives were let go in several rounds of extensive and brutal firings, some senior executives forced out just months before the full vesting of their pensions.[25] In the midst of the crisis, the board replaced Greenbury with a company outsider, Belgian Luc Vandevelde. He immediately put pressure on M&S's traditional suppliers to absorb more of the company's losses, and many responded by breaking ties to the company that had been in place for decades. Vandevelde then attempted to right the ship by moving upscale, introducing designer brands and abandoning most of the St Michael product line, thus further alienating M&S's traditional customer base.[26] After that, the company was forced to sell several subsidiaries in an effort to fight off a hostile takeover bid. Over the next three years the company employed a rapid succession of ineffective strategies (and short-term chairmen), all to no avail.

"In 2004," said a Marks & Spencer manager, "the company was broken. We had the wrong leaders, high prices, we weren't listening to our customers, our suppliers were unhappy and we were slow to market."[27] That year Marks & Spencer's board hired a new chairman, Stuart Rose, an experienced executive with a track record of fighting off takeover bids and reviving struggling companies. In the 1970s and '80s, Rose had served as a junior executive at M&S before leaving to become chief executive at another prominent British retailer, so he was familiar with the practices that once had made the company one of the UK's most respected firms. While successfully fending off the takeover bid, Rose introduced a plan to refocus the company "on the core values that had made M&S an icon," including offering quality goods at low prices and stressing customer service. Two years later, he introduced the "Look Behind the Label" campaign to highlight the company's numerous ethical and environmentally sustainable practices, such as offering fair-trade products, clothing made with environmentally sound dyes, and fresh fish obtained from sustainable stocks. Along with reintroducing the St Michael brand, the company became a leader in informational labeling of its products, disclosing the sources of, and ingredients in, each. Rose also committed the company to meeting ambitious long-term goals of working with its customers and suppliers "to combat climate change, reduce waste, safeguard natural resources, trade ethically, and build a healthier nation."[28] At the same time he addressed employee morale problems that his predecessors had left to fester, increasing compensation, rewarding performance and customer service, and offering more training opportunities. When Rose retired in 2011, the company had returned to full profitability and was being cited, along with Unilever and the John Lewis Partnership, as a British national leader in its social and environmental policies.

It appeared that Marks & Spencer had avoided the fate so many companies experience after the death or retirement of enlightened leaders, or the loss of ownership control by founding families. The practices developed by Michael Marks's heirs seemed to be firmly back in place at M&S as late as 2015. Yet, as we have seen, they were nearly lost; if it hadn't been for the fortuitous rehiring of a person who understood the significance of those practices, M&S might well have become just another subsidiary of a traditionally managed retail conglomerate—or out of business entirely. Despite their three generations of admirable leadership, the Marks family might be legitimately criticized for having failed to take steps to ensure the continuity of the ethical culture they had created and nurtured. Michael Marks died before he had given any thought to his succession or legacy, and his son and grandnephew after him seem to have done too little to institutionalize the company's culture, values, and practices. Unlike Spedan Lewis, they did not encourage extensive employee ownership, didn't write a constitution, and didn't create a board of directors committed to maintaining and defending the practices that distinguished Marks & Spencer from its competitors.

In 2018, M&S's leaders were once again under shareholder pressure to radically change its business model to focus on its most profitable product lines. Under its new chairman, the widely respected Archie Norman, the company announced it would close one hundred stores over the next four years, in addition to the thirty-five it had recently shuttered. As it had been under William Chapman's leadership from 1910 to 1917, the company was struggling anew to find a successful strategy, unsure of what business it was in—clothing or food—or who its customers were. With its business model in flux, its enlightened culture was once again imperiled.

Marcus Sieff and Bob Haas were the last heirs of the pioneering enlightened capitalists; they also were among the first of a new generation of corporate leaders in Britain and America to introduce enlightened practices during what, at the time, seemed a golden era of business social responsibility. Between roughly 1970 and 1990 many observers—myself among them—were convinced it was just a brief matter of time before those practices became the norm among corporate executives.[29] Our optimism on that score would prove to be a misreading of how investors and their business peers would receive the behavior of the leaders profiled in the next section.

PART II

THE GOLDEN ERA

10

Leadership as an Art

MAX DE PREE (1924–2017)

In 1919, Herman Miller lent his son-in-law, Dirk Jan (D.J.) De Pree, a few thousand dollars to purchase a controlling interest in the Star Furniture Company, where D.J. was employed as a clerk. The company had been manufacturing traditionally styled home furniture for fifteen years, but D.J. refocused its strategy on making high-quality, high-margin office furniture, a change that almost immediately improved its financial performance. In 1923, D.J. renamed the now highly successful company in appreciation for his father-in-law's generous demonstration of faith in his untested business acumen. The freshly named Herman Miller Company was then—and still is today—headquartered in Zeeland, Michigan, a frosty little town with no bars, no restaurants, no pool halls, and no movie theaters. Zeeland, like its nearby neighbor Holland ("a city of churches"), was settled by members of the Dutch Reformed Church, a morally strict, no-frills Calvinist religion to which the De Prees were fervent adherents. As it was with the families of J. C. Penney, James Lincoln, Milton Hershey, and John Eagan, deeply held religious convictions motivated D.J.—and later his sons Hugh and Max—to adopt the virtuous practices they would put into place at Herman Miller during the three-quarters of a century in which they led the company.

D.J., a part-time minister in his church, explained how his religious beliefs informed his business philosophy: "If you believe that all people are created equal under God, there are tremendous implications regarding how you manage them."[1] He thus set out during the workweek to put into practice what he preached on Sundays, a linking of the spiritual and the material that his son Max would later expand into a full-fledged philosophy of leadership he only half-jokingly called "theory fastball." Max and that philosophy are the focus of this chapter—but, as he acknowledged, he owed it all to his dad, D. J. De Pree.

D.J.'s Legacy

There was never any doubt in the minds of Zeelanders that D.J. was a devoutly religious man; yet it would have been a mistake for them to have viewed him simply as pious and otherworldly. Once he'd gained control of the town's furniture company, he quickly demonstrated his entrepreneurial skills, establishing a reputation as an able businessman with a knack for manufacturing fashionable, high-quality products that sophisticated urban business executives wanted for their offices—not just for their undeniable utility but equally as displays of good taste and conspicuous consumption. D.J. understood his own strength (management) and weakness (product design). To compensate for the latter, he realized he would need to "abandon himself to the wild ideas of others"—namely, the greatest furniture designers of the twentieth century. By promising the likes of George Nelson, Gilbert Rohde, Charles Eames, and Robert Propst a free hand in designing what Eames called "good goods," D.J. lured them to backwater Michigan, where he protected them from the pesky managers, salespeople, and engineers who in the typical company want to "make little changes here and there" in the designs of applied artists.

In addition to abandoning himself to the ideas of those designers, D.J. did the same with the ideas of the workingmen and -women in his factory responsible for turning the designers' ideas into shippable products. The Herman Miller Company was one of the first in America to adopt the Scanlon plan, a form of gainsharing in which employees are financially rewarded for their efforts and ideas to improve productivity and product quality. The plan was named after Joe Scanlon, a former steelworker and union leader who developed it while teaching at MIT's business school. Scanlon's ideas were based on his own workplace experiences and the teachings of Douglas McGregor, perhaps the most influential management thinker of the twentieth century and the scholar credited with creating a formal theory that encompasses many of the humanistic practices of our idealistic capitalists. In 1950, when one of Scanlon's MIT graduate students, Carl ("Jack") Frost, became a professor at Michigan State University (not far from Zeeland), D.J. hired him to design a managerial system for Herman Miller that would be every bit as forward-looking as the product designs of Eames and his peers. Frost organized Herman Miller employees into committees to identify ways to reduce costs, increase output, and improve quality. The system was different from Lincoln Electric's piecework model, with one major exception: worker compensation was based on prenegotiated performance standards, and thus not subject to post hoc, or arbitrary, managerial evaluations. Thanks to Frost's intervention, participatory management became the core of the human-centered organizational culture that evolved at Herman Miller over the next half century.

Under D.J.'s leadership, everything undertaken at Herman Miller was done with the intent of showing "respect for individuals"—whether the individual was a worker, designer, or user of its products. In describing D.J.'s legacy, his son Max often told a story about the death of a millwright who had labored diligently in a Herman Miller factory for many years. After the millwright's funeral, D.J. visited the man's home to pay condolences to his widow and family. As he was leaving, the grieving woman presented him with a printed collection of poetry her husband had composed over the years he had been employed in the plant. On reading the poems, D.J. discovered that the worker he had viewed simply as a skilled machinist was also an accomplished poet. D.J. then vowed to begin treating every Herman Miller employee as a whole person—that is, as an individual with unique talents deserving to be recognized, developed, and encouraged to use. Max wrote that the lesson he drew from D.J.'s story was, "When we think about leaders and the variety of gifts people bring to corporations and institutions, we see the art of leadership lies in polishing and liberating, and enabling those gifts."[2] In practical terms, that translated into career-long education and training for all Herman Miller employees.

It also meant sharing the wealth the company produced with everyone who had contributed to its making. In the 1970s D.J. and his eldest son, Hugh, established an employee stock ownership plan before they took the company public to raise capital needed to fund its growth. D.J. led that effort, even though he had technically "retired" in 1961, when he was succeeded by Hugh as Herman Miller's chief executive. However, idle retirement was not a part of D.J.'s DNA, so he actively served as the company's chairman (and later chairman emeritus) for three decades, coming into his office almost until the day he died at age ninety, and having lived to see Max become the third De Pree to head the company, after Hugh's retirement.

Max's Turn at the Helm

Everything D.J. and Hugh had initiated coalesced under Max's leadership. By the late 1980s, Herman Miller was ranked ninth on *Fortune*'s annual America's Most Admired Corporations list—quite a feat, considering that it placed only 457th when ranked by sales. Moreover, the company was highly profitable: between 1977 and 1987, its total average return to investors was over 27 percent annually, seventh highest on the Fortune 500.[3] Throughout the 1980s, the company annually ranked high on the list of best places to work.[4] Because Max De Pree was the CEO when the company earned all those kudos, he was regularly featured on the cover of business magazines, and hailed as one of America's top corporate leaders.[5]

The company also won awards left and right for quality, product design, and the architecture of its facilities.[6] It was perhaps best known for the artistic beauty of its innovative products: Herman Miller's Eames lounge chair and Noguchi table found their way into the permanent collection of New York's Museum of Modern Art; its Aeron and Ergon chairs introduced the science of ergonomics to the office place; and the company's open-office cubicles became ubiquitous (if frequently unloved) in American businesses. Herman Miller's enlightened practices were unique in its industry, although competitor Steelcase, located a stone's throw away in Grand Rapids, also had a good record of product quality and working conditions. But Herman Miller was far and away the furniture industry's leader in the amount it invested in research and development, and in dedication to the "human environmental design" its products and manufacturing facilities evidenced. In 1982 the *Journal of the American Institute of Architects* published a feature article on a Herman Miller plant, calling it "a splendid workplace" bathed in natural light and "designed and built with the individual worker in mind."[7]

In 1989 De Pree wrote a remarkable little book, *Leadership Is an Art*, which became a surprising bestseller. The vocabulary Max employed in this book's pages can appear more than a bit "soft" to those trained in the hardheaded dollars-and-cents business tradition, and off-putting to those not raised in fundamentalist Christian settings. He used spiritually laden words—*love, warmth, beauty,* and *joy*—and such biblical concepts as "stewardship" and "covenants." He called his relationship with Herman Miller employees "covenantal" (as opposed to legal or contractual) because it was based on them being "volunteer" members of a community with shared values and goals, and he often communicated by way of parables and homilies—what he called "tribal story telling."

That's where theory fastball came into play. Max told a story about his brother-in-law, a famed major-league baseball pitcher, from whom he learned that every great pitcher needs a great catcher. The brother-in-law told Max that Sandy Koufax was such an intimidating presence on the mound that the very sound of his fastball made hitters timid—

indeed, the only thing that could have slowed those pitches down was an incompetent catcher. Max saw the story as a parable about the interdependent relationship between leaders and followers: "In baseball and business, the needs of the team are best met when we meet the needs of individual persons. By conceiving a vision and pursuing it together, we can solve our problems of effectiveness and productivity."[8] From that premise, Max concluded that, at least sometimes, a titular leader needs to "play catcher" when employees are "pitching"—for example, by providing the resources his designers need to produce "good goods," then limiting his role to supporting them in their self-directed efforts. Similarly, he understood that he needed to delegate the tasks of accounting, sales, manufacturing, marketing, and finance to people who were more knowledgeable than he on such matters, and not attempt to "manage" their efforts. In that fashion, he limited his role as leader of Herman Miller to the exercise of three tasks and responsibilities at the heart of theory fastball:

- "The first responsibility of a leader is to define reality." By that, Max meant that leaders need to define what business a company is in, and what it needs to accomplish in innovation, product quality, and customer service—and earn in profits—to successfully compete and survive financially. Then leaders need to show individual employees and teams how what they do makes a necessary contribution toward that success.

- The last task is "to say thank you." That is, leaders need to accurately assess the performance of employees, then reward them with fair and appropriate compensation for their contributions.

- "In between the two, the leader must become a servant." De Pree assumed that if people know clearly what is expected of them, and are rewarded fairly for their efforts, they will endeavor to make their best contribution to the organization. When (or if) they fail to do so, the cause is a failure of leadership, not willful disobedience. Max believed there are five possible reasons people underperform: they have been assigned the wrong tasks given their talents or abilities; their tasks have been unclearly or incorrectly defined; they are being rewarded for doing the wrong things; they have been inadequately trained; or they lack the resources (staff, money, machines, tools) to do their jobs. Providing those necessary things—that is, creating the conditions under which people can do their jobs effectively—is the task and responsibility of the "catcher" (leader).[9]

In sum, De Pree defined the art of leadership as "liberating people to do what is required of them in the most effective and humane way possible," a practice he called "servant leadership."

Theory Fastball Applied

All of that may sound a bit hokey and impractical. I was skeptical myself when, in the early 1980s, I first heard about De Pree's unusual leadership philosophy. Deciding to discover for myself what was going on in Zeeland, I cold-called Max, and he graciously invited me to visit the company's facilities and speak with the people employed in them, even offering to put me up for a night at Herman Miller's conference center. After the visit I reported—a bit gushingly, as I now see—that I "was given *carte blanche* to go anywhere and to talk to anyone, managers and workers. The only problem was that I couldn't tell one from the other! People who seemed to be production workers were engaged in solving the 'managerial' problems of improving productivity and quality. People who seemed to be managers had their sleeves rolled up and were working, side by side, with everybody else in an all-out effort to produce the best products in the most effective way."[10]

I knew that Max had written, somewhat cryptically, "The measure of leadership is not the quality of the head, but the tone of the body. The signs of outstanding leadership appear primarily among the followers:

Are the followers achieving their potential? Are they learning? Serving? Do they achieve the required results?" In Zeeland I saw how that translated into the practical world of manufacturing—and how the avuncular Max qualified as a great leader by his own measure.

I learned a lot more in Zeeland—for example, that the company's Scanlon plan had provided bonuses averaging 10 percent of employee salaries between 1953 and 1983, and that in the 1980s, those bonuses more than paid for themselves: employee suggestions annually generated some $12 million in cost savings (about $3,000 per employee).[11] All employees also participated in profit-sharing and stock-ownership plans (100 percent of regular employees who worked there for at least a year were granted company stock, and over 50 percent regularly purchased shares in addition to those that came as a benefit of employment).[12] Richard Bennett, a Herman Miller middle manager in that era, explained the significance of extensive employee stock ownership: "As an owner, you approach your job in a different way, a more responsive way."[13] As Max said, "Around here the employees act as if they own the place."[14] And creating that attitude was the intent of the company's bonus, profit-sharing, and stock-ownership plans:

> Nothing is being given. Ownership is earned and paid for. The heart of it is profit-sharing, and there is no sharing if there are no profits. Risk and reward are connected logically and fairly. There is no smug condescension at play here. Rather, there is a certain morality in connecting shared accountability as employees with shared ownership. This lends a rightness and a permanence to the relationship of us to our work and to each other. . . . There are also some clear implications. There is risk personally and there is risk corporately. While it is great to work for gains, one also has to be ready for losses.[15]

It would be a mistake to minimize the impact of that risk on the company's culture. Employees often mentioned that Herman Miller's participative managerial processes generated much discussion and dis-agreement, and on occasion even conflict among employees with differ-ing views. As one manager explained, "When I came to Herman Miller I felt I had an obligation to speak my mind on topics that I felt were im-portant. It's gotten me into a lot of trouble emotionally, you know, you put a heavy emotional commitment into [this] kind of thing because it's your company."[16] After all, the Scanlon plan guaranteed only that every employee would have a say, not that all would have their own way. Indeed, because their own money was at risk when employees made de-cisions, the decision-making process was slow and often contentious, much as it was at Lincoln Electric. Of course, the company also offered a full menu of other employee benefits and perks—including day care, rehabilitation services, and college tuition reimbursement—but no al-cohol, not even at the annual Christmas party.

Central to Max's philosophy was the universal ethical principle of respecting people, which on one level meant not being judgmen-tal toward sinners, but more to the point, meant that Herman Miller hired people based solely on their skills and character, with no atten-tion paid to their religion, political views, age, color, or gender. In the mid-1980s, the company hired Michelle Hunt, an African American from Washington, DC, to serve as its Vice President for People, at a time when Zeeland was lily-white, and the idea of a woman execu-tive was almost as unthinkable as having a black neighbor. It was all part and parcel of recognizing people as individuals—a commitment graphically illustrated in the company's 1985 annual report, whose first twenty-two pages were devoted to a spread of photos of 2,900 of its 3,265 employees, each depicted in ways reflecting their individual personalities and interests.

Hunt's unusual title—VP for People—reflected Max's belief in re-specting the dignity of individuals: he abhorred the practice of think-ing of employees as "human resources" and "human capital," arguing that they were *people* and should be thought of, and treated, as such. Every individual, in his Christian view, had been created in the image of his or her Maker; thus, each was entitled to due respect and dignity. From that premise, he deduced that every human had been endowed with basic rights and that, since those rights derived from God, they could not be abridged or rescinded by mortals—including employers and bosses. Those unalienable rights included, in Max's language, the rights to be needed, to be involved, to understand, to affect one's own destiny, to be accountable, to make a commitment, and to appeal.[17]

It is instructive to see how meeting those rights played out in practice at Herman Miller. In the 1980s, a severe economic recession led to a precipitous drop in demand for the company's products. The recession hit Herman Miller especially hard because so many of its high-end products were seen as luxury goods, and thus their purchase could readily be postponed. The consequence was a river of red ink in the company's books. For the first time in decades, it was losing large sums. With no end to the recession in sight, executives at other manufacturing firms across America were laying off workers to stay afloat. But Max responded differently. Because he had committed the company to honoring the rights of its workers to be involved, be informed, be needed, and affect their own destiny, he and his top management team assembled the company's workers to give them a thorough briefing on the company's financial situation, along with an explanation of what that meant for its ability to pay bills, meet payroll, fund pensions and other benefits, and survive in the long term. The executives then presented a range of possible actions that might be taken to restore profitability, none of which was particularly attractive in the short term, and all with negative consequences for the company's employees and owners.

The people in that room were, of course, both employees and owners, and they were accustomed to wearing both those hats. For many years, managerial and financial data had been routinely shared with them at the company's regular monthly meetings. The workers had been known to use those occasions to aggressively query top management, demanding, for example, to know why the value of shares of "their" company had dropped a dollar or so.[18] So when the employees were asked what actions they thought the company should take during the recession, they were prepared to deal with the challenge. After much discussion—some of it heated—a consensus emerged that there should be no layoffs. In order to preserve the company's cherished sense of community and mutual respect, all employees agreed to be paid for a four-day workweek, and if the recession continued, they were willing to further share the sacrifice and go on a three-day paid week, all the while continuing to put in five days on the job. In addition, some production workers volunteered to hit the road as sales reps in geographical areas the company wasn't currently serving, and others organized themselves into teams to develop lower-cost products that might open new markets and perhaps not be as vulnerable to changing economic conditions as the current line of furniture. Others volunteered to undertake deferred maintenance, and some worked on finding opportunities for cost reduction. As manager Marg Mojzak explained, "Herman Miller puts a lot of demands on employees, and the employees rise to the occasion."[19]

Max's "soft" philosophy was played out in hard terms in other ways, as well. At a time when executives in other companies were arranging golden parachutes for themselves, Herman Miller introduced "silver parachutes" for all employees with over two years of service. In the event of an unfriendly takeover leading to the termination of their employment, the plan offered a soft landing for a level of employees whose welfare most executives placed far below their own. Most radically, the company introduced the principle that its chief executive could not be paid more than twenty times the average wage of its line workers, doubtless the narrowest salary ratio among Fortune 500 companies.

Additionally, Herman Miller demonstrated concern for the environment by becoming an early leader in energy and water conservation and waste recycling. It also was known for its excellent relationships with its dealers, suppliers, and customers, offering the latter a five-year guarantee on its products, as opposed to the one-year industry standard. Most impressive was the degree to which Herman Miller's values-based culture was embraced throughout the company's ranks, even at the blue-collar level. For example, in 1984, a recently retired production worker confessed to a reporter that whenever people asked where she had been employed, she would answer proudly "Herman Miller," then carry on with details about how wonderful the company was. Her husband would interrupt and say, "They only asked you where you worked, you don't have to sell them the company."[20] But she wasn't the company's only "salesperson." In 1988, a group of my MBA students visited Herman Miller's West Coast facility, where furniture was reassembled for delivery to its California customers. The students came back amazed to have found the same culture in that remote outpost that I had found in Zeeland. One student reported: "I talked to one manual worker who sounded exactly like Max does in his book."

A Shockingly Bad, and Surprising, End

In 1989 the Herman Miller Company was highly profitable, netting $47 million on $765 million in sales; known as a great place to work; renowned for high ethical standards; admired for the quality and design of its products; and exalted for its socially responsible behavior. Furthermore, its future looked brighter than ever. Max turned sixty-five that year, and decided the moment was propitious for him to step down and pass leadership of the company on to its first non–De Pree CEO. The company's board chose Richard Rauch, a thirty-three-year Herman Miller employee, to be Max's successor. He was reluctant to accept the post; nonetheless, he was the obvious choice, favored by his fellow vice presidents for the job, and "an absolute believer" in the company's values and practices.

Alas, Rauch turned out to be ill-suited for the role of chief executive, a fact that he himself had suspected. Within a year, he asked the board to accept his resignation. The board then worked with the company's management to draw up an exacting list of sixteen characteristics they were seeking in a new CEO, including proven leadership ability; being in sync with Herman Miller values and culture; being a skilled delegator outstanding at selecting, nurturing, and assigning top-quality talent; and commitment to participative management, employee ownership, and the Scanlon plan. They then launched a national search, ultimately selecting an individual who seemed ideal on paper and had said all the right things to those who interviewed him.

Once on the job, the new CEO started off on the right foot—but it soon became apparent to the company's close-knit top management team that their new leader was, if anything, less well equipped for the position than his predecessor. He was uncomfortable with the company's values-based culture, unable to work with the executive team, and out of his depth dealing with the complexities of managing international design and manufacturing operations. Moreover, the new CEO had inherited a problem that had gone relatively unnoticed during Max's tenure: the company's rapid growth had outpaced its ability to manage it. When Max assumed the leadership of Herman Miller, it had been basically a medium-sized family-run business with organizational systems and structures appropriate to its relatively limited scale of operations. But quite suddenly it had become a major Fortune 500 company with extensive and complex international operations, and was now within the purview of Wall Street investors, who were paying increasing attention to its short-term profitability. When economic conditions then turned bad, the new CEO undertook a series of actions intended to deal with declining profit margins. Unfortunately, those steps were aligned less with the company's values than with practices in traditionally managed corporations.

I have found considerable disagreement among former Herman Miller employees about the details of what occurred at the company under the new CEO's leadership. However, several informants told me that, not long after the executive had assumed office, company morale ebbed to an all-time low, and several key employees decided to leave in search of greener pastures. The turmoil that followed led to declining productivity, sales, and profitability. The CEO—unsure how to respond to the looming crisis—hired a compensation consultant, who in effect assumed the role of co–chief executive. After a quick study of the situation, she gave the CEO what turned out to be poor advice, concluding that the most effective way to quickly cut costs was to fire a large number of long-term executives and managers who, she felt, had grown stale in their jobs. Claiming that they had become unproductive because too little had been demanded of them in terms of bottom-line performance, she advised the CEO to replace many of the company's top management team, which he agreed to do—but only on the condition that she did the actual firing! In the first round of firing, she axed a number of key individuals who, between them, averaged twenty-eight years of experience with the firm. She did those mass firings by voice mail, then assembled all headquarters-based employees in the company's auditorium, where she summarily announced that many more would soon follow. When she made good on that promise, the upshot was an almost immediate rupture of the bonds of trust that the De Prees had nurtured over decades. What had taken so long to create was rapidly lost, and the essence of the company's culture became critically imperiled. The board's subsequent decision to remove the CEO came too late. The damage had been done.

In hindsight, it seems that the Herman Miller board, despite its stated commitment to finding a chief executive who would be a perfect fit with the company's unique character, had failed in their due diligence, overlooking the candidates' lack of relevant leadership experience. Moreover, they had never interviewed anyone who had worked with the new executive, or for him. Had they done so, they might have learned that he was uncomfortable with team leadership, chronically indecisive, and, when he did act, had often displayed questionable judgment.

Max then retired from the board; he would be the last De Pree to work in what had been a family business for seven decades. Over the years, the family had been gradually selling its holdings in the company, and by then they were no longer majority shareholders. With no De Prees on the Herman Miller board, and having lost control of its ownership, Max and his family no longer had any influence over the company's direction.

Herman Miller Today

Some two decades and two subsequent CEOs later, by 2016 Herman Miller appeared to have regained at least some of the cultural features that had made it great in the 1980s. In 2015 it won awards for its human rights and conservation efforts, and it continues to place strong emphasis on reducing its environmental impact. In 2000 it had become one of the first companies to issue a sustainability report, and since announced the goal of achieving zero levels of air emissions, water use in manufacturing, and hazardous waste by 2020. The company has recently diversified with the acquisition of furniture retailer Design within Reach (the chain's staff are not treated as Herman Miller employees). In 2015 it was profitable on nearly $2 billion in sales. Although most employees are no longer shareholders, and the Scanlon plan is no longer used, the company does offer profit sharing and excellent employee benefits. But the word from Zeeland is that the company is "not the way it used to be," and working there now is "just a job." Its absence from current lists of best places to work seems to confirm those judgements.

Shortly before his ninetieth birthday, I called Max to ask him why he thought the company's culture had proved unsustainable. He found it understandably difficult to discuss the bad decisions made in choosing his successors—choices he had had a hand in making, and for which he acknowledged personal responsibility. He was neither critical of the company's current leadership nor surprised that many of the practices he had pioneered were no longer in place. Managing the Scanlon plan was extremely difficult, he explained; maintaining intimate relationships with workers is hard and time-consuming; and it is far from easy for the nominal boss of a company to continually share power and financial information with employees. He suggested that those were the reasons why so many executives decide enlightened leadership isn't worth the extra effort.

Eventually, he concluded, all companies "lose their souls." As he saw it, that regrettable phenomenon is the result of what he called "organizational entropy." As with the laws of nature, he believed organizational practices, even the most virtuous and successful ones, inevitably deteriorate over time. He reminded me that, in 1989, he had called attention to that process, writing that people in large organizations "often fail to see the signs of entropy" around them— dark tensions among key people; leaders who seek to control rather than to liberate; pressures of day-to-day operations that push aside concern for vision and ethics; a growing orientation toward the dry rules taught in business schools, as opposed to a values orientation that takes into account such things as contribution, spirit, excellence, beauty, and joy; an urge to establish ratios and quantify both history and visions of the future; and leaders who rely on organization manuals and structures instead of people.[21]

I went back to his book, where I discovered that he also had written that the most important thing he personally needed to work on as a leader was "the interception of entropy." While he did so many other things so well, like many leaders cited in this book, he failed at that important task.

11

Too Much of a Good Thing

WILLIAM C. NORRIS (1911-2006)

A believer in reincarnation might well become convinced that Robert Owen had made a second appearance on this blue orb as William Norris, founder of the Control Data Corporation. Both were brilliant, farsighted entrepreneurs committed to helping those most in need— and equally messianic, deaf to the opinions of others, and, in the end, destructive of the companies they created and of their own reputations as well.

Norris and his twin sister, Willa, were born and raised on a cattle, hog, and corn farm in Nebraska in the second decade of the twentieth century. Together they attended a one-room rural elementary school, along with their older sister and seven other children. Norris later recalled the experience of being helped at the school by older students who taught him the value of working in teams—a lesson he seems often to have forgotten in his later career.[1] After high school (where his sister claimed he knew more about physics than his science teacher), he matriculated at the University of Nebraska, where he obtained a degree in electrical engineering. Final examinations in his senior year were taken on the fly when he was forced to rush home to assume management of the family farm after his father's sudden death. Despite that trauma, he had no trouble passing with flying colors. In the terrible Dust Bowl winter that followed, he saved the family's cattle from starvation by feeding them Russian thistle, against the advice of fellow farmers who believed the weed fatal for cows. When those farmers' cows subsequently died over the ensuing windy, freezing months, and Norris's survived (in remarkably healthy condition, no less), he seems to have drawn the somewhat less than logical conclusion that "the majority is always wrong." Thereafter, he invariably played the role of maverick in whatever context he found himself.

During World War II, Norris served in a top-secret US Navy cryptology unit engaged in breaking Japanese and German codes. Like their more famous British counterparts, Alan Turing and his colleagues at Bletchley Park—notably depicted in the 2014 film *The Imitation Game*—Norris and his navy colleagues made several technological breakthroughs that after the war proved invaluable in the development of digital computers. Leaving the navy in 1945, Norris worked for a variety of companies involved in the creation of mainframe computers, and in 1955 was named vice president and general manager of the Univac division of Sperry Rand. Less than two years later, saying that he'd "had a belly full" of top-management decisions he disagreed with, he joined twelve other dissatisfied Univac colleagues in a mass defection from Sperry Rand.[2]

Control Data

Within a matter of weeks, those engineers had started a new company, soon to be incorporated as the Control Data Corporation (CDC), with forty-six-year-old William Norris as its president. Norris was not the most creative engineer among the company's dozen founders; that distinction went to the youngest of them, thirty-one-year-old Seymour Cray, who years later has become recognized as a highly significant figure in the development of computers. One of the biggest leadership challenges Norris faced at CDC was taming Cray, "a brilliant person who marches to his own tune." Cray hated organizations of any kind, manifesting a passionate disregard for such standard administrative processes as planning, budgeting, and communicating.[3] Only after Norris repeatedly nagged him to prepare a business plan did Cray submit the following:

Five-year goal: Build the biggest computer in the world.
One-year goal: Achieve one fifth of the above.

What his plan lacked in details, Cray more than compensated for in execution. In 1960 CDC delivered a supercomputer to the US Navy that was more powerful, faster, and cheaper—at a bargain $600,000— than anything IBM offered at the time (a second computer was soon sold to the British government agency that had managed the Bletchley Park codebreaking). Control Data was on its way to becoming the manufacturer of the world's largest, most powerful, and highest-speed computers. In 1962, IBM's legendary chairman, Thomas J. Watson Jr., testily asked his executive team how they had allowed the Control Data Corporation to gain the lead in superconductors: "Contrasting this modest effort [of Cray's laboratory] with 34 people including the janitor with our vast development activities, I fail to understand why we have lost our industry leadership position by letting someone else offer the world's most powerful computer."[4]

For the next decade, CDC turned out a succession of ever faster, more powerful computers. In 1969, IBM, reeling from continually being bested by CDC, announced it was about to introduce a computer as fast as CDC's fastest model. The effect on CDC's sales was calamitous, as would-be customers sat on the sidelines for a year awaiting the release of the new IBM model. However, there was a serious problem with the new IBM computer: *it didn't exist*. A furious Norris dubbed IBM's unethical marketing tactic "FUD"—fear, uncertainty, and doubt—and brought an antitrust suit against Big Blue. No one expected CDC to win in court, and Norris's colleagues advised him not to sue, warning that all he would gain from the exercise was unconscionably high legal bills that their chronically cash-strapped company could ill afford. True to character, he proceeded with the legal action, and when IBM settled the case by offering a package of concessions amounting to $80 million, a gloating Norris called the suit "one of the best management decisions in our history."[5]

But none of CDC's accomplishments satisfied Seymour Cray. He harbored the ambition of building a colossal computer, with capabilities beyond the imagining of most engineers at the time—and far exceeding the demands of CDC's customers. But Cray was frustrated: existing circuit technology was insufficient to meet the needs of his dream machine, and getting the technology he wanted would require capital—lots of it. Norris, on his part, was reluctant to bet all CDC's marbles on superconductor development; the profit potential simply wasn't there. In fact, the bulk of CDC's income was by then coming from its growing computer services businesses. He could not justify giving Cray the large sums he requested for what, increasingly, looked like a vanity R&D operation. Moreover, Norris knew Cray well enough to suspect that he would never be content working in a large organization, no matter how generous his budget. After a short tug of war between two rather immovable individuals, Norris and Cray amicably agreed to part company, and in 1972 the latter launched his own start-up, Cray Research. To help get it off the ground, CDC bought $300,000 worth of Cray Research stock (later sold for a threefold profit).[6] Within a few years, Cray Research would be CDC's major competitor in the supercomputer business, but the organizational growth that came with this success only rankled Cray. Less than ten years after founding his company, he resigned from it to do research of his own liking in a small lab—funded, naturally, by Cray Research.

Acquisitions and Diversifications

Unwilling to become dependent on either a single product line or CDC's own internal R&D capabilities, Norris continually hunted for small companies with promising technologies that might fuel CDC's growth and diversification. Between 1960 and 1979 the company acquired eighty-eight businesses, all through the exchange of equity. The largest acquisition, the Commercial Credit Corporation, was purchased in 1968 with three-quarters of a billion dollars of CDC stock. That marriage of a traditional financial institution to an unconventional technology company was not quite as bizarre as it may seem: CDC was in constant need of cash, and Commercial Credit came with a $3.4 billion dowry. *Businessweek* called the acquisition "marrying for money," which was largely true; nonetheless, Norris claimed the long-term goal was to find ways to use computers to deliver the many financial services Commercial Credit offered. Although that promise was never realized, Norris did support the early development of electronic funds transfer, a process still in use today. Some of CDC's acquisitions turned out to be "dogs," as Norris put it, yet in total they paid off handsomely. By 1970, CDC was a flourishing international business in which thirty thousand employees generated $1 billion in revenue, up from ten thousand workers and $160 million in sales less than five years earlier.

Commercial Credit proved its value as a ready source of cash, allowing Norris to move into fields more closely related to CDC's primary computer business, most successfully as an original equipment manufacturer. The OEM market for such peripherals as data-storage devices, disk drives, printers, and monitors emerged about the time CDC entered those businesses, and then ripened with the introduction of smaller computers, ultimately bearing full fruit with the advent of desktop models. In 1982, the year the company celebrated its twenty-fifth anniversary, CDC's peripherals were a billion-dollar business, and the company had a half share of the world's disk-drive market.[7] It also dominated the data services market (since most companies could not afford to own mainframes, they remotely stored and processed their data on CDC's supercomputers), and had introduced several successful computer-based customer-service businesses, such as Ticketron, a box office and lottery business, and Arbitron, a radio and television rating system.

During the 1970s, CDC was a Wall Street glamour stock. From its inception, the company's shares had been widely held: it had initially been funded by selling six hundred thousand shares at $1 per share to some three hundred investors, and its ownership subsequently was spread broader with each company it acquired.[8] Since Norris's total personal investment was only $75,000, he was never the company's controlling stockholder; nonetheless, he ran Control Data as if he were its sole proprietor. More precisely, he managed the company as if its shareholders—and the stock market itself—didn't exist. Unlike most other enlightened corporate leaders, Norris had no interest in employee stock ownership, arguing that workers didn't want to own stock, and they didn't (couldn't?) fully understand the complexity of share ownership. Most important, he was unwilling to expose his own employees to the vagaries of the stock market. At base, there was nothing about the market he liked. He was particularly outspoken on the subject of hostile takeovers, arguing that technology companies suffered greatly from the defection of their most creative employees when they became takeover targets. He also believed that executives were unwilling to make costly but necessary long-term investments because they feared that the consequent decrease in earnings would make their companies vulnerable to takeovers—an opinion he was not reluctant to share with investors. Norris had an opinion about almost everything, and was never shy about expressing it. For example, he didn't believe there was any value in doing market research, arguing that everything CDC needed to know about consumer needs could be found in a newspaper. Indeed, he didn't much care what CDC's customers wanted.

Norris on the Road to Damascus

Even his closest colleagues said Norris was imperious, autocratic, willful, and stubborn. When I met with him several times in the early 1980s, I found him to be curmudgeonly, curt, irascible, and argumentative. Still, I rather liked him, or more precisely, I admired and respected his boldness, candor, and willingness to be an iconoclast and nonconformist. His most often quoted line was "When I see everybody going south, I have a great compulsion to go north."[9]

And go north he did, beginning in early 1967, when he attended a seminar moderated by Whitney Young, head of the Urban League, one of the nation's most influential civil rights groups. That year's "long hot summer" was marked by a series of riots in several of America's largest cities, including Minneapolis, where CDC was headquartered. After the violent Minneapolis uprising, which had led to the destruction of a large swath of the city's Northside area, Norris flew to New York to discuss with Young ways in which Control Data might help to avoid a repetition of such violence. "Jobs," Young replied. "Until these young blacks have jobs, until they have something to look forward to and work for, you're going to have trouble in Minneapolis and everywhere else."[10]

Norris returned to Minneapolis a changed man—literally a man on a mission. And that mission was for CDC to provide jobs for African Americans. Later, CDC's mission would evolve and expand, becoming "to address society's major unmet needs as profitable business opportunities." By the late 1970s, Norris had developed, and largely implemented, a business model for CDC in which it endeavored to serve society directly through the goods and services it offered. This was radical stuff. Norris came to believe that meeting a company's social responsibility should not be separate from its basic business functions. A few years earlier, US Steel's chairman had declared, "The duty of management is to make money. Our primary objective is not to make steel." In effect, Norris turned that statement on its head: CDC was not in the business of making money; instead, *its business was serving society.* The *Wall Street Journal* labeled this strategy "far out," vilifying Norris as "eccentric."[11] At the same time, he was criticized by some on the left who portrayed him as a wolf in sheep's clothing seeking to profit from poverty and social misfortune. Norris's answer to such criticism was characteristically blunt and provocative: "No one objects to a reasonable profit on a can of beans. Why should there be objections to making a profit meeting the needs of disabled persons?"

The implementation of Norris's new strategy had significant organizational implications. Unlike other progressive companies, CDC had no need for a special department of social responsibility or community outreach programs; in particular, it would not engage in corporate philanthropy. Norris was particularly contrarian on the subject of philanthropy, utterly rejecting the activity that was the special pride of his fellow leaders in the Minneapolis business community. In the early 1980s, forty-five Twin Cities companies were members of the "Minnesota 5 Percent Club," each donating at least 5 percent of its profits to community organizations (another twenty-five local firms donated at least 2 percent). Norris made no friends among his peers by refusing to join their club, arguing that philanthropy never solved a social problem, nor could it: "Foundation after foundation, you look at their reports, and hell, there are hundreds of little projects, $10,000 here and $5,000 there, and what have they got to show for it? You can see, Christ, they're not really accomplishing much."[12]

Norris believed traditional corporate philanthropy—donations amounting, on average, to roughly 1 percent of profits—might be commendable, but it was far from adequate. In 1984 he explained to me, "In order to bridge the gap created by the [recent] Reagan administration budget cuts, corporate giving would have to increase by something like 150 percent." Hence, he concluded that corporate giving was about as useful as "pissing in the ocean" when it came to addressing major social issues such as poverty, unemployment, and job training: "So we [CDC] abandoned the traditional do-gooder concept because it was too narrow, in favor of one that says we should address society's unmet needs as profitable business opportunities. In that way, you're not worrying about doing good or doing well. You're really doing what needs to be done. And solving social problems is no longer a peripheral (and thus expendable) add-on to your business—it *is* your business. Now, it's true that addressing major unmet needs is longer term than the traditional [business] strategy. But the traditional strategy is not working well these days."[13]

The longer-term approach CDC developed had its inception in 1967, shortly after Norris's visit with Whitney Young, when the company opened a hiring office in Minneapolis's predominantly African American Northside neighborhood. Because Northside was some distance from CDC's largest plant in suburban Arden Hills, Norris initiated a shuttle bus service to take newly hired people to and from work. But when few ghetto residents signed up for the distant jobs, Norris decided to bring the jobs to them. He rented a vacant Northside facility to serve as a temporary plant until an attractive new facility could be constructed in the same neighborhood. In 1969, that modern factory—built, in the main, by minority contractors—opened for business with a workforce composed of Northside locals, hiring preference given to the chronically unemployed, school dropouts, and in particular, unemployed women who were heads of households. Because Norris did not want the plant to be an act of charity, over the vociferous objections of the company's manufacturing managers he directed it to produce peripheral controllers—at the time, a key part of CDC's product line. He also didn't want the plant to be seen as "an experiment," believing that things done on a trial basis are doomed to fail ("If you leave room for failure, you're very likely to fail").[14] As a top CDC executive later explained, peripheral controllers were "a vital part of our business. We had no choice but to make it [the plant] work or we were out of business as a company."[15]

In subsequent years, opinions on the extent to which the plant was a success or failure would vary. From the start, there had been problems. Community leaders assumed that CDC was opening a plant in the ghetto simply to burnish its public image. Few neighborhood residents applied for jobs; many feared that whites would be too biased to hire them, and some who wanted to apply didn't have the standard identity documents, educational records, and references the company typically demanded of new hires. Once those preliminary hurdles were overcome and a workforce assembled, training became an issue for the company's supervisors, almost all of whom were white, and few with backgrounds supervising adults with little or no prior work experience. Skilled jobs at other CDC facilities were filled by employees with either experience or formal training, but the Northside workers lacked both. Hence, Control Data found itself in the business of offering the equivalent of an on-the-job technical-high-school education.

Over the next three years, the company was forced to deal with a raft of issues not found in its other facilities. Many Northside workers were unaccustomed to the discipline of showing up for work on time (or every day). Employees brought personal problems to work ranging from domestic violence to legal run-ins (on Monday mornings, a CDC manager routinely went to the local jail to bail out employees who had run afoul of the law over the weekend). No matter the problem, Norris was undaunted. "When you come to an obstacle," he told his managers, "you don't say you can't do it, you just overcome the obstacle and do it."[16] For the most part, CDC was able to overcome the obstacles to the plant's success. When it became clear that single mothers who worked in the plant frequently had to stay home to watch their sick children—or to care for them when friends or relatives who usually did so were unavailable—CDC opened a neighborhood day-care center, making the facility available to non-CDC employees as well. Somehow—often due to Norris's sheer willpower—the plant eventually became an efficient and profitable part of CDC that he was proud to boast about, and boast he did, to all who would listen (as well as to those who would not). He was particularly proud of the day-care center, which he often visited, and where he was said to have been "absolutely enthralled by the children."[17] Like Robert Owen in New Lanark, Norris seemed to have had the rapport with children he lacked with adults.

Even before the Northside plant was running smoothly, Norris told his staff, "Let's try one in Washington. There are a lot of blacks there who need jobs, too."[18] It took heroic efforts on the part of its managers, but a profitable CDC plant was eventually up and running a stone's throw away from Capitol Hill. Norris then turned his attention to the other Twin City, opening a peripherals plant in a high-unemployment area of St. Paul. The plant was uniquely organized to provide jobs for those who couldn't work full-time: a four-hour shift for mothers during the hours their children were in school, followed by a four-hour shift for teenagers after school, and a final shift in the evening for people seeking a part-time late shift. Unfortunately, when the plant was almost ready to open, demand for computers fell drastically due to a sudden, deep recession, and CDC found itself with the problem of overcapacity. But Norris was not deterred: the plant was quickly reconfigured to serve as a bindery for the company's numerous manuals and other printed materials needing to be assembled, bound, and shipped.

In 1970, Norris decreed all new CDC plants were to be located in high-poverty areas, a fiat poorly received by his bitterly complaining operations managers. Norris not only held firm but doubled down, proclaiming, "You know, on our next poverty thing, we ought to try some burned out coal mining town somewhere in Appalachia."[19] And they did, opening a facility in Campton, Kentucky, the second-poorest American county at the time. That was followed by a new plant in San Antonio, Texas, where a predominantly Hispanic workforce was recruited and trained. Each of the new plants provided employees with extensive training, counseling services, and wellness programs. Based on what CDC had learned in its own facilities about training hardcore unemployed people, it then created a for-profit subsidiary—the Employment Preparation Service—which provided training in fifty centers across the nation on a contract basis for public agencies and private employers.

By 1980, Control Data's long-term strategy of "addressing society's major unmet needs as profitable business opportunities" was firmly in place. New divisions, subsidiaries, and product lines were being introduced almost as fast as Norris could invent them. Among these was the City Venture Corporation, a cooperative enterprise involving business, professional, governmental, and religious organizations dedicated to finding holistic solutions to urban problems. City Venture supported the formation and growth of new small businesses in run-down urban areas, offering residents a share of ownership in those enterprises. Operating in Toledo, Philadelphia, Baltimore, Miami, and, of course, Minneapolis, City Venture attempted to provide health care, job training, transportation, and affordable housing to the communities it sought to revitalize. But Norris wasn't simply interested in revitalizing blighted urban areas. He also formed Rural Ventures, Inc. to bring the efficiencies of large-scale agribusiness via computers to small family farms like the one he'd grown up on. That was followed by Medlab, a mobile pathology laboratory that served isolated areas such as Indian reservations, and then Fair Break, a job-training and career-counseling program for high-school dropouts. And on, and on . . .

PLATO

Among all those initiatives Norris's favorite, his pièce de résistance, his obsession (as many would say), was PLATO. His love affair with PLATO technology began in the 1960s, when a CDC salesman told him about an interesting experiment in the application of computer technology to the field of education. Professors at the University of Illinois had recently developed a computer-based system of instruction they called Programmed Logic for Automated Teaching Operations, aka PLATO. Norris immediately saw the potential of computer-based teaching systems not only for classroom use but also for occupational training. When he subsequently learned that the University of Illinois scientists were running their program on a clunky computer they had built themselves, he offered to lend the university one of CDC's supercomputers rent-free. The professors then spent the better part of a decade perfecting PLATO's computer programming and developing academically authoritative courseware for elementary and high schools, colleges, and universities, in subjects ranging from foreign-language instruction to mathematics and such business disciplines as accounting and finance. PLATO's university-based developers were pioneers of what came to be known as CMI (computer-managed instruction) or CBE (computer-based education), the essence of which was a capacity for interaction between a machine and an individual student. The beauty of CMI was that it allowed each student to progress at his or her own pace, thus individualizing instruction. That's what Norris loved about it: he felt CMI captured the best aspects of his old one-room schoolhouse, in which each student had been able to learn at his or her own rate. According to James Worthy, a longtime member of CDC's board, Norris was the first business leader to recognize "that instead of dehumanizing the teaching/learning experience, the computer can be a means of humanizing it."[20] Convinced that PLATO represented the future of education, Norris entered into a partnership with the University of Illinois to develop and market it.

In 1973 CDC began to use PLATO internally in its digital computer training course for new hires, subsequently adding more advanced classes. A million dollars in software development later, Control Data Institute (CDI) learning centers began marketing a series of three courses leading to state accreditation in the field of digital computing. Six years later, CDI was offering a smorgasbord of technical and vocational subjects, all delivered on drone PLATO terminals located in its learning centers. In 1981 Norris claimed that PLATO had been "proven" to be cost and educationally effective in teaching basic academic subjects. As useful as PLATO was, alas, no studies actually existed to support his boast.[21]

All the computing power for PLATO was centralized at CDC's superconductor facilities and distributed by phone lines to CDI's network of learning centers in twenty-five American cities. Unfortunately, almost as soon as CDC perfected its distributed delivery of PLATO courseware, competitors began to introduce more cost-effective delivery of CMI on self-contained microcomputers and desktops. Norris, never willing to say die, directed his sales force to concentrate on serving school systems and colleges, where he felt it was still more efficient to use cheap drone terminals remotely connected to supercomputers. That might have been the case at the time, but few educational institutions had the financial wherewithal to cover CDC's high fees for delivering PLATO. Moreover, few educators were experienced or comfortable with computer-assisted learning. About that time, the unorthodox partnership between the for-profit CDC and the nonprofit University of Illinois began to show signs of strain, so Norris ended the partnership agreement and hired his own team of academics to develop PLATO courseware. The cost of their salaries then was added to CDC's ever-increasing investment in the development of PLATO.

Norris, creatively desperate in his search for markets for PLATO, decided to develop a program for high-school dropouts between sixteen and twenty-four years old. After a time-consuming—and expensive— period of development, the only market CDC could find for the program was in two prison systems. Looking farther afield, Norris set his eye on the nation of Iran, where the then-reigning shah was attempting to modernize and industrialize his country. Sure enough, the shah signed on. Unfortunately, while CDC was developing Farsi-language PLATO courseware, the shah was deposed. His successor, the Ayatollah Khomeini, had extremely limited interest in computers—or much of anything developed after the fourteenth century—and that venture ended as yet another write-off. An even more embarrassing error was CDC's decision to sell PLATO technology to the apartheid-era South

African government, which used it as a tool in the infamous passbook system used to enforce racial segregation. Norris, never willing to acknowledge a mistake, insisted that PLATO was used only to educate black South Africans.[22]

Nonetheless, Norris kept inventing new uses—and new markets—for PLATO: corporate training, agribusiness, the long-term unemployed, and homebound handicapped people. All were well intended, yet few proved economically viable. Norris continued to believe that the best use of CMI was in the classroom, and in hindsight, he was correct; nonetheless, he had the wrong technology with which to deliver it. PLATO's el-hi courseware was first-rate, but CDC's staff had a trained incapacity to adopt it for use with the inexpensive Apple and PC desktop computers that school systems were beginning to purchase. CDC's programmers tried their best to convert PLATO courseware for delivery on the floppy disks used in those machines, but never managed to make the transition. Desperate to meet the growing PC challenge, CDC contracted with Texas Instruments (TI) to market PLATO courseware programmed for use with the personal computers it manufactured. A year later, TI exited the PC business, and CDC was back at square one. In 1984 Norris tried one last time to find a way to get PLATO into the nation's classrooms, forming a wholly owned CDC subsidiary, United School Services of America, to reach the K-12 market. Like previous efforts, that one fizzled out, disappearing with nary a whimper. In all, CDC spent about $1 billion on PLATO and never turned a profit.

While Norris was becoming ever more deeply involved in the execution of CDC's social mission, the company's traditional lines of business continued to expand both domestically and internationally. The company's customers included the US government, state and local agencies, foreign governments, corporations, engineering firms, and universities. With Norris occupied on other matters, someone was needed to manage all of that. Control Data was fortunate to have two long-term employees, Norbert Berg and Robert Price, whom Norris trusted. Berg, hired as Norris's personal assistant in 1959, and Price, hired as a computer programmer in 1961, greatly respected (and were loyal to) Norris; more important, they were tolerant of his cantankerous disposition. Increasingly, Norris entrusted them with the day-to-day management of the corporation—Price running operations, and Berg dealing with areas in which the people skills Norris noticeably lacked were requisite. Berg appears to have been the only person who could speak freely to Norris, thus becoming the go-to individual for Control Data's managers and outsiders who sought him out as an intermediary in their dealings with the notoriously difficult CEO. Indeed, if it could be said the antisocial Norris had a friend, that person was Norbert Berg. Fortunately, what Norris lacked in friends, he made up for in family. He and his wife, Jane Malley Norris, had eight children and twenty-one grandchildren.

Too Much of a Good Thing?

Over time, engineer William Norris—who had played a key role in the development of computers and been a pioneer in applying digital technology to the requirements of science, engineering, and industry—left all that behind to become a full-time business reformer, activist, and public scold. Like Robert Owen nearly two centuries earlier, Norris drifted away from his entrepreneurial, technical, and managerial roots as he became more and more concerned with alleviating human misery. Much like Owen, Norris never believed governmental action was sufficient, or efficient enough, to adequately provide the number of jobs, quality of health care, and levels of education needed by modern societies. Both Norris and Owen believed that enlightened capitalism was the best, and perhaps only, way to solve such social problems, although both also believed that government needed to be an active and supportive partner in such efforts. And both appreciated the fact that no one enlightened company—or even several—no matter how positive or virtuous their actions, could make more than a dent in such massive problems as poverty and joblessness. Ergo, at the height of their respective companies' successes, both men turned their attention outward in attempts to convince fellow capitalists to adopt social missions.

Much as Owen had done before him, in the early 1980s Norris began to devote most of his waking hours to writing articles, giving speeches, testifying before legislative bodies, granting press interviews, and meeting privately with corporate leaders in fevered attempts to convert others to his secular religion of addressing social problems as business opportunities. He argued that all the charity in the world could not end poverty, and that adequately funding government antipoverty programs would require confiscatory taxation. Thus the only effective and economically viable course was for business leaders to transform solving social problems from costly activities consuming capital into profitable actions that created it. Sounding like a biblical prophet, Norris beseeched corporate leaders to see the light, exhorting them "to take the initiative and provide the leadership for planning and managing the implementation" of business activities that created social and financial capital. He repeatedly urged business leaders to join him in this common cause, because "no other sector of society has such capabilities for effectively planning, assembling the resources for, and managing the large and diverse programs necessary today."[23] Like Owen's similar efforts, Norris's largely fell on deaf ears.

Assuming Norris was correct, why did no other prominent business leaders enlist in his cause? It could be argued that many were convinced they were already engaged in solving society's ills by addressing them as business opportunities; after all, isn't identifying a need and filling it the essence of entrepreneurial capitalism? Alternatively, many business leaders may have been put off by Norris's confrontational—and often condescending—know-it-all attitude. But the most probable explanation is that CDC's poor financial performance made Norris's arguments unconvincing. In the end, few of Norris's social initiatives succeeded, and those rare successes were short-lived. Yet he oversold his ideas, too often believing that the dreams he envisioned had been realized when in fact they had not yet been implemented. And once he had launched an initiative, he almost invariably lost interest in it, PLATO being the exception. In the early 1980s skeptics had begun to take note of the short half-life of Norris's initiatives, many of which seemed simply to disappear after ballyhooed launches.

That record might have gone unnoticed were it not for the unmistakable fact that, beginning in 1984, CDC's primary computer businesses were in serious financial and competitive straits—the result of growing competition from Japanese companies and nascent Silicon Valley firms. That year, CDC was forced to spin off what once had been its core business, supercomputers. The next year the company lost $400 million. After defaulting on its short-term debts in 1986, Control Data's board removed Norris from office, although they allowed him a face-saving "retirement." In a clear rebuke, the board named Robert Price as CEO over Norbert Berg, who had been Norris's choice. To keep CDC afloat, Price sold off at least half a dozen major CDC subsidiaries, most prominently Ticketron, Arbitron, and the Commercial Credit Corporation (the latter acquired by Sandy Weill, who subsequently made it a major component of Citigroup). Price soon was replaced by Lawrence Perlman, who promptly sold several more subsidiaries, including PLATO and the Control Data Institute. Most of CDC's inner-city plants were closed, and many thousands of workers were laid off, though a few plants were saved by selling them to their managers and community groups. Over the next decade, the remaining bits and pieces of the company were either sold piecemeal or simply shut down. Today, vestigial parts of CDC continue to exist at Syntegra, part of the BT Group, and a Minneapolis peripherals facility acquired by Seagate in 1988 remains in operation.

Two competing views suggest why Control Data imploded so dramatically and disappeared so completely. The majority view, as expressed in *Businessweek*, is that the company's problems stemmed from Norris's "frittering away resources on offbeat social schemes and letting grand visions overcome the day-to-day details of running a business for profit."[24] The minority view, advanced by former CDC board member James Worthy, is that "less than 5 percent of the company's assets were employed in the so-called societal needs areas," so the unprofitability of those programs could not have been responsible for CDC's massive financial crisis. Instead, Worthy puts blame on the red ink generated by the company's basic businesses, including peripherals, computer systems, and data services.[25] Yet neither Worthy nor any other of Norris's admirers claimed that PLATO ever turned a profit on the $1 billion that CDC invested in its development, or that any of Norris's other social initiatives proved viable for more than the short term.

My own perspective is that for many years Norris's attention was almost exclusively focused on CDC's social mission, and a great many of the company's executives and managers were similarly distracted from the day-to-day operations of the company's core businesses. In effect, CDC's leaders had taken their eyes off the ball, and as a result the company lost its ability to compete effectively in the rapidly changing world of computers where technological leads vanish in the blink of an eye. Control Data thus stands as the only major corporation ever to have failed as the result of its commitment to enlightened business practices.

So what to make of Norris? Even his harshest critics admit that he was farsighted and, in areas such as the development of PLATO, a step ahead of his time. Even though he suffered from overweening optimism, he might have gone down in history as a great business leader had he limited his social initiatives to those directly related to CDC's computer businesses, and devoted as much time and energy to renewing the company's technology as he did to its social mission. During the late 1980s and early '90s, the collapse of CDC was frequently advanced as a cautionary example to business leaders tempted to believe their corporations had a role to play in solving social problems. By the turn of the century, however, memories of Norris and the Control Data Corporation had faded, and few business leaders today know much, if anything, about either. At the time of Norris's retirement, he told an interviewer that he "had accomplished maybe 10 percent of the work he plan[ned] to do in this world."[26] In fact, he was a burnout case; after his retirement, the world relegated Norris to an irrelevancy. At age ninety-five, he died in a suburban Minneapolis nursing home after a long struggle with Parkinson's disease.

Coda: A Story Much Too Sad to Be Told

Control Data has the distinction of being the sole example of a publicly traded corporation that failed as a consequence of its virtuous practices; however, it is not the only company to have suffered such a sad fate. In 2001, privately owned Malden Mills, a textile manufacturer located in Lawrence, Massachusetts, filed for bankruptcy when it was unable to pay its creditors. Six years earlier the company had made headlines after the largest fire in the state's history destroyed its three factory buildings. The company's CEO-owner, Aaron Feuerstein, then became something of a national hero when he rebuilt the facilities, rehired all his three thousand employees, and paid their full salaries during most of the period of reconstruction. During that time he paid those men and women some $25 million, in the process earning the endearing soubriquet "the Mensch of Malden."

Feuerstein's benevolent actions generated disbelief from his peers in the textile industry. They pointed to the hundred or so abandoned mills in the American Northeast that had either gone belly-up or moved operations to Southeast Asia to secure cheap labor. Like most informed businesspeople, they were certain there was no future for their industry in high-wage New England; thus, they counseled Feuerstein to cut his losses and reinvest the $300 million he was due in insurance money in more verdant pastures. But he was of a different mind: he told CBS's Morley Safer he had no intention of leaving his employees to fend for themselves, nor walking away from the economically devastated town. Citing the Torah as his ethical guide, he said he "felt a responsibility for all my employees to take care of them and give them jobs." So he borrowed heavily to build a modern worker- and eco-friendly mill in which he put his unionized employees back to work, making its signature product, Polartec.[27]

Alas, Polartec was not patented, and soon low-cost operators were undercutting the price Malden Mills needed to charge to cover costs. Then, after a couple of unusually warm winters reduced demand for the product, Feuerstein was left unable to service the $140 million in debt he had incurred during the rebuilding. His creditors took control of the company, pushed him out the door, laid off half the workforce, and by cutting other costs allowed the mills to limp along until making a final shipment in 2007. When Feuerstein was asked what words he would like engraved on his tombstone, he answered "He Done His Damnedest." In truth, there was nothing more he could have done. Out of principle, he had refused to read the handwriting that had been on the wall for decades: unionized American textile workers could not compete against cheap foreign labor.

About the time of Feuerstein's relatively unnoted death in 2015, the CEO of the arts and crafts company Etsy was axed when investors tired of his benevolent business practices. His successor CEO explained the reasoning behind the dismissal: "Being good doesn't cut the mustard."[28] That judgment would have made a fitting epitaph for Feuerstein, Norris, and a good number of other enlightened capitalists who failed to produce sufficient profits to keep the wolves of finance at bay.

12

Business Mavericks

KEN IVERSON (1925–2002),
ROBERT TOWNSEND (1920–1998),
HERB KELLEHER (1931–),
BILL GORE (1912–1986),
and TERRI KELLY (1963–)

While all the enlightened capitalists made a habit of swimming upstream, the business leaders profiled in this chapter earned reputations for being alpha salmon: they didn't simply buck the current of
established management practices, they discarded nearly every tenet
of received wisdom and rejected almost everything taught in business
schools. It is thus somewhat of an understatement to label the men profiled in this chapter as "mavericks," nor does the term do justice to the
sui generis way in which the first woman CEO to appear in these pages
is leading her company today. As the song goes, they did it their way.
Moreover, they did so without William Norris's maniacal tendency to
take good things to self-destructive extremes.

Ken Iverson, Man of Steel

During the 1980s and '90s, one of the world's most progressive companies was to be found, rather improbably, in one of the most outmoded

industries: steel. There is nothing glamorous about the pouring of molten metal. The work is hot, hard, dirty, and dangerous—and as bad as work in a steel mill can be, that is among the least significant reasons why the American steel industry appeared moribund in the late twentieth century. From the late nineteenth century through the mid-twentieth, things had been different in the industry. Back then, Big Steel was emblematic of the nation's rise as a global military and economic power, and Andrew Carnegie was widely viewed as the iconic industrial titan thanks to the millions of tons of steel, and millions of dollars of profit, his Pittsburgh-based Carnegie Steel (later US Steel) produced between 1880 and 1901. Yet by the late 1970s the steel industry had become better known for giving an unenviable name to a vast, depressed swath of middle America: the rust belt. Between 1960 and 1990, roughly half of American steelworkers lost their jobs permanently as the result of, among other factors, the failure to invest in new technologies, the rise of competition from nations with lower labor costs, poor labor relations that resulted in union demands for higher wages not matched by increases in productivity, bloated layers of management, and increasingly stringent environmental standards. Optimists during that era thought the industry might survive until the turn of the century; pessimists saw it already good as dead.

NUCOR

The company most responsible for the resuscitation of American steel production, Nucor, wasn't a significant player in the industry until well into the 1970s. In 1965 Nuclear Corporation, as it was then called, was an irrationally diversified conglomerate losing $400,000 on sales of $20 million. The company was an offshoot of the Reo Motor Car Company, founded by Ransom Olds in 1906 (his previous venture, Oldsmobile, had been acquired by General Motors). The Reo automobile was a brief success, but after that promising start the company struggled for well over half a century as successive generations of managers tried their hands at a smorgasbord of relatively unprofitable ventures. In 1955 Reo merged with the Nuclear Corporation of America, makers of nuclear-related medical devices and Geiger counters; then, in 1962, Nuclear acquired Vulcraft, a manufacturer of steel joists and girders that soon became the only profitable business in the firm's odd concatenation of companies.

The head of the Vulcraft division was Ken Iverson, a Cornell-educated engineer who stressed job safety and good working conditions in the plants he managed. Iverson's division proved so profitable that the company began to concentrate on the production of steel, changing its name to Nucor Corporation in 1978. Between 1965, when Iverson become Nucor's president, and 1995, when he retired, the company's return on invested capital was three times greater than at General Electric during the era when GE was headed by the legendary Jack Welch.[1] By 1998 Nucor had become America's largest steel company, with seven thousand employees and sales of $3.6 billion, widely recognized as the industry leader thanks to its use of new technologies, farsighted management practices, and impressive (if occasionally mixed) safety and environmental records. A great part of Nucor's success was attributable to the company's innovative use of electric-arc "mini-mills" that offered it numerous competitive advantages over the traditional integrated steel mills that employed energy-intensive blast-furnace technology. Mini-mills are roughly a tenth the size of integrated mills, require less capital to construct, are more flexible in terms of introducing new technologies, use cheap scrap metal instead of iron ore, and can be located close to their markets. In toto, mini-mills were far more efficient than Big Steel's giant traditional mills. Nonetheless, the person responsible for Nucor's adoption of mini-mills, Ken Iverson, contended that the company's comparative competitive advantage resulted more from its unusual corporate culture than from its technological edge: "It is 70% culture and 30% technology."[2]

RECIPROCAL FAIRNESS

Iverson, a self-described business maverick, consciously rejected the business-as-usual practices that had led to America's industrial decline in the late twentieth century, in their stead creating "an alternative set of assumptions and approaches for running a business."[3] Iverson was a thirty-seven-year-old engineer when he joined Nuclear in 1962, and was still a relatively inexperienced corporate manager when the company's board appointed him its president three years later. "I wasn't flattered," Iverson later explained. "No one else wanted the job. It was mine by default."[4]

When Iverson assumed leadership of the company, he was convinced that the only way it could succeed in the long term was to remain union-free. Seeking to avoid the fate of Big Steel, he decided to fight unionization fair and square, by making it in the self-interest of Nucor employees to reject union attempts to organize them. He thus introduced an employee-centered philosophy, one aspect of which was the principle of "reciprocal fairness": the company committed to profit sharing with employees during good times, and to "pain-sharing" when times were bad. Curiously, this arrangement was identical to the one the young Andrew Carnegie had proposed to his steelworker's union—a deal they accepted, and on which he later reneged. Much as had Carnegie's, Iverson's arrangement was soon put to the test. During the severe 1981–82 recession, the company's production was cut in half, leading Iverson to worry that Nucor would be the next American mill to fall silent. But unlike Carnegie, he did not respond by laying off workers; instead, he reduced their workweeks to three or four days, cutting their take-home pay by some 25 percent. That might have been seen as unfair had Nucor's managers not taken salary cuts of up to 40 percent; its officers, 60 percent; and Iverson himself 75 percent, his annual salary reduced to $110,000, making him the lowest-paid CEO on the Fortune 500 list. In stark contrast, that same year the CEO of Bethlehem Steel received a 37 percent raise even though the company's net income was down 59 percent, and it had lost $309 million and laid off scores of workers. The difference between the ways Nucor and Bethlehem shared the financial pain during that recession helps to explain why the former company went on to greater growth and profitability, while the latter, once the nation's second-largest steel producer, shrunk to the size of a pea before going bankrupt in 2001.

What saved Nucor—and allowed it to prosper over the next two decades—was Iverson's James Lincoln–esque commitment, in the words of one steel industry observer, to "get workers to identify their own interests fundamentally with those of management."[5] Iverson basically agreed with that assessment, although he took objection to its hint of paternalism, if not Machiavellianism: "That makes it sound like we tricked or manipulated employees into pushing their interest aside." Instead, Iverson said, "We've joined with our employees to pursue a goal we can *all* believe in: long-term survival. We run Nucor first and foremost to ensure that, a decade or two from now, there will still be a place for our children and grandchildren to work without being laid off. That is our higher cause."[6]

The means to achieving the company's goal of sustainable full employment was, in Iverson's reckoning, its "long-term perspective." Yet he denied that that focus was altruistic: "Our executives worry about profitability as much as those in any company." The basic reason why his competitors were not as successful as Nucor, he felt, was that they were too willing to satisfy the demands of Wall Street for short-term profit. Like James Lincoln, Iverson saw stock speculators as the major cause of mismanagement, not only in the steel industry but in corporate America in general. He argued that leaders of publicly traded corporations needed to choose which master to serve, "the investor or the speculator."[7] The duty of professional managers, he believed, was to reward patient investors with long-term growth in equity. More unusual than that belief (which many corporate leaders appear to share, at least in principle) was Iverson's willingness to express it before a group of stock analysts on Wall Street, in remarkably strong and plain language:

Many of you, with your short-term view of corporations, remind me of a guy on drugs. You want that quick fix, that high you get from a big spike in earnings. So you push us to take on more debt, capitalize start-up costs and interest, and slow down depreciation and write-offs. All you're thinking about is the short term. You don't want to think about the pain of withdrawal that our company will face later on if we do what you want. Well, Nucor isn't going to respond to that kind of thinking. We never have and we never will.[8]

And the company didn't. Nonetheless, during Iverson's tenure Nucor rewarded its long-term shareholders with a steady increase in the value of their stock. On Iverson's watch, Nucor's sales increased 150-fold, earnings grew from negative $2.2 million to positive $274.5 million, and stockholder equity increased from $760,000 to $3.8 billion (roughly 1,800 times).[9]

Freed from the enslaving need to produce quarterly results for speculators, Nucor's executives managed their company in unusual ways. When Iverson assumed its leadership, the company had been a traditionally structured hierarchy with a bloated headquarters staff and numerous layers of management separating the CEO from the front line. Iverson delayered the organization, reducing it to four levels of management, with only twenty-two people in the company's headquarters. Relatedly, it became highly decentralized, with twenty-one independently operated businesses—each having its own marketing strategy, buying its own raw materials, serving its own customer base, setting its own production quotas, and hiring, training, and managing its own workforce. The managers of those businesses were simply required to generate at least a 25 percent return on the assets they controlled, to abide by common ethical standards, and to follow a few general rules that they collectively set for themselves; otherwise, they were free to operate as they saw fit.

The autonomy enjoyed by Nucor's divisions was extreme by the standards of most corporations. Iverson tells the story of the general manager of a division in South Carolina who decided to expand his scrap-metal-melting operations by using induction furnaces instead of the arc furnaces used in Nucor's other units. Although they weren't certain about it, most of the company's managers thought their Carolinian colleague was making a mistake, and offered him reasons for their misgivings. Nonetheless, the company gave the manager the $10 million he needed to install the furnaces. After all, it was his call. Later, when it became clear that the new mills hadn't worked as intended, the decision was made to remove them. Significantly, *that* decision also was made locally, by the same Carolina manager. Iverson explained, "So we live with it, good and bad." A division manager put it more positively: "We are honest-to-god autonomous."

Yet Nucor was clearly a single company, with a strong common culture and shared values. What kept the company from flying apart due to the centrifugal forces of autonomy was a process of continual and candid communication. Three times a year all the company's officers and division managers came together to shape the policies of Nucor as a whole. The meetings were designed to facilitate open discussion between the managers, and to give them an opportunity to tell executives at headquarters what was on their minds. The rule of thumb was to speak up and speak honestly. "There's a healthy tension to these meetings, too," Iverson explained. "People yell. They wave their arms around and pound on tables. . . . Put that many confident, headstrong personalities in a room together and sparks are bound to fly. I think that's a good thing. In fact, I worry when the sparks *don't* fly."[10]

A steady stream of new ideas emerged from those meetings. In addition to ideas for continuous technological improvement, managers shared their best organizational practices with their peers and, based on their own experiences, offered suggestions to those who were encountering human and technical problems. Several unique and effective practices evolved out of those free exchanges of ideas, among which was a decision not to have central R&D and engineering departments.

Instead, the goal was for each unit constantly to experiment with new things, then share their learnings with the others. (By Iverson's reckoning, roughly half of Nucor's investments in new ideas and technologies yielded positive results.) If each division was to function as an experimental laboratory, it was necessary to keep them small. Each had no more than four to five hundred employees, following the example of W. L. Gore & Associates, which—as we will see later in this chapter—Iverson acknowledged as the model for much of what Nucor attempted to do.

SMALL-TOWN BIAS

Again building on the Gore example, Nucor's facilities were widely dispersed geographically to enhance their autonomy. Additionally, to generate a sense of community, they were located in small towns or rural areas. Iverson, like Robert Wood Johnson, believed that people in small towns are more likely to know one another off the job than are those in big cities, and hence more willing to engage in mutual help and, as in the 1980s recession, mutual pain-sharing. Iverson himself had been a small-town boy, growing up in Downers Grove, Illinois, not far from the farm on which his mother was raised. His paternal grandfather was a Yellowstone lumberman, and Iverson's family had spent their summers in the Big Sky region of Montana. He obviously had a small-town bias, but it was a bias with factual validity: it is worth noting that the lion's share of high-performing divisions of the manufacturing companies reviewed in this book were located in small towns or rural areas, and few had more than five hundred workers.

Stanford University economist Kathryn Shaw has examined the managerial practices at mini-mills organized à la Nucor; a key to their productivity, she has found, is the amount and frequency of communication between workers, and between workers and managers. Unlike employees in traditional mega-mills, those in mini-mills stay on the job after their shifts have ended to interact with workers on the next shift, thus facilitating effective transfer of experience and knowledge.[11] When a Nucor manager was asked by a Canadian researcher what the biggest problem was in his plant, he replied that he couldn't think of any major issues. When pushed to cite a problem, he offered this surprising answer:

> The second shift ends at midnight and everybody goes home. What happens is that there are a couple of groups of employees that go out and stay in the parking lot at midnight. After everybody leaves, they'll sneak back in and they keep working. They are off the clock and not getting paid. What they are doing is building up their parts pool, and this makes their bonus higher. I have told their supervisors that this fouls up our bonus calculation. Now the supervisors and I pretend to be leaving and, when these guys try to come back, we run them off.[12]

It is the rare manufacturing facility in which the biggest problem is people working overtime without pay, but there are many such stories at Nucor. One employee told the Canadian researcher that he knew a team of employees who put in extra work to cover for a team member whose productivity had fallen off badly as the result of a painful divorce. More remarkable was another Nucor team that demanded the firing of a relatively new hire because he didn't "pull his weight" on the job and had nearly caused an accident that could have seriously hurt them. When the supervisor refused the request on grounds that the worker was entitled to a full ninety-day trial in which to prove himself, the team reluctantly agreed to grant the additional time. But at the end of the new worker's allotted three-month trial, the team returned with the same demand for termination, to which the supervisor acceded. One team member was overheard complaining, "Damn old Nucor management; they drag their feet and finally have done something we told them to do three months ago. . . . Now, they better get us someone who can really work with us, someone who really wants to work."[13]

Nucor's small-town workers' strong ties to their local communities led to a desire to make their mills behave as good citizens. By their very nature, the modern technologies employed at Nucor's mini-mills were far less energy-intensive and environmentally damaging than methods used at traditional mills (Nucor was essentially in the recycling business). In addition, Nucor appears to have made unusual efforts to limit the negative effects of production on the environment of its host communities. Nevertheless, several environmental problems surfaced after Iverson's tenure that had their genesis on his watch. For example, years after Nucor had sold off an Arizona subsidiary, that state filed a pollution claim against the company. Significantly, Nucor promptly agreed to a settlement. Sam Siegel, the company's finance chief, explained Nucor's unusual reaction to what many companies would have seen as an unfair regulatory ruling: "We believed it was better to furnish funds to the State to help them take care of the problem rather than (like most companies) spend funds for attorneys and consultants."[14]

The company has been ranked among the best in its industry for employee safety, although there, too, its record has had blemishes. In 1991 the *Wall Street Journal* ran a story claiming that Nucor's employee accident and death rates were highest in its industry: between 1980 and 1990, three of the company's steelworkers died as the result of on-the-job accidents, and seven others were killed in trucking accidents and while constructing Nucor facilities. Because of the way statistics are kept, it is unclear how the company's industrial safety record actually ranked, but to its credit, the company's head of personnel publicly owned up to the problem, admitting that "one fatality is unacceptable. We've had ten and we are working on it." Subsequently Nucor seemed to make every effort to improve worker safety.[15]

Community relations were a major concern—and challenge—for Iverson during his lengthy Nucor career. When he became manager of a mill in a small southern town in the mid-1960s, he was forced to deal with the racial segregation pervasive in the region. He writes that it was relatively easy to end the practice of separate Christmas parties for black and white Nucor workers, and to tear down the wall separating the white from black locker rooms, but changing deeply ingrained racial attitudes was a more difficult matter. He attempted to deal with it directly, but because he was a northerner, white employees resented his efforts, and they led nowhere. Then, instead of dealing with racial discrimination head-on, Iverson switched tactics and worked to create an egalitarian culture in his division. He began by eliminating invidious distinctions between management and labor, doing away with such executive perks as a private lunchroom, reserved parking spaces, company-paid limos, and country club memberships. Everywhere he looked, he found hierarchical class distinctions, down to the wide range of colors of the hard hats every worker in a steel mill must wear (naturally, gold helmets were at the top of the pecking order). Iverson ruled that, henceforth, all helmets would be white. Most important, he introduced merit-based hiring and promotion and objective measures of performance evaluation. By thus stressing egalitarian meritocracy across the board, he gradually changed the culture of the company, eventually even with regard to race.

AN ETHICAL CULTURE

Iverson stressed the importance of treating all workers with respect. He saw that as central to Nucor's culture of fair play: "Each day we all face situations that require us to exercise our own moral judgement. . . . We want to do what is equitable and right because we strive to be ethical people and to treat each other fairly."[16] Nonetheless, he was a realist:

> The world of business is loaded with temptations. There are so many ways to cut corners that seem to offer such easy roads to whatever you may want [that] your conscience can be overwhelmed by that mighty tag team, the ego and the id. In fact, all the primary rewards in business—prestige, power, money— appeal to our base cravings. The whole system is designed to fuel

the fires of temptation. And while there are many good people in business, there are precious few saints. For all these reasons and more, behaving ethically in business can be very hard work. But it is work you *must* take on.[17]

Iverson cited his family upbringing and small-town background as the sources of his ethical, human-centered management philosophy. "Once, my older brother took coupons for a free ice cream cone from every newspaper in the neighborhood," he wrote. While it was doubtful any of those neighbors would either have noticed or cared, Iverson's father told his son to take them back. More than that, he was told to knock on the neighbors' doors, explain to them what he had done, and apologize. Iverson says the early impression made by that lesson—rather than religious teachings—informed his decision to create an ethical corporate culture based on fairness, equity, honesty, and respect. The company's ethical commitments extended to all its constituencies. Shareholders were assured that they could trust the accuracy of the financial results the company published, and that it would never distort earnings or put a "spin" on the numbers. Iverson and Siegel reduced the company's financial statements to four simple and easily comprehensible pages. Nucor promised customers that the prices it published were the same for everyone, and that it would never offer discounts, nor would a member of its sales force "take you to dinner" or "offer you a ride on his ore boat."[18] To the broader society, Nucor pledged not to hire lobbyists, make political contributions, participate in PACs, or accept government subsidies.[19]

The rule of thumb at Nucor was "Tell employees everything." Since its workers were essentially self-managing, they needed access to all managerial data if they were going to be held responsible—and subsequently rewarded—for controlling costs and increasing productivity. Iverson's successor, John Correnti, explained the risks involved in that commitment to transparency: "Obviously some of the information we share flows to the street. . . . But the value of sharing everything with our employees is much greater than any downside there might be to some information getting out. It hasn't hurt us through 27 years of profitable growth in an industry that hasn't consistently done well."[20]

One way Nucor demonstrated respect for employees was to involve them directly in decisions affecting their work. All the company's production workers were organized into self-managing teams, then left free to organize their own tasks, even making decisions about the technology they used. Workers at all levels were encouraged to innovate, and rewarded for doing so. In 1995, at the end of Iverson's tenure, the average production worker earned $60,000 per year, much of that in the form of weekly bonuses amounting to 100–200 percent of base pay. In addition, workers were eligible for profit sharing, while managers and executives were not. In all, Nucor workers were the highest paid in their industry, including unionized workers; a few of its most productive workers earned more than their supervisors. Their annual income placed them—many of whom had no more than a high-school education—among the world's highest-paid blue-collar workers, albeit a bit behind Lincoln Electric's manufacturing employees.

The company also offered generous scholarships to the children of employees, applicable for either four years of higher education or post-high-school vocational training. When the scholarship program was introduced in 1974, only seventy-six children of Nucor employees were attending college; twenty years later, over six hundred were enrolled.[21] The meritocratic ethos of the company showed respect to production workers, which encouraged them to rise into the ranks of management, regardless of the level of their education. As in other companies reviewed in these pages, the development of the skills of Nucor's workforce was a high priority that, in Iverson's words, meant "shaping a work environment that stimulates people to explore their own potential."[22] As at Herman Miller, Nucor employees had clearly defined rights, including the right to be treated fairly, the right to appeal if they felt unfairly treated, the right to their jobs (if they did them properly), and the right to earn according to their productivity. A high degree of managerial trust in employees was evidenced by the absence of time clocks, job descriptions, and performance appraisals.

What differentiated Nucor's human resources practices from most of the other companies in this book was the absence of significant employee stock ownership. Although the company often awarded shares of its stock as bonuses, regularly gave each employee five shares of stock for every five years of service, and contributed 10 percent of the purchase price of Nucor stock, the bulk of employee compensation came in the forms of salary, gainsharing, cash bonuses, and a company-funded retirement plan. Given Iverson's chronic and deep distrust of the stock market, it is not surprising he chose not to reward employees by making them overly invested in Nucor stock. He summarized what he called Nucor's "Higher Cause" by saying, "At Nucor, people get what they *ought* to get from their work: Good pay. Real job security. Interesting challenges. Respectful treatment. The chance to accomplish something every day. A fair and equitable workplace. The pride of being a part of a very successful enterprise."[23]

AFTER IVERSON

By all accounts, Iverson made good on that pledge; moreover, his enlightened policies appear largely to have been sustained by his successor CEOs. (Iverson was forced to retire in 1995 due to chronic ill health. He died in 2002.) The most significant blot on the company's record occurred five years after he had stepped down from the company's leadership. In 2000, Nucor paid the US government $95 million to resolve allegations that it had failed to adequately control emissions of toxic chemicals at several of its mills. If Iverson had a blind spot, it was with regard to air and water pollution; doubtless he should have been more attentive to those issues. In his otherwise enlightening and inspirational book, *Plain Talk: Lessons from a Business Maverick*, he fails to mention any real environmental concerns. The good news is that after the settlement with the government, Nucor appears to have become a leader in environmental performance. In 2013 the company—now the nation's largest steel producer, with some twenty thousand employees—not only touted its record of never having laid off an employee during bad financial times but also proudly proclaimed, "We are cultural and environmental stewards."

Beginning in the middle of the first decade of this century, Nucor's leaders found themselves in the news as critics of US trade policy on steel imports. In particular, the company's executives have accused China of "dumping" steel at below cost. The Chinese government, which owns some 80 percent of that country's steel manufacturing capacity, appears to subsidize its state-owned mills to provide jobs for its workers. That subsidized steel finds its way into American markets, where it drives the price of steel well below the cost of production at Nucor and other American steel companies. Hence, Nucor's executives have claimed that if the US government doesn't actively enforce anti-dumping laws, including tariffs, the company will not be able to sustain its enlightened labor practices. Indeed, American steel companies might even be driven completely out of business.

That threat appears to have triggered President Donald Trump's 2018 threatened trade war with China. Ken Iverson, who had pledged that Nucor would not engage in government lobbying, might well have been dismayed to see the company's current CEO, John Ferriola, sitting beside the president and cheering him on when he announced the imposition of tariffs on foreign steel—even though Nucor has been relatively unaffected by foreign imports, reporting pretax profits of $1.75 billion in 2017, up 35 percent from the previous year.[24] Prior to Ferriola, every leader cited in these pages, beginning with Robert Owen, had been an advocate of free trade. Of course, Nucor's executives continued to say that they favored free trade, but only on "a level playing field," and thus, because of "dumping," they had no choice but to petition the government for protection. Taking them at their word that they were being harmed by cheap imports, perhaps they might have had more options had Iverson been a proponent of employee stock ownership. If Nucor's workers had a greater ownership stake in the company, they might have had more incentives to find competitive ways to meet the Chinese challenge. Nucor's executives also might have been able to better ignore the Wall Street investors demanding more profits if they, their workers, and retirees owned a controlling block of company stock.

Ken Iverson had his critics on Wall Street, in the steel industry, and in the labor union movement. Anyone as inclined as he to publicly offer irreverent and contrarian opinions was bound to invite detractors. He once said, "My goal is to make the right decision sixty percent of the time." In the evaluation of many business experts, he fared far better than that. Leadership scholar Warren Bennis recalled that he had "written a half-dozen books about Ken Iverson" before he realized he was writing about him! "Ken," he wrote, "is in many ways the leader I've portrayed in the abstract, here in the flesh."[25]

Bob Townsend, Executive Funnyman

Another of Bennis's favorite business leaders, Bob Townsend, was every bit as much of a maverick as Iverson. In the 1960s, Hertz dominated the auto rental business in the commanding way that US Steel had ruled its industry. Then things suddenly changed: as US Steel's preeminence was usurped by mini-mills, Hertz's lead was similarly challenged—albeit by little more than a mere advertising slogan. Circa 1963, the upstart car rental firm Avis boldly proclaimed on radio, television, and in magazine and newspaper ads, "We're Only #2, But We Try Harder." The phrase "We try harder" caught on, and soon most American adults were familiar with it, often appropriating the phrase for use in their own business and personal situations. If Bob Townsend is remembered for nothing else, history records that he coined that unforgettable commercial slogan when he led Avis.

Townsend also deserves to be remembered for other, and far more important, contributions. His 1969 bestseller *Up the Organization:*

How to Stop the Corporation from Stifling People and Strangling Profits was the first shot in what would become a revolution in the way large organizations are managed. In that slim volume, Townsend challenged decades of corporate shibboleths, while irreverently slaying dozens of business sacred cows. *Harper's Magazine* called it "the sagest (and even most outrageous) book ever written about how business should be run." In it, Townsend bashed bureaucracy, hierarchy, rule-based management, and executive privilege, among other things. His courageous stances—both in the book and as a business leader—would over the next five decades lead to a radical rethinking of the roles that corporate executives and board members play.

Robert Chase Townsend was an unlikely candidate for the part of establishment scourge. He was born into a life of privilege, went to the Lawrenceville prep school and Princeton, and in his salad days enjoyed the good life as part of the Long Island sailing set. Yet, as his son Tuna wrote after his father's death, Bob Townsend "would always evince some ambivalence about growing up in advantaged surroundings; he exhibited an egalitarian streak and resented any displays of ostentation, nepotism, or elitism. He was quoted as saying, 'Too much inherited money is a birth defect.'"[26] Nonetheless, Townsend pursued a conventional career as a Wall Street securities analyst while studying for an MBA at night at Columbia University. Along the way, he married Joan Tours, who, throughout a long and happy marriage, he always referred to as "Saint Joan." In 1950 he went to work for American Express, where, so he claimed, for the next fifteen years he learned how *not* to run a corporation. He did, however, learn a few useful things about the rental car business when he managed an American Express joint venture with Hertz, which successfully transformed the latter into a global company. He called that two-year project "Operation Mars," because it required him to be on the road so much he "might as well be on a trip to Mars."

In the early 1960s the legendary André Meyer of Lazard Frères hired Townsend to head the then moribund Avis rent-a-car company, telling him he would be paid $50,000 annually (about $500,000 in current dollars). Characteristically, Townsend replied, "No I won't. As an about-to-be-substantial stockholder I insist the President be paid $36,000 because that's the top salary for a company that [has] never earned a nickel for its stockholders."[27] Worse, overpaying him would be "defeating my crusade for a just compensation system" based on merit.

At Avis, Bob Townsend became one of the first American corporate chieftains to put into practice what, fifty years later, is now being widely advocated with regard to executive perks: no reserved parking spaces, no executive dining rooms and washrooms, no company planes, no golf club memberships or yacht clubs, no chauffeur-driven cars, and no fancy offices or other invidious privileges. On the positive side, he introduced stock options (never backdated) for every employee, generous rewards for performance, authentic delegation of authority, "honesty as the only policy," the encouragement of healthy dissent, commitment to product (service) quality, and above all, the virtue of putting customers first. More than anything, Townsend hated bureaucracy and bloated central-headquarters staffs, famously demanding "Fire the Personnel Department." Ditto the law, purchasing, advertising, and PR departments! He was opposed to staffs headed by "VPs of," believing that such supernumeraries not only produced little at great expense but often put obstacles in the way of operating employees, who in fact added true value to a company. Similarly, he railed against unproductive boards: "Directors are usually the friends of the chief executive put there to keep him safely in office." Never able to resist an opportunity to poke a finger in the eye of the indolently powerful, he added, "Be sure to serve cocktails and a heavy lunch before the [board] meeting. At least one of the older directors will fall asleep (literally) at the meeting and the consequent embarrassment will make everyone eager to get the whole mess over as soon as possible."[28] In a serious vein, he actively resisted Wall Street pressures for short-term profits, instead reinvesting heavily for Avis's long haul. When he initially accepted André Meyer's job offer, Townsend did so on the condition that they would not mention the stock price for two years. And he did all that more than a decade before Ken Iverson would take similar actions at Nucor.

GUERRILLA WARFARE

Townsend argued that symbolic organizational "guerrilla warfare" was necessary to awaken the "walking dead" who constituted much of the American corporate workforce from the executive suite down to the mailroom:

> They are docile, they are bored, and they are dull. Trapped in the pigeonholes of organization charts, they've been made slaves to the rules of private and public hierarchies that run mindlessly on and on because nobody can change them.
>
> So we've become a nation of office boys. Monster corporations like General Motors and monster agencies like the Defense Department have grown like cancer until they take up nearly all the living work-space. Like clergymen in Anthony Trollope's day, we're but mortals trained to serve immortal institutions.[29]

Townsend could have been more politic in his choice of words, but he admittedly didn't care what people thought about him personally; what he cared about was creating organizations that were profitable, ethical, and exciting places to work. He sought to improve people's lives by involving and energizing them in the process of creating better futures for their companies. Based on his experience as an employee at American Express, and later as head of Avis, he created "a survival manual for successful corporate guerrillas . . . a book about how institutions—groups of people working together for a common purpose—*ought* to conduct themselves."[30] In a nutshell, he sought to improve the lives of employed Americans by giving managers guidance on how to change their organizations, and the courage to act on their convictions. His advice, invariably delivered with great humor, was always practical: "Before you hire a computer specialist, make it a condition that he spend some time in the factory and then sell your shoes to the customers. A month the first year, two weeks a year there-after. This indignity will separate those who want to use their skills to help your company from those who just want to build their know-how on your payroll."[31]

While at Avis, Townsend established a course to train the red-jacketed front-line agents who staffed the company's rental desks. It was taught by employees themselves, women who had proved the company's best at providing customer service. "It was a tough school, at O'Hare airport, with an exam every night. I made the whole man-agement go through it; it was an absolute condition of employment. We had to study and we had to spend two or three hours renting cars at the airport."[32] Parenthetically Townsend added, "I once saw the Ph.D. who was responsible for all Avis systems panic and run from an O'Hare rental counter at the approach of his first real customer."[33] Townsend took the course himself, finding the front-line job embar-rassingly hard to do well: "I tell you when we got back to headquarters we were so proud of those ladies out there on the firing line and the difficult job that they were doing that we started wearing red jackets in the executive office as a sign that we were part of their team." After Bob's death, the editor of *Up the Organization*, the renowned Robert Gottlieb, concluded, "I believe the secret of the book's success was that everything Bob said and advised exactly reflected the way he be-haved."[34]

Townsend's bottom line was the degree to which the organization he led treated all its constituents justly and fairly. He called corporate secrecy "a child's garden of diseases. . . . It defeats the crusade for jus-tice, which doesn't flourish in the dark."[35] Yet Townsend admitted that it was hard for a leader always to do the right thing, so he anointed the equivalent of a king's jester at Avis, whom he empowered to adamantly remind him whenever he was going astray. He modeled the role on an assistant to Billy Graham "who yells 'Horseshit'—however you say that in Baptist—at him whenever he takes himself too seriously."[36]

Townsend believed that the only excuse for having large organizations is that they provide opportunity for everyone in them to grow in their jobs. Like Ken Iverson, he did what he could to keep Avis from becoming unionized on the grounds that unions hinder the kind of development opportunities he hoped the company would provide its workers. Unionism "has deteriorated into a kind of industrial police force that also sells insurance," he concluded, believing that the best way to avoid unionization was to give his people the "chance to realize their potential (and get recognition for their contribution) in helping the company reach its objectives."[37]

Skeptics at the time claimed that Townsend's humanistic philosophy of management was impractical and counter to the profit-maximizing purpose of corporate capitalism. Yet Townsend's record at Avis indicates otherwise: in the thirteen years prior to his arrival in 1962, the company had never made a profit. When he left three years later, annual sales had increased from $30 million to $60 million, and Avis had posted $5 million in profits while investing heavily to provide for future growth. Townsend had turned that trick without laying off employees, adding only two executives from the outside, and growing the company without benefit of acquisitions. Avis's financial record was so impressive that the company attracted the attention of Harold Geneen, whose giant conglomerate ITT was actively on the prowl for promising companies to acquire. Geneen made an offer for the company that proved too generous for Avis stockholders to refuse, and presto, Avis was a part of ITT's unfathomably diverse portfolio of businesses. Geneen, who prided himself on being the world's most effective (and toughest) manager, immediately introduced his patented management-by-the-numbers practices at Avis, thus prompting Townsend to clean out his desk and look for his next opportunity to transform a company.

Townsend was only forty-five at the time, and other corporations might well have been expected to immediately vie for the services of an executive with such an impressive turnaround record. But such offers never came: the author of *Up the Organization* was viewed either as a madman or a pariah in the nation's boardrooms. Instead, he embarked on a decade of helping troubled small and midsize companies to transform themselves into profitable human-centered enterprises. His influence spread as he became a regular on the "rubber chicken" lecture circuit and on nighttime television: after an appearance on the *Tonight Show* in which he flippantly criticized the management of RCA, owners of NBC, he was effectively banned from further engagements on that network.

A SECOND LIFE

In 1974 Bob and Joan moved to California with an eye toward retirement, briefly living on a sailboat moored in Marina del Rey. A few years later their daughter Claire, an executive at 20th Century-Fox, introduced her dad to Alan Ladd Jr., the studio's head. Ladd then coaxed Bob to become, in effect, his corporate court jester, assigning him to keep the hands of the "suits and bean counters" off the creative process of filmmaking. In the 1980s Townsend served on the board of a few midsize companies, and in 1991 he asked me if I would be interested in serving with him on the board of Radica, a small electronic-games manufacturer about to have its initial public offering. The first thing he told me about the company was that it was "clean," and he would work to keep it that way—nonetheless, he added, we should both be ready to resign at the first sign of unethical behavior. The second thing he mentioned was that the company's CEO, Bob Davids, wanted to create the kind of organization described in *Up the Organization*.

Davids would later recall that Townsend "was an invaluable asset on the board; although he was not chairman, he was the natural soul of the group and set the tone. He forbade anyone to mention "the 'S word'—stock price."[38] Townsend mentored Davids, helping him to develop his leadership skills and to implement many of the progressive practices that Townsend advocated. Over the nearly nine years that Townsend served on the Radica board and Davids led the company as its CEO, it practiced almost everything that Townsend advocated. However, once the two Bobs were out of the picture, Radica's board quickly became dominated by finance-oriented men who sought to "dress up" the company's books with an eye toward selling it to a large toy company, and in the process, the legacy of the Bobs wilted faster than a prom corsage. Radica was soon acquired by Mattel, where it subsequently disappeared.

Bob Townsend did not live to witness the sad denouement of the once-promising Radica story. A few years earlier, he and Saint Joan had gone on their annual Caribbean sailing trip. One balmy night, while Bob was swapping fish tales with the ship's captain, he suddenly closed his eyes and peacefully passed away. He knew how to finish a great story.

Bob had never retired fully, having spent his last decades as an adviser or board member at several small companies. Given the fates of Avis and Radica, one might be tempted to conclude that he had failed in his mission to change the corporate world. Yet in fact he influenced the leaders of many companies, including Chaparral Steel, a mini-mill competitor of Nucor, whose CEO, Gordon Forward, practiced Townsendian "management by adultery"—that is, treating employees like adults by encouraging them to be self-managing. (Forward offered mini-sabbaticals to blue-collar front-line workers who wanted to travel out of state and out of country to study best practices at other manufacturing facilities.) In Paris in the 1980s, Jacques Raiman was CEO of GSI Corporation, a computer company that practiced very un-French bureaucracy bashing and employee involvement. When asked where he had learned to lead in such a non-Gallic mode, Raiman was known to reach into his pocket and pull out a dog-eared copy of *Up the Organization*. In 2007 Warren Bennis summed up Townsend's contribution by pointing out that the practices Bob advocated had gained more adherents and robustness over the years with a new vocabulary of "HR talk" like empowerment, transparency, agency, and so forth. And there are more enlightened and emboldened leaders and scholars making some headway toward creating cultures of growth and learning. But it will always be a struggle. And we need, *seriously* need, more Bob Townsends. More leaders and scholars who make us nervous with their ideas, who bother us, bother the hell out of us. . . . Bob Townsend was one helluva botherer, always reminding us of what's important. Unlike those other ephemeral botherers of the Sixties, his songs live on and on.[39]

Bennis wasn't the only management expert to extol Bob Townsend's practices. On reading *Up the Organization*, Tom Peters wrote, "Townsend shouldn't just be read, he should be memorized."

Herb Kelleher: A Wee Nip of Wild Turkey at Forty Thousand Feet

In 1967, Rollin King saw the future of the airline industry, and thought he could make it work in Texas. He had taken a flight on Pacific Southwest Airways (PSA), which then served the San Francisco, Burbank, and San Diego airports. Every Californian of a certain age remembers PSA as Poor Students' Airline because it offered cheap, no-frills discount flights that even impecunious undergrads could afford (in 1959 I flew PSA from San Francisco to L.A. for $9.99). Duly impressed by PSA's informal flight crews (they joked with passengers), its daringly attired stewardesses (as they were then called), and its ease of ticketing (flight tickets were simple cash-register receipts), King wanted an airline just like that for his home state, so he asked his lawyer to apply for the necessary permits to start one to serve Houston, Dallas, and San Antonio. The lawyer, Herb Kelleher, told King he thought the idea

was crazy—quickly adding that he wanted to invest $20,000 in the
new business. King put up about $130,000, and assumed that he soon
would own an airline. King understood that discounting interstate air-
fares was prohibited by federal law at the time, but because the feds had
no authority over intrastate carriers such as PSA, he was confident that
creating a Texas-only airline was well within reach. Theoretically he
was right, but the world of commerce seldom conforms to theory—and
that's why businesspeople need lawyers.

Irish American Herb Kelleher was an unusual kind of lawyer—a
chain-smoking, whiskey-swilling, charming, folksy risk-taker. After
earning an undergraduate degree in English from Wesleyan, followed
by a JD from NYU, he shucked his proper Back East ways and headed
west to Texas, where he quickly earned a reputation as a corporate lawyer willing to take on cases others in his profession rejected as losing
propositions. The process of getting the necessary approvals for King's
airline was just such a case. The established airlines pulled out all the
available legal, regulatory, and legislative stops to prevent the launch
of a discount competitor they feared would drive down their profits,
if not drive them out of business. Years later, King called those acts "a
perversion of what America is supposed to be about."[40] But at the time,
he was so discouraged by the amount of energy, legal talent, and money
that big airlines were willing to invest to kill his nascent dream, he confessed to Kelleher that it might make sense to throw in the towel. But
quit wasn't a word in Herb Kelleher's vocabulary. Energized by the prospect of a battle royal and appalled by the anticompetitive tactics of the
big airlines, Kelleher told Rollin that he would take on the fight without
charge—a rare concession from a corporate lawyer. Four years, several
higher-court rulings, and God only knows how many unbilled hours
later, Kelleher won final approval to proceed with Rollin King's airline.
King then surprised Kelleher by asking him to become the founding
chief executive of Southwest Airlines (SWA), naming himself its executive vice president.

SOUTHWEST TAKES OFF

In 1971 SWA began flying passengers from Houston, its corporate headquarters, to Dallas and San Antonio, copying every innovation introduced by PSA—with the exception of its profitability. Southwest lost money during the first two years of operation, at one point down to only $148 in the till. But by 1973 SWA was running in the black, and it has stayed there ever since. Moreover, in subsequent years Southwest improved greatly on PSA's no-frills: SWA uses just one type of airplane (the Boeing 737), has a user-friendly reservation system, and operates in accordance with the simple philosophy of putting employees first, customers second, and shareholders third. In other words, Kelleher believed that if SWA served the needs of its employees, they would then take good care of passengers, who in turn would become satisfied repeat customers, thus providing profit for the airline's shareholders.

Kelleher became known for his fervent commitment to the belief that SWA's success hinged completely on the performance of its employees, one of the first of whom was his former legal secretary, Colleen Barrett. Briefly serving in a variety of positions, Barrett ultimately became the company's long-term head of customer service, and later its president. Because customer service was the prime responsibility of the airline's employees, Barrett's job became the linchpin of SWA's success. Over her forty years at the airline she became the "keeper of the culture," known informally as its "corporate mom." As Barrett explains,

> We've talked to our employees from day one about being one big family. If you stop and think about it for even 20 seconds, the things we do are the same things that you would do with your own family. We try to acknowledge and react to any significant event in our brothers' or sisters' lives, whether it's work-related or personal. We do the traditional things like sending birthday cards or cards on the anniversary of their date of hire. But if employees

have a child who is sick or a death in the family, we do our best to acknowledge it. We celebrate with our employees when good things happen, and we grieve with them when they experience something devastating.[41]

And celebrate they did. Actually, they partied at every possible opportunity: hot dogs and beer to mark milestones, and big shindigs like the annual Halloween party where every employee—including top executives—came dressed in zany costumes. In the past, passenger parties even broke out on airplanes (the Los Angeles–Las Vegas route was known for its Friday-night bashes). Herb Kelleher was SWA's party animal in chief, inevitably pictured with a glass of Wild Turkey whiskey in one hand and a cigarette in the other. Kelleher believed in turning everything into an excuse for having fun—even lawsuits. In 1992, when Stevens Aviation sued the company for trademark infringement of its motto "Just Plane Smart," Kelleher responded by challenging Stevens's CEO to an arm-wrestling match in a Dallas arena. Kelleher then made a promotional video showing him training for the "Malice in Dallas" event by doing sit-ups, with—naturally—a cigarette in one hand and a glass of whiskey in the other.

Fun and games aside, Southwest's treatment of its employees has been exemplary by any standard. They have been the highest paid in the airline industry, earning 25 to 40 percent more per annum than their peers. For example, in 2006 Southwest pilots earned $186 per hour (taking home, on average, $171,000 per year), while their counterparts at United Airlines were paid $131 per hour.[42] That was particularly remarkable because Southwest flights were considerably less expensive than those of competitor airlines. The explanation for that phenomenon was that Southwest was better managed than United, Delta, American, and most other major airlines. As at Lincoln Electric, Southwest's leaders understood the difference between unit labor costs and total labor costs: at United, the goal was to keep unit labor costs (what workers are paid per hour) as low as possible, whereas at Southwest the goal was to keep total labor costs (the sum of all the wages and benefits paid to its workforce) as low as possible. The result was that Southwest's cost of doing business was lower than United's, even though United paid lower hourly wages. Southwest's advantage was higher productivity: its employees worked more efficiently, more effectively, and often harder than their counterparts at United and elsewhere. The better scheduling of pilots at Southwest allowed the company to pay them for actually working, not for time on the ground, as was often the case at United. Moreover, flight crews at Southwest helped ground crews to clean planes, thus reducing the time needed to ready a plane for its next flight, which meant more revenue-generating time in the air for SWA's fleet. All that was true despite the fact that most Southwest employees, like their counterparts at United and other airlines, were unionized.

Southwest employees made extra efforts to increase customer satisfaction and improve productivity largely because it was in their self-interest: senior flight attendants earned as much as twice the annual take-home pay of United's attendants. Moreover, they benefited from a generous profit-sharing plan, most of it paid in company stock. In 2006 a number of active flight attendants each owned Southwest stock valued at over $1 million. One of those attendants, Linda Pinker, told a reporter that one consequence of such ownership was that "you have a tendency to work a little harder."[43] Another result: Southwest employees did not demand the restrictive work rules which limited the ability of their counterparts at other unionized airlines to pitch in and help others do whatever was needed to get a plane in the air on time.

CULTURE COMMITTEES

But money was not the sole motivator at Southwest. There was also a high degree of employee involvement in management. Instead of controlling employee behavior through rules and formal structure, Southwest facilitated communication, coordination, and change through employee participation on cross-functional committees, the most unusual of which was its company-wide culture committee, buttressed by local culture committees at all SWA locations. The purpose of these committees was to find better ways to put the company's stated values into practice, and to identify practices in need of improvement. The committees were not only charged with identifying problems but empowered to form teams to develop solutions. For example, one team addressed the problem of employee burnout among those with long tenure at the company.

Consistent with Barrett's focus on SWA as "family," current CEO Gary Kelly describes the essence of the company's culture as "taking care of each other," which, he says, requires three things of every employee: working hard, treating people with respect, and having a positive attitude. All of those, he adds, involve practicing the Golden Rule. Of course, not everyone is game for Kumbaya in the workplace, and that is why SWA has been highly selective in its hiring practices, looking for people who are cheerful, positive, and with a customer-oriented attitude. Since the company figures that it is harder to find such individuals than it is to train them to be flight attendants or ticket agents, SWA's recruitment strategy is to "hire for attitude; train for skills."

However, it was not always thus. In the early days, Kelleher and King copied PSA's practice of hiring attractive young "stewardesses" and putting them in uniforms featuring orange hot pants and vinyl go-go boots, adopting PSA's "Long Legs and Short Nights" theme, and retaining the services of the person who recruited stewardesses for Hugh Hefner's airline. In 1981 Southwest was sued successfully for its practice of hiring only women flight attendants; the hot pants and boots were abandoned shortly thereafter.

Although a tad sexist at the start, Southwest has become a model employer of women and people of color: in 1980 the company hired its first black pilot, Louis Freeman, who went on to become SWA's chief pilot in 1992. Long before it was common for a Texas-based company to do so, Southwest provided equal employment opportunities to Hispanic and African American workers. Walls at the company's headquarters were covered with over a hundred thousand photos of employees of all ethnicities celebrating at the company's numerous festivities, parties, and theatricals, at which top executives were routinely roasted. Employees were never an afterthought; instead of employing professional actors in its television commercials and professional models in its print ads, Southwest featured the actual men and women who flew, cleaned, repaired, and served on its airplanes.

EXEMPLARY PRACTICES

Apart from its employment practices, most of the other aspects of Southwest—advertising, flight scheduling, information technology, finance—have been equally well managed. For example, in the late 1990s, then-CFO Gary Kelly engaged in shrewd airline-fuel hedging, giving SWA a significant cost advantage over its competitors when the price of jet fuel soared in the early part of this century. Critics argued that, without Kelly's "lucky bet," Southwest's performance over the last decade would not have been nearly so impressive. While acknowledging that it has not hurt SWA to have lower fuel bills than its competitors, the company's defenders claim, in fact, that the airline's long suit has been its customer service. For example, in 1995 it became the first airline to have a website. While most airlines have since gone online, none has been able to match the ease and simplicity of buying tickets on southwest.com. Southwest's travel rewards program is similarly simple (although it recently became a bit more complicated). Perhaps the most consumer-friendly aspect of ticket purchasing is the ability to easily change flight plans without incurring fees. Moreover, when other airlines began charging passengers to check their luggage, Southwest answered with its "Bags Fly Free" promise. And small things count: along with providing free pretzels, SWA offers adult passengers another in-flight benefit: it sells premium-brand booze (including, naturally, Wild Turkey whiskey) at reasonable prices. While all those goodies are important, Colleen Barrett claims that they are secondary to the way

SWA employees treat passengers: "The type of customer service I'm talking about doesn't cost a lot of money. Most of my things are service from the heart. They're attitudinal, they're behavioral."[44]

It is difficult to write about Southwest without sounding like a hired PR flack, but there are many demonstrable reasons why the airline has perennially ranked high on *Fortune*'s Most Admired Corporations list. Nonetheless, like all companies, its behavior has not been perfect. In 2008, the Federal Aviation Administration alleged that Southwest violated regulations regarding the frequency of safety inspections. After voluntarily grounding several planes, the company paid $7.5 million in fines. In an audacious act of hypocrisy, in 1991 Southwest prevented the development of a high-speed rail system that would have linked Dallas, Houston, and San Antonio, using much the same arguments and tactics that its competitor airlines had used in their unsuccessful attempts to keep SWA out of business—tactics Rollin and Kelleher had branded "unfair" and "un-American."

SWA TODAY AND TOMORROW

Although Southwest's stock has never been a favorite on Wall Street (the price of its shares dropped by 18 percent between 2005 and 2010, even as it was gaining market share), the company's unique practices have been admired and studied closely by management scholars, consultants, gurus, and managers from companies around the globe. Yet unlike many other enlightened leaders profiled in these pages, Kelleher never engaged in serious efforts to convince other business types that he had discovered the best way to manage, or advocate that they should do as he did. The reason for his relative lack of zealotry is that he doesn't believe Southwest has discovered a secret sauce. He agrees with Barrett that SWA's success is all "attitudinal": "Everyone is looking for a formula in business like $E = mc^2$. . . . But it's not a formula. It's got to be emotional, spontaneous, and from the heart . . . basically, we've said there are some things that you can't quantify—intangible things that are exceedingly valuable and that are, in some cases, more valuable than the tangibles."[45]

If there is no formula behind Southwest's success, then what is there to pass on to subsequent generations of company leadership? The airline's "attitude" would seem to have derived from the unique leadership traits of founders Kelleher, King, and Barrett. So what happens after them? Kelleher, who personally began phasing out of day-to-day involvement in company management in the late 1990s, argues that the company's culture allows it to continually adapt, change, and grow without being dependent on him or any other individual in a leadership position:

> The fact that I cannot possibly know everything that goes on in our operation—and don't pretend to—is a source of competitive advantage. The freedom, informality, and interplay that people enjoy allows them to act in the best interests of the company. For instance, when our competitors began demanding tens of millions of dollars a year for us to use their travel agents' reservations systems, I said, forget it: we'll develop an electronic, ticketless system so travel agents won't have to hand-write Southwest tickets—and we won't be held hostage to competitors' distribution systems. It turned out that people from several [SWA] departments had already gotten together, anticipated such a contingency, and begun work on a system, unbeknownst to me or the rest of our officers. That kind of initiative is possible only when people know that our company's success rests with them, not with me.[46]

Since becoming CEO in 2004, Gary Kelly has hewed to the values and business model of the founders with regard to SWA's customers and employees, building on those to include the company's external constituencies. An advocate of corporate transparency, he introduced the *Southwest Airlines One Report*, an annual social audit of its financial, social, and environmental performance that adheres to standards established by the Global Reporting Initiative for "triple bottom line" reporting. In 2012 the report noted that Southwest employees logged over 137,000 hours of volunteer service in their communities. The company also documents actions the company has taken to reduce its greenhouse emissions, carbon footprint, and overall environmental impact. However, SWA's accomplishments in that regard amount to small potatoes: after all, there is no such thing as environment-friendly air travel. And the steps the airline has taken to reduce fuel consumption can be seen simply as prudent management.

In 2016 Southwest was the world's most profitable airline, and America's largest, with fifty thousand employees annually serving more domestic passengers than any company in its industry. Yet it is far from certain that its future will be as rosy as its past. Other airlines have been adopting its business model, presenting more effective competition than it heretofore has faced. Moreover, opportunities for growth beyond the places where it currently flies appear limited. Hawaii is the only major American market it doesn't serve, and although SWA has signaled intentions to begin flying there, it has been unable to do so because the length of the flight is beyond the range of its Boeing 737s. Introducing new, bigger planes to its fleet would require a major change in the company's business model, so the plan has been on hold for years, but is now scheduled for 2019. SWA has begun flying internationally to Mexico, Belize, the Dominican Republic, and Cuba, but there are few other places within range of its current planes with enough passenger traffic to justify serving them. Expansion would thus require SWA to adopt a business model radically altered from the one that has guided its fortunes for forty years.

Significant changes appear in the offing. Rollin King retired from the board in 2006, and Herb Kelleher stepped down as chairman two years later (the same year Colleen Barrett retired from the board and as SWA's president). After serving as the company's controller and chief financial officer for eighteen years, Gary Kelly became Southwest's second CEO in 2004, and its chairman in 2006. In 2018 he turned sixty-four, and he is the last of the founding generation still in the company. His successor will not have the same historical ties to SWA's founders. Over the last twenty years, I have chatted with Southwest employees on the many flights I have taken on the airline, finding them to be extremely knowledgeable about all aspects of the business. To a person, they have volunteered how much they love working at SWA. But over the last couple of years, several have expressed concern about the airline's future. Recent acquisitions have proved hard to digest; the feeling of family is being lost as the company grows; other airlines have learned how to compete more effectively by offering in-flight amenities SWA can't afford without raising prices; and there is uncertainty over what happens after Gary Kelly retires.

Bill Gore and Terri Kelly, "Unmanagers" Extraordinaire

Wilbert L. (Bill) Gore was a chemist whose main invention helped to make today's electronic age possible. In the 1950s, while working in DuPont's research lab on a polymer called PTFE, Gore surmised that the supersubstance could be used to coat metal wires. Today, when almost all electrical wires are plastic-coated, his insight may no longer seem like much of a technological breakthrough—but it was so revolutionary back then that DuPont's research managers could not fathom what Gore was proposing. At the time, wires used in electronic devices (refrigerators, radios, televisions, phonographs, and so forth) were coated in thick black rubber. Those wires were coded in silver paint to help technicians tell them apart while making and repairing devices. The problem was that the bulky wires took up a lot of space, and technicians needed eagle eyesight to read the silver code against a black background. Gore showed his superiors at DuPont that PTFE could be dyed any color, and that when a wire was dipped into it, a thin coat of insulation could be made to adhere. He demonstrated that thin, color-coded wires would make the complex wiring of computers more practical, and allow for the gradual miniaturization of those then-new machines. After his idea had been vetted by several layers of committees, DuPont's bosses told Gore, "Sorry, pal, we'll take a pass on developing that idea."[47]

So in 1958, on the day they celebrated their twenty-third wedding anniversary, Bill Gore and his wife, Vieve, decided to develop the product on their own, starting in their basement lab and using their life savings as capital. In addition to making PTFE-coated wires, Gore wanted to create a business with two overarching goals. First, it would be dedicated to innovation; and second, it would be a place where management would encourage and reward employees for their creativity and intellectual risk-taking. In short, W. L. Gore & Associates would become a place where no one with a wild idea would be treated as Bill Gore had been at DuPont. So he set out to design an organization devoid of the barriers, structures, and bureaucratic nonsense that hamper the free play of imagination, creativity, and initiative.

THE LATTICE

Over subsequent decades, Gore designed an organizational system that came to be known as "unmanagement," in which there were no titles, no bosses, no job descriptions, no ranks, and no rules. To avoid the deadly pyramidal hierarchies found at DuPont and other big companies, Gore's organization had a "lattice" structure. Picture an organization chart shaped much like a square, slatted garden lattice with no top or bottom: everyone in it is equal. Since there were no bosses, if Gore associates wanted to put a title on their business cards, they were free to invent one. One imaginative young associate titled herself "Supreme Commander."[48] Whenever new Gore associates were hired, they were simply told to "go find something useful to do."

Understandably, most new hires were a bit uneasy about such an open-ended assignment, craving more structure and clarity about what exactly they were supposed to be doing. They would ask, "How much authority do I have?" and "What are the limits to what I can do?" Gore would help them out by sticking a piece of butcher paper on a wall, on which he drew a stick-figure boat floating on a wavy-line sea, explaining, *The boat is the company, and that's the waterline. Every associate has full authority to try anything, take any risk, make any decision, as long as it is above the waterline. That way, if a mistake is made, we can easily patch up the figurative hole and our ship can sail on without permanent damage. However, no one has authority to make below-the-waterline decisions that risk sinking our company ship.*

Gore pointed out that the company might well choose to take a bet-the-ship risk, but it would have to be a decision taken collectively because the consequences could affect all the crew members. That was helpful, but obviously not enough guidance for most associates, who then were likely to ask, "O.K., Bill, but where's the waterline in our business?" Gore would smile and reply, "That's the question!" Because the risk-taking waterline is subjective in any company, and dependent on varying circumstances, Gore would enter into a dialogue with his people, analyzing the various real and hypothetical situations they would posit, engaging with them for as long as it took for a shared consensus to emerge on what constituted a waterline decision. Such discussions took a long time; in fact, they were ongoing at W. L. Gore & Associates. One purpose of those Socratic dialogues was to allow Gore to communicate and reinforce the company's principles, purpose, and philosophy. In effect, it was through such continuing discussions that Gore's associates came to understand fully why the company was structured as it was, and what they should do to make it succeed without the need of constant supervision or time-wasting approvals from higher-ups. Gore believed that when his people understood what he was trying to achieve, they would act in any given situation as he himself would act. With that confidence, he was able to put full trust in them—without hampering their creativity with bureaucratic rules. One company long-timer recalled that Gore was loved by his associates because he trusted them, allowing them to make mistakes, appreciating that was how they learned and grew. As Gore said, "Maybe it's not a mistake. Maybe it's an invention." When a group made a mistake that ended up wasting costly material, Gore told them, "Try it again tomorrow. I know you can do it."[49]

Because one of Gore's goals was the development of his associates, all new hires were assigned senior individuals who served as their "sponsors"—that is, mentors and coaches—but definitely not bosses. After eventually getting their bearings in the company's unstructured environment, associates then were free to choose their own sponsors. Along the way, Gore developed his theory of emergent leadership: one becomes a leader by attracting followers. For example, when an associate had an idea for a new product or project, the first step was to enlist others to work on it, too. Once a team was assembled and a project proposal written, the effort would be funded. If, after a time, the project didn't work out, there would be a small celebration, the team would disband, and the former leader might join a new team headed by another emergent and temporary leader. Each team was self-managing, and each set its own work schedules. Finally, to make the time needed for creativity, each associate was given 10 percent "free time" to work on new projects.

Gore understood that his company's unique structure needed to be reinforced by a complementary system of rewards and compensation. Pay was determined by what he called "contribution ranking," a procedure in which all members of a team listed all their fellow members in order of the value of their contributions to a project—whether through their ideas, effort, skill, or leadership. That was supplemented by profit sharing, which rewarded groups who brought products to market or made research breakthroughs helping other teams. In addition, the company contributed 13 percent of each associate's salary to their stock ownership plans, and an additional 3 percent to their 401(k) retirement plans. Over the decades, employees have come to own greater and greater percentages of the nontraded company stock, in partnership with the Gore family. And it literally was a partnership, with Bill, Vieve, and their son Bob working side by side with their associates.

Bill Gore served as the company's president until he was succeeded by son Bob in 1976, and in 2000, long-term Gore employee Charles Carroll became president when Bob stepped up to become chairman of the company's board. Bill died in 1986, but Vieve continued her work at the company until she died in 2005, at ninety-one!

As the company grew, Bill Gore—believing that knowing one's fellow workers fostered informal communications and created a needed sense of community in the absence of more formal structures—became concerned that gargantuan operations would undermine his system. Since any one associate could probably identify only about two hundred other individuals by name or face, he reasoned that as soon as a company facility reached 150 to 250 workers, he would open another facility. Later he clustered related units in the same town to encourage cross-functional communication.

In 1969 Gore's system bore its first fruit when son Bob discovered that PTFE was stretchable and expandable when rapidly heated. That breakthrough allowed PTFE to be made into the miracle material widely known as Gore-Tex, for which teams of Gore associates then found applications ranging from breathable fabrics used in shoes and jackets to synthetic blood vessels used in surgery to guitar strings and dental floss. The company became known as both an incubator of innovative products and processes and a great place to work, ranked among *Fortune*'s 100 Best Companies to Work For every year since the list first appeared in 1998.

BREAK IN THE GLASS CEILING

Gore was an especially good place for women associates, perhaps due to Vieve Gore's influence. The company made it a practice to recruit women, and because of its egalitarian nature, many worked their way into leadership positions. Since academic credentials and previous leadership experience were irrelevant at Gore, women—underrepresented as a group in university science and technology programs, and often passed over for leadership positions in most technology companies—had a better shot at achieving prominence. Terri Kelly was one such woman. She started to work at Gore & Associates in 1983, immediately after graduating from the University of Delaware with an undergraduate degree in engineering. In 2005 she was named the company's fourth president and chief operating officer—remarkably, at the age of forty-two. Under her leadership, the company grew to a $3.2 billion business in 2015, with over 6,500 employees at fifty facilities in five countries. As she told a *Fortune* reporter, she is most proud of the fact that Gore has been steadily profitable, year after year, and relatively free of the boom-and-bust cycles that plague most companies: "You can have a blip, a one-off good year. But for us it's all about sustaining that over time." That consistency is reflected in the company's low 3 percent full-time voluntary turnover rate.

Kelly, a low-key, unassuming leader, practices inclusion because she believes her role is to "empower the individual. That scares a lot of companies because you think you'll lose control." For example, when the company received a rare adverse legal ruling regarding a patent issue, Kelly shared all the information with employees that lawyers typically advise clients to closely hold. "Transparency builds trust," she explained. "Some companies try to keep [information] protected. You end up filtering so much, your people are really disconnected."[50] Kelly has worked to preserve the essence of the no-rules culture Bill Gore created, hewing faithfully to the four cardinal principles of fairness, freedom, commitment, and waterline he articulated, and to which each Gore associate agrees to observe:

- Try to be fair. Sincerely try to be fair with each other, our suppliers, our customers, and all persons with whom we carry out transactions.
- Allow, help, and encourage associates to grow in knowledge, skill, scope of responsibility, and range of activities.

- Make commitments—and keep them.
- Consult with associates before taking actions that might be "below the waterline" and cause serious damage to the enterprise.

While Kelly has endeavored to preserve the company's values, she has also tried to continually adjust its practices to respond to an ever-changing competitive and technological environment. To refresh the company's strategy, employment practices, and openness to new technologies, she has enlisted the ideas of the company's youngest associates. She also has added a modicum of organizational structure at its European operations to comply with governmental regulations—for example, German laws requiring foreign companies to have "country managers" and boards of directors with worker members. Those changes appear to have been made without losing the essence of the company's American culture: Gore has been regularly ranked as one of the best companies to work for in Britain, Germany, Italy, Sweden, and France. Kelly has also had to find ways to bring a touch of formal discipline into the company's American business units as the result of its continued growth, and the need to cope with the difficult environmental problems it faces by the very nature of its chemical-based business. She remains a calming force at the eye of the Gore organization's innovative hurricane. When asked the secret for coping with chaos, she replied: "Grow up."

Some sixty years after its founding, and three presidents later, by all accounts Gore & Associates has preserved its innovation-generating culture of unmanagement—which makes it one of the conspicuous outliers among the companies examined in these pages. In my view, the company's ability to maintain Bill Gore's enlightened practices has been due to three factors: it has continued to be privately held (its ownership shared by associates and the Gore family); Bill Gore's carefully designed system has turned the difficult trick of being both flexible and enduring; and Terri Kelly has not felt the ego-driven need to change things simply to prove her leadership chops.

13

The Patricians

THORNTON BRADSHAW (1917–1988),
J. IRWIN MILLER (1909–2004),
EDWIN LAND (1909–1991),
JOHN WHITEHEAD (1922–2015),
and ROY VAGELOS (1929–)

Business mavericks Iverson, Townsend, Kelleher, and Gore unsettled the stodgy corporate world by developing liberating practices that were effective, efficient, and ethical. Indeed, during the 1990s such influential management thinkers as Tom Peters and Warren Bennis were inclined to believe that the best—perhaps only—path to creating organizations that didn't "stifle people and strangle profits" was to follow the mavericks' lead and introduce one form or another of free-flowing "unmanagement." Because I felt that way myself at the time, I failed to take sufficient notice of the fact that not every enlightened leader during the golden era of business social responsibility was a maverick intent on thumbing a nose at Wall Street, or taking an ax to the venerable commandments of corporate management. There were also a few prominent virtuous businesspeople who were accepted by the financial and corporate establishment and, to some extent, actually led it. Among those patrician leaders were the oilman, industrialist, scientist, financier, and physician profiled in this chapter.

Thornton Bradshaw, Oilman

It is strange how the most virtuous corporate leaders often suffer the greatest criticism; among those executives, Thornton F. Bradshaw was perhaps the most maligned in modern business history. Bradshaw served as president of the Atlantic Richfield Corporation (Arco) from 1964 through 1981, when it was one of America's most successful energy companies. During his Arco tenure, Bradshaw was widely recognized as a brilliant manager (he was a pioneer in the application of quantitative forecasting techniques), while at the same time earning a reputation as a corporate statesman. *Time* magazine wrote in 1976 that Bradshaw would "make as able a candidate for [US] President as the politicians who have declared themselves in the running."[1] Yet three years later he would find himself reviled by his peers in the oil industry, and subject to harsh criticism by executives in other businesses as well.

Bradshaw was known for being unfailingly mild-mannered and gentlemanly, with just a hint of a patrician air about him. Educated at Phillips Exeter Academy, and holder of two Harvard degrees, he could easily have passed as scion of an old-wealth New England family. In fact, he came from a modest background and attended those prestigious institutions on scholarships. After earning his MBA, he taught corporate planning at Harvard Business School, then worked briefly as a management consultant before joining the Atlantic Refining Co. in 1956. There he began a long association with the company's chairman, CEO, and largest shareholder, Robert O. Anderson. They seemed to have had little in common, other than both being intellectually inclined. Anderson's family was wealthy, and he had been classically educated at the University of Chicago, yet he affected Western clothing (boots and Stetson to business meetings) and the casual manner of a cowboy. In fact, with a cattle ranch in New Mexico bigger than several states, for a time Anderson was said to be the largest private landowner in America. He was an entrepreneur by temperament and showed little interest in mastering the intricacies of corporate leadership. Unlike the polished, careful, and analytical Bradshaw, Anderson did business by bluster, daring, and intuition. As head of the Philadelphia-based Atlantic refinery, he had acquired several small petroleum companies and then forged a mega-merger with Los Angeles–headquartered Richfield Oil, creating Arco. As CEO of Arco, Anderson made some spectacular—and risky—bets with the company's capital, including leasing and purchasing untested oil fields (most successfully, in 1967, those at Prudhoe Bay, Alaska).

But Anderson was not always lucky. After he acquired the Anaconda copper mines on a whim in 1977, it became clear that he had paid too much for them, and they would subsequently require investment of hundreds of millions of Arco capital in an ultimately unsuccessful attempt to make them profitable. Characteristically, only *after* having completed the Anaconda purchase did Anderson direct Arco's staff to undertake an analysis of the financial implications of the deal. The staff joked that Anderson specialized in "post-planning." While Anderson was engaged in making bold strategic moves, Bradshaw worked to humanize the image of the company externally while internally creating a robust corporate culture, which he described in this way: "It must all be of a single fabric. From the company's social posture, through the way it treats its employees, to the care it takes in the artistic décor of its buildings, *everything* must manifest a commitment to quality, to excellence, to service, and to meeting the needs and aspirations of our owners, workers, consumers and the broader society."[2]

Bradshaw did just that, continually taking into account the claims of Arco's sundry stakeholders:

> Every decision made at my desk is influenced by some, and at times many, of the following: the possible impact on public opinion; the reaction of environmental groups; the possible impact on other action groups—consumers, tax reform, antinuclear, pro-desert,

pro-recreational vehicles, etc.; the constraints of government—
DOE, EPA, OSHA, FTC, etc.—and the states and the municipal-
ities; the effect on inflation and labor union attitudes; the OPEC
cartel. Oh yes, I almost forgot the anticipated economic profit, the
degree of risk, the problem of obtaining funds in a competitive
market, the capability of our organization, and—when there is
time—the competition.[3]

Under Bradshaw's leadership, Arco became the only American oil
company to earn broad-based public respect. In the 1970s and '80s, it
was the first in its industry to introduce state-of-the-art environmental practices in its drilling, refining, transportation, and other operations. Bradshaw and his colleagues worked closely with the likes of
the Sierra Club and Jacques Cousteau to ensure that Arco's environmental practices and standards were among the highest in the world.
In the early 1980s it became the first oil company to invest in solar
technology—although that investment proved as unsuccessful as its
Anaconda venture. Arco's company foundation became known for its
creative philanthropy, hiring professional administrators to manage
its charitable efforts instead of letting its executives support their favorite charities (then, as now, the corporate norm). Bradshaw explained
the decision to entrust professionals with what theretofore had been
an executive task: "Corporate officers are not chosen for their skills
in judging [public]-sector needs or in giving money away—quite the
contrary."[4]

Beginning in the early 1970s, Arco moved positively on many social fronts: building a new headquarters in rapidly decaying downtown
Los Angeles when other major businesses were fleeing to the suburbs;
initiating a carpooling program used by 60 percent of its employees;
becoming the first major corporation to offer health and other benefits
to same-sex partners of employees; donating $1 million to the Nature
Conservancy to enable the purchase of Santa Cruz Island off the coast
of California to create a nature preserve; removing its advertising from

a thousand billboards to help end visual pollution; and sponsoring Town Hall Los Angeles, a forum for serious, nonpartisan discussion of the city's many urban problems. Bradshaw also worked to make Arco a model of good corporate governance, appointing a board composed of all but two outside members, and pioneering in the inclusion of women and minority directors.

When the company's reputation for social responsibility was at its peak, Bradshaw launched several initiatives to keep its managers from succumbing to smugness and complacency. The most unusual of those efforts was the commissioning of an annual "audit" of the company's social performance: in Bradshaw's words, "a balance sheet of the year's activities (both debits and credits)." Arco hired noted ethicist Kirk Hanson, then on the faculty of the Stanford Graduate School of Business, to undertake the audit and write an independent report. As Bradshaw insisted, "The arrangement precludes editing by the corporation and guarantees publication."[5] Hanson's charge from Arco was simply to tell the truth and not pull punches, and the audits he produced were far from straight-A report cards. Indeed, Arco was not a perfect corporate citizen. The company had few women managers; it demolished the old Art Deco Richfield building in downtown Los Angeles, one of the city's most architecturally significant edifices; it was widely criticized for the way it handled the closing of the Anaconda facilities in Wyoming; and the management of its Alaskan pipeline was constantly questioned by environmentalists. Bradshaw insisted that the company closely and objectively examine those and all other aspects of its social performance, facilitating the process by establishing a seminar for its senior managers at which university-based scholars were invited to offer critiques of Arco's record and engage in a free-flowing discussion with company participants. (Disclosure: On several occasions I served in the capacity of outside critic at those Arco seminars, alternating with Stanford's Hanson and the University of California's David Vogel. The only complaints we profs received from Bradshaw about our efforts were his concerns that we were "going too soft" on the company.)

Under Bradshaw, Arco listened to its critics. When it was criticized for having few minority employees, the company "made a management commitment to a new hiring rule"; as Bradshaw explained, "if two people applied for a job, both equal in capability, but one black and the other white, the black was to be hired."[6] At the Arco seminars, Bradshaw continually reinforced a basic ethical message: the need for openness and candor both internally and externally. When lower-level managers confronted him with the charge that the company's practices were inconsistent with its stated values, Bradshaw's reaction was not to punish the messengers but to improve the practical application of the company's principles and philosophy. Candor was also the rule with external stakeholders, and even the press. Bradshaw told his managers that if a journalist called about a potential issue with the company's social performance, they should never stonewall. Instead, he insisted that they had authority to tell whatever they knew, and if they didn't know, they should refer the reporter to someone who did.

Thanks to Bradshaw's leadership, the company took courageous public stands—courageous for an oil company, at least. Arco played a leading role in the advocacy of public transportation and energy conservation, for example, advocating the diversion of highway (gasoline) taxes to mass transit. Bradshaw spoke in favor of increasing the tax on gasoline to encourage conservation and fund clean-energy research, repealing the oil depletion tax allowance, and, most controversially for an oil executive, introducing national energy planning. On the latter, he wrote that "the free market mechanism has never worked for oil," particularly since OPEC "controls the price." Needless to say, Bradshaw's name became anathema in the petroleum industry, prompting petro-heir Charles Koch to pen a lengthy letter to *Fortune* in which he claimed that "most of Thornton Bradshaw's major contentions are wrong-headed and blatantly self-serving."[7]

It is unclear if Bradshaw's position proved right in the long term, but it is a fact that he advanced such arguments from a realism born of necessity. He advocated limited national energy planning from the viewpoint of an enlightened capitalist who recognized that it was in the self-interest of business to work with government to do things corporations acting alone could not do, and that it was better to work with government to make sensible rules than work against it and end up being overregulated. He never varied from his position that every action Arco undertook was in its own long-term interest. For example, when he proposed ending the windfall profits tax on petroleum companies, he also called for a quid pro quo removal of federal oil price controls. Koch and his fellow critics (who all but accused Bradshaw of socialism) failed to acknowledge the capitalist core of Bradshaw's philosophy: "First and foremost, the corporation must be an effective economic institution or it can be nothing at all. Wherever else the future may take it, the corporation must continue to respond to the marketplace, producing quality goods at the lowest possible cost, allocating resources efficiently, distributing its products, and earning an acceptable profit for its shareholders."[8] Libertarian Koch also failed to note that Arco's general counsel at the time—and one of its chief public spokesmen—had been nominated twice by the Libertarian Party as their candidate for president of the United States, once with David Koch, Charles's brother, as his vice presidential running mate. Some socialists!

In addition to profitability, Bradshaw continually stressed another basic business role: innovation. Under his leadership, Arco was among the most innovative companies in its industry, introducing such products as cleaner-burning gasoline and mini-marts at its service stations (later, it was the first to take the "service" out of the stations when it introduced self-service gas pumps). The company was also the first American corporation to embrace two-way teleconferencing as a way to reduce its carbon footprint.

Bradshaw and Arco took public stands that alienated them from the broader California business community, most notably when they opposed Proposition 13, a cap on state property taxes. When the company announced that it would cease paying its executives' dues at private Los Angeles clubs with discriminatory racial practices, the local business community was aghast. In 1979 Bradshaw's actions came back to haunt him when he was a finalist for the presidency of the University of Southern California. Although he was the front-runner for the position, influential members of the university's board of trustees—some of whom were oil heirs, and others members of clubs Arco had singled out as discriminatory—made it clear that they would blackball his candidacy. He politely withdrew his name from consideration.

In the early 1980s Arco weathered the increasing criticism directed toward it, but the rogue behavior of CEO Anderson set the stage for the company's eventual undoing. When it became known that Anderson had donated several million dollars of Arco company funds to the Los Angeles County Museum of Art to erect a building named in his honor, and for many years had underwritten the sizable debts of the Aspen Institute using company money, Arco's board fired him on the grounds that he had spent shareholders' money for personal reasons. If nothing else, Anderson's actions were a violation of Arco's stated principle of leaving decisions about corporate charitable contributions in the hands of its professional philanthropic staff.

About that time Bradshaw, then contemplating retirement, was unexpectedly named CEO of the financially struggling RCA Corporation. In 1981 he moved to New York, where over the next four years he deftly restored the prestige of the company's NBC division and brought RCA back to financial health. He then presided over the company's sale to General Electric in a move that was a financial boon to RCA shareholders, while securing the operating independence of NBC, a matter of great importance to its lauded news operation. Bradshaw then retired and, in apparent good health, died suddenly at age seventy-one in the office of a Manhattan dentist. On his death, GE chairman Jack Welch said, "America has lost a great business leader." The head of NBC, Grant Tinker, recalled, "If there was a fairer, nicer, total gentleman than Brad, I've yet to meet him. He left an exemplary legacy." CEO of CBS Laurence Tisch added that Bradshaw "was a gentleman and a giant in our industry. He was a creative force in television, in finance and in the cultural world. His influence was widespread. His impact will be lasting."[9] Sadly, that was not to be. Bradshaw's career is all but unrecorded in the annals of American business. There are no Harvard Business case studies about him, or about Arco under his leadership; no biography of him has yet been written; and in what today passes for the ultimate definition of obscurity, he lacks a Wikipedia entry.

Meanwhile, out in Los Angeles, Arco was imploding in the late 1980s. The culture Bradshaw created survived briefly under the leadership of Lodwrick Cook, the CEO who succeeded Anderson, but the company reeled under subsequent management (and mismanagement). Insiders started calling Arco the Great Shrinking Oil Company as it laid off employees and sold off assets. Gradually it retreated from most, if not all, the virtuous practices initiated by Bradshaw, in the end becoming all but indistinguishable in its social policies from other American oil companies. Arco was acquired by British Petroleum in 1999, which, given its sterling environmental record under Bradshaw, provides an ironic ending to the Arco story in light of BP's disastrous later handling of the 2010 Gulf of Mexico oil spill.

In 1999, when Arco announced that it was closing its Los Angeles headquarters and ceasing to operate as an independent company, UCLA political scientist Xandra Kayden penned an op-ed piece in the *Los Angeles Times* outlining what the loss of the company meant for the Southern California community: "Arco was more than a leading oil company on the West Coast: It was a leading citizen. It consciously defined 'corporate citizenship' for many U.S. companies, and many U.S. communities as well. The local economy probably doesn't need a lot of corporate headquarters to survive, but the question of leadership for the city remains: Having the resources to invest is one thing, but understanding how to help and encouraging others to follow suit is quite another. That is where Arco excelled."[10] Fund-raising at many nonprofit organizations in Southern California suffered when the area's most generous corporate foundation closed its doors. (A similar problem occurred about that time in San Francisco when locally based Bank of America, the area's largest supporter of nonprofits, closed its California headquarters after being acquired by a North Carolina bank.) The phenomenon of nonprofit overdependence on business donations highlights one of the shortcomings of corporate philanthropy: the boom-and-bust nature of business organizations, and the prevalence of mergers and acquisitions, put NGO financing at considerable risk. That is one reason why some enlightened corporate leaders in the past— and more today—have concluded that the most important social role a company can play is through engaging in virtuous business actions, leaving philanthropic decisions to their individual managers and employees (perhaps matching those with corporate contributions). Indeed, as Xandra Kayden noted, Arco's behavior under Bradshaw was laudable not primarily as a result of its generosity but for the leadership examples it set. Bradshaw showed that it was possible for a company in any industry—even one as widely reviled as the oil business—to act, in his words, as "good neighbors."[11]

J. Irwin Miller, Industrialist

The headline on the cover of the October 1967 issue of *Esquire* read, "This man ought to be the next President of the United States," above a photo of one J. Irwin Miller. I recall asking myself a question the majority of the magazine's readers doubtlessly were also pondering: Who is this guy? Reading the article, I not only discovered who he was but began to suspect that *Esquire's* editors might be right: J. Irwin Miller probably would be a great president. Alas, he wasn't interested in the job. As chairman of the Cummins Engine Corporation, first lay president of the National Council of Churches (which he had helped to establish), trustee of Yale University, the Museum of Modern Art, and the Ford Foundation, and mastermind behind the effort to turn Columbus, Indiana, into a showcase for the world's finest modern architects, his plate was sufficiently full as it stood. Instead of running for president, Miller persuaded Nelson Rockefeller to run, then served as his campaign chairman.

Joseph Irwin Miller was the son of Nettie Irwin Sweeney and Hugh Thomas Miller, the latter a professor and sometime politician. J. Irwin was raised in the mansion of his great-uncle, Will G. Irwin, the family patriarch and prominent Indiana businessman. In 1919 Uncle Will had invested in his chauffeur Clessie Cummins's start-up diesel engine business. Unfortunately, Clessie proved more adept at technological development than business management. After running up fifteen straight years of red ink, Uncle Will finally decided that the time had come to recruit someone capable of turning the business around. Will had just the man in mind for the job: his twenty-five-year-old grand-nephew J. Irwin Miller (who, conveniently, was also heir to the Irwin family fortune). In addition to possessing the right pedigree, the young man had the requisite smarts: degrees in classical philosophy from Yale and PPE (philosophy, politics, and economics) from Oxford, along with deep knowledge of the fields of theology, architecture, and music (he played a Stradivarius fiddle in his spare time). He also had a bit of business experience, having worked for a spell in the family's grocery store chain.

Miller joined Cummins Engine as its vice president and general manager in 1934, and two years later the company posted its first profits. He developed a corporate strategy for Cummins focused on improving diesel technology, increasing product quality, and prudent cost cutting, insisting that the company's managers constantly "obsolete our own products before our customers do it."[12] Cummins Engine grew steadily until World War II, when demand for diesel engines increased exponentially (diesels provided the high horsepower needed to drive heavy-duty military vehicles). After the war, diesel technology proved perfectly fitted to the needs of the large trucks, tractors, and construction equipment fast replacing less powerful vehicles propelled by conventional engines. In a thrice, chauffeur Clessie's little company had become a big business.

In 1947 J. Irwin Miller assumed the presidency of Cummins, shortly thereafter expanding its operations overseas by opening efficient modern plants in Europe, Asia, and South America to supplement its growing number of manufacturing facilities in America. By the end of the 1950s, Cummins was America's premier manufacturer of high-quality diesel engines. But it wasn't simply the company's technology that made it stand out from its competitors; what caught the particular attention of the greater public was its ethics-focused organizational culture— especially its relationship to Columbus, Indiana, the small prairie town where it was headquartered. In 1957 Miller promised Columbus's civic leaders that the Cummins Engine Foundation would pay the commissions needed to attract top architects to design new public buildings for the town. Over the next decade Richard Meier, Eero Saarinen, I. M. Pei, and dozens of other noted architects created fifty modernistic churches, schools, and government buildings—even a knock-your-socks-off new jail—far surpassing William Lever and Milton Hershey's earlier accomplishments. And, unlike them, Miller was careful to avoid any hint of paternalism: all decisions with regard to the town were left to its denizens.

A generous philanthropist, Miller gave away so much of his personal wealth that little of it was left at the end of his life. But his greatest accomplishments were achieved at the company he led for the better part of five decades. Under Miller's leadership, Cummins Engine became known for treating its customers, dealers, and suppliers fairly and honestly, heavily reinvesting its profits for the long term, making heroic efforts to minimize the environmentally damaging impact of its products, and being a great place to work. It also made a lot of money for its investors: during Miller's tenure, Cummins was profitable for forty-one years in a row, annually increasing the value of shareholder equity by 12 percent year after year.[13]

J. Irwin Miller's first priority was to run an ethical business. A deeply religious man and an astute student of Aristotle's virtue-based ethics, he believed that "business ethics are really an effort to do good long-term planning. In that sense, I'd say the fundamental reason for business ethics is to say, 'What will I wish I had done if I could be around fifty years from now?'"[14] In the 1970s, Cummins appointed an ethics officer long before ethics and compliance officers became de rigueur in American corporations. At Cummins, ethical practices began with the way the company treated its employees. To create a sense of community among its workers, no Cummins facility had more than five thousand employees (a large number, but small for diesel factories). In 1936, when CIO union organizers attempted to enlist the workers in Columbus's largest companies, Miller rejected his fellow industrialists' concerted efforts to prevent unionization; he even refused to join the Indiana Chamber of Commerce because it backed so-called right-to-work legislation. His reason: "We don't feel right fighting our own people."[15] Years later, after Cummins workers had rejected the CIO bid and formed their own Diesel Workers Union, Miller remarked, "I wouldn't know how to run a big business without a strong union. The unions are management's mirror. They tell you things your own people won't admit."[16]

Miller, like William Norris and Walter Haas, was a business pioneer in the 1960s struggle for civil rights. An early supporter of Martin Luther King Jr. (Miller helped King to organize the famous 1963 March on Washington), Cummins became the first company in its region to recruit, hire, and train African American employees for nonjanitorial jobs, ultimately promoting many into supervisory, managerial, and executive positions, which necessitated a battle with Columbus city officials to end housing segregation. When Reverend King called Miller "the most progressive businessman in America," the honor earned him a spot on Richard Nixon's "Enemies List."[17]

Charles Powers, the executive most responsible for formalizing ethics training at Cummins, proudly explained, "We were always prepared to be pariahs on matters of real principle."[18] That was the case, most controversially, with regard to the company's environmental policies. When most industrialists were fighting environmentalists' calls for legislation to curb air pollution, Cummins worked with them and members of Congress to devise reasonable emission standards. (In sharp contrast, the Diesel Engine Manufacturers Association refused to provide information to the government.) Miller felt a moral obligation to part company with his peers on that issue: "We supported the Clean Air Act because the problem of smog in the major urban areas is obviously going to be very dangerous in the future."[19] In fact, Cummins helped draft a section of the Clean Air Act that caused the company to reduce emissions from its own diesel products. Years later, Miller showed no regrets at having had a hand in greatly increasing its own regulatory burden: "It ended up great for the industry because it converted us from a relatively low-technology industry to an extremely high-tech industry. We learned more about engines than we ever would have, had we not been under this pressure. We actually improved fuel consumption as well as reduced emissions, something we couldn't do to start with."[20]

Miller was intent on creating a company—and an ethical culture—that would last beyond his lifetime. When investors attempted a hostile takeover of Cummins in 1989, Miller and his sister, Clementine, spent $72 million of their own money to buy the raiders' shares, paying a $5 million premium over the going stock price. In addition, Cummins invested more than $1 billion in new plants and equipment during the 1980s when foreign competitors were making significant inroads into the American market.[21]

A leader in much the same mold as Max De Pree, Miller advocated "servant leadership," stressing the centrality of employee involvement and development at Cummins. "A leadership that is concentrated on the ideas of one person is very limited," he explained. "Genuine leadership involves getting all the wisdom that is available in a group, and helping that group come to a better decision than any one of its members would have been able to achieve himself. The servant-leader is the person who gets the unsuspected best out of his group of people."[22]

Miller sought to create a cadre of servant-leaders, recruiting well-educated graduates of liberal arts colleges and Ivy League universities to fill the managerial ranks of Cummins. Miller mentored one such recruit, Henry Schacht (degrees from Yale and Harvard), who in 1973 became the company's CEO when Miller assumed the role of chairman. Unlike Max De Pree, Miller got the process of succession right: for the next twenty years, Schacht faithfully adhered to Miller's values and commitment to servant leadership, doubling down on both by becoming one of the nation's leading advocates of corporate social activism. But Cummins did not achieve the same level of financial success under Schacht that it had enjoyed under Miller. In the 1980s it faced significant competitive challenges from Japanese imports and such domestic manufacturers as Caterpillar and Detroit Diesel. In weakened financial condition, Cummins was confronted with the threat of a second hostile takeover in 1990, and was saved thanks to a $250 million investment by three of its largest customers. During the turmoil of the early 1990s, Schacht made numerous changes in the composition of the top management team at Cummins and then, in 1994, surprised the business world when, at age sixty-four, he announced his retirement from the company. (He later served as the first chief executive of Lucent Technologies when the company was spun off from AT&T in 1995.)

Cummins was also plagued by an increasing number of environmental challenges during Schacht's tenure, challenges that continued to bedevil both the company and its competitors throughout the 1990s. After years of negotiation, in 1998, Cummins and other American manufacturers of heavy-duty diesel engines signed a consent decree with the EPA that required them to greatly reduce emissions of oxides of nitrogen (NOx). During the fifteen-month period that companies were granted to implement the tough new standard, customers and competitors pressured Cummins to pay a nonconformance penalty rather than complying. There were several compelling reasons not to comply: Cummins would save the considerable expense of developing a new, cleaner, more expensive engine that in all probability would lose out to the cheaper, more polluting products of its competitors; it had turned a profit in only two years during the 1990s, while accumulating over a billion dollars in debt; its market share had fallen from

60 to 30 percent, and its stock price had dropped to its 1972 level. In all, Cummins was poorly positioned to assume the risk of developing a new, untested diesel engine. On the other hand, Cummins had a tradition of living up to its commitments, of working cooperatively with government, and of endeavoring to reduce its products' negative environmental effects. And there was no doubt that NOx emissions had an adverse impact on ground-level ozone, acid rain, global warming, and water quality, and contributed to health problems affecting children and people with asthma. The decision was thus an extremely difficult one, requiring careful balancing of the interests of the company's various stakeholders. After much deliberation, Cummins complied with the consent decree.

A decade later, after Cummins had been hit hard during the 2007–9 recession, it faced yet another decision that tested its commitment to then recently deceased J. Irwin Miller's principles and values. In 2010, the company needed a massive facility where it could efficiently manufacture a new line of high-horsepower engines. The choice of sites came down to two contenders: Pune, India, and Seymour, Indiana, a small town twenty miles south of Columbus. In making the choice, there were many logistic, financial, and social factors to consider. The advantages of Pune were largely financial (inexpensive labor and construction costs), while the arguments in favor of Seymour were primarily social (Miller's commitment to providing good jobs to the people of his home state). In the end, financial considerations prevailed, and the factory was built in Pune (Seymour got a much smaller facility). In 2016 Cummins's CEO surprised the business community when he announced that the company was abandoning its historical commitment to free trade, and supporting the effort to introduce protectionist measures designed to shield American manufacturers from competition with goods imported from low-wage nations. Those two not terribly dramatic decisions illustrate and encapsulate the life cycle of enlightened business practices at most companies: they don't end suddenly; instead, as Max De Pree noted, they gradually erode away.

Edwin Land, Scientist

As millions of the people who owned a Polaroid Land Camera once knew, instant photography was invented by Edwin H. Land. Fewer people are aware that Land was "the man who inspired Steve Jobs"— which is as ironic as it is an interesting tidbit of techno-trivia.[23] For it was Apple's Jobs who perfected and successfully marketed the digital photographic technology that Land stubbornly resisted to the point of losing control of the company he'd founded.

Land was a nonobservant Jew born into a Connecticut family just wealthy enough to send him to a semiprivate prep school, and then to Harvard. That background, plus a distinguished New England accent and Cary Grant good looks, misled many to believe that he was a patrician WASP. He studied chemistry at Harvard just long enough to become so bored that he dropped out and headed for New York City. There he taught himself optical physics and chemistry in the reading room of the New York Public Library during the day, while conducting research in the Columbia University labs he sneaked into at night, after students and faculty had gone home. Somehow he also found time to get married. His early experiments in optical physics were so successful that by age nineteen he had invented a filter capable of polarizing light, the immediate value of which was to reduce glare. A brilliant and prolific inventor, he would go on to hold 535 US patents.[24]

Land moved back to Cambridge, Massachusetts, where, in partnership with his former Harvard chemistry professor, he established a company to commercialize his polarization breakthroughs by making filters for sunglasses and camera lenses. Renamed the Polaroid Corporation in 1937—with Land now sole owner—the company would turn out one after another application of sheet polarizers, including 3-D glasses for color movies. Thanks to Land's work in Polaroid's research labs, the company made significant contributions to the US military effort during World War II, inventing a stereo-optic photo system used to spot camouflaged enemy fortifications from the air.

But it was the Polaroid camera that made Land famous. In 1943 his three-year-old daughter had asked him why she had to wait days to see the pictures he took of her. (Note to readers under thirty: at the time, exposed color film had to be sent to a lab to be developed and then printed, a process that could take a week or more.) As the story goes, Land then and there conceived of the instant camera. Three years later he demonstrated the first working model, and the next year he began marketing Polaroid Land Cameras in Boston's Jordan Marsh department store. The first day it was on sale, customers gobbled up the company's entire inventory of fifty-six cameras, along with its only demonstration model. In the 1960s and '70s, the camera became nearly as ubiquitous as the iPhone today: a Polaroid camera could be found in half the households of America. Fame ensued for Land in the form of simultaneous *Time* and *Life* magazine cover stories, an honorary doctorate from Harvard (where he never had completed his undergraduate education), a street named after him in Cambridge near MIT, and the Presidential Medal of Freedom. Like the largely self-educated "Dr." Samuel Johnson during the eighteenth century, autodidact Edwin Land would come to be known by all as "Dr." Land, America's most recognized and respected scientist-inventor. He was said to have performed an experiment every day, and until near the end of his life, he remained dedicated to scientific research. Indeed, he viewed profits from Polaroid products as the means to support the real purpose of his company: research and invention.

There was more to Land than science: he was also a humanist of the first order. He built one enormous instant camera the size of a phone booth, capable of making a life-size print of a standing human, and about a dozen hand-built cameras that produced twenty-by-twenty-four-inch prints. Because it was unnecessary to enlarge those prints, they had none of the distortions that result from enlarging a photo captured by regular film, and the colors produced were richer, deeper, and truer than Kodak and Fuji films were capable of capturing. Land made those giant cameras available, gratis, to such esteemed photographers and artists as Ansel Adams, Chuck Close, William Wegman, and Andy Warhol, and many of the photos they took with the large-format cameras made their ways into permanent collections of such top museums as the Museum of Modern Art in New York.

When I visited the company in the early 1980s, it was widely seen as a model of enlightened business management. For example, Land made it a practice to hire and train women for managerial and professional research positions, and the company's history is replete with names of women who had graduated from liberal arts colleges, given crash science courses, and then gone on to make significant technical contributions as members of Polaroid research teams. One such hire with a degree in art history, Meroë Morse, became one of Polaroid's top-level research managers, leading teams that created some of its first instant photo products. At Polaroid women were regularly promoted into managerial and technical posts, and there was a liberal maternal leave policy long before those were common in industry. As a result, the company became known as the best large company in America for female employees.[25]

Much like William Norris, Walter Haas Jr., and J. Irwin Miller, Land was profoundly moved by the 1968 assassination of Martin Luther King Jr. Beginning that year, he started to train inner-city Boston youth for technical jobs in manufacturing, creating a Polaroid subsidiary, Inner City Inc., where for the next two decades the company prepared 250 unemployed or underemployed minority men and women each year for jobs at seventy Boston-area firms. They were paid while they learned and worked in a plant that manufactured Polaroid components. Significantly, Inner City Inc. was never intended to be a charitable operation: it started to break even five years after its founding, and during subsequent years, beginning in 1973, it turned a modest profit. Because of the program's emphasis on job placement for its graduates, nearly all who apprenticed at Inner City found employment, and their first-year retention rates were on the order of 80 to 90 percent. Some 65 percent of the class of 1968 was still working at Polaroid thirteen years later, several in managerial positions.[26]

Polaroid was recognized as a great place to work because Land encouraged his management team to attempt to enrich jobs so they would become learning experiences instead of drudgery. Viewing the company as a scientific think tank, Land would hire talented people and give them labs and staff to work on projects that interested them, thus anticipating the practice later introduced at Gore facilities. Land urged his fellow industrialists to join Polaroid in devoting 5 percent of their budgets to R&D. That would not only ensure the continuation of American technological leadership, he argued, but also create good jobs for millions: "Our national scene would change in the way, I think, all Americans dream of. Each individual will be a member of a group small enough so that he feels a full participant in the purpose and activity of the group. His voice will be heard and his individuality recognized."[27]

Like Milton Hershey, Land worked alongside his employees in the lab, often putting grueling hours into attempting to perfect a product or conduct an experiment. Unlike Hershey, Land let his workers go home when they were exhausted, bringing in a fresh shift to labor on with him throughout the night. At a time when Max De Pree's humanistic practices were viewed as impractical in most of American industry, he was welcomed as a speaker at Polaroid, where his philosophy found a receptive audience. Indeed, there were many similarities between Herman Miller and Polaroid: the former hired great designers like Charles Eames as consultants and contractors; the latter hired such great photographers as Ansel Adams to test and critique its products. (Eames and his wife, Ray, even made a documentary film about Polaroid's technology.)

Following the introduction of the SX-70 color-print camera in 1972, everyone from John Lennon to Woody Allen "had to have" a Polaroid camera. (Allen's use of the camera to take nude photos of his stepdaughter precipitated the end of his marriage to Mia Farrow.) Although the company's sales, profits, and stock price soared, Land had his critics on Wall Street who claimed that the company had invested too much in developing the SX-70—estimates ranged as high as three quarters of a billion dollars—and that it spent too much on research that didn't lead to marketable products.[28] The company also was faulted for paying too little attention to business details, which had led to expensive product recalls and shortages of film. In the words of Land's biographer Christopher Bonanos, Land "was a perfectionist-aesthete, exhaustively obsessive about product design. The amount spent on research and development, on buffing out flaws, sometimes left Wall Street analysts discouraging the purchase of Polaroid stock, because they thought the company wasn't paying enough attention to the bottom line. (When a shareholder once buttonholed Land about that, he responded, 'The bottom line is in heaven.')"[29]

Looking to create the next great technological advance, in 1977 Land introduced Polavision, the instant moving picture system he had been dreaming about for years. The system was technically brilliant, but badly flawed from the consumer's perspective: only one person at a time could view a three-minute soundless video. Believing that the system would sell in the millions, Land invested some $500 million in its development. As it turned out, only sixty thousand or so units were sold, and the company was forced to take a $68 million write-down.[30] About then, friends and critics began to urge Land to appoint a chief operating officer to handle day-to-day company operations. When it became clear that he would not give up total control—as its chairman, chief executive officer, and head of research and development—several promising top executives chose to leave the firm. One of those whom many had viewed as Land's likely successor, Tom Wyman, left to become CEO of Green Giant, where he earned a reputation as an enlightened executive and a leader of Minneapolis's progressive business community. From that point on, Polaroid's fortunes began to wane, and it never fully regained its magic touch.[31]

At the core of Polaroid's difficulties in the late 1970s were Land's deep commitment to chemical technology, and his fixation on the value of hard-copy photographic prints. During previous decades, those commitments had been appropriate, given the state of technology and what consumers then wanted from a camera. But in the words of Sony founder Akio Morita, Polavision was "too late" by the time Land marketed it.[32] Indeed, the hour would prove too late even for Sony's Betamax videotape system and, subsequently, the VHS system that supplanted it. By then, it was clear that the future belonged to digital technologies. Out in the San Francisco Bay Area, young techies like Steve Wozniak, Steve Jobs, and countless students at Stanford and the University of California, Berkeley, were hard at work creating the technological revolution that eventually put the power of instant photography in the pockets of people around the world.

Nonetheless, as late as 1982, Land was still assuring Polaroid's shareholders that his chemical-based technology produced higher-quality images than digital systems. In a way, he was right: the quality of resolution and the purity of the colors in photos taken on the large-format Polaroid cameras used by professional photographers remains, to this day, superior to anything yet to emerge from Silicon Valley. But his claim was also irrelevant from a business perspective: there was no money to be made in large-format professional cameras, while a fortune was waiting for those who could put instant, no-fuss photography in the hands of the masses. Three years later Land was gently ousted (controlling only about 8 percent of the stock, there was little he could do about it) from leadership of the company he had founded. He tried hanging on in a research capacity but soon realized that he had lost all influence with the company's board and top management. At age seventy he retired to work in a private, nonprofit lab he funded. He promptly sold off his Polaroid stock, and five years later declined an invitation to attend the fiftieth-anniversary celebration of the founding of the company. Shortly after his death in 1991, at age eighty-one, Land's private papers were destroyed as he had wished.

Polaroid briefly caught a second wind with new, low-priced cameras in the 1980s, but the poor quality of the prints they produced earned the company a bad reputation among consumers. The company then lost focus, trying to enter new lines of business, eventually finding itself in dire financial straits. In 1990 Polaroid was bailed out when it won a nearly billion-dollar award in a highly publicized patent-infringement lawsuit against Kodak (later reduced to $36 million). But the die had long since been cast. In 1978, Polaroid had over twenty thousand employees; the year after the company won the judgment against Kodak, it was down to a five-thousand-member workforce. By then the company was on life support, and over the next decade it gradually disintegrated. In 1988 Shamrock Holdings (a private equity company owned by the Disney family) made an offer to purchase the company, which Polaroid's then-CEO Mac Booth fought off by establishing a large employee stock-ownership plan. The ploy, designed to make it nearly impossible for Shamrock to obtain a controlling interest in the firm, worked, and the takeover was averted. Booth may have won that battle, but he then lost the war. He had ignored the real purpose of employee stock plans: namely, to give workers a sense of ownership and motivation to make a company in which they own stock succeed. But employee effort alone cannot save a company, like Polaroid, that is struggling as the result of mismanagement. Moreover, it is unconscionably risky to compensate workers with stock in such an enterprise. In the end, Polaroid's now-embittered workers received a measly nine cents per share of stock once traded as high as $47 a share.[33]

Between 2001 and 2009, Polaroid twice declared bankruptcy, and it was resold on three separate occasions. One of those buyers was arrested for fraud (in a case unrelated to the company) while at the helm of Polaroid and sentenced to a federal prison. Having purchased Polaroid for $426 million, he auctioned it off for a paltry $86 million before serving his fifty-year jail term. The new buyers then sold 1,200 of the company's most valuable large-format photo prints, many of which had been donated by such photographers as Chuck Close with the understanding they would be part of a permanent public collection, to Sotheby's. When the company stopped making film for its cameras in 2008, it was all but defunct.

KODAK, TOO

The lessons to be taken from the decline and fall of Polaroid are muddied by the fact that conventionally managed Kodak underwent a similarly spectacular decline at roughly the same time, and for roughly some of the same reasons. In the late 1980s, Kodak had dominated the photographic film industry, with some 145,000 employees; by 2012, the year it filed for bankruptcy, its workforce had shrunk to 20,000. (For the record, in 2018 a resuscitated remnant of Kodak was back in business, bizarrely selling a photo-based cryptocurrency.) For too long, both Polaroid's and Kodak's leaders had convinced themselves that digital technology would never overtake chemical-based processes, and when they finally faced reality, it was too late to catch up with high-tech competitors. It is accurate to say that Polaroid—like countless conventionally managed companies before and since—was the victim of technological change that had been resisted, ignored, or came as a surprise. The lesson is that enlightened companies often fail for the same reasons that conventionally managed companies fail. But that isn't the whole story. It is important to note that, despite Land's similarities to Control Data's William Norris, Polaroid didn't fail as the result of taking enlightened managerial practices to extremes. Doubtless, Land was every bit as stubborn as Norris with regard to technology, but he never went overboard with his commitment to social causes. Polaroid failed neither because of its social commitments nor as the result of spending too much on R&D. It failed largely because of Land's technological myopia. Perhaps the worst societal consequence of Polaroid's demise was that it was a major setback for those who advocated the spread of enlightened business practices and had pointed to Land as a model for emulation.

Curiously, fifty years earlier Kodak had similarly been cited as a model employer and generous benefactor to the community of Rochester, New York, where the company was headquartered. And, like Polaroid, its labs had made numerous significant photochemical breakthroughs. Yet in later decades it was not known for the enlightened practices its founder, George Eastman, had pioneered in the early part of the century. In that regard, Polaroid was different from Kodak. While Land was running the company, it continued to lead its industry in scientific research and never lost its commitment to its employees, the arts, and the broader society. Up to the day Land was forced out, Polaroid remained one of America's most respected companies. It is thus tempting to speculate what might have happened if Land had been a bit more flexible and turned day-to-day operations over to a manager like Tom Wyman with greater interest in making the company profitable, and then personally concentrated on leading the company's scientific and social efforts. Polaroid might well have succeeded and continued to serve as a model for other companies—but that was not how the story ended. Sadly, Land lost sight of the fact that Polaroid could not fulfill its humanistic, artistic, and scientific missions without the financial wherewithal to pay for them.

Ironically, Land's legacy is today found in Silicon Valley, where skilled technicians work on teams in relatively unstructured organizations with cultures that encourage innovation. As Land's biographer Bonanos notes, Steve Jobs drew inspiration from Land. Moreover, both men were visionary, obsessive, committed to making the "next great thing," intent on creating a work environment that fostered creativity and innovation, and devoted to great product design. Nonetheless, the differences between the two were as important as their similarities. Unlike the colossally egocentric Jobs, Land was a humanist who was never interested in getting rich, an employer who treated his colleagues and employees with respect, a man of great ethical integrity, and one dedicated to the greater social good. Yet it is Jobs who is remembered as a great leader.

John Whitehead, Financier

Like his contemporaries Bradshaw and Land, John Whitehead was raised in a middle-class family and yet, thanks to acquired Ivy League credentials and the ability to blend in easily with those of inherited wealth, was widely assumed to have been born into the patrician class. Indeed, newspaper columnist Liz Smith once described Whitehead as "chairman of the establishment."[34] Unlike the other businesspeople profiled in these pages, Whitehead's entire thirty-seven-year business career was spent on Wall Street in the field of finance. He thus came from an industry in which—at least for the last forty years—few leaders have earned the mantle of "enlightened." Yet, on his death, the *New York Times* saluted him in a glowing editorial, saying "he represented the best of Wall Street."[35]

How the WASP son of a midlevel phone company manager became cochairman of Goldman Sachs is as improbable a story as it is exemplary. Whitehead grew up in Montclair, New Jersey, where he attended public schools, raised racing pigeons, and learned to play the violin. His father's life savings were wiped out in the Depression; worse, he lost his job at AT&T, eventually finding work selling furniture. Whitehead thus grew up in less-than-patrician financial circumstances, although he remembered that his loving mother provided wonderful meals of macaroni and cheese. He was raised as a not terribly devout Episcopalian, and had a record for mischievous behavior in school where he showed few signs of leadership potential, although he did become an Eagle Scout. Fortunately, his poor grades in deportment were offset by just enough top marks in academics to allow him to matriculate at Haverford College. There he came into his own as a student, earning a bachelor's degree in economics. Equally important, he was influenced for the rest of his life by that Quaker school's emphasis on ethics.

After graduation, Whitehead enlisted in the US Navy only days after the Japanese attack on Pearl Harbor and was assigned to a troop carrier as a junior officer. Appalled by the second-class treatment of the large number of African American sailors on board the ship, and "possibly inspired by my nascent Quaker ideals," Whitehead used the little power a junior officer has to improve the living conditions of his black shipmates.[36] It was his first recorded act of leadership. The second was when, as skipper of a landing craft during the D-Day Allied invasion of Normandy, he delivered two boatloads of soldiers to Omaha Beach while under heavy fire from the entrenched German army. He would go on to similar heroics during the allied invasion of southern France and, later, during the storming of Iwo Jima in the South Pacific.

Near the end of the war, Whitehead was sent to Harvard Business School to teach basic administration to navy supply officers. After he was demobilized, he was accepted in the HBS's MBA program, where he concentrated on accounting and finance. On graduation in 1947, he was hired by a "small, little-known and rather genteel" investment banking firm.[37] He was Goldman Sachs's only hire that year, with the handsome starting salary of $3,600 per annum. One of the few gentiles in the firm, Whitehead seems to have been fully accepted by the company's Jewish leaders.

Goldman Sachs was in many ways still the family firm it had been under founder Marcus Goldman (his daughter had married Sam Sachs, a lad who so impressed his father-in-law that he was made name partner in the firm). The small Goldman Sachs investment bank became successful serving as middlemen between buyers and sellers of stocks, bonds, and commercial paper—mostly for companies headed by such Jews as Sears Roebuck CEO Julius Rosenwald. When Whitehead joined the company, it was headed by the legendary Sidney Weinberg. The diminutive and self-educated Weinberg—who would have a sixty-two-year career with the firm—had been there long enough to have worked with Sam Sachs. Weinberg was as skilled as the founders in building personal relationships that led to profitable business deals; nonetheless, the firm was much smaller than competitors Morgan Stanley, Lehman Brothers, Kuhn Loeb, and Dillon Read. In 1947,

Goldman had only five partners; when Whitehead retired thirty-seven years later, it had over two hundred and fifty, and was one of the largest investment banks in the world, if not the largest.[38]

Much of the growth was attributable to the efforts of John White-head. Soon after joining the firm, he had caught the eye of Weinberg, who was impressed by Whitehead's Harvard MBA and, more particularly, his ability to quickly make accurate calculations on a slide rule in the midst of fast-paced negotiations. Whitehead recalled that Weinberg never quite mastered the knack of using a slide rule: "'C'mere,' he'd say, 'show me how to use this damn thing.'"[39] In no time, Whitehead was personal assistant to the head of the firm, and at age thirty-four he was trusted to handle Ford Motor Company's initial public offering, then the largest ever. After nine years he was made partner, with a salary of $25,000 and a quarter of 1 percent of Goldman profits.

Worried that the firm in which he was a partner was overly dependent on its septuagenarian rainmaker Weinberg, Whitehead reorganized it. His creation of a new-business department, with managers assigned to regional areas, allowed the firm to expand nationally and beyond the contacts in Weinberg's impressive but East Coast–limited Rolodex. He launched other departments—investment banking services, equity sales—and entered several new lines of business, in essence creating a formal organization at Goldman, which to that point had been managed informally as a small partnership with little specialization among its staff. By the end of the 1960s Goldman was a national firm, one of the "big five" investment banks. In 1976 Whitehead was named co-chairman, along with Sidney Weinberg's son John. Then Whitehead led the successful effort to transform Goldman, as he put it, into "the first truly international banking firm."[40]

Although Whitehead, more than any other person, was responsible for making Goldman Sachs Wall Street's preeminent firm, he is better remembered as the finance industry's last impeccably ethical leader. As Goldman started to grow, Whitehead feared the eventual loss of its reputation for integrity earned over several decades of "gentlemanly" financial dealings based on personal trust. He thus enunciated a set of twelve J. C. Penney–like "Business Principles" which he felt should inform the firm as it grew. Some of them were:

- Our client's interests always come first.
- Our assets are our people, capital, and reputation.
- We take great pride in the professional quality of our work.
- To breach a confidence and use confidential information improperly or carelessly would be unthinkable.
- Integrity and honesty are at the heart of our business. We expect our people to maintain high ethical standards in everything they do.[41]

Whitehead fleshed out each of these points so all Goldman Sachs professionals would understand clearly what was required of them, and established formal training sessions at which the principles were presented to new hires. Additionally, he introduced recruiting procedures in which the character of new hires was weighted as heavily as the GPAs on their résumés. Most important, he led by example, practicing what he called "quiet leadership." He was known as a courteous, patient, and thoughtful listener, solicitous of the opinions and ideas of everyone in the firm—behavior manifesting his conviction that his self-interest, as he put it, included the interests of his colleagues.[42] Although he had zero tolerance for employee dishonesty, his brand of leadership was respectful rather than commanding, persuasive rather than belligerent, encompassing rather than divisive, and idealistic rather than ideological. And by the example of his own numerous civic activities, he encouraged Goldman colleagues to have a sense of responsibility to their communities, quietly asserting, "I am convinced that a social conscience is sound business practice."[43]

In all, Whitehead devoted nearly forty years of his life to making Goldman Sachs a great company he was proud to be a part of. Yet it was not always easy sledding. He worked long days and missed out on most weekends and vacations, suffering two failed marriages as the result of his day-and-night dedication to the firm. In the early 1980s, while attending a many-hours-long budget review session, he found himself thinking, "My God, I don't think I can do this one more time." He retired in 1984 at age sixty-two—only to then begin two decades of distinguished public service. In his first such post, as deputy secretary of state under George Shultz, he worked with East European Communist nations to develop their economies in exchange for improving their human rights records. As number two in the State Department, he earned a reputation for speaking truth to power. Nonetheless, he recognized that, as a progressive Rockefeller Republican, he was a fish out of water in the conservative Reagan administration, and successfully found a graceful way to make an early exit from Washington.

Whitehead then presided over such prestigious nonprofit institutions as the Andrew Mellon Foundation, the United Nations Association, the Brookings Institution, and the National Gallery of Art (my wife recalls him as a "highly respected and beloved" member of the board of the Getty Museum, where she was general counsel). He also served as unpaid chairman of the Federal Reserve Board of New York and, toward the end of his life, with great distinction as chairman of the Lower Manhattan Development Corporation, working to rebuild downtown New York after the 9/11 terrorist attacks.

In his 2005 autobiography, Whitehead wrote that when shares of his old firm went on public sale for the first time in 1999,

> I worried that, with the transformation to a publicly owned company, some of the intangible things about Goldman Sachs that I had treasured and tried to follow might be lost: the emphasis on always acting in the client's interest, the importance of teams, on holding high ethical standards. As I see what happened, I think I was wrong to worry. . . . As to the intangible values that were and are so important, I believe the firm has maintained them pretty well; better than my fears had led me to imagine and, on the whole, better than the others.[44]

He doubtless would not have drawn that conclusion a few years later when, in the aftermath of the 2007–8 recession, it was revealed that Goldman partners had systematically betrayed nearly all the ethical principles he had stood for, most brazenly by unloading toxic derivatives the firm owned on its unwitting clients. In the decade since, the name Goldman Sachs has, in the public eye, come to stand for all that is venal on Wall Street. That assessment may not be totally fair, but it is undeniably true that the firm's reputation for integrity, which Whitehead called one of its greatest assets, has been seriously eroded. There appear to be many reasons why the culture of Goldman Sachs changed so dramatically in the years after Whitehead's retirement: going public destroyed the bonds of partnership that had served as ethical rudders; the firm grew so large that it became impossible for all in it to share the same values; its leaders failed to emphasize the centrality of integrity; and, probably most important, there was just so much money sloshing around in the firm that greed became its dominant value.

In his autobiography Whitehead noted that after he had retired from Goldman Sachs, "I started a book tentatively called *The Social Responsibilities of Business*, intended to present case studies of companies doing good works while they made money for their stockholders."[45] After finishing one chapter and getting an advance from a publisher, he was called to service in Washington and never finished the book. I like to think, just perhaps, that this might be the book Whitehead had wanted to write.

Roy Vagelos, Physician

Merck & Co. was founded as a pharmacy in the seventeenth century in Darmstadt, Germany, by Friedrich Jacob Merck. In the 1890s his descendant Georg Merck immigrated to the United States, where he started an American subsidiary of the family's pharmaceutical business. During World War I, the US government nationalized the company to sever its ties with Germany, and then reestablished it as a publicly traded American corporation headed by George W. Merck, Georg's son. George led the company until 1946, leaving behind a legacy of ethical business behavior. In George's words, "We try never to forget that medicine is for the people. It is not for the profits. The profits follow, and if we have remembered that, they have never failed to appear. The better we have remembered it, the larger they have been."[46]

In the early 1970s Merck was known for its advanced research capabilities, which led to the development of numerous lifesaving and life-enhancing drugs: the first vaccines for mumps and rubella, the first statins, and the first diuretics that alleviated hypertension. It was the kind of company that attracted talented young medical researchers, such as physician Roy Vagelos. Pindaros Roy Vagelos grew up in a Greek-speaking household in small-town New Jersey, where his immigrant parents ran the Rahway Lunchette. As soon as he was old enough, Roy (as he preferred to be called) went to work as a soda jerk there. After much later graduating from Columbia University Medical School, in 1951 he returned to Rahway, where he briefly interned at the Merck Sharp and Dohme research labs. From there he worked as a researcher and practicing physician on the staffs of several major hospitals and at the National Institutes of Health before returning to Merck in 1975 as director of research.

Almost as soon as he had assumed his position at Merck, Vagelos faced an extremely difficult business decision, one with significant ethical implications. In a memo to Vagelos, a senior researcher who was working on a drug to treat parasites in animals hypothesized that, if reformulated, that drug could be used to kill human parasites—specifically, the worm *Onchocerca volvulus*, which caused the dreaded disease river blindness. In some thirty-five developing-world countries, millions of people living near rivers were at risk of contracting the disease when bitten by blackflies carrying the parasitic worm. When the worm grew inside a human, it gave birth to millions of microscopic offspring that quickly spread throughout the host's body, leading to itching so severe that it often drove people to suicide. In time the tiny worms spread to people's eyes, eventually leading to blindness. In 1978 some eighteen million people were infected with the parasite, over three hundred thousand of them blinded by it.

Vagelos was intrigued by the prospect of finding a cure for river blindness, but he was well aware of the enormous amounts of time and money involved in developing drugs for human use. He reckoned it would take a dozen years, and cost over $200 million, to bring this drug, Ivermectin, to market. Then there was the considerable risk involved in testing a veterinary drug on human subjects. Moreover, there was no market for Ivermectin; those who suffered from river blindness were too poor to pay for it. Despite all that, Vagelos—recalling George Merck's conviction that "Medicine is for the people"—felt a moral obligation to proceed with the project, at least to the next step.

Vagelos directed his research team to develop a pill safe for humans while strong enough to kill the dreaded parasite. That accomplished, in 1980 he convinced the World Health Organization to conduct human trials of the drug (in 1985, while the trials were being undertaken, Vagelos was named Merck's chief executive officer). In 1987 the drug, renamed Mectizan, was finally approved for human use. Now the problem was how to pay for—and distribute—it. Vagelos assumed he could find funding from private donors and international health organizations, but after months of knocking on doors, he found no person or group willing to commit to a program that could, he reckoned, cost up to $20 million a year for many years to come. However, he did get close with the US government, thanks to an intervention by John Whitehead, then serving as deputy secretary of state in the Reagan administration. Whitehead was so enthusiastic about the project that he took Vagelos to meet the director of the USAID program, telling the agency head, "We have to do this program." The director was sympathetic, but explained to Whitehead, "Mr. Secretary, we don't have any money."[47]

After nearly a decade, Vagelos—who had spent hundreds of hours personally trying to get Mectizan to those who needed it—finally accepted the fact that no institution was willing and able to take on the responsibility for distributing it. He understood why: the task was daunting, considering that millions of those suffering from river blindness lived in remote villages, far from hospitals, pharmacies, and health professionals who could administer the drug. Mectizan was in fact a miracle drug: it was safe and efficient, and a single tablet taken once a year killed the parasite. Nonetheless, it was necessary to explain the medication to people who almost invariably were illiterate, and responsible medical practice dictated that records must be kept, and follow-up testing conducted. Mectizan could not simply be handed out to people who might inadvertently overdose, or not follow up with annual doses. If no organization could be found to do all that, Vagelos concluded that Merck would not only be giving the drug away but assuming the expensive responsibility of ensuring its effective distribution.

Vagelos faced opposition to giving Mectizan away from managers both inside Merck and at competing pharmaceutical companies who believed the donations were "setting a bad precedent." If Merck could afford to give this drug away, they feared, it would establish an expectation that other drugs used in the developing world could similarly be provided for free. Such opposition was in part legitimate; free distribution would remove the economic incentive to develop drugs to treat diseases prevalent in impoverished nations. The financial community also was not pleased with a decision that in the long run would amount to over $200 million that could have gone to Merck's bottom line (and to shareholders).

In 1987 Merck announced its intention to supply Mectizan, gratis, to all who needed it for as long as people suffered from river blindness. Such open-ended generosity was unprecedented in business history: What company had ever given away its products? But because the related animal drug, Ivermectin, was earning something like $300 million per year, Vagelos reasoned, Merck could afford to provide Mectizan to people free. Still, the problem of distribution remained. To ensure that distribution was accomplished in a professional manner, Merck funded the independent Mectizan Expert Committee, charged with establishing rules and procedures for getting the drug promptly to those who needed it in a process free of commercial, bureaucratic, or political influence or interference. In the end, the program was a success: by 1996, over fifty-five million people had been treated, and the disease was no longer a major threat in areas where it had been prevalent.

When Vagelos was asked in the early 1990s why Merck continued to spend millions to make the drug available, he answered, "When I first went to Japan fifteen years ago, I was told . . . that it was Merck that brought streptomycin to Japan after World War II, to eliminate tuberculosis which was eating up their society. We did that. We didn't make any money. But it is no accident that Merck is the largest American pharmaceutical company in Japan today."[48] Echoing George Merck, Vagelos added that doing the right thing "somehow . . . always pays off." That same philosophy informed his 1986 decision to sell Merck's patented technology for making hepatitis B vaccine to China at a time when liver cancer resulting from hepatitis was a major cause of death among young Chinese men. Merck sold the technology at a fraction of its cost because, Vagelos explained, he believed China would one day become an active player in the world economy, and then "the Chinese will remember that it was the Merck vaccine that saved all those kids."

Diseased, poor people of the world were not the only beneficiaries of the company's enlightened practices. Despite the costs involved in helping others, Merck's shareholders also did well. During Vagelos's tenure the company was one of the most profitable in the pharmaceutical industry, and a leader in developing new drugs. Moreover, Merck's tens of thousands of employees around the world took great pride in being a part of such an organization, and the river-blindness program reinforced the company's values and George Merck's belief in its higher purpose. Merck became known as a company in which employees demonstrated high levels of loyalty and commitment.

In 1994 Vagelos was forced to retire from Merck at the mandatory age of sixty-five. After that, the company gradually regressed to the norm in its industry with respect to addressing pressing public health issues. To its credit, Merck did not abandon the Mectizan program, although after 1996 the program required a much smaller financial contribution on the part of the company, thanks to a commitment by the World Health Organization and the World Bank to use their resources to eliminate river blindness in Africa. Unfortunately, Merck's new CEO, Ray Gilmartin—a Harvard Business School graduate with little background in health care—was not interested in going beyond the river-blindness program to preserve the company's legacy of corporate beneficence. (Personal observation: When I met Gilmartin, he impressed me as an insecure manager overwhelmed by the daunting task of living up to his predecessor's platinum reputation. In trying to get out from behind Vagelos's shadow, Gilmartin seemed to reflexively choose to do the opposite of whatever Vagelos might have done if faced with a similar situation.)

Speculation about motives aside, there is no doubt that the company's formerly unblemished ethical record was badly besmirched during Gilmartin's tenure. In 2004 Merck was forced to withdraw Vioxx, a treatment for arthritis, when it was discovered that the drug increased the risk of heart attack and stroke. Some fifty thousand individuals would subsequently sue Merck on grounds that they, or family members, had had heart attacks or strokes while on Vioxx. Such suits are, of course, risks all pharmaceutical companies face—but Merck turned an unfortunate situation into a legal and ethical morass by continuing to sell the drug for several years after they knew of its dangers, and by funding bogus studies to "prove" its effectiveness. In 2009 a lawsuit was brought in Australia concerning a sham medical journal that Merck funded that had reported favorably about Vioxx. During the hearing it was revealed that the company had compiled a "hit list" of physicians who had been critical of Vioxx, along with an internal Merck email that read: "We may need to seek them out and destroy them where they live."[49] Gilmartin retired shortly after Vioxx was withdrawn from the market. He then joined the faculty of Harvard Business School as an adjunct professor, teaching "management practice" (alas, fact is often more bizarre than fiction). In 2008 Merck agreed to pay $4.85 billion to settle the civil suits; three years later it pleaded guilty to criminal charges related to the marketing and sales of Vioxx, paying $950 million in fines and penalties.[50] That same year, the company paid $650 million to settle a claim with regard to Medicaid overbilling, and in 2013 it settled a $27 million class action suit with 1,200 plaintiffs who alleged that its drug Fosamax caused a rare, dangerous condition of the jawbone.

Given Merck's constant legal difficulties under Gilmartin, the company's board seems to have concluded that the most appropriate qualification for its next CEO was a law degree. In 2011 the board named Harvard-educated attorney Kenneth C. Frazier as Merck's chief executive. That appointment speaks volumes about the devolution of the pharmaceutical industry: Merck had been led by a physician focused on bringing lifesaving drugs to the world, then led by an MBA whose prime interest was serving investors, and was now led by a lawyer charged with keeping it out of the courts. There is a silver lining: under Frazier, the company continues to be profitable and to develop promising new drugs, and it has recommitted to spending on long-term R&D.[51] And, possibly with a nod toward the legacy of Vagelos, Frazier has been actively involved in international organizations concerned with environmental and health issues. In 2017 he also emerged as an outspoken champion of corporate responsibility with regard to racial justice.[52]

Perhaps Vagelos's most lasting legacy is found in the behavior of other major pharmaceutical companies: the publicity surrounding Merck's Mectizan program encouraged, or perhaps shamed, others in its industry to make drugs affordable—and sometimes free—for people in the developing world. Beginning in 2008, the Dutch Access to Medicine Foundation (funded largely by the Bill and Melinda Gates Foundation) has published a biannual ranking of the twenty largest pharma firms, ranked by the degree to which they make drugs accessible in the world's 107 poorest countries. For the record, Merck ranked fifth in 2016, up from seventh place two years earlier.

When Vagelos reluctantly retired from Merck, he was still vigorous and interested in developing useful drugs. Fearing he would become bored, he agreed to become chairman of the board of start-up Regeneron Pharmaceuticals and to buy six hundred thousand shares of its stock. Over the next two decades, he helped the company develop numerous drugs while delivering a 16,000-percent return to its shareholders, personally earning over $1 billion in compensation for his efforts. Still active at age eighty-eight, he has become known for his generous philanthropic support of numerous educational and medical institutions. Author of over a hundred scientific papers, Vagelos was elected to the American Academy of Arts and Sciences, the National Academy of Sciences, and the American Philosophical Society. As he put it, "my fears about retirement were unwarranted."[53]

In hindsight, Roy Vagelos was to the pharmaceutical industry what John Whitehead was to Wall Street: its last great statesman. Today financial and pharmaceutical firms account for the lion's share of articles in the business press about ethical misbehavior and violations of legal compliance, and neither industry has produced another generation of leaders as enlightened as those two eminently practical patricians.

14

Environmentalists or Capitalists?

ANITA PERELLA RODDICK (1942–2007) and TOM CHAPPELL (1943–)

Enlightened capitalism requires, by definition, the rare ability to maintain a delicate balance between virtue and greed. For example, there are capitalists who have been willing to engage in environmentalism up to the point that corporate profitability is diminished, and environmentally oriented entrepreneurs who have sacrificed some profitability to achieve ecological ends, but few business leaders have been able (or willing) to maintain an equal commitment to both. Anita Roddick and Tom Chappell came as close as any prominent business leader ever has to pulling off that oxymoron-defying feat. Yet at the ends of their careers, even Roddick and Chappell found themselves favoring one end more heavily than the other. Their respective struggles to be both environmentalists and capitalists are the subject of this chapter.

Anita Roddick: The Mosquito Who Pestered the Corporate World

Only recently have women had opportunities to head major businesses, and Anita Lucia Perella Roddick was one of the first of her gender to have led a successful global corporation. She is remembered as founder of the Body Shop, an international chain of stores making and marketing natural products to "cleanse, polish, and protect the skin and hair." Her entrepreneurial skills, along with her dedication to environmental causes and human rights, led the Queen of England to name her Dame Commander of the British Empire in 2003.

Roddick was an unlikely candidate for the role of corporate executive and British dame. Her life story was anything but conventional; her autobiography reads more like the script for a soap opera than the résumé of the business pioneer she was. Born in an English bomb shelter during World War II to a dysfunctional family of Italian immigrants, she didn't learn who her real father was until she was eighteen years old. Her mother, Gilda, came from a small village near Cassino, Italy, at a time when arranged marriages were common in that part of Europe. Her parents thus thought nothing of sending their daughter off to England in the 1930s as the fiancée of Donny Perella, a man she had never met. The marriage, not unexpectedly, was an unhappy one, and Gilda soon fell in love with Donny's cousin, Henry Perella. For several years Gilda and Henry carried on a clandestine love affair while Donny, literally, was out minding the store (actually, a café in the seedy seaside town of Littlehampton). Gilda bore two love children with Henry—Anita and her younger brother, Bruno—and the unwitting Donny assumed that they were his own progeny, and raised them as such. When Gilda refused to divorce Donny on religious grounds, heartbroken Henry embarked to America. Several years later, Henry returned to Littlehampton with a few dollars in his pocket, bought the café from Donny, and then Gilda (ultimately opting for love over the dictates of the Roman Catholic Church) filed for divorce and married Henry. Not long after the marriage, "Uncle" Henry died of tuberculosis, leaving Gilda with the children and the café. Anita later recalled that in her youth, she felt guilty about having loved her "uncle"-cum-stepfather Henry more than her "father" Donny. It took Gilda nearly a decade after Henry's death to screw up the courage to tell Anita and Bruno who their real father was.

Anita grew up helping her mother in the family café, surrounded by relatives and friends in a close-knit immigrant community culturally more Italian than British. She attended a Catholic convent primary school, where she became an avid reader. At age ten, she read a photo book about the Holocaust and was left aghast at the visual evidence of man's inhumanity. As she later explained, "That kick-started me into a sense of outrage or sense of empathy with the human condition."[1] Indeed, she would spend the rest of her life engaged in a variety of activities motivated by either outrage or empathy, sometimes both. Even at an early age, she found the dictates of Catholicism too confining, and when she switched to a public secondary school, she blossomed into a serious student with a questioning mind. Her academic record earned her entry into a local college, where she studied to be a teacher, while longing to become an actor. With Anita busy studying, Gilda grew tired of running the café alone, so she sold it and opened a Latin American–themed nightclub.

Anita spent her early to mid-twenties as a free spirit traveling around the world, living and (briefly) working in Israel, France, Switzerland, and England as a schoolteacher. Her unconventional educational philosophy was simple: learning should be fun. Acting on that belief made her a successful and popular teacher, but a menace in the eyes of school administrators, who were quick to give her the ax. Anita spent those formative vagabond years ("I am such a _____ing nomad") in youthful rebellion and participation in a variety of progressive— sometimes radical—political causes.[2] At age twenty-six, on returning to Littlehampton for a brief visit, she discovered that her mother had been grooming a potential beau for her. Over many months, Gilda had been entertaining Gordon Roddick at her nightclub, giving him food, drink, and motherly advice—along with a daily dose of stories about her daughter, whose letters to home she had been encouraging him to read.

While her own mother had been unlucky at matchmaking, Gilda apparently had a magic touch: Anita and Gordon fell instantly in love. Anita found her soul mate in Gordon, a part-time poet with a comparable case of wanderlust. She moved into his apartment, they had a baby out of wedlock, and when she was pregnant for the second time, they took a trip they couldn't afford to San Francisco, which in the late 1960s was a counterculture mecca attracting hippies and would-be hippies such as Anita and Gordon. From there they drove with their baby to Nevada to gamble with money they didn't have. While in Reno, Anita recalled, "We decided, on the spur of the moment, to get married."[3]

Returning to Littlehampton, Anita and Gordon bought a run-down eight-room hotel that over the next few years would serve as both their home and their prime source of income. While running the B&B, they discovered that they had strong entrepreneurial proclivities, which they further exercised by opening a health-food-themed Italian restaurant. That proved to be an unwise strategic decision in a working-class seaside resort where fish 'n' chips passed for gourmet cuisine. But when they changed the menu to American-style burgers and steaks, they soon were catering to a full house—and discovering that success often comes at a price. In Anita's words, "Running a successful restaurant is one of the most exhausting and time-consuming occupations in the world."[4] Anita and Gordon were working such long hours that Gilda had to sell her nightclub to care full-time for her grandchildren.

Working until midnight seven days a week also took a toll on Anita and Gordon's marriage. In 1976 Gordon suddenly announced that he wanted to sell their restaurant and go off, alone, to South America, where he intended to ride on horseback from Buenos Aires to New York, a 5,300-mile trip he estimated would take two years to complete. Nonetheless, he insisted that he wasn't asking Anita for a divorce, and wasn't planning to abandon her: before departing, he promised to help her get established in a new business. Doubtless most married women would be considerably upset—if not absolutely furious—were their husbands to inform them of such unilateral and consequential plans. But Anita Perella Roddick was not like most women. One can only suppose, given the odd ways in which her life had developed to that point, that nothing could unnerve her. Instead of erupting in anger, Anita simply told Gordon she planned to open an environmentally conscious cosmetic shop.

THE BODY SHOP

As an ardent feminist and believer in natural products, Anita had long been enraged by the practices of the world's dominant cosmetics companies, which she viewed as both demeaning to women and unhealthy. In particular, she found the images of idealized feminine beauty used in cosmetics advertising to be damaging to the self-esteem of ordinary women, concluding that it made them feel dissatisfied with their looks and bodies. With utter contempt, she quoted Leonard Lauder, CEO of Estée Lauder, as saying his company catered to "the kept woman mentality."[5] Further, she believed most cosmetics products were rip-offs—overpriced, overhyped, and ineffective—and railed against the millions spent on cosmetics packaging and advertising. She especially detested cosmetic advertising that made such outlandish claims as "You'll look and feel years younger."[6] While traveling in Tahiti years earlier, Roddick had observed how healthy the skin of Polynesian women appeared, even though they spent most of their lives exposed to the merciless South Seas sun. When she asked a Tahitian woman what her secret was, the woman showed Anita how to make a skin conditioner from cocoa butter. From that moment, she believed it possible to make all personal care products from natural materials.

So when Gordon asked her what business she might like to try, she was ready with an answer: a little shop "that sold cosmetics products in different sizes and in cheap containers," the way some health-food stores sold whole foods in bulk.[7] Gordon then located a small (three hundred square feet) store for rent in nearby Brighton; borrowed £4,000 from a local bank (putting their hotel-house up as collateral); helped Anita to source batches of jojoba oil, almond oil, cocoa butter, rhassoul clay, and aloe vera; served as her *sous chef* in their kitchen while she engaged in soap and cosmetics R&D; and then worked with her to find manufacturers to make the products she concocted. In 1976, two months after the store opened, he took off for Argentina.

Anita cheekily called her little store the Body Shop, after the auto repair garages she had seen in the United States. It offered a line of twenty-five natural hair- and skin-care products. As she recalled in her 1991 memoir *Body and Soul*, when she opened the store, she'd had no intention either of getting rich or starting a global chain: "My sole object was to survive, to earn enough to feed my kids."[8] Nonetheless, from the start the Body Shop was unlike any commercial enterprise the developed world had seen. The place had the casual feel of a country store in which customers were encouraged to bring their own bottles of any size to fill with soaps and conditioners, many of which they were free to mix from a variety of ingredients Roddick offered in recycled jugs: "If they wanted to make their own eau-de-toilette, I told them to mix it with Vodka."[9]

Elizabeth Arden once wrote that the cosmetics business is "the nastiest in the world."[10] But from the get-go, Roddick set out to create an ethical business based on compassion, caring, and candor. The Body Shop's one-sentence mission statement read, "We will be known as the most honest cosmetics company around." Unlike Estée Lauder and Elizabeth Arden, Anita Roddick believed that "the cosmetics industry should be promoting health and well-being," and that would become the intent of the Body Shop's products and practices. While under Roddick's leadership, every item the company sold was biodegradable and made from ingredients "as close to the natural source as possible"; no aerosol containers were used, and everything from the bottles containing cosmetics to the labels on them—even the company's annual report—was recycled and recyclable. The company even offered refunds to customers who returned packaging.[11] All the company's products came with a full list of ingredients, and the Body Shop advertised only to provide information. Roddick admitted that, initially, she knew nothing about business in general, or the cosmetics trade in particular: "There was a grace when we started—the grace you didn't have to bullshit and tell lies. We didn't know you could. We thought we had to be accountable. How do you establish accountability in a cosmetics business? We looked at the big companies. They put labels on the products. We thought what we printed on the label had to be truthful. I mean, we were really that naive."[12]

The store came close to being an immediate success, so much so that Anita was able to open a second Body Shop less than a year after launching the first, this one managed by one of her friends. To finance it, she sold half of the entire business to an investor for £4,000—which turned out to be the worst business decision she made in her life. Eight years later, that investor's stake was worth £4 million (and, by 1991, £140 million). Gordon then returned unexpectedly from South America, having completed two thousand miles on horseback, but now soured on the adventure after the death of his favorite steed. Anita, elated to have Gordon back, promptly turned over the financial and legal operations of the business to him, thus freeing herself to focus on the overall leadership of the growing, and thriving, business. Gordon managed the books in such a way that the company soon was able to finance the opening of several more stores without the help of outside investors. With neighborhoods all over Britain, and then in Continental Europe, clamoring for more Body Shops than the Roddicks could open using their own capital, Gordon came up with the idea of franchising stores. By 1982 they were opening two new shops a month, and charging a £3,000 up-front licensing fee to franchisees, who were contractually obliged to buy all their products from the Body Shop, attend extensive training sessions, and operate in accord with the company's strict environmental, health, and humanistic employment practices. Within a few years the Roddicks were faced with the challenge of choosing new franchisees from over five thousand applicants. By 1990, the Body Shop's licensing fee had increased to as high as £25,000.[13]

In 1984, with thirty-eight shops in the United Kingdom and fifty-two abroad, the company went public.[14] On the day of the initial public offering, Body Shop shares opened at 95 pence; by market closing they were selling at £1.65.[15] As the value of the stock soon soared by 500 percent, they became known as "the shares that defy gravity."[16] The first year after the company went public, its profits doubled, and fifty new stores were opened. By 1991 the company (some 90 percent of its stores franchisees) had a market value of some £300 million. The Roddicks were rich, but they felt their wealth came with obligations. Anita explained that she and Gordon had early on recognized that "a function of profits was to create jobs and provide security and prosperity for our employees. That was fine, but then what?"[17] The "what" turned out to be a range of environmental and human rights initiatives unprecedented in British and European business in the early 1980s. Anita began by using Body Shop stores to promote Greenpeace's efforts to stop dumping hazardous waste in the North Sea, an effort soon followed by a "Save the Whales" campaign. Then, working with Friends of the Earth, the company became leaders in the battle to end acid rain. About that time, Anita joined with the Social Venture Network in the United States, which included such like-minded enterprises as Ben & Jerry's and Patagonia, formed to enlist other companies in similar efforts to raise public consciousness about social and environmental issues. To ensure that the Body Shop's own social performance was up to snuff, the company commissioned an environmental audit of all its operations—including packaging, waste, and effluents—and insisted that its suppliers conform to the same strict standards.[18] Around then, Anita's social agitation was becoming increasingly controversial. For the previous five years, the Body Shop had been requiring its own suppliers to vouch that they never engaged in animal testing, but in 1989 Anita began to lead an effort to ban all animal testing in the European cosmetics industry.

SOCIAL AGITATOR

Anita Roddick soon became a highly visible advocate of an entirely new business philosophy. "My passionate belief," she said, "is that business can be fun, it can be conducted with love and [be] a powerful force for good."[19] When critics said that a small company like hers could have no significant impact on the world's environmental and human rights issues, she retorted, "If you think you are too small to have an impact, try going to bed with a mosquito." In many ways, she became the mosquito who pestered the business world into acknowledging its role in preserving the environment. Not only did Roddick insist that the Body Shop become the world's leader in its own environmental and employment practices, but she also set out to encourage, cajole, and hector other businesses to follow suit. When the Body Shop was named company of the year by the Confederation of British Industries in 1985, her acceptance speech was "a blistering attack" on traditional business values. When invited to address the British Marketing Society, she delivered a talk those advertising managers didn't want to hear: "Why I Would Never Use an Advertising Agency."[20]

All the while Roddick never let up with her relentless criticism of nearly every standard practice in the cosmetics industry. As she famously asserted, "Its main products are packaging, garbage and waste."[21] She condemned the industry's low ethical standards: "They were prepared to sell false hopes and unattainable dreams; I was not. . . . They sold through hype: I was so innocent I didn't even know what hype was. They thought packaging was important; I thought it was totally irrelevant. They all had huge marketing departments; I never fully understood what marketing was. . . . They talked about beauty products; I banished the word 'beauty.'"[22]

In fact, she was quoted as saying her concept of beauty was "Mother Teresa and not some bimbo."[23] Not since Robert Owen had a major British business leader been so openly critical of his or her peers. Moreover, she boasted that she was getting under the skin of many of her fellow businesspeople: "I have the reputation of being Ms. Mega-Mouth."[24] In particular, she was unsparing in her criticism of stock speculators, heaping scorn on those who ran the largest financial institutions in London's City. "I have never kow-towed to the speculators or considered them to be my first responsibility," she openly stated. "They play the market without much concern for the company or its values. Most are interested only in short-term and quick profit."[25]

That said, Anita Roddick was no antibusiness radical. As she put it, "I think profits are jolly good." As if to prove it, the Roddicks became millionaires many times over and lived in comfort in a large castle in Scotland. Where they differed from their business peers was in their insistence on sharing their wealth with impoverished communities, and using company resources to address global problems. Anita believed that the Body Shop could do good and yet "still play the game according to the City, still raise money, delight the institutions, and give shareholders a wondrous return of investment."[26] To reassure investors that the Body Shop wasn't simply, in Anita's words, "a flaky organization led by a mad woman with frizzy hair," Gordon served as the company's "calm presence," managing the financial end of the business.[27]

While making money for themselves and their shareholders, the Roddicks accelerated the company's community-based activities. As Anita explained, "Not a single decision is ever taken in The Body Shop without first considering environmental and social issues."[28] Employees in each of the company's shops were required to undertake community service projects on company time (a Body Shop in Melbourne, Australia, organized five hundred people to plant fifty thousand trees, and the staff in an Edinburgh, Scotland, store volunteered as social workers in a woman's prison). The Body Shop was among the first to promote fair trade in the developing countries whence it sourced raw materials, making sure that the profits that indigenous locals derived from those sales were used for community development projects, ranging from schools to health care. The company's Trade Not Aid program (now Community Trade) initiated imaginative job-creation projects among destitute populations in Asia, Africa, and South America, many of which turned out to be embarrassing failures. For example, it contracted with the Kayapo tribe of Amazon Indians for handicrafts to be sold in Body Shops in Britain and Europe, a venture that unraveled when the tribe's chief sued over the use of his image in Body Shop advertising. And the company's highly touted Boys Town program in India—in which poor and homeless boys were said to be trained to make wooden Footsie Rollers for the company—backfired when it became known that the work was being subcontracted to a local sweatshop.[29] Nonetheless, the Roddicks came to be seen as heroes in parts of Brazil, thanks to their efforts to save the Amazonian rain forest. (In a related activity, the Body Shop also became the first company to hire a staff anthropologist to catalog the world's disappearing tribes and the methods they used for skin and hair care.)

In Britain, the company trained and hired minority immigrants to work in its shops, and in 1989 it opened a soap factory in Easterhouse, a Glasgow suburb where the unemployment rate was 70 percent. By 1991 the soapworks were employing over a hundred people, with 25 percent of its profits dedicated to projects benefiting the local community. But even there, controversy lurked. After Roddick described the Scottish neighborhood as pretty much a slum "where angels fear to tread," a critic retorted, "To hear her speak . . . you might think The Body Shop was the only industrial employer in Easterhouse," and pointed out that her small plant was in fact surrounded by many large, busy factories. Characteristically, she replied, "Cynics—up yours!"[30]

While engaging in such external activities, Roddick claimed she never lost sight of the company's primary responsibilities to its customers and employees. She insisted that the company keep the price of its products low to serve average consumers, stressing the importance of treating all Body Shop customers with respect. To that end, she made a humorous employee-training video entitled *Smile, Dammit, Smile*, and offered employees "Anita's 20 second crash course on Customer Care": "Never treat customers as enemies, approach them as potential friends. Think of customers as guests, make them laugh. Acknowledge their presence within 30 seconds: smile, make eye contact, say hello. Talk to them within the first 3 minutes. Offer product advice where appropriate. Smile. Always thank customers and invite them back. Treat customers as you'd like to be treated!"[31]

Roddick actively recruited store workers whose attitudes were much like her own: "We want people in our shops who care, who are enthusiastic, who like trading [commerce], who enjoy rapping, and don't mind wrapping."[32] She trained the staff never to push a product but instead to give customers all the facts, then leave them to decide what, if anything, to purchase. In 1985 she opened the Body Shop School in London to encourage the fuller development of employee talents and skills, offering free classes on such diverse topics as sociology, aging, and AIDS. "Conventional retailers trained for a sale; we trained for knowledge," she explained, adding, "You can train dogs. We wanted to educate people."[33] Sticking with her fundamental belief that, above all, learning should be fun, the school offered a course on "management by humor." As she explained her business philosophy to employees, "First you have to have fun. Second, you have to put love where your labor is. Third, you have to go in the opposite direction to everyone else."[34]

Anita Roddick was a principled advocate of employee participation and organizational openness. She encouraged Body Shop employees "to challenge the rules, to question the status quo and things we took for granted, and never accept that a manager, simply because he or she was a manager, necessarily knew better."[35] To ensure that employee voices were heard, she established a system by which, if need be, they could bypass management and communicate directly with members of the company's board. She loved it when employees pushed back against bad company policies and ideas, even when those were her own. When members of the sales staff complained about the uniforms they had been given to wear on the job, Anita asked them, "Then why the _____ are you wearing them?"[36] She believed all Body Shop employees (75 percent of whom were women under the age of thirty) should be treated as adults. Influenced by Brazilian business leader Ricardo Semler—whose employees set their own work hours and hired their managers—she established a system in which her workers evaluated the effectiveness of their supervisors.[37] To encourage employees to submit suggestions on any subject, she initiated a Department of Damned Good Ideas (DODGI), offered bonuses for innovative ideas, and was proud of the many that were implemented.

In 1988 the Body Shop opened its first store in the last developed country not to have one: the United States. The Roddicks had been reluctant to enter the world's largest, most competitive commercial market because previous attempts by British retailers to do so had mostly ended in failure. As Anita explained, "It was Gordon's view that, while the United States offered The Body Shop the greatest potential for growth, it also represented the greatest potential for disaster."[38] To begin, the Body Shop trademark was already owned in America by another party, who eventually agreed to sell it to the Roddicks for $3.5 million.[39] Furthermore, American regulators often played hardball: for example, the company's long-standing practice of refilling customers' cosmetics bottles was declared verboten. And once the Body Shop was established on American soil, domestic competitors proved to be tougher than any it had previously encountered. Almost the moment the Body Shop established that there was demand in America for natural products, Leslie Wexner (founder of retailer the Limited) opened the knockoff Bath & Body Works chain, whose shops were near-exact replicas of Body Shops, carrying a similar line of goods down to the loofah back scrubbers, potpourri, and aromatic soaps that were hallmarks of the British firm. The Roddicks replied with legal action. "People think we're a flaky New Age company," Anita roared. "But by God, we defend ourselves like lions."[40] By 1994, the Body Shop was a $500 million company operating in forty-four countries, with America its major growth market.

RODDICK'S CRITICS

For all the Body Shop's admirable environmental efforts and financial success, Anita Roddick faced a continual barrage of criticisms from left, right, and center, many casting doubt on the sincerity of her efforts. An influential 1994 article by Martha Nichols in the *Harvard Business Review* dismissed Roddick's book *Body and Soul* as a utopian New Age screed, paternalistic at best. Nichols challenged Roddick's assumption that Body Shop employees all shared her values: "Entrepreneurs like Roddick often confuse themselves—their goals, political beliefs, dreams and considerable talents—with the companies they create and the people who work for them."[41] In 1991, Roddick had admitted as much: "I realized I did not necessarily have the right to speak for The Body Shop on every issue. . . . I accepted that principle—and completely ignored it, I have never been able to separate Body Shop values from my own personal values."[42] Nichols also condemned Roddick for "false humility":

> At their worst, New Age morality tales mix up an individual's drive for power with a higher purpose. In Roddick's case, the story goes like this: Innocent hippie teacher and poet husband know nothing of the evil world of business, forge ahead because, she says, "my sole object was simply to survive, to earn enough to feed my kids." She opens her first shop in Brighton, England, in 1976, never loses her vision of selling cosmetics with natural ingredients at reasonable prices, and never loses sight of her customers. . . . Roddick's tale, by turns flippantly direct and disingenuous, is representative of the contradictions that suffuse New Age writing.[43]

According to Nichols, those "contradictions" included the undeniable fact that the Roddicks—and other entrepreneurs who shared their philosophy—"benefit disproportionately" from the profits of their companies while piously espousing the interests of employees, and that Anita's rejection of advertising was a sham because "the media attention Roddick thrives on is part of a larger promotional scheme that has helped mold a strong brand image." Furthermore, "Roddick's iconoclastic business approach and politically correct image . . . are savvy sales tools, not just a gauntlet thrown in the face of 'borrowing bankers.'"[44] In effect, Nichols argued, Roddick had simply come up with an effective, au courant marketing strategy. Nichols went on to claim that, even if the efforts of Roddick and her ilk in the personal care and consumer goods industries were well-intentioned, they nonetheless didn't "map to most industries" involved in "selling consequential products like cars, computers, or commodities such as steel."[45]

Exasperated by Nichols's criticism, Roddick replied that the cosmetics and fashion industries were in fact real businesses, and far from financially inconsequential, noting that in the United States alone, they accounted for more than $20 billion in annual sales.[46] She also rejected the charge that she was a New Age utopian, saying that she was "fully aware that running a skin- and hair-care product company with more attention to values won't solve the world's problems. It can, however, be one step in the right direction. We at The Body Shop are using the modest tools at our disposal to make things a little bit better." With regard to the sincerity of her beliefs, Roddick answered,

> Nichols suggests that my company's values are nothing but a marketing tool because I let my customers know about them. I *do* think our values should make people feel better about buying from us. As a customer, I shop for goods that are well made in all senses of the word: functionally, environmentally, ethically. I have always assumed others would do the same. I see no fundamental contradiction between my values and my entrepreneurial success. . . . Nichols wants me to choose between being a values-oriented businessperson and a street-smart entrepreneur. I refuse to simplify myself in that way.[47]

It is worth noting that prior to the Nichols article, the *Harvard Business Review* had seldom, if ever, published direct and personal criticism of the beliefs or behavior of business leaders. Previously, the journal's editorial policy seemed to preclude printing anything but positive comments about specific individuals. One is left to wonder why an exception was made for Roddick. Had the perceived "radical" nature of her business philosophy prompted the attack? Yet in fact her views were neither antibusiness nor socialist. Her stated belief that "enlightened capitalism is the best way of changing society for the better"[48] is consistent with the philosophy of today's libertarian-minded "conscious capitalists," as was the Body Shop's commitment to "trade not aid." Instead, she appears to have been seen as fair game because "Ms. Mega-Mouth" repeatedly violated the corporate executive's so-called Eleventh Commandment: Never say anything bad about one's fellow business leaders. Nearly two hundred years after Robert Owen criticized the British business community, Roddick found herself similarly rejected by her peers, and for much the same reasons.

At other times and in other forums, Roddick was criticized for inconsistencies in the Body Shop's environmental and product purity standards (the company acknowledged that, indeed, it had used some synthetic preservatives and artificial colors).[49] Similarly, she was accused of hypocritical "green-washing," taking advantage of cheap third-world labor, underpaying her own employees, "maternalistically" imposing her political views on the company and customers, being an imperious manager, not returning enough to her shareholders, and making too much profit for her husband and herself. She received her most negative reviews when, in 2006, she sold the company for $1.2 billion to L'Oréal, a giant corporation whose values seemed inconsistent with the Body Shop's. She countered the accusation that she was "selling out," claiming that her intention was to become a Trojan horse inside the acquiring behemoth, and pledging to work to change the industry from the inside: "Instead of the dinosaurs in pin-stripes determining our future . . . we will be teaching L'Oréal to introduce community trade throughout their business."

The L'Oréal takeover caught both Anita's friends and critics by surprise. No one could make sense of why the Roddicks had "sold out."

Indeed, it is not altogether clear why they agreed to sell the company to the very kind of major cosmetics competitor Anita had spent years mocking. However, there is some evidence that the Roddicks had become increasingly concerned about their company's future. Anita had for years understood that its success was due, in great part, to the enthusiasm and passion of the people who worked in its stores. She admitted, "I'd never get that kind of motivation if we were just selling shampoo and body lotion,"[50] recognizing that it was the higher purpose of the business that had fired the intense commitments made by the young people who "wo-manned" her shops. And doubtless it was Roddick herself, with all her wild and noble environmental and social causes, that had served as the company's primary source of energy and electricity. But could the company's next leader provide such a spark? As early as 1991 Roddick commented to Harvard Business School professor Christopher Bartlett that "leadership of a company should encourage [the] next generation not just to follow, but to overtake.... The complaint Gordon and I have is that we are not being overtaken by our staff."[51]

Ironically, for all Anita Roddick's commitment to staff development, she had failed to groom a viable successor. It is not clear if she ever admitted that fact; nonetheless, she seems to have concluded that not having a successor meant she had to ensure the sustainability of the organization by institutionalizing the passion she had personally inspired: "What's imperative is the creation of a style that becomes a culture." In Gordon's words, "The thing we now have to do is reduce the dependence of the business on Anita and Gordon [and] create a structure where they are pleased to see you, but they can do without you. That is our aim."[52] Apparently, the Roddicks concluded that this aim could best be achieved if the Body Shop became part of a larger, more formal organization. We can only take Anita Roddick at her word that she was committed to ensuring that her company's spirit would survive in a corporate environment, and that its values would become contagious, ultimately infecting the acquiring company.

The extent to which the Body Shop had that effect inside L'Oréal is unclear, but there is no doubt that a great number of its stores were closed after the acquisition, and the commitment to community service all but disappeared. The Body Shop ceased being active in environmental and human rights causes, although in 2014 L'Oréal joined a few environmentally conscious firms in signing a pledge to reduce, and ultimately end, the clearing of tropical forests to grow palm oil. Sadly, we will never know if Anita Roddick would have made good on her pledge to change L'Oréal from within: in 2007, she died from a brain hemorrhage caused by lingering hepatitis C she had contracted from a blood transfusion after the birth of her second child. On learning she still had the disease after many decades, she characteristically said, "It's a bit of a bummer, but you groan and move on." To the end she maintained a positive outlook, firmly believing in a brighter tomorrow, no matter how bleak today's forecast. From the beginning of her career, Roddick had been an optimist with regard to the future of business behavior. In 1991 she had predicted that "by the year 2000 any company that does not operate like The Body Shop will have a hard time operating at all."[53] She was wrong about the specifics of her forecast; it remains to be seen if her general optimism will ultimately be justified.

In 2017 L'Oréal sold what was left of the Body Shop chain to Brazil's Natura Cosmetics for €1 billion, less than the French giant had paid for it a decade earlier. Natura's cochairman, Luiz Seabra, vowed that his environmentally focused company would return to its founding roots: "We want to reconnect the company with its own soul, with the values of Anita, and we think that through that we can bring in an important revitalization."[54]

Throughout her career, Anita Roddick built a reputation for being angry, combative, outspoken, impolitic, and pushy. (On the one occasion when we met, I found her to be charismatic, bursting with self-confidence, and totally exhausting company.) In short, she was as flawed a human being and business leader as were the other individuals profiled here. What seems also to be true is that the traits her critics criticized in a woman executive were often viewed more positively as "tough, firm, single-minded, and courageous"—if a bit quirky—when found in men. All the leaders we have considered faced criticism and resistance, but it is no exaggeration to say that Anita Perella Roddick received more than her fair share of both.

Tom Chappell: For God, or Profit?

As we have seen, Max De Pree's motivation to create an ethically virtuous company was rooted in deep religious convictions, as it was for James Penney, James Lincoln, John Eagan, and the individual whose career we now examine, Tom Chappell, cofounder of Tom's of Maine. In Chappell's case, the linking of business and religious principles came almost as an afterthought; but when it came, it fundamentally changed the way Chappell led his company. Chappell has told the story himself in a painfully personal account that illustrates how daunting managing the tensions between idealism and practicality is for leaders who wish to serve both Mammon and their Maker.

In 1970, twenty-seven-year-old insurance company manager Chappell came to the realization that he was an unrequited entrepreneur with a hankering to start his own business, in partnership with his wife, Kate. The couple decided to take the entrepreneurial plunge by producing environmentally safe cleaning and personal hygiene products. Working in their kitchen, they developed the first nonpolluting liquid laundry detergent and, not long after, the first toothpaste made with "all natural ingredients" (and unsweetened, to boot). By 1981, Tom's of Maine was reaping $1.5 million in sales from a line of natural soaps, shampoos, mouthwash, skin lotion, and shaving cream, products developed by what Tom called "intuition" (as opposed to analytical R&D).

It was a good start, but the company was too small to expand beyond its local New England customer base, and without a significant advertising budget, its products had no foreseeable pathway to the shelves of large national retail chains. Wanting their company to grow, Tom and Kate decided to get serious about the business end of their enterprise, particularly finance and marketing (Kate was a whiz at new product development, and Tom had eco creds, so they were set on those fronts). Having set ambitious goals for increased sales and profits, the Chappells hired a handful of experienced sales and marketing managers who had honed their skills in such big companies as General Mills and Procter & Gamble. With the help of those young MBAs, five years later the company was bringing in close to $5 million in sales. They were on their way financially; yet Tom was unhappy, and wasn't sure why. After a visit with his Episcopalian priest, he did something unprecedented in the history of business leadership: he enrolled in the Harvard Divinity School as a graduate student in theology, and commuted to his company headquarters in Maine to spend two and half days a week.

GOD AND MAMMON

Chappell had always been a devote Episcopalian, but he had kept his business interests separate from his spiritual life. That changed in 1986 after a series of disagreements with his hired professional managers over what constituted "success" in their business. They were certain success was measured by profit margins, but Tom wasn't so sure that was all there was to it. He was certain that he liked making money; nonetheless, he wanted something more from his business than just wealth. In the remarkably frank account of his spiritual-cum-business journey, *The Soul of a Business*, Chappell writes that he discovered the missing element while at Harvard. His book is not just the typical executive memoir, recounting how its author succeeded and what readers can learn from his experience, although it more than thoroughly covers such matters; it is also a soul-searching account of Chappell's personal struggle to find a way to "do good while doing well." In some passages there is a confessional, Saint Augustinian quality to his attempts to free himself from the clutches of Mammon (*but, dear Lord, please not yet!*)

and embrace a righteous path. Chappell admits he wanted to have it both ways, as the book's subtitle indicates: *Managing for Profit and the Common Good*. At times the reader senses the presence of Francesco Datini's uneasy sixteenth-century pairing—"For God and for profit"— which, over the ensuing centuries, has cast a shadow of doubt on the way most Christian business leaders have ordered their priorities. But where Datini put his emphasis squarely on profit, Chappell says he emerged from his spiritual ordeal focused on "the common good."

That outcome would not have surprised anyone who knew Chappell. Unlike Penney and Eagan, he is a modern mainstream Christian more at home quoting Martin Buber, Immanuel Kant, T. S. Eliot, and Lao-Tzu than citing holy scriptures as inspiration for his good works. Moreover, he is very much a secular child of the 1970s, proudly active in social movements calling for greater equality for women and minorities, world peace, and a healthy planet. Of course, he also came to own a yacht and a big pad in Kennebunkport!

Chappell convinced himself that he could square the circle: at divinity school he decided he would be "a capitalist, but also a moralist."[55] There, he committed himself and his company to treat all their constituencies—customers, employees, suppliers, financial partners, government, the community, and environment—"with respect." Back from Harvard, he informed his team of MBAs that the company's primary emphasis henceforth would be not on profit but, instead, on serving its customers by offering healthy and environmentally safe products:

> I now began to understand that the tensions at Tom's of Maine between me and my young MBAs were a symptom of our different visions of business, of our clash of values. No matter how much those young professionals wanted to work at Tom's of Maine and be "different" from their fellow business school graduates, they had been trained the same way, indoctrinated into the same business principles, taught to ask the same questions: What will the

numbers be this time next year? How do we get the numbers we want? To make those numbers, to get more market share from our competitors, to give us that edge on the crowded supermarket shelves, they were more inclined than I to change, even if ever so slightly, those things that made us different.[56]

However, it wasn't practical to simply sack those talented professionals—at least, not if he wanted the business to be a financial success. He explains, "I began to think about how I could transform Tom's of Maine into a company that could live its values—*my* values—and continue to grow."[57] Ergo, he attempted to bring his team around to his way of thinking through the same process that had allowed him to clarify his own values and priorities: education. He launched an educational process that would go on for years, holding frequent meetings in which he would bring guest speakers into the company, taking his managerial team on weekend off-sites, gathering informally—using all those occasions as opportunities for his managers to honestly discuss how they wanted to shape the identity and culture of the company. Like Robert Wood Johnson at J&J, Chappell worked with his key executives to define the company's responsibilities to its constituencies, jointly writing the "Tom's of Maine Statement of Beliefs." Among other things, that company credo stated, "We believe that people bring different gifts and perspectives to the team and that a strong team is founded on a variety of gifts."[58] And, as James Burke had done at J&J, Chappell urged his people to regularly challenge the company's principles and values until they were clear and accepted by all—and then repeat the process until those concepts were institutionalized in its culture and incorporated in its business strategy. In the end, a consensus formed around the idea that the company's mission was "to serve our customers by providing safe, effective, innovative, natural products of high quality."[59]

Then they attempted to "live that mission." But it wasn't easy. Tom's team kept slipping back to thinking the way they had been taught at

B-school: "I just hadn't realized how ingrained the utilitarian spirit had become."[60] But the slow process of "letting the mission seep down" eventually bore fruit, and the company began to act with a common purpose. It should be mentioned that, while all this was going on, Tom's of Maine was a very small company: in the late 1980s it had a total of eighty-five employees, all located in Kennebunkport. Chappell's organizational challenge was thus nowhere near as daunting as Burke's at J&J, where he had led a global workforce of a hundred thousand. Yet Burke had J&J's enormous resources at his disposal, while Tom faced the nail-biting monthly challenge of meeting payroll.

THE GROWTH IMPERATIVE

Chappell knew the greatest barrier standing in the way of his company's success was its small size. Tom's of Maine had no financial margin for error, a vulnerability that was exposed when, striving to become ever greener, the company substituted a vegetable-based ingredient for a petroleum-derived substance in its popular deodorant. Its customers rebelled, bombarding Kennebunkport with irate complaints that the new formula conked out halfway through the day, leaving them smelling less than flowerlike. A painful decision was then taken to recall the product—to the tune of $400,000, some 30 percent of expected profits for the year. In doing so, the company admirably lived up to its values, but the decision necessitated either forgoing or reducing needed capital expenditures, which created operating problems over the next few years. At J&J, a $400,000 recall would have amounted to a rounding error.

Chappell worked diligently to meet the company's responsibilities not only to its customers but to its employees, introducing such benefits as retirement and profit-sharing plans, parental leave, and child care—all costly for such a small organization. At his insistence, the company became a leader in hiring women and minorities. But its most progressive policy was philanthropic: the company's theologian-CEO insisted that it engage in "corporate tithing." He started by giving 5 percent of pretax profits to local charities and nonprofits, and then, not long thereafter, began to donate 10 percent—perhaps the highest level of giving at any American company. Tom justified this extreme generosity in religious terms, but even from a purely business perspective, it was hard for anyone to criticize the policy; Tom and Kate owned the vast majority of company stock. It might be argued that those charitable donations could have gone to employees in the form of higher salaries or more generous benefits, yet most of the company's workers took pride in its support of organizations serving their home community. (Although Tom and Kate involved employees in some decisions on which local organizations to support, they seemed to have made most such calls on their own.)

Chappell had a deeply philosophical take on business. As a capitalist, he recognized that almost all companies do "good" for society by creating wealth, jobs, and new technology, and by providing the products and services people want and need. However, he noted, those "goods" come about as the unintentional by-products of the desire to make a profit: "Most businesses, however, do not *intend* to do good; it isn't their primary goal." He contrasted that goal with his own business beliefs and practices: "Our ideas for new natural products have been intentional acts of doing good."[61] He believed that differences in intention lead to differences in behavior: for example, if a company's intent is simply to increase sales, it will use hype in advertising; but if its intent is to bring healthy products to customers, it will use factual, informational advertising. The sum of Chappell's argument is that *intentionality* is the key to distinguishing business virtue from business as usual. In making the case, Chappell used much the same religious vocabulary Max De Pree employed: the words *grace, respect, goodness, virtue, faith,* and *gifts* appeared frequently when both explained their business philosophies.

Similar to De Pree, Chappell was a firm believer in the power of storytelling to convey the culture of an organization and to create a sense of "community"—another word used often by both leaders.

Chappell told the story of one longtime manager who had lost passion for his work, becoming such a chronic underperformer that his fellow employees pressed Tom to fire him. Instead, Tom worked long and hard to "unlock" this person's "creative self" by giving him new challenges that, in due course, reignited his passion. Chappell told the story to illustrate the importance of treating each employee as a unique individual deserving of respect, much as De Pree told the story of the millwright poet. Indeed, both De Pree and Chappell frequently personalized their messages, referring to specific examples of individual employees when explaining company policies, rather than, as most executives do, using abstract financial and organizational constructs such as "rationalizing" and "retraining." To both leaders, business was about creating an ever-expanding community of individuals, each worthy of respect, that included employees, customers, and residents of the localities where their operations were situated.

It was the goal of "ever-expanding" that would constantly bedevil Tom's of Maine. Chappell was ambivalent about growth. On the one hand, he said, "The reason big companies buy small companies is that the giants lose their capacity to be creative and innovative. They are too burdened by rationality and analysis."[62] On the other hand, he wanted the company to grow so more people could benefit from its healthy products; moreover, it would then have more profit to spread around philanthropically. Indeed, the company's tithing became an increasingly major focus. Soon the company was supporting arts, educational, environmental, and social welfare organizations, not only locally but nationally. Those donations often had nothing to do with the company's line of business; American Indians and public television were among Chappell's favorite causes. By 1993, according to Tom, the company was spending "more than $300,000 on public education and community organization sponsorships—absolutely separate from our tithed, donations budget."[63] Additionally, he introduced a policy that encouraged employees to engage in community service during 5 percent of their paid work time.

Yet, again, Tom Chappell was a businessman: with Kate acting as the company's director of R&D, it introduced a top-selling line of children's toothpaste and a nonpolluting cleaner that came in a returnable container. The latter was the first such example of modern-era product recycling (although milk, beer, and soda bottles had once been recycled, that time had long since passed in the American throwaway culture that emerged in the 1950s). The Chappells even figured out how to derive fluoride naturally from the sea for use in toothpaste. However, for every mention Chappell made of the company's success in developing environmentally safe products, he reiterated his desire for growth: more profits, increased sales, a national market for the company's goods, and being able to compete with the "big guys" for market share. "I'm very competitive," the avowedly environmentalist CEO confessed, somewhat apologetically.[64]

CONTRADICTIONS GALORE

Throughout its history, the company stressed the value of participative management. But Tom Chappell was a man of many contradictions and paradoxical tensions between the two sides of his often-conflicted self. For example, he worked hard to keep his temper and impatience in check, and to learn to listen to his people and involve them in decisions he was tempted to make on his own. On one page of his book, he protested, "Personally, I don't value that kind of power, unless I'm able to share it," while on the next page admitting, "Yet no one was more reluctant to yield power. Even when I thought I had become one of the most magnanimous CEOs in the land [a company board member] reminded me that my view of autonomy might not be the same as that of my executives or employees."[65] Reminding Chappell that he sat at the top of the company, where he almost always insisted on having the last word, the board member asked him, "What's it like for others in the hierarchy? . . . Do you and your managers grant others in the company the freedom to serve?" He was forced to admit, "I had kept the managing control of the company right in my lap."[66] Almost every page of Chappell's book manifests his ongoing, near-Manichean struggle between wanting to keep control and realizing he needed to delegate. For a self-proclaimed moralist, he obsessed over maintaining control, constantly referring to the fact that he and Kate needed to control the majority of company shares. As much as he struggled to trust his people to make decisions, he never seems to have let control get far from his office, let alone his lap. He made it clear that, when push came shove, he was the chief, the boss, the decider. After all, Episcopalians are led by bishops!

By the 1990s, Tom's of Maine was gaining a national market and recognition for its pioneering environmental efforts. In 1991, Chappell shared CNBC's Entrepreneur of the Year award with Anita Roddick. Two years later, he and Kate won Maine's Governor's Award of Business Excellence. About then, the company sought to raise the capital needed to reach its goal of $100 million in sales, the amount its managers figured would be necessary to compete nationally with Bristol-Myers, Johnson & Johnson, and Procter & Gamble. But Kate was uneasy about the potential consequences of reaching that goal: "I have concerns about how such a rapid growth to $100 million would offset the culture we've labored to create in living a mission that respects other people's dignity, [and one] that respects nature and communities."[67] Indeed, as the company increasingly focused on expansion, Kate found her interest in managing the business waning. She had served the company since its inception as its creative spark, inventing new products and lines of business (for which, Tom admitted, he often failed to give her due credit), but now, as her "intuitive" approach to innovation was being replaced by formal management processes, the fun was going out of the work. She decided to step aside from the company to pursue a career as an artist.

CHAPPELL AGONISTES

Tom Chappell had earlier posed a major question he still needed to answer: "Are we going to remain a lifestyle company in which Tom and

Kate govern kindly over their kingdom, or are we going to claim our rightful share of the personal-care market in America?" In trying to decide which it would be, he felt that, "like a boatman navigating a swirling river, Tom's of Maine [has] to steer between analysis and intuition, between our goals of profit and social responsibility, between hardball and softball."[68] Being Tom, he characteristically decided not to choose one path or the other, but instead to take both. Henceforth, the company would adopt what he termed "the middle way" of pursuing "profit and the common good," sticking with his goal of growth—but now with "compassion." He believed that conclusion was not paradoxical; in fact, he argued that the company's most effective strategy would be to demonstrate to customers that it was a business with a soul. If the company managed to do that, he rationalized, customers would come. Believing that there was a growing "market for virtue," he set the goal of capturing it. When he was finally convinced the company could both do good *and* do well—indeed, do well *by* doing good—he claimed to have experienced a sense of newfound freedom. Yet he realized that his have-it-both-ways strategy might sound a tad idealistic: "I can read your mind. 'He thinks he can compete,' you're wondering, but where is this guy going to get the money?"[69]

Tom didn't have an answer to his question. As he openly acknowledged, the company had been forced to postpone needed capital expenditures as the result of its $400,000 product recall, a shortfall subsequently compounded by declining sales during a national economic recession. It had insufficient cash on hand, or coming in, to self-finance growth. Moreover—and this was a fact he seems not to have acknowledged—he had recently chosen to increase the company's charitable donations, in effect giving away hundreds of thousands of dollars that could have been reinvested to generate the desired growth. So where *would* the money come from? A loan was out of the question: no bank would lend millions to a small company with few assets. Selling equity was unthinkable; that would mean forgoing the Chappells' cherished control of the firm's ownership. In sum, there was no obvious avenue to the capital needed to pursue Tom's goal of expansion.

About that time, as Chappell recalled, "three of our major competitors—three really big boys—came calling. The conversations went something like, 'You're doing well. We like what you are doing. We'd like to buy your business.'" To all three, he answered, "No way!" When they then proposed entering into a strategic alliance in which they would market Tom's of Maine's products, he "turned them all down—no sale today, thank you." Chappell was worried that if they got a foot in the door, the next step would be a complete takeover.[70] Nonetheless, he fantasized about what it would be like if Tom's of Maine were to become a subsidiary of a large corporation and he stayed on as its president. In that scenario, he would have the capital he needed; at the same time, he imagined the reaction of the corporation's CEO if he were to walk into his office and tell him he'd just given away $150,000 to community groups: "Before showing me the door, I suspect the . . . [CEO] would point out that $150,000 was more than enough to launch new Tom's of Maine products, or test the power of television in a selected market share—two products that have been on hold for a while now at Tom's for lack of time and money."[71]

Again, no way! The most important thing, he concluded, was to maintain the company's autonomy, or what he called the necessity of "self-rule"—which, of course, meant his personal freedom to run the show as he saw fit. Despite not having figured out how to raise the requisite capital, Tom had become convinced (or had convinced himself) that he could now manage the tension between profit and good works effectively. Hence, in 1993, he pledged to stay the course: "My family will continue to control the company. We need our autonomy to keep calling our own shots. Family control gives us the chance to be a new model of a successful business, an inspiration to other corporations who also want to change the face of American business."[72]

Looking forward, he waxed philosophical about his "new-found autonomy": "My goal in life has become perfecting this *freedom to serve* my employees, my customers, my community, and the natural environment that houses and nurtures us all. The Hindus call it *moksa*—a personal mastery and caring less for material things and more for others. . . . Now I would like to become an entrepreneur committed to others. . . . Managing for profit and the common good—it works."[73]

A SURPRISING END

Thirteen years after Chappell decided that his company would remain independent, the Colgate-Palmolive Company bought a controlling 84 percent of Tom's of Maine for $100 million, the Chappells retaining the remaining 16 percent. What had happened between 1993 and 2006? The company had continued to grow slowly, although never breaking into the mass market; it had continued to make excellent products, and to share its profits generously with nonprofit organizations, much as Tom had wished and planned. Colgate's motivation for buying the company was clear: the company's management wanted to enter the growing market for natural products, and it was safer to bet on Tom's of Maine's established reputation than to introduce its own line of products and then try to convince informed eco-shoppers that Colgate had "gone green." Moreover, a little greenwashing was in order at any company dependent on forest-destroying palm oil plantations as prime suppliers.

But the stakes were different for Tom Chappell. He had those same discerning customers *to lose* if he were seen as selling out to an uncaring global giant with a mixed environmental record. Yet from a business point of view, if growth was the goal, it made sense for Tom's of Maine to be acquired. According to two business school professors who examined the company's financial and sales performance after it became a part of Colgate, "While Tom's was . . . able to lower costs of some production inputs due to Colgate's larger purchasing volumes, even more significantly it gained greater access to and bargaining power with the distribution channels. It also had larger resources to invest in market research and new product development."[74]

In addition, Chappell could proudly point to the fact that he had negotiated an agreement with Colgate by which Tom's of Maine would be treated as a relatively independent subsidiary, and he would continue for three years as its president, reporting to the CEO of the parent company. In effect, he had accepted an arrangement nearly identical to the one he had rejected out of hand some ten years earlier. It is not clear what had changed in the interim, but it is logical to assume that Tom and Kate simply decided to pursue the same exit strategy followed by most business founders: reap a hard-earned reward by selling their company to a corporation with deep pockets. If so, the Chappells' behavior was consistent with the entrepreneurial aspect of their personalities they had displayed throughout their careers. Indeed, most entrepreneurs eventually get bored with managing the businesses they create, seeking to free themselves of them to once again feel the adrenaline rush of starting a new business. In fact, after selling Tom's of Maine, Tom started Ramblers Way, a company that makes wool undergarments using a carbon-neutral process—wool undies apparently being a necessity in chilly Maine.

While it is impossible to fully understand the motives of others, I believe Tom could rightly claim that he had achieved most of his goals for his company, and it was time to move on. Moreover, by selling it, he would achieve his goal of bringing a line of healthy, eco-friendly products to the mainstream market. He also acted responsibly by making sure that key Tom's of Maine employees retained their positions after the acquisition. And, most important to Tom and Kate, Colgate agreed to allow the subsidiary to continue its generous charitable activities. As a fillip, Tom could boast he had achieved something Anita Roddick failed to do at L'Oréal: Colgate-Palmolive absorbed at least a degree of Tom's of Maine's environmentalism and social responsibility, and now issues an annual "social audit," highlighting a growing number of enlightened societal activities. In sum, Chappell could claim to have struck a good deal for all involved.

So, what's not to like about the sale? To begin, Chappell, like Anita

Roddick, lost credibility with many enlightened businesspeople who, rightly or wrongly, believe that virtuous practices are inherently incompatible with the central tenet of corporate capitalism: maximizing shareholder value. To achieve that goal, skeptics argue, all giant corporations are forced to standardize their organizational policies, systems, and structures to realize the efficiencies needed to justify the cost of the acquisitions they make. Thus it is merely a matter of time before Colgate has a bad quarter, and its leaders then feel compelled to "make some efficiencies" at their high-operating-cost subsidiary in Kennebunkport. On another level, some critics felt betrayed by Chappell's volte-face on his pledge to remain independent. "We need our autonomy to keep calling our own shots," he had said. "Family control gives us the chance to be a new model of a successful business, an inspiration to other corporations who also want to change the face of American business." After the sale, critics felt the company could no longer serve as such a role model. Indeed, it appears that Chappell never truly managed the company after the acquisition, nor did Colgate establish an independent governance structure for the subsidiary. Moreover, the claim that all the ingredients in Tom's of Maine's products are made from "natural" sources has come under scrutiny by environmentalists. Despite repeated attempts, Chappell declined to speak with me about what happened after the sale.

But Tom Chappell's personal reasons for selling his company are not the main issue in the eyes of corporate watchdogs. Business school professor Sandra Waddock criticizes the increasing trend among large corporations of acquiring "values-driven" companies (such as the Body Shop and Tom's of Maine), arguing that more is at stake than simply putting the latter's social agendas at risk. She suggests that it is difficult—if not impossible—for big companies to maintain the community-sensitive cultures found at small, enlightened ones; the uniquely valuable "quirkiness" of those "social icons" is bound to be lost as they are digested in the maw of corporate behemoths.[75] She sees little reason to be confident that Tom's of Maine's "naturalist and organic approaches to product development"—or its commitment to fair trade and community projects in the developing world—can survive intact for long in Colgate's traditional business model. To preserve what is unique in their culture, Tom's of Maine's managers would find it necessary to engage in "uneconomical" practices, and occasionally put meeting their subsidiary's long-term social mission ahead of reaching Colgate's short-term financial goals. Those uneconomical practices represent what Waddock calls a "fairly radical departure from mainstream business logic,"[76] and she doubts that large corporations are capable of dealing with such deviations from the norm. Thus large companies must eventually force their "iconic" acquisitions into the corporate mold, in the process losing the very "quirky" factors that made the acquired company attractive to them. Then, paradoxically, what looked like a profitable acquisition may turn out, in the long term, to have been a bad investment by the parent corporation: "Acquisition carries real risks of losing over time what made the smaller company special in the first place, not to mention alienating the stakeholders who helped build the special character of the blended companies, who may have liked the feeling of being special when they consumed the company's products."[77]

Finally, Waddock questions Tom Chappell's assumption that his company needed to grow in order to survive and carry out its social mission. It is not clear why Tom's of Maine could not have continued as a small, independent family-owned company, satisfied with modest growth and profits and proud of the positive relationships it maintained with its various constituencies. After all, many small and medium-sized family-owned businesses have done as much over several generations (as we will see in chapter 16). And if Tom's of Maine needed a capital infusion, it might have created an employee stock option plan (ESOP) to put cash in the bank, at the same time making the company an even better place to work. Perhaps there were other options, as well.

It is impossible to say for certain whether Tom Chappell made the right decision, and whether Tom's of Maine will thrive or perish in the long run as a Colgate subsidiary. Colgate does have a record of granting some autonomy to its various divisions, and in 2017 Tom's was still operating with considerable independence. Nonetheless, it was now governed in much the same way Colgate manages its many other brands. In sum, the story of Tom's of Maine illustrates the many difficulties and complexities that founders encounter in attempting to maintain virtuous practices as their companies grow. And Tom Chappell is living proof of how hard, indeed, it is to do good.

15

Lever Redux

BEN COHEN (1951–)

An improbable event occurred at the White House in 1988: President Ronald Reagan bestowed the National Small Business Person of the Year Award on Ben Cohen and Jerry Greenfield, the famously hirsute founders of Ben & Jerry's. The beliefs of the conservative chief executive and those of the counterculture ice cream moguls were diametrically opposed on almost every subject (with the possible exceptions of a fondness for good ice cream, and belief in the merits of entrepreneurship). History does not record how the president felt about honoring individuals who stood for everything he didn't like about the American progressive movement (although someone in attendance did capture the chief executive's single unscripted remark: "Which one is Jerry?"). The award did nothing to bridge the ideological divide between the parties; shortly after the event, Ben & Jerry's introduced a new product, Peace Pops, as part of a campaign to reduce the defense budget that Reagan was in the process of increasing.

Cohen and Greenfield were in the mode of Anita Roddick, unlikely capitalists whose business successes not only surprised those "who knew them when" but probably came as a shock to the individuals themselves. Ben and Jerry were born in the same year and met as classmates in junior high school on Long Island. Both were decidedly on the chubby side. The nerdish Jerry was the better student, but highly energetic Ben had the more outgoing personality. Ben matriculated at

Colgate, and then dropped out during his sophomore year; Jerry graduated from Oberlin but was not accepted at the medical schools to which
he had applied. Both drifted between jobs for a few years before recon-
necting in Saratoga Springs, New York, where, faute de mieux, they
decided to start a business using Jerry's savings of $4,000 and Ben's
$2,000 (the latter intending to borrow an additional two grand to make
them equal partners).[1]

Since both liked to eat, Ben and Jerry naturally opted to go into the
food business, at first leaning toward bagels, then settling on ice cream.
They sent off $5 to Pennsylvania State University to enroll in a corre-
spondence course on how to make homemade ice cream, and with that
rigorous preparation under their extra-large belts, were set to go into
business. But someone had beaten them to the punch by recently opening an ice cream parlor in Saratoga Springs. Concluding the town too
small to support two such enterprises, they moved to Burlington, Vermont, an unpromisingly frigid place for would-be ice cream merchants
to set up shop. There they edited a business plan an acquaintance had
used to solicit investors in a New York City pizza joint—substituting
"ice cream" for "pizza" in the text—and took it to a local banker, who
offered them the sensible advice of complementing their proposed
product line with something hot to sell in winter. After they decided
on crepes as their cold-weather offering, the banker helped Cohen and
Greenfield secure a $20,000 loan from the Small Business Adminis-
tration. Once they had found a suitable location, they were good to go.

Orgasmic Flavors

An unheated, uninsulated, abandoned gas station was the best Cohen
and Greenfield could afford. After installing a stove, hiring a hippie
plumber to bring the restroom and kitchen up to code, and building two
wooden tables themselves, they opened for business in 1978. Employing used kitchen and ice-cream-making equipment, they experimented

with various recipes and flavors, dumping all manner of fruits, nuts, extracts, cookies, and candies into assorted mixes. Jerry liked his ice cream thick, with a high fat content, so that's how they made it. After a few months they had concocted a line of "Orgasmic Flavors," or so they advertised.[2] Some flavors offered (like Honey Apple Raisin Oreo) failed to find favor among even the most adventurous of Burlington's gourmands, but enough satisfied customers frequented the converted gas station to convince the partners that their ice cream was good enough for the business to succeed.

It was the business part of the business that tripped them up. While Jerry was adept as an ice cream maker, and Ben a brilliant marketer, they proved inept at all other aspects of business management, from customer service through bookkeeping—especially the latter. Two months after opening, they were forced to close shop for a day to huddle with an accountant, hanging a handwritten sign on the door: "We're Closed Today So We Can Figure Out If We Are Making Money." They weren't. So they looked for ways to increase profits, such as sales promotions (including Jerry's "Dr. Inferno" fire-eating act, during which he set his beard aflame) and diversifying their product offerings (for example, broccoli mushroom bread).[3] They introduced a new company slogan, "Lick It," a double entendre that stirred controversy among members of the local lesbian community who had adopted the scoop shop as a hangout.[4] Ben quickly switched the slogan to "Vermont's Finest," a modest claim in the nation's only state without a Baskin-Robbins franchise.

When the store was still in business a year after opening, Ben and Jerry celebrated the anniversary with a "free cone day" and twelve hours of live music at the shop. Ben wrote a flyer promoting the event, which included a statement that would become the company's basic philosophy: "Business has a responsibility to give back to the community from which it draws its support."[5] Jerry added these words: "If it's not fun, why do it?" Making good on both those commitments would be as difficult for the founders as turning a profit.

Nonetheless, the company appeared ready to start making money after Ben hit the road and began selling wholesale ice cream to restaurants in Vermont, New Hampshire, and upstate New York. That venture was sufficiently promising to prompt the Small Business Administration to advance another loan, enabling B&J's to open a larger manufacturing facility. Alas, they ended up producing more ice cream than Ben could sell to restaurants, leading them to open seasonal scoop stands as additional outlets. That worked in the summer, but didn't completely solve the problem. Then Ben hit on the idea of packaging their ice cream in pint containers for sale in supermarkets. To draw attention to their products, they offered to refund the cost of a pint to any unsatisfied customer. Next, they started to franchise scoop shops, and to contract with commercial distributors in four New England states.

Throughout this long, tough slog Ben proved his mettle as a marketing maven, devising one clever (and inexpensive) way after another to promote their products, from creating the world's largest ice cream sundae to sending Jerry on a cross-country tour in a funky, ancient van that died halfway along the drive home. Still, they couldn't make a financial go of the business. They went from one managerial faux pas to another, hiring and trusting the wrong people, mispricing their goods, and inefficiently manufacturing them. As one longtime B&J's manager recalled, "When I started at Ben & Jerry's we didn't work smart, we worked very, very hard, and sure, we wasted tons of products and tons of money." Another employee added, "There was a lot of money wasted because we didn't have a sense of the economics involved."[6] Ben and Jerry were not only incapable of getting their arms around their business problems; they couldn't agree on the least consequential of matters. They disagreed so heatedly on how many cookies they should put in their popular Oreo Mint ice cream that they decided to divide their managerial responsibilities, Jerry in charge of production, Ben handling sales. (Ben, a stickler for quality, also served as the company's taster-in-chief, once sampling 144 variations of a single flavor before approving one for production.)[7]

Not only weren't they making money, they were also falling short on realizing Ben's avowed social mission, and failing abysmally to meet Jerry's pledge to make working at B&J's fun. Their employees were toiling long hours, and conflict was brewing between those who thought the company should concentrate on making a profit and those who felt its prime purpose should be serving society. Neither Ben nor Jerry knew how to address those issues effectively, let alone resolve them. After all, they couldn't even figure out how to get along with each other.

At the end of their third year in business, Ben and Jerry were working sixteen-hour days, seven days a week, and Jerry was sixty pounds overweight. Realizing that they were both burned out, Jerry decided to follow his longtime girlfriend to Arizona, where she planned to enroll in a PhD program, and Ben opted to sell the company and retire. A purchaser came along with a satisfactory offer, and the deal appeared done. But suddenly Ben got cold feet. Fearing that the company's culture and social mission were at risk, he backed out of a deal that, in the eyes of the buyer, had been completed. The would-be buyer sued, but after a prolonged legal battle, Ben eventually prevailed in court on a narrow technicality. Ben then sold Jerry's half of the business by private offering to friends, acquaintances, and local Vermonters who shared his values. (Jerry retained a small ownership position and agreed to continue to participate in promotional events.) The sale amounted to an early exercise in crowdsourcing.

Enter Chico

Ben was now in control, but the company was in trouble. For all his marketing brilliance and admirable commitment to social causes, he was a terrible manager, by turns autocratic and indecisive. As a result, his hardworking employees were not having the fun Jerry had promised, and their already poor morale was in decline. Ben knew the company needed a professional manager.

He was lucky enough to find a capable one living right in Burlington. Ben had been hanging out at a local bar and nightclub where Fred "Chico" Lager was manager and part owner. Chico had recently received his MBA from the University of Southern California's business school (where, incidentally, he was one of my first students). Impressed by Chico's credentials, values, and sense of humor, Ben asked if he might be available to work half-time as B&J's general manager. It became clear almost immediately that the job was full-time (and more), so in 1982 Chico sold his share of the bar, bought a block of B&J's stock, and soon became its president and subsequently CEO (aka "Chief Euphoria Officer").

Chico set to work putting the company's finances in order, filing for incorporation, and negotiating a deal to buy Heath Bars—necessary to make one of B&J's most-popular flavors, Heath Bar Crunch—in bulk. The company then introduced a successful branding campaign featuring "two real guys" who lived in Vermont, the land of "black and white cows." Ben kept proving his marketing genius as a modern-day heir to William Lever's pioneering advertising efforts, including the art of jingle writing. The company bought radio time to broadcast its "Two Real Guys" ditty:

> There ain't no Häagen, there ain't no Dazs,
> There ain't no Frusen, there ain't no Glädjé,
> There ain't nobody named Steve at Steve's
> But there's two real guys at Ben & Jerry's.

As the saying goes, you had to have been there and heard it for yourself.

Soon the company found itself on the road to profitability. Then it hit a pothole: its prime competitor, the giant Pillsbury Company, told supermarkets that if they sold B&J's ice cream, they couldn't also carry Pillsbury's Häagen-Dazs brand. B&J's growing retail business seemed dead in the water: Häagen-Dazs had a 70 percent market share at the time, and Pillsbury supported the brand with the kind of heavy pro-

motion that makes products move quickly off supermarket shelves—
and puts profits in the hands of retailers.[8] While such "exclusive dealing
agreements" are frequently voided by the courts, B&J's faced the prospect of years of expensive legal actions against a corporation that easily
could afford a protracted battle—one it probably would win through
attrition, if not legal merit.

So instead of suing, B&J's decided to fight with a clever public relations campaign, an arena in which little David had better odds against
mighty Goliath. Ben & Jerry's placed a $250 ad in *Rolling Stone* maga-
zine, headlined "What's the Doughboy Afraid Of?" (referring to Pillsbury's corporate symbol). The ad explained Pillsbury's tactics and
asked readers to send a dollar to receive more facts and a pro-B&J's
bumper sticker. The company also bought space on a billboard on
the main highway around Boston, also asking "What's the Doughboy
Afraid Of?" Soon tens of thousands of people who never heard of Ben
& Jerry's were supporting the company in its battle against Pillsbury—
and moreover, they now wanted to buy B&J's ice cream. In light of the
bad publicity, Pillsbury backed away from the exclusivity agreements.
As Calvin Trillin wrote in a 1985 *New Yorker* article, not only had B&J's
slingshot hit the bull's-eye at Pillsbury, but the company had also gar-
nered millions in free publicity, which then led to inroads into Häagen-
Dazs's formidable market share.

Although the company's future was brightening, all was not well in
Burlington. The long-standing tension between the company's social
and economic missions had never been resolved, and employees at all
levels expressed confusion about the purpose of the business. Eventually this low-grade confusion festered into open conflict, prompting
B&J's top management to formalize a three-pronged mission statement
built around the concept of "shared prosperity":

> Product Mission: To make, distribute, and sell the finest qual-
> ity all natural ice cream and related products in a variety of inno-
> vative flavors made from Vermont dairy products.

Social Mission: To operate the company in a way that actively recognizes the central role business plays in the structure of society by initiating innovative ways to improve the quality of life of a broad community: local, national and international.

Economic Mission: To operate the company on a sound financial basis of profitable growth, increasing value for our shareholders and creating career opportunities and financial rewards for our employees.

Underlying the missions of Ben & Jerry's is the determination to seek new and creative ways of addressing all three parts, while holding a deep respect for individuals outside the company, and for the communities of which they are a part.

The company's purpose thus clarified, in 1985 Ben & Jerry's went public with an initial listing on NASDAQ, its share price rising from $13 to $21 in the first month. Ben and Chico subsequently amused themselves watching their company's share price rise and fall with no correlation to how well it was performing. In a *Wall Street Transcript* interview, a reporter asked Ben, "How do you react to the way the stock market has been treating you in general and vis-à-vis other companies in your line?" He answered candidly: "I think the stock market goes up and down unrelated to how a company is doing. I never expected it to be otherwise. I anticipate that it will continue to go up and down, based solely on rumor and whatever sort of market manipulation those people who like to manipulate the market can accomplish."[9]

Chico somehow managed to edit Ben's impolitic answers before they reached print, having him say instead, "We try and focus our energy on the company itself rather than preoccupying ourselves with what the market is doing." When B&J's stock went on public sale, the company had announced its policy of "linked prosperity" in the prospectus, explaining to would-be investors that "as the company grew and prospered, the benefits would accrue not just to shareholders, but also to our employees and the community."[10] In the beginning, that commitment would be carried out through the Ben & Jerry's Foundation, chaired by Jerry (now back in Burlington) and endowed with fifty thousand shares of company stock. In so doing, the company pledged to contribute 7.5 percent of its pretax profits to the foundation. (At the time, only a minuscule handful of companies donated as much as 5 percent, and most gave on the order of 1 percent.) In Chico Lager's candid and amusing 1994 account of the company's early days, *Ben & Jerry's: The Inside Scoop*, he noted that the foundation also served as an antitakeover device, after the percentage of company stock held by insiders decreased following the public offering.[11]

The company then introduced the first in a series of measures designed to make its promise of "shared prosperity" a reality for employees, the most radical of which was the introduction of a five-to-one salary ratio; executives could not earn more than five times the salary of entry-level workers (a few years later, the ratio was raised to seven to one). All employees also shared in a bonus pool of 5 percent of pretax profits. In 1986, employees received a onetime bonus of company stock valued at 1 percent of their salaries, and subsequently they could buy stock at 85 percent of market value.[12] Around that same time, a high standard of company ethics was introduced with regard to the treatment of customers, suppliers, and franchisees: B&J's employees and managers were forbidden to receive any gifts from outsiders (even inexpensive pen and pencil sets had to be placed in the "graft box" in Chico's office).[13]

Not Easy Being Green

Over the years, Ben & Jerry's frequently found itself in alliance with environmentalist and other groups dedicated to improving the quality of life. To avoid even the odor of hypocrisy, in 1988 the company began to "green up" its practices. Chico challenged the company's employees to come up with ideas on how to improve its environmental performance. One of the first to offer suggestions was Chico's own adminis-trative assistant, Gail Mayville. Growing up on a Vermont dairy farm, Mayville had learned that "you better put back what you take from the land, or it's not going to be able to sustain you for very long."[14] Believing that B&J's wasn't "being as pro-active as we might be in managing our solid waste and conserving our resources," she approached Chico with a list of actions the company should take to become an environmen-tal paragon, starting with the prodigious amount of high-fat residue produced in the manufacture of ice cream. Dumping this sludge into Burlington's municipal sewer pipes placed a heavy burden on the city's water treatment systems, creating a growing problem the city was ill-equipped to handle. After careful analysis, Mayville concluded that the most ecological solution was to feed the waste to pigs. There were no pig farms nearby, so she approached a farmer who had several hundred unproductive acres of land with a proposition he couldn't refuse: B&J's would set him up in the pig business if he would purchase all their waste for swine food. She later reported that the pigs "like all of it except for Mint Oreo."[15] By 1990 the company had constructed its own sewage pretreatment lagoons, which eliminated the pollution problem.

From there, Mayville figured out how to recycle the ten bales of cardboard the company was dumping each week, saving $17,500 an-nually in the process. After that, she discovered a "technically impos-sible" way to recycle the fifty thousand 4.5-gallon plastic buckets the company used every year to hold ice cream ingredients, thus saving 70 percent of the cost of dumping, not to mention tons of landfill. And on she went, each activity requiring moral and entrepreneurial imagina-tion to turn social costs into company savings and profits. She found ways to reduce the amount of paper and plastic in product packaging, to use recycled paper in everything from the company's copying ma-chines to its annual report, and inspired a fellow worker to take similar initiatives with regard to the company's energy use. Today, many com-panies engage in similar efforts, but in 1988, Mayville's programs were extraordinarily far ahead of their time. In 1990 she was presented with a Business Enterprise Trust Award for "vision, integrity, and courage" in management.

Troubles in Burlington

Alas, at Ben & Jerry's no good deed went unpunished. Although many at the company—including Ben, Jerry, and Chico—were proud of Mayville's accomplishments, and pleased that she was receiving national recognition, a few employees were resentful that she was being personally lauded for what they felt were company-wide efforts. Moreover, she was criticized for having taken many initiatives without consulting with, or involving, her coworkers in an organization whose culture supposedly was built around teamwork. In hindsight, Mayville saw that the criticism was largely deserved. Chastened, Chico appointed her the company's environmental program development manager, a role in which she created a "Green Team" composed of nineteen employees interested in working on sustainability issues. The company also began to publish an unvarnished annual social audit of its environmental record, community service activities, and ingredient-sourcing practices in the developing world, empowering an independent outsider (à la Arco) to document and evaluate not only its successes but shortcomings, as well.

Being socially responsible proved to be no mean task at Ben & Jerry's, since their main product, high-butterfat ice cream, isn't exactly a health food, at least in large quantities. Since B&J's inception, the company has had to wrestle with the paradox of preaching virtue while promoting a product that, when not used in moderation, can clog arteries and lead to obesity. As much as it has tried over the years to square that circle, it has never really succeeded, often finding itself subject to criticism from one health group or another.

After Jerry had returned from Arizona with his newly PhD'd wife, he went back to work at the company full-time. While never as active in its management as Ben, he was deeply involved in the company's community outreach activities and marketing campaigns, adding a personal handwritten note to every piece of customer correspondence. With Jerry back on board, Chico at the helm, and Ben dreaming up new promotional schemes almost daily, the company was growing and, finally, profitable. Perhaps Ben's most successful brainchild was the Cherry Garcia flavor, which sent sales through the roof; the company had to scramble to keep up with growing demand. Still, not everybody was having fun. One B&J's manager characterized the company as "a sweatshop in a pastoral setting."[16] Facing up to the problem, Ben and Jerry began to meet regularly with employees in informal meetings where they stressed the company's culture and values and listened to their ideas about how to make their work fun. Collectively, a consensus emerged that the prime values of the company's "hippie and funky" culture were hard work and tolerance of diverse dress, lifestyles, and personalities.

But the waters were never calm for long in Burlington, and the one who most often roiled them was Ben. He could not stop injecting himself into operational decisions, second-guessing company policies, offering contradictory ideas, and insisting on having his own way. As one B&J's manager put it, "Ben was a crazy man—that's ok—crazy men are sometimes how things get moving in the world."[17] Because he was the company's largest shareholder, owning 40 percent of its stock, he believed everything it stood for should reflect his progressive business philosophy. For the most part, it did: as one former employee explained, "I think Ben was not questioned—he was treated as the social mission king. Ben for years was the driving force of the company."[18] But Ben needed constant reconfirmation of the company's dedication to its social mission. At one point he went so far as to suggest employees sign a kind of loyalty oath, in effect pledging commitment to the company's progressive values. He backed off after it was pointed out that such a pledge was contradictory to the company's stated value of tolerance of diversity.

Influenced by Anita Roddick's social activism, Ben became involved in a broader international movement to encourage other companies to adopt progressive causes. Like Robert Owen and William Norris, he evolved from enlightened business leader to social reformer—and the consequences of that shift proved similarly damaging. Ben became enamored with a political movement that advocated diverting 1 percent of the US defense budget to activities promoting peace between America and the Soviet Union. He managed to convince B&J's board to rename an existing product Peace Pops, donating 1 percent of profits from it to peace-advocacy activities as part of a broader national "1% for Peace" campaign. But not all B&J's employees, nor every member of its board, were willing to go as far as Ben wanted to promote social causes. Although most were sympathetic with the causes Ben advocated, many—perhaps the majority—believed that the company's social mission needed to be tied directly to its business mission. It made perfect sense for B&J's to promote the well-being of Vermont's dairy farmers, they believed, but shelling out half a million in company money to clean up one New York City subway station was beyond the company's remit and resources. It started to become clear to even Ben's greatest admirers (of whom there were many) that he had drifted away from the original commitment of ice-cream-related community service into the realm of trying to solve the world's most intractable problems. Increasingly, Ben and Chico found themselves on opposite sides of issues, with Ben stressing the company's social mission, and Chico arguing that it first needed to be profitable.

The Challenge of Succession

But the conflicts were not simply about defining the limits of the company's social mission. As B&J's grew, and its competition with Häagen-Dazs for market share became more intense, business issues common to all organizations arose, problems relating to manufacturing capacity, distributor relations, and introduction of new products. In Chico's words, the company may have been "fumbling successfully," but it had become evident to the board that it lacked the business processes and management systems needed for efficient organizational coordination and financial control. Thus, the decision was taken to begin the process of transitioning from leadership by the founders to professional management. Even Ben said he agreed.

Choosing a new CEO at Ben and Jerry's turned out to be as fraught a process as it was at many of the other companies discussed in these pages, and with similarly dismal results. For several years previous to the search for his successor, Chico had a quote clipped from *Forbes* taped to his desk: "The true mark of greatness in a CEO is how well he chooses his successor." As Chico later admitted, he failed by that measure.[19] The company's board (including Ben, Jerry, and Chico) chose an insider, Chuck Lacy, to be its next chief executive. He was chosen because he knew the business and shared the founders' values. In 1990 Chico retired (though he stayed on as a member of the board), and Lacy assumed responsibility for day-to-day business operations— with the exception of marketing, which he turned over to Ben. For the next three years the company continued to grow, and in each of those years it was named one of *Forbes*'s 200 Best Small Companies in America. In 1992 B&J's reported a profit of $6.7 million on $132 million in sales, prompting Ben to write in a letter to the company's shareholders, "The most amazing thing is that our social values—that part of our company mission that calls us to use our power as a business to improve the quality of life in our local, national and international communities—have actually helped us to become a stable, profitable, high-growth company."[20]

At the end of 1992, with a growing national market share (35 percent, compared with Häagen-Dazs's 47 percent) and happier employees (93 percent of whom said they liked working for the company, and 84 percent of whom said they felt its social mission was important to its success), B&J's finally appeared to have found stability after fourteen years of sailing on troubled seas.[21] Yet again Ben overreached, and Lacy couldn't control the founder's instinctive need to create turmoil. Ben's admirers said of him that he always had ten new ideas—three or four of which were awful and needed to be shelved before they turned into disasters. But Lacy failed to sufficiently channel Ben's marketing genius, apparently admiring him to such a degree that he couldn't say no to any of his ideas. Suddenly things started to go wrong: after a decade of double-digit growth, the company slowed to 6 percent in 1993, and the value of its stock plummeted as investors began to worry about what was going on in Burlington. In 1994, with the company veering out of control, and no firm hand on the helm, the board decided it needed a new CEO. They sacked Lacy and launched a search, this time looking for an experienced outsider.

During that eighteen-month process, Chico returned to run B&J's operations and manage its next leadership transition. The company, being Ben & Jerry's, undertook the search for a new chief in a most unorthodox fashion: it launched an essay contest—"Why I would be a great CEO for Ben & Jerry's"—in which the person writing the most convincing hundred words would win the prize post. There were twenty thousand entries, and the winner, as might reasonably be expected, turned out to be the wrong person for the job. After less than two years, he resigned, and the board was once again searching for a new leader. After heated discussion, the much-divided board decided—improbably—to appoint a top executive from a nearby gun manufacturer.

B&J's for Sale

This time the board's choice proved more than just a mistake. Over the objections of Ben and a minority on the board, the new CEO opted to dress up the company's financials in order to sell it. As one longtime employee recalled, "The worst time was when Ben & Jerry's was scrubbing up to sell itself—that was a terrible time because it kept bringing in people into marketing and CEOs that were purely looking at the bottom line."[22] About that time, Chico—who had stayed on the board until near the end of the 1990s—decided that the company had become so dysfunctional that he had to walk away.[23] But the financial scrubbing had worked. Soon there were three bidders for the company: Unilever, Dreyer's, and a consortium of Ben's progressive friends who wanted to take the company private. To Ben's chagrin, the board opted to go with Unilever, the highest bidder at $326 million. As Chico recently has noted, if "benefit corporation" charters (see chapter 18) had been available in the late 1990s, B&J's board probably would have opted to reincorporate using that mechanism rather than be acquired.

Unilever bought 100 percent of B&J's shares and retained a few of the company's key managers and employees. As a sop to Ben, it also agreed to create a separate board for the Ben & Jerry's Foundation and to empower it with maintaining the company's culture and social mission. Unfortunately, the first executive chosen to head the Ben & Jerry's division, Yves Couette, a French executive from the parent company, failed to appreciate the countercultural significance of the B&J's brand. Hence, almost as soon as Unilever was able to do so, its corporate management took control of the acquired company's marketing and manufacturing operations and began to change its policies to conform with those of its many other divisions. (After B&J's old "fun-and-funky" website was junked, Ben and Jerry refused to allow their likeness to appear on its corporate-designed replacement.) One B&J's employee recalled, "When Yves came—there were two hundred people that lost their jobs—and it wasn't a grand time—and then it really was about the economic mission and people were going around and taking the social mission off the wall because it really didn't matter anymore."[24] Over the next couple of years, tension continued to build between Unilever's European leadership and B&J's American managers and workers and the foundation's board, until Couette was finally replaced by an American whose values were more simpatico with those of the founders. Nonetheless, the tensions continued.

A Happy Ending?

For the next decade, Unilever attempted to manage B&J's as simply another acquired company, one in need of being folded completely into
its portfolio of brands and run according to its global operational policies and standards. Much as the Body Shop and Tom's of Maine had
been swallowed by their corporate acquirers, it appeared that the once-
enlightened practices of B&J's would vanish in the powerful embrace of
Unilever. Philip Mirvis, a consultant first to B&J's and later to Unilever,
recalled the scene in Burlington after the takeover:

> The main manufacturing plant—and site of the brand build-
> ing and [the top] Vermont tourist attraction factory tour—was
> severed from B&J's control and reported into Unilever's North
> American Ice Cream division in Green Bay, Wisconsin. This
> began months of political power plays where the [Unilever] ice
> cream division diluted ingredients (smaller chunks, more air),
> challenged longstanding commitments to pay dairy farmers a
> premium to sustain them through tough times, fought against
> further use of organic and fair trade ingredients, reduced the scale
> and costs of tour operations, and pushed constantly to increase
> margins.[25]

Unilever argued that such changes were necessary because the cost
of producing ice cream was considerably higher at B&J's than at its
American competitors. Which it was. But that was the rational, economic justification for the imposed changes; the executive desire for
personal recognition seems also to have played a significant role. After Chico stepped down, his six successor CEOs each tried to stamp
their own marks—or Unilever's corporate identity—on the company,
attempting to get their personal reputations as leaders out from behind
Ben Cohen's bulky shadow. They attempted to distinguish their vari-

ous tenures by trying almost everything but the things that had been key to B&J's success under its founders: high-quality ice cream, public service, and a culture of fun. As recently as 2005, most observers believed that B&J's story would have the kind of sad, bad end that has been the fate of so many other acquired companies whose enlightened practices proved unsustainable under new management.

Yet that may not be the way things will turn out. As described at the end of chapter 3, in 2010 Unilever's new CEO, Paul Polman, began returning the giant, global enterprise company back to the values of its founder, William Lever. One step in that direction has been the appointment of Norwegian Jostein Solheim as head of Ben & Jerry's. Solheim has managed the division much as if it were an independent company, with its own board, culture, managerial policies, and social practices, all reflecting the values of B&J's founders—and Lever Bros.' founder, as well. Solheim encouraged Cohen and Greenfield to reengage with the company, and they began to participate in promotional and community-service activities. The company is once again involved in supporting Vermont social and cultural institutions, and once again viewed as a leader in environmental protection, energy conservation, fair trade, and sustainable sourcing in the developing world. In 2018 it launched a new line of low-fat, low-calorie ice creams, finally responding to its health-oriented critics after forty years in business. All of which meld nicely with Polman's plans for the rest of Unilever.

Perhaps the most important development at Unilever has been the articulation of a new corporate strategy that integrates the company's social and economic missions. As at Tom's of Maine, throughout B&J's first thirty years in business there had been a never-resolved debate concerning how to strike the right balance between its social and economic missions. In hindsight, there is evidence that, when conceived in those terms, it may be impossible to satisfactorily strike such a balance. The promise inherent in Polman's strategic reconceptualization of the issue is that instead of treating social and economic concerns as separate and discrete entities, Unilever is attempting to integrate ethics, environmental concerns, and global social responsibility as inseparable parts of its overall business strategy. Central to the success of that integration is Unilever's ability to seamlessly and systemically incorporate all those factors in a financially viable way.

If that end can be achieved at B&J's, Unilever's Vermont-based ice cream maker might then serve as a model for the parent corporation's numerous other divisions. In 2016, Ben Cohen had a consulting relationship with Unilever; there is a chance he might once again surprise the world (and, most likely, himself) by accomplishing what Anita Roddick never lived to do at L'Oréal: act as a catalyst for change in a large global corporation. When recently asked about B&J's on national television, Ben proudly referred to it as "my company." That represented a remarkable change in the relationship between the founder and the acquiring corporation, and if it continues, the story of William Lever might well come full circle as Ben Cohen helps Paul Polman, a hundred years after the fact, to realize Lever's vision at Unilever.

Addendum: On April 18, 2016, Ben Cohen and Jerry Greenfield, both sixty-five years old, were among three hundred people arrested at the US Capitol, charged with unlawful demonstration while protesting to protect voting rights and against the Supreme Court's Citizens United ruling. Later that year, Unilever came under threat of a hostile takeover, a subject explored in chapter 18.

16

Capitalists of a Different Stripe

YVON CHOUINARD (1938-),
JACK STACK (1949-),
ROBERT BEYSTER (1924-2014),
and OTHERS

Investors and financiers have been the bugbears of enlightened capitalists from the day Robert Owen had his first run-in with the non-managing majority owners of *his* New Lanark mills. Likewise, J. C. Penney, William Lever, William Norris, and Edwin Land all lost control of their companies to conventionally minded executives favored by shareholders. To avoid that fate, James Lincoln, Milton Hershey, Robert Wood Johnson, Spedan Lewis, J. Irwin Miller, and Ken Iverson all fought career-long battles to keep the wolves of Wall Street (and London's City) at bay. Ditto the heirs of Michael Marks and Levi Strauss. Most recently, Tom Chappell, Anita Roddick, and Ben Cohen sold their firms to corporate behemoths headed by executives with little interest in social engagement. For anyone who believes in the promise of enlightened capitalism, that pattern bodes ill for the future.

Yet the historical record is far from monochromatically bleak. While investor-owned companies have been generally inhospitable to virtuous leaders, other forms of capitalism have been more receptive and nurturing. If capitalism is defined as a system in which privately owned enterprises compete for customers in a market economy, then there are in fact many forms of capitalism. Indeed, shareholder-owned corporations represent only a small percentage of all the capitalist enterprises in the United States and United Kingdom. A vast majority of companies in those nations are owned by individuals, families, and employees. Among those are many businesses—but by no means, all—known for their enlightened practices, a few of which are described below.

Sole Proprietorships and Family-Owned Businesses

Throughout history, most businesses have been small enterprises owned by their founders and later passed down to their descendants, often for generations. A family in Japan has owned an inn since AD 718, and the Antinori family has been in the wine business in Tuscany since 1385 (the year Francesco Datini celebrated his fiftieth birthday in nearby Prato). As we have seen with Milton Hershey, James Lincoln, and Bill Gore, when business leaders own outright the companies they founded—or maintain uncontestable financial control—they are free to manage them in any way they wish. That, of course, can be either a good or bad thing. At least anecdotally, successful founders typically treat employees well, often retaining them on payrolls for years, if not decades. Loyal workers often come to be seen, and treated, almost as part of founders' families. At family-owned Wegmans Food Markets, each of the company's forty-three thousand employees sports a name tag citing the number of years of his or her "incredible service." Minnesota's Marvin Windows and Doors has been family-owned for four generations, and many of its four thousand employees are second- and third-generation descendants of Marvin workers. The company was founded in 1912 with the purpose of providing work for chronically unemployed residents of host town Warroad, snuggled hard against the Canadian border. Today, Marvin Windows' workforce easily outnumbers the town's total population, but the company is still dedicated to full employment. During the 2007–8 recession, when the market for custom-made doors and windows shrank drastically, no one at Marvin was laid off. The sense of loyalty and community was so strong that older, higher-paid employees voluntarily reduced their work hours so their younger, lower-paid peers could maintain their incomes.[1]

There are, of course, notable exceptions to the behavior of the Marvin and Wegman families: marginal mom-and-pop concerns often lack resources to provide their workers with decent pay, benefits, or job security, and some small businesses take advantage of their size exemption from governmental regulations to exploit employees, even exposing them to unsafe and unhealthy working conditions. But larger, successful second- and third-generation family businesses often have excellent reputations as employers and citizens of the communities hosting their operations. Most singularly, they are known for making the kinds of long-term investments typically frowned on by stock speculators.[2] A company that comes to mind here is Nordstrom, the family-owned American department-store chain known for its exceptional customer service and employee benefits, and willing to make long-range investments its publicly traded competitors view as too risky.

In the United States, privately held companies (which accounted for the lion's share of the nation's total employment in 2011) productively reinvested more than twice as much annually as the public ones, despite earning only 20 percent of total profits. Where public companies invest as little as possible, returning the rest to shareholders while reducing costs via outsourcing and cutting corners on quality, smaller, private companies are often crucibles of innovation, job creation, and product quality. As *Financial Times* columnist Rana Foroohar notes, "The private company business model also has the advantage of being more humane. Shorter supply chains bring capitalists and workers closer to one another, and as everyone knows, when you have to look someone in the eye every now and again, you are much less likely to treat them badly. Pay differentials between managers and workers go down. Wages and growth at a regional level go up."[3]

Alexis de Tocqueville made a similar point in 1835, when he predicted that the incipient process of industrialization would create "an aristocracy of manufacturers" and thus destroy the unique American condition of rural equality. In towns and villages at the time, businesses were small, and owners worked side by side with their employees, lived nearby, attended the same churches, and sent their kids to the same schools—thus creating a sense of shared community among capitalists and laborers. But in an urban factory, Tocqueville observed, there is "no real bond" between the owner and the worker: "These two men meet in the factory but know not each other elsewhere; and whilst they come into contact on one point, they stand very wide apart on all others. The manufacturer asks nothing of the workman but his labor; the workman expects nothing from him but wages. The one contracts no obligation to protect, nor the other to defend; and they are not permanently connected either by habit or duty."[4]

Today there is an aristocracy of professional executives at the top of large global corporations, people who live in gated communities, send their progeny to private schools, attend elite universities, and have little to no contact or bond with the domestic employees they endeavor to replace with foreign workers willing to labor for a pittance. It is thus not surprising to learn that a high percentage of the manufacturing companies on Fortune's 100 Best Companies to Work For list, like Nucor, Herman Miller, and Gore, have facilities located in small towns with strong senses of community.

Something like 19 percent of Fortune 500 companies are said to be family controlled, defined as an individual or family having the largest ownership stake—with a minimum of 18 percent—and the ability to name its chief executive officer. One of the largest such American firms is Mars, makers of chocolate bars, M&M's, and prepared foods for humans and pets. When still in his prime, founder Forrest Mars handed 100 percent of the company's ownership to his two sons and daughter, then retired three thousand miles away from the company's headquarters. The family has owned and led Mars over the many decades since, in the process earning a much-deserved reputation for farsighted investments, enlightened management, and in particular progressive employee- and management-development practices. Based on personal dealings with Mars executives between 1973 and 1993, I would have ranked the company among the best-managed American firms of the era—that is, *if* the Mars family had not been so obsessively, and quirkily, secretive about their practices. Nonetheless, the company's management philosophy recently received what amounted to external validation when investor Warren Buffett partnered with the Mars family to acquire chewing-gum manufacturer Wrigley, another family-owned business. The 106-year-old Mars company now employs eighty thousand people worldwide and has sales of $35 billion annually. In 2017 the company's nonfamily CEO, Grant Reid, called on his peers in industry to greatly increase their efforts to fight climate change, pledging to spend $1 billion on renewable energy such as wind farms, and vowing to cut Mars's greenhouse emissions 27 percent by 2025, and 67 percent by 2050. In addition, the company has introduced a line of healthy snacks and vows to cut back on the amount of salt, fat, sugar, and butter in its chocolate products. Reid says being a family-owned company makes it easier for him to make such costly long-term commitments.[5]

Of course, not all family-owned businesses practice enlightened management. Walmart and Ford are two of America's largest and most successful family-controlled firms, yet neither has a sterling record of dealing with its stakeholders, employees in particular. In contrast, the S. C. Johnson family, makers of household cleaning products, and the Sulzbergers, owners of the *New York Times*, have positive records of social engagement. Among the heirs of the enlightened capitalists, the Johnson, Haas, Marks, and Sieff families retained their forbearers' virtuous social practices for several generations, only to lose effective control of their companies when the last of their lines serving in active managerial capacities retired. That issue—coupled with struggles over leadership succession among descendants, and squabbling among family members over sharing of profits—eventually comes to bedevil most family-owned companies. Nonetheless, family ownership provides immunity from the inevitable conflict that arises in publicly traded corporations between shareholders and professional managers—a fact not lost on Yvon Chouinard.

"Capitalist Cat"

Chouinard, founder and owner of Patagonia—the first company of significant size to have a business model focused on environmental issues—wants everyone to know he hates Wall Street in particular, and financiers in general. He avers that socially responsible companies such as his need to remain privately held, adding for emphasis that "Venture Capitalists are such assholes."[6] Chouinard, who grew up in a French-speaking Quebecer community in Northern Maine, didn't speak English until his family moved to Southern California in the 1940s, when he was in grade school. Thus handicapped linguistically, he never became much of a student; instead, he spent his teens chasing high surf in his 1939 Chevrolet. In 1957 he invented reusable, high-quality, rock-climbing pitons that he fashioned himself, and then sold out of the back of the old Chevy. Over the next dozen years his business grew and, after adopting the Patagonia name in 1972, morphed into one of America's premier suppliers of innovative sports gear and apparel. In 2015 Patagonia had $600 million in revenue, and was known for its eco-consciousness, quality products, and unusual employment practices. The company perfected the use of all-organic cotton in its apparel, and has the jaw-dropping policy of allowing workers at its beachfront headquarters in Ventura, California, to set aside their tasks to hit the beach when the surf is up.

In his eighties today, Chouinard was an avid surfer, rock climber, and kayaker when younger, and is now an inveterate fly fisher. As a purist who uses a reel-less rod, he identifies himself more as an outdoorsman and eco-warrior than businessman ("I've never respected the profession"). Arguing that far too many companies today are engaged in greenwashing than in truly eco-friendly business activities, he is proud to point out that Patagonia invests large sums in research and development to make its apparel better for not only its customers but the environment. For example, it developed Synchilla fleece, a breathable, warm, lightweight fabric made from recycled plastic soda bottles. In 2013 the company launched its "$20 Million and Change Fund" to invest in eco-friendly start-ups, and the following year it began selling fair-trade-certified apparel. It also helped start a consortium of retailers—including Macy's, Walmart, and the Gap—involved in creating a method to grade the sustainability of the raw material used in the apparel they sell. Annually, Chouinard donates 10 percent of Patagonia's profits to environmental causes. It is clear why Chouinard has been called the "eminence green."[7]

As with most businesses, not all has been smooth sailing for Patagonia. In the early days it found itself stuck with an unsalable load of poor-quality rugby shirts made in Hong Kong. Then the company expanded too rapidly in the 1990s, forcing it to lay off 20 percent of its workforce and nearly go bankrupt. ("We were just growing for the sake of growing, which is bullshit," Chouinard explains.) Around that time, the company was taken to task by human rights activists over poor working conditions in its suppliers' Asian factories. But today Patagonia is profitable and a model contractor: like Levi Strauss, it has trained seventy-five employees to serve as inspectors in supplier factories, where they enforce a strict code of conduct, including a generous living-wage provision. Yet trenchant criticism has been leveled against Chouinard on the grounds that Patagonia's products are "lifestyle" goods that only the wealthy can afford, and thus appeal to a class of people who engage in conspicuous consumption, an end not in keeping with the company's avowed ecological raison d'être. In 2011 Chouinard answered the charges with a Patagonia ad that read, "Don't Buy This Jacket. . . . The environmental cost of everything we make is astonishing. . . . Don't buy what you don't need."[8] Q.E.D.

Chouinard's management practices reflect an admixture of Zen, Scandinavian, and New Age influences. They also entail a great deal of his wife's influence. Malinda helped him start Patagonia, and in subsequent years was quietly the Chouinard most responsible for managing its day-to-day operations. Today, neither Chouinard participates actively in the details of company management; yet at the start and over the years, they worked together to create, in Yvon's words, the conditions in which "work must be enjoyable on a daily basis. . . . We needed to be surrounded by friends who could dress whatever way they wanted, even barefoot. We all needed to have flextime to surf the waves when they were good, or ski the powder after a big snowstorm, or stay home and take care of a sick child. We needed to blur the distinction between work and play and family."[9]

Today Patagonia's two thousand employees play beach volleyball in the company's sandpit, tend to a shed full of recuperating raptors, and dine in an organic café. Most strikingly, they drop their kids off at an on-site child-care facility, the Great Pacific Child Development Center. Created by Malinda, the center's twelve thousand square feet of buildings, lawns, and fruit trees is watched over by a staff of twenty-eight.

What Patagonia's employees *can't* do is participate in its ownership: the company is owned by Chouinard and his family, down to the last fleece pullover in its inventory. He claims that's necessary because, if ownership were someday to become widely distributed, the company's environmental goals might be put at risk.[10] He thus plans to leave Patagonia to his daughter and son, both of whom are employed by the company in midlevel positions. As he told *New Yorker* reporter Nick Paumgarten, "Going public would be the death of this company. . . . It is impossible to be a public company and be responsible. My kids realize that. They are taking over more and more."

When asked how the financial community viewed his practices, Chouinard once replied, "One time I made a big mistake and I talked to about fifty bankers. They didn't get it. They just stood there stony-faced. They don't get that the world is changing."[11] Nonetheless, the "eminence green" has also been dubbed the "capitalist cat," the billionaire (according to *Forbes*'s reckoning) leader of a successful company, and the man who says "If we wish to lead corporate America by example, we have to be profitable."[12] But unlike his peers Tom Chappell and Anita Roddick, Chouinard has never looked to sell his company to pocket a bundle. He disdains the dominant practice among capitalists who, in the centuries-old tradition of Francesco Datini, wait until retirement to get religion: "The capitalist ideal is you grow a company and focus on making it as profitable as possible. Then you cash out and become a philanthropist." In distinction, he believes that an entrepreneur has a responsibility to behave virtuously all along, not wait until he or she retires before acting "for the sake of the employees and sake of the planet." Chouinard says, "Everybody tells . . . me that we could grow this business like crazy and then go public and make a killing. . . . But that would be the end of everything I've wanted to do. It would destroy everything I believe in." His friend and fellow environmentalist Tom Brokaw quotes Chouinard as saying, "I don't want a Wall Street greaseball running my company."[13]

It is thus consistent with Chouinard's beliefs that Patagonia would become the first company in California to apply to the state for "benefit corporation" status. As explained in chapter 18, twenty-seven American states grant benefit corporation charters that allow companies to be legally structured so that their officers and directors are permitted to make decisions benefiting society, even if those actions are not in the immediate interest of shareholders. Thus, at least theoretically, benefit status shields socially engaged companies from the threat of activist shareholder suits based on the doctrine of shareholder primacy. It is testament to Chouinard's deep commitment to social and environmental causes—and, equally, his distrust of investors—that he filed for benefit status. After all, it was completely unnecessary for him to have done so, given that Patagonia has no shareholders! Well, one can never be too careful.

A Social Entrepreneur

Chouinard's adamant commitment to family ownership is rare, even among the for-profit companies that are part of the fast-growing "social enterprise" movement. According to Daniel Lubetzky—founder and CEO of KIND—for-profit social entrepreneurs like himself "detect problems in society and try to find solutions to improve the world."[14] Such entrepreneurs are engaged in a wide range of socially worthwhile endeavors, from manufacturing inexpensive water treatment devices for use in the developing world to providing jobs for inner-city residents. The purpose of Lubetzky's company is not quite so noble, yet more typical of the genre: KIND makes healthy snack bars. He argues that, given the world's manifest social and environmental problems, companies can no longer operate under the assumption that they can, or must, choose between doing good and doing well. The argument is far from new—all the enlightened capitalists have advanced it—but it has become the fundamental premise of the social enterprise movement. In Lubetzky's book, *Do the KIND Thing*—a how-to leadership text aimed directly at budding social entrepreneurs—he describes his operating philosophy: business today must be a matter of "and," not "or." Applied to his business, that means making snacks that are both "healthy *and* tasty, convenient *and* wholesome, economically sustainable *and* socially useful." And Lubetzky appears to have done that. The stuff tastes good, and he has earned transparency kudos for packaging it in clear wrappers to symbolize the company's openness to sharing almost everything about its products and practices with its stakeholders.

Lubetzky's background—as a corporate lawyer at Sullivan & Cromwell and consultant at McKinsey & Co.—may seem odd for one committed to demonstrating to business leaders that they need to start thinking in social as well as economic terms. Indeed, in some ways his thinking still reflects those formative traditional experiences, and that is why the story he tells would be familiar to all entrepreneurs, social minded or not. For example, he documents the trials and tribulations he underwent when starting his business and, later, attempting to raise the capital needed to finance its growth. And once the company had established a niche for itself at many national grocery chains, Lubetzky admits to more than once having been tempted to sell it, or a large share of it, to investors—only to back away when it became clear that they were asking for too large a say in its management.[15] He says he has to keep reminding himself of the cautionary tale of Balance Bars, which in the 1990s was the first company to produce healthy (or relatively so) snacks. The company's founders sold it to giant Kraft Foods in 2000 for the impressive sum of $100 million. Almost immediately, Kraft managers chased easy profits, altering the product to the point the brand lost its health creds. Unable to make a financial go of it, Kraft sold the company in 2009.

Despite that risk, Lubetzky makes no bones about the fact that his ultimate goal is to reap a windfall by being acquired by a company, like Kraft, capable of writing big checks—but, he adds, preferably, a company that shares his values. As we have seen, that's far easier said than done. While many social entrepreneurs are making useful contributions to society, the subtext of Lubetzky's book is that, like Anita Roddick and Tom Chappell, in the final analysis he is willing to sacrifice his "and, not or" philosophy for a pot of gold. Ergo, while social entrepreneurs like Lubetzky crow about their desire to "make the world a better place," few seem as committed to their espoused social and environmental values as Yvon Chouinard. There is, however, a form of ownership in which the temptation to be acquired by a large organization is all but nonexistent.

Employee Ownership

Many of the companies we have reviewed benefited from significant degrees of employee ownership, including J. C. Penney, Lever Bros.,

John Lewis Partnership, ACIPCO, Lincoln Electric, Herman Miller, Southwest Airlines, and W. L. Gore. Although it is unclear whether employee ownership was a cause or consequence of the enlightened practices found at those firms, high levels of insider ownership offered them a degree of protection from hostile takeovers, allowing their managers to make longer-term investments, and spend more on employee development, than is typically possible in investor-dominated corporations.

The degree and influence of employee ownership at those companies has varied widely over time, as have the forms it has taken. Indeed, employee ownership comes in a wide range of types, each with different purposes, benefits, and shortcomings. Among those several forms, the two most common in America are the direct holding of shares by employees, and employee stock ownership plans, ESOPs, a complex way of financing employee purchase of a firm from its founder-owner. In effect, employees borrow money to purchase the shares of a company's stock, which then are placed in a trust. Over a period of decades, the loan is paid off from company profits and the stock then theoretically becomes "owned" by the employees, who, in effect, sell it back to the trust when they retire, in exchange for what amounts to a generous pension. Not surprisingly, the performance of companies with simple, direct ownership has proved better than those with complex, indirect ESOP ownership, probably for the same reason that stock options have little effect on company performance: the holders of such options never really "own" their shares.

Three of the most highly regarded engineering and construction giants—Parsons, CH2M Hill, and PCL Construction—have benefited from direct employee ownership for decades, as has Graybar Electric (America's largest distributor of electronic products), Round Table Pizza, and the Publix supermarket chain. The high percentage of employee ownership at those companies is significant because research shows that the greater the financial stake employees have in a company, the more likely they will be productive, loyal, committed, and ethical.[16]

"The Great Game"

Employee-owned SRC Holdings—with a mixture of ESOP and direct stock holding—has had a consistently impressive record of financial performance and authentic worker participation in company management. In 1982, plant manager Jack Stack and 119 of his workers and managers bought the failing Springfield ReManufacturing Corp from their employer, International Harvester, for $9 million, $8.9 million of which was borrowed. Immediately on becoming the company's CEO, Stack realized that he was faced with servicing an enormous debt and meeting a payroll without the advantages of capital, a solid customer base, advanced technology, or a sophisticated workforce. Not sure where to begin addressing those shortcomings, Stack decided to start with his workers, many of whom lacked even a high-school education. "They're fantastic people," he later recalled, "but no one had ever given them the tools to do the job right."[17]

The most important of those tools, Stack reasoned, is information—not an obvious conclusion in the grungy old-line business of rebuilding diesel engines for the used truck and tractor markets. Still, he believed that if his people knew how their own performance translated into the company's overall ability to compete—and if they had the authority to act on that knowledge—workers would start to think like managers, and everyone would start to act as if they owned the business (which they did). In his book *The Great Game of Business*, Stack describes the practice of "open-book management" he developed at SpringfieldRe: every employee is given access to all managerial information. Not only do they see the company's income and cash-flow statements and balance sheet, they are taught how to read, interpret, and then apply that information. Blue-collar workers, office staff—everybody in the company—is given the equivalent of a college business education. Stack describes how the system works with respect to cost control: "You don't become the least-cost producer by issuing edicts from an

THE ENLIGHTENED CAPITALISTS

office, or by setting up elaborate systems and controls, or by giving pep talks. The best way to control costs is to enlist everyone in the effort. That means giving them the tools that allow them to make the right decisions. Those tools are our magic numbers."[18]

So it's management-by-the-numbers at SpringfieldRe—rows and columns of hard-edged numbers everyone generates daily and feeds to the finance department, where they are aggregated, crunched, and distributed weekly to all company departments. Then everybody analyzes the data to see how they are doing and where they can do better. Because everyone owns a share of the business, and all participate in gainsharing, each and all care about waste, productivity, and profitability. Hence, Stack's leadership philosophy is simple: "The best, most efficient, most profitable way to operate a business is to give everybody in the company a voice in saying how it is run, and a stake in the financial outcome, good or bad." In essence, his approach is ethical and efficient. And it contains a lesson that can be drawn from the successes and failures of all the companies considered in these pages. For worker participation to be effective and legitimate, two things must occur. First, employees must participate in the decisions that affect their own work; and second, they must participate in the financial gains that come as the result of their efforts. Participation in decision making alone is unethical, because workers then see the fruits of their efforts reaped by others (executives and investors); and participation in financial gains alone is ineffective, because workers are then powerless to influence the things that determine their paychecks. Therein lies the genius of Stack's "great game of business": worker ownership is coupled with authentic participation in management. As journalist Art Kleiner notes, Stack has also "found a way to reconcile two subcultures of American Business whose partisans almost never see eye to eye. On one side are the financiers who demand higher and higher productivity. On the other side are the nurturers of human capital, who coach people to continually achieve better performance by improving themselves. Mr. Stack is both."[19] Kleiner also praises Stack for having created a system that "solved some of the most entrenched problems of entrepreneurial capitalism, such as the perennial need to raise 'exit money' so key shareholders won't bankrupt the company when they leave and cash in their shares."[20] One of the several ways in which that is done is to stretch out the stock buyback process over ten years.

At the close of SpringfieldRe's first decade of business, the company's stock, worth ten cents a share at the time of its founding, was valued at more than $18, and seven hundred new shareowners had been added to the payroll in a rust-belt city where most other manufacturers were downsizing or going out of business. Over the years since, employees at SRC Holdings (as the company is now called) have identified thirty-nine new business opportunities that the company has funded as entrepreneurial start-ups. A dozen or so of those companies have been spun off to generate the capital needed to pay down the original 1982 ESOP loan, and two dozen are now part of what has become a diversified mini-conglomerate of original equipment manufacturers. In recent years the company has engaged in joint ventures with several large manufacturers, started non-capital-intensive businesses, established a community bank, and launched a new industrial park. In 2017 SRC Holdings had grown to 1,500 employees, who are proud owners of stock now worth $435 a share. Not incidentally, those employees are active volunteers in over a hundred community organizations. Indeed, not only has SRC Holdings created countless jobs, its financial success has transformed Springfield from a moribund rust-belt town into a vibrant, prosperous community with a high quality of life.

How *Not* to Run Employee-Owned Firms

Employee ownership stories don't always end so happily. For decades, package shipper UPS was entirely owned by forty thousand of its managers and sixty-six thousand of its full-time employees, with the preponderance of shares held by the former. The company was known for the egalitarian nature of its culture, illustrated by the fact that the route to the executive suite always began in the drivers' seats of the company's classic brown delivery trucks: that is, the only way to get to the top of the organization was to work one's way up from the bottom. UPS was a good place to work even for those who didn't own stock: at the time it became a publicly traded company in 1999, it was spending $250 million annually on tuition reimbursement, a great deal of which went to seasonal and part-time student employees who were rewarded for their willingness to work long hours over holidays and serve on night shifts. While the initial public offering of UPS's stock was a financial boon to its employee-owners at the time, at least some of the company's vaunted sense of community appears to have been lost in the longer term—as indicated by a rather large number of lawsuits filed by employees alleging racial and gender discrimination, poor working conditions, and problems relating to health care and disability benefits. Today employees own only a minority of shares, and they do not participate appreciably in company management. Thus, unlike SRC Holdings, UPS has failed to reap the full advantages of employee ownership.[21]

While many ESOP companies have been successful (35 percent of the initial funding at SpringfieldRe came in the form of an ESOP), a few have been highly publicized failures—most notably the 1983 purchase of West Virginia's Weirton Steel Company by its seven thousand managers and workers. With the cooperation of the company's unions, Weirton's employees bought the mill (by way of ESOP funding) when its owner, the National Steel Company, announced plans to close the financially troubled operation. Although the employee-owned company managed to eke out two decades of marginally profitable operations, it was never able to achieve sufficient profitability to pay off its ESOP loan, nor gain the extensive capital investments needed to make it truly viable. Additionally, the indirect nature of ESOP ownership, which functioned like a retirement fund, may have hampered efforts to create a culture in which workers felt they were, in fact, the company's owners. Weirton Steel struggled for two decades, finally filing for bankruptcy in 2003. That failure seems not to have been the result of employee ownership, but instead stands as a singular demonstration that ESOPs are not panaceas for companies in severe financial straits. Former McKinsey partner Ronald Bancroft studied Weirton and other ESOP companies during the first decade after the legislation creating them was enacted, concluding that the record "has not been particularly encouraging. . . . In practice, it seems most new ESOPs in mature industries have struggled to remain afloat, with little opportunity to use their tax advantages, and with too little cash to be able to reinvest in needed equipment."[22]

The shortcomings of ESOPs are an inadvertent by-product of the process by which they were created. Looking to find a just alternative to communism in the early 1950s, philosopher Mortimer Adler and lawyer Louis Kelso teamed up to devise and promote ESOPs. They found a receptive audience in Louisiana senator Russell Long, who saw employee ownership as a way to make good on the dream of his deceased father, populist governor Huey Long, of providing the nation's working class with their shares of the American dream. Kelso, Adler, and Long each had admirable intentions; unfortunately, none had Jack Stack's experience in business management, and thus they were naive about the nature of employee motivation, and unaware that workers need a voice in the management of companies they are said to own. The lack of attention to those factors in the law that established ESOPs has led to an ongoing flaw in their performance.

The governance and management of all forms of employee-owned firms is particularly complex: Should top management be elected by employees? Who should serve on the executive board? What programs, policies, and practices should be voted on? How should employee-owners be involved in making managerial decisions? Should managers be paid on a different scale than shop-floor workers? All this is tricky business, as United Airlines discovered in the 1990s when, threatened with bankruptcy, it was rescued by its pilots, machinists, and other employees who took a 55 percent stake in the company in exchange for pay cuts (UA's flight attendants chose not to participate). The existing executive team stayed in place, and the company continued to be managed and governed as before, with the addition of two union representatives on its board of directors. At first employee morale and productivity improved. Machinists worked more efficiently and cooperatively, and pilots took pride in "their airline," welcoming passengers to "employee-owned United" and offering to serve them in any way they could. While United's employee-owners adjusted productively to their new status, top management found it nearly impossible to alter their past behavior. They continued to treat pilots and machinists as employees, and failed to listen to their suggestions for improving operations, let alone engage them in decision making. Moreover, it eventually became clear to the pilots and machinists that having union representation on the board fell far short of authentic employee participation in management. Within a couple of years, United's employees came to view their ownership stake as merely a good pension plan, and labor-management relations returned to being more adversarial than cooperative. United filed for bankruptcy in 2002, and while it made a comeback after a merger with Continental, today it is plagued by high levels of employee dissatisfaction, which have led to poor customer service.

Some eleven thousand companies in the United States are owned by employees, yet the prospects for a marked increase in worker ownership appear limited. Although employee-owned firms perform well—in fact, they outperform publicly traded companies—the problem is that they don't conform to received wisdom with respect to business ownership. In the eyes of most American corporate managers and investors, worker-owned companies don't fit into their perception of capitalist enterprises and, thus, are viewed as irrelevant. Among other things, that means worker-owned firms have problems raising start-up capital and obtaining operating loans. Worse, they are widely perceived as inefficient, resistant to change, and insufficiently imbued with the profit motive to be truly successful financially. Yet, to the extent that is true, it is due primarily to mismanagement and poor governance. The sad end to the SAIC employee-ownership story is a case in point.

The Governance Challenge

In 1969 physicist Robert Beyster and a handful of his colleagues founded Science Applications International, a technology-based consulting and research firm headquartered in San Diego, California. Beyster, with a PhD from the University of Michigan, began his career as a research physicist at the Los Alamos National Laboratory and later, head of the Accelerator Physics Department at the General Atomic corporation. He raised the funds to start SAIC by selling the company stock he had accumulated at General Atomic, and by financial contributions made by SAIC's initial employees. From the start, then, SAIC was completely owned by its workforce, who were compensated, in part, with company stock, received bonuses in the form of stock, and had the opportunity to purchase additional shares at a discounted price. The shares were traded on an internal "stock exchange" in which only employees and retirees were allowed to participate. The stock turned out to be a great investment: a share of SAIC purchased for $100 in 1970 was worth $3.5 million circa 2004. (By then, CEO Beyster owned 0.4 percent of its stock.)[23] Thirty-seven years after its founding, SAIC had $8 billion in annual revenues and, with some forty thousand employee-owners, was one of the largest worker-owned firms in America. By every measure the company was a success: it had satisfied customers, it was innovative, worker morale and productivity were high, and it was known for its impeccable ethical standards.[24] In 2005, independent observers concluded that employee ownership at SAIC was successful thanks to the large amount of financial information about the company made available to all employees, and the fact that employees played a direct role in management through an elected advisory committee reporting to the company's leaders, à la Lincoln

Electric.[25] (Founder Beyster credited James Lincoln for the managerial and organizational template on which SAIC was structured.)

Then the unthinkable occurred: in 2004, the company's board of directors, the majority of whom were outsiders, pushed founder Beyster into involuntary retirement; two years later, they voted to take the company public and shortly thereafter abolished its employee advisory committee. The company's then-publicly traded stock languished, and after seven years of little to no growth under three different CEOs, the board voted in 2013 to split the company in two parts to make it more attractive to investors.

Why would SAIC's board have chosen to destroy what had been a model of employee ownership? The answer is complicated, but Beyster later wrote that he was largely to blame for what occurred. He admitted, in hindsight, that he had appointed the wrong people to the board, believing it useful to have it filled with prominent people from the worlds of finance and industry, and especially those with military and government service on their résumés (the federal government was the company's largest customer). Unfortunately, those outsiders "were not committed to our unique culture of employee ownership." Applying conventional investor logic, the board believed SAIC was worth more as a publicly traded company. Ignoring the company's unique purpose of serving its employees, the board appears not to have asked, "Worth more to whom?" Shortly before Beyster's death in 2014, he rued not having made commitment to the company's core values a prime requisite for board membership, as at the John Lewis Partnership. He realized too late that, in addition to the board's roles relating to fiduciary oversight and strategy formation, their most important task should have been "to protect the company's unique employee-ownership culture, which I believed was central to making it an economic success."[26]

Fortunately, there is yet another form of employee ownership, one less susceptible to the pressures SAIC and Beyster experienced.

Cooperatives

In 1844 a group of struggling English workers and tradesmen, many of whom were disciples of Robert Owen, founded the Rochdale Society of Equitable Pioneers, a wholesale and retail trade cooperative, pledging not only to sell affordable wares to their members but "to commence the manufacture of such articles as the Society may determine upon, for the employment of such members as may be without employment, or may be suffering in consequence of repeated reductions in their wages."[27] The cooperative movement remains very much alive and well in Britain, America, and many other countries: according to the International Co-operative Alliance, 250 million people are employed in them worldwide. Yet their existence is largely ignored by the financial media and business schools, and they are all but invisible to the public at large. While cooperatives come in many shapes and forms, in most instances their business practices are oriented toward serving their members and collaborating with their local communities. Consider a few examples:

- Co-Opportunity Natural Foods in Santa Monica, California, is a consumer cooperative grocery store governed by a democratically elected board of community residents. Founded in 1974, the store offers low prices, health-oriented, high-quality, and environmentally sustainable products, and supports community-oriented activities and organizations in its neighborhood. Profits are redistributed as rebates to community members.
- Recology—a trash collector in California, Oregon, and Washington—has been employee owned since 1921, when Italian immigrants founded the Sunset Scavengers to collect garbage in San Francisco. Today the company is recognized as the nation's leading recycling innovator, its 2,200 employee-owners known

for their attentive customer service and high productivity. While growing up in San Francisco, I observed Scavengers literally running from one trash bin to the next! Once a month, they would all put on sports coats and neckties and then go door-to-door collecting fees for their services. Significantly, the Scavengers were respected in San Francisco as independent businessmen, not demeaned as "garbagemen." Today, of course, Recology's billing is done electronically.

- Denver-based $92 billion behemoth CoBank has been named "one of the world's fifty safest banks"[28] thanks to its resolute focus on a mission of providing financial services to the thousands of farmers who are its owners.

The cooperative movement is active in many industries and with several distinct purposes: consumer co-ops such as sports equipment giant REI are designed to serve their customer-owners; producer co-ops manage marketing and distribution for their manufacturing and agricultural owners; and, within a radius of fifteen miles of where I live, thirty-four co-ops are active in such diverse lines of business as printing, bookselling, and groceries (I buy pizza from the co-op Arizmendi— the name is explained below—a bakery providing healthy food at four locations around San Francisco). In addition, there are numerous artists' cooperatives across America.

Cooperatives are often portrayed as placing too much emphasis on idealism and not enough on practicality. Thanks to occasional over-heated claims about their potential to create a worker paradise, some of that skepticism has been deserved. Witness retailer Bradford Peck's 1900 utopian novel, *The World a Department Store*, which depicted a futuristic American co-op-based economy in which all citizens enjoyed "a delightful existence" of great abundance sans "wasted energy and social and commercial dishonesty." Peck went so far as to predict co-ops would disprove the common cynical belief that humans will "never give up their selfish ambitions."[29] Obviously, such misty-eyed boosterism invites criticism from realists, let alone cynics. In fact, co-operatives are not perfect: these nontraditional enterprises tend to grow slowly, and to not be technologically innovative. They also are difficult to govern: it is devilishly hard for co-op managers to give direction to employees, who, after all, are their peers and co-owners. Similarly challenging is the ongoing effort needed to reconcile the differing needs, desires, and opinions of members of organizations with deep roots in the principles of democracy, equality, and mutual support.

The financing of cooperatives is a particular challenge, and not merely confined to the task of raising start-up capital. It is worth noting recent news from Mondragón, Spain, home to a group of 289 worker-owned cooperatives employing some eighty thousand employee-owners. Founded in 1941 by Basque priest José Arizmendiarrieta (hence the name of San Francisco's Arizmendi bakery), the Mondragón co-ops are often cited as the most successful alternatives to both state ownership and shareholder capitalism. Yet in 2013, when one of the largest Mondragón companies—5,600-employee Fagor appliance manufacturer—announced that it might soon file for bankruptcy, there was widespread concern in Spain that such a filing would trigger the downfall of dozens of other companies in the financially integrated group. Because the local Mondragón economy is overdependent on this one form of business organization, the entire community found itself at risk financially. The Mondragón group ultimately was forced to let Fagor go under.[30] Around the same time, Britain's Co-Operative Bank—a prime source of capital for the UK's cooperative movement—was hit with heavy losses incurred making bad property loans (the problem was compounded by a juicy sex scandal involving the bank's top executive). After a temporary bailout by American hedge funds, the bank was put up for sale.

Despite such pitfalls and shortcomings, the cooperative movement has lasted for an impressive century and three-quarters and appears to be vital as ever, constantly taking on new challenges and morphing in creative ways. In 2016, 220,000 people were employed in 6,797 co-ops in the United Kingdom, including 160 at Sana, a profitable business selling a line of vegetarian, organic, and ethically sourced foods ranging from baked beans to beer. Sana's sales (much of it international) topped £50 million in 2017, the year it received a coveted Queen's Award for Enterprise. All of the democratically governed company's worker-owners are paid the same £16-per-hour rate, including the co-op's leader, Stephen Newton, who says he feels a heightened sense of responsibility to carefully consider his decisions relating to allocation of company resources: "That money is my peers' money. It means I have to really focus on what I am doing and have to justify everything."[31] That fraternal attitude is rare in publicly traded corporations.

In Cleveland, the second-poorest major American city (a notch ahead of Detroit), locals at the Evergreen Co-operative Corporation are attempting to deal with at least a bit of the area's persistently high rates of poverty and unemployment. With start-up funding from the Cleveland Foundation, Evergreen has launched three co-ops employing 125 workers. Modeled after Spain's Mondragón group, the co-ops do laundry for local hospitals and provide fresh lettuce and herbs (grown in a three-acre hydroponic greenhouse built on an abandoned lot) to the Cleveland Clinic. Evergreen's workers are paid about $14 an hour—enough to have enabled twenty-three of them to purchase rehabilitated houses, thanks to loans from Evergreen. Workers can own their homes free and clear in five years. However, the work they do is extremely hard, the hours they put in are long, and they have limited prospects of promotion or higher salaries. Nonetheless, as one laundry worker explained, "I used to be poor.... I might not make a lot of money, but I've got a job, I've got a family, and I don't have to be looking over my shoulder. From where I come from, it's night and day. What I've got that I didn't have [before] is hope." Following what is now known as the Cleveland Model, similar cooperative groups have been formed in Albuquerque, New Orleans, Richmond, and Rochester. In all, two hundred new cooperatives were founded in the United States between 2000 and 2016. Albeit not a large number, the increase indicates the movement is far from passé.[32]

Then there are credit unions, the most visible and successful form of cooperatives. Federally and state-chartered credit unions are consumer co-ops, each traditionally serving a specific group or community: a church, workplace, college, labor union, or town. The first credit union was founded in New Hampshire in 1908, and subsequently, their numbers grew rapidly, reaching a peak of 23,866 in 1969. In 2016, American credit unions served some 100 million members, and employed over 240,000 people. In general, credit unions have had a sterling record of providing services to their members, notably making credit available to low- and medium-income individuals and members of minority groups who have historically had problems obtaining mortgages from regular banks. With only a couple of exceptions, the nation's credit unions weathered the 2007–8 financial crisis by avoiding the wildly risky behavior of the Wall Street banks against whom they compete in the mortgage market. Again, no organizational form is perfect: some credit union executives have taken advantage of their federal charters, accentuating the practical over the idealistic aspects of their businesses by paying themselves egregiously high salaries and even converting their organizations into regular banks to treat themselves to financial windfalls.

Mutual companies are another cooperative structure. Technically owned by their policyholders, most large life insurance companies in America were originally chartered as mutuals, including Mutual of Omaha, Prudential, and Guardian Life. On the whole, they have had admirable records of social and financial performance—although there has been a recent trend among mutual top executives to follow the lead of their peers in credit unions and "take their companies public" to enrich themselves.

A Few Good, Happy Endings

The existence of several viable forms of ownership which are not vulnerable to the vagaries of stock markets, shareholder short-termism, or the necessity to sell socially engaged companies to large corporations, should give enthusiasts of enlightened capitalism reason to cheer. If nothing else, these alternatives to shareholder ownership—sole and family proprietorships, social enterprises and benefit corporations, employee-owned firms, and co-ops—provide promising opportunities for socially minded businesspeople to practice their values. Moreover, this brief examination of some less visible forms of capitalism brings our review of the stories of the enlightened capitalists to an end on a relatively positive note.

When considered in total, the stories recounted in these pages constitute a rich body of experience to draw on as we now move to consider questions posed at the beginning of the book: Can businesses do both good and well? What were the motivations of leaders who introduced enlightened practices? Why have so few companies maintained virtuous practices and, in the instances where they were sustained, what did the leaders do that differed from the actions of those who did not succeed? What were the errors of those who failed? Will investors support leaders of companies that engage in addressing social problems? Given how hard it has been to sustain enlightened corporate practices, are there reasons to believe the task will be easier in the future? And, finally, the meta question: Are socially virtuous business practices compatible with shareholder capitalism?

In the chapters that follow, we look back to see what we have learned from our many stories, and forward to weigh the future prospects of enlightened corporate leadership.

PART III

YESTERDAY, TODAY, AND TOMORROW

17

Looking Back

WHAT WE HAVE LEARNED

In the late 1970s and early '80s, many observers—myself among them—were convinced that a golden era had arrived and the enlightened capitalists whose stories we have reviewed were the vanguard of a new way of thinking about the role of business in society. Hence, we concluded, their virtuous practices would soon become the corporate norm. That prediction proved premature. Indeed, I still have egg on my face from the 1980s, when I advanced, as models to be emulated, twenty-four American firms with impressive records of socially responsible, ethical, and environmentally conscious behavior. Alas, today only three of those companies have maintained their admirable practices—the others having abandoned or greatly de-emphasized them in the 1990s as the result, variously, of being acquired by conventional firms, going bankrupt, or changes in leadership, all three typically prompted by pressures from investors for increased short-term profit.[1]

By the mid-1990s, the brief golden-era wave of social responsibility had crested, and traditional modes of business thinking were once again ascendant—possibly with a stronger hold on the assumptions of corporate leaders than at any time since the pre-Depression 1920s. A variety of factors accounted for this shift in thinking. The first was the increasing influence of scholars ideologically aligned with the University of Chicago school of economics. As disciples of Milton Friedman, they believed that the sole purpose of a corporation is to

American Vanguard Corporations in 1985

Arco [A]	Honeywell [L, A]
Chaparral Steel [A]	Johnson & Johnson [L]
Control Data [X]	Kollmorgen [A]
Cummins Engine [L]	Levi Strauss [L]
Dana [L]	**Lincoln Electric**
Dayton-Hudson (now Target)	Lord Corporation [L]
Deere [L]	Motorola [L]
Digital Equipment (DEC) [X]	Olga [A]
Fel-Pro [L, X]	Polaroid [X]
W. L. Gore	TRW [L, A]
Herman Miller [L]	Weyerhaeuser [L]
Hewlett-Packard [L]	Xerox [L]

[A] = Acquired or merged
[X] = Out of business
[L] = Change in leadership resulting in loss, or considerable lessening, of commitment to social
    engagement
Bold = Enlightened practices still largely in place

make a profit, and the concept of social responsibility is wrongheaded, if not abhorrent. That belief was buttressed by business school finance professors who were vocal advocates of agency theory. According to that theory, professional managers of publicly held corporations are "paid agents" (employees) of the legal owners (shareholders) of firms. As such, corporate managers are said to have fiduciary duties to produce the maximum profits possible for their employers. An implication of both those concepts is that managers who use corporate funds to benefit employees, communities, or the natural environment are, in effect, appropriating their employers' capital (unless, of course, shareholders explicitly approve such "unprofitable" uses of the money). The prevalence of those theories, about which more is said below, lent intellectual license to corporate executives bent on abandoning social activities that, they concluded, reduced shareholder profits and wealth. With such diminished interest in the corporate community, a great many American business schools retreated from their 1980s pro-social-responsibility curriculums. For example, in the MBA program where I taught between 1973 and 1992, students were offered as many as five different electives on such subjects as business ethics, business and society, business and government, and corporate social responsibility. By 1993, none of those courses was being offered.

Perhaps as significant, the booming economy during the Clinton administration was seen as proof that shareholder-first corporate capitalism was the surest road to wealth creation and national prosperity. That conclusion was accompanied by a shift in editorial emphasis at such publications as *Fortune, Businessweek,* and the *Harvard Business Review,* which in the 1980s had touted corporate social engagement, but in the '90s either lost interest in the subject or cynically mocked it. In that era of fast-rising incomes, high profits, low unemployment, and rapid technological progress, corporate executives felt little pressure to address social problems that, at the time, the broader society was also largely ignoring. It wasn't that issues related to corporate conduct entirely disappeared or dissipated: revelations about working conditions in the factories of Nike's contractors led to calls for improving health and safety and elimination of child labor in Asian workshops; Starbucks and other retailers began to introduce fair-trade policies for imports of coffee and other agricultural products; Western corporations divested their operations in apartheid South Africa; social investment funds were introduced; and environmentalists began calling for the reduction of greenhouse gases. Nonetheless, those trends had little influence on the internal operations of most large corporations or on the levels of their societal engagement. And so, in the waning decade of the twentieth century, the brief golden era of corporate social enlightenment whimpered to a conclusion.

Lessons from Experience

The shift in thinking at the end of the millennium offers a convenient historical vantage point from which to look back and reflect on what was learned from the experiences of the enlightened capitalists. Perhaps the most obvious conclusion is that enlightened business practices have proved difficult to introduce and to maintain everywhere they have been tried, and in all eras. It has been far simpler, the record shows, for business leaders to focus solely on the goal of profitability—a large enough challenge as it is—without also attempting to address societal ills. That is probably why most business leaders have concentrated on purely business matters, with some salving their consciences, or boosting their reputations, by way of philanthropic activities requiring little more effort than writing a check.

As we have seen, socially focused business endeavors often came a cropper for reasons related to investor greed, executive ego, and hubris. In reality, more than one of those factors invariably was implicated, as was the contributing element of mismanagement. Somewhat arbitrarily, we might say that enlightened practices were not maintained because: investors wanted higher returns on their capital (New Lanark, Lever Bros., Levi Strauss, Marks & Spencer, Polaroid, Ben & Jerry's, Goldman Sachs); founders sold their companies to increase their own personal wealth (Roddick, Chappell); and the insecure egos of successor executives led to the erasure, or de-emphasis, of their predecessors' legacy programs, actions often justified as necessary to increase profits (J. C. Penney, Johnson & Johnson, Herman Miller, Arco, Avis, Cummins, Merck, SAIC). More than a few of the enlightened capitalists' own egos led them to overreach and, in a few instances, to self-destruct (Owen, Penney, Lever, Hershey, Land, Norris, Roddick, Cohen). Doubtless each of those individuals had enemies, yet they themselves contributed to the woes they encountered and endured. At a minimum, it can be said that the enlightened practices at all the companies suffered the fate of what Max De Pree called "organizational entropy," although it is too soon to make a final judgment on Southwest, Gore, SRC Holdings, and Patagonia.

On the positive side, few companies found themselves in financial straits as the direct result of engaging in socially beneficial activities.

Of the cases reviewed, arguably only at Control Data and Malden Mills did a company's social mission undercut its ability to make a profit. Indeed, virtuous conduct proved compatible with profitability at all the companies, starting with the New Lanark mills on down to Ben & Jerry's—yet those efforts were often abandoned despite their evident success. It is hard to escape the fact that, regardless of the extent to which virtuous practices contributed to productivity, the reputation of firms, or increases in the quality of the lives of workers, customers, and host communities, they were *seldom embraced* by investors, trade unionists, academics, business competitors, the business press, and successor managers. Moreover, there was never strong, concerted public demand for corporate social engagement in either the United States or the UK. Historically, nothing more was expected from business leaders than wealth creation and obeying existing laws. On that score, I find it telling that so many of the enlightened capitalists' stories have been forgotten.

The record also shows that corporate virtue was particularly hard to maintain consistently, even under the best economic conditions. The enlightened leaders continually faced pressures to make trade-offs that would have entailed abandoning their principles and practices in order to shore up profits, or to cope with changing technological and competitive conditions. When times were bad, they often lost control of their firms (Lever, Norris, Land), and the legacy of none survived the aftermath of a merger or acquisition (Lever, Roddick, Bradshaw, Townsend, and perhaps Cohen and Chappell). Most singularly, enlightened practices were put at risk after changes in leadership: when founders died, retired, or resigned, "new brooms swept clean"—if not immediately, within the span of two successions of leadership (Owen, Penney, Lever, Hershey, Burke, De Pree, Whitehead, Vagelos, Townsend, Miller, Burke, Iverson, Roddick, Beyster).

On the positive side of the ledger, we found examples of practical idealism in a wide variety of industries, in companies large and small, during almost every era between 1815 and 2000. We saw that the motivations of our idealistic capitalists were many and diverse, including religious principles (Penney, Hershey, Eagan, Chappell, Miller, and the Marks and Sieff families), laissez-faire ideology (Lincoln, Lewis, Robert Wood Johnson, Stack), and progressive political ideology (Owen, Haas, Roddick, Chappell, Cohen, Chouinard). Some idealists believed they had a moral obligation to do the right thing based on humanistic Enlightenment values (Owen, Lever, Bradshaw, Land, Townsend), while some were business pragmatists who simply believed the most effective way to do well is to do good (Whitehead, Vagelos, Gore, Kelleher, Beyster). Most appear to have been motivated by a combination of such factors—and others; after all, we mustn't slight the undoubtedly profound influence that ballroom dancing had on the philosophies of Owen, Lever, Hershey, and Robert Wood Johnson!

In all, only a few valid generalizations can be made about enlightened capitalists in toto: none was primarily a philanthropist; none started with the intent of using his or her business to do good works (instead, they adopted that goal gradually); all were committed to the development of employees; and all were dedicated to ethical dealings with their constituencies (specifically, by treating them with respect). And no matter how noble their principles and practices may have been, they succeeded only to the extent their businesses succeeded. No amount of virtue was enough to compensate for instances of mismanagement, or failure to keep their eyes on their economic missions. Absent strategic flexibility and adaptability with regard to changing products, technology, and competition—and not least, ongoing profitability—not one succeeded.

Quite remarkably, given that they were all committed capitalists, none of our enlightened leaders was driven to do good by market demand: their virtuous actions were seldom, if ever, in response to customer desire for responsible corporate behavior. And there is a clear explanation for why those practical businesspeople ignored (at least in this regard) the dictates of Adam Smith's invisible hand. In a 2006 review of corporate attempts to do good while doing well, business scholar David Vogel found that "the market for virtue" was, at best, a small one, with precious little evidence that consumers opted to buy products based on the admirable deeds of the companies that made them, or that companies reaped financial gain from acts of social responsibility.[2]

And there is even less evidence that shareholders reward ethical leaders. In 2014, the *Economist* examined the flip side of the question, concluding that corporate *mis*conduct is forgiven quickly by investors—provided the company engaged in wrongdoing recovers quickly and delivers high profits.[3] Hewlett-Packard's stock promptly recovered after revelations of accounting irregularities, Wells Fargo's share value increased after revelations the bank had bilked several million of its unwitting customers, VW rebounded after it was caught in an emissions-rigging scandal,[4] BP remained profitable even after paying billions to settle damages incurred in the Clearwater disaster, and Mylan's share price was not affected for long by damning front-page stories documenting how it had charged hundreds of dollars for a lifesaving drug that cost only a few dollars to produce. The bad publicity attendant on such corporate misbehavior may have led to some short-term decrease in sales among a few consumers unwilling to reward unethical behavior, yet as long as such downturns in profitability were minor and of brief duration, the preponderance of investors were unfazed. The stock market is, after all, an amoral mechanism that neither punishes misbehavior nor rewards virtue. That is a fact that all the idealistic men and women whose careers we have studied were practical enough to understand. In effect, unlike traditional business leaders who expect their performance to be measured by the sole metric of profitability, the enlightened leaders were eager to *also* be evaluated by an ethical yardstick. If nothing else, that made their jobs twice as hard to do well.

While all our idealistic leaders shared a number of core characteristics, they nonetheless were—each in their own way—different from the others. Aside from their manifest differences in personality and backgrounds, three broad factors may be said to account for most of their differences in philosophies and practices: namely, the historical and intellectual contexts in which they worked; the degree to which they institutionalized their practices and values; and the ownership structure of their respective companies. As we see below, those three complexly interrelated factors may also have influenced the degrees to which they each succeeded or failed in the long term.

Intellectual Influences and Historical Contexts

Enlightened capitalism is neither an ideology nor an established canon of beliefs and practices. As the name I have given them implies, the enlightened capitalists shared a common philosophy only to the extent that their beliefs are rooted in the ideas of eighteenth-century Enlightenment thinkers. Even if they had not read Rousseau, Locke, and Jefferson, those idealistic leaders were indirectly inspired by the Enlightenment notion that men and women can improve the condition of society through the application of reason. While most of the enlightened capitalists wrote books outlining their philosophies (with the notable exceptions of Lever, Hershey, and Norris) they seldom cited specific intellectual influences, and they only occasionally offered nods in the direction of virtuous leaders who had preceded them. In the rare instances when they did acknowledge a debt to a great thinker or prominent business progenitor, they seldom cited the same individuals: Owen makes passing mention of Bentham, Spedan Lewis does the same for Owen, De Pree credits Peter Drucker and Carl Frost, Townsend acknowledges his debt to Douglas McGregor, Robert Wood Johnson cites papal encyclicals, Beyster tips his hat to James Lincoln, and Lincoln, more than any of the others, draws heavily on early-twentieth-century economic and management theorists. Hershey clearly put the ideas of F. W. Taylor into practice (even if he didn't write about them).

In their various writings and practices, astute readers can find reflections of Henry Gantt's early-twentieth-century teachings about the importance of sharing profits to bridge the gap between labor and management; applications of Maslow's hierarchy of needs (itself derived from Aristotle's thoughts about human development); examples of the economic concept of "internalizing" costs that company actions impose on society and the environment; and, most clearly, the influence of McGregor's Theory Y on post–World War II practices. Nonetheless, our leaders seldom, if ever, acknowledged those intellectual influences. Why that is so is a matter for speculation. It may be they suffered from the egocentrism that afflicts so many executives (enlightened and otherwise), a condition that prevents them from acknowledging the contributions of others to their success. Or perhaps they merely recognized that useful intellectual theories are often derived from the observed practices of business leaders; hence, scholars deserve credit only for later naming what practitioners had earlier created. For example, if Peter Drucker's writings about corporate social responsibility were based on the practices of Julius Rosenwald (at Sears) and the Marks and Sieff families, then why acknowledge a debt to Drucker?

So where did the enlightened capitalists' ideas come from? Keynes doubtless put his finger on the source when he famously wrote,

> Practical men, who believe themselves to be quite exempt from intellectual influences, are usually the slave to some defunct economist. Madmen in authority, who hear voices in the air, are distilling their frenzy from some academic scribbler of a few years back.[5]

Or, in the case of the enlightened capitalists, some defunct philosopher, psychologist, pope, or management theorist.

Whatever their intellectual influences, the fact is all of them were products of their times. From Owen in the early 1800s to Chappell at the turn of the twenty-first century, they acted in response to the major social problems of their eras. The farsighted workplace practices of Owen, Lever, Hershey, Eagan, and Lincoln were in response to the horrors of the Industrial Revolution and the continuing harsh nature of factory work in its aftermath. During those years, there were glaring needs for safe factories and decent worker housing, and the enlightened capitalists met those admirably and effectively. The markedly different practices employed by enlightened capitalists who led retail and services companies in the early twentieth century reflected social and demographic changes then occurring in Britain and America—specifically, the growth of a white-collar workforce and a burgeoning middle class. At roughly the same time, fear that Marxist communism was finding a toehold in the liberal democracies led several large corporations to introduce a form of corporate socialism: such Manhattan department stores as Lord & Taylor and Wanamaker's offered employees lunchrooms, libraries, and medical clinics.[6] By the 1920s, the National Cash Register Corporation, Kodak, Sears, AT&T, General Electric, and later IBM were providing pensions, health benefits, training, and job security. In that light, the generous employee benefits offered by J. C. Penney, the John Lewis Partnership, Johnson & Johnson, Levi Strauss, and Marks & Spencer appear something less than radical.

Starting in the 1960s, the effects of the civil and women's rights movements and the advent of the counterculture—and, in particular, the waxing influence of every breed and ilk of psychologist who descended, en masse, on workplaces—were reflected in policies and practices employed at Polaroid, Ben & Jerry's, the Body Shop, and Tom's of Maine. Today, the issue of climate change dominates the zeitgeist. Because the importance of environmental concerns is now seen to outweigh all other business-related issues, global warming has become the focus of most enlightened practices being introduced in Britain and America. Significantly, the growing recognition of the need to address environmental issues has led advocates of enlightened capitalism to conclude that a new golden era of business virtue is nigh, and that even publicly traded corporations will embrace it. (In the following chapter, we examine that encouraging possibility.)

Given the different eras in which the enlightened capitalists lived and worked, and the sundry intellectual influences exerted on them, it is no wonder they employed different practices. Yet there was one thing upon which they agreed, and one policy they all attempted to implement: they all expressed a sense of unease about, if not dread of, shareholder capitalism, and all used every method at their disposal to avoid taking their companies public. Even after she listed her company on the London exchange, Anita Roddick expressed disdain for financial investors, and John Whitehead's Goldman Sachs partners were loath to list their firm publicly, correctly fearing the negative effects on its ethical culture that, indeed, would come. Which brings us to the related issues of governance and ownership.

Governance

Only four of the companies reviewed here managed to sustain virtuous practices over more than two generations of leadership: the John Lewis Partnership, ACIPCO, Lincoln Electric, and W. L. Gore. Significantly, the first two of those are owned by trusts the boards of which are legally bound to preserve their founders' values and ensure that employees now and in the future are prime beneficiaries of all profits earned, after reinvestment. Lincoln Electric and Gore are largely owned by family foundations and employees. Although such ownership structures have proved central to sustaining virtuous practices at those companies, those forms are neither a guarantee of admirable behavior nor easy to fund, design, and implement, as the mixed legacy of Milton Hershey's trust demonstrates. Indeed, John Spedan Lewis and John Joseph Eagan spent years— and fortunes on legal fees—to construct ironclad documents binding future generations of trustees to conform to the intent of their wills. In contrast, Hershey personally, and to some extent cavalierly, dictated the terms of his trust, terms that continue to give insufficient guidance to the trust's directors and, worse, offer them perverse behavioral incentives.

That is not to condemn Milton Hershey. After all, if the observed reluctance among many men and women to prepare wills is a reliable indicator, few people are eager to contemplate the aftereffects of their own mortality. And as directors who have served on corporate boards can attest, one of their most difficult chores is to convince a CEO or founder to engage in succession planning. Executives, like monarchs, find no pleasure in imagining another soul occupying their chairs (or thrones). Rather perversely, then, it must have seemed a bit strange, if not bizarre, to those around Spedan Lewis when he devoted decades to preparing for what would come after him, as it must have seemed normal to Hershey's associates that he would dash off the will creating the Hershey Trust in the matter of an afternoon.

Although company ownership by family trusts is common in the United States, independent trusts such as Hershey's and ACIPCO's are rare (but not unheard of: until a decade or so ago, the publisher of the *Encyclopaedia Britannica* was an independent company owned by a trust of which the University of Chicago was sole beneficiary, somewhat akin to the relationship between the Hershey company, trust, and school). In England, the tea company Camellia PLC is governed by a foundation holding 52 percent of its stock, with the remainder closely held by its founder and a few others. The terms of that foundation bind its trustees for a hundred years, during which they must continue to provide housing, schools, and hospitals for the company's seventy-nine employees on tea plantations in Kenya, India, and Bangladesh.

Many of Continental Europe's largest corporations (including IKEA, Carlsberg, and Bertelsmann) are owned by foundations, a primary purpose of which is to maintain company values (and to make hostile takeovers virtually impossible).[7] Scholar David Ciepley documents how ownership by a trust or foundation can offer enormous organizational, social, and economic benefits; nonetheless, he notes how difficult it has been to create industrial foundations in the US since 1969 when "Congress passed tax legislation that effectively prohibited a non-profit from owning more than 20% of the voting shares in a corporation."[8] Hence, use of the form to preserve enlightened practices is unlikely to grow appreciably in America unless the law is changed. Not only is the creation of such structures hampered by mind-addling legal and tax complexities, there is also understandable reluctance on the part of company founders to, in effect, give away a major part of their descendants' inheritances. Nonetheless, intellectually resourceful founders can identify other, less drastic and expensive tools to protect the social missions of their enterprises after their departure. For example, the American J. M. Smucker Company employs a shareholder voting system in which those who have owned shares for over four years have ten votes per share, while other stockowners have only one, thus reducing the power of speculators and activists to influence corporate direction.[9] In England, the 174-year-old *Economist* magazine has a board of independent trustees charged with safeguarding its corporate and editorial independence from the whims of whomever should come to own it.[10] Doubtless Robert Beyster went to his grave regretting that he had failed to create such a structure at SAIC.

Nearly all the enlightened capitalists attempted, in one form or another, to institutionalize their practices—as it were, to bake them into their organizations' cultures. Indeed, Penney, Hershey, De Pree, Burke, and the Haas, Marks, and Sieff families appear to have believed they had successfully done so. Alas, most of the enlightened leaders either neglected that task or were inept at the nuts and bolts of building the infrastructures needed to preserve valued legacies. Even the more recent leaders who were well aware of their responsibilities to shape company culture did little to convince their boards to create legal and governance barriers to hostile takeovers, and the abandonment of their companies' basic values and higher purposes by later generations of professional managers. Boards, of course, are reluctant to engage in this planning, fearing that such restrictions will hamper a company's future ability to make necessary strategic changes. But as Margaret Thatcher rightly noted, it is the responsibility of leaders to constantly adjust strategies, tactics, and policies in response to changes in the environment, but to change their values? "Never!" Thus, one of the greatest weaknesses of the enlightened leaders was their collective failure to educate their boards on the importance of their role in protecting legacies of virtue.

A major conclusion to be drawn from our stories is that, when corporate practices were viewed as personality-dependent—particularly in the cases of Owen, Penney, Lever, Hershey, Townsend, Whitehead, Vagelos, Roddick, and Cohen—successor executives found few impediments to excising their predecessors' virtuous programs and policies. Conversely, such practices were more likely to be sustained when they had become thoroughly institutionalized in organizational cultures and rules of governance, as at Lincoln Electric, the Lewis Partnership, and W. L. Gore. That said, a well-designed governance structure, in and of itself, may be insufficient to guarantee the sustainability of enlightened practices. Indeed, it might better be considered a prerequisite for a more potent element: control of ownership.

The Ownership Factor

After studying the careers of enlightened capitalists for the better part of my career, I have concluded that ownership is far and away the most significant predicator of virtuous business practices, and especially the key to their sustainability. As history demonstrates, the virtuous practices of Owen, Penney, Lever, Roddick, Norris, Cohen, and Beyster—as well as the Haas, Johnson, Marks, and Sieff families—came to an end once they lost financial control of the organizations they founded. In contrast, as just noted with respect to governance, the cultures of stewardship at ACIPCO, Lincoln Electric, the John Lewis Partnership, and W. L. Gore have been sustained, in large, because control of those companies has remained in the hands of the founder's descendants and employees (as guaranteed by their governance structures and strictures). Moreover, the nature of company ownership was a prime determinant of the long-term sustainability of enlightened practices at all the companies discussed in these pages.

When we think about the ownership of business organizations, we tend to focus on two clearly distinguishable constructs: privately held, and publicly traded, companies. The former—in the guise of small and medium-sized businesses—serve as society's primary engines of innovation and job creation, while the latter—in the form of giant corporations—harness the vast amounts of capital required to grow and to compete globally. While both types play essential roles, they are also sources of different kinds of economic instability (small businesses have high failure rates; large corporations engage in high-risk mergers, pursue short-term profit across national boundaries, have a tendency toward cycles of boom and bust, and engage in investment-sapping share buybacks). To the extent that the latter engage in virtuous practices, they tend to do just enough to appear to be good corporate citizens; the former typically have too few resources for any but the most minimal forms of social engagement.

Because small, privately held businesses are seldom profitable enough to compensate their entrepreneurial founders for the hard work and long hours they invested in creating them, their founders typically seek to garner payoffs for their efforts in one of two ways: like Anita Roddick, by selling their companies to big corporations, or like William Norris, by selling shares to investors. As we have seen, either way founders risk losing control. Even entrepreneurs who continue to own and manage their companies often find it necessary to sell equity in them to finance growth. That act often turns out to be a devil's bargain: when founders' (or their families') ownership is diluted, they begin to lose control of how a company is managed. And when shares are bought and sold on financial markets, investors inevitably gain the upper hand; eventually founders or their families lose influence as their companies come to be led by professional managers. When that occurs, investor demand for short-term profit increases, and the sustainability of virtuous practices becomes imperiled.

Recently deceased law professor Lynn Stout argued that the perceived need to maximize shareholder value drives many directors and
executives—often unwillingly and against their better judgment—to
focus almost exclusively on increasing profits in order to raise stock
prices: "In the quest to 'unlock shareholder value' they sell key assets,
fire loyal employees, and ruthlessly squeeze the workforce that remains; cut back on product support, customer assistance and research
and development; delay replacing outworn, outmoded and unsafe
equipment; shower CEOs with stock options and expensive pay packages to 'incentivize' them; drain cash reserves to pay large dividends
and repurchase company shares, leveraging firms until they teeter on
the brink of insolvency."[11]

The problem does not arise simply from pressures by investors in
public stock exchanges—as we saw, shares of Robert Owen's and William Lever's companies were not publicly traded; nonetheless, they
came into conflict, respectively, with their nonmanaging partners and
outside investors. As previously noted, that conflict between managers
and investors became institutionalized in 1919 when, in *Dodge v. Ford
Motor Company*, a Michigan court ruled that "a business corporation is
organized and carried on primarily for the profit of the stockholders.
The powers of the directors are to be employed for that end."[12] That
ruling—actually a "dicta," or a nonbinding aside made by a judge—has
since been accepted as gospel by investors, and shareholder primacy
has become an ingrained tenet of corporate capitalism in America and,
to only a slightly lesser extent, in Britain. That remarkable phenomenon is an exercise in either collective delusion or willful ignorance.
For as legal scholar Stout documented, the oft-stated principle that the
law requires directors to maximize shareholder value is nowhere to
be found in American law, nor has the principle ever been cited by the
Delaware court that hears the preponderance of cases relating to corporate governance. Yet the notion that corporations exist to maximize
shareholder profit is unquestioningly accepted by most lawyers, law
professors, investors, corporate executives, and business journalists,

along with professors of economics, finance, and accounting in both the United States and the United Kingdom.

Simply put, the business community, *writ large*, is enthralled by the notion of shareholder primacy, which, as noted above, is buttressed by agency theory and Milton Friedman's oft-quoted doctrine that the only responsibility of business is to increase its profits.[13] However, a close reading of Friedman reveals that he hedged on the terms of his own doctrine, arguing that it was permissible for corporate managers to support local schools and colleges that supply a company with trained workers and educated managers; offer employees good pay and benefits that lead to increases in loyalty and productivity; and engage in community and social activities that result in enhanced brand image or corporate reputation. Even if a polluting company engaged in hypocritical environmental "greenwashing," that too would be fine and good as long as its managers justified the expenditures in terms of the bottom line. In short, Friedman opposed only corporate social activities undertaken for virtuous reasons! What he specifically opposed was corporate philanthropy. When executives used shareholder money to support causes of their choosing, he claimed that they were spending shareholders' money without permission. Those significant hedges have been largely overlooked by both Friedman's critics and supporters, and thus his doctrine has been applied indiscriminately across the board to any and all corporate deeds not directly contributing to short-term profit.

It has mattered not a whit that shareholder primacy is a legal myth, or that the originator of agency theory, Michael Jensen, later repudiated it, or that Friedman's doctrine is an exercise in garbled reasoning and deplorable morality. *Most players in the system believe the purpose of a corporation is to maximize shareholder profit.* Moreover, a great many corporate executives *act* on that belief—and as long as they do, it is doubtful that they will embrace virtuous practices that are seen as appreciably diminishing profit. To my mind, that conclusion is as discouraging as it is an inescapable takeaway from the stories of the enlightened capitalists. The only silver lining lurking behind that dark cloud is the existence of alternative forms of ownership such as trusts, foundations, and others discussed in the previous chapter, all of which lend themselves more readily to initiating and maintaining enlightened business practices than does public ownership.

Conclusion

The record shows that few publicly traded companies in the twentieth century were able to sustain enlightened practices over time and through changes in leadership. The companies faring best have been owned by families, trusts, foundations, employees, and in some cases professional partnerships. Hence, it is reasonable to conclude that businesspeople wishing to create sustainably virtuous organizations are more likely to succeed in companies with those forms of ownership than in investor-owned ones. However, as *Financial Times* management columnist Andrew Hill cautions, "Co-ops, mutuals, and employee-owned organizations, for all their ideals, are still prone to volatile business cycles, venality, and common-or-garden [variety] mismanagement."[14] That caveat noted, Hill nevertheless concludes that co-ops, in particular, have earned a place in modern economies, providing stability during eras of boom and bust. Nonetheless, putting all an economy's financial eggs in one structural basket is far too risky, as the recent financial crisis at the Mondragón co-ops illustrates. Moreover, companies with different forms of ownership have mutually compensating strengths and weaknesses, and no single form can provide a modern nation with all it needs to ensure the prosperity of its people. Smaller, privately held companies create jobs and innovation better than large publicly held companies, but those behemoths are capable of producing the economies of scale that make goods and services readily available to all economic classes, and can amass the capital needed for large-scale industrial projects and efficient global commerce. Big banks provide the operating capital that businesses need, and credit unions can't provide; yet credit unions do a better job than big banks when it comes to providing home and car loans to the middle and working classes. As Hill notes, "The financial crisis showed that when a single ownership model starts to dominate the economy, systemic risks increase."[15]

Based on my own reading of history, an economy with a healthy mix of private, public, and nonprofit organizations—and a business sector with a robust mix of ownership forms—offers the best prospect for prosperity and a just society. In light of that, I believe there is ample room in the American and British economic systems to accommodate a great many more trusts, foundations, employee-owned firms, cooperatives, benefit corporations, and mutual organizations—and that society would be the better for it.

Still, we are left with unanswered questions: Is enlightened leadership compatible with shareholder capitalism? If not, can it be made compatible? And what is the likelihood that it will become more so in the future? In the next chapter we explore the degree and extent to which leaders of publicly traded organizations might be expected to behave virtuously in the future. Those corporations represent the "commanding heights" of capitalist economies, and as such, have the capacity to do both the most social harm *and* the most good. After all, they are where the money is.

18

Looking Forward

THE PROSPECTS FOR ENLIGHTENED CORPORATE LEADERSHIP

As the evidence shows, virtuous business practices can be, and have been, successfully implemented, although such leadership feats have proved difficult to achieve, particularly in publicly traded corporations. Even when such practices have been implemented, they have had relatively short half-lives in most corporations—despite the benefits they have produced, and the fact that they have had only minor, if any, negative effects on profitability. The historical record also reveals that most executives have simply not been interested in assuming the task of social engagement, while others have believed that their shareholders opposed such practices. Those are rather discouraging findings for those, like me, who want to believe that corporate capitalism can, and should, be conducted virtuously. Nonetheless, many contemporary advocates of social responsibility are not discouraged by the historical record; instead, they optimistically point to what they foresee is a brighter future. In the words of entrepreneur-environmentalist Paul Hawken, "If you meet the people who are working to restore this earth and the lives of the poor, and you aren't optimistic, you haven't got a pulse."[1]

Optimists believe that conditions have changed so radically in the twenty-first century—particularly with regard to the environment and global warming—that past experience cannot be taken as indicative of future events. In their view, a historical inflection point has been reached, and now corporate executives have no choice but to act to save the planet. Assuming a historical discontinuity, advocates of enlightened management thus argue that even executives in publicly traded firms are now poised to embrace social responsibility, citing a steady stream of books published since 2000 profiling companies that are "making doing good an integral part of doing well," "delivering value with values," and deriving "profit with passion and purpose."[2]

Optimists see a major shift in the way some corporate leaders are beginning to respond to environmental and social challenges they previously viewed as outside their remit:

- Some corporations are integrating ethical considerations, social responsibility, and environmental sustainability into their corporate strategies, changing product mixes and production methods to reduce environmental impact, and addressing social issues and human needs.
- Some corporations are sourcing fair-traded and certifiably sustainable raw materials and agricultural commodities, while addressing such issues as land rights, pollution, and community development wherever in the world they operate.
- A handful of corporations are attempting to use social engagement activities to gain a competitive advantage with customers and to attract qualified employees.
- A few corporate leaders appear to be abandoning the traditional, unidimensional goal of maximizing profits for shareholders, instead espousing the belief that there is no necessary trade-off between profitability and social responsibility.[3]

Those developments are said to offer encouragement to corporate leaders waiting on the sidelines, as yet reluctant to take action themselves. To wit, if they now choose to initiate socially responsible practices, they at least have precedents to cite as cover when skeptical investors object. Nonetheless, a significant triple-barreled question remains: How many of those uncommitted executives can be expected to enlist in the nascent movement, to what extent will they participate, and under what conditions? The idealist in me wants to believe that "things are different now," but my realist side has difficulty believing that the expectations of investors have changed in the last twenty years, when they had not changed over the seven centuries since the days of Datini and Fugger. As in Thomas Jefferson's famous debate between his head and his heart, I am torn between what I think will happen, and what I want to happen. In this chapter I try to reconcile that tension as objectively as possible while assessing the likelihood that six emerging trends will become the norm in publicly traded corporations over the next two decades. For if these trends were to continue, I believe there would be a brighter future for enlightened corporate leadership.

Trend One: An Emerging Generation of Enlightened and Effective Business Leaders

My heart is drawn to evidence that a new generation of enlightened capitalists has emerged in recent years—a generation of men and women as committed to social engagement as their forbearers, but more sophisticated and skilled, and thus more likely to be able to create sustainable legacies. Among the contemporary chief executives often mentioned in this regard are Starbucks' Howard Schultz, Salesforce's Marc Benioff, Apple's Tim Cook, PepsiCo's Indra Nooyi, Campbell Soup's Denise Morrison, Merck's Kenneth Frazier, and, especially, Unilever's Paul Polman and Whole Foods' John Mackey. Because they all lead large, publicly traded corporations, optimists posit that those CEOs are on the verge of finally proving that shareholder capitalism and enlightened business practices are fully compatible. As sincerely as I hope they succeed, my head is drawn to some inconvenient facts concerning the recent experiences of Polman and Mackey.

In 2017, Unilever—widely considered the world's leader in terms of socially responsible behavior—was threatened with a hostile take-over by a corporation manifesting no interest in maintaining Polman's global efforts to produce safe and healthy goods in an environmentally sound manner. Polman called the $143 billion bid from Kraft Heinz "clearly a clash between a long-term, sustainable business model for multiple stakeholders and a model that is entirely focused on share-holder primacy."[4] As we saw in chapters 3 and 15, Polman had pledged to make and sell safe and healthy goods while offering well-paying jobs and decent benefits to the men and women Unilever employs on five continents. When introducing those policies, he had warned that it would take the better part of a decade for Unilever to fully implement them, cautioning investors that some short-term profits might be sac-rificed before the company became the model global corporation he envisioned. Although the attempted takeover of Unilever was averted, investors had grown impatient with Polman's long-term plans; thus, he was forced to take actions to boost quarterly profits—for example, purchasing the highly profitable cosmetics company Carver Korea for seven times its annual revenue. Unilever probably would not have made that purchase if it weren't under pressure from investors to immedi-ately increase earnings. In order to further boost profit margins, be-tween 2015 and 2017 Unilever acquired eighteen companies for nearly €9 billion, paying a sizable premium for most of them. By making such acquisitions—and buying back €5 billion worth of its stock, increas-ing its dividend by 12 percent, and doubling its planned budget cuts—Unilever has limited its ability to realize the transformation Polman hopes to achieve.[5]

In 2018 Polman publicly admitted as much at a conference of insti-tutional investors: "We had to make some practical compromises . . . which frankly I would not have done."[6] He then asked those asset managers to stop demanding reductions in corporate social and envi-ronmental programs and, instead, to start asking themselves why they "have the courage to destroy . . . this wonderful planet." A few days later, Unilever announced that it would cease its century-long legal structure as a joint Dutch-British company, and unify its headquarters in Rotterdam. Polman made it clear that the major reason was to protect the company against the threat of hostile takeovers that are far more easily achieved under British (and American) law than in Europe. Alarmingly, British institutional investors then revolted and blocked the move.

The full effects of the aborted Unilever takeover are yet to be documented; nonetheless, they were felt almost immediately at the corporation's Dollar Shave American subsidiary. In 2016, Unilever had acquired the zany California e-commerce start-up from its founder, Michael Dubin, for $1 billion, along with the promise to keep Dubin's management team intact and grant them the level of managerial autonomy from corporate headquarters recently given the leaders of its Ben & Jerry's subsidiary. Dubin, in turn, agreed that Dollar Shave would be governed by a board consisting of three Unilever executives and himself. At the time of the acquisition, Unilever assured Dubin that it was making a long-term investment in Dollar Shave in the belief the subsidiary would eventually increase its US customer base and expand its operations internationally. But after the 2017 takeover threat, the actions taken by Polman to shore up Unilever's near-term profits trickled down in the form of pressure on Dollar Shave to tighten up its casual and "cheeky" culture, lay off key staffers, expand more quickly overseas, and introduce new products to generate domestic profits. Dollar Shave's budget became the subject of close scrutiny by Unilever's finance team, leading to concern among Dubin's managers that this was the first step toward the multinational exerting greater control over all its operations. Indeed, with Unilever under the gun from investors, it is unclear how long it will be patient with Dollar Shave before selling it or, perhaps, letting it go under. The significance of this example is *not* that such short-termism is unusual; rather, that it is par for the course in publicly traded corporations. What is significant is that it has happened at the global corporation most committed to a patient, long-term plan to implement enlightened practices.[7]

About the time Unilever was under threat of a hostile takeover in Britain, America's Whole Foods Corporation faced a similar challenge from activist investors dissatisfied with its rate of financial return. Like Unilever, Whole Foods was known for its stakeholder-oriented and environmentally sensitive practices. Again, like Unilever, it was profitable—but not *profitable enough* for the activist investment firms holding large blocks of the company's stock. Citing what they perceived as Whole Foods' too rapid expansion and insufficiently profitable mix of products, in 2017 those investors demanded changes in company management or, failing that, its sale to a traditionally managed grocery chain. The company's combative founder and CEO, John Mackey, characterized the activist investors as "a bunch of greedy bastards running around exploiting people, screwing their customers, taking advantage of their employees, dumping their toxic waste in the environment, acting like sociopaths." Fearing the effects of a hostile takeover, he arranged a lightning-fast sale of the company to the mammoth Amazon corporation, believing that offered the best chance of preserving Whole Foods' culture and practices.

After the sale was announced, Mackey tried to make the best of a bad situation by praising the courage of Amazon's managers to "resist the drumbeat of short-term, quarterly earnings" which, he said, had pressured Whole Foods to take steps inimical to the company's long-term interest (Mackey had been under near-constant pressure from one or another group of activist investors since 2009). Although he acknowledged that significant changes were likely under Amazon's ownership, he failed to mention what everyone knew: unlike Whole Foods' employee-centered practices, Amazon had a reputation for mercilessly driving its employees and managers to increase efficiency and productivity and cut costs. As pleased as Mackey was about being acquired by Amazon, he nonetheless cautioned his staff, "There are no guarantees in life. Some marriages end up badly." The week after the acquisition was made final, Amazon began to change Whole

Foods' pricing policies and business model to integrate the subsidiary into its larger operations. As we have seen, the record shows that most such "marriages" result in the eventual loss of the kind of practices Mackey sought to preserve by being acquired by Amazon.[8] Indeed, even being acquired by a company noted for its social conscience is no guarantee that a company's virtuous practices will be maintained. In 2012, Starbucks acquired bakery chain La Boulange, makers of healthy organic products. Three years later, Starbucks closed the bakeries but retained the brand name for use on its own range of baked goods.

It's hard not to be pessimistic when considering these two examples. I become even more pessimistic when I recall that the lion's share of corporate executives' compensation comes in the form of stock options, which gives them an almost irresistible temptation to do whatever it takes to give share prices a boost, including selling their companies to the highest bidder.[9] That is *not* because corporate executives oppose virtue. Based on dozens of conversations I have had with top executives over the years, I believe many would choose to adopt more enlightened, ethical, and socially responsible practices. Nevertheless, they realistically conclude that the financial community will tolerate only those amounts of social engagement that directly enhance a company's reputation, and keep protest-prone environmental, consumer, and workers' rights groups at bay. And those executives doubtless have drawn sobering lessons from the experiences of Polman, Mackey, and other idealistic capitalists, understanding full well that investors welcome no amount of social engagement at companies deemed insufficiently profitable. Hence, while my heart is attracted by the prospects of a new generation of enlightened business leaders, my head says they are likely to run into the same buzz saw of investor resistance their predecessors faced. Indeed, Campbell's CEO Morrison was recently sacked by her board on the grounds that the company was insufficiently profitable.

Trend Two: The Emergence of New Forms of Enlightened Practices in the Tech World

As discouraging as the experience at Unilever and Whole Foods may be, my heart reminds me that, in some industries, it has become increasingly common for corporate executives to engage in enlightened practices, particularly in high-tech organizations. For example, companies like Google and Apple are hailed as harbingers of a bright future of employee-friendly work environments. Many high-tech firms provide their workers with all the comforts of home (free and unlimited food and drink, daybeds where they can catch a quick nap) along with the services found in residential neighborhoods (laundry and dry cleaning, gymnasiums, and more), all designed to make it unnecessary to go home, or waste time running neighborhood errands. Those perks are truly impressive, yet my head finds something disturbingly unethical about the ways in which the paternalistic practices of the past have morphed into the hot-tub cultures found at Google and other high-tech organizations. To my mind, there is an enormous ethical difference between the well-meaning paternalism practiced by the likes of Owen and Lever, on the one hand, and the instrumentalist manipulation of workers practiced at some places in the tech world.

The most thoughtful criticism of Silicon Valley's management practices is found in Dave Eggers's dystopian 2014 novel *The Circle*, eerily set in the very near future.[10] The fictitious Circle is a high-tech company that has taken Google's management practices to the next logical level. If the Circle were a real company, it would sit atop *Fortune*'s 100 Best Companies to Work For list, thanks to its platinum-level medical insurance, free gourmet lunches, health club, pet sitting, luxury commuter buses, and the opportunity for employees to spend more time working productively, and less time managing their personal lives and "wasting time" with friends and family (and, presumably, reading long novels like *The Circle*). But the Circle doesn't stop with perks currently available in Silicon Valley firms; it elevates those goodies to the next level, satisfying not only employee needs but also their wants: first-class live entertainment, boozy parties, on-campus housing (with opportunities for sex), social clubs—even a sense of community and social purpose.

Because almost everything the Circle does is, on its face, positive for employees, customers, and society, the novel's protagonist initially finds her job there exhilarating. The catch is that she becomes locked into the company, eventually giving up her freedom, humanity, and individualism. She is gradually transformed from a loving, idealistic young woman into an unquestioningly loyal "true believer" willing to betray her friends and lover to advance the Circle's goal of taming "the chaos of an orderless world." The Circle is governed by a founding troika of Guardians, recognizable variations on the charismatic, visionary, self-confident, brilliant, and obsessively single-minded leaders found in abundance in the tech world. As in Plato's Republic, creating such a well-ordered organization ultimately requires its members to abandon their freedom to these Guardians, "who know better than they do" what is good for them because, as Circlers assert, "We are the future."

Eggers is not the only writer to have spotted the dangers inherent in the privacy-invading technology emerging in Silicon Valley, but he was the first to offer a premonitory tale about the potential consequences of SV's corporate cultures run amok. Alarmingly, in 2017 Google's parent company, Alphabet, announced plans to create an entire "city of the future" called Quayside in a run-down dock area in Toronto to demonstrate the benefits of a technology-enabled city, a "laboratory for innovation on an integrated basis," a testing ground for new approaches to infrastructure, transportation, governance, and social policy.[11] Thus, the day of Eggers's dystopia may arrive sooner than he thought: North American business now stands poised to cross the fine ethical line between the comparatively benign paternalism that spawned company towns a century or so ago and the compellingly powerful, potentially manipulative, and societally out-of-control twenty-first-century tech-dominated world. I find that prospect greatly disturbing.

Trend Three: The Advent of Consortia of Enlightened Capitalists

The first time enlightened business leaders teamed together to address social issues was in the mid-1960s, in the wake of major rioting in several American inner cities, notably Los Angeles, Newark, and Detroit. In response, Ford Motor's Henry Ford II created the National Alliance of Businessmen to provide job training and placement services for "hard-core" unemployed men and women. Hundreds of company executives (among them William Norris, Walter Haas Jr., and Edwin Land) gave time and money to the effort; however, as ethicist Kirk Hanson concludes, "the track record of the NAB was mixed, though it limped along until the 2000s" (before quietly dying).[12] That effort was followed by the Social Venture Network, in which Anita Roddick and Ben Cohen played major roles. It is all but defunct today. In 1988, the Business Enterprise Trust (BET) was founded by Norman Lear, James Burke, and a half dozen other prominent men and women to chronicle, honor, and inspire business social engagement (SpringfieldRe's Jack Stack and Ben & Jerry's Gail Mayville were BET honorees). Ethicist Hanson was the first executive director of the trust, which after a few years of notable service, petered out in the 1990s as the result of the general decline in interest in corporate social responsibility. Then, in 2000, UN secretary Kofi Annan launched the UN Global Compact in which some eight thousand firms worldwide pledged to adhere to ten core ethical and social principles and to report annually on their progress in achieving them. Alas, over the subsequent decade, some two thousand of those companies were delisted for failing to file reports (the Global Compact now rewards "Lead Companies" who take their social responsibilities seriously).

Although the sustainability of such consortia has been poor, today some dozen such organizations exist around the world to promote corporate ethics, social responsibility, and especially environmental sustainability. The Caux Round Table, for example, is an international network of "principled business leaders working to create a moral capitalism." The organization brings businesses and governments together to design strategies, management tools, and practices that better serve the global community. More active in Europe and Asia than in America, Caux hosts international conferences and issues informative reports. Similarly, the Skoll World Forum assembles social entrepreneurs annually at Oxford's Said Business School. Such activities lend credence to the belief that the future of social engagement promises to be brighter than its past.

Executives who have participated in these business consortia have tended to be from the center-to-progressive end of the ideological spectrum, and therefore representative of only a minority of business leaders. The exception has been the Conscious Capitalism (CC) movement founded by Whole Foods' John Mackey, a libertarian who has recruited corporate executives from the ideological right to participate in the organization. Mackey calls the CC movement a "new paradigm" for business designed to "elevate humanity." Writing a chapter in a book ambitiously subtitled *How Entrepreneurs and Conscious Capitalists Can Solve All the World's Problems*, Mackey argued that CC can, and must, "save Capitalism": "It's as if there were a wall. And on one side of the wall is the belief that not-for-profits and government exist for public service and that they're fundamentally altruistic, that they have a deeper purpose, and they're doing good in their work, and they have pure motives. On the other side of the wall are corporations. And they're just selfish and greedy. They have no purpose other than to make money. They're a bunch of psychopaths. And I'd like to tear that wall down."[13]

Mackey's "wall destruction" plan is to encourage corporate leaders to adopt CC's four principles of Conscious Business: higher purpose, stakeholder interdependence, conscious leadership, and conscious culture. Significantly, those principles appeal greatly to advocates of social engagement from the opposite end of the political spectrum of many, if not most, of CC's participants—thus offering hope of bridging the divide between groups on the two sides of Mackey's ideological wall. That would be promising news if it weren't for Mackey's insistence on making allies only on his own terms. He is a purist who insists his movement is philosophically different from the practices of the enlightened capitalists, which he dismisses as mere "corporate social responsibility." While most other business consortia promote business enlightenment on moral grounds, he claims that "conscious capitalism is not primarily about virtue or doing good." Instead, it is "holistic and integral with deeper comprehensive purposes," which constitute such an entirely new way of thinking about business that the distinction between doing good and doing well entirely disappears.[14] Nor is CC about ethics, libertarian Mackey argues, because he finds capitalism already to be inherently ethical: "This ethical foundation of business doesn't necessarily mean that everything any particular business does is always ethical, but that voluntary exchange for mutual benefit is itself an ethical process."[15] His commitment to free-market capitalism is so strong that he objected when he was complimented for being a modern-day Robert Owen: "This is a highly unflattering comparison to me since Owen was a Utopian Socialist who disapproved of capitalism, while I consider myself highly pro-capitalism with strong libertarian convictions."[16] Mackey goes so far as to claim that if (when?) CC becomes the norm, there will be little to no need for government regulations, or such social welfare programs as health benefits for the uninsured, because conscious capitalists understand that it is in their self-interest to be self-regulating and provide for the needs of their workers.

Regardless of one's ideological bent, the educational outreach of the CC movement has made a useful contribution by encouraging fence-sitting executives to adopt enlightened business practices, and Mackey so far is unique among his generation of CEOs in that he has developed a fully fleshed-out business philosophy. In 2011 my colleague David Vogel and I offered praise for the movement in an article cheekily titled "Two and a Half Cheers for Conscious Capitalism."[17] We explained why we hesitated to give CC the additional half hurrah, pointing out that its goal of "elevating humanity" wasn't easy to meet; that those who had previously tried to do so had not succeeded; and that a great many executives were unlikely to buy into CC's principles. We also doubted that business self-regulation could ever negate the need for government regulation, and questioned the proposition that all virtuous activities can be made profitable. We noted that many smaller businesses lack the resources to provide employees with health insurance, even if their owners would like to provide the benefit, and thus it was unrealistic to claim that there would be no need for a governmental role in health care provision if all companies were to embrace CC. We also suggested that some CC advocates risked ruining the movement's credibility with overblown talk about "solving all the world's problems" (for example, one active participant in the CC movement, Gary Hirshberg, CEO of Stonyfield Farms, offered a standard lecture called "How to Make Money and Save the World").[18] When we called attention to how difficult it is to sustain good practices in publicly traded companies, citing the examples of what happened when Ben & Jerry's and the Body Shop were acquired, CC's academic leader, Rajendra Sisodia, offered this rejoinder: "We do not believe that the equity markets are a major constraint on conscious businesses. We have studied a large number of publicly traded companies that are conscious businesses and have found that they are able to operate in a conscious manner despite the short-term pressures that may come from certain analysts on Wall Street."[19] Sisodia added, "It is indeed the case that conscious businesses must exercise great care when merging with larger companies . . . they must ensure that the Board of Directors of the acquiring company understands what makes them special, and that they commit to maintaining those qualities." He then cited two major CC companies that he claimed had successfully managed that near-impossible feat: Stonyfield

Farms (acquired by Danone), and the Container Store (purchased by a private equity firm, then publicly listed).

Sadly, since then things have not turned out quite as Sisodia had hoped. Hirshberg sold organic yogurt maker Stonyfield to the French firm Danone because it offered three things he was looking for: a generous $35 million payday for himself, sufficient capital to grow the company, and a compatible culture. While he successfully obtained those good things, he also found himself running a subsidiary of a large, publicly traded company that, in 2017, found itself under the same pressures to increase short-term profits that Whole Foods' Mackey and Unilever's Polman were painfully attempting to address. After the publicly traded Danone forecast a slowdown in profit growth, American activist hedge fund Corvex pressured the firm to cut costs, replace its chairman (who is the champion of the company's enlightened practices), and, if the company wasn't then sufficiently profitable, consider selling it.

As for the Container Store, its CEO, Kip Tindell, had entered into a financial partnership with a private equity firm in 2007 under the condition that its "beloved culture and customer service" be preserved. When the partnership failed to provide enough capital to finance the company's expansion into smaller cities—and to increase the number of employees owning company stock—Tindell decided to go public in 2013. When store sales subsequently declined by 3.5 percent, and the stock price plummeted by 25 percent, Tindell expressed dismay at his new obligation to appease shareholders in the short term.

With Whole Foods recently joining Stonyfield in the acquired status, there are now more tests of Sisodia's optimism that acquiring publicly traded corporations will make—and keep—pledges not to interfere in the operations of their subsidiaries. That Whole Foods and Stonyfield have been the largest companies (along with the Container Store) actively involved in the Conscious Capitalism movement is an indication that the future of even the most successful enlightened businesses may be as parts of publicly traded corporations, with all the negatives that entails. Vogel and I ended up applauding CC's practices (with two and a half hands), offering the idealistic hope that many businesspeople would join the movement in the future—while realistically recognizing that a great many would not. We concluded that the movement's "creation of a common ground for progressives and libertarians is no mean feat" and its "creative squaring of the circle was why the movement is increasingly seen as so attractive."[20] In sum, CC and other business consortia are positive omens, but their influence is limited to the like-minded, and they are unlikely to change the practices of investor capitalism that threaten the cultures of enlightened companies.

Trend Four: Social Entrepreneurship and Benefit Corporations

Conscious Capitalism is closely related to two other movements that gladden my idealistic heart: social entrepreneurship and benefit corporations. Recent years have witnessed the rapid growth of "social enterprises," an increasing number of which are for-profit businesses (such as Daniel Lubetzky's KIND), although many are not. The term *social entrepreneur* appears to have been coined by American Bill Drayton, founder of Ashoka, an organization that supports over three thousand such individuals in ninety-some-odd nations. Although the movement is headquartered in America, it is currently in vogue in Britain as well. John Bird—who now sits in the House of Lords—was raised in an orphanage, yet went on to become financially successful after outgrowing his youthful Marxist days. In 1991 he funded a magazine that employs street people as vendors, and since 2005 he has invested some £30 million in social enterprises designed to help the disadvantaged.[21]

In a great many ways, the social enterprise and Conscious Capitalism movements overlap: leaders of for-profit social enterprises, like conscious capitalists, face the same issue of if, when, and how to be acquired. While many social entrepreneurs are making useful contributions to society, I remain ambivalent about the movement's for-profit companies. Too many of the social entrepreneurs I have met have struck me as motivated a bit more by the prospects of getting the big acquisition payday Lubetzky dreams of than by creating sustainable organizations (although it feels a bit churlish to question the motives of those who do good). Nonetheless, I also sense something a bit too self-congratulatory in the habit of many social entrepreneurs to crow about their do-goodism and commitment to "make the world a better place." Unlike the enlightened capitalists—who seldom engaged in such public piety and self-promotion—listening to some social entrepreneurs, I am at times tempted to agree with the cynical proposition, "You can trust a business that merely wants to run a profit in a way you cannot quite trust one that wants to change the world."[22] That said, most of the signs point to a bright future for the movement: social enterprises are popping up around the world (there is a Social Enterprise Business Centre in Hong Kong, serving locals as well as mainland Chinese students), and several business schools now offer master's degrees in social entrepreneurship, most notably the Skoll Centre for Social Entrepreneurship at Oxford's Said B-school. Nonetheless, the idealist in me has a bit more confidence in the depth of the social commitments of leaders of B corporations.

The fast-growing "B corporation" movement has fueled optimism about the future of business enlightenment. Although all B (for benefit) companies are committed to achieving social as well as economic goals, they come in two varieties, the largest of which are the more than seventeen hundred companies certified by the nonprofit B Lab as practicing socially responsible levels of workplace wellness, transparency, environmentalism, community service, and philanthropy. With the exception of a few companies (Plum Organics, Clif Bar & Company, Etsy, and Method), the vast majority of B-certified organizations have fifty or fewer employees, and hardly any are publicly traded.

Several things about the B movement appeal to my optimistic side. It has proved to be a particularly congenial home for women entrepreneurs like Sheryl O'Loughlin, former CEO of Clif Bar & Company, cofounder and CEO of Plum Organics, and now CEO of healthy beverage company REBBL; and the increasingly large number of certified companies—including cooperatives and employee-owned firms—indicates that a spirit of practical idealism is alive and well, even if not residing in publicly traded corporations. Moreover, B-certification has become for enlightened management what LEED certification stands for in buildings, and fair trade signifies with regard to coffee.[23]

While B-certification is not a legal designation, twenty-seven American states grant "benefit corporation" charters that allow companies, such as Patagonia, to be structured in such a way that their officers and directors are permitted to make decisions benefiting society *even when those actions are not in the immediate interest of shareholders.* Indeed, such chartered companies have a positive duty to provide benefits to society, including protecting the environment, bringing goods and services to poor communities, and promoting the arts and science. What that means, legally, is that their managers and boards could be sued by shareholders if they *failed* to act in a socially responsible manner—but shareholders *cannot* sue when companies engage in such activities, even if the wherewithal comes out of their pockets. While Lynn Stout and other legal scholars argue that such protection is unnecessary (see previous chapter), some 860 companies had filed for benefit status by 2014, apparently believing that they needed an extra layer of protection in the event of an acquisition or change in leadership. Ryan Honeyman, the author of *The B Corp Handbook,* explains that "in a time of crisis, such as the recent financial collapse, or under a leadership change, social and environmental values can get pushed aside if they are not embedded in the company's legal structure. The benefit corporation legal structure provides entrepreneurs, owners, and investors with the assurance that the company's social and environmental values will remain equally important to making a profit—no matter what."[24]

The advent of benefit corporations leads one to speculate that the sad, bad ends experienced at many companies reviewed in this book might have been happier if they had had the option of becoming benefit corporations. Nonetheless, the emergence of benefit corporations cannot be taken as an indicator of a positive future for enlightened *corporate* leadership; after all, the designation was created to shield virtuous businesses from the grasp of publicly traded acquirers.

Trend Five: A Change in Investor Attitudes

One positive harbinger of a rosier future is the growing market for the eco-friendly "green bonds" floated by utilities and other companies to finance projects benefiting the environment—such as the construction of energy-efficient buildings and wind farms. In 2017, investors bought over $120 billion of such securities, 20 percent more than in the previous year.[25] As good news as those bonds are to optimists, there is an even more potent and promising financial trend: namely, the growth of ethical investing, particularly by university endowments, union and public-employee pension funds, and national sovereign funds. For example, in 2017 the Ford Foundation announced its intention to invest its $12 billion endowment in stocks of companies promising social as well as financial returns.

The first so-called social investment fund was launched as early as 1971; by 2017, there were over two hundred such funds active in the United States, with collective assets of $77 billion (a large number, but one that pales to insignificance when taken as a percentage of the $41 trillion in assets held by pension funds worldwide). The future of those funds, now called "impact" or ESG (environmental, social, governance) investors, depends on finding answers to two fundamental questions. The first is, How to define corporate virtue? That sounds like a simple question, but, it turns out, ethical investing presents challenges every bit as difficult as enlightened company leadership. Unable to find an acceptable measure of overall corporate social responsibility, an increasing number of funds are specializing: one invests only in companies where women are in leadership positions, another avoids investing in companies "that do not align with Biblical values," including "the LGBT lifestyle," yet another only invests in companies dedicated to boardroom diversity and favors Exxon-Mobil stock, while yet another won't invest in oil and gas companies.[26] Another version of social investing, such as a fund offered by Goldman Sachs, doesn't exclude companies on any moral criterion other than selling tobacco. Hence, coal companies can be included if they have good governance and treat their employees well.[27] And the highly activist Norwegian national sovereignty fund, which does not invest in coal, is now considering divesting its holdings in oil and gas companies—a rather controversial subject, given that the source of the fund's $1 trillion in assets is North Sea oil and gas![28] It is clear why managers of ESG funds are in need of guidelines when choosing which corporate stocks to buy and which to divest: Is clean-car-maker Tesla a virtuous company even though it has a terrible employee-safety record? Are the baddies the makers of cigarettes, whiskey, and firearms? What about fossil fuel companies and gambling casinos? Does one draw the line at diamond mines, or bottlers of sugary drinks?

The second question is every bit as difficult, and one almost every investor asks: Are the returns for investments in ESG funds higher, lower, or the same as those for more broadly based funds? The findings of researchers who have attempted to answer that question have been mixed—although there is some rather unsettling evidence that sin investing (in the stock of gambling, alcohol, and tobacco firms) pays rather handsomely.[29] Until those questions are answered definitively, it is unlikely there will be a great rush among the majority of investors to risk their money on virtue.

Nonetheless, in 2015 CalPERS (the California Public Employees' Retirement System) announced that it would actively press companies whose stocks it held to emphasize environmental issues, workplace diversity, and good corporate governance. The fund's board deleted a sentence in its charter that had stated it should focus its investment strategy on companies that optimized "performance, profitability, and returns to share owners," replacing it with a section acknowledging the need to invest in companies engaged in "responsible conduct" with regard to the environment, climate change, and "social" factors such as fair labor practices and board diversity. After the directors had pledged to pay greater attention to social and environmental issues—perhaps even at the expense of profitability—CalPERS' senior portfolio manager explained that the fund now had a fiduciary duty to "optimize" its returns over multiple generations, and not an obligation to "maximize corporate profits."[30] It is far from certain that CalPERS will, or can, follow through and implement the new policy. To do so would require clear definitions of what constitutes "responsible conduct," and hard-to-quantify trade-offs between profits and environmental protection. But if CalPERS and other funds find a path through those thickets, the pressure on corporate executives to adopt virtuous practices would greatly increase.

As noted in the preface to this book, there are signs that some private investment firms may be ready to follow the example of the Ford Foundation and CalPERS. In 2018 Laurence D. Fink, founder and chief executive of BlackRock, a firm that manages $6 trillion in savings and retirement funds, announced that his firm would use its clout to encourage corporate boards to "not only deliver financial performance, but also show how [their companies make] a positive contribution to society" with regard to such issues as the environment, automation, and worker retraining.[31] Weeks later, Fink's comments were echoed at the annual World Economic Forum at Davos by Bill McNabb, chairman of Vanguard asset managers. A few months later, both Fink's and McNabb's pledges were put to the test in the wake of the horrific school shooting in Parkland, Florida, when it was revealed that both Vanguard and BlackRock held stock in gun manufacturers. In fact, BlackRock turned out to be the largest index investor in gun company stock. BlackRock subsequently announced that it had "reached out to the major publicly traded civilian firearms manufacturers to engage in a discussion of their business practices," but as of the time this book went to press, BlackRock had not divested from its gunmaker stock. As noble as the intentions of Fink and McNabb may be, they raise a serious question: Is it in the public interest for a few managers controlling trillions in assets to be deciding what corporate actions are virtuous, and which are not?

Because corporate boards are said to represent the investors in publicly traded companies, they would seem to have the greatest leverage over the behavior of executives who, in theory, report to them. Yet to date, most boards have remained passive at best in matters of corporate social engagement. In fact, the social activities of many enlightened executives have met with board hostility. At least in the United Kingdom, there are some signs that may be changing in the aftermath of the collapse of the mammoth Carillion corporation. That company's board turned a blind eye when its executives took highly questionable financial steps to boost its stock price.[32] Such short-termism caused the light of publicity to shine on Britain's new Stewardship Code, which encourages boards to take a more active role in matters of governance and corporate culture. In addition, the UK's Financial Reporting Council has called on boards to support increased corporate engagement with stakeholder groups. Clearly, the prospects for enlightened corporate behavior would be profoundly enhanced if the attitude of boards were to become more positive with regard to social engagement, but it remains to be seen if such pressure on boards will continue to grow. *Financial Times* columnist Rana Foroohar suggests that one of the most important things boards should do, echoing Robert Owen's two-centuries-old plea, is to encourage executives to "manage human resources as well as they manage capital."[33] Alas, in America, an unintended consequence of the Dodd-Frank legislation was an enormous step backward in that regard. To comply with the act's stringent financial reporting rules, boards have become overpopulated by men and women with backgrounds in finance and accounting—in general, people whose technical training leaves them unlikely to be comfortable dealing with matters of culture, values, and employee development.

Trend Six: Public Concerns

The odds favoring increased corporate social engagement also would be greatly improved if there were strong public demand for it, strong public support (and praise) for executives who behave virtuously, and resolute condemnation of those who behave unethically and irresponsibly. Recent polls indicate that Americans—younger ones in particular—want corporate executives to speak out publicly on important social and political issues. In 2018 the Global Strategy Group released the results of a poll indicating that two-thirds of Americans believe corporations have a responsibility to address major political and social issues.[34] And more executives are doing just that. In recent years, Howard Schultz has called on his fellow CEOs to hire more military veterans, Paul Polman has spoken eloquently on the issue of climate change, and Kenneth Frazier has called attention to the lingering problem of racism. Such "executive activism" has thus far been tolerated by investors because it is relatively cost-free. Yet, there is the risk that customers might become so put off by such public pronouncements that they boycott the offending company's products. (When executives at coffee-machine maker Keurig Green Mountain stopped advertising on a television network that had defended a politician accused of sexually assaulting teenagers, irate consumers posted online videos of themselves smashing Keurig machines.)

While I join the chorus in praise of executives who want to hire veterans, fight global warming, and stamp out racism, my head reminds me that such advocacy can be a mixed blessing. Mounting evidence that influential CEOs like Apple's Tim Cook have the power to sway public opinion raises alarms because big company executives already wield disproportionate political power through their personal wealth, the financial clout of the corporations they lead, and the influence of lobbyists in their employ. Is it then good for society if they *also* exercise the considerable power of the bully pulpit that comes with their position? Moreover, when such power is used with regard to sensitive political or religious issues, it is unlikely to be universally appreciated. For example, when Tim Cook spoke in favor of gay marriage, his pronouncement was greeted positively by those on the left, but negatively by those on the right; similarly, when Chick-fil-A CEO Dan Cathy took the opposite stand, the right cheered, and the left jeered.[35]

The issue is where to draw the line between legitimate and illegitimate use of executive bully pulpits. The experiences of the enlightened capitalists lead me to conclude that it is acceptable for CEOs to speak out when a social or political issue directly affects their companies, or when their companies' actions directly affect an issue. And it makes sense for executives to speak out when they have special knowledge, or unique expertise, that adds value to public discourse. Failing those tests, executive activism is generally unwise and unwarranted. For example, when Starbucks' Howard Schultz instructed his tens of thousands of employees to engage their customers in conversations about race, as well-intentioned as that was, the campaign backfired; such dialogues were unrelated to the making or drinking of coffee, and the company's baristas had no special competence in the thorny patch of race relations. It is worth remembering that Owen, Lever, Hershey, Norris, Roddick, Cohen, and Robert Haas never received more criticism than when they ventured into the public arena.

My head thus concludes that the most desirable future would be one in which executives left politics to citizens and politicians, and concentrated on making things better for their employees, customers, owners, and society through enlightened business practices. If CEOs focused their efforts on that task, I suspect they collectively would make a greater contribution to the general welfare than if they became voices of political morality. In short, I believe Theodore Roosevelt was correct in concluding that Andrew Carnegie would have made a greater social contribution by treating his workers fairly than he did with his public antiwar pronouncements.

Corporate leaders are also becoming more engaged in addressing pressing social issues via personal philanthropy. Indeed, in the eyes of many executives—and the general public—"social responsibility" in business is becoming synonymous more with philanthropy than with virtuous corporate practices. Many executives are following the example of Bill Gates by making as much money as possible while in office, and then engaging in philanthropy after they retire. If horse racing was once the sport of kings, philanthropy is now the preferred pastime of retired chief executives—in particular, among retired financiers and high-tech entrepreneurs who often displayed little hint of virtue in their business dealings. Many Goldman Sachs partners, for example, put their social consciences on hold while they amass personal fortunes at work, then turn to a second career in philanthropy when they retire—often as young as in their forties.

Who can blame them? Enlightened corporate leadership, as they well know, is a demanding endeavor involving constant trade-offs between the needs of various stakeholders, each applying pressures of one form or another to achieve their diverse, often incompatible, ends. Virtuous corporate executives must therefore constantly ask themselves challenging questions: Am I paternalistically imposing my values on others? When is it right to compromise the economic mission of my enterprise? How far should I go in pursuing a social objective? How much time and effort should I demand of my staff to achieve those objectives? Am I seen as behaving consistently? How do I determine what is the ethically right thing to do? In the end, the majority of wealthy executives seem to conclude that philanthropy is easier.

Like most people, I believe philanthropy is noble and virtuous—particularly when it is done anonymously and not to gain tax advantages. However, in some quarters the charitable activities of billionaires are viewed negatively because the wealth such individuals command is so great that they can wield personal power to rival that of many governments, and thus make decisions greatly affecting society without the checks and balances of democratic processes. In addition, there is the related issue of inconsistency, if not hypocrisy, when executives give money to worthy causes to compensate for the social costs their companies created—for example, when retired executives from fossil fuel industries donate to environmentalist organizations, or when former Walmart executives give to hospitals whose emergency rooms are crowded with uninsured Walmart clerks. Similarly, when executives at Pfizer boast publicly about "embracing our responsibility to society," loftily claiming that the pharma giant works proudly with NGOs and "other global stakeholders" to improve health care in the developing world, it is gobsmacking to watch that same company engage in a "tax inversion" to avoid paying its fair share of domestic taxes. Some of that tax money, not incidentally, would have gone to support health care in America and contribute to the millions of dollars in federal grants that subsidize Pfizer's drug research.[36] Corporate philanthropy is particularly prone to acts of self-serving and hypocrisy. A recent study found that many "Firms deploy their charitable foundations as a form of tax-exempt influence seeking"; for example, by donating to the favorite charities of powerful members of Congress. And one can't help but lapse into cynicism when one remembers that all the time that Enron's top management was cooking the company books, they were making a show of donating large sums to a variety of charitable causes.

Here, once again, the realist in me comes to the fore. All the issues I've just raised are primarily concerns of social activists, professors, and some members of the media. The public, in general, appears uninterested, apathetic, and unfazed by these, and almost all, issues relating to corporate virtue and social responsibility. Here are some facts that are hard for idealists to swallow: no one (except a few ethics professors) boycotted Mylan's pharmaceutical products when it was revealed that the company was gouging purchasers of its EpiPen, and putting lives at risk for those who couldn't pay hundreds of dollars for a product that cost under $5 to make and market; no one (except trade union activists) avoids shopping at Walmart because the company doesn't provide its lower-level workers with health insurance; no one (except environ-

mentalists) spoke out against General Electric when its plastics division was dumping PCBs into the Hudson River.

That is not to say that the public is in favor of acts of corporate misbehavior, or opposed to socially beneficial business programs and policies. But the harsh fact is that there is not now, nor has there ever been,
deep and wide public demand for greater corporate enlightenment.
Author Richard Conniff bemoans the fact that "we don't vote with
our wallets." He pleads guilty himself, admitting he buys books online
from Amazon even though he dislikes the e-giant for putting book-
stores out of business and driving down the income of publishers and
writers. But as long as Amazon delivers the book we want that very day,
or the next—and at a 40 percent discount—the natural tendency for us
all is to think like consumers, and worry later (but not too hard or too
much) about the social and moral consequences of our actions. Significantly, consumerist behavior overrides social conscience among those
on the right, as well as those on the left. Business professor Brayden
King studied the purchasing behavior of conservatives who pledged
to boycott Starbucks when, after President Trump's immigration plan,
the company committed to hiring ten thousand refugees, and found no
correlation between what they said and what they bought.[37]

There are, however, some business issues about which the general
public feels strongly. In Britain and America, most people disapprove
of the low ethical standards and greed-driven misbehavior found in finance and banking; public opinion polls indicate wide-scale support
for corporate efforts to reduce global warming and improve air and
water standards; and, perhaps to a lesser degree, most people believe
that executive compensation is excessive. Because executives see public opinion as important, those three areas are likely to become foci of
their attention in the future:

Finance ethics. It is evident why the public is concerned about finance
industry ethics: In 2007, the excesses of "Wall Street" put the mortgages of millions of homeowners at risk, and led to foreclosures for tens
of thousands. Understandably, the public is deeply worried that it could

happen again. But financial shenanigans are not limited to risky mortgages, credit default swaps, and derivatives, or even to such blatantly
unethical actions as the millions of false customer accounts fabricated
at Wells Fargo. The Enron scandal, followed by Bernie Madoff's Ponzi
scheme, has highlighted the fact that more ethical misbehavior occurs
in finance than in any other industry or in any other aspect of corporate
management. Significantly, because financial ethics is one arena where
the public interest and the interests of investors are often in sync—and
because nothing is more important than money—it is safe to predict
continuing public demand for greater accountability and transparency
from bank executives and corporate financial officers.

Environmental issues. As complex as they are, environmental issues
are among the *least* controversial arenas of corporate social responsibility: no one favors pollution. They are also among the easiest aspect
of social engagement to address and to measure. For example, to spruce
up its corporate image, and perhaps deflect criticism of its employment
policies, Walmart has introduced a high-profile company-wide effort
to reduce its energy use. By doing such simple things as swapping out
incandescent and fluorescent light bulbs for LEDs, and more efficiently
routing delivery trucks to reduce fuel consumption, Walmart has been
able to document in hard numbers the positive impact those actions
have had on the environment. As a fillip, the efforts more than paid
for themselves in lower utility and petroleum bills. The bottom line is
that it has been relatively easy for Walmart to buff up its reputation—
and basically for free. And "cheap and easy" are two reasons why there
is less resistance from Walmart's investors, directors, and executives
to capturing low-hanging energy savings than there is to, say, the far
more costly effort of providing employee health insurance (an activity
that doesn't yield as much in the way of image enhancement), and easier than ending its environmentally damaging practice of using hard-
plastic packing shells to limit product theft.

On the positive side, it is worth noting that executives are not just
businesspeople: in their private lives they want clean air and water for

themselves and their families, so many see it in their self-interest to embrace environmentally sound policies. Another positive sign is the growing corporate practice of encouraging employees to volunteer in their communities, a relatively cost-free and easy-to-do form of social engagement offering high image-enhancement returns. Significantly, some of the strongest pressure on executives to adopt socially responsible programs comes from employees who desire to work for companies that do good, and want to be seen by their friends and families as working for ethical and community-spirited organizations—especially ones that don't foul the air they breathe and water they drink. That is why Salesforce and other technology companies are increasingly using community outreach programs as recruiting tools.[38] In all, the odds are good that corporations will continue to make environmental programs and employee volunteering main thrusts of their social engagement in the future.

Executive pay. As the gap between the richest members of society and the average citizen has widened in most Western economies, the spread between CEO compensation and the median pay of employees has expanded to an even greater degree. In the United Kingdom during the 1990s, chief executive salaries were about twenty times those of the average worker; in 2015, the multiple had grown to 150 times, leading to demands in Parliament for publicly traded firms to annually release their compensation ratios. It was argued that such public disclosure of obscenely generous executive compensation would shame corporate boards into reining in excessive pay packages. That's a noble idea, but not one likely to change behavior—although such shaming appears to have been more successful when reporting the differences between men's and women's pay became obligatory in 2018 in Britain.

In America, the Securities and Exchange Commission has for years required public disclosure of top executive compensation, and such publications as *Fortune* and the *Wall Street Journal* regularly publish tables listing CEO pay. Far from shaming those ranked at the top, those lists serve as scorecards in a race to the top among CEOs! The numbers keep escalating: in 2018, the CEO of Aptiv took home $13.8 million, some 2,500 times the median earnings of his 130,000 employees, and the head of Del Monte pocketed 1,465 times the median earnings of his workforce of 39,000. While both those companies have many low-paid workers in the developing world, Jamie Dimon's $30 million compensation was 364 times the median salary ($78,000) of his highly paid, largely domestic staff at JPMorgan.[39] Indeed, Wall Street is the capital of excessive compensation: in 2017, securities professionals were paid average *bonuses* of $184,000. Despite public outcries, boards of directors (and the investors they are said to represent) have shown little interest in curbing unconscionable executive compensation—even in instances where the ratio of pay between a CEO and the median worker is as large as 1,188 to 1, as it is at Walmart.[40] Investment firm BlackRock seldom, if ever, votes against excessive executive pay packages. Perhaps that's because its "reformer" chief, Larry Fink, was ranked twenty-sixth on a recent list of most overpaid bosses.[41]

As long as companies are making money, shareholders care not a whit how much executives pocket for themselves. In one respect that attitude is understandable: if a CEO is delivering billions in returns to them, investors view rewarding executives with a mere few million or so more in compensation as well worth the expense. Rather shockingly, investors show far greater concern about the cost of providing low-level employees with health insurance than they do when executives treat themselves to such expensive perks as country club memberships, private jets, and opera boxes. A few recent exceptions to this rule include the State Street Global Advisors, a Boston-based $2.8 trillion assets management firm, and Norway's sovereign wealth fund, both of which announced in 2018 that they planned to vote against excessive proposed pay increases in a few companies in which they are major investors. And in 2018, 52 percent of Disney shareholders voted to nix a $100 million bonus the company's board had voted to pay the CEO because, reportedly, he wasn't happy having to show up at the office.

The problem is not strictly one of responsible corporate governance; it is foremost a social problem. As the gap between the rich

and everyone else in society grows, so too do radical, populist political movements that threaten democracy and social cohesion. Almost
all the enlightened capitalists saw a clear link between how employers compensated workers and the degree to which the public viewed
the capitalist system as fair. That is why they drew reasonable salaries
for themselves—seldom more than twenty times that of their average
employees. Equally, they tried not to create the invidious social distinctions between managers and workers that destroy the sense of
community in organizations and in society.

There are, of course, two basic ways to close the executive-employee
wage gap. The first is to limit the compensation of those at the top—
which boards are unwilling to do, and most citizens see as an inappropriate use of governmental power. The second is to raise the wages of
everyone else, and the only economically viable way to do that is by increasing the productivity and profitability of an organization. That was,
of course, the approach most often used by the enlightened capitalists.
They understood that raising everyone's pay as profits increased set a
virtuous cycle in motion, in which it became in the self-interest of employees to work more efficiently and effectively. When that happened,
everyone from the top to bottom of a company *earned* higher salaries.

That's probably what Dan Price, CEO of Seattle's Gravity Payments,
had in mind when in 2015 he cut his own income in order to pay every
one of his 120 employees a whopping $70,000 per year. Unfortunately,
things didn't turn out as planned for the credit-card processing company owned by Price and his cofounder brother (who owned a 30 percent share). Soon after Price announced the plan, his brother sued him,
local business leaders attacked him for making them look stingy by
comparison, some corporate clients dropped Gravity on the grounds
that their employees would demand the same deal, and conservative
critics in the media condemned the pay scheme as creeping socialism.
All that might have been expected, but what came as a surprise was the
reaction of Price's own employees: a lot of them didn't like it. Several
more experienced workers complained that it was unfair to pay them

and new hires the same amount, and some more productive ones said that the pay scheme would reward the less-deserving.[42]

Price had acted generously and in good faith after hearing about the economic hardships some of his employees were experiencing while trying to pay off college loans and support families on $45,000 per year. He also hoped the example he was setting would call attention to the problems of inequality in American society—especially the plight of minimum-wage workers and the struggling middle class in high-cost-of-living cities like Seattle. So he tried the simplest and fastest way to bring a bit of economic security to his employees. Unfortunately, the simplest and fastest method was not the best. He might have achieved his goal had he taken the time to first ask his employees what *they* wanted and needed, then involved them in devising a productive and equitable pay plan. And he definitely would have been better off had he explored such proven methods of equitable compensation as stock ownership, profit sharing, gainsharing, and the Scanlon plan. All the best intentions in the world don't excuse the failure to draw on, and learn from, the experiences of others.

Price's botched salary experiment rather succinctly sums up a major theme of this book: *it is hard for businesspeople to do good.* Alas, as this chapter also illustrates, it is especially hard for the leaders of publicly traded companies. When I think objectively about the emerging trends just reviewed, I find reason to be hopeful about the prospects of a few of them. Yet it would require a prodigious degree of optimism that I am incapable of mustering to conclude that the behavior of corporate leaders will change appreciably in the near future. In particular, my head will not allow my heart to disregard, or discount, the historical behavior of investors. That said, I also find it ethically unacceptable to discourage corporate executives from attempting to buck the odds by adopting enlightened practices. Thus, no matter what the pessimist in me says, I am unwilling to argue that businesspeople should not do the right thing simply because virtue is hard to put into practice. What, then, do I conclude?

CONCLUSION

Difficile Est Bonum Esse

Success is not final, failure is not fatal. It is the courage to continue that counts.
—*Winston Churchill*

As I gaze into my crystal ball, hoping for a sign that will reveal the future of enlightened corporate capitalism, I find my view particularly opaque with respect to one highly significant element: *the future of the corporation itself.* It is quite possible that a great many corporations—as currently constituted—will no longer exist in coming years. Yet throughout these pages I have assumed that companies are actual places in which people work, often side by side. My premise has been that managers and employees take a part of their identities from their participation in such workplaces, and by investing their time and energy in them, achieve a sense of membership in a community, and satisfaction from helping those organizations to succeed. In return, organizations respect those employees as contributing members, and reward them fairly and appropriately for their loyalty, commitment, and productive efforts.

But those assumptions are wrong when applied today to such varied corporations as Uber, Universal Pictures, and Hewlett-Packard. Those companies, and many others found in a variety of industries, are increasingly hollowed-out organizations that accomplish tasks by employing contractors, subcontractors, freelancers, and part-timers who come together only for as long as it takes to accomplish a task. Then the workers disband and wait for another hollow corporation to place them on other ad hoc teams—perhaps ones that conduct meetings remotely and never meet in person. Such contingent workers have no security, no benefits, no sense of participation in a community, and no identification with an organization. As a result of this unprecedented transformation in the nature of organizations, some workers gain modicums of freedom and choice; however, they all lose the incalculably valuable benefits of job, career, and personal development. Beginning with Robert Owen, the use of workplaces as crucibles for human development has been at the heart of the philosophies of the enlightened capitalists. By more than a century, Owen anticipated the modern economic concept of human capital in which employers see investment in the development of workers as essential as investment in machines. Unlike modern economists, however, Owen and other enlightened leaders viewed investing in employee development as necessary not merely for business reasons but, more important, because they believed they had a moral responsibility to provide workers with the opportunity to pursue happiness through fulfilling their individual potentials at work. In Jeffersonian terms, the enlightened capitalists considered employee development a human right.

But why would Uber pay for the development of its drivers? After all, they might go to work for Lyft tomorrow. And why would Hewlett-Packard—once a leader in employee skill and career development—invest in the training of its contingent workforce, whose next gig will probably be at a competitor hollow organization? And why would Universal Pictures plan for full employment, or engage in community-building activities, when the movies it produces are made by freelancers? Thus, in sharp contrast to the times when nearly everyone who worked at major corporations was a full-time employee, a growing number of companies today have no incentive to provide developmental opportunities to their workforces, the majority of whom are contractors, nor do they have any reason to think about creating ethical organizational cultures at what, in essence, are virtual organizations. And the problem isn't confined to America. In Britain there has been comparable growth in the use of workers provided by employment agencies, often replacing regular employees, even at such unionized companies as carmaker Jaguar Land Rover.[1] In this new world, the ties linking employees to organizations are sundered; thus, workers are unlikely to have much loyalty to their employers—why would employees show loyalty to employers who show no loyalty to them? The absence of employee loyalty has profound negative consequences for organizational productivity, product quality, customer service, and ethical behavior.

It is alarming to consider that few of the practices of our enlightened leaders are applicable in a world of hollow virtual corporations. And I have not even mentioned the looming negative effects of automation on tomorrow's workforce, nor dealt with the problem of foreign outsourcing. And, to offer a specific example, I have failed to examine the consequences for former taxi drivers of the upheaval in their lives caused by the advent of Uber and Lyft. Many of those men and women had been members of long-standing worker cooperatives offering health insurance and a sense of community. Then there is the unsettling fact that most new jobs being created today are in low-paying industries—in hotels, restaurants, and discount retailing—where worker skills are seldom developed and such benefits as health insurance are rare.[2] Taken together, these trends threaten to leave countless people in Britain and America without meaningful employment in traditional organizations.

Contemporary philosopher Edmund Phelps has described the psychological toll being exacted by the way work is evolving in Western societies. He speaks of "not only a loss of income but a loss of *inclusion*— access to jobs offering work and pay that provide self-respect." He explains that people want, and need, something more fulfilling in life than just leisure and consumption: "They desire to participate in a community in which they can interact and develop." Indeed, most research about work and life satisfaction conducted over the last half century highlights the needs people have to achieve mastery at work, to exercise initiative and creativity, and to learn and develop not only as workers but as human beings.[3] Phelps hypothesizes that the observed declines in productivity and job satisfaction in America are due to "a critical loss of indigenous innovation in the established industries like traditional manufacturing and services that was not nearly offset by the innovation that flowered in a few new industries—digital, media, and financial. In the vast heartland of America, the loss of dynamism is almost palpable."[4]

But not all good jobs have been, or are being, lost. As Phelps points out, the best new jobs in America are being created in Silicon Valley. That would be good news if it weren't that the number of jobs there amounts to a small percentage of total national employment. Moreover, not all jobs at large SV corporations are good ones—witness HP's contingent workers. And if Dave Eggers's high-tech dystopia is the wave of the future, even jobs that pass as "good work" by Phelps's definition could turn out to be more psychologically damaging and freedom-sapping than traditional assembly-line jobs.

Fortunately, that is not the whole story. The optimistic, idealistic side of me draws great encouragement from the continued existence of such high-involvement organizations as Lincoln Electric, SRC Holdings, ACIPCO, the John Lewis Partnership, Patagonia (and other benefit companies), and scores of worker-owned firms and cooperatives. I am cheered by their consistent records of high productivity, exemplary customer service, good environmental records, ethical behavior, and long-term sustainability. Because the compensation of executives in those companies is not measured in bloated multiples of average employee pay, they have little incentive to take wild financial risks or engage in nonproductive "deals" that can shake the entire economy. Thanks to these companies, I suspect that the legacy of the enlightened capitalists will be sustained in coming years, even if it doesn't expand.

My pessimistic-realist side remains skeptical about the prospects for greater enlightenment among publicly traded corporations— although, even there, I would not completely rule out the possibility. Certainly, public pressure with regard to environmental concerns, ethical financial dealings, and possibly executive pay may lead many large companies to comply with existing laws and regulations, and doubtless many will engage in philanthropic acts to enhance their brand images and corporate reputations. And odds are there will continue to be a few maverick corporate CEOs here and there who, in the mold of James Burke, Thornton Bradshaw, J. Irwin Miller, Robert Townsend, Ray Vagelos, and, today, Paul Polman, will have the moral courage to ignore pressures from investors and use the resources of the publicly traded companies they lead for positive social purposes. But as long as financial markets operate as they do, and the motives of investors remain as they have been, I would not expect much more than a continuation of the present behavior of public corporations. Of course, as we saw in the previous chapter, there is some evidence that I may well be wrong about that. With all my heart I hope I am, because society desperately needs a new generation of virtuous corporate leaders willing to offset the disturbing trends emerging in virtual workplaces in Britain and America. The crowning irony is that the efforts of organizations with the greatest resources, and thus the greatest capacity to benefit society, are those most constrained by the dictates of stock markets.

What matters, of course, are not my conclusions about the future, but what business leaders draw from the experiences of the enlightened capitalists. The future will be determined by the lessons they take from those stories and apply in their own careers and at their own companies. My intent in telling the stories has been to provide the next generation of business leaders with information they need to avoid making the same mistakes as our idealistic leaders. I hope many of them, particularly younger ones, will have become inspired to steer their companies on socially beneficial courses, and not be discouraged by the regrettable fact that virtuous practices have so often proved unsustainable. As mentioned in the preface, the enlightened capitalists are my heroes, even though so few of their practices were maintained in the long term. What counts ethically is that—against long odds and often at considerable personal cost—they had the moral courage to do the right things.

In sum, I wish to encourage leaders of businesses small and large, publicly traded and privately owned, to draw inspiration and guidance from these stories—and then go on to create profitable organizations that address the most profound human needs. My concern, as expressed at the end of the last chapter, is that by presenting the unvarnished truth about the past, I may inadvertently discourage some leaders from acting virtuously in the future. With regard to that risk, I believe the odds on their success will be far better if they understand how difficult their task will be *before* they attempt to accomplish it. And no important task is ever easy. Without doubt, it is extremely difficult for business leaders to do good, but that fact is no excuse for not trying to do so. I trust that by understanding how hard it is to behave virtuously, the next generation will succeed where many of the pioneers failed. If so, may those brave salmon forever swim on upstream—and may they spawn many future generations of enlightened capitalists!

Finally, the time has come for me to take a stand on the meta-issue raised in the preface: Based on the experiences of our enlightened leaders, do I believe virtuous corporate leadership is, or can be, compatible with shareholder capitalism?

On that question I come down firmly in the camp of my favorite living philosopher (cracker-barrel style), Garrison Keillor, who in his novel *Pontoon* concludes, "You get old and you realize there are no answers, just stories."

ACKNOWLEDGMENTS

Because I have been noodling about this book's subject matter since 1970, it is impossible to acknowledge all the individuals who, over the ensuing decades, have influenced my thinking about enlightened capitalism. I have been fortunate to have had many marvelous mentors, including the late Mortimer Adler, Peter Drucker, Warren Bennis, and Robert Townsend, and the living Charles Van Doren and Keith Berwick. I am eternally grateful to them all for never having hesitated to tell me when I was wrong (and for encouraging me when, on occasion, I was on the right track). Ditto the generous colleagues who offered helpful comments on a draft manuscript of this book: Gary Cook, Michael Higgins, Edward Lawler, and David Vogel. Special thanks go to Philip Mirvis, who not only provided detailed suggestions on an early partial draft but four years later did the same with the full manuscript—in both cases helping me immensely to shape my conclusions and the final structure of the book. And, of course, I am indebted to the enlightened capitalists whom I had the pleasure of learning from directly: Walter Haas Jr., Marcus Sieff, William Norris, Thornton Bradshaw, Anita Roddick, Robert Beyster, and Max De Pree (all now deceased), and Robert Haas, who generously gave his time in a recent interview.

I first wrote about enlightened capitalism in the 1972 "Work in America" report prepared for the distinguished public servant Elliot L. Richardson (then secretary for the Department of Health, Education and Welfare in the Nixon administration). I have since revisited the topic—and written about many of the virtuous leaders profiled in these pages—in one form or another in a dozen subsequent books, most directly in *Vanguard Management* (published by Doubleday in 1985); *Leading Change* (Jossey-Bass, 1995); and in *Corporate Stewardship*, a volume I edited with Susan Mohrman and

Edward Lawler (Greenleaf, 2015). I recently found it instructive to look back at what I had written in those books, noting how my thinking had evolved and, in some cases, changed radically with regard to how I now evaluate the contributions of some enlightened capitalists. I would say the same with regard to my articles about virtuous business leaders that appeared in the *California Management Review* in 1991 ("Do Good, Do Well") and 2013 ("Two and a Half Cheers for Conscious Capitalism"), as well as in blogs, articles, and book reviews published in *Strategy+Business* over the last two decades. My thanks to *CMR*'s editor David Vogel and to *S+B*'s editor Art Kleiner for giving me the opportunity to write for their fine publications. In preparing the chapters here about William Lever, Milton Hershey, and James Lincoln, I drew heavily on recent biographies by, respectively, Adam Macqueen (*The King of Sunlight*), Michael D'Antonio (*Hershey*), and Frank Koller (*Spark*). I highly recommend those excellent books to readers interested in learning more about Lever, Hershey, and Lincoln.

Thanks are due to Helga Haraldsson, head librarian at the University of Southern California's Marshall School of Business, who taught me how to use the Internet when doing research when I was shocked and saddened to find the drawers that once held USC's card catalog are now empty. John Mills of Cummins and Andrea Hicklin of Levi Strauss kindly helped me find information about their respective companies. I also received invaluable research help from three marvelous students: Kristin Friedery and Leigh Rogers (University of Denver) and Sobrina Hodjati (University of California, Berkeley). And I greatly appreciate the support and encouragement offered by my former University of Denver colleagues, professors Bruce Hutton, Don Mayer, and Buie Seawell, during the six years I was at the university's Daniels College of Business working on the first drafts of this book. The book began to take final shape between 2015 and 2017 while I served as Founding Director of the Neely Center for Ethical Leadership at USC's Marshall School of Business. I am most grateful for the support the center's donor Jerry Neely gave me during the three years I had the pleasure of working with him, and to the center's current director, Ali Abbas, for his continued support. Likewise, I extend heartfelt thanks to the staff of USC's Center for Effective Organizations for their help at several stages in the writing of this book, especially Nora Hilton, who formatted the manuscript. Erin O'Toole provided much-appreciated assistance in obtaining permission to use illustrations in the photo section, and Christine Burrill not only took the photograph of Anita Roddick but also generously snapped the author's photograph for the book's jacket.

I am extremely fortunate to have, in my opinion, not only the best literary agent in New York, Jim Levine, but also the finest editor, Hollis Heimbouch. My appreciation goes to everyone at the Levine Greenberg Rostan Literary Agency, and to the entire cast and crew at HarperCollins who have flawlessly shepherded this book from manuscript into print, notably Rebecca Raskin. Finally, and most significantly, I gratefully acknowledge the saintly patience, wise counsel, and unwavering support that my wife, Marilyn Burrill O'Toole, has given me over the last fifty-two marvelous years during which we have jointly produced two lovely daughters and two perfect grandchildren (and twenty-odd books). I am lucky, indeed, to have such wonderful colleagues, mentors, friends, and family members.

NOTES

Preface: The Good Unearthed

1. James O'Toole, *Vanguard Management* (New York: Doubleday, 1985).
2. "Business Must Help Fix the Failures of Capitalism," editorial, *Financial Times,* October 23, 2017.
3. "A Better Deal between Business and Society," editorial, *Financial Times,* January 2, 2018. Report on Davos executives and McNabb quote in Gillian Tett, "Passive Investing Goes Active," *Financial Times,* February 2, 2018; Fink quote in Andrew Ross Sorkin, "A Demand for Change Backed Up by $6 Trillion," *New York Times,* January 16, 2018, Business Day.
4. Quoted in David Reid, *The Brazen Age* (New York: Pantheon, 2016), 426.

Introduction and Background: Why It Is Hard to Do Good

1. Iris Origo, *The Merchant of Prato* (London: Penguin, 1963).
2. Charles Handy, "Best Business Books 2002: Management's Renaissance Man," *Strategy+Business,* October 16, 2002.
3. Origo, *Merchant of Prato,* 10.
4. Origo, 12.
5. Origo, 221.
6. Greg Steinmetz, *The Richest Man Who Ever Lived: The Life and Times of Jacob Fugger* (New York: Simon & Schuster, 2016).
7. Martha Howell, "The Amazing Career of a Pioneer Capitalist," *New York Review of Books,* April 7, 2016, 55–56. See also John T. Flynn, *Men of Wealth* (New York: Simon & Schuster, 1941).
8. Document found in the archives of the Atlantic Richfield Corporation in the late 1970s.
9. "Rockefeller, Jr., to Get Out of Standard Oil," *New York World,* May 22, 1905.
10. Vincent Curcio, *Henry Ford* (New York: Oxford University Press, 2013), 114.
11. Curcio, 168–69.
12. David Nasaw, *Andrew Carnegie* (New York: Penguin, 2006).
13. Nasaw, 167.
14. Nasaw, 358.
15. Nasaw, 647.
16. Nasaw, 750.
17. Adam Smith, *An Inquiry into the Nature and Causes of the Wealth of Nations* (London: W. Strahan and T. Cadell, 1776), 1:17.

18. Stanley Fish, "Are the Studios in the Morality Business?" *Los Angeles Times*, February 28, 2016.

19. Milton Friedman, *Capitalism and Freedom* (Chicago: University of Chicago Press, 1962).

20. Smith, *Wealth of Nations*, 4:35.

21. Quoted in *Businessweek*, February 26, 2001, 101.

22. Edward E. Lawler III and Jay A. Conger, "The Sustainable Effectiveness Model: Moving Corporations Beyond the Philanthropy Paradigm," *Organizational Dynamics* 44, no. 2 (2015): 97–103.

23. Susan Albers Mohrman, James O'Toole, and Edward E. Lawler III, eds., *Corporate Stewardship: Achieving Sustainable Effectiveness* (Sheffield, UK: Greenleaf, 2015).

24. John Mackey and Raj Sisodia, *Conscious Capitalism* (Cambridge, MA: Harvard Business School Press, 2013).

25. Sunil Bharti Mittal, "There Is a Case for World Trade—If Only Business Could Make It," *Financial Times*, July 25, 2017.

26. Notably, Unilever in Britain and Whole Foods in America. A fuller review of this issue can be found in chapter 18 of this volume.

27. Niccolò Machiavelli, *The Prince*, trans. Luigi Ricci (New York: Mentor, 1952), ch. 15.

28. Quoted in Sydney Blumenthal, *Wrestling with His Angel* (New York: Simon & Schuster, 2017).

29. Stephen Greenblatt, *The Swerve* (New York: W. W. Norton, 2011), 149.

30. As noted historian Douglass Adair wrote, "It has been said that history itself is a dialogue in the present with the past about the future." Adair, *Fame and the Founding Fathers*, ed. Trevor Colburn (New York: W. W. Norton, 1974), 34.

31. Kate Maltby, "What Did Luther Ever Do for Us?" *Financial Times*, October 31, 2017.

32. Charles Handy, "What's a Business For?" *Harvard Business Review*, December 2002, 49–55.

Chapter 1: The First Business Reformer: Robert Owen (1771–1858)

I have written about Robert Owen in several other published works, most extensively in *Leading Change: Overcoming the Ideology of Comfort and the Tyranny of Custom* (San Francisco: Jossey-Bass, 1995). My conclusions about Owen have changed considerably since then, in part due to a visit I made to New Lanark, where I came to appreciate more fully all that he had accomplished.

1. Robert Heilbroner, *The Worldly Philosophers*, 6th ed. (New York: Simon and Schuster, 1986), 44. Readers who note echoes of Heilbroner in the first few pages of this chapter will appreciate the debt this book owes to *The Worldly Philosophers*, in my opinion the finest nonfiction work of the twentieth century. That collection of profiles of great economists provided the inspiration for this volume. I would note, in passing, that Heilbroner's worldly philosophers were often less worldly and less philosophical than some of my idealistic capitalists. Both books review the contributions of Robert Owen, doubtless the only political economist who ever met a payroll.

2. Robert Dale Owen, *Threading My Way: Twenty-Seven Years of Autobiography* (New York: G. W. Carleton, 1874), 246–48nn.

3. G. D. H. Cole, *Robert Owen* (London: Ernst Benn, 1925), 13.

4. See especially Cole, *Robert Owen*; Joseph McCabe, *Robert Owen* (London: Watts, 1920); A. L. Morton, *The Life and Ideas of Robert Owen* (New York: International, 1969); Margaret Cole, *Robert Owen of New Lanark, 1771–1858* (New York: Oxford University Press, 1953); Frank Podmore, *Robert Owen: A Biography* (New York: D. Appleton, 1907); Elbert Hubbard, "Robert Owen," in *Great Business Men*, vol. 11 of *Little Journeys to the Homes of the Great* (New York: Wm. Wise, 1928).

5. G. D. H. Cole, *Robert Owen*, 320.

6. Cole, 41.

7. Cole, 46.

8. Owen, *Threading My Way*, 48.

9. McCabe, *Robert Owen*, 9.

10. Margaret Cole, *Owen of New Lanark*, 53.

11. G. D. H. Cole, *Robert Owen*, 94–95.

12. Podmore, *Robert Owen*, 79.

13. G. D. H. Cole, *Robert Owen*, 91–92.

14. Cole, 98.

15. Robert Owen, *The Life of Robert Owen* (London: G. Bell and Sons, 1920), 86–88.

16. Owen, 87.

17. G. D. H. Cole, *Robert Owen*, 106.

18. Robert Owen, *A New View of Society and Other Writings*, ed. G. D. H. Cole, Everyman's Library (New York: Dutton, 1927).

19. G. D. H. Cole, *Robert Owen*, 98.

20. McCabe, *Robert Owen*, 35.

21. Owen, *New View of Society*, 8–9.

22. Owen, *Life of Robert Owen*, 84, 86.

23. G. D. H. Cole, *Robert Owen*, 166–67.

24. Owen, *Threading My Way*, 108.

25. Owen, 79.

26. Margaret Cole, *Owen of New Lanark*, 40.
27. Podmore, *Robert Owen*, 146.
28. G. D. H. Cole, *Robert Owen*, 104–5.
29. Cole, 215.
30. Cole, 126–27.
31. Podmore, *Robert Owen*, 275.
32. Owen, *New View of Society*, 24.
33. Owen, *Life of Robert Owen*, 186.
34. G. D. H. Cole, *Robert Owen*, 18.
35. Cole, 167.
36. McCabe, *Robert Owen*, 40.
37. McCabe, 21.
38. T. J. Ward, "Owen as a Factory Reformer," in *Robert Owen: Prince of Cotton Spinners*, ed. J. Butt (Newton Abbot: David & Charles, 1971), 110.
39. W. H. Fraser, "Robert Owen and the Workers," in Butt, *Robert Owen*, 13.
40. Morton, *Life and Ideas of Robert Owen*, 232–35.
41. Owen, *Life of Robert Owen*, 157.
42. Heilbroner, *Worldly Philosophers*, 112.
43. G. D. H. Cole, *Robert Owen*, xiii–xiv.
44. R. H. Tawney, *The Radical Tradition* (New York: Minerva, 1964), 37–38.
45. Owen, *Threading My Way*, 201.
46. Podmore, *Robert Owen*, 325.
47. Bob Blaisdell, *The Communist Manifesto and Other Revolutionary Writings* (Mineola, NY: Dover, 2003), 101.
48. Owen, *Threading My Way*, 291.
49. McCabe, *Robert Owen*, 119.
50. *The Complete Works of Ralph Waldo Emerson*, vol. 10 (Boston: Houghton, Mifflin, 1904), 347.

Chapter 2: Man with a Thousand Partners: James Cash Penney (1875–1971)

1. Norman Beasley, *Main Street Merchant: The Story of the J. C. Penney Company* (New York: McGraw-Hill, 1948), 8.
2. J. C. Penney, *Fifty Years with the Golden Rule* (New York: Harper & Brothers, 1950), 24.
3. Penney, 25.
4. Penney, 26.
5. Mary E. Curry, *Creating an American Institution: The Merchandising Genius of J. C. Penney* (New York: Garland, 1993), 29.
6. Curry, 38.
7. Penney, *Fifty Years*, 36.
8. Penney, 26.

9. Curry, *Creating an American Institution*, 93.
10. Penney, *Fifty Years*, 52.
11. Penney, 54.
12. Beasley, *Main Street Merchant*, 150.
13. Beasley, 71.
14. Penney, *Fifty Years*, 95.
15. Penney, 73.
16. Penney, 95.
17. Beasley, *Main Street Merchant*, 94.
18. Beasley, 86.
19. Curry, *Creating an American Institution*, 122.
20. Penney, *Fifty Years*, 70.
21. Penney, 119.
22. Beasley, *Main Street Merchant*, viii.
23. Curry, *Creating an American Institution*, 152.
24. Beasley, *Main Street Merchant*, 90.
25. Beasley, 95.
26. Beasley, 216.
27. Beasley, 80.
28. Curry, *Creating an American Institution*, 147.
29. Curry, 150.
30. Curry, 152.
31. Penney, *Fifty Years*, 103.
32. Curry, *Creating an American Institution*, 171–72.
33. Beasley, *Main Street Merchant*, 100.
34. Curry, *Creating an American Institution*, 214.
35. Curry, 191.
36. Curry, 107.
37. Curry, 112.
38. Curry, 111.
39. Curry, 242.
40. Curry, 214.
41. Curry, 145.
42. Curry, 270.
43. Curry, 149.
44. Curry, 151.
45. Curry, 277.
46. Curry, 310.
47. Penney, *Fifty Years*, 232.
48. Curry, *Creating an American Institution*, 306.
49. Jennifer Reingold, "J. C. Penney: How to Fail in Business While Really Trying," *Fortune*, April 7, 2014, 82.

Chapter 3: The Businessman Who "Cleaned Up the World": William Lever (1851–1925)

Lever was a high-profile public figure during his life, hence his career is well documented. In this chapter I draw heavily on his most recent biography, Adam Macqueen's *The King of Sunlight: How William Lever Cleaned Up the World* (London: Bantam, 2004). The book is well written and easily obtainable. I recommend it to readers wishing to learn more about Lever.

1. Charles Wilson, *The History of Unilever: A Study in Economic Growth and Social Change*, 2 vols. (London: Cassell, 1954), 1:9.
2. Friedrich Engles, *The Condition of the Working Class in England* (German original 1845, English trans. New York, 1887), ed. David McLellan (Oxford: Oxford University Press, 1993).
3. Adam Macqueen, *The King of Sunlight: How William Lever Cleaned Up the World* (London: Corgi, 2005), 23.
4. Macqueen, 39.
5. Macqueen, 43–44.
6. Macqueen, 52.
7. Wilson, *History of Unilever*, 40.
8. Wilson, 37.
9. Wilson, 36.
10. Macqueen, *King of Sunlight*, 4.
11. Macqueen, 127.
12. Macqueen, 226.
13. Macqueen, 5.
14. Macqueen, 79.
15. Wilson, *History of Unilever*, 157.
16. Wilson, 290.
17. Macqueen, *King of Sunlight*, 54.
18. Macqueen, 69.
19. Wilson, *History of Unilever*, 142.
20. Macqueen, *King of Sunlight*, 81.
21. Macqueen, 136.
22. Macqueen, 143–50.
23. Macqueen, 233.
24. Macqueen, 262.
25. Wilson, *History of Unilever*, 150.
26. Wilson, 267.

27. Geoffrey Jones, *Renewing Unilever* (New York: Oxford University Press, 2005), 248.
28. Philip Mirvis, "Unilever's Drive for Sustainability and CSR—Changing the Game," in *Organizing for Sustainability*, vol. 1 of *Organizing for Sustainable Effectiveness*, ed. Susan Albers Mohrman and Abraham B. (Rami) Shani (Bingley, UK: Emerald, 2011), 46–50.
29. Scheherazade Daneshkhu and David Oakley, "Unilever Under Pressure to Step Up Growth Rate," *Financial Times*, February 10, 2015.
30. David Gelles, "Smaller Footprint. Giant Task," *New York Times*, November 22, 2015, Sunday Business.
31. Gelles, 9.
32. Gelles, 8.
33. Gelles, 9.
34. Daneshkhu and Oakley, "Unilever Under Pressure," 13.

Chapter 4: Kisses Sweeter Than Wine: Milton Snavely Hershey (1857–1945)

Like William Lever, Hershey lived a public life, seemingly adoring public attention and admiration. He is the subject of several biographies, but none as readable and objective as Michael D'Antonio's *Hershey: Milton S. Hershey's Extraordinary Life of Wealth, Empire, and Utopian Dreams* (New York: Simon & Schuster, 2006). It is worth noting that D'Antonio is also the author of an unauthorized biography of Donald Trump. I will leave it to readers to decide if the two larger-than-life protagonists had anything in common.

1. Michael D'Antonio, *Hershey: Milton S. Hershey's Extraordinary Life of Wealth, Empire, and Utopian Dreams* (New York: Simon & Schuster, 2006), 10.
2. Mary Malone, *Milton Hershey: Chocolate King* (Champaign, IL: Gerrard, 1971).
3. D'Antonio, *Hershey*, 55–59.
4. "M. S. Hershey Dead; Chocolate King, 88," *New York Times*, October 14, 1945.
5. D'Antonio, *Hershey*, 65.
6. D'Antonio, 93–94.
7. "M. S. Hershey Dead."
8. D'Antonio, *Hershey*, 112, 137.

9. D'Antonio, 137.

10. D'Antonio, 166.

11. "M. S. Hershey Gives $60,000,000 Trust for an Orphanage," *New York Times*, November 9, 1923.

12. D'Antonio, *Hershey*, 130, 180–81.

13. D'Antonio, 221.

14. Mike King, *Quakernomics: An Ethical Capitalism* (London: Anthem, 2014).

15. D'Antonio, *Hershey*, 205.

16. Joseph Richard Snavely, *Milton S. Hershey, Builder* (Hershey, PA: Hershey Press, 1935), 67.

17. D'Antonio, *Hershey*, 218.

18. D'Antonio, 198.

19. Stephen Greenhouse, "Resentment as Workers Strike in a Town Built on Chocolate," *New York Times*, May 18, 2002.

20. Michael J. de la Merced, "Hershey Trust Reaches Tentative Deal with Pennsylvania on Governance," *New York Times*, July 22, 2016, Deal Book.

21. See chapter 18 for a fuller discussion of the attempted Unilever takeover.

22. Leslie Picker, Stephanie Strom, and Michael J. de la Merced, "Trust Holds the Key to Whether a Bid for Hershey Succeeds This Time," *New York Times*, June 30, 2016, Deal Book.

23. David Segal, "Chocolate-Covered Conflict," *New York Times*, July 31, 2016, Sunday Business.

24. Segal.

25. Segal.

26. For details of Hershey company takeover attempts and the role of the trust's board, see Nelson D. Schwartz, "Hershey Overhauls Its Board of Directors," *New York Times*, November 12, 2007, Business Day; Andrew Ross Sorkin, "Market; Court Ties Up Hershey Deal, for Time Being," *New York Times*, September 5, 2002, Business Day; Frances X. Clines, "Whiff of Chocolate, and the Sweet Smell of Success," *New York Times*, September 19, 2002, Business Day; David Segal, "Back-Stabbing and Threats of a 'Suicide Parachute' at Hershey," *New York Times*, July 30, 2016, Deal Book; and Steven Davidoff Solomon, "Another Hershey Deal May Come Unwrapped. Maybe It Should," *New York Times*, July 6, 2013, Deal Book.

27. D'Antonio, *Hershey*, 205.

Chapter 5: Creating an Enduring Enterprise: James Lincoln (1883–1965)

1. Horace Mann, "The Importance of Universal Free, Public Education," in *Lectures and Annual Reports on Education*, ed. Mary Mann, vol. 3 (Boston: Horace P. Fuller, 1867), 668–70.

2. Raymond Moley, *The American Century of John Lincoln* (New York: Duell, Sloan and Pearce, 1962).

3. Virginia P. Dawson, *Lincoln Electric: A History* (Cleveland: Lincoln Electric, 1999), 32.

4. Dawson, 32.

5. Dawson, 3.

6. James Lincoln, *Incentive Management* (Cleveland: Lincoln Electric, 1951), 4–5.

7. Frank Koller, *Spark: Lessons from Lincoln Electric's Unique Guaranteed Employment Program* (New York: Public Affairs, 2010), 15.

8. Koller, 52.

9. James O'Toole and Edward E. Lawler III, *The New American Workplace* (New York: Palgrave Macmillan, 2006), 158–63.

10. Dawson, *Lincoln Electric*, 79.

11. Journalist Frank Koller's blog carries annual reports on Lincoln's financials, including the amount of its annual bonuses. His 2015–16 reports showed slightly lower bonuses as the result of reduced construction activity. http://frankkoller.com.

12. Jamie O'Connell, "Lincoln Electric: Venturing Abroad," HBS case 9-398-094 (Boston: Harvard Business School Publishing, 1998), 7.

13. Koller, *Spark*, 29–31.

14. Koller, 76.

15. Koller, 66.

16. Dawson, *Lincoln Electric*, 90.

17. Mitchell Fein, *Motivation for Work* (New York: American Institute of Industrial Engineers, 1971).

18. Koller, *Spark*, 40.

19. James O'Toole, *Work in America* (Cambridge, MA: MIT Press, 1973), 25.

20. Dawson, *Lincoln Electric*, 36.

21. Dawson, 65–66.

22. Dawson, 85–86.

23. Dawson, 86–87.

24. *Dodge v. Ford Motor Company*, 170 NW 668 (Michigan 1919).

25. Lincoln, *Incentive Management*, 9.

26. Norman Fast, "The Lincoln Electric Company," HBS case 9-376-028 (Boston: Harvard Business School Publishing, 1983).

27. Lynn Stout, *The Shareholder Value Myth: How Putting Shareholders First Harms Investors, Corporations and the Public* (San Francisco: Berrett-Koehler, 2012), 37–38. This issue is treated more fully in chapter 17.

28. Dawson, *Lincoln Electric*, 118.

29. Dawson, 118.

30. Koller, *Spark*, 171.

Chapter 6: New Forms of Incorporation and Governance: John Spedan Lewis (1885–1963) and John Joseph Eagan (1870–1924)

1. John Spedan Lewis, *Partnership for All* (London: Ker-Cross, 1948), 7.
2. John Spedan Lewis, *Fairer Shares: A Possible Advance in Civilization and Perhaps the Only Alternative to Communism* (London: Staples Press, 1954), v.
3. Allen Flanders, Ruth Pomeranz, and Joan Woodward, *Experiment in Industrial Democracy* (London: Faber and Faber, 1968), 23.
4. Lewis, *Partnership for All*, 55.
5. Lewis, v.
6. Lewis, ix.
7. Lewis, xv.
8. http://www.johnlewispartnership.co.uk/about/our-founder/bbc-broadcast.html.
9. Lewis, *Fairer Shares*, 3–4.
10. Lewis, 4.
11. The Lewis Partnership's constitution is found at http://www.johnlewispartnership.co.uk/about/our-constitution.html.
12. Lewis, *Fairer Shares*, 226.
13. Flanders, Pomeranz, and Woodward, *Experiment in Industrial Democracy*, 46.
14. Flanders, Pomeranz, and Woodward, 17.
15. Lewis, *Fairer Shares*, 11.
16. Flanders, Pomeranz, and Woodward, *Experiment in Industrial Democracy*, 19.
17. http://www.johnlewispartnership.co.uk/about/our-founder/bbc-broadcast.html.
18. Lewis, *Fairer Shares*, 43.
19. Lewis, 45.
20. Flanders, Pomeranz, and Woodward, *Experiment in Industrial Democracy*.
21. Lewis, *Fairer Shares*.
22. Flanders, Pomeranz, and Woodward, *Experiment in Industrial Democracy*, 114.
23. Flanders, Pomeranz, and Woodward, 222.
24. Flanders, Pomeranz, and Woodward, 193.
25. Lewis, *Fairer Shares*, 12.
26. Lewis, 3.
27. "The Feeling Is Mutual," *Economist*, January 21, 2012, 62.
28. "Read All About Us," *Economist*, August 1, 2015, 58.
29. Robert E. Speer, *John J. Eagan: A Memoir of an Adventurer for the Kingdom of God on Earth* (Birmingham, AL: American Cast Iron Pipe Company, 1939), 31.
30. Speer, 23.
31. Speer, 24.
32. Speer, 141.

33. Speer, 76.
34. Speer, 80.
35. Speer, 142.
36. Speer, 180–81.
37. Speer, 182–83.
38. Speer, 140.
39. Speer, 111.
40. Speer, 112.
41. Speer, 114.
42. Speer, 147.
43. Speer, 7.
44. Speer, 9.
45. Speer, 152.
46. Speer, 170.
47. Speer, 149.
48. Speer, 142.
49. Speer, 225.
50. Speer, 215.
51. "The McWane Story—Two Companies, Two Visions," *Frontline*, 2003, http://www.pbs.org/wgbh/frontline/shows/workplace/mcwane/two.html.
52. Speer, *John J. Eagan*, 200.

Chapter 7: Johnson & Johnson's Roller-Coaster Ride: Robert Wood Johnson (1893–1968) and James Burke (1925–2012)

1. Lawrence G. Foster, *Robert Wood Johnson: The Gentleman Rebel* (State College, PA: Lillian, 1999), 26.
2. Foster, 53.
3. Foster, 81.
4. Foster, 428.
5. Foster, 111.
6. Foster, 186.
7. Foster, 195.
8. Foster, 94.
9. Foster, 208.
10. Foster, 226.
11. Foster, 224.
12. Foster, 230.
13. Foster, 233.
14. Foster, 98.
15. Foster, 247.
16. Foster, 272.
17. Foster, 284.

18. Robert Wood Johnson, *Or Forfeit Freedom* (New York: Doubleday, 1947).
19. Johnson, 5.
20. Johnson, 7.
21. Johnson, 12.
22. Johnson, 17.
23. Johnson, 21.
24. Johnson, 50.
25. Johnson, 51.
26. Johnson, 67.
27. Johnson, 191.
28. Johnson, 81.
29. Johnson, 254.
30. Johnson, 78.
31. Johnson, 253.
32. Foster, *Robert Wood Johnson*, 109.
33. Johnson, *Or Forfeit Freedom*, 141.
34. Johnson, 161.
35. Johnson, 174.
36. Johnson, 115.
37. Johnson, 130.
38. Foster, *Robert Wood Johnson*, 284.
39. Foster, 379.
40. Lawrence G. Foster, *A Company That Cares: One Hundred Year Illustrated History of Johnson & Johnson* (New Brunswick, NJ: Johnson & Johnson, 1986).
41. Foster, *Robert Wood Johnson*, 358.
42. Foster, 614.
43. Richard S. Tedlow and Wendy K. Smith, "James Burke: A Career in American Business (A)," HBS case 9-389-177 (Boston: Harvard Business School Publishing, 1989; rev. 2005), 1.
44. Tedlow and Smith, 4.
45. Tedlow and Smith, 9.
46. Tedlow and Smith, 9.
47. Tedlow and Smith, 11.
48. Tedlow and Smith, 11.
49. Tedlow and Smith, 12.
50. "Our Credo," Johnson & Johnson company video, 1975.
51. Francis J. Aguilar and Arvind Bhambri, "Johnson & Johnson (A): Philosophy and Culture," HBS case 384-053 (Boston: Harvard Business School Publishing, 1986), 6.
52. Aguilar and Bhambri, 1.
53. Foster, *Company That Cares*, 143.

54. Tedlow and Smith, "James Burke," 16.
55. Natasha Singer and Reed Abelson, "Can Johnson & Johnson Get Its Act Together?" *New York Times*, January 16, 2011, Sunday Business.

Chapter 8: Great Genes: Levi Strauss (1829–1902) and His Heirs

Much of the information in this chapter came to me as the result of interviews with Walter Haas Jr., Robert Haas, Peter Thigpen, and other longtime Levi employees.

1. Remarkably, a full-scale, authoritative biography of Levi Strauss has not been written until recently. See Lynn Downey, *Levi Strauss: The Man Who Gave Blue Jeans to the World* (Cambridge: University of Massachusetts Press, 2016).
2. Ed Cray, *Levi's: The "Shrink-to-Fit" Business That Stretched to Cover the World* (Boston: Houghton Mifflin, 1978), 35.
3. Cray, 30.
4. Cray, 78.
5. Cray, 100.
6. Cray, 129.
7. Cray, 157.
8. Cray, 168.
9. Cray, 200.
10. Cray, 190.
11. Cray, 212.
12. Cray, 252–53.
13. Cray, 219.
14. Cray, 220.
15. Cray, 221.
16. Cray, 229–30.
17. Cray, 237.
18. Cray, 240.
19. I was so filled with admiration that, in a book I wrote the following year, I cited Levi Strauss as one of eight "vanguard corporations" that, I proclaimed, were "redesigning the corporate future" of America. James O'Toole, *Vanguard Management* (New York: Doubleday, 1985).
20. Katherine Rudolph Bose, "Levi Strauss & Co.," SGSB case E-350 (Stanford, CA: Stanford Graduate School of Business, 2009).
21. Robert Howard, "Values Make the Company: An Interview with Robert Haas," *Harvard Business Review*, September–October 1990, 135.
22. David Bollier, *Aiming Higher: 25 Stories of How Companies Prosper by*

Combining Sound Management and Social Vision (New York: American Management Association, 1996), 344.

23. Nina Monk and Jane Hodges, "How Levi's Trashed a Great American Brand: While Bob Haas Pioneered Benevolent Management, His Company Came Apart at the Seams," *Fortune*, April 12, 1999.

Chapter 9: Marks & Sparks: Michael Marks (1863–1900) and the Marks and Sieff Families

1. Goronwy Rees, *St Michael: A History of Marks & Spencer* (London: Littlehampton, 1969), 12.
2. Rees, 10.
3. Rees, 53–54.
4. Rees, 61.
5. Rees, 86.
6. Rees, 93.
7. Rees, 226–27.
8. K. K. Tse, *Marks & Spencer: Anatomy of Britain's Most Efficiently Managed Company* (Oxford, UK: Pergamon Press, 1985), 115.
9. Tse, 117–20.
10. Tse, 120.
11. Marcus Sieff, *Don't Ask the Price* (Weidenfeld and Nicolson, 1986), 84.
12. Sieff, 64.
13. Drucker, *Management: Tasks, Responsibilities, Practices* (New York: HarperBusiness, 1993), 53.
14. Sieff, *Don't Ask the Price*, 210.
15. Sieff, 210.
16. Tse, Marks & Spencer, 35.
17. Sieff, *Don't Ask the Price*, 201.
18. Sieff, 146.
19. Sieff, 339.
20. Sieff, 255.
21. Sieff, 223–24.
22. Sieff, 250.
23. "Lord Sieff of Brimpton," obituary, *Telegraph*, February 24, 2001.
24. Tse, *Marks & Spencer*, 5, 183.
25. Joseph L. Bower, "Marks & Spencer: The Phoenix Rises," HBS case 9-303-096 (Boston: Harvard Business School Publishing, 2005), 5.
26. Bower, 7.
27. Quoted in David Bell, Nitin Sanghavi, and Laura Winig, "Marks and Spencer: Plan A," HBS case 9-509-029 (Boston: Harvard Business School Publishing, 2009), 3.
28. Bell, Sanghavi, and Winig, 4.

29. See, for example, Mary Scott and Howard Rothman, *Companies with a Conscience* (New York: Birch Lane Press, 1992). Scott and Rothman profiled twelve small companies that they saw "as typifying a new era of 'caring capitalism.'" A decade later, when they revised the book, only two of those companies were still on their list: Ben & Jerry's and Patagonia (both of which are also profiled here). Mary Scott and Howard Rothman, *Companies with a Conscience*, 3rd ed. (Radnor, PA: Publishing Cooperative, 2003).

Chapter 10: Leadership as an Art: Max De Pree (1924–2017)

1. Ralph Caplan, "The Design of Herman Miller," *Design*, 1976, 14.
2. Max De Pree, *Leadership Is an Art* (New York: Doubleday, 1989), 10.
3. Carol Davenport, "America's Most Admired Corporations," *Fortune*, January 30, 1989, 58–81.
4. Robert Levering, Milton Moskowitz, and Michael Katz, *The 100 Best Companies to Work for in America* (Reading, MA: Addison-Wesley Publishing, 1984), 217–20.
5. Kenneth Labich, "Hot Company, Warm Culture," *Fortune*, February 27, 1989, 74–78.
6. Robert J. McClory, "The Creative Process at Herman Miller," *Across the Board*, May 1985, 9–15.
7. Levering, Moskowitz, and Katz, *100 Best Companies*, 217.
8. De Pree, *Leadership Is an Art*, 35.
9. De Pree, 11.
10. Foreword to De Pree, xxii.
11. Levering, Moskowitz, and Katz, *100 Best Companies*, 218.
12. De Pree, *Leadership Is an Art*, 96.
13. Herman Miller, Inc., *1985 Annual Report*, 42.
14. De Pree, *Leadership Is an Art*, 100.
15. De Pree, 98.
16. Levering, Moskowitz, and Kate, *100 Best Companies*, 219.
17. De Pree, *Leadership Is an Art*, 36–42.
18. McClory, "Creative Process at Herman Miller," 12.
19. Herman Miller, *Annual Report*, 15.
20. Levering, Moskowitz, and Katz, *100 Best Companies*, 219–20.
21. De Pree, *Leadership Is an Art*, 110–12.

Chapter 11: Too Much of a Good Thing: William C. Norris (1911–2006)

1. James C. Worthy, *William C. Norris: Portrait of a Maverick* (Cambridge, MA: Ballinger, 1987), 16.
2. Worthy, 32.

3. Worthy, 39.
4. Worthy, 43.
5. "Computers: A Settlement for IBM," *Time*, January 29, 1973.
6. Worthy, *William C. Norris*, 46.
7. Worthy, 64.
8. Worthy, 35.
9. Worthy, 5.
10. Worthy, 108.
11. "Far-Out Firm: Seeking to Aid Society Control Data Takes on Many Novel Adventures," *Wall Street Journal*, December 22, 1982.
12. Norris, interview by author, in James O'Toole, *Vanguard Management* (New York: Doubleday, 1985), 367.
13. Norris, 368.
14. Worthy, *William C. Norris*, 110.
15. Worthy, 111.
16. Worthy, 117.
17. Worthy, 117.
18. Worthy, 117.
19. Worthy, 121.
20. Worthy, 102.
21. Elizabeth Van Meer, "PLATO: From Computer-Based Education to Corporate Social Responsibility," *Iterations*, November 5, 2003, www.cbi .umn.edu/iterations/vanmeer.html.
22. Van Meer.
23. Worthy, *William C. Norris*, 137.
24. Worthy, 203.
25. Worthy, 204.
26. Worthy, 224.
27. Rebecca Leung, "The Mensch of Malden Mills: CEO Aaron Feuerstein Puts Employees First," CBS News, July 3, 2003, https://www.cbsnews.com /news/the-mensch-of-malden-mills/.
28. Quoted in Andrew Hill, "Why It Can Be Cruel to Be Too Kind in the Workplace," *Financial Times*, December 4, 2017.

Chapter 12: Business Mavericks: Ken Iverson (1925–2002), Robert Townsend (1920–1998), Herb Kelleher (1931–), Bill Gore (1912–1986), and Terri Kelly (1963–)

1. Bryan J. Poulin, "Nucor Corporation 1995: After 30 Years of Success, What Next?" Faculty of Business Administration, Lakehead University, Ontario Canada, September 2008, 1, https://www.slideshare.net /homeworkping4/239744610-nucorcase.

2. Ken Iverson, *Plain Talk: Lessons from a Business Maverick* (Hoboken, NJ: John Wiley & Sons, 1998), 75.
3. Iverson, 4.
4. Iverson, 8.
5. Iverson, 16.
6. Iverson, 16–17.
7. Iverson, 18–19.
8. Iverson, 18.
9. Poulin, "Nucor Corporation," 32.
10. Iverson, *Plain Talk*, 45–46.
11. Kathryn Shaw, "The Value of Innovative Human Resource Management Practices," in *America at Work*, ed. Edward E. Lawler and James O'Toole (New York: Palgrave Macmillan, 2006), 233.
12. Poulin, "Nucor Corporation," 12.
13. Poulin, 11.
14. Poulin, 21.
15. Jeffrey L. Rodengen, *The Legend of Nucor* (Fort Lauderdale, FL: Write Stuff Enterprises, 1997), 119.
16. Iverson, *Plain Talk*, 171.
17. Iverson, 175.
18. Iverson, 181.
19. Iverson, 171.
20. Iverson, 67.
21. Rodengen, *Legend of Nucor*, 74.
22. Iverson, *Plain Talk*, 2.
23. Iverson, 24.
24. Ed Crooks, "Leading Steelmaker Chief on Trump, Tax and the Case for Protection," *Financial Times*, March, 14, 2018, 4.
25. Iverson, *Plain Talk*, vii.
26. Robert Townsend, *Up the Organization: How to Stop the Corporation from Stifling People* (San Francisco: Jossey-Bass, 2007), 170.
27. Townsend, 102.
28. Townsend, 26.
29. Townsend, xxvii.
30. Townsend, xxxvi.
31. Townsend, 15.
32. Townsend, 165.
33. Townsend, 15.
34. Townsend, xxiii.
35. Townsend, 115.
36. Townsend, 54.
37. Townsend, 61.

38. Townsend, xxi.
39. Townsend, x.
40. Joseph Guinto, "Rollin On," *Southwest Airlines Spirit*, June 2006, 141.
41. Jeffrey Pfeffer, "Working Alone: Whatever Happened to the Idea of Organizations as Communities," in Lawler and O'Toole, *America at Work*, 8.
42. Jeff Bailey, "On Some Flights, Millionaires Are Serving the Drinks," *New York Times*, May 15, 2006.
43. Bailey, A6.
44. Joseph Guinto, "Mom Knows Best," *Southwest Airlines Spirit*, June 2006, 122.
45. Joseph Guinto, "Wheels Up," *Southwest Airlines Spirit*, June 2006, 117.
46. Guinto, 117.
47. Michael J. Milne, "The Gorey Details," *Management Review*, March 1985, 16–17.
48. Lucien Rhodes, "The Un-Manager," *Inc.*, August 1982, 34–43.
49. Robert Levering and Milton Moskowitz, *The 100 Best Companies to Work for in America* (New York: Plume, 1993).
50. Robert Safian, "Terri Kelly, the 'Un-CEO' of W. L. Gore, on How to Deal with Chaos," *Fast Company*, October 29, 2012.

Chapter 13: The Patricians: Thornton Bradshaw (1917–1988), J. Irwin Miller (1909–2004), Edwin Land (1909–1991), John Whitehead (1922–2015), and Roy Vagelos (1929–)

1. Paul Richter, "Ex-Arco, RCA Chief Thornton Bradshaw Dies," *Los Angeles Times*, December 7, 1988.
2. James O'Toole, notes taken at meeting with Arco executives in Santa Barbara, California, in the early 1980s.
3. O'Toole.
4. Thornton Bradshaw, introduction to *Corporations and Their Critics*, ed. Thornton Bradshaw and David Vogel (New York: McGraw-Hill, 1980), xxiii.
5. Bradshaw, xxii.
6. Thornton F. Bradshaw, "The Corporation Executive's View of Social Responsibility," *Financial Analysts Journal* 27, no. 5 (Sept.–Oct. 1971): 31.
7. Charles Koch, "Let's Try a Free Market in Energy," https://MasterResource.org/about/.
8. Bradshaw, *Corporations and Their Critics*, xviii.
9. Marilyn Berger, "Thornton F. Bradshaw Dies at 71; Led RCA until Purchase by G.E," *New York Times*, December 7, 1988.
10. Xandra Kayden, "The Loss of a Corporate Citizen," *Los Angeles Times*, April 4, 1999.

11. Bradshaw, "Corporation Executive's View," 31.
12. Joseph L. Bower and Michael Norris, "Cummins, Inc.: Building a Home Community for a Global Company," HBS case 9-313-024 (Boston: Harvard Business School Publishing, 2014), 3.
13. David Bollier, *Aiming Higher: 25 Stories of How Companies Prosper by Combining Sound Management and Social Vision* (New York: American Management Association, 1996), 305.
14. Bollier, 312.
15. Bollier, 303.
16. Bollier, 303.
17. Bollier, 310.
18. Bollier, 311.
19. Bollier, 311.
20. Bollier, 311.
21. Bollier, 305.
22. Bollier, 302.
23. Christopher Bonanos, "The Man Who Inspired Jobs," *New York Times*, October 7, 2011.
24. Victor K. McElheny, *Insisting on the Impossible: The Life of Edwin Land* (Cambridge, MA: Perseus, 1998).
25. McElheny, chapter 12.
26. "Polaroid 'Develops' Job Skills," *Industry Week*, August 10, 1981, 27.
27. Christopher Bonanos, *Instant: The Story of Polaroid* (Princeton, NJ: Princeton Architectural Press, 2012), 54.
28. Bonanos, 13.
29. Bonanos, "Man Who Inspired Jobs."
30. Bonanos, *Instant*, 117.
31. Peter T. Kilborn, "Polaroid President Appointed by Land," *New York Times*, January 23, 1975.
32. Bonanos, *Instant*, 117.
33. Bonanos, 160.
34. Douglas Martin, "John C. Whitehead, Who Led Effort to Rebuild After 9/11, Is Dead at 92," Obituaries, *New York Times*, February 9, 2005.
35. "John C. Whitehead, A Giant of Postwar Finance and Public Service in New York," editorial, *New York Times*, February 9, 2005.
36. John C. Whitehead, *A Life in Leadership* (Basic Books, 2005), 43.
37. Whitehead, 72.
38. Whitehead, 77.
39. Whitehead, 92.
40. Whitehead, 128.
41. Whitehead, 108–9.
42. Whitehead, 276.

43. Whitehead, 277.
44. Whitehead, 130–31.
45. Whitehead, 137.
46. David Bollier, Stephanie Weiss, and Kirk O. Hanson, "Merck & Co., Inc.,"
    Business Enterprise Trust Case 90-013, Stanford California, (A) 3.
47. Bollier, Weiss, and Hanson, (B)4.
48. Bollier, Weiss, and Hanson, (D)3.
49. Milanda Rout, "Vioxx Maker Merck and Co. Drew Up Doctor Hit List,"
    Australian, October 6, 2009, www.theaustralian.com.au/news/drug . . .
    /story-e6frg6n6-1225693586492.
50. Duff Wilson, "Merck to Pay $950 Million Over Vioxx," *New York Times*,
    November 22, 2011, Business Day.
51. "Making Merck Work," *Economist*, February 24, 2018, 56.
52. David Geller and Katie Thomas, "Merck's Leader Speaks Out and Leaves
    a Panel, and 2 More Chiefs Follow," *New York Times*, August 15, 2017,
    Business Day.
53. Caleb Melby and Doni Bloomfield, "Boardroom Compensation Made This
    Man a Billionaire," *Bloomberg*, October 29, 2015, https://www.bloomberg
    .com/news/articles/2015-10-29/regeneron-makes-a-boardroom
    -billionaire-in-vagelos-s-second-act.

Chapter 14: Environmentalists or Capitalists? Anita Perella Roddick (1942–2007) and Tom Chappell (1943–)

1. Anita Roddick, *Body and Soul: Profits with Principles* (New York: Crown,
    1991), 39.
2. Roddick, 25.
3. Roddick, 59.
4. Roddick, 64.
5. Roddick, 12.
6. Roddick, 11.
7. Roddick, 69.
8. Roddick, 7.
9. Roddick, 82.
10. Roddick, 9.
11. Christopher A. Bartlett, "The Body Shop International," HBS case 9-392-
    032 (Boston: Harvard Business School Publishing, 1995), 8.
12. Bartlett, 3.
13. Bartlett, 4.
14. Roddick, *Body and Soul*, 110.
15. Roddick, 106.
16. Bartlett, "Body Shop International," 3.
17. Roddick, *Body and Soul*, 109.

18. Roddick, 242.
19. Roddick, 7.
20. Roddick, 215–16.
21. Bartlett, "Body Shop International," 7.
22. Roddick, *Body and Soul*, 20.
23. Bartlett, "Body Shop International," 3.
24. Roddick, *Body and Soul*, 98.
25. Roddick, 22.
26. Roddick, 24.
27. Roddick, 236.
28. Roddick, 23.
29. Bartlett, "Body Shop International," 9.
30. Bartlett, 10.
31. Roddick, *Body and Soul*, 147.
32. Roddick, 219.
33. Bartlett, "Body Shop International," 7.
34. Roddick, *Body and Soul*, 128.
35. Roddick, 148.
36. Roddick, 149.
37. Roddick, 228.
38. Bartlett, "Body Shop International," 11.
39. Roddick, *Body and Soul*, 133.
40. Bartlett, "Body Shop International," 12.
41. Martha Nichols, "Does New Age Business Have a Message for Managers?" *Harvard Business Review*, March–April 1994, 8.
42. Bartlett, "Body Shop International," 11.
43. Nichols, "Does New Age Business," 8.
44. Nichols, 9.
45. Nichols, 9.
46. Anita Roddick, letter to the editor, *Harvard Business Review*, May–June 1994, 144–45.
47. Roddick, 145.
48. Roddick, *Body and Soul*, 27.
49. Bartlett, "Body Shop International," 5.
50. Bartlett, 6.
51. Bartlett, 13.
52. Bartlett, 13.
53. Roddick, *Body and Soul*, 27.
54. Andres Schipani, "Body Shop's Owners Pick British Chief," *Financial Times*, September 13, 2017.
55. Tom Chappell, *The Soul of a Business: Managing for Profit and the Common Good* (New York: Bantam, 1993), 16.

56. Chappell, 18.
57. Chappell, 24.
58. Chappell, 141.
59. Chappell, 33.
60. Chappell, 39.
61. Chappell, 90–92.
62. Chappell, 126.
63. Chappell, 201.
64. Chappell, 175.
65. Chappell, 172.
66. Chappell, 162.
67. Chappell, 180.
68. Chappell, 185.
69. Chappell, 195.
70. Chappell, 158.
71. Chappell, 158.
72. Chappell, 216.
73. Chappell, 217.
74. James Austen and Herman B. "Dutch" Leonard, "Can the Virtuous Mouse and the Wealthy Elephant Live Happily Ever After?" *California Management Review* 51, no. 1 (Fall 2008): 77–102, 87.
75. Sandra Waddock, "Of Mice and Elephants," *California Management Review* 51, no. 1 (Fall 2008): 103.
76. Waddock, 104.
77. Waddock, 105.

Chapter 15: Lever Redux: Ben Cohen (1951–)

1. There are several published accounts of the Ben & Jerry's story, including Brad Edmondson's *Ice Cream Social* (San Francisco: Berrett-Koehler, 2014), and the founders' own account: Ben Cohen and Jerry Greenfield, *Ben & Jerry's Double Dip* (New York: Simon & Schuster, 1997). I have drawn most heavily on Fred "Chico" Lager, *Ben & Jerry's: The Inside Scoop* (New York: Crown, 1994).
2. Lager, *Inside Scoop*, 25.
3. Lager, 34.
4. Lager, 31.
5. Lager, 36.
6. Julie Bayle-Cordier, Philip Mirvis, and Bertrand Moingeon, "Projecting Different Identities: A Longitudinal Study of the 'Whipsaw' Effects of Changing Leadership Discourse About the Triple Bottom Line," *Journal of Applied Behavioral Science* 51, no. 3: 349.
7. Lager, *Inside Scoop*, 149.
8. Lager, 109.

9. Lager, 125.
10. Lager, 126.
11. Lager, 128.
12. Lager, 230.
13. Lager, 129.
14. David Bollier, *Aiming Higher: 25 Stories of How Companies Prosper by Combining Sound Management and Social Vision* (New York: American Management Association, 1996), 256.
15. Bollier, 260.
16. Lager, *Inside Scoop*, 178.
17. Bayle-Cordier, Mirvis, and Moingeon, "Projecting Different Identities," 348.
18. Bayle-Cordier, Mirvis, and Moingeon, "Projecting Different Identities," 348.
19. Lager, *Inside Scoop*, 211.
20. Lager, 225.
21. Lager, 227–28.
22. Bayle-Cordier, Mirvis, and Moingeon, "Projecting Different Identities," 354.
23. Lager, *Inside Scoop*, 20.
24. Bayle-Cordier, Mirvis, and Moingeon, "Projecting Different Identities," 356.
25. Philip H. Mirvis, "Can You Buy CSR?" *California Management Review* 51, no. 1 (October 2008): 112.

Chapter 16: Capitalists of a Different Stripe: Yvon Chouinard (1938–), Jack Stack (1949–), Robert Beyster (1924–2014), and Others

1. "A Window Company's Clear Vision," *CBS News Sunday Morning*, September 3, 2017, https://www.cbsnews.com/news/marvin-windows-a-company-with-clear-vision/.
2. "To Have and to Hold," Special Report on Family Companies, *Economist*, April 18, 2005.
3. Rana Foroohar, "Why America's Tax and Trade Debate Is Wrong," *Financial Times*, September 24, 2017.
4. Alexis de Toqueville, *Democracy in America*, trans. Henry Reeve (New York: G. Dearborn, 1838), vol. 2, ch. 20.
5. Anna Nicolaou, "Mars Eyes Healthy Snacks and Pet Food to Sweeten Sales," *Financial Times*, September 11, 2017, 16.
6. Nick Paumgarten, "Patagonia's Philosopher-King," *New Yorker*, September 19, 2016.
7. Dara O'Rourke and Robert Strand, "Patagonia: Driving Sustainable Innovation by Embracing Tensions," Berkeley-Haas Case Series B5853, February 16, 2016.
8. Paumgarten, "Patagonia's Philosopher-King."
9. Yvon Chouinard, *Let My People Go Surfing* (New York: Penguin, 2005), 45.

10. Yvon Chouinard and Vincent Stanley, *The Responsible Company* (Ventura, CA: Patagonia, 2012), 98.
11. Patt Morrison, "Yvon Chouinard: Capitalist Cat," *Los Angeles Times*, March 12, 2011.
12. Chouinard, *Let My People Go Surfing*, 160.
13. Susan Casey, "Eminence Green," *Fortune*, April 2, 2007, 70.
14. Daniel Lubetzky, *Do the KIND Thing* (New York: Ballantine, 2015), 11.
15. Lubetzky.
16. Joseph Blasi, Douglas Kruse, and Richard Freeman, "Shared Capitalism at Work," in *America at Work*, ed. Edward E. Lawler III and James O'Toole (New York: Palgrave Macmillan, 2006).
17. David Bollier, *Aiming Higher: 25 Stories of How Companies Prosper by Combining Sound Management and Social Vision* (New York: American Management Association, 1996), 169–82.
18. Bollier, 176.
19. Art Kleiner, "Jack Stack's Story Is an Open Book," *Strategy+Business*, July 1, 2001.
20. Kleiner.
21. Kenneth N. Gilpin, "Workers Ready to Cash In as U.P.S. Goes Public," *New York Times*, November 11, 1999.
22. Ronald Bancroft, "Employee Ownership at Weirton Steel," *New Management* 2, no. 2 (1984): 50–54.
23. Joseph Blasi, *Employee Ownership* (New York: Harper Business, 1990), 225–31, 268–69.
24. Robert H. Rosen, *The Healthy Company* (Los Angeles: Tarcher, 1992), 99–104.
25. Rosen, 104.
26. J. Robert Beyster (with Peter Economy), *The SAIC Solution* (La Jolla, CA: Foundation for Enterprise Development, 2014), 193.
27. G. D. H. Cole, *Robert Owen* (London: Ernst Benn, 1925), 228.
28. www.gfmag.org.
29. Andrew Hill, "Twitter Should Not Crush the Idealists and Their Co-Op Dream," *Financial Times*, February 13, 2017.
30. "Trouble in Workers' Paradise," *Economist*, November 9, 2013, 72.
31. Jennifer Thompson, "Workers' Co-Operative Unites World's Vegetarians," *Financial Times*, April 21, 2017.
32. Dale Maharidge, "American Ballad," *Smithsonian*, December 2016, 81–87.

Chapter 17: Looking Back: What We Have Learned

1. James O'Toole, *Vanguard Management* (New York: Doubleday, 1985).
2. David Vogel, *The Market for Virtue* (Washington, DC: Brookings Institution Press, 2006).

3. "Schumpeter: Sailing Through a Scandal," *Economist*, December 20, 2014, 104.
4. Patrick McGee, "VW Shakes Off Diesel Scandal to Hit Sales Record in 2017," *Financial Times*, January 18, 2018, Companies and Markets section, 1.
5. John Maynard Keynes, *The General Theory of Employment, Interest, and Money* (San Diego: Harcourt, Brace & World, 1964), 383.
6. Ralph Blumenthal and Sandra Huff, "When Luxury Department Stores Delivered Babies and Set Broken Bones," *New York Times*, March 5, 2018, A22.
7. In Scandinavia, such large companies as Carlsberg, Novo Nordisk, and Maersk are owned by foundations. Swedish furniture giant IKEA is owned by foundations located in the Netherlands and Liechtenstein, established by its founder, Ingvar Kamprad, to give the company "eternal life," and, of course, to evade Swedish taxes. The Dutch brewery Heineken is also owned by a trust, as is the German publishing giant Bertelsmann. All those companies boast impressive, if sometimes inconsistent, records of social engagement. "Scandinavia Leads the Way in Foundation-Building," *Financial Times*, February 15, 2017.
8. David Ciepley, "Can Corporations Be Held to the Public Interest, or Even to the Law," *Journal of Business Ethics* (forthcoming), https://papers.ssrn.com/abstract=3173810, 43.
9. "Takeover Defences Will Not Stop Short-Termism," editorial, *Financial Times*, April 11, 2018.
10. "A New Chapter," *Economist*, August 15, 2015.
11. Lynn Stout, *The Shareholder Value Myth* (San Francisco: Berrett-Koehler, 2012), 3.
12. Stout, 26.
13. The citation usually referenced for the Friedman is "The Social Responsibility of Business Is to Increase Its Profits," *New York Times Magazine*, September 1970. In fact, Friedman first pronounced the doctrine in 1962 in his book *Capitalism and Freedom* (Chicago: University of Chicago Press, 1962).
14. Andrew Hill, "Twitter Should Not Crush the Idealists and Their Co-op Dream," *Financial Times*, February 13, 2017.
15. Hill.

Chapter 18: Looking Forward: The Prospects for Enlightened Corporate Leadership

1. Paul Hawken, "Commencement: Healing or Stealing," 2009 commencement address, University of Portland, http://www.up.edu/commencement/default.aspx?cid+9456.
2. See especially Marc Benioff and Karen Southwick, *Compassionate*

Capitalism: How Corporations Can Make Good an Integral Part of Doing Well (Franklin Lakes, NJ: Career Press, 2004); Ira Jackson and Jane Nelson, *Profits with Principles: Seven Strategies for Delivering Value with Values* (New York: Doubleday, 2004); Fred Kofman, *Conscious Business: How to Build Value Through Values* (Boulder, CO: Sounds True, 2006); and Rajendra Sisodia, David Wolfe, and Jagdish Seth, *Firms of Endearment: How World-Class Companies Profit from Passion and Purpose* (Philadelphia: Wharton School, 2006). A 2007 *Businessweek* special report, "Beyond the Green Corporation," was subtitled "Imagine a World in Which Eco-Friendly and Socially Responsible Practices Actually Help the Company's Bottom Line. It's Closer Than You Think." Pete Engardio, "Beyond the Green Corporation," *Businessweek*, January 29, 2007, 51–64.

3. Countless books and articles published in recent years have advocated greater corporate social engagement and documented exemplary practices—particularly with regard to climate change, pollution, and working conditions in the developing world. See especially C. K. Prahalad and S. L. Hart, "The Fortune at the Bottom of the Pyramid," *Strategy+Business*, no. 26 (2002): 54–67; Andrew W. Savitz, *The Triple Bottom Line: How Today's Best-Run Companies Are Achieving Economic, Social and Environmental Success—and How You Can, Too* (San Francisco: Jossey-Bass, 2006); E. Freya Williams, *Green Giants: How Smart Companies Turn Sustainability into Billion-Dollar Businesses* (New York: AMACOM, 2015); and John Mackey and Raj Sisodia, *Conscious Capitalism* (Cambridge, MA: Harvard Business School Press, 2013). Also see chapters by Sandra Waddock, Chris Laszlo, Philip Mirvis, Stuart Hart, Jette Steen-Knudsen, Bruce Hutton and Tricia Olson, and Andrew Hoffman and John Ehrenfeld in *Corporate Stewardship: Achieving Sustainable Effectiveness*, ed. Susan Albers Mohrman, James O'Toole, and Edward E. Lawler III (Sheffield, UK: Greenleaf, 2015).

4. Scheherazade Daneshkhu and Lionel Barber, "Foiling a Hostile Takeover," *Financial Times*, December 4, 2017.

5. Scheherazade Daneshkhu, "Unilever Uses Deals Strategy to Enter Niche Markets," *Financial Times*, December 1, 2017.

6. Andrew Edgecliffe-Johnson, "Unilever Chief Regrets Wooing Investors," *Financial Times*, February 28, 2018.

7. Pasresh Dave, "At Dollar Shave, a Struggle to Stay on Cutting Edge," *Los Angeles Times*, September 3, 2017.

8. Andrew Hill, "Complacency Will Eat the Heart Out of Whole Foods," *Financial Times*, May 1, 2017.

9. Eduardo Porter, "Motivating Corporations to Do Good," *New York Times*, July 16, 2014.

10. Dave Eggers, *The Circle* (New York: Knopf, 2013).

11. Leslie Hook, "Alphabet Draws Up Plans to Build City of the Future," *Financial Times*, September 15, 2017.
12. Kirk O. Hanson, "The Long History of Conscious Capitalism," *California Management Review* 53, no. 3 (Spring 2011): 77.
13. John Mackey, "Creating a New Paradigm for Business," in Michael Strong, *Be the Solution: How Entrepreneurs and Conscious Capitalists Can Solve All the World's Problems* (Hoboken, NJ: John Wiley & Sons, 2009).
14. Quoted in Nick Paumgarten, "Food Fighter: Does Whole Foods' C.E.O. Know What's Best for You?" *New Yorker*, January 4, 2010.
15. John Mackey, "What Conscious Capitalism Really Is," *California Management Review* 53, no. 3 (Spring 2011): 86–87.
16. Mackey, 90.
17. James O'Toole and David Vogel, "Two and a Half Cheers for Conscious Capitalism," *California Management Review* 53, no. 3 (Spring 2011): 60–76.
18. Gary Hirshberg, "How to Make Money and Save the World," address given at "Conceptualizing Conscious Capitalism" conference, Bentley College, Waltham, MA, May 24, 2010.
19. Rajendra Sisodia, "Conscious Capitalism: A Better Way to Win," *California Management Review* 53, no. 3 (Spring 2011): 105.
20. O'Toole and Vogel, "Two and a Half Cheers," 73.
21. Alice Troy-Donovan, "The Homeless and the Upper House," *Financial Times*, House and Home section, 13–14, January 12, 2018.
22. Eduardo Porter, "Motivating Corporations to Do Good," *New York Times*, July 16, 2014.
23. James Surowiecki, "Companies with Benefits," *New Yorker*, August 4, 2014, 23.
24. Ryan Honeyman, *The B Corp Handbook* (San Francisco: Berrett-Koehler, 2014), 174.
25. Andrew Ward, "Green Bonds Boom Brings Growing Pains," *Financial Times*, 2017.
26. Paul Sullivan, "How to Invest with a Conscience (and Still Make Money)," *New York Times*, March 17, 2018; Ron Lieber, "Why It's So Hard to Invest with a Social Conscience," *New York Times*, March 3, 2018.
27. Andrew Ross Sorkin, "A Feel-Good Index Now Has a Fund," *New York Times*, June 12, 2018, B2.
28. "More Ethical Dilemmas for Norway's Oil Fund," *Financial Times*, March 8, 2018.
29. "Not Its Own Reward," *Economist*, September 23, 2017, 67.
30. Stephen Davidoff Solomon, "The Thorny Task of Advocating Good Corporate Behavior," *New York Times*, March 24, 2015.
31. Andrew Ross Sorkin, "Big Investors Could Sway Gunmakers," *New York Times*, March 6, 2018.

32. Jonathan Ford, "Shareholder Primacy Lies at Heart of Modern Governance Problem," *Financial Times*, March 5, 2018.
33. Rana Foroohar, "The Backlash against Shareholder Value," *Financial Times*, March 5, 2018.
34. Foroohar.
35. Aaron Chatterji, "The Power of C.E.O. Activism," *New York Times*, April 3, 2016; Jena McGregor, "Millennials Want CEOs Talking on Social Issues," *Los Angeles Times*, July 30, 2017.
36. Schumpeter, "Social Saints, Fiscal Fiends," *Economist*, January 2, 2016, 52.
37. Richard Conniff, "Why We Don't Vote with Our Wallets," *New York Times*, October 22, 2017, Sunday Review.
38. Philip H. Mirvis, "Stewardship and Human Resources Management: From Me to We to All of Us," in Mohrman, O'Toole, and Lawler, *Corporate Stewardship*, 134–55.
39. Patrick Jenkins, "Gaping Pay Divide between Head Honchos and the Hired Help," *Financial Times*, March 27, 2018.
40. David Gelles, "Want to Make Money Like a C.E.O.? Work for 275 Years. A Telling Look at Income Inequality," *New York Times*, Sunday Business, May 27, 2018, 1.
41. Attracta Mooney, "Managers 'Asleep at the Wheel' over Executive Pay," *Financial Times*, March 5, 2018.
42. Patricia Cohen, "The Raise That Roared," *New York Times*, August 2, 2015, Sunday Business.

Conclusion: *Difficile Est Bonum Esse*

1. Sarah O'Conner, "Jaguar Land Rover Lay-Offs Highlight the Plight of UK's Temporary Workers," *Financial Times*, May 2, 2018, 9.
2. James O'Toole and Edward E. Lawler III, *The New American Workplace* (New York: Palgrave Macmillan, 2006).
3. James O'Toole, *Work in America* (Cambridge, MA: MIT Press, 1973).
4. Edmund Phelps, "What Is Wrong with the West's Economies?" *New York Review of Books*, August 13, 2015, 54–56.

INDEX

Adair, Douglass, 484n30
Adams, Ansel, 322, 323
Adams, John Quincy, 4–5
Adler, Mortimer, 411
agency theory, 424, 439
Albert, King of Belgium, 59–60
Alger, Horatio, 33
Allen, Woody, 323
Amazon, 447–48, 467
American Cast Iron Pipe Company
    (ACIPCO), 135–44, 476
    African American workers at, 141, 142
    board of directors, members of,
        140–41
    company ownership and, 139–40, 406,
        433, 436
    company's constitution, 140–41, 143
    competitor McWane's OSHA
        violations and, 142
    co-op store, 138
    Eagan as first president, 136
    Eagan's philosophy of business
        stewardship and, 136, 138
    Eagan's three principles and, 138
    employee advisory board, 138, 141
    employee benefits, 138, 140
    employee housing, 138
    employee medical services, 142–43
    employee ownership, 139–40, 406
    employees on board of directors, 138,
        140
    employee training and education, 142
    employee turnover, 142
    employer-employee relations, Golden
        Rule applied, 138
    ethical values and principles, 141
    on Fortune's 100 Best Companies to
        work for list, 142
    governance, 140–41
    Great Depression and, 141
    growth, 141
    guaranteed employment, 138
    legacy of, 138
    paying a living wage, 138, 139
    profit-sharing and, 139

    rediscovery by media and public,
        141–43
    reinvestment of profits at, 140
    sustainability of business model,
        143–44, 433
    women workers, 138
    work day and, 138
    working conditions, 138, 142
American Express, 280, 282
Anderson, Robert O., 305–6, 311
Annan, Kofi, 451
Antinori family, 396
Apple, 444, 449, 463
Aptiv, 469–70
Arco (Atlantic Richfield Corporation),
    305–13, 424, 426
    acquired by BP, 312
    Bradshaw as president, 305, 306–13
    CEO Anderson's rogue behavior and,
        311
    CEO Cook and, 312
    community relations, 312
    corporate governance, 308
    creation of, 306
    creative philanthropy of, 307, 311, 312
    employee benefits extended to same-
        sex partners, 307
    environmental practices, 307–8
    ethics audit at, 308, 386
    headquarters, Los Angeles, 307
    implosion of, 312
    innovation and, 310
    long-term thinking and, 310
    profitability and, 310
    public positions of, 309–11
    social responsibility, 307–9
    Town Hall Los Angeles, 308
    women, minorities, and, 308, 309
Arden, Elizabeth, 347
Aristotle
    humans as "social animals," xxii
    thoughts about human development,
        431
    virtue-based ethics, 315
Arizmendi, 416, 417

Arizmendiarrieta, José, 417
Arkwright, Richard, 4, 9
Ashoka, 456
automation, 475
Avis rent-a-car company, 279, 426, 427
    acquired by ITT, 284
    annual sales and profits, 284
    employee stock ownership plan, 281
    employee training, 283
    humanistic philosophy of
        management, 284
    stock price, 282
    Townsend and famous commercial,
        279, 280–81
    Townsend and just compensation
        system, 281
    Townsend heads, 281, 282–84
    Townsend leaves, 284–85
    Townsend's business practices, 281
    Townsend stops executive perks, 281

Balance Bars, 404
Bancroft, Ronald, 411
Bank of America, 312–13
Barrett, Colleen, 289–90, 292, 293–94, 296
Bartlett, Christopher, 358
Batten, William, 48, 49
B Corp Handbook, The (Honeyman), 458
B corporation movement, 403, 456–59. See
    also Benefit corporations
Belgian Congo, 59–60
Ben & Jerry's, 65, 349, 376–94, 426, 427,
    432, 497n29, 504n1
    battle with Pillsbury, 381–82, 388
    Burlington, Vt. and, 377
    CEOs under Unilever, 392–93
    Cherry Garcia flavor, 387
    Cohen's marketing and, 379, 381, 389
    community relations, 378, 383, 386,
        387, 388, 393
    company ownership and, 380, 387, 436
    early stumbles, 378–80
    employee compensation, 384
    employee complaints, addressing, 387
    employee satisfaction and, 389
    environmental practices and, 384–86
    ethics and, 384
    first location, 377–78
    Forbes's 200 Best Small Companies in
        America list and, 389
    founding of, 377
    franchising scoop shops, 379
    Greenfield returns full-time, 386–87
    "Green Team," 386
    growth of, 379, 389
    Lacy as CEO, 389–90
    Lager as president and CEO, 381, 383,
        389
    leadership search at, 390
    line of low-fat, low-calorie ice creams,
        393
    line of "Orgasmic Flavors," 378
    mission statement, 382–83
    products, 376, 381
    profitability and, 382–83, 384, 387,
        388, 389
    promise of "shared prosperity,"
        383–84
    public offering of stock, 383
    selling to supermarkets, 379
    social audit, 386
    social responsibility and, 383–84,
        387–88, 393
    Solheim as CEO and return to values,
        393–94
    transition to professional management,
        388–90
    Unilever takeover of, 390–94, 454
Ben & Jerry's Foundation, 384, 391
Ben & Jerry's: The Inside Scoop (Lager), 384,
    504n1
Benefit corporations, 391, 403, 456–59
Benioff, Marc, 444
Bennett, Richard, 234
Bennis, Warren, 279, 304
    on Townsend, 286–87
Bentham, Jeremy, 27, 30, 430
Berg, Norbert, 257–58, 260
Bertelsmann publishing, 434, 507n7
Bethlehem Steel Company, 267–68
Beyster, Robert, 395, 413–14, 427, 428, 430,
    435, 436
Bharti Enterprises, xxxix
Bill & Melinda Gates Foundation, xxxviii,
    340
Bird, John, 456
B Lab, 457
BlackRock, xiv, 461, 470
    gun company stock and, 461–62
Body and Soul (Roddick), 347, 355
Body Shop, 346–59, 432
    Body Shop School, 353

community relations, 351, 352, 359
community service and employees, 351
Community Trade program, 351–52
customers and, 352–53
employees and, 351, 352, 353–54
environmental audit and, 349
fair-trade sourcing, 351
first store and products, 346–47
first U.S. store, 354
franchising, 348
honest labels, 347–48
inner-city factory opened, 352
L'Oréal sells to Natura Cosmetics, 359
L'Oréal takeover, 357–59, 392, 395, 454
minority hiring at, 352
mission statement, 347
profitability and, 349, 351
public offering of stock, 348–49
recruitment and, 353
sales and earnings, 354, 356
second store, 348
social responsibility and, 349–54
stock price, 349
Bolt, Robert, *A Man for All Seasons*, xlii
Bolton, UK, 52, 56–57, 64
Bonanos, Christopher, 324, 328
BP (British Petroleum), 312, 429
Bradshaw, Thornton, 427, 428, 477
    accolades for, 311–12
    Arco and, 305–13
    background and personal life, 305–6
    capitalism and, 310
    as CEO of RCA Corporation, 311
    death of, 311
    long-term thinking and, 310
    public positions of, 309–11
    on what influences his decisions, 306–7
Brinkley, Ian, 133
Brokaw, Tom, 403
Buffett, Warren, 399
Bunn, John, xliii
Burke, James, 163–74, 364, 427, 451, 477
    background and personal life, 164–65
    board member, various companies, 174
    Bob Johnson and, 165, 166
    Catholic ethical teachings and, 164
    Credo Challenge, 163, 167–71, 172
    death of, 174

early years at J&J, 165–67
    Fortune ranking, 174
    Harvard Business School and, 164–65
    institutionalization of practices, 435
    J&J corporate culture and, 174
    J&J growth under, 173
    as J&J president and CEO, 167–74
    leadership philosophy of, 171
    Medal of Freedom award, 174
    Tylenol crisis and, 165–66, 171–74
    virtuous behavior, 164
Burlington, Vt., 377, 385
Burnham, Daniel, 76, 77, 78
Business and Sustainable Development Commission, xl
    Better Business, Better World, xl
Business Enterprise Trust (BET), 451
business orthodoxy through history, xxi–xxxviii
    businesses as small, xxii
    caste hierarchies, xxii
    common motivation for all great business figures, xxxiv
    division of labor, xxi–xxii
    feudal systems, xxii
    in medieval Europe, xxii
    merchant of Prato and the dominant mode of business thought, xxiii–xxvi
    philanthropy, late-career, xxvi–xxxiii
    profit motive and, xxiii, xxiv, xxvi, xxxiv
    proto-capitalist activities, xxii
    realists' case against business enlightenment, xxxiv–xxxviii
    in the Renaissance, xxii, xxiii
    trade and craft guilds, xxii
    trading and bartering, xxi–xxii
BusinessWeek, 425
    why CDC failed, 261–62

Cadbury, George
    chocolate factory, 84
    model town: Bournbrook, 84
    as Quaker, 77, 84
Callahan, Tom, 34
CalPERS (the California Public Employees' Retirement System), 460–61
Calvinism, 11, 17–18, 31
Camellia PLC, 434
Campbell Soup, 444, 448

capitalism
    benefits for society, xxxv
    Bradshaw and, 310
    "caring capitalism," 497n29
    Continental European and Asian, xv
    creation of wealth and advancement of
        civilization, xxxiv–xxxv
    defined, 395
    "exit money" and, 409
    Fugger's contribution, xxv
    Lewis's new type of, 122–23, 132
    Lincoln and, 132
    Mackey's CC and saving, 452–53
    Mill and, 132
    Owen's reforms and non-exploitive
        capitalism, 6, 16, 22, 132
    profit motive, xxxiv, xxxv, xxxvi, 16–17,
        21, 113–14
    proto-capitalist activities in the
        Renaissance, xxii, xxiii
    rioting in 1877 against practices, 31
    Shaw's *Major Barbara* and, 70
    types of, xv, 396
Carillion corporation, 462
Carlsberg, 434, 507n7
Carnegie, Andrew, xxvii, xxix–xxxiii, 81,
    265, 267, 464
    Eagan influenced by, 136
    economies of scale and, xxx
    "The Gospel of Wealth," xxxi–xxxii
    Homestead strike and, xxxii
    late-life philanthropy of, xxxiii, xxxvii
    motivation for philanthropy, xxix,
        xxxii
    paternalism and, xxxvii
    as "The richest man who ever lived,"
        xxxiii
    as union buster, xxix, xxxi, xxxii
    US Steel and, xxx–xxxii
Carroll, Charles, 301
Cartwright, Edmund, 9
Carver Korea, 445
Cathy, Dan, 464
Caux Round Table, 452
CH2M Hill, 406
chain stores, 34
    A&P grocery chain, 35
    J. C. Penney and, 34–35
    John Lewis Partnership, 120
    manager partnerships, 35–37
    Marks & Spencer and, 210

    origins of, 35
    Woolworths, 210
    See also specific companies
Chaparrel Steel, 286, 424
Chapman, William, 209, 223
Chappell, Kate, 360, 365, 366–67, 368, 372
Chappell, Tom, 342, 404, 428, 431
    attempts to "do good while doing
        well," 361–64, 365
    awards and kudos, 368
    Christian values and managerial
        philosophy, 360, 361, 428
    company ownership and, 365, 368,
        369–70
    compared to De Pree, 365–66
    contradictions of, 367–68
    critics of, 373–74
    intentionality of business virtue, 365
    "the middle way" of pursuing "profit
        and the common good," 368–70
    motive for selling the business, 372
    Ramblers Way, 372
    sells to Colgate, 371–75, 395, 403, 427
    The Soul of a Business, 361–62, 367–68
    storytelling to convey company
        culture, 365–66
    Tom's of Maine and, 360–75
    "Tom's of Maine Statement of Beliefs,"
        363
Charles V, Emperor, xxv, xxvi
Chicago World's Columbian Exposition, 76
    Machinery Building, 77
Chick-fil-A, 464
child labor
    Asian subcontracting and, 203
    fortunes built on, 23
    J&J's prohibition on, 148
    Lever Bros. prohibition on, 57
    Nike's contractors and, 425
    Owen's reforms and, 13, 22–23
    textile mills and, 3–4, 5–6, 12
Chouinard, Malinda, 402
Chouinard, Yves, 395, 404, 428
    as billionaire, 403
    as the "capitalist cat," 403
    critics of, 401
    the "eminence green," 401, 403
    management practices, 402
    Patagonia and, 400–403
Churchill, Winston, 59, 473
Ciepley, David, 434

Circle, The (Eggers), 449–50
Citigroup, 260
City Beautiful movement, 78
City National Bank, Miami, Fla., 44, 45
Clemens, Samuel, xxxii
    "The Gilded Age," 31
Cleveland, Ohio, 418–19
Clif Bar & Company, 457
Clinton, Bill, 174
Close, Chuck, 322, 326–27
CoBank, 416
Cohen, Ben, 376–94, 426, 427, 428, 436,
    464
    background and personal life, 376–77
    Cherry Garcia flavor, 387
    company ownership and, 380, 436
    discord and, 390
    founding of Ben & Jerry's, 377
    handles sales of Ben & Jerry's, 379
    hires Fred "Chico" Lager, 381
    learning the business, 377–79
    as marketing maven, 379, 381, 389
    social activism and, 387–88, 394, 451
    social responsibility and, 383
    Unilever and, 394
Cole, Margaret, 18
Coleridge, Samuel Taylor, 10
Colgate-Palmolive Company
    acquires Tom's of Maine, 371–75, 392
    short-termism of executives, 374
    "social audit," 372
    traditional business model, 374
Collins, David, 168, 170, 172
Columbus, Ind., 313, 315
    architects designing buildings for, 315
community relations
    Arco and, 312
    Ben & Jerry's and, 378, 383, 386, 387,
        388, 393
    Body Shop and, 351, 352, 359
    CDC and, 250, 252
    cooperatives and, 415
    Friedman on, 439, 507n13
    Hershey and, 83, 90
    J&J and, 157, 161
    John Lewis Partnership and, 122, 131,
        132
    Kodak and, 328
    Levi Strauss and, 183–85, 200, 201–2
    Lincoln Electric and, 110, 113, 116
    Marks & Spencer and, 213

Nucor and, 273
Penney and, 46
SRC Holdings and, 409
SWA and, 296
Tom's of Maine and, 362, 365, 366,
    370, 371, 374
Unilever and, 66
Wegman's Food Markets and, 397
Companies with a Conscience (Scott and
    Rothman), 497n29
competitive advantage
    economies of scale and, 37
    employee benefits and, xlii
    ethical behavior and, xlii
    Kelleher and SWA's culture, 295
    Nucor's "mini-mills," 266
    Penney's and, 37–40, 48
    social engagement activities as, 443
*Condition of the Working Class in England,
    The* (Engels), 5
Conniff, Richard, 467
Conscious Capitalism (CC) movement,
    xxxix, 452–56
"consensus management," 126
Container Store, 455
contingent workforces, 473–76
Control Data Corporation (CDC), 243–63,
    395, 424
    acquisitions and diversifications,
        247–48
    antitrust suit against IBM, 245–46
    Berg and management of, 257–58
    City Venture Corporation created, 254
    Commercial Credit Corporation and,
        247, 260
    community relations, 250, 252
    Control Data Institute (CDI) learning
        centers, 255–56
    Cray departs, 246
    employee day-care center, 252–53
    Employment Preparation Service
        created for training, 253–54
    expansion and growth, 257
    failure as a consequence of virtuous
        practices, 260–62, 327, 427
    failure of company, 260–61, 395
    Fair Break, 254
    founding of, 244
    gaffs in Iran and South Africa, 256–57
    headquarters, Minneapolis, 248
    incorporation of, 244

Control Data Corporation (CDC) (*cont.*)
    inner-city plants closed, 260
    layoffs at, 260
    Medlab, 254
    minority hiring at, 251–54
    Norris leaves, 258–60
    Norris's attention on social mission,
        261
    Norris's business model, 249–54
    Norris's ideas and, 248
    peripherals of, 247–48
    Perlman as CEO, 260
    plants opened in high-poverty areas,
        251–54
    PLATO education technology,
        254–57, 260, 261
    poor financial performance, 259
    Price and management of, 257–58, 260
    profits and, 250
    remnants of the company, 260
    Rural Ventures, Inc., 254
    selling off of subsidiaries, 260
    size, revenue, and profits (1970), 247
    social responsibility and, 249, 250–51,
        254
    stock of, 248
    success of, 245
    Ticketron and, 248, 260
    training and, 252, 253–54, 255
    United School Services of America
        and, 257
    women hired at, 251, 252
Cook, Lodwrick, 312
Cook, Tim, 444, 463–64
Cooper, Francis D'Arcy, 64
Co-Operative Bank, 417
cooperative movement, 29, 41, 133, 415,
    417–18
cooperatives, 415–19, 440, 476
    artist co-ops, 416
    B corporation movement and, 458
    business practices of, 415
    Cleveland Model, 418–19
    community relations, 415
    consumer co-ops, 416
    credit unions, 419
    critics of, 417
    employment numbers, 418
    examples of, 415–16
    financing problems for, 417
    governance issues, 417

    idealism and, 416–17
    ignored by financial media and
        business schools, 415
    Mondragón, Spain and, 417, 418, 440
    mutual companies, 419
    new, in the U.S., 419
    in the UK, 418
Co-Opportunity Natural Foods, 415
corporate citizenship, 312, 439, 443
    consortia of enlightened capitalists
        and, 451–56
corporate philanthropy, 54, 250, 307, 311,
    312–13, 439, 466
corporations/corporate capitalism, xi, xii,
    xiii, xiv, xx, xxxvi, xxxix, 46, 396, 437
    activist investors and, xli, 447
    agency theory and, 424, 439
    Anglo-American vs. Continental
        European and Asian capitalism, xv
    aristocracy of top executives, 398
    compatibility of virtuous business
        practices and, 420, 441, 442,
        444–48, 454–55, 478
    consequences for democracy of
        corporate do-goodism, xxxvii
    contingent workforces, 473–76
    criticism of the film industry and,
        xxxvi
    deliberate cessation of successful,
        socially desirable practices, xiii (*see
        also* Body Shop; J. C. Penney; Lever
        Bros.; Levi Strauss & Co.; Tom's of
        Maine; Whole Foods)
    Dodd-Frank legislation, impact on
        board members, 462
    Dodge v. Ford Motor Company and,
        113–15, 438
    economic growth and standard of
        living, xxxv
    economies of scale and, 440
    environmental issues, responses to,
        443, 459
    ethical investing and, 459
    future of, 473
    history of, xxii
    hollow virtual corporations, 473–75,
        477
    "impact" or ESG (environmental, social,
        governance) investors, 459–60
    Johnson's *Or Forfeit Freedom* and,
        153–55

new social contract for, xiv–xv
opposition to corporate do-goodism,
    xxxvi, xxxvii
"primacy of shareholder value," xli,
    113–14, 373, 395, 423–24, 425,
    438–39
proponents of corporate do-goodism,
    xxxviii–xl
separation of "ownership" from
    professional management and, 47
shareholder response to corporate
    misconduct, 429
short-termism of executives, xiv,
    67–68, 113, 115, 116, 197–98, 268,
    281, 395, 423, 446
socially virtuous practices and, xiii, xiv,
    xxxvi, xlii, 373, 438, 476
Up the Organization and management,
    280
*See also specific business leaders; specific
    companies*
Correnti, John, 275–76
Costco, 197
    controlling labor costs at, 101
Couette, Yves, 391
Cousteau, Jacques, 307
Cray, Seymour, 244–45, 246
Cray Research, 246
credit unions, 419
Crompton, Samuel, 4, 9
Cummins Engine Corporation, 313, 314–19,
    424, 426
    company ownership and, 317, 395
    environmental practices, 316–17
    ethics-focused organizational culture,
        315–16
    expansion of, 315
    financial and environmental problems
        under Schacht, 318–19
    headquarters, Columbus, Ind., 315
    hiring practices, 316, 317–18
    labor unions and, 316
    minority hiring at, 316
    "organizational entropy" and, 319
    profitability and, 315
    Schacht as CEO, 318
    test of values (2010), 319
customers
    Body Shop and, 352–53
    corporate social responsibility and,
        xxxviii–xxxix

Herman Miller Company and, 237
John Lewis Partnership and, 128
Lewis and, 122
Lincoln's philosophy and, 96
Marks & Spencer and, 210, 211–12,
    213–17
no consumer demand for virtue, 429
Nucor and, 275
Owen's ethical practices and, 8, 19
Penney and Penney Principles, 33,
    37–39, 45–46
SWA and, 293–94

Dale, David, 11–12, 27
Dalton, John, 10
Dana, 424
D'Antonio, Michael, 80, 92, 489n
    Hershey, 489n
Datini, Francesco (the Merchant of Prato),
    xxii, xxiii–xxv, xxxvii, xlii, 362, 396, 444
    double-entry bookkeeping, xxiii
    foundation established by, xxv
    historical record of, xxiii
    motto of, xxiii
Davids, Bob, 285–86
Davis, Jacob, 176–77, 179
Davis, Simon, 179–80
"Davos Conscience," xii
Davos World Economic Forum, 461
    2018: social responsibility discussion,
        xiv
Dayton-Hudson (now Target), 424
Deere, 424
Deere, John, xxxiii
Defoe, Daniel, 3, 4
Della Femina, Jerry, 172
Del Monte, 470
De Pree, Dirk Jan (D.J.), 227–30
    entrepreneurial skills, 228
    founding of Herman Miller Company,
        227
    human-centered organizational
        culture and, 229–30
    legacy of, 228–30
    religious motivation for virtuous
        practices, 227–28
De Pree, Hugh, 230
De Pree, Max, 318, 323, 427
    Chappell compared to, 365–66
    Christian values and managerial
        philosophy, 227–28, 231, 360, 365

De Pree, Max (*cont.*)
    employee relationships as
        "covenantal," 231
    ethical principle of respect, 235–36
    Herman Miller Company and, 227–42
    institutionalization of practices, 435
    intellectual influences on, 430
    Leadership Is an Art, 231
    "organizational entropy" and, 242,
        319, 426
    retirement from the Herman Miller
        board, 240
    "servant leadership" and, 233, 317
    "theory fastball" (philosophy of
        enlightened leadership), 228,
        231–38
    "tribal story telling," 231, 365, 366
Dewhirst, I. J., 207, 211
Digital Equipment Corporation (DEC), 424
Dillon Read & Company, 330
Dimon, Jamie, 470
Disney, 470
Dodge, John and Horace, 114
Dodge v. Ford Motor Company, 113–15, 438
Dollar Shave, 446
Don't Ask the Price (M. Sieff), 217
Do the KIND Thing (Lubetzky), 404
"Dough Boy" (Johnson), 155
Drayton, Bill, 456
Drucker, Peter, 154, 214, 430, 431
Dubin, Michael, 446
Dupont, 297–98
Durgin, Kit, 194
Dutch Access to Medicine Foundation
    ranking of pharma firms, 340–41
Dutch East India Company, 46–47

Eagan, John Joseph
    ACIPCO and, 135–44
    African Americans and, 137, 141, 142,
        143
    background and early career, 135–36
    Carnegie's influence, 136
    Christian values and managerial
        philosophy, 136–37, 139, 141, 360,
        428
    company ownership and, 144
    death of, 143
    establishes Commission on Interracial
        Cooperation (CIC), 137–38
    Golden Rule and, 137, 138

    health problems, 139
    lasting legacy of, 143–44
    leaves his company stock in trust for
        employees, 139–40, 433
    legacy of, 138
    legal arrangements to cap maximum
        payout to shareholders, 139
    profit-sharing and, 139
    on the purpose of business, 141
    as social reformer, 137
    stakeholder approach to management,
        138–39
    workplace practices, reason for, 431–32
Eames, Charles, 228, 231, 323
Eames, Ray, 323
Eastman, George, 328
Eastman Kodak, 112
"Economic Possibilities of Our
    Grandchildren, The" (Keynes), xxxv
economic progressivism, 33
Economist
    corporate misconduct, response to,
        429
    criticism of John Lewis Partnership,
        133, 134
    governance and ownership, 435
    Owen's ideas and, 20
Edison, Thomas, xxxiii, 146
    social contributions of, xxxviii
education
    ACIPCO training and tuition
        remission, 142
    Body Shop School, 353
    CDC's PLATO and, 254–57
    CDC training, 252, 253–54, 255
    Herman Miller Company career-long
        education and training, 230
    Hershey and tuition-free community
        college, 88
    Hershey Industrial School, 82–83, 86,
        87, 89
    human capital and, 15
    John Lewis Partnership adult
        education program, 127
    Johnson on, 159–60
    Lever's free courses, 57
    Marks & Spencer and, 212
    Nucor's scholarship program, 276
    opposition to worker education, 23
    Owen's reforms and, 13, 15–16, 23, 27
    Penney's free courses, 43

Rowntree and tuition-free schooling, 84
SRC Holdings and, 407
Eggers, Dave, *The Circle*, 449–50, 476
Ellison, Larry, xxxviii
Emerson, Ralph Waldo, 29
employee ownership, 117n, 123, 405–20, 476
ACIPCO and, 139–40, 406
Avis and, 281
B corporation movement and, 458
benefits of, 406
cooperatives, 415–19
critics of, 133
direct ownership, 406
ESOPs (employee stock ownership
plans), 406, 410–11, 472
failures, 410–11, 413–14
governance challenge, 411, 413–14
Herman Miller Company and, 230,
234, 406
how *not* to run employee-owned firms,
409–13
J. C. Penney and, 35–37, 406
John Lewis Partnership and, 124–28,
132, 406
Lever Bros. and, 58–60, 405
Levi Strauss and, 189, 192, 193
Lincoln Electric, 8, 101–3, 406
number of U.S. companies, 412
perception of, 412
performance of, 412
Polaroid Corporation and, 326
SAIC and, 413–14
SRC Holdings and, 407–9
SWA and, 290, 406
types of, 406
UPS and, 409–10
W. L. Gore & Associates and, 300–301,
406
See also profit-sharing
employees, xiv
ACIPCO and, 138, 139–40
American companies introducing
enlightened labor practices, 112
Arco and, 307, 308, 309
Avis and, 281
Ben & Jerry's and, 384, 387, 389
Body Shop and, 351, 352, 353–54
British textile mills, 3–5
Carnegie's workers, xxxii
community service and, 185, 213, 218,
296, 351, 409, 469

companies providing health care vs.
companies that do not, xlii
contingent workforces, 473–76
corporate socialism and, 432
egalitarian work environments, 274
family-owned businesses and, 396–97
Ford's workers, xxviii
globalization and, xl
group life and health insurance for,
112, 138, 212, 307, 454, 470
Herman Miller Company and, 234–37,
241
human development and, 15–16, 23,
96–97, 100, 474
J&J and, 159–60
job security or guaranteed
employment, 13, 40, 81, 94, 95, 97,
103–5, 111, 112, 118, 154
John Lewis Partnership and, 124–30
Lever and, 57–58
Levi Strauss and, 178, 181, 183,
185–86, 196, 199–200, 202
Lincoln Electric and, 94–95, 98
Lincoln's "the development of latent
ability" and, 96–97, 100
Marks & Spencer and, 210, 211, 212,
216, 219
Marvin Windows and Doors, 396–97
Merck & Co., 338
Nucor Corporation, 267–68, 271–72,
274–77
Owen's ethical practices and, 8, 13–14,
18, 20, 27
Patagonia and, 400, 402
paying a living wage and, 85, 138, 139,
150, 154, 157, 401
Penney and, 38–40
pensions/retirement homes, 18, 112,
138, 183
Polaroid Corporation and, 323
pressure from for ethical and
community-spirited organizations,
469
Scanlon plan and, 228–29
social engagement by, 469
SRC Holdings and, 407–9
SWA and, 289–93, 296
Tom's of Maine and, 365, 366, 372
Wegman's Food Markets, 396
W. L. Gore & Associates and, 298–300
Encyclopaedia Britannica, 434

Engels, Friedrich, 5, 6
  on Bolton, UK, 52
  The Condition of the Working Class in England, 5
  criticism of Owen, 6–7, 25
  "immiseration" of mill workers, 5
  as wealthy capitalist, 25
enlightened capitalists, xii, xv, xvii
  advent of consortia of enlightened capitalists, 451–56
  American companies introducing enlightened labor practices, 112
  American companies withdrawing enlightened labor practices, 112
  American Vanguard Corporations in 1985 (list), 424
  arguments against, 119
  balance between virtue and greed, 342, 404
  business publications and shift in editorial emphasis, 425
  change in investor attitudes, 459–62
  characteristics of, xii, xix–xxi
  commitment of, xxi
  common fear of, 433
  compatibility with shareholder capitalism, 420, 441, 442, 444–48, 454–55, 478
  "Difficile est bonum esse," xliii–xliv, 426, 472, 473–78
  doing good and doing well, xii, 251, 361, 404, 420, 428, 443, 453
  emergence of new forms of enlightened practices in the tech world, 449–51
  emerging generation of enlightened and effective business leaders, 444–48
  ethical compasses of, xii, xx
  failure to produce sufficient profits and, 263
  future prospects for, 442–72, 473, 478
  generalizations about, 428–49
  governance of companies and, 433–36
  historical perspectives on, xliv
  as iconoclasts, xxi
  idealists' case for, xxxviii–xl
  institutionalization of practices, 435–36
  intellectual influences and historical contexts, 430–33
  investor resistance, 446–48

  MBA programs and, 424–25
  McGregor's ideas and, 229
  motivations for, xvi, xx, 420, 427–28
  as the new norm, xl
  new social contract for, xv
  no consumer demand for virtue, 429
  "organizational entropy" and, 242, 319, 426
  ownership of companies and, xli, 16–17, 46, 64, 427, 433, 436–40
  policies underlying, xvi
  as practical idealists, xli
  practices of, not adopted by others, 427
  primary value of, xx
  private companies and, 396–420
  profitability and, 442
  public concerns and increasing social engagement, 463–72
  questions for business leaders, xli–xliii
  realists' case against business enlightenment, xxxiv–xxxviii
  reasons for unsustainability, 426, 427
  Roddick's statement on, 357
  salaries of, 471
  Shavian perspective, 68–70
  shift toward traditional modes of business thinking, reasons for, 423–44
  social entrepreneurship and benefit corporations, 404–5, 456–59
  social mission and company failure, 426–27
  as solution to social problems, 258–59
  Stieff and Haas as last of the pioneers, 223
  strategies of, xvi
  sustainability of business model, xiii, xvi, xxi, 50, 241–42, 420, 423, 424, 433, 437, 440
  sustainability of business model: ACIPCO, 143–44, 433
  sustainability of business model: John Lewis Partnership, 120–35, 433
  sustainability of business model: Lincoln Electric, 94–119, 424, 433
  sustainability of business model: Nucor, 277–79
  sustainability of business model: W. L. Gore & Associates, 302–3, 424, 433

three factors accounting for differences
  in philosophies and practices,
  429–30
Unilever and, 65–68
unusual business philosophies, xvi, xx
what history shows, 423–41
"What's a business for?" queried, xliv
See also specific business leaders
Enlightenment ideas, 8–9, 10, 11, 15, 430
Enron, xvii, 466, 468
environmental issues, xi, xiv, xv, xx, xxxviii–
  xxxix
  Arco and, 307–8
  Ben & Jerry's and, 384–86, 393–94
  Chappell and Tom's of Maine and, 342,
    360, 367, 368
  Cummins Engine Corporation and,
    316–17, 318
  diesel engines and EPA rules, 318
  global warming, xxxviii, xl, 432, 442
  "green bonds" and, 459
  greenwashing, 371, 401, 439
  Herman Miller Company and, 237, 241
  John Lewis Partnership and, 132
  Johnson on, 157
  large corporations rejection of, 425
  Lever and, 56–57
  Levi Strauss and, 205
  Marks & Spencer and, 222
  Mars and, 399
  Nucor and, 266, 273, 277–78
  Patagonia and, 400–403
  Polman and, 463
  profit vs. virtue and, xl
  public concern about, 468, 476
  Roddick and, 342–60
  SWA and, 295–96
  Unilever and, 65–66, 393–94
Esquire magazine, article on J. Irwin Miller,
  313
ethical business practices
  in an amoral world, xlii
  Arco and, 308
  Ben & Jerry's and, 384
  business leaders vs. unethical
    competitors, xlii
  code of, xi
  Cummins Engine Corporation and,
    315–16
  enlightened capitalists and, xii, xx
  John Lewis Partnership and, 127–28

Levi Strauss and, 181, 187, 205
  Merck & Co. and, 335–39
  Owen and, 8
  Penney and, 32
  pharma firms and misbehavior, 341
  public concern about finance ethics,
    467–68, 476
  self-interest and, xlii
  Townsend and, 285
  virtue vs. profit, xlii
ethical investing, 459–62
  CalPERS and, 460–61
  "impact" or ESG (environmental,
    social, governance) investors,
    459–60
  returns on, 460
Ethics of the Fathers, The (Sieff), 218
Etsy, 263, 457
Evergreen Co-operative Corporation, 418
executives
  aristocracy of, 398
  compensation as stock options, 448
  compensation of, 384, 469–70, 471,
    476
  consortia of enlightened capitalists
    and, 452, 453
  critics of executive social activism,
    xxxvii
  current leaders turning good
    intentions into practice, xxxix
  doing good and, xiv, xxxvi, xxxvii
  emerging generation of enlightened
    and effective business leaders,
    444–48
  "executive activism," 463–64
  highest paid, 469–70
  investors and the addressing of social
    problems, xlii
  Machiavelli's advice to, xlii
  mavericks, 264–303, 304, 477
  paternalism and, xlii
  perks for, 470
  personal philanthropy and, 465–66
  public concern about executive pay,
    469–70, 476
  public demand for social engagement
    and, 463
  questions about enlightened
    capitalism, xli–xliii
  separation of "ownership" from
    professional management and, 47

executives (*cont.*)
    short-termism, xiv, 67–68, 113, 115,
      116, 197–98, 268, 281, 446
    social responsibility and, 448
    as "stewards" of their organizations
      and of the physical environment,
      xxxix, 132, 161–62
    Townsend's "management by
      adultery," 286
    Up the Organization and management,
      280, 286, 287
    virtuous, questions for, 465
    See also specific people
Exxon, 173

fair-trade sourcing, xl, 66, 222, 351, 401,
  425, 443
family-owned businesses, 396–97
    company ownership by family trusts,
      434
    leadership succession problems,
      399–400
    long-term thinking and, 399
    Patagonia, 400–403
    percentage of Fortune 500 companies,
      398
    See also specific companies
Fel-Pro, 424
Ferriola, John, 278
Feuerstein, Aaron, 262–63
Financial Times, 397
    on board responsibility, 462
    caution on private or co-op businesses,
      440
    new social contract editorial, xiv–xv
Fink, Larry, xiv, xv, 461, 470
Fish, Stanley, xxxvi
Fisher, Isaac, 143
Forbes
    on Chouinard, 403
    200 Best Small Companies in America,
      389
Ford, Henry, xxvii, xxviii–xxix, xxxiii, 81,
  157
    employees and, xxviii, xxix, 19–20, 113
    Ford Foundation, xxix
    Fordlandia utopian "social
      experiment," xxviii–xxix
    industrial practices of, 96, 112–13
    late-life philanthropy of, xxix, xxxvii
    motivation to increase sales, xxviii

paternalism of, xxxvii, 113
    as world's first billionaire, xxviii
Ford, Henry, II, 451
Ford Foundation, 459, 461
Ford Motor Company, xxviii, xxxviii,
  112–13, 331, 399
    Dodge v. Ford Motor Company, 113–15
foreign outsourcing, 475
Foroohar, Rana, 397, 462
Fortune magazine, 425
    America's Most Admired Corporations
      list, 230, 294
    on Bob Haas, 205
    Burke on 10 Greatest CEOs of All
      Time list, 192
    CEO pay tables, 469–70
    Iverson lowest paid CEO, 267
    Kelly on W. L. Gore & Associates, 302
    Koch's letter complaining about
      Bradshaw, 309
    "Levi Strauss Burst Its Britches," 192
    100 Best Companies to Work For list,
      142, 301, 398, 449
Forward, Gordon, 286
Foster, Lawrence G., 151
Frazier, Kenneth C., 340, 444, 463
Freeman, Louis, 292
free market economics, 21, 59, 111, 278, 453
Frick, Henry Clay, xxx–xxxi, xxxii
Friedman, Milton, xxxvi, 423, 439, 507n13
Friends of the Earth, 349
Frost, Carl "Jack," 229, 430
Fuerza Unida, 200
Fugger, Jacob, xxv–xxvi, xxx, 444
    "The richest man who ever lived," xxvi,
      xxxiii
    self-penned obituary, xxvi
Fulton, Robert, xxxiii, 10

gainsharing, 229, 277, 408, 472
Gantt, Henry, 431
Gap, 401
Gates, Bill, xxxiii, 465
    late-life philanthropy of, xxxvii–
      xxxviii
Geneen, Harold, 284
General Electric (GE), 42, 112, 311, 466–67
General Motors, xxix, 282
George, Henry, 115
Gerstner, Lou, 174
Gilded Age, 31

Gilmartin, Raymond, 339
    Vioxx scandal and, 339–40
Gladstone, William Ewart, 61
Glasgow, Scotland, 352
Global Strategy Group, 463
Golden Rule stores, 34–35
Goldman, Marcus, 330
Goldman Sachs, 330–34, 426, 433, 460
    growth of, 331
    loss of ethical principles, 334
    public offering of stock, 333
    second careers in philanthropy, 465
    Whitehead's "Business Principles," 332
    Whitehead's concerns about, 333–34
    Whitehead's "quiet leadership," 332
Goodwin, Sir Fred, 133
Google, 449
    Alphabet's Quayside, 450–51
Gore, Bill, 264, 304, 396, 428
    as beloved by associates, 299–300
    at Dupont, 297–98
    organizational system of
        "unmanagement," 298–99
    PTFE and, 297–98
    theory of emergent leadership, 300
    W. L. Gore & Associates and, 298–303
Gore, Vieve, 298, 301
"Gospel of Wealth, The" (Carnegie), xxxi–
    xxxii
Gottlieb, Robert, 283
Graham, Billy, 284
Gravity Payments, 471
Graybar Electric, 406
Great Depression, xi
    ACIPCO and, 141
    Hershey Chocolate Company and, 86,
        88, 103
    J&J and, 149–50
    J. C. Penney and, 45
    Johnson and, 150–52, 154
    Levi Strauss and, 181
    Lincoln Electric and, 100, 103
    Marks & Spencer and, 213
    "Try Reality" (Johnson), 150–51
Great Game of Business, The (Stack), 407
"green bonds," 459
Greenbury, Richard, 220–21
Greenfield, Jerry, 376
    background and personal life, 376–77
    as Ben & Jerry's Foundation chair, 384
    founding of Ben & Jerry's, 377

    learning the business, 377–79
    returns to Ben & Jerry's, 386–87
    sells his half of Ben & Jerry's, 380
    social activism and, 394
    takes charge of production of Ben &
        Jerry's, 379
Greenpeace, 349
Grunbaum, Milton, 180, 182
GSI Corporation, 286
Guardian Life, 419

Haas, Elise Stern, 180
Haas, Peter
    business downturn and, 192
    Levi Strauss and, 182–84, 192, 194
    philosophy of enlightened leadership
        and, 182–84
    quality of goods and, 187
Haas, Robert "Bob," 194–203, 399, 428, 464
    AIDS crisis and, 201–2
    background and personal life, 194–95
    family values and, 195
    heads Levi Strauss, 195–203
    idealism and, 205
    institutionalization of practices, 435
    Jewish culture and philanthropy, 195
    Levi Strauss taken private with LBO,
        198, 201, 436
    mission and aspirations statements
        (1987) and, 201
    social responsibility, ethics, and,
        195–96
Haas, Walter, Jr. "Wally," 316, 322, 451
    company values and Thigpen, 192
    lesson about responsibility to workers,
        182
    at Levi Strauss, 182–94
    in NAB, 184
    philosophy of enlightened leadership
        and, 182–84
    quality of goods and, 187
    social responsibility of business and,
        186–87
Haas, Walter, Sr., 180–82, 193
Hale, John, 33
Hamilton, Alexander
    views on British industrialism, 5
    views on manufacturing and child
        labor, 3–4
Hamilton, Mo., 33, 43
Handy, Charles, xxiii, xliv, 134

Hanson, Kirk, 308, 451
Hargreaves, James, 4, 9
Harmon, Sidney, 107–9
    piecework experiment of, 108–9
Harmsworth, Alfred (Lord Northcliffe),
    61–62
Harvard Business Review
    editorial emphasis, shift in, 425
    editorial policy, 356–57
    Nichols article criticizing Roddick,
        355–56
    "What's a business for?" queried in, xliv
Harvard Business School (HBS), 164–65,
    182, 194, 330, 340
Haverford College, 329
Hawken, Paul, 442
health care, xlii
    ACIPCO and, 142–43
    Arco and, 307
    group life and health insurance for
        employees, 112, 138, 212, 307,
        454, 470
    Hershey Foods and, 89–90
    M&S and, 212
    Owen and, 23
Hearst, William Randolph, 177
Heilbroner, Robert, *The Worldly
    Philosophers*, 485n1
Heineken, 507n7
Herman Miller Company, 227–42, 323,
    424, 426
    acquisition of Design within Reach,
        241
    America's Most Admired Corporations
        list, 230
    awards and kudos, 230–31, 241
    bad, and surprising, end, 238–41
    cap on CEO compensation, 237
    career-long education and training,
        230
    customers and, 237
    employee benefits and, 235, 241
    employee compensation, 229, 232
    employee rights, 276
    employee stock ownership plan, 230,
        234
    employee stock ownership plan
        shelved, 241
    environmental issues, 237, 241
    Fortune's 100 Best Companies to Work
        For list, 398

    founder, D.J. De Pree, 227–30
    Frost and, 229
    great furniture designers and, 228
    growth outpacing management, 239
    headquarters, Zeeland, Mich., 227,
        398
    human-centered organizational
        culture, 229–30
    "human environmental design," 231
    innovative products, 231
    lack of sustainability and, 241–42
    last De Pree at and loss of control,
        240–41
    manufacturing facilities, 231
    Max's leadership, 230–38
    nonfamily CEOs and problems,
        238–41
    "organizational entropy" and, 242
    participatory management, 229
    profits and, 230, 238, 241
    public offering of stock, 230
    recession of 1980s and employee input,
        236–37
    regaining of culture at today, 241–42
    religious motivation for business
        practices, 227–28
    Scanlon plan adopted at, 228–29, 234,
        235
    Scanlon plan shelved, 241
    "silver parachutes," 237
    social responsibility, 238
    "theory fastball" and leadership of,
        231–38
    value-based culture at, 237–38
    Vice President for People, 235–36
    women at, 235
    worker committees, 229
Hershey, Catherine "Kitty" Sweeney, 76, 80,
    81, 82, 83
Hershey, Fanny Snavely, 71–73, 74, 75, 80,
    85
Hershey, Henry, 71–73, 74, 75, 76, 78, 80
Hershey, Milton Snavely, 71–93, 119, 143–
    44, 323, 395, 396, 426, 427, 436, 489n
    as autocratic, 87, 89
    Burnham's influence on, 76–77, 78
    business practices, 74
    childhood, 71–73
    chocolate experiments, 76–80
    chocolate manufacturing and, 79, 80
    City Beautiful movement and, 76, 78

contradictory character and behavior, 71, 80–81
cooperative movement and, 86–87
costly pleasures of, 76, 80, 85
in Cuba, 85
dancing and, 152, 428
detractors, 86–88, 464
earlier chocolate makers and, 77
early career, 73–75
employees and, 80–81, 87
giving away his fortune, 82, 83, 88
Great Depression and, 86, 88
Hershey's Milk Chocolate, 78
Hershey Trust and, 83, 89, 90, 434, 507n
incorporation of company, 85–86
Industrial School established by, 82–83, 86, 87
Lancaster Caramel Company and, 75–76, 78
legacy of, 89–93
legacy of Hersey trust, 89–93, 433–34
living conditions of workers and, 80
marriage to Kitty, 76, 80, 81, 83
model town: Central Hershey, Cuba, 85
model town: Hershey, Pa., 78–79, 81, 82, 85–86, 88, 315
paternalism and, 87
Pennsylvania Dutch and, 71–72, 76, 84, 428
philanthropy and fame, 81–82
politics of, 83–84
revered by employees, townspeople, and public, 88
Taylorism and, 81, 430
wealth of, 76
workers' education and, 88
workplace practices, reason for, 431–32
Hershey Chocolate Company, 395
    advertising and, 89
    Amish and Mennonite men working in, 80
    CEO Lenny and changes at, 89–90, 92
    community relations, 83, 90
    Cuba sugar plantation and mill, 85
    environmental issues and global sustainability efforts, 89
    factory built, Lancaster county, 78–79
    "Field Ration D," 88
    Hershey Trust and ownership of, 89–93, 433–34, 507n

incorporation of, 85
institutionalization of practices, 435
job security and, 81, 86, 103
labor unions and, 87–88, 90
NLRB rulings and changes in pay policies, 88
profits and, 82, 86, 89
profit-sharing at, 82
recent news and stain on, 71
school trustees and scandal, 90, 91–92
"scientific management" system, 81, 107
social responsibility today and, 89
takeover attempts, 90–91, 92, 490n26
uncertain future of, 92
wages and, 80–81, 87, 92
working conditions at, 81
Hershey Foundation, 86
Hershey Industrial School, 82–83, 86, 87
    endowment for, 89
    renamed Milton Hershey School, 89
Hershey Trust, 83, 89, 90, 434, 507n
Hertz, 279, 280
Hewlett-Packard, 424, 429, 473, 474, 476
Hill, Andrew, 440–41
Hirshberg, Gary
    "How to Make Money and Save the World," 454
    sale of Stonyfield Farms to Danone, 455
Hockney, David, 56
Hoffman, Philip, 163
Honeyman, Ryan, The B Corp Handbook, 458
Honeywell, 424
Hoover, Herbert, 149
"How to Make Money and Save the World" (Hirshberg), 454
human capital, 15, 408, 474
Hunt, Michelle, 235

IBM, 112, 174
    Norris labels unethical marketing tactic as "FUD," 245–46
idealism
    cooperatives and, 416
    corporate social responsibility and, xxxviii–xl
    Credo Challenge meeting and, 167–69
    enlightened capitalists as practical idealists, xli

idealism (*cont.*)
  hard facts for, 466–67
  history's support of, xliii
  increased corporate interest in social
    responsibility and, 443–44
  Levi Strauss and, 205
  Lewis and, 131, 134–35
  Lincoln and, 131
  motivations for, 427–28
  Owen and, 26, 131
  practical, examples of, 427
  realism vs., xxxvi
  tensions with practicality, 360
IKEA, 434, 507n7
Imitation Game, The (film), 244
incentive management, 97–105
income inequality, 123, 469–72
independent trust and foundation-owned
    companies, 434–35, 507n
India, caste hierarchies in, xxii
Industrial Revolution, xi, 51, 68, 432
  effect on Britain's economic and social
    order, 4–5
  in England, 206
  growth of cities and slums, 5
  Manchester, UK and, 9
  movement from farms to cities, 5
  Owen's reforms and non-exploitive
    capitalism, 6
innovation, xvii, xxxviii
  Arco and, 310
  cultures that encourage, 328
  De Pree on, 232
  employee mobility and, 133
  Google's Quayside and, 450
  Herman Miller Company, 231
  Hershey and, 74
  John Lewis Partnership and, 132
  Land and, 328
  Lever and, 51, 53, 58
  Lewis's system and, 133, 134
  Lincoln Electric, 94, 95, 102, 109–12
  loss of, 476
  Nucor and, 266
  smaller private companies as crucibles
    of, 397, 437, 440
  SWA and, 289
  Tom's of Maine and, 368
  W. L. Gore & Associates and, 298, 303
International Co-operative Alliance, 415
International Harvester, 407

Irwin, Will G., 314
Iverson, Ken, 264–79, 304, 395, 427
  background and personal life, 265,
    267, 271
  business practices, 267–71
  community relations and, 273–74
  culture of fair play and, 267–68,
    274–77
  distrust of the stock market, 268–69,
    277
  fighting unionization, 267, 284
  human-centered organizational
    culture, 275
  Nucor and, 266–77
  Nucor's "Higher Cause," 277
  Nucor's organizational structure and,
    269–70
  opposition to short-termism, 268–69
  *Plain Talk: Lessons from a Business
    Maverick*, 277
  as president of Nucor, 266, 267
  retirement of, 277
  success of, 279

Jaguar Land Rover, 475
James, Charlotte, 136
Japan
  "consensus management," 126
  family-owned businesses, 396
  Merck provides streptomycin and,
    338
J. C. Penney (Penney Company), 31–50,
    112, 211, 426
  as America's largest retail business, 41
  community relations, 46
  copycatting, failure and, 48, 49
  decline of, 47–50
  drift from philosophical
    underpinnings, 46, 48, 395
  employee benefits and job security,
    39–40
  employee education and, 43
  expansion, 1908 to 1920, 36
  Golden Rule name changed to, 40
  growth, 40, 41, 43, 45
  headquarters, 41, 42
  incorporation of, 40–42
  institutionalization of practices, 435
  manager partnerships, 35–37, 406
  Penney Principles, 37–40, 45, 332
  profitability, 45

as world's largest retailer, 45
See also Penney, James Cash
Jefferson, Thomas, 4, 430, 474
 Enlightenment ideas, 15
 head vs. heart debate, 444
 Owen and, 28
 "pursuit of happiness," xx, 15, 123
Jensen, Michael, 439
J. M. Smucker Company, 434–35
Jobs, Steve, xxxiii, 320, 325, 328
 social contributions of, xxxviii
John Lewis Partnership, 120–35, 222, 414, 476
 acquisition of grocery store chains, 128, 131
 bonuses paid in 2014, 132
 community relations, 122, 131, 132
 company's constitution, 123–24, 125, 132, 133
 as "constitutional monarchy," 125
 criticism of trade unions, 129
 critics of, 133–35
 employee benefits and, 127
 employees compared to unionized workers, 129–30
 environmental stewardship, 132
 ethical behavior and, 127–28
 five-day-workweek issue, 126–27
 Gazette, anonymous letters and, 128
 governance and ownership, 121, 124–28, 433, 434, 436
 growth, 128–29, 132
 innovation, 132
 institutionalization of practices, 436
 as one of Britain's largest retail chains, 120
 ownership structure, 124–28
 partner participation, 123, 124–28, 132, 406
 proponents of, 134
 questionnaires on providing "happiness" to partners, 128–31
 recruitment and, 131
 responsibility to stakeholders, 124
 social contract (1929 covenant), 123
 statement of purpose, 123, 125, 126
 sustainability of business model, 120, 122, 132, 134–35, 143–44, 395, 433
Johnson, Edward Mead, 145
Johnson, Guy, 34

Johnson, James, 145, 146, 149
Johnson, Robert Wood, 65, 145–46, 271
Johnson, Robert Wood, II "Bob," 146–62, 363, 428
 advertising and, 147, 151
 advocating improved labor-management relations, 150, 153–54
 advocating paying workers a living wage, 150, 154
 background and personal life, 147, 148, 149, 152, 162
 contradictions of, 147
 controlling shareholder in J&J, 148
 customers and, 157
 dancing and, 152, 428
 death of, 162
 "Dough Boy," 155
 on employee wages, 157, 158
 encyclical *Rerum Novarum*: "On the Condition of the Working Classes" and, 155–56
 environmental sustainability and, 157
 ethical thinking based on the church, 147, 155–56, 158, 430
 FDR and, 152
 FDR's New Deal and, 147
 as "the General," 153
 as J&J president, 149
 as J&J's first board chairman, 152
 J&J stock left to his foundation, 162
 Johnson New Brunswick Foundation founded by, 152
 labor movement and, 156–57
 Lever's influence, 148
 long-term thinking and, 172
 management style of, 151–52
 managerial philosophy, 158–60
 model town built by, 148
 Or Forfeit Freedom, 153–55, 159
 organizational decentralization, 158–59
 "Our Credo," 161
 "Our Management Philosophy" (servant leadership), 161
 philanthropy of, 147
 philosophy of, central tenets, 155–62
 philosophy of "corporate social responsibility.," 150–51, 157–58
 politics of, 147, 149, 151
 primed for career in the business, 147

Johnson, Robert Wood, II "Bob," (cont.)
    progressive business ideas and
        practices, 148
    as protégé of Doc Kilmer, 147–48
    quality of goods and, 157
    quirky or eccentric ideas, 162
    respect for American workers and, 160
    successor search, 162
    "Try Reality," 150–51
    World War II and, 152–53
Johnson, Robert Wood, III "Bobby," 162,
    166–67
Johnson, Ron, 49–50
Johnson & Johnson (J&J), 145–75, 399,
    424, 426
    Bob Johnson as first board chairman,
        152
    Bob Johnson's explication of
        stewardship philosophy and
        implications for employee
        behavior, 161–62
    Bob Johnson's leadership, 146–62
    Burke as president and CEO, 163–74
    community relations, 157, 161
    cooperation with government
        agencies, 146
    corporate culture pillar 1: industrial
        decentralization, 159
    corporate culture pillar 2: "Our
        Credo," 161, 163, 166–67
    corporate culture pillar 3: long-term
        thinking, 172, 174
    Credo Challenge, 163, 167–71, 172,
        175
    design of factories, 148, 149
    employee engagement and work
        satisfaction, 159
    employee job security, 149, 150
    employee training and education,
        159–60
    employee wages, 149–50
    executives as major shareholders, 153
    foreign expansion, 148–49
    founding of, 145
    governance, 153
    Great Depression and, 149–50
    growth under Burke, 173
    headquarters, New Brunswick, 163
    Hoffman as CEO, 163
    internationalization of, 147
    living conditions of workers, 148

    location of mini operating units, 159
    marketing, 146, 151
    McNeil Pharmaceuticals and, 165–66,
        168, 170, 172, 175
    post-Burke changes: sad, bad end, 175
    products, 145–46
    profits and, 170, 172, 175
    Propulsid withdrawal, 175
    public offering of stock, 153
    research and development, 146
    safety packaging introduced by, 173
    Sellars as CEO, 163, 167, 170
    shareholder lawsuit against, 175
    social responsibility and, 170
    surgical products available, gratis, in
        war and natural disasters, 146
    Tylenol crisis and, 165–66, 171–74
    working conditions and, 148
Johnson New Brunswick Foundation, 152
Jones, Geoffrey, 65
JPMorgan, 470

Kamprad, Ingvar, 507n7
Kayden, Xandra, 312, 313
Keillor, Garrison, 478
Kelleher, Herb, 264, 287–97, 304, 428
    background and personal life, 288
    founding of SWA and, 287–88
    hiring mistakes, 292
    lack of zealotry, 294
    phasing out of day-to-day involvement
        in SWA, 295
    retirement of, 296
    as SWA CEO, 288–94
    SWA's culture behind its success,
        294–95
Kelly, Gary, 292, 293, 295, 296–97
    Southwest Airlines One Report
        introduced by, 295–96
Kelly, Terri, 264, 302–3
Kelso, Louis, 411
Kemmerer, Wyo., 34–35
Kent, Duke of, 20
Keurig Green Mountain, 463
Keynes, John Maynard, 431
    case against business virtue, xxxv
    "The Economic Possibilities of Our
        Grandchildren," xxxv
Kilmer, Fred "Doc," 146, 147–48
Kilmer, Joyce, 147–48
    "Trees," 148

KIND, 404–5, 456
King, Brayden, 467
King, Martin Luther, Jr., 316, 322
King, Mike, *Quakernomics: An Ethical Capitalism*, 84
King, Rollin, 287–88, 292, 294, 296
"King of the River" (Kunitz), xix
King of Sunlight, The (Macqueen), 61–62, 488n
Kleiner, Art, 408–9
Koch, Charles, 309, 310
Koch, David, 310
Kodak, 326, 327–28
Koller, Frank, 99, 117, 491n11
Kollmorgen, 424
Koshland, Daniel, 180, 181, 193
Koufax, Sandy, 231–32
Kraft Foods, 404
Kraft Heinz, 445
Kuhn, Loeb & Company, 330
Kunitz, Stanley, "King of the River," xix

labor unions
    American companies introducing enlightened labor practices and, 112
    criticism of "industrial democracy," 129
    Cummins Engine Corporation and, 316
    employee shareholders criticized by, 189, 192
    Harmon's piecework experiment and, 108–9
    Hershey Chocolate Company and, 87–88
    Iverson and Nucor opposing, 267
    John Lewis Partnership criticized by, 134
    Johnson and, 154
    Johnson's call to, 156–57
    Lever Bros. (Unilever) and, 64
    Levi Strauss and, 181–82
    Lincoln Electric and, 105–9
    Owen and, 28–29
    piecework system opposed by, 106–9
    Townsend and Avis opposing, 284
La Boulange bakeries, 448
Lacy, Chuck, 389–90
Ladd, Alan, Jr., 285
Lager, Fred "Chico," 381, 383

Ben & Jerry's: The Inside Scoop, 384, 504n1
    conflict with Cohen, 388
    environmental practices and, 384–85
    retires from Ben & Jerry's, 389
    returns to Ben & Jerry's, 390
    walks away from Ben & Jerry's, 391, 392
Land, Edwin H., 328, 426, 428, 451
    background and personal life, 320
    civil rights and, 322–23
    death of, 325
    fame of, 321
    as humanist, 321–22, 328
    legacy of, 328
    ousted from Polaroid, 325, 395, 427
    Polaroid and, 320–27
    as perfectionist, 324
    technological myopia of, 327
Lauder, Leonard, 346
Lazard Frères, 280
Leadership Is an Art (De Pree), 231
Lear, Norman, 451
Lehman Brothers, 330
Lehmann, J. M., 77
Lenney, Richard H., 89–90, 92
Lennon, John, 323
Leopold II, King of Belgium, 60
Leo X, Pope, xxv
Leo XIII, Pope, 156
    encyclical *Rerum Novarum*: "On the Condition of the Working Classes" and, 155
    Johnson aligned with, 155–56
Lever, Elizabeth Hulme, 52, 55, 59, 60, 61, 62, 64
Lever, James (brother), 52, 53, 55, 62
Lever, James (father), 51–52, 53
Lever, William Hesketh, 51–70, 96, 119, 141, 393, 426, 427, 428, 436, 488n
    advertising and mass marketing, 53–54
    African trips, Congo copra farms, 60, 63, 66
    bar soap invented by, 51
    business losses, 63–64
    company ownership and, 64, 395, 427, 436, 438
    co-partnerships, 58–60
    dancing and, 57–58, 152, 428
    death of, 64

Lever, William Hesketh (*cont.*)
  detractors, 61–62, 464
  early years of, 51–52
  education of workers and, 57, 160
  efficient management practices, 52
  elected to Parliament, Liberal Party, 59
  enlightened capitalism, advocating for, 60–61
  environmental issues and, 56–57
  failed Hebrides project, 62–63
  as free-trader, 59
  gender equality and, 57, 66
  granted a peerage, 61
  interests and enthusiasms, 56
  Johnson influenced by, 148
  living conditions of workers and, 54–55
  marketing genius of, 53–54
  marriage and family, 52, 55, 56, 59
  model town: Port Sunlight, 55, 58, 63, 315
  as paternalistic and autocratic, 56, 58, 449
  personal losses, 62
  philosophy of, 60–61
  product packaging innovation, 53
  profits, use of and, 114
  sad, bad end, 62–65
  soap manufacturing business begun, 53
  social conscience and, 51–52
  working conditions in plants, 57
  workplace practices, reason for, 431–32
Lever, William Hulme, 55, 64–65
Lever Bros. (now Unilever), 51, 222, 426
  acquisitions to boost profit margins, 445
  after Lever, 65–68
  Ben & Jerry's acquired, 390–94, 446
  brands, 59, 65, 67
  business losses, Great Depression, and, 63–64
  ceasing of joint Dutch-British structure (2018), 446
  community relations, 65, 66
  company ownership and, 64, 395, 427
  continuing saga, 68
  copra farms in the Congo, 59–60, 66
  corporate philanthropy and, 54
  critics of, 68
  culture built on "doing the right thing," 66–67
  current workforce, 65
  diversification, 59, 63
  Dollar Shave American subsidiary, 446
  economies of scale and, 58
  employee benefits, 57–58
  employee co-partnerships, 58–60, 405
  environmental practices, 65–66, 89
  ethical behavior and, 65
  fair-trade sourcing, 66
  first global corporation, 59
  gender equality and, 57, 66
  growth, 54
  Hellmann's mayonnaise as certifiably sustainable, 67
  hostile takeover threat, 394, 445–46
  incorporation of, 56
  innovation and, 58
  Lever and micromanagement, 56
  Lever cedes control of, 64, 395
  merger with Margarine Unie, 65, 427
  oilseed operation, Nigeria, 63, 64
  Polman as CEO, 66–68, 393–94, 444–46
  profits, 58, 445
  profit-sharing, 58–59
  reduction of workday, 57
  share price, 68
  social responsibility and, 65–68, 393, 444–45
  Sunlight soap, 53
  Sustainable Living Plan, 66, 68
  working conditions in plants, 57
  as world's largest soap producer, 58
Levi Strauss & Co., 176–205, 424, 426, 495n19
  acquisitions, 196
  AIDS crisis and, 201–2
  Asian subcontracting, 202–3
  Blackstone, Va. plant, integration of, 183–84
  Blackstone, Va. plant, shutdown of, 200
  boycott of, 200
  campus headquarters, Embarcadero, San Francisco, 193
  community relations, 183–85, 200, 201–2
  company ownership and, 184, 193, 198, 201, 436
  cultural change at, 193–94
  Davis, Jacob, and, 176–77, 179

Davis, Simon, and, 179–80
diversification of workforce at, 196
downturn in business, business model
    and, 190–92
employees, 178, 183, 188, 199–200
employee bonuses, 180–81
employees as philanthropists, 185
employee shareholders, 189, 192, 193
employee turnover, 185
environmental issues, 205
ethics and, 180–81, 187, 192, 193,
    195–96, 200, 205
focus on middle market, 196
foreign operations, 191, 193, 196
goal of all-around excellence, 184, 186
Great Depression and, 181
growth, 179, 184, 193
guidelines for global product sourcing,
    202–3, 204
Haas, Bob, heads, 194–203
Haas, Sr., heads, 180–82, 193
Haas brothers head, 182–89
handicapped workers hired, 185
homosexual employees and, 202, 204
job losses at, 198
Koshland as president, 193
labor practices, 178
labor unions and, 181–82
legend of, 176
long-term thinking and, 196–97
minority hiring, 183, 189, 203
minority-owned stores and suppliers,
    184, 203
mission and aspirations statements,
    201
new factory and industrial design, 179
nonfamily CEOs and current state,
    204–5
ownership structure, 201
passes billion-dollar mark, 193
paternalism and, 178
pensions and, 183
plant closings, 198–99, 201
product quality department, 184
products, 177, 179, 190, 196, 198
profits and, 185, 192
promoting blue-collar workers to
    management, 189
public offering of stock, 188–89
quality of goods and, 401
rivet patent for jeans, 177, 179

San Francisco earthquake and, 179
Santone factory, 196, 198–99
severance packages, 199–200
social responsibility, 178, 184, 186–89,
    195–96, 202–3
Stern heads, 178–81
stock granted to key employees, 183
stock price, 192–93
Strauss and, 176–79
Strauss's heirs and, 178
"suggested pricing" issue, 187–88
Thigpen and, 191–92
tsuris (trouble) at, 197–200
wages and benefits, 185, 190
women workers, 185, 189
Levi Strauss Foundation, 184, 185
Lewis, John Spedan, 120–35, 219, 428
    as capitalist, 131–32
    commitment to free speech, 128
    company ownership and, 144, 395
    customer care and, 122
    death of, 125
    early career, 120–21, 123
    economies of scale and, 122
    employee committees and, 120–21,
        138
    employee well-being and wages, 121,
        122
    experiment in industrial democracy
        and, 121–22
    income inequality and, 123
    John Lewis Partnership and, 120,
        123–35
    lasting legacy of, 143–44
    legal framework of governance and
        ownership developed by, 121,
        124–28, 433, 434
    motivation for a virtuous enterprise,
        122
    Owen's ideas and, 430
    personality of, 121–22, 127
    political-economic philosophy, 131
    sustainability of business model, 120,
        122, 132, 134–35
Lewis, John, Sr., 120–21
Limited stores, 354
Lincoln, Abraham, xliii
Lincoln, James, 150, 268, 396, 428
    about, 95–96
    as advocate of his philosophy, 96–97,
        111–12

Lincoln, James (*cont.*)
  arguments against his system, 118–19
  as capitalist, 131–32
  Christian values and managerial
    philosophy, 110–11, 137, 360
  "classless society" vision of, 112, 123
  congressional questioning of, 102–3
  customer service and, 96
  death of, 116
  "the development of latent ability" and,
    96–97, 100
  durability of system, 112–16, 395
  ethics and, 111
  Ford's influence on, 96, 112–13
  as free-trader, 111
  idealism of, 131
  incentive management, 94, 97–105, 111
  influence of, 430
  innovation and, 109
  intellectual influences on, 430
  Lincoln Electric and, 94–119
  management style of, 115–16
  message of, 96
  as outspoken, 96, 116
  product innovation and, 109–12
  profound insight of, 95
  reconciling the antagonistic interests
    of workers and owners, 94
  study of management by, 96
  system as alternative to socialism, 97
  system not adopted by any other major
    company, 117, 117n
  trust of workers, 113
  workplace practices, reason for, 431–32
Lincoln, John Cromwell, 95, 109, 110, 115
Lincoln Electric, 290, 406, 424, 476
  advisory board, 97–98, 100, 106, 138,
    413
  average earnings, 100
  community relations, 110, 113, 116
  company today, 94, 116–19
  critics of, 118–19, 134
  culture of, 98–99
  diversification resisted, 109–10
  egalitarian work environments, 98
  employee bonuses, 94, 102, 491n11
  employee communication and
    participation, 97–99
  employee retention, 104, 185
  employee self-management and lowest
    total labor costs, 101
  employee wages and benefits, 94–95,
    98, 99–101, 158, 276
  ethical behavior and, 111
  expectations of employees, 104–5
  foreign expansion, 98, 102
  founding of, 95
  Great Depression and, 100, 103
  growth, 110
  guaranteed employment/job security,
    94, 95, 103–5, 111
  incentive management, 97–105
  influence on SAIC, 413–14
  innovation and, 94, 95, 109–12
  institutionalization of practices, 436
  merit-based bonus, 101–3
  number of employees, 94
  ownership structure, 115, 116–17,
    433, 436
  piecework compensation, 99–101,
    106–7, 117n, 229
  productivity, 99–101
  profits (2017), 94
  profits reinvested, 109, 110
  profit-sharing, 98, 101–3, 406
  public offering of stock, 117
  recent acquisitions, 117
  recruitment and, 131
  sustainability of business model,
    134–35, 395, 433
  trade union objections, 105–9
  working conditions, 98
  world's largest manufacturer of electric
    arc-welding machines, 94
Lindt, Rodolphe, 77
Lister, Joseph, 145
living conditions of workers, xi
  ACIPCO housing, 138
  Britain's textile mills and, 6
  Carnegie's workers, xxxii
  Ford and, 113
  Ford's Fordlandia, xxviii
  Hershey and, 78–79, 80, 82, 85, 86
  J&J and, 148
  Lever and, 54–55, 56–57
  Lever Bros. in the Congo and, 60
  M&S employee lunchrooms and, 212
  Miller and, 315
  model towns, 18–19, 54–56, 78–79, 82,
    84, 85, 113, 148, 315, 450
  Owen and, 12, 13, 18–19
  Pullman's company town, 77

Locke, John, 9
Locke, Robert, 430
London Stock Exchange, 47
Long, Russell, 411
Lord & Taylor, 432
Lord Corporation, 424
L'Oréal, 357–59, 392, 394
Los Kass, 35
Lubetzky, Daniel, 404–5, 456, 457
    Do the KIND Thing, 404
Luce, Henry, 154
Lucent Technologies, 318
Lyft, 474, 475

Macauley, Thomas, 7, 154
Machiavelli, Niccolò, xlii
Mackey, John, 444, 447, 448, 455
    Conscious Capitalism (CC)
        movement, 452–53
    as pro-capitalism with libertarian
        convictions, 453
Macqueen, Adam, The King of Sunlight,
    61–62, 488n
Macy's, 401
Madoff, Bernie, 468
Maersk, 507n7
Major Barbara (Shaw), 69–70
Malden Mills, 262–63, 427
    Polartec and, 263
Maltby, Kate, xliv
Manchester, UK, 5, 6, 8–10, 11, 208
    as center for the Industrial Revolution,
        9
    Enlightenment ideas in, 9
    Owen in, 8–10
Manchester Literary and Philosophical
    Society, 10
Manchester University, 210
Man for All Seasons, A (Bolt), xlii
Mann, Horace, 94
Margarine Unie, 65
Marks, Hannah Cohen, 207
Marks, Michael, 206–9, 395
    death of, 209, 223
    ethics and, 210, 222, 428
    Leeds market stalls and, 207
    marriage and family, 207
    novel retail practices, 207
    partnership with Spencer, 208
Marks, Miriam Sieff, 209
Marks, Simon, 209, 431

    as Baron Marks of Broughton, 217
    birth of, 207
    concept of "superstores," 210–11
    death of, 217
    economic philosophy, 209–10
    friendship with Israel Sieff, 208, 209
    institutionalization of practices, 435
    as Marks & Spencer CEO, 209–17
    marriage and family, 209
    paternalism and, 213
    personality of, 214, 215
    Weizmann's influence on, 210, 211, 428
Marks & Spencer (M&S), 206–23, 426
    acquisitions, 220
    bad decisions at, 220
    as Britain's dominant retailer, 211
    business model, 210
    Chapman heads, 209
    community relations and, 213, 216
    company ownership, 209, 211, 399,
        436
    crisis of 1999 and reorganization, 221
    customer base, loss of, 221
    customers and, 211–17
    domestic sourcing of products, 214
    employees and, 210, 216, 219
    employees' education and training,
        212
    employees' health care, 212
    employees' lunchrooms, 212
    employees' profit-sharing and stock-
        ownership program, 212, 221
    employment policies, 219
    environmental practices, 222
    ethical lapses and, 220
    ethical standards, 210
    first private brand in British retailing
        (St Michael), 213–14, 216, 221, 222
    food sales, 214
    founding of, 208
    Greenbury as CEO and loss of business
        model, 220–21
    growth, 211
    incorporation of, 208
    industrial research and, 211
    as leader in informational labeling, 222
    as limited liability corporation, 211
    "Look Behind the Label" campaign,
        222
    management, 215–16
    in Manchester, 208

Marks & Spencer (M&S) (*cont.*)
    Marks, Simon, heads, 209–17
    as "Marks and Sparks," 211
    nonfamily CEOs and current state,
        220–23
    Norman as CEO and imperiling of
        enlightened culture, 223
    paternalism and, 213
    Penny Bazaars, 208
    philosophies and practices (list), 216
    philosophy of employment policies,
        212
    product line, 215
    profits and, 220
    Rayner as CEO, 220
    refocus on core values, 222
    relationships with manufacturers,
        211, 216
    reputation for quality, 215
    Rose as CEO, 221–22
    Sieff, Israel, leadership of, 209–10, 217
    Sieff, Marcus, as CEO, 217–19
    social responsibility, 210, 213, 216, 218
    social responsibility and, 222
    stock and lost value, 220–21
    store closings, 223
    transforming British retailing, 210
    Vandevelde as CEO, 221
    wages and benefits, 211, 212, 219
    women managers and, 212
    Woolworths as competitor, 210
    World War II and, 214
Mars, 398–99
    environmental practices, 399
    line of healthy snacks, 399
    long-term thinking and, 399
    management philosophy, 399
    number of employees, 399
    progressive employee-and
        management-development
        practices, 399
    Reid as CEO, 399
    sales and earnings, 399
    Wrigley acquired by, 399
Mars, Forrest, 398–99
Martineau, Harriet, 27
Marvin Windows and Doors, 396–97
Marx, Karl, xi, 5, 25, 432
    criticism of Owen, 6–7
    redistribution of wealth and, 132
Maslow, Abraham, 160, 431

Mattel, 286
Maximilian I, Emperor, xxv, xxvi
Mayo, Elton, 154
Mayville, Gail, 385–86, 451
    "Green Team," 386
Mazzei, Ser Lapo, xxiv–xxv
McGregor, Douglas, 160, 229, 430
    Theory Y, 431
McKinsey & Co., 194, 411
McNabb, Bill, xiv, xv, 461
McWane, J. R., 138–39, 143
McWane Inc., 142
Meier, Richard, 315
Merck, Friedrich Jacob, 334
Merck, Georg, 334
Merck, George W., 335
    ethical business practices and, 335,
        336
Merck & Co., 334–41, 426, 444
    company history, 334–35
    cure for river blindness and free
        distribution, 335–38, 339
    employees, 338
    ethical business practices and, 335,
        336
    Fosamax and, 340
    Frazier as CEO, 340
    Gilmartin as CEO, and besmirching of
        ethical record, 339–40
    in Japan, streptomycin and, 338
    legacy of corporate beneficence,
        curtailing under Gilmartin, 339
    Mectizan Expert Committee, 338
    Merck Sharp and Dohme research
        labs, 335
    profitability and, 338
    sells China technology for hepatitis B
        vaccine, 338
    Vagelos and, 335–39
    Vagelos legacy, 340–41
    Vioxx scandal and, 339–40
Method, 457
Meyer, André, 280, 281
Microsoft, xxxviii
Mill, John Stuart, 30
    capitalism and, 132
    On Liberty, 30
    "tyranny of custom," 30
Miller, Bernard, 125
Miller, Herman, 228. *See also* Herman
    Miller Company

Miller, J. Irwin, 313–19, 427, 428, 477
  background and personal life, 314
  civil rights and, 316, 322
  Clean Air Act and, 317
  Columbus, Ind. and, 313
  Cummins Engine Corporation and,
    313, 314–19
  National Council of Churches and, 313
  paternalism avoided by, 315
  philanthropy of, 315
  "servant leadership" and, 317–18
  sustaining strategies for Cummins
    and, 317, 395
Mirvis, Philip, 392
Mitsui, 35
Mittal, Sunil Bharti, xxxix–xl
Mobil Oil Corporation, 186
Modern Times (film), 81
Mojzak, Marg, 237
Mondragón, Spain, 417, 418, 440
  Fagor appliance manufacturer, 417
Montgomery Ward, 37, 47, 48, 49
Morgan, J. P., xxxii
Morgan Stanley, 330
Morita, Sony, 325
Morrison, Denise, 444, 448
Morse, Meroë, 322
Motorola, 424
Murdoch, Rupert, 61
mutual companies, 419
Mutual of Omaha, 419
Mylan, 429
  EpiPen price gouging, 466

National Alliance of Businessmen (NAB),
  184, 451
National Association of Manufacturers, 150
National Council of Churches, 313
Natura Cosmetics, 359
Nelson, George, 228
Nestlé, Henri, 77
New Harmony, Ind., 27–28, 44
New Lanark, Scotland, 11, 12, 113
  Owen's initial view of, 12
  Owen's model community and, 18–19
  as UNESCO World Heritage site, 29,
    55
  workers' living conditions in, 12
New Lanark Mills, 6, 11–14, 18, 20, 27, 426,
  427
  child labor and, 12, 13, 22–23

  conflict over control of company
    ownership, 16–17, 46, 395
  Owen's reforms, 11–14, 23
  profits from, 16, 21, 22
  quality of goods, 21
Newman, Edwin, 168–69
"New Nationalism" (T. Roosevelt), 157
Newton, Stephen, 418
New York Times, Sulzberger family
  ownership, 399
Nike, 425
Nixon, Richard, 316
Nooyi, Indra, 444
Nordstrom, 397
Norman, Archie, 223
Norris, Jane Malley, 258
Norris, William C., 327, 426, 464
  background and personal life, 243–44
  CDC and, 243–63
  CDC board removes, 260, 395, 427,
    436
  CDC stock, 248, 437
  commitment to minority jobs, 249,
    251–52, 316, 322, 451
  compared to Owen, 243, 253, 258–59
  credo of, 249–50
  death of, 262
  evaluation of, 261
  as full-time reformer, 258–60
  marriage and family, 258
  as maverick, 244
  as opposed to philanthropy, 250
  personality of, 249, 258
  PLATO education technology and,
    254–57, 261
  social responsibility and, 249, 250–51
  at Sperry Rand, 244
  unsuccessful spreading of his ideas,
    259–60
Norwegian national sovereignty fund, 460,
  470
Novo Nordisk, 507n7
Nucor Corporation, 265–79
  absence of significant employee stock
    ownership, 277, 278–79
  as America's largest steel producer, 266
  Chinese dumping of steel and, 278–79
  commitment to transparency, 275–76
  community and, 273–74, 398
  continual and candid communication
    at, 270–71, 275

Nucor Corporation (*cont.*)
    corporate culture of, 266, 270, 274–77
    Correnti heads, 275–76
    customers and culture of fairness, 275
    egalitarian work environments, 274
    employee-centered philosophy and
        "reciprocal fairness," 267–68,
        274–77
    employee rights, 276
    employees and, 271–72
    employee self-management, 275, 276
    environmental issues, 266, 273,
        277–78
    ethics and, 274–77
    Fortune's 100 Best Companies to Work
        For list and, 398
    free market economics and, 278
    goal of sustainable full employment,
        268
    history of company, 265–66
    Iverson as head of Vulcraft division,
        266
    Iverson as president, 266–77
    Iverson pay cut at, 267
    Iverson retires, 277
    Iverson's business model at, 267–71
    labor unions and, 267
    long-term thinking and, 268–69
    management practices, 266
    merit-based hiring and promotion, 274
    meritocratic ethos, 276
    "mini-mills" and, 266, 271–72, 286
    number of employees, 266
    organizational decentralization,
        269–71
    performance evaluation, 274
    pretax profit, 2017, 278
    profitability under Iverson, 266
    profitable growth, long term, 276
    response to 1981–82 recession, 267–68
    safety and working conditions, 266,
        273
    sales and earnings, 266, 269
    scholarship program, 276
    small-town bias for facilities, 271–74
    stock value increase, 269
    success of, reason for, 268
    sustainability of business model,
        277–79, 395
    technological edge, 266
    wages, average, 276

Olds, Ransom, 265
Olga, 424
O'Loughlin, Sheryl, 457–58
On Liberty (Mill), 30
"open-book management," 407
Oracle, xxxviii
Or Forfeit Freedom (Johnson), 153–55, 159
"organizational entropy," 242, 319
O'Toole, James, "Two and a Half Cheers for
    Conscious Capitalism," 454
Owen, Caroline Dale, 11, 12, 17–18, 27
Owen, Robert, xliv, 3–30, 96, 103, 119, 122,
    131, 141, 150, 157, 350, 357, 426, 427,
    431, 436, 462, 484n
    admirers, 7, 20, 27
    adoption of ideas in Britain and
        America, 29–30
    as anti-communist/anti-revolutionary,
        25
    attempts to spread his methods, 19–20,
        21, 22–23, 67, 117, 219
    Bentham and, 27, 30, 430
    as capitalist, 6, 131–32
    company ownership and, 16–17, 46,
        395, 436, 438
    cooperative movement and, 29, 86,
        133, 415
    criticism's effect on and end of life,
        26–28
    critics of, 6–7, 21–25, 52, 464
    dancing and, 7, 24, 152, 428
    death of, 29
    early years of, 7–10
    end of his experiment and profits,
        24–25
    Enlightenment ideas, 8–9, 10, 11, 15,
        428, 430
    ethical practices, 8, 19
    founding of the *Economist* and, 20
    as free-trader, 21, 59
    Grand National Consolidated Trades
        Union and, 28
    history's view of, 6–7
    idealism of, 26, 131
    immigration to America, 27
    Jefferson and, 28
    legacy of, 28–30
    making a profit while improving
        working conditions, 6
    manufacturing in his times, 3–6
    marriage and family, 11, 12, 17–18

mystery of why industrialists failed to
emulate his methods, 6, 22
the New Lanark Mills, 6, 11–14, 18, 20,
27, 484n
Norris compared to, 243, 253, 258–59
paternalism and, 19, 24, 25, 449
paying workers, 19–20
personal fortune of, 21–22, 25
philosophy of, human development,
15–16, 23, 474
profit motive and, 16
Quakers adoption of his business
practices, 84
reduction of workday, 18
social movements championed by, 26
unemployment proposals, 25
utopian communities and, 26, 27–28
"What's a business for?," 15
work day and, 13
worker evaluations, 19
workers' community established by,
18–19
workers' education and, 13, 23–24,
27, 160
working conditions and, 13, 19
workplace practices, reason for, 431–32
Owen, Robert Dale, 10, 18, 27, 28, 29
as American abolitionist and U.S.
diplomat, 28
Smithsonian Institution and, 28
Oxford University, Said Business School
Skoll Centre for Social
Entrepreneurship, 457
Skoll World Forum at, 452

Pacific Southwest Airways (PSA), 287, 289
Parsons, 406
Patagonia, 349, 400–403, 426, 476, 497n29
"benefit corporation" status, 403, 458
business model focused on
environmental issues, 400
employment practices, 400
family ownership of, 402
management practices, 402
number of employees, 402
percentage of profits donated, 401
quality of goods and suppliers, 401
R&D investment, 401
sales and earnings, 400
sustainability of raw materials,
consortium of retailers and, 401

"$20 Million and Change Fund," 401
working conditions, 402
Paumgarten, Nick, 402
PCL Construction, 406
Peck, Bradford, The World a Department
Store, 416
Pei, I. M., 315
Penney, Bertha Hess, 34, 41
Penney, James Cash, 31–50, 96, 119, 141,
426, 427, 436
"cash and carry" policy, 35, 37
Christian values and managerial
philosophy, 31–33, 360, 428
City National Bank, Miami, and, 44,
45
in Colorado, 34
company ownership and, 46, 395, 436
competitive advantage, 37
cooperatives and "spirit of cooperation," 41–42
customer service, 37–38
the Dynamo, 42–43
early years of, 31–33
employee benefits and, 39–40
employee education and, 43, 160
ethics of, 32, 33, 48–49
favorite sayings and mantra, 38
financial woes, emotional problems, 45
focus on selection and training of
managers, 42
Golden Rule stores, 34–35
Great Depression and, 44–47
hiring by, 36
incorporation of business, 40–43
losing interest in Penney Company,
43–44
manager partnership, 34–37
mansion on Belle Isle, Fla., 44, 45
marriages and family, 34, 41, 43
Penney Company decline, 47–50
Penney Principles, 37–40, 45–46
philanthropy, Christian causes, 44
politics of, 32
quality of goods and, 38, 157
resigns as president, 42
social responsibility and, 39
unconventional streak, 34, 41, 43
utopian community: Penney Farms,
44–45
values of, 32–33, 41–43, 137
PepsiCo, 444

Perlman, Lawrence, 260
Peters, Tom, 287, 304
Pfizer, 466
Phelps, Edmund, 475–76
philanthropy, late-career, xxvi–xxxiii
    Carnegie and, xxix–xxxiii
    Datini and, xxv
    Ford and, xxviii–xxix
    Fugger and, xxvi
    as means of redemption, xxvii
    Rockefeller and, xxvii–xxviii
Pillsbury's Häagen-Dazs, 381–82, 388, 389
Pinker, Linda, 290
Pius XI, Pope, 156
    encyclical *Quadragesimo anno*: "On
        the Reconstruction of the Social
        Order," 156
Plain Talk (Iverson), 277
Plato, xxii
Plum Organics, 457, 458
Polaroid Corporation, 320–27, 395, 424,
    426
    difficulties at, 324–25
    digital technologies and demise of,
        325–27
    employees and, 323
    employee stock-ownership plan, 326
    enlightened business management,
        322, 323
    Herman Miller compared to, 323
    Inner City Inc. and minority jobs,
        322–23, 432
    Land's control of and loss of top
        executives, 324
    large-format camera, 321–22, 325,
        326–27
    Polavision, 324, 325
    R&D at, 321, 323, 324, 328
    SX-70 color-print camera, 323–24
    women at, 322
    working conditions, 323
Polman, Paul, 66–68, 393, 444, 448, 455,
    477
    on climate change, 463
    hostile takeover threat and, 445–46
    as most vocal advocate of socially
        responsible business practices,
        67–68
    opposition to a ninety-day reporting
        cycle, 67–68
Port Sunlight, 55, 58, 64, 113, 315

poverty, xii, 11, 12, 31
    CDC plants opened in high-poverty
        areas, 251–54
    enlightened capitalism as solution to,
        258–59
    Evergreen Co-operative Corporation
        and, 418
    Johnson and, 156
    Marxist revolution and, 70
    Mill on, 132
    Norris and, 250, 253, 259
    Owen's "human development"
        approach, 15, 20
    Protestant Federal Council of
        Churches on, 156
    Shaw's *Major Barbara* and, 69, 70
    social Darwinism and, 155
    Tory view of, as workers' fault, 11
Powers, Charles, 316
Price, Dan, 471–72
Price, Robert, 257–58, 260
private company business model, 397, 437
    advantages of, 397
    payoffs for founders, two forms, 437
    Tocqueville on, 297–98
Procter & Gamble, 112, 165
productivity
    Costco vs. Walmart's Sam's Club, 101
    employee wages and, 157, 158
    Harmon's piecework experiment and,
        108
    labor costs vs. total labor costs and,
        290–91
    labor unions and, 156
    Lincoln Electric, 94
    Owen's philosophy and, 15, 20, 21
profit-sharing, xi, 58–59, 112, 472
    ACIPCO and, 139
    Gantt's teachings and, 431
    Herman Miller Company and, 234
    Hershey Chocolate Company and, 82
    John Lewis Partnership and, 127
    Lever Bros. (Unilever) and, 58–59
    Lincoln Electric and, 94, 98, 101–3
    Marks & Spencer and, 212, 221
    SWA and, 290
Progressive Era, 160
Propst, Robert, 228
Protestant Federal Council of Churches,
    Social Creed of 1908, 155–56
Prudential, 419

Publix supermarket chain, 406
Pullman, George, 77, 81
Pure Food and Drugs Act (1906), 146

Quadragesimo anno: "On the Reconstruction
    of the Social Order" (Pius XI), 156
Quakernomics: An Ethical Capitalism (King),
    84
Quakers, 17
    Haverford and John Whitehead,
        329–30
    Owen's business practices and, 84
    Rowntree and Cadbury families, 77, 84

Radica, 285–86
Raiman, Jacques, 286
Ramblers Way, 372
Rauch, Richard, 238
Rayner, Derek, 220
RCA Corporation, 311
Reagan, Ronald, 376
realism
    Bradshaw and, 309–10
    Credo Challenge meeting and, 167–69
    expectations of investors and
        corporate behavior, 444
    history's support of, xliii
    public as uninterested in corporate
        social responsibility, 466–67
REBBL, 458
Recology, 415–16
Regeneron Pharmaceuticals, 341
regulations, 454
    diesel engines and EPA rules, 318
    European countries and, xv
    Johnson on, 155
    Miller and the environment, 317
    in the UK, changes proposed, xv
REI, 416
Reid, Grant, 399
Rerum Novarum: "On the Condition of the
    Working Classes" (Leo XIII), 155–56
Richardson, John Grubb, 84
robber barons, 31, 81
Robert Wood Johnson Foundation, 162
Rochdale Society of Equitable Pioneers, 415
Rochester, N.Y., 328
Rockefeller, John D., xxvii–xxviii, xxxiii, 81
    image of Standard Oil and, xxvii
    late-life philanthropy of, xxvii–xxviii,
        xxxvii

Warden's proposals for fairer treatment
    of suppliers, customers, and
    employees, xxvii
Rockefeller, John D., Jr., xxvii
Rockefeller, Nelson, 314
Roddick, Anita, xi, 342–60, 368, 372–73,
    376, 388, 394, 404, 426, 427, 428, 433,
    436, 464
    background and personal life, 343–46
    Body and Soul, 347, 355
    Body Shop and, 346–59
    Brazil's rain forest and, 352
    business mistake of, 348
    business philosophy, 349–50, 353
    as capitalist, 351
    commitment to an ethical business,
        347–48
    criticism of stock speculators, 350–51
    criticism of the cosmetics industry,
        350
    critics of, 354–57
    death of, 359
    effort to ban all animal testing in
        cosmetics, 349
    on enlightened capitalism, 357
    environmental and human rights
        initiatives, 349
    influence of Semler, 353
    named Dame Commander of the
        British Empire, 343
    Nichols's criticism countered by, 356
    sale of Body Shop to L'Oréal, 357–59,
        395, 403, 427, 436, 437
    Social Venture Network and, 349, 451
Roddick, Gordon, 345–46, 347, 348, 351
Rohde, Gilbert, 228
Roosevelt, Franklin Delano (FDR)
    Bob Johnson and, 149, 151
    Four Freedoms, 154
    Lincoln's system as alternative to
        social welfare, 111, 114
    New Deal, 111, 147
Roosevelt, Theodore, xxxviii, 83
    on business leaders and doing good,
        xliii
    criticism of Carnegie, xxxiii, 464
    environmental issues, 157
    "New Nationalism," 157
    Square Deal, 154
Rose, Stuart, 221–22
Rosenwald, Julius, 330, 431

Rothman, Howard, *Companies with a Conscience*, 497n29
Round Table Pizza, 406
Rousseau, Jean-Jacques, 9, 430
  The Social Contract, 9
Rowntree, Joseph, 77, 84
    chocolate factory in New Earswick, 84
    education of workers and, 84
    employee benefits and, 84
    living conditions of workers and, 84
    working conditions and, 84
Royal Bank of Scotland, 133
Rykens, Paul, 65

S. C. Johnson, 399
Saarinen, Eero, 315
Sachs, Sam, 330
SAIC (Science Applications International), 117n, 413–14, 426, 435
Salesforce, 444, 469
Salt, Titus, 55, 56
Saltaire, West Yorkshire, UK, 55–56
Sams, Earl Corder, 35–36, 40, 41, 42, 45, 46, 49
Sana, 418
Scanlon, Joe, 228–29
Scanlon plan, 228–29, 234, 235, 471
Schacht, Henry, 318
Schultz, Howard, 444, 463, 464
Schumacher, E. F., 134
"scientific management" system, 81, 106–7
Scott, Mary, *Companies with a Conscience*, 497n29
Seabra, Luiz, 359
Seagate, 260
Sears, Roebuck and Company, 37, 47, 48, 49, 112, 211, 330
Sellars, Richard, 163, 167, 170
Semler, Ricardo, 353
"servant leadership," 136–37, 161, 233, 317–18
Shakespeare, William, *Julius Caesar*, xi
Shamrock Holdings, 326
Shaw, George Bernard, 68–70
    Major Barbara, 69–70
Shaw, Kathryn, 271
Shultz, George, 333
Sieff, David, 220
Sieff, Edward, 217
Sieff, Ephraim, 208
Sieff, Israel, 209, 214, 431

    as Baron, 217
    economic philosophy, 209–10
    employee lunchrooms and, 212
    friendship with Simon Marks, 208, 209
    institutionalization of practices, 435
    marriage and family, 209
    paternalism and, 213
    retirement of, 217
    Weizmann's influence on, 210, 211, 428
Sieff, Marcus, 212, 214, 215, 399
    business practices, 218–19
    CEOs reject his practices, 219
    Don't Ask the Price, 217
    The Ethics of the Fathers, 218
    as future Marks & Spencer CEO, 215
    as Lord Sieff of Brimpton, 217
    as Marks & Spencer CEO, 217–19
    personality of, 218–19
    socializing with the rich and famous, 217–18
    social responsibility and, 218
    wealth and upbringing, 217
    Weizmann's influence on, 218
Sieff, Michael, 217
Sieff, Rebecca Marks, 209
Siegel, Sam, 273, 275
Sierra Club, 307
"single tax" theory, 115
sin investing, 460
Sisodia, Rajendra, 454–55
60 Minutes (TV show), 171–72
Skoll World Forum, 452
Smith, Adam, 154
    business as human commonality, xxi
    case against business idealism, xxxiv
    free markets and, 21
    invisible hand, 428
    opposition to corporate do-goodism, xxxvii
    The Wealth of Nations, xxxiv, 7
Smith, Liz, 329
Snavely, Mattie, 73, 74, 75
Social Contract, The (Rousseau), 9
social Darwinism, xxxi, 155
Social Enterprise Business Centre, 457
social enterprise movement, 404
social entrepreneurship, 456–59
social investment funds, 459
socialism, 7, 21, 59, 432
    Lincoln's system as alternative to, 97, 111, 114

social responsibility, xi, xii, xv, xvi, xvii, xx, 497n29
  Arco and, 307–9
  Ben & Jerry's and, 383, 387–88, 393–94, 497n29
  CDC and, 249, 254, 261
  changing investor attitudes and, 459–62
  company failure, relationship of, 426–27
  consortia of enlightened capitalists and, 451–56
  consumerist behavior overriding social conscience, 467
  of corporate capitalism, xxxviii–xl
  critics of, 424
  Davos 2018 and, xiv, 461
  Drucker on, 431
  ethical compasses and, xx
  Friedman on, 439, 507n13
  future prospects for, 442–72
  global in scope, xxxix–xl
  Herman Miller Company and, 238
  Hershey Chocolate Company and, 89
  as job of government not business, xxxvi
  John Lewis Partnership and, 132
  Johnson and, 150–51, 157–58
  large corporations rejection of, 425
  Levi Strauss and, 178, 184, 186–89, 202
  Levi Strauss's global sourcing guidelines, 202–3, 204
  Marks & Spencer and, 210, 213, 216, 218, 222
  MBA programs and, 424–25
  no financial gain from, 429
  opposition to corporate do-goodism, xxxvi, xxxvii, xli, 462
  Patagonia and, 400–403, 497n29
  paternalism and, xxxvii, xlii
  Penney and, 39
  Polman as outspoken advocate, 66–68
  profit vs. virtue and, xl–xli
  promotion of diversity and, xxxvi
  proponents of corporate do-goodism, xxxviii–xl
  public demand for, 463–72
  questions business leaders need to ask, xli–xliii
  Roddick, the Body Shop, and, 349–54
  SWA and, 295–97
  Tom's of Maine and, 372
  Unilever and, 65–68, 393–94, 444–45
  Weizmann and, 210
Social Venture Network, 349, 451
sole proprietorship, 396
Solheim, Jostein, 393
Sony, 325
Soul of a Business, The (Chappell), 361–62, 367–68
Southwest Airlines (SWA), 117n, 426
  big airlines oppose creation of, 288
  business model, 289, 296
  culture committee, 291–93
  customer service and, 293–94
  employee focus of company, 289–93
  employee volunteers, 296
  environmental issues, 295–97
  exemplary practices, 293–94
  FDA fine, 294
  Fortune's Most Admired Corporations list, 294
  future of, 297
  hiring women and people of color, 292–93
  Kelleher as CEO, 288–94
  Kelly as CEO, 292, 295, 296–97
  Kelly as CFO, 293
  management and employee involvement, 291–93
  profitability and, 289, 296
  social responsibility and, 295–97
  Southwest Airlines One Report, 295–96
  stock ownership plan, 290, 406
  stock price, 294
  wages, 290
Spencer, Herbert, xxxi, 155
Spencer, Thomas, Jr., 209
Spencer, Thomas, Sr., 208–9
  partnership with Marks, 208
  retirement, 208–9
Sperry Rand, 244
Springfield, Mo., 409
SRC Holdings, 407–9, 426, 476
  business education at, 407
  community relations, 409
  cost control at, 407–8
  employee ownership, 407
  employees and, 407–9
  number of employees, 409
  "open-book management," 407
  share price, 409
  Springfield Re and, 407, 408, 409, 410

Stack, Jack, 395, 407–9, 411, 428, 451
    "exit money" and, 409
    The Great Game of Business, 407
    leadership philosophy of, 407
    "open-book management," 407
stakeholder benefits, xii
Standard Oil, xxvii
Starbucks, 425, 444, 464, 467
    acquisition of La Boulange, 448
State Street Global Advisors, 470
Stern, David, 176, 177
Stern, Sigmund, 178–79, 180
Stevens Aviation, 290
stock exchanges, 46–47
Stonyfield Farms, 454–55
Stout, Lynn, 438, 458
Strauss, Levi, 176–79, 495n1
    death and estate of, 178
    heirs of, 177, 395
    philanthropy of, 178
Sulzberger family, 399
Sumner, William Graham, 155
Sunset Scavengers, 415–16
Syntegra, 260

Tawney, R. H., 27
Taylor, Frederick W., 430
    Taylorism, 81, 106–7
Tesla Motors, 460
Texas Instruments (TI), 257
textile mills
    Britain's exports of cloth and, 4–5
    child labor, 5
    child labor in, 4–5
    closing of British, 1806, 14
    creation of wealth and, 4
    Defoe's description, 4
    "immiseration" of mill workers, 5
    J&J's cotton mill, 148
    Johnson advocates minimum wage, 151
    living conditions of workers, 5
    Owen's reforms at New Lanark mills,
        6–30
    power loom, 9
    spinning jenny, 4, 9
    spinning mule, 4, 9
    water frame, 4, 9
Thatcher, Margaret, 435–36
Theory Y, 431
Thigpen, Peter, 191, 192
    Santone factory closing and, 198–99

Thompson, J. Walter, 146
Time magazine, on Bradshaw, 305
Tindell, Kip, 455
Tinker, Grant, 311
Tisch, Laurence, 311–12
Tocqueville, Alexis de, 395–96
Tom's of Maine, 360–75, 432
    Colgate-Palmolive Company buys
        controlling interest in, 371–75,
        392, 395
    community relations, 362, 365, 366,
        370, 371, 374
    company credo, 363, 365
    company ownership and, 365, 368,
        369–70
    company's mission, 362–64
    "corporate tithing," 364–65, 366, 372
    education on values and priorities, 363
    employees, 365, 366, 372
    environmental practices, 360, 367, 368
    expansion and growth, 361, 364–67
    future of, 374–75
    hiring women and minorities, 364
    need for capital, 369–70, 374
    participative management, 367
    product recall, 364, 369
    products, 367
    recycling and, 367
    size of, late 1980s, 364
Townsend, Claire, 285, 286
Townsend, Joan Tours, 280, 285
Townsend, Robert "Bob," 264, 279–87, 427,
    428, 436, 477
    American Express and, 280, 282
    as Avis head, 281, 282, 283–84
    background and personal life, 280
    Bennis on, 286–87
    business philosophy at Avis, 281
    commercial slogan for Avis, 279
    death of, 286
    ethics and, 285
    fighting unionization, 284
    humanistic philosophy of
        management, 284
    influence of, 286–87
    intellectual influences on, 430
    ITT acquires Avis, 284–85
    life after Avis, 285–87
    long-term thinking and, 281–82
    "management by adultery," 286
    "Operation Mars," 280

organizational "guerrilla warfare" and,
282–85
Radica and, 285–86
Up the Organization, 279–80, 283,
285, 286
"Trees" (Kilmer), 148
Trillin, Calvin, 382
Trollope, Anthony, 282
Truman, Harry, xvi
Trump, Donald, 278, 467, 489n
TRW, 424
"Try Reality" (Johnson), 150–51
"Two and a Half Cheers for Conscious
Capitalism" (O'Toole and Vogel), 454,
455–56

Uber, 473, 474, 475
UN Global Compact, 451
Unilever. *See* Lever Bros.
Union Carbide, 173
United Airlines, 290–91, 411–12
United Auto Workers, 108
United Garment Workers of America
(UGWA), 181
United Kingdom (UK)
bathing habits and Lever, 51, 53
Bolton, 52, 56–57, 64
Brexit, 446
"British disease," 215
changes to economic order proposed, xv
chief executive salaries in, 469
child labor in, 22, 23
chocolate makers, 84
contingent workforces and virtual
workplaces in, 474–75, 477
cooperative movement, 29, 415, 417, 418
corporate capitalism and profit
primacy in, 438
effect of industrialization in, 4
eighteenth century working
conditions, 8
exporting cloth, 4–5
finance and banking, public concern
about misbehavior in, 467
Financial Reporting Council, 462
gender pay inequity and, 469
global warming concerns and
enlightened business practices, 432
history of textile mills in, 3–4
John Lewis Partnership among largest
retail chains, 120

labor unrest (1960s), 129
Manchester, 5, 6, 8–10, 11, 208
Marks & Spencer as dominant retailer,
211
middle class growth in, 432
no demand for socially responsible
companies, 427
old-age pensions law, 59
social entrepreneurship and, 456
socialized medicine, 212
Stewardship Code, 462
tabloids, 61
welfare-state and, 129
See also Lewis, John Spedan; Lever,
William; Owen, Robert; Roddick,
Anita
United States
contingent workforces and virtual
workplaces in, 473–75, 477
corporate capitalism and profit
primacy in, 438
declines in productivity and job
satisfaction, 476
Dodd-Frank legislation, 462
finance and banking, public concern
about misbehavior in, 467
first stock exchanges, 47
Gilded Age, 31
global warming concerns and
enlightened business practices, 432
large manufacturing facilities
encouraged by Hamilton, 3–4
largest retail business, 41
middle class growth in, 432
new cooperatives in, 419
no demand for socially responsible
companies, 427
public disclosure of top executive
compensation required, 469
rioting in 1877 against capitalist
practices, 31
social entrepreneurship and, 456
tax legislation prohibiting industrial
foundations, 434–35
See also specific companies
Universal Pictures, 473, 474
University of California
Berkeley, 194
Hass School of Business, 182
Levi Strauss scholarships, 178, 182
"unmanagement," 298–99, 304

UPS, 409–10
Up the Organization (Townsend), 279–80,
    283, 285, 286, 287
US Steel, xxx, 249, 265
utilitarianism, 21, 27
utopian communities
    Google Alphabet's Quayside, 450–51
    Hershey and, 79
    Owen's New Harmony, 27–28, 44
    Owen's "villages of co-operation," 26
    Penney's Penney Farms, 44–45
    See also living conditions of workers

Vagelos, Roy, 334–41, 427, 428, 436, 477
    accomplishments, 341
    background and personal life, 335
    cure for river blindness and, 335–38,
        339
    decision to sell vaccine patent to
        China, 338
    legacy of, 340–41
    Merck and ethical business practices,
        335–39
    Merck retirement, 338–39
    opposition to giving away Mectizan, 337
    philanthropy of, 341
    Regeneron Pharmaceuticals and, 341
Vanderbuilt, Cornelius, xxxiii
Vandevelde, Luc, 221
Vanguard investment fund, xiv, 461
Victoria, Queen, 20
Vogel, David, 308, 429
    "Two and a Half Cheers for Conscious
        Capitalism," 454, 455–56
Volkswagen, 173, 429

Waddock, Sandra, 373–74
wages
    ACIPCO and, 138, 139
    Avis and, 281
    Ben & Jerry's and, 384
    British textile mills, 5
    Carnegie's philosophy on paying the
        minimum, xxxiii
    executive-employee wage gap, 469–72
    Ford's $5 a day, xxviii, 20, 113
    Herman Miller and, 228–29, 232, 234
    "iron law" of, 21
    J&J and, 149–50, 157
    labor costs vs. total labor costs and,
        290–91

Levi Strauss and, 190
Lincoln Electric, 94–95, 98, 99–101
link between compensation and
    perception of fairness, 471
living wages, 85, 138, 139, 150, 154,
    157, 401
Nucor, average yearly, 276
Owen's philosophy and, 20, 21
Patagonia and, 401
proven methods of equitable
    compensation, 472
Scanlon plan, 228–29, 234, 472
SWA and, 290–91
well-paid workers and productivity,
    157, 290–91
W. L. Gore & Associates and, 300
Waitrose Limited, 128, 132
Wallace, Mike, 171–72, 173
Wall Street Journal, CEO pay tables, 469–70
Walmart, 197, 399, 401, 466, 468
    Sam's Club, controlling labor costs
        at, 101
Wanamaker's, 432
Warden, William, xxvii
Warhol, Andy, 322
Warroad, Minn., 396
Watson, Thomas J., Jr., 245
Wealth of Nations, The (Smith), xxxiv, 7
Wegman, William, 322
Wegman's Food Markets, 396, 397
    community relations, 397
Weill, Sandy, 260
Weinberg, John, 331
Weinberg, Sidney, 330, 331
Weirton Steel Company, 410–11
Weizmann, Chaim, 210, 211, 218
Welch, Jack, 42, 311
Wells Fargo, 173, 429, 468
Wexner, Leslie, 354
Weyerhaeuser, 424
Whitehead, John, 329–34, 336, 341, 427,
    428, 433, 436
    autobiography, 333
    background and personal life, 329–30,
        332
    as "best of Wall Street," 329
    "Business Principles," 332
    Goldman Sachs and, 330–34
    Haverford and emphasis on ethics,
        329–30, 331
    HBS and, 330, 331

nonprofits headed by, 333
  in public service, 333, 334
  "quiet leadership," 332
  retirement, 333
  The Social Responsibilities of Business
    (unpublished), 334
Whole Foods, 444, 452
  activist investors and hostile takeover
    threat, 447
  sale to Amazon, 447–48, 455
Winchell, Walter, 153
W. L. Gore & Associates, 271, 298–303, 426
  Carroll as president, 301
  community and, 398
  company ownership and, 303, 433, 436
  European operations, 303
  Fortune's 100 Best Companies to Work
    For list ad, 301, 398
  four cardinal principles of fairness,
    302–3
  Gore-Tex and, 301
  institutionalization of practices, 436
  Kelly as COO, 302
  "lattice" structure, 298–301
  profitability and, 302
  self-management at, 300
  small units and, 301
  stock ownership plans, 300–301, 406
  sustainability of business model, 424,
    433
  transparency and, 302
  "unmanagement" and, 298–99
  wages and "contribution ranking," 300
  women associates at, 301–3
women in the workplace
  at ACIPCO, 138
  B corporation movement and, 457–58
  Lever and gender equality, 57, 66
  at Levi Strauss, 185
  Marks & Spencer and women
    managers, 212

pay inequity and, 469
Polaroid Corporation and, 322
textile mills and, 4, 5
W. L. Gore & Associates and, 301–3
Woolworths, 210
Work Foundation, 133
working conditions, xi, xii
  ACIPCO and, 138, 142
  Bolton, UK, 52
  British textile mills, 5
  Carnegie's steel workers, xxxii
  Herman Miller Company and, 231
  Hershey Chocolate Company and,
    81, 432
  Industrial Revolution and, 432
  J&J and, 148
  Johnson and, 154
  Lever Bros. in the Congo and, 60
  Lever Bros. plants and, 57, 432
  Levi Strauss factory and, 179
  Lincoln Electric and, 98, 432
  Nike's contractors and, 425
  Nucor and, 266
  Owen and, 12, 18, 23, 432
  Patagonia and, 402
  Polaroid Corporation and, 323
  tech companies and employee-friendly
    work environments, 449
World a Department Store, The (Peck), 416
Worldly Philosophers, The (Heilbroner),
    485n1
Worthy, James, 255, 262
Wozniak, Steve, 325
Wrigley Company, 90, 399, 490n26
Wyman, Tom, 324, 328

Xerox, 424

YMCA/YWCA, 44
Young, Whitney, 248, 251

ABOUT THE AUTHOR

JAMES O'TOOLE is Professor Emeritus at the University of Southern California's Marshall School of Business, and Founding Director of the Neely Center for Ethical Leadership. At USC he held the University Associates' Chair of Management, served as Executive Director of the Leadership Institute, and edited *New Management* magazine.

O'Toole received his doctorate in social anthropology from Oxford University, where he was a Rhodes Scholar. He was Chairman of the Task Force on Work in America and Director of Field Investigations for the Commission on Campus Unrest during the Nixon administration. He served on the Board of Editors of the *Encyclopaedia Britannica*, was editor of *The American Oxonian* magazine, and is currently a contributing editor to *Strategy+* magazine. He has been Executive Vice President, and later the Mortimer J. Adler Senior Fellow, at the Aspen Institute, and Chairman of the Booz/Allen/Hamilton Strategic Leadership Center. He is currently a Senior Fellow at Santa Clara University's Markkula Center for Applied Ethics.

O'Toole's research and writings have mainly been in the areas of leadership, ethics, and corporate culture. Among his nineteen books, *Vanguard Management* was chosen as "One of the best business and economics books of the year" by the editors of Business Week. He has won a Mitchell Prize for a paper on economic growth policy, named one of the "100 most influential people in business ethics" by the editors of *Ethisphere*, and one of "the top 100 thought leaders on leadership" by *Leadership Excellence* magazine.